The CHINUA ACHEBE
Encyclopedia

The **CHINUA ACHEBE** Encyclopedia

Edited by M. KEITH BOOKER

Foreword by Simon Gikandi

GREENWOOD PRESS
Westport, Connecticut • London

Library of Congress Cataloging-in-Publication Data

The Chinua Achebe encyclopedia / edited by M. Keith Booker ; foreword by Simon Gikandi.
    p. cm.
  Includes bibliographical references (p.) and index.
  ISBN 0–325–07063–6 (alk. paper)
    1. Achebe, Chinua—Encyclopedias. 2. Authors, Nigerian—20th century—Biography—
Encyclopedias. 3. Nigeria—In literature—Encyclopedias. I. Booker, M. Keith.
PR9387.9.A3Z459 2003
823'.914—dc21   2003049203

British Library Cataloguing in Publication Data is available.

Library of Congress Catalog Card Number: 2003049203
ISBN: 0–325–07063–6

First published in 2003

Greenwood Press, 88 Post Road West, Westport, CT 06881
An imprint of Greenwood Publishing Group, Inc.
www.greenwood.com

Printed in the United States of America

∞

The paper used in this book complies with the
Permanent Paper Standard issued by the National
Information Standards Organization (Z39.48–1984).

10 9 8 7 6 5 4 3 2 1

Contents

Photos follow page 160

Foreword: Chinua Achebe and the Institution of African Literature

Simon Gikandi

The appearance of this encyclopedia (in a series that has previously devoted volumes to such authors as Emily Dickinson, William Faulkner, and Toni Morrison) represents still another step in the inexorable rise of Chinua Achebe to canonical status in world literature. While Achebe's enshrinement in the company of such Western authors has its problematic aspects, the critical attention that Achebe has received in the West has, by and large, been a positive development in the sense that it has brought needed recognition and respect to African literature and culture as a whole. Indeed, Achebe's leadership in this respect is only one of the many ways in which he might be said to have founded and invented the institution of African literature.

ACHEBE AND THE IDEA OF AN AFRICAN CULTURE

I have never met Chinua Achebe in person, but every time I read his fiction, his essays, or his critical works, I feel as if I have known him for most of my life. If the act of reading and re-reading establishes networks of connections between readers, writers, and context, and if texts are indeed crucial to the modes of knowledge we come to develop about subjects and objects and the images we

associate with certain localities and institutions, then I can say without equivocation that I have known Achebe since I was thirteen years old. I can still vividly recall the day when, in my first or second year of secondary school, I encountered *Things Fall Apart*. It was in the early 1970s. We had a young English teacher who, although a recent graduate of Makerere University College, which was still the bastion of Englishness in East Africa, decided to carry out a literary experiment that was to change the lives of many of us: instead of offering the normal literary fare for junior secondary school English, which in those days consisted of a good dose of abridged Robert Louis Stevenson novels, Lamb's *Tales from Shakespeare*, and Barbara Kimenye's popular readers, we were going to read *Things Fall Apart*. We would read a chapter of the novel every day, aloud in class, until we got to the end. Once I had started reading *Things Fall Apart*, however, I could not cope with the chapter-a-day policy. I read the whole novel over one afternoon, and it is not an exaggeration to say that my life was never the same again, for reading *Things Fall Apart* brought me to the sudden realization that fiction was not merely about a set of texts that one studied for the Cambridge Overseas exam, which, for my generation, had been renamed the East African Certificate of Education; on the contrary, literature was about real and familiar worlds, of culture and human experience, of politics and economics, now re-routed through a language and structure that seemed at odds with the history or geography books we were reading at the time.

At the center of the transformation engendered by my reading of Achebe's first novel was nothing less than the figure of the yam. Yes: the figure of the yam had been bothering me even before I read *Things Fall Apart*. As (post) colonial subjects of my generation may recall, the yam had been making its way into the standard geography books in Anglophone Africa since the modernization of the curriculum in the late 1950s, ostensibly in anticipation of independence. In the 1960s and the early 1970s, the major geography primers were the *Geography for Africa* series, published by Oxford University Press and written by a certain McBain, graduate of Oxon or Cantab (I forget which); these works were primarily concerned with mapping the movement, or non-movement, of the African from primitive production to modernization. Somehow, the yam seemed to occupy a central position in this narrative of the modernization of the African.

In McBain's *Geography for Africa* for standard four, for example, young minds were informed that the yam was essential to agricultural production among the Igbo of Eastern Nigeria and that, together with palm-oil, it had been a major part of the regional economy before the discovery of coal at Enugu. In those days it made sense to see African life as the movement from primitive (agricultural) practices to industrial production, and we were thus not interested in questioning the logic of this narrative of modernity; still, for those of us growing up in the highlands of East Africa, the yam was as alien as the proverbial apple that opened

all English readers. Having never seen a yam in our lives, we were hard-pressed to understand its value. Indeed, it is now clear to me, in retrospect, that McBain of Oxon/Cantab did not explain the notion of commodity value well enough for us to overcome the distance between Nairobi and Enugu. But in reading *Things Fall Apart*, everything became clear: the yam was important to Igbo culture, not because of what we were later to learn to call use-value, this time at the University of Nairobi, but because of its location at the nexus of a symbolic economy in which material wealth was connected to spirituality and ideology and desire. The novel was teaching us a fundamental lesson that old McBain could never comprehend. *Things Fall Apart* provided us with a different kind of education.

I begin these reflections on the significance of Chinua Achebe to the institution of African literature and culture by noting the transformative power of *Things Fall Apart* for two reasons. The first one is to call attention to an interesting phenomenon that I have noticed in conversations with many Africans of my generation, both inside and outside academia, on the role of literature in the making of African subjects. I have noticed that when the debate turns to questions of culture, of literature, and of the destiny of Africa, subjects that concern many of us as we get older and the problems of the continent seem to multiply with our aging, we seem to clamor for those Pan-African moments that defined our identities as we came of age in the 1960s and 1970s. These debates and questions crystallize around many of the tragic and triumphant events that stand in our memories—the Mexico City Olympics or the civil war in Nigeria, for example—but while these events generate disagreement, the transformative nature of *Things Fall Apart* is undisputed. Like one of these momentous events that one is bound to remember, like where one was when John F. Kennedy was assassinated, many of us recall where we were when we first read Achebe's first novel. But, of course, such acts of recall make sense only for a generation that has come to feel, rightly or wrongly, that it shared a common cultural project. Whatever questions we may now have about this project (was the 1960s the golden age of African independence, or does it appear to be so only through the prism of bourgeois nostalgia and against the background of postcolonial failure?), there is consensus that *Things Fall Apart* was important for the making and marking of that exciting first decade of decolonization. There also seems to be consensus that the production of the novel, as well as its reading and (re)reading, and its circulation within the institutions of education came to define who we were, where we were, and as Achebe himself would say, where the rain began to beat us.

My second point, however, is that the association of a text such as *Things Fall Apart* with a certain generational project or even a foundational moment of literary history also marks the gap between the text and those readers removed from its moment of irruption into the world; those are the readers who are bound to be baffled by the claims to monumentality adduced to the novel itself. Scholars and readers of my generation, people who often take the monumentality of Achebe's work for granted, are constantly frustrated when their young students seem unable to comprehend the historic nature of his intervention in the field of African literature, which was, in the 1950s, in a state of flux and, in my judgment, crisis. I am often taken to task for having claimed, or rather repeated the claim, that Achebe was the person who invented African literature.

From the perspective of literary history, as I argued in *Reading Chinua Achebe* (London: Currey; Portsmouth: Heinemann; Nairobi: Heinemann Kenya, 1991), Achebe had important precursors on the African scene, and the more I re-read the works of such figures as René Maran, Amos Tutuola, Paul Hazoumé, and Sol Plaatje, the more I am convinced of their significance in the foundation of an African tradition of letters. Still, none of these writers had the effect Achebe had on the establishment and reconfiguration of an African literary tradition; none of them were able to enter and interrupt the institutions of exegesis and education the same way he did; none were able to establish the terms by which African literature was produced, circulated, and interpreted. So the question that needs to be addressed in any tribute to Achebe is not why he was the person who invented African literature as an institutional practice but what exactly accounted for the foundational and transformative character of his works, not to mention its monumentality. Why must *Things Fall Apart* always occupy the inaugural moment of African literary history? From the perspective of a literary critic rather than a common reader, I came to discover the significance of Achebe's novels in the shaping of African literature through a negative example. Sometime in the late 1970s, as an apprentice editor at the Nairobi office of Heinemann Educational Books, I was asked by my senior colleagues, Henry Chakava and Laban Erapu, to review a manuscript by a certain Dambudzo Marechera and, specifically, to address the concerns of the "London Office," whose managers were not sure that *The House of Hunger* could be published and marketed as African literature. I did not have to ask what exactly was construed to be African literature. It was assumed that it was something akin to Achebe's novels, especially *Things Fall Apart*, and this seemed to exclude many forms of experimental writing. My first impulse was to react against this tendency to equate African literature with Achebe's works, a tendency that had produced what I felt were many poor imitators in the Heinemann African Writers Series, books about village life and the crisis of change whose titles we no longer need to mention. My second impulse was to read Marechera's manuscript as an attempt to break out of what I then thought was an ill-advised over-determination of the series by its first—and most important—writer.

But as soon as I started reading *The House of Hunger*, I realized that the question of over-determination was more complicated than I initially thought. Marechera's "avant-garde" fiction could not simply be juxtaposed against Achebe's works; on the contrary, it existed in a productive relation to it, so much so that one could not argue for the newness of the title story or novella ("The House of Hunger") without invoking its relationship with Achebe's project. Even a cursory reading of Marechera's fiction indicated that his protagonists had been reading Achebe and other African writers; these African writers were important tools in their struggle against the culture of colonialism in Rhodesia/Zimbabwe. What was even more remarkable about Marechera's subjects was the fact that they took the existence of this African literature for granted and considered it inseparable from the idea of an African identity and a Pan-African culture. Like many Africans of my generation, Marechera's characters paid homage to African literature by taking it for granted as something that didn't need to be rationalized or justified; more importantly they were leading their lives according to the dictates of a Pan-African, rather than, or in addition to, the colonial, library. If I were writing that review of Marechera's manuscript today, I would say that the soon-to-be gadfly of African letters was important to the tradition not because he was writing a different fiction than Achebe, but because he had taken Achebe's fictional world as an integral part of what it meant to be African. Achebe's novels had become an essential referent for the African cultural text.

However, when I said that Achebe had invented African literature, I was thinking about something more than the existence of his novels as the Ur-texts of our literary tradition; what I had in mind then was the tremendous influence his works have had on the institutions of pedagogy and interpretation and the role his fictions have come to play in the making and unmaking of African worlds. Like most émigré African intellectuals, I am ambivalent about the institutionalization of *Things Fall Apart* and the wisdom of using it as supplement for African culture or the authorized point of entry into Igbo, Nigerian, or African landscapes. Within Africa, itself, I have sometimes wondered why the institutions of power have been so keen to place Achebe at the center of the curriculum. I am reminded of an episode that took place in Kenya sometime in the 1980s when the state, in its eagerness to isolate Ngugi wa Thiong'o, whom it then considered to be the single most important threat to its cultural hegemony, sought to return to a colonial literary curriculum, one in which Shakespeare would once again occupy a place of honor. The Kenyan state was eager to purge the curriculum of radical writers, I am told, but still the president and the then minister of higher education wanted Achebe retained because, in spite of their hankering for the colonial days, they wanted students to have a dignified sense of African culture. Ironically, when he was detained at the end of 1977, Ngugi was in the middle of teaching a course focused on Achebe's work as a mirror of the transformation of African history from the pre-colonial past to the neocolonial present. If the Kenyan state associated Achebe's fiction with the idea of a dignified African culture, its radical opponent read the same fiction as a critique of decolonization.

Given the appeal he has had for different kinds of readers and factions, the institutionalization of Achebe raises some important questions: what is it about his novels that enabled them to play their unprecedented role as the mediators of the African experience and the depository of a certain idea of Africa? Why is it that when the term "African culture" is mentioned, Achebe's works almost immediately come to mind? Achebe is the person who invented African culture as it is now circulated within the institutions of interpretation. It is my contention that his intervention in the already existing colonial and Pan-African libraries transformed the idea of Africa and that his project has indeed valorized the idea of culture in the thinking of African worlds. The argument can be made that the valorization of culture as the medium of thinking the African was already under way when Achebe started writing his novels. After all, is there a more profound valorization of culture than the one we encounter in Senghor's Negritude? Perhaps not. But for reasons that are too complicated to discuss here, the valorization of culture in Senghor's work—and indeed the writings of early Pan-Africanists—was so closely associated with European ideas or sought to reconcile the African to the dominant European discourse about race and culture, that they could not seriously be invoked in radical gestures of dissociation from Eurocentric ideas about Africa. I will not be audacious enough to claim that Achebe's work is not indebted to European ideas of Africa or to the culture of colonialism (they carry powerful signs of these entities); but I think the claim can be made that these works have been read—or at least render themselves to being read—as counterpoints to the colonial library.

A brief context can help clarify the argument I am trying to make here: we have now come to associate the idea of an African culture with the whole discourse of decolonization that we forget, too often perhaps, that there was a time when the narrative of African freedom was predicated on the negation of what we have come to call tradition. This negation is the fulcrum in key texts of Pan-Africanism for most of the nineteenth and twentieth centuries. The Pan-African elite might have celebrated the greatness of African cultures, but as even a cursory reading of their sourcebooks will show, their celebration of "classical" Africa was a flight from the barbarism associated with the "tribal," those whom Achebe's parents would have called the people of darkness. Up until the 1950s, the education of Africans was predicated on their relocation from the darkness associated with the "tribal" to the sweetness and light of colonial institutions. When African culture entered literary texts, it did so either as the European idea of Africa or as a sign of lack. *Things Fall Apart* is as anxious about its colonial context as other texts from this period; at the same time, however, it seems determined to exist in excess of this context; for a novel written within colonialism, it seems confident about its ability to represent its African background as it is of its power to manage the colonial anxieties that generated it in the first place. I would argue, then, that this confidence is precisely what enabled Achebe to shift the idea of Africa from romance and nostalgia, from European primitivism, and from a rhetoric of lack, to an affirmative culture. It is in this sense that Achebe can be said to have invented, or reinvented, the idea of African culture.

ACHEBE AND AFRICAN LITERARY HISTORY

It is likely that Achebe may be frustrated by the attention and amount of critical energy given or devoted to *Things Fall Apart* often to the neglect of his other works, including

Arrow of God, his stated favorite. Yet it is difficult to ignore the significance of this first novel, either in the making of African cultures and reading communities, as discussed above, or in its dominant role in African literary history, where it serves as an important reference for many novels written in the last decade of formal colonialism in Africa and the first decade of independence. At the same time, however, it is important to recognize the influential role Achebe's other novels, *No Longer at Ease* (1960), *Arrow of God* (1964), *A Man of the People* (1967), and *Anthills of the Savannah* (1987), spanning a significant period of postcolonial Africa, have played in mapping out the nature of African culture and the institutions of literary interpretation. Considered together, these novels occupy such a crucial diachronic role in the history of an African literature almost always driven by the desire to imaginatively capture the key moments of African history from the beginning of colonialism to what has come to be known as postcoloniality. In both their subject and their aesthetic concerns, then, Achebe's major novels are located at the point of contact between European and African cultures and are concerned with the political and linguistic consequences of this encounter.

In this respect, Achebe's novels can be divided into two categories. First, there are those works that are concerned with recovering and representing an African precolonial culture struggling to retain its integrity against the onslaught of colonialism. *Things Fall Apart* and *Arrow of God* belong to this category: they are narrative attempts to imagine what pre-colonial society could have looked like before the European incursion and the factors that were responsible for the failure of Igbo or African cultures in the face of colonialism. These novels are themselves cast in a dual structure, with the first part seeking to present a meticulous portrait of Igbo society before colonialism and the

second part narrating the traumatic process in which this culture loses its autonomy in the face of the colonial encounter. Unlike some of his contemporaries, however, Achebe does not seek to recover the logic of a pre-colonial African culture in order to romanticize it, but to counter the colonial mythology that Africans did not have a culture before colonialism. As he noted in an influential essay called "The Role of the Writer in a New Nation," Achebe's works were concerned with what he considers to be a fundamental theme "that African people did not hear of culture for the first time from Europeans; that their societies were not mindless but frequently had a philosophy of great depth and value and beauty." At the same time, however, these narratives are often attempts to explore the fissures of pre-colonial culture itself in order to show why it was vulnerable to European colonialism.

In his second set of novels, *No Longer at Ease*, *A Man of the People*, and *Anthills of the Savannah*, Achebe turns his attention away from the past to diagnose and narrate the crisis of decolonization. While the novels dealing with the past have been influential for showing that Africans had a culture with its own internal logic and set of contradictions and hence derive their authority from their capacity to imagine an African past derided or negated in the colonial text, the second set of novels have been popular because of their keen sense of the crisis of postcoloniality and, in some cases, a prophetic sense of African history, the attendant promise of decolonization and its failure or sense of discontent. From another perspective, both Achebe's early and later novels have been influential because of their acute capacity to map out the cultural fault in which African cultures and traditions have encountered the institutions of modern European colonial society. In fact, it could be said that Achebe's early novels were the first to popularize the tradition/modernity paradigm which, though constantly questioned in many theoretical works, continues to haunt the study of African literature and culture.

But as has been the case for most of his writing career, Achebe has been able to produce novels that both set up paradigms and deconstruct them. While *Things Fall Apart* derives most of its power from the ability to position pre-colonial Igbo society in opposition to an encroaching colonial culture, it is also memorable for the way it problematizes the nature of Igbo society and deprives it of any claims to cultural purity. In this novel, it is those who seek to protect the purity of culture, most notably Okonkwo, the hero of the novel, whose lives end up in ignominy. In *No Longer at Ease*, the subjects who had subscribed to the logic of colonial modernity are increasingly haunted by the choices they make, wondering where they stand in the new dispensation, and in *Arrow of God*, clearly one of the major novels on the colonial situation, attempts to subscribe to the idiom of tradition arc shown to be as lacking as the logic of colonization itself.

Although Achebe is now considered to be the premier novelist on the discourse of African identity, nationalism, and decolonization, his main focus, as he has insisted in many of the interviews he has given throughout his career, has been on sites of cultural ambiguity and contestation. If there is one phrase that sums up Achebe's philosophy of culture or language, it is the Igbo proverb: "Where one thing falls, another stands in its place." The complexity of novels such as *Things Fall Apart* and *Arrow of God* depends on Achebe's ability to bring competing *cultural* systems and their languages on to the same level of representation, dialogue, and contestation. In *Arrow of God*, for example, the central conflict is not merely a racial one between white Europeans and black Africans, or even an epistemological encounter be-

tween an Igbo culture and a colonial polity, but also a struggle between idioms and linguistic registers. Although the novel is written in English, as are all of Achebe's works, it contains one of the most strenuous attempts to translate an African idiom in the language of the other. Although we read the world of the Igbo in English, Achebe goes out of his way to use figures of speech, most notably proverbs and sayings, to give readers a sense of how this culture might have represented itself to counter the highly regimented and stereotyped language of the colonizer.

In the end, the authority of Achebe's works has depended on their role as cultural texts. This does not mean that they are not imaginative works, or that their formal features are not compelling, or that they are valuable primarily as ethnographic documents; rather, Achebe's novels have become important features of the African literary landscape because they have come to be read and taught as important sources of knowledge about Africa. For scholars in numerous disciplines, such as history and anthropology, *Things Fall Apart* and *Arrow of God* are read as exemplary representations of African traditional cultures at the moment of the colonial encounter. Although *No Longer at Ease* has not had the same cultural effect as these other novels, it is clearly indispensable in the mapping out of the space of transition from colonialism to postcolonialism. For students trying to understand the violent politics of postcolonial Nigeria, especially the period of corruption and military coups in the mid-1960s, there is perhaps no better reference than *A Man of the People*. The parallel between Achebe's works and their historical and social referents is so close that it is difficult not to read his major novels as significant documents of the African experience. For this reason, Achebe's novels are notable for their sense of realism.

Indeed, while a novel like *Anthills of the*

Savannah is unusual in its bringing together of techniques drawn from realism, modernism, and what has come to be known as magic realism, rarely does Achebe's work reflect an interest in formal experimentation for its own sake. The use of a multiplicity of forms in this novel can be connected to the author's desire to account for a postcolonial crisis that cannot be contained within one feature of novelistic discourse. It is perhaps because of his commitment to realism that Achebe's novels have tended to be out of fashion in institutions of interpretation dominated by theories of structuralism and poststructuralism. And yet, Achebe's sense of realism, as a technique and mode of discourse, is not that of the nineteenth-century European novel with its concern with verisimilitude, the experiences of a unique bourgeois subject undergoing the process of education, and a language that seeks to make communities knowable, although Achebe's novels do seek to make African communities knowable. As he himself has noted in an early essay called "The Novelist as a Teacher," he started his career envisioning the role of writing as essentially pedagogical—"to help my society regain belief in itself and put away the complexes of the years of denigration and self-abasement." Achebe is attracted to realism because it enables him to imagine African cultures, especially postcolonial cultures, possible and knowable.

Nevertheless, Achebe's novels operate under the shadow of modernism and modernity for two closely related reasons. First, his early novels were written in response to a set of modern texts, most notably Conrad's *Heart of Darkness*, in which African "barbarism" was represented as the opposite of the logic of modern civilization. Since he was educated within the tradition of European modernism, Achebe's goal was to use realism to make African cultures visible while using the ideology and techniques of modernism to counter the colonial novel in its own terrain. Second, modernity was an inevitable effect of colonization in Africa. As Achebe was to dramatize so powerfully in *Things Fall Apart* and *Arrow of God*, the disruption of the African polity was made in the name of colonial modernity; it was also in the name of being modern that some African subjects would defect from their own cultures and identify with the new colonial order. Indeed, Achebe's "postcolonial" novels are concerned with the consequences of colonial modernity. The sense of instability that characterizes the process of decolonization in *No Longer at Ease* arises as much from doubts about the future of the imagined community of the Nigerian nation as the main character's entrapment between the culture of colonialism, represented by the shaky idiom of Englishness, and the continuing power of what were once considered to be outdated customs such as caste. Similarly, behind the comic mode of *A Man of the People* is a serious questioning of the nature of power once it has been translated into a nationalist narrative that is unclear about its idiom and moral authority.

But the continuing influence of Achebe's works and their now classical status go beyond their topicality and their role as sources of knowledge about Africa. Achebe's novels are cultural texts to the extent that they have an imaginative relationship to the African experience and hence cannot be properly interpreted outside the realities and dreams of an African political configuration. This concern with the meaning of the past in the pressure of the moment of writing is pronounced in Achebe's short stories (*Girls at War and Other Stories*) (1972) and his two collections of poems (*Beware Soul Brother and Other Poems*, also published as *Christmas in Biafra and Other Poems*) (1972/1973), many provoked by the Nigerian Civil War. In all these works and four collections of essays, Achebe has been responsible for making the African experience, in a historical and cultural perspective, the center of an African literature. He has been persistent in his claim that the main concerns of an African literature arise from a fundamental engagement with what he would consider to be the stream of African history and consciousness. In formal terms, Achebe's literary works, like his own life, reflect the variety of influences that have gone into the making of African literature, ranging through the folk traditions of the Igbo people of Eastern Nigeria, the idiom of the Bible and the culture of the Christian missions, colonial education, the university and the institutions of English literature.

NOTE

Most of the material in this foreword is derived from a slightly revised combination of two previously published works. The first part is from "Chinua Achebe and the Invention of African Culture," *Research in African Literatures* 32.3 (Fall 2001); the second part is from *The Encyclopedia of African Literature* (London: Routledge, 2002).

Preface

Chinua Achebe is, without question, the single author who has been most responsible for the rise of the African novel as a global cultural phenomenon in the past half century. Indeed, as Professor Simon Gikandi notes in his foreword to this volume, there is a very real sense in which Achebe can be said to have invented African literature, at least insofar as it exists as an internationally recognized cultural institution. Achebe's first novel, *Things Fall Apart* (1958), is generally thought of as the first real novel to have been produced by an African writer in the English language. The impressive achievement of that book—plus its subsequent critical and commercial success—blazed a trail followed by numerous other African novelists. With Achebe in the lead, these novelists have been able, within the seemingly Western genre of the novel and generally in Western languages (especially English), to find an eloquent and effective mode for the expression of the particular social, historical, and cultural situation of modern Africa. Achebe himself was among those authors who built upon the impressive achievement of *Things Fall Apart*, producing a sequence of powerful novels that together tell the story of the history of modern Nigeria from the traumatic moment of first colonization to the era of postcolonial

political turmoil. Achebe's body of work has received considerable attention from Western critics, and in this sense he has also led the way for other African novelists. But Achebe has also been an important and outspoken critic in his own right, courageously condemning the colonialist biases of canonical Western classics such as Joseph Conrad's *Heart of Darkness*, while at the same time explaining to Western audiences the crucial factors that both link the African novel to its Western predecessors and identify the African novel as an altogether different cultural phenomenon.

Given the extensive nature of Achebe's work as a novelist, poet, short-story writer, critic, political commentator, and international ambassador for Africa and African culture, it should perhaps come as no surprise that there is now a vast body of information available about him and his work. This volume represents an attempt to pull much of that information together in a single place, providing a convenient starting point at which those interested in Achebe and his work can find a substantial amount of information of various kinds, while also learning where to go to seek additional material. In this sense, the volume is intended to be accessible to those with little or no knowledge of Achebe and his work. However, because of its broad scope, it should also be useful even to those who have substantial experience with Achebe or African literature.

The chronology at the beginning of the volume is intended to give a quick overview of the highlights of Achebe's life and career. Similarly, the bibliography at the back of the volume contains numerous sources from which additional information can be obtained. All of these bibliographic entries are referred to in at least one of the individual entries that form the heart of the volume. These entries fit into a variety of categories, though they are, for convenience of reference, arranged in a single alphabetical list. Central emphasis has been placed on Achebe's production as a novelist, and the entries include extensive critical introductions to each of his novels. There is also a wide variety of brief entries that identify and explain the various characters, locations, and concepts that figure in the novels.

Achebe's books of poetry, short stories, and nonfiction are also each discussed in their own entries, though those entries are less extensive than the ones devoted to the novels. There are also entries describing adaptations of Achebe's writing to other media, such as film and television. Similar entries are included describing the most important book-length critical discussions of Achebe's work, and biographical entries are included for Achebe's most important critics. Similar biographical entries are included for Achebe himself and for friends, family, and associates who have played a prominent role in his

career. Historical, geographical, and cultural entries provide useful background for readers who may need such material to help them understand the Nigerian context of Achebe's writing. There are also entries on specific issues and critical debates concerning this context and the ways in which postcolonial literature (such as the novels of Achebe) needs to be approached differently than Western literature. Finally, there are also entries for specific authors or works of literature that have been important to Achebe in his career or about which Achebe has provided important critical commentary. The various entries are cross-referenced using a system of bold-facing; any item in boldface within a given entry is also covered in an entry of its own.

The various entries have been provided by expert scholars who work in the field to which the entries are relevant. Many of these scholars have, in fact, themselves made important contributions to Achebe's growing critical reputation over the years. In that sense, the information provided is the best that could be obtained. However, the length restrictions inherent in a work such as this one require that the information included here is merely a starting point and should not be taken as complete and comprehensive. In this sense, readers interested in more complete and detailed information should pay serious attention to the suggestions for further reading that are included with the more substantial and complex entries and should consult the sources in the bibliography for further information.

Chronology

1909	Marriage of Isaiah Okafor Achebe and Janet Anaenechi, Achebe's parents.
1930	Achebe born on November 16 at Ogidi, just east of Onitsha in the Eastern Region of Nigeria. He is christened Albert Chinualumogu Achebe.
1944–1948	Achebe attends Government College, Umuahia.
1948–1953	Achebe attends University College, Ibadan.
1954	Achebe begins work for the Nigerian Broadcasting Corporation.
1956	Achebe trains with the BBC in London.
1958	*Things Fall Apart* published by Heinemann.
1960	Nigeria gains independence from British colonial rule on October 1. *No Longer at Ease* published.
1961	Achebe marries Christie Chinwe Okoli.
1962	*The Sacrificial Egg and Other Stories* published. Achebe becomes founding editor of the Heinemann African Writers Series. Daughter Chinelo born.
1963	Nigeria becomes a republic with Nnamdi Azikiwe as the first president.
1964	*Arrow of God* published. Son Ikechukwu born.
1966	*A Man of the People* published. An Igbo-led military coup establishes Major General Johnson T. U. Aguiyi-Ironsi as head of the government in January. A second coup, led by Hausa officers, results in the killing of Ironsi and establishes Lieutenant Colonel Yakubu Gowon as the head of the new government in July. Massacres of Igbo in the North are part of a crisis that causes Achebe to leave Lagos and return to Eastern Nigeria.
1967	Biafra secedes from Nigeria on May 30, triggering the Nigerian civil war. Nigerian poet/activist Christopher Okigbo killed in the subsequent fighting. Achebe's son Chidi born.
1970	Biafra surrenders and rejoins Nigeria. Achebe's daughter Nwando born.

1971   *Okike: An African Journal of New Writing* begins publication. *Beware, Soul Brother* (poems) published.

1972   *Girls at War and Other Stories* published. *Beware, Soul Brother* wins the Commonwealth Poetry Prize.

1972–1975   Achebe serves as Visiting Professor of Literature at the University of Massachusetts at Amherst.

1975   Achebe delivers lecture "An Image of Africa." *Morning Yet on Creation Day* (essays) published. Gowon deposed in a coup that places General Murtala Muhammad as the head of the government.

1975–1976   Achebe serves as Visiting Professor of Literature at the University of Connecticut, Storrs.

1976   "An Image of Africa" published in *Massachusetts Review*. Muhammed assassinated and replaced by General Olusegun Obasanjo as head of the military government. Achebe returns to Nigeria and becomes Professor of Literature at the University of Nigeria, Nsukka.

1979   Alhaji Shehu Shagari elected head of a civilian government. Achebe receives the Nigerian National Merit Award and the Order of the Federal Republic. He is elected Chairman of the Association of Nigerian Authors.

1982   *Aka Weta* (a volume of Igbo-language verse edited by Ache-

be and Obiora Udechukwu) published.

1983   *The Trouble with Nigeria* published. Shagari re-elected but deposed by a military coup a few months later. Death of Mallam Aminu Kano, leader of the People's Redemption Party. Achebe elected Deputy National President of that party. A military coup on December 31 establishes General Buhari as head of the government.

1985   Another military coup establishes the regime of Major General Babangida.

1986   Achebe appointed Pro-Vice-Chancellor of the State University of Anambra in Enugu.

1987   *Anthills of the Savannah* published. It is short-listed for the Booker Prize for that year.

1987–1988   Achebe serves as Visiting Fellow at the University of Massachusetts at Amherst.

1988   *Hopes and Impediments* (essays) published.

1989   Achebe serves as Distinguished Visiting Professor at the City College of New York. He is nominated for the presidency of PEN International.

1990   Celebration of Achebe's sixtieth birthday at Nsukka. Achebe badly hurt in a near-fatal accident. Achebe accepts a position as Charles P. Stevenson Professor of Literature at Bard College in New York.

1991   Abuja becomes new capital of Nigeria.

1993   A joint civilian-military government is installed and elections are held. It is deposed a few months later in a coup led by General Sani Abacha. Abacha voids subsequent elections and declares himself head of the government.

1995   Ken Saro-Wiwa executed amid growing domestic tensions in Nigeria.

1998   Abacha dies.

1999   Elections install a new civilian government, led by Obasanjo.

2000   *Home and Exile* (essays) published.

A

ABAME, a village near **Umuofia** in *Things Fall Apart*. The men of Umuofia regard Abame as having "upside-down" customs. In chapter 15, we learn that the village of Abame has been destroyed by British-led troops in reprisal for the killing of a white man. The story is based on the fate of the actual town of **Ahiara**, which was largely wiped out by British-led troops in 1905 after the killing of an Englishman, **J. F. Stewart**. The village of Abame also figures prominently in *Arrow of God*, in which we learn that the six villages of **Umuaro** originally banded together as a single unit in order to defend themselves against raids by Abam warriors.

FURTHER READING

Robert M. Wren, *"Things Fall Apart* in Its Time and Place."

M. Keith Booker

ABAZON, a region in the northern part of the fictional African state of **Kangan** in *Anthills of the Savannah*. While Abazon has, at the time of the novel's action, been restored to Kangan, it had previously seceded and thus recalls the situation of **Biafra** in **Nigeria**. The uneasy position of Abazon within Kangan suggests the way in which postcolonial African nations were typically yoked together by their European rulers rather than evolving through an organic historical process based on shared cultural and political traditions. Meanwhile, the woes of Abazon are compounded in the novel by a severe, long-term drought that has brought famine to the region, which continues to occupy a problematic political position because of its recent refusal, as a region, to approve a recent referendum declaring **Sam, the President** to be president for life of Kangan.

M. Keith Booker

ABUJA, the capital city of **Nigeria**, located near the center of the federal capital territory and of Nigeria itself. The land of Abuja was the southwestern part of the ancient kingdom of Zazzau (Zaria). The name "Abuja" was derived from that of Abu Ja, a brother to Muhammadu Makau, the last Hausa ruler of Zaria. In the early nineteenth century, Makau had left Zaria after being defeated by the Fulani and settled in the area now known as Abuja. In 1825 his brother Abu Ja succeeded him as the sixty-second King of Zaria.

The old town of Abuja was built into a modern city between 1976, when plans for the new capital were approved, and December 1991, when it officially became the capital of Nigeria, replacing **Lagos**. At that time, the population of Abuja was just over 370,000. The population of the city was estimated at 440,000 in 1997.

M. Keith Booker

ACHEBE, CHINUA (1930–   ). Achebe's contribution as a novelist, essayist, and poet to the development of a literary tradition in Africa is well acknowledged. A Nigerian whose now classic first novel *Things Fall Apart* (1958) has sold more copies than any other African novel and been translated into several international languages, Achebe is the most popular African writer worldwide of the twentieth century. His pioneering role as founding editor of Heinemann's **African Writers Series** and the Nigerian-based journal *Okike* has accentuated his prominence and his international stature, particularly in the English-speaking world. Indeed, Achebe's global importance as a spokesman for African culture and for Africa in general goes well beyond his considerable importance as a writer and critic.

Born November 16, 1930, at Ogidi, just east of **Onitsha** in the Eastern Region of **Nigeria**, in an area that was first colonized by the British at the end of the nineteenth century, Achebe was christened Albert Chinualumogu Achebe. The son of Christian evangelists, he was educated in colonial schools, attending Government College at Umuahia from 1944 to 1948 and **University College, Ibadan**, from 1948 to 1953. The Ibadan of this time was an institution in which Achebe's "formal studies in English literature would have been very similar to those of a British undergraduate," for, in "those days the new British-style universities in Africa were intended to transplant on African soil what established academic circles in England regarded as the best features of English universities, without much regard for the special needs of the countries where they were set up" (Ravenscroft 7). Achebe's Iba-

dan years occurred at the height of Nigerian anticolonial nationalist activity and the struggle for self-determination and independence from British colonial rule. His writing career thus conjoins with what he describes as the age of the "crossroads" or the epochal encounter between African and European cultures (Achebe, ***Hopes and Impediments*** 22).

The beginning of the twentieth century was "a period of sweeping and complex changes" in Igboland and Nigeria (Ohaeto 1). Achebe's novels of the colonial encounter in Igboland—*Things Fall Apart* and **Arrow of God**—confront this historical moment and thematize the Igbo/Nigerian experience with imperialism and colonialism in a manner that speaks directly to the circumstances of many colonized African peoples. The acute historical realism and symbolic resonance of *Things Fall Apart* and *Arrow of God* have ensured the place of these novels as "foundation texts in the African literary tradition" (Akwanya 60). Achebe's chronicling of Igbo, Nigerian, and African history explores the transition of Africa into a new world order wrought by colonialism and captures developments within the pre-colonial, colonial, and postcolonial moments. His early writings, particularly *Things Fall Apart* and *Arrow of God*, are programmatic novels of nationalist self-assertion that interrogate the Eurocentric assumptions of colonial writing on Africa.

After his education at Ibadan, Achebe joined the Nigerian Broadcasting Corporation in 1954 and remained there until 1966, when violence against Igbos in Northern Nigeria began to accelerate to proportions that eventually triggered the **Nigerian Civil War** of 1967–1970. During the period prior to the Civil War, Achebe explored the question of post-independence nationalism in such novels as *No Longer at Ease* (1960) and *A Man of the People* (1966). These novels represent a shift in narrative posture from the chiefly oppositional anticolonial counter-discourses of *Things Fall Apart* and *Arrow of God*. They illustrate Achebe's recognition of the "limitless possibilities" of the novel for "inventing a new national community" (Gikandi, *Reading Chinua Achebe* 3). Engaging primarily with Africa's contemporary socioeconomic and political situation, they imagine Nigeria as a national community simultaneously as they dramatize the crises of post-independence that the nation embodies. Questions discussed in these works include political corruption, tribalism, ethnicity, the relationship between individuals and groups within the Nigerian nation, and the general abuse of power in Africa.

However, the civil war had a crucial impact on the evolution of Achebe's career and of his attitudes toward Nigerian nationalism. All of his explorations of the post-independence phase of Nigerian history capture the paradoxes and ambiguities of Nigerian history after the demise of colonialism. But, while he initially affirmed faith in the idea of a Nigerian nation, he would subsequently express complete disenchantment with it in his post–civil war work. Earlier on in his self-conception as a nationalist writer, Achebe had argued that "[a]fter the elimination of white rule shall have been completed, the single most important fact in Africa in the second half of the twentieth century will appear to be the rise of the individual nation-states" (*Morning Yet on Creation Day* 93). However, during the political turbulence of the period 1967–1970, Achebe abandoned the project of nation-building, joining the unsuccessful struggle to free **Biafra** from the rest of Nigeria.

Achebe's involvement in the Biafran cause affected the form of his writing significantly. Subsequently, Achebe's artistic imagination entered a new phase—the contemplative state that produced his first collection of poems, **Beware, Soul Brother** (1971), and the short story collection **Girls at War and Other** *Stories* (1972). He would not publish another novel until **Anthills of the Savannah** (1987), his most complex and nuanced fictional treatment of postcolonial politics. In the meantime, his commentary in **The Trouble with Nigeria** (1983) indicates a turn back toward an engagement with problems of the Nigerian nation; the ideological blueprint and political manifesto for reforming Nigeria's political system that Achebe provides in this volume offer definitive evidence that he had once more embraced the concept of a united Nigeria after the debacle of Biafra. Achebe's most recent collection of essays, **Home and Exile** (2000), adds to the existing *Morning Yet on Creation Day* and *Hopes and Impediments* as an impressive body of nonfiction commentary on various issues related to postcolonial culture.

During the latter decades of the twentieth century, Achebe held a number of teaching positions at universities in Nigeria and the United States. During this time, his growing international stature was acknowledged by the increasing critical attention to his work and by the numerous prizes and awards he received from organizations worldwide. In February 1990, Achebe was honored at a symposium at **Nsukka**, Nigeria (see *Eagle on Iroko*); however, a month later, he was seriously injured in an automobile accident near **Awka**, Nigeria, resulting in his subsequent confinement to a wheelchair. In September 1990, he accepted a position as the Charles P. Stevenson Professor of Literature at **Bard College** in New York. He remains at Bard College as of this writing, still active as a writer, speaker, teacher, and ambassador for African culture.

A chronology of Achebe's life and career can be found at the beginning of this volume. Achebe has also been the subject of two book-length biographies, including Ezenwa-Ohaeto's well-documented **Chinua Achebe: A Biography** and Phanuel Egejuru's **Chinua**

Achebe: Pure and Simple, an "oral" biography based on extensive interviews.

FURTHER READING

Amechi Akwanya, "Ambiguous Signs"; Phanuel A. Egejuru, *Chinua Achebe*; Ezenwa-Ohaeto, *Chinua Achebe: A Biography*; Edith Ihekweazu, ed., *Eagle on Iroko*; C. L. Innes, *Chinua Achebe*; Arthur Ravenscroft, *Chinua Achebe*.

Kwadwo Osei-Nyame Jr.

ACHEBE, DR. CHRISTIE CHINWE, wife of Chinua Achebe, came from Umuokpu village in **Awka**, Anambra State of **Nigeria**. She and Chinua met at **Enugu** in 1958. At that time Chinua was the controller of the **Nigerian Broadcasting Service (NBS)**, Eastern Region, while Christie had come from Ibadan University to do a vacation job at NBS, Enugu. Thus, their initial meeting was "on official business." They eventually fell in love and got married in 1961. Christie and Chinua have four children, two boys and two girls. Christie went back to the university for graduate studies in education after having her children. She received her Ph.D. in education counseling from the **University of Massachusetts at Amherst**. Upon their return to Nigeria in 1976, she joined the faculty of the **University of Nigeria, Nsukka**. Christie was forced to leave her position at Nsukka to take care of her husband, who was involved in an automobile accident that left him in a wheelchair in March 1990. In the fall of 1990, Christie and Chinua joined the faculty of **Bard College** in Annandale-on-Hudson, New York. Christie's support has clearly helped shape and determine her husband's literary career.

FURTHER READING

Phanuel A. Egejuru, *Chinua Achebe: Pure and Simple* (pp. 98–117); Ezenwa-Ohaeto, *Chinua Achebe: A Biography*.

Phanuel Akubueze Egejuru

ACHEBE, ISAIAH OKAFOR, the father of Chinua Achebe, was born in the late nineteenth century in the village of **Ikenga** in the town of Ogidi in present-day Anambra State, **Nigeria**. Okafor Achebe lost his mother when he was about two years old. Consequently, he was raised by his maternal uncle Udo of Ikenga village in Ogidi. Okafor was still a very young man when the Church Missionary Society of the British Anglican Church came to Ogidi in 1892. Like other curious young men of his village, Okafor went to listen to the **missionaries** as they went preaching and singing round the villages. Okafor was so captivated by the zeal and ardor of the evangelists that he started following them wherever they went. His uncle, who disliked the mournful hymns of the missionaries, was not aware that his nephew had become a regular "follower" of the preachers. However, when he eventually found out, he encouraged Okafor to continue so as to keep him informed of whatever "plot" the "crazy" missionaries were hatching. In the end, Okafor was baptized and named Isaiah. In 1904, he was sent for training at St. Paul's Teachers' College, **Awka**, the first of its kind in Eastern Nigeria. He met his future wife, **Janet Anaenechi**, at Awka while he was a student at St. Paul's College. Upon his graduation as a catechist, Isaiah returned to Ogidi and founded St. Paul's Anglican Church at Ikenga, Ogidi. Later he collaborated with David Okoye to build St. Philip's, a larger church for all Ogidi, at Akpakaogwe, Ogidi. Isaiah worked as a church teacher or catechist in several towns in Igboland until his retirement in 1935. Isaiah was a very devout Christian who raised his children under very strict Christian tradition. He refused any compromises between Igbo traditional ways and Christian ways. By the time of his death in 1962, Isaiah had relented in his outright condemnation of all things traditional as heathenish. He seemed to have re-alized the distinction between Christianity as an organized religion and a people's way of life.

Phanuel Akubueze Egejuru

ACHEBE, JANET ANAENECHI, the mother of Chinua Achebe, was the daughter of Iloegbunam of Umuike village in **Awka** town of Anambra State, **Nigeria**. Achebe's father, **Isaiah Okafor Achebe**, met Janet while he was a student at St. Paul's Teachers' College, Awka. Without wasting time, Isaiah told his family that he had found a girl to marry. Traditional marriage protocols soon followed, and the young couple became of-ficially engaged. In 1905, Janet was sent to St. Monica's school, the first Victorian fin-ishing school in Eastern Nigeria. Janet ex-perienced firsthand the comportment of a Victorian woman when she lived in the same house with and served Miss Warner, the prin-cipal of her school. After her training, Janet and Isaiah were married in 1909. Their wed-ding was conducted by the famous mission-ary, **G. T. Basden**, who would become the model for **Mr. Brown** of *Things Fall Apart*. Janet and her husband had six children: four sons and two daughters. Chinua is the last of the boys and the last but one of the six chil-dren. Janet believed strongly in giving chil-dren hands-on experience in housework even if the parents could afford paid house help. Her favorite dictum was: "She who leaves all the house chores to the servant is raising the servant and not her own children." Janet sur-vived her husband by five years; she died in 1967 during the **Nigerian Civil War**.

FURTHER READING

Phanuel A. Egejuru, *Chinua Achebe: Pure and Simple* (pp. 3–7); Ezenwa-Ohaeto, *Chinua Ache-be: A Biography*.

Phanuel Akubueze Egejuru

ACHEBE, REV. JOHN CHUKWUE-MEKA, the second son of **Isaiah** and **Janet Achebe**, played a crucial role in Chinua's ed-ucation. John persuaded their parents to al-low him to take Chinua to live with him at Nekede, where he was then teaching. Asked why he deemed it necessary to remove his brother from Ogidi, John said: "Why I came to take him was that I knew what God had told my father about the child. I knew that it was necessary to be careful over him. I found out somehow that he needed guidance." Thus, Chinua went to live with John at Nek-ede Central School. He read standard six there in 1943. It was from there that he took the entrance examinations to Government College Umuahia and to Dennis Memorial Grammar School (DMGS), Onitsha. Chinua gained admission to both schools. Their fa-ther wanted Chinua to attend DMGS where his other sons had studied. However, John insisted that Chinua should attend the Gov-ernment College, and he did. From Umuahia, Chinua gained entrance with a major schol-arship to **University College, Ibadan**, in 1948. When Chinua switched his field of study from medicine to arts, he lost his major scholarship. His brother John and his imme-diate elder brother, Augustine, teamed up and paid his fees. Chinua later received a schol-arship to finish up his studies in the arts. In effect, John was like a second father to Chinua, not only in directing the course of his education but in other intimate ways. John died in March 2000.

Phanuel Akubueze Egejuru

ACHEBE AND THE POLITICS OF REP-RESENTATION (2001), by Ode Ogede, is a critical study written late enough to be able to factor in several decades of the critical re-ception of Achebe's work. To a certain ex-tent, Ogede goes against the grain of much of this critical tradition by arguing that the immensely positive critical reception of *Things Fall Apart* has worked to the detriment of our appreciation of Achebe's other fiction, which, for Ogede, is actually superior to *Things Fall Apart* in a number of ways. In particular, Ogede finds that Achebe's first novel remains thoroughly trapped within Western intellectual and aesthetic traditions, thus limiting its effectiveness as a work of literary resistance to the legacy of European colonial domination of Africa. In his concern about the inability of *Things Fall Apart* to move beyond Western models, Ogede echoes the work of other critics, such as Michael Valdez Moses, who has been concerned that Achebe's first novel seems informed by a Hegelian sense of the historical inevitability of the Western colonial domination of Africa. In addition, Ogede calls attention to widely debated questions concerning the danger that English-language novels in general are in danger of perpetuating the Western cultural domination of Africa in the postcolonial era. Finally, Ogede wonders if the extremely positive reception of *Things Fall Apart* in the West might be at least partly due to the fact that it is so Western in its own outlook.

Ogede sees colonialism and its aftermath as the central historical events that most centrally conditioned the development of African literature. He grants that *Things Fall Apart* played a crucial role in establishing the African novel as a viable form and in encouraging other Africans to write. However, he feels that *Things Fall Apart* relies so crucially on the model of Greek tragedy in the construction of its plot that it is unable to offer genuine alternatives to the colonialist legacy. Ogede concludes that Achebe's reliance in his early work on such colonialist forms often undermines his own anticolonialist intentions. On the other hand, Ogede also concludes that this and other limitations of *Things Fall Apart* may derive largely from limitations in Achebe's early vision and, in

particular, from Achebe's inability to move beyond the lingering effects of his own colonial education at this early stage in his career.

More radical African writers, such as **Ngugi wa Thiong'o**, Ousmane Sembéne, and Festus Iyayi, have, for Ogede, been more successful in transcending colonialist forms, though Ogede also grants that such writers drew significant inspiration from Achebe's example. Also, Ogede argues that Achebe himself, in his short stories and later novels, begins to move in innovative directions that genuinely challenge the legacy of colonialism. *Anthills of the Savannah*, which Ogede sees as an "ideological breakthrough" toward a more effective political mode of writing, is a particularly crucial text in this regard. In addition, Ogede is very enthusiastic about the aesthetic value and political effectiveness of Achebe's short stories, which he feels have not received nearly as much critical attention and respect as they deserve. For Ogede, these stories portray an Africa that is beginning to move beyond the legacy of colonial domination and thus "constitute precious documents which portray socio-political, cultural, and economic changes of the community" (102). Indeed, Ogede's principal point is not to detract from the critical reputation of *Things Fall Apart* so much as to call attention to Achebe's short stories and later novels and thus to bring those works out of the critical shadow of Achebe's first novel.

FURTHER READING

Michael Valdez Moses, *The Novel and the Globalization of Culture*; Emmanuel Ngara, "Achebe as Artist"; Ngugi wa Thiong'o, *Decolonising the Mind*.

M. Keith Booker

ACHEBE THE ORATOR: THE ART OF PERSUASION IN CHINUA ACHEBE'S NOVELS (2001), by Chinwe Christiana Okechukwu, approaches Achebe's novels as arguments with specific didactic intentions, exploring the rhetorical strategies through which those intentions are largely fulfilled. Okechukwu is from the same **Igbo** village in Ogidi as Achebe, and she occasionally notes Achebe's use of modes of argument derived from traditional Igbo oral culture. Her principal emphasis, however, is on reading Achebe's techniques of argumentation within Western rhetorical traditions from Aristotle onward, including an occasional appeal to modern literary theorists such as Kenneth Burke and Mikhail Bakhtin. Nevertheless, Achebe's arguments, according to Okechukwu, are aimed primarily at an Igbo audience in a desire to overcome the legacy of colonialist indoctrination and to teach the Igbo that they have a rich history filled with social and cultural traditions of which they can be proud. For Okechukwu, "Achebe sees himself as a teacher who uses his novels to teach his people to recognize the source of their problem in order for them to stop accepting the notion of racial inferiority" (7).

Noting that Achebe's five novels together "encompass the entire sociohistorical and political experience of Nigeria, from precolonial times to the present," Okechukwu begins with a brief overview of her vision of Achebe's mission as a writer (2). She then devotes one subsequent chapter to each of the five novels, followed by a conclusion that summarizes the findings of the earlier chapters. Chapter 2, on *Things Fall Apart*, argues that, in his first novel, Achebe presents a thoroughly convincing argument that traditional Igbo society and culture were highly sophisticated and at least as worthy as the Western society and culture that shattered and replaced them with the coming of colonialism. Particularly interesting is Okechukwu's exploration in this chapter of Achebe's representation of Igbo oratory and of the way in which the coming of the British to the Igbolands initiates a breakdown in com-

munication and in the traditional function of language.

Okechukwu continues this theme of the breakdown of rhetoric in the chapter on *Arrow of God*. In particular, she argues that this novel deals centrally with the disastrous consequences of the failure of the Igbo leadership to exercise rhetoric properly in the face of the British invasion of Igboland. Focusing on the confrontation between **Ezeulu** and **Nwaka**, Okechukwu concludes that Ezeulu's arguments have the force of truth but lack persuasion because they are not presented with the proper rhetorical strategies. Nwaka, on the other hand, exercises these strategies effectively, but in support of a false argument. In contrast, British and Christian leaders such as **John Goodcountry** use rhetoric both effectively and appropriately, resulting in a victory of Christianity over traditional Igbo religion.

In chapter 4, Okechukwu counters the frequent critical view that *No Longer at Ease* is one of Achebe's weaker novels. Focusing on the novel's use of rhetoric and treatment of rhetorical themes, she concludes that it is, in fact, a highly effective novel that well achieves Achebe's goal of exploring the predicament of the young elite in postcolonial Nigeria in ways that both condemn corruption and dispute the stereotype that African societies and people are somehow inherently corrupt. In particular, for Okechukwu, this novel convincingly links postcolonial corruption to the legacy of colonialism, attributing the corruption of postcolonial Nigeria to structures and attitudes put in place during and by British colonial rule. For one thing, she shows that the diverse groups yoked together in postcolonial Nigeria are forced to use English as a common language of communication. However, the words of this foreign language lack moral force as well as authenticity because the speakers who use them are not organically connected to them.

In addition, Okechukwu's exploration of rhetoric and oratory in the novel is used to demonstrate the incompatibility between inherited African cultural traditions and the Western education received by postcolonial leaders such as **Obi Okonkwo**, an incompatibility that places such leaders in an extremely difficult situation that lends itself directly to corruption.

The chapter on *A Man of the People* continues this exploration of the ways in which the legacy of colonialism continues to haunt the social, political, and cultural landscape of modern Nigeria. Here, the rhetorical tools wielded by politicians, largely inherited from colonialism, are shown to be effective as a means of gaining power for the politicians but entirely ineffective as a means of uniting the people of Nigeria and leading them to a better future. The false and self-serving nature of this rhetoric leads to a situation that seems rectifiable only by the extreme cleansing measure of a military takeover.

In this sense, as Okechukwu notes in chapter 6, *Anthills of the Savannah* can be seen as a direct sequel to *A Man of the People*, demonstrating the pitfalls of this military rule, which, rather than cleansing the rhetorical landscape, turns out to use many of the same false rhetorical strategies as the politicians but now backs them up with the force of arms, resulting in an even worse situation. In this novel, meanwhile, Achebe also indicts Nigerian intellectuals for their failure to make a positive contribution to overcoming this situation, largely because their arrogance separates them from the people and interferes with their ability to construct arguments that the people will find convincing. In addition, Achebe identifies the modern media as a culprit in the continuing decay of rhetoric in postcolonial Nigeria, authoritarian one-way broadcasts having replaced the dialogue and discussion that were so crucial to traditional Igbo culture.

In her conclusion, Okechukwu reiterates these arguments, concluding that Achebe's very effective deployment of Aristotelian rhetoric is especially appropriate because it is also consonant with the "traditional praxis" of Igbo society, which placed great emphasis on rhetoric and oratory (148). All of Okechukwu's readings of Achebe's novels emphasize both his own use of rhetoric and argumentation and his treatment of rhetorical themes in his novels. The effectiveness of his arguments is, for her, a great achievement that makes his novels powerful and important, while at the same time demonstrating the inappropriateness of occasional critical complaints that Achebe's didacticism diminishes the value of his art.

FURTHER READING

Aristotle, *Art of Rhetoric*; Mikhail M. Bakhtin, *The Dialogic Imagination;* Wayne Booth, *The Rhetoric of Fiction*; Kenneth Burke, *Language as a Symbolic Action*; Kalu Ogbaa, *Gods, Oracles, and Divination*.

M. Keith Booker

ACHEBE'S WORLD: THE HISTORICAL AND CULTURAL CONTEXT OF THE NOVELS OF CHINUA ACHEBE (1980), by **Robert M. Wren**, provides a wealth of background historical, social, and cultural information useful to an understanding of Achebe's first four novels and some of the short stories. This information is consistently grounded in the fictional work it serves to explain so that the reader is never far from plot and fictional context, adrift in detail that does not serve the literary work's purposes. Indeed, Wren's book is not merely a compendium of information: it is directly aimed at explication of specific aspects of Achebe's writing. Thus, one might describe Wren's as a combination of old-style historical criticism and enduring *explication du texte*.

Wren works from a central assertion that art is experience transformed by a sort of dialectic, which clearly speaks to and illuminates Achebe's commitment as writer and teacher. Wren himself provides a substantial appreciation of Achebe's aesthetics, though his demonstration of the richness of Achebe's engagement with his historical and cultural context is particularly valuable in making the reader more deeply aware of the realities of Achebe's artistry. Of particular note are Wren's lengthy and well-informed political discussions. The reader is given more than a passing knowledge of the politics of those Nigerians to be considered the founding fathers of the Nigerian state: among them, Dr. M. I. Okpara, Chief Sam Akintola, Tafawa Balewa, Dr. **Nnamdi Azikiwe**, and Chief Obafemi Awolowo. The reader learns that **Lord Frederick Lugard**'s notion of British **indirect rule** did not work well in **Nigeria**, although Lugard continues to be lauded in Great Britain for this innovation in imperial rule.

Wren's sociocultural discussions of mission schools, **pidgin English**, cannibalism, and European perceptions of Africans are particularly useful, preparing the reader for Wren's depiction of what he calls "Achebe country," which he discusses in detail. In this discussion Wren clarifies for the non-African reader ideas of community and social order that may be confusing given Achebe's leaving these to contextual explanation within the early novels. There is further discussion of the efforts of European **missionaries** with the explanation of the role of the Church Missionary Society. Most noteworthy is the discussion of archival records of European sources so influential in formulating European ideas of Africa and Africans.

Also of special interest is Wren's discussion of **Joyce Cary**'s novel *Mister Johnson* with its claim that the character Rudbeck is a precursor for Gulley Jimson in Cary's *The Horse's Mouth*. This discussion accurately exposes those things in Cary's novel that are objectionable for their racism and ethnocentrism while making the very important point that the African world depicted in the book "is recognizably the world of ordinary affairs, and yet still beyond the colonial officer's understanding" (108–9).

In addition to his explication of the sociopolitical and historical contexts of Achebe's early novels and stories, Wren provides his reader with numerous and telling illustrations, maps, and photographs, as well as a glossary, lengthy bibliography, and notes on names, money, and pidgin English. Wren's is a critical work replete with implicit suggestions for further research in Nigerian literature. Even the experienced teacher of Achebe's fiction will find Wren's book essential reading, whatever his or her own critical approaches to literary works.

Susan Williams

ADAMMA, a young nursing student who is a passenger on the northbound bus on which **Chris Oriko**, **Braimoh**, and **Emmanuel Obete** attempt to flee to **Abazon** late in *Anthills of the Savannah*. The amorous Obete unsuccessfully tries to pick her up on the bus, but Obete and Adamma later become friends and members of the circle of survivors and friends of Oriko and **Ikem Osodi**.

M. Keith Booker

ADEYEMI, MR., a lawyer who gets into trouble with **Mr. Justice William Galloway** at the trial of **Obi Okonkwo** at the beginning of *No Longer at Ease*. He arrives late for court because his car breaks down on the way.

M. Keith Booker

ADEZE, **Ezeulu**'s and **Okuata**'s eldest daughter, who is married and lives in **Umuezeani** (*Arrow of God*, chapter 7).

Rachel R. Reynolds

AFO. See **Market days**.

"AFRICA AND HER WRITERS." Achebe essay. See *Morning Yet on Creation Day*.

THE AFRICA THAT NEVER WAS (1970), by Dorothy Hammond and Alta Jablow (reissued in 1977 with revisions, as *The Myth of Africa*), is a study of British representations of Africa that convincingly demonstrates the ways in which these representations have arisen more from Western fantasies about Africa than from material facts about African reality. Chapters on ten separate patterns of stereotypes (such as "The Dark Labyrinth" and "The Strange Woman") are preceded by an introduction and followed by an extremely extensive and useful bibliography of British writings about Africa. Covering more than 400 years of both fiction and nonfiction, Hammond and Jablow find that British writings about Africa are informed by a very consistent pattern of primitivist myths in which Africa and Africans emerge as the polar opposite of Britain and the British. It thus becomes clear that negative and denigrating stereotypes about Africa have the function of helping the British to envision themselves positively as noble, honorable, and sophisticated.

To a great extent, then, *The Africa That Never Was* can be seen as an important founding text of **postcolonial studies**, predating **Edward Said**'s *Orientalism* (often seen as the crucial founding text of colonial discourse analysis) by eight years. However, Hammond and Jablow employ more conventional anthropological and psychological methodologies and ideas than does Said, whose work is crucially informed by the post-structuralist discourse theories of Michel Foucault. In particular, Hammond and Jablow envision British stereotypical representations of Africa and Africans as arising from individual projections of shared unconscious fantasies into the real world. This vision of the stereotyping of Africa also differs from that of Robinson and Gallagher, who preceded Hammond and Jablow in 1961 with their study of the ways in which British visions of Africa in the late nineteenth century worked in the interest of official power. Other forerunners of Hammond and Jablow include Philip D. Curtin's *The Image of Africa* (1964) and Es'kia Mphalele's early *The African Image* (1962), which studies Western fictional representations of Africa from an African perspective. Finally, the work of Hammond and Jablow also serves as a forerunner to the more recent work of the African philosopher V. Y. Mudimbe (again significantly influenced by Foucault) on the imaginative construction of "the idea of Africa" in Western thought.

Achebe cites the work of Hammond and Jablow in **Home and Exile**, noting the value of their demonstration of how "a body of fantasy and myth about Africa developed into a tradition with a vast storehouse of lurid images to which writers went again and again through the centuries to draw 'material' for their books" (26–27). On the other hand, later in this same book, Achebe is a bit perplexed by the generosity with which Hammond and Jablow express appreciation for the "skill and subtlety" of writers such as **Joseph Conrad** and **Graham Greene** in their literary manipulation of British stereotypes about Africa. For Achebe, "literature is always badly served when an author's artistic insight yields place to stereotype and malice" (41).

FURTHER READING

Philip D. Curtin, *The Image of Africa*; John Cullen Gruesser, *White on Black*; G. D. Killam, *Africa in English Fiction*; Es'kia Mphalele, *The African Image*; V. Y. Mudimbe, *The Idea of Africa* and *The Invention of Africa*; Ronald E. Robinson and John A. Gallagher, *Africa and the Victorians*; Edward Said, *Orientalism*.

M. Keith Booker

"AFRICAN LITERATURE AS RESTO-RATION OF CELEBRATION." See *Chinua Achebe: A Celebration*.

AFRICAN SHORT STORIES (1985) is a collection of short stories edited by **Chinua Achebe** and **C. L. Innes** and first published in the Heinemann **African Writers Series** (AWS 270), then republished by Heinemann in 1987. Subtitled "Twenty Short Stories from Across the Continent," the volume contains five stories from West Africa—by Sembene Ousmane, **Ama Ata Aidoo**, Odun Balogun, David Owoyele, and Chinua Achebe ("Civil Peace," originally published in *Okike* 2, 1971); five stories from East Africa—by Jomo Kenyatta, Grace Ogot, Abdulrazak Gurnah, Leonard Kibera, and **Ngugi wa Thiong'o**; three stories from North Africa—by Alifa Rifaat, Tayeb Salih, and Mohamed El-Bisatie; and seven stories from South Africa—by B. L. Honwana, Nadine Gordimer, Ahmed Essop, Dambudzo Marechera, Ezekial Mphahlale, Bessie Head, and Mafika Gwala. Some of these writers are familiar names as novelists; others are less well known. All of the stories illustrate, as Achebe notes in his introduction to the volume, that the short story, like the novel, has "achieved distinctiveness in the hands of its practitioners" among African writers (vii). In the introduction, Achebe makes a number of points about the collection and the choice of authors and their stories. The stories reveal their indebtedness to African oral traditions, a fact that has been generally acknowledged since African writing in English first appeared. This being so, "there is no necessity to demonstrate the link further by including traditional tales" in the collection (vii). The editors have aimed to demonstrate the "rich contrasts" that exist between the broad geographical regions of Africa the stories represent (vii). More important than the contrasts, however, in Achebe's view is "a striking

spirit of unity which is more than a political cliché" (vii–viii). Achebe briefly characterizes the content of several of the stories—by Kenyatta, Aidoo and Rifaat—to suggest why this is so. Achebe commends the book to both the general reader and students and teachers as a way into an acquaintance with the art and world of African fiction generally.

The book includes brief biographical notes on the writers of the stories.

Douglas Killam

"THE AFRICAN WRITER AND THE BIAFRAN CAUSE." See *Morning Yet on Creation Day*.

"THE AFRICAN WRITER AND THE ENGLISH LANGUAGE." See *Morning Yet on Creation Day*."

AFRICAN WRITERS SERIES. The publication in 1958 of Achebe's first novel, *Things Fall Apart*, and its immediate success in Britain and North America were the undisputed catalysts for the creation of the African Writers Series (AWS) by Heinemann Eductional Books (HEB). In 1959, the director of HEB, **Alan Hill**, went to Nigeria, where news of Achebe's novel was greeted initially with much skepticism, to find and publish new African authors. His travel extended through several sub-Saharan countries and confirmed a general lack of publishing of works by African writers. In 1960, Hill contracted Van Milne, a West African specialist, and the idea for the series was born. It was launched in 1962 with the publication of four books: Achebe's *Things Fall Apart* and *No Longer at Ease*, Kenneth Kaunda's *Zambia Shall Be Free*, and Cyprian Ekwensi's *Burning Grass*. Achebe was appointed general editor and advisor to the series, a role that he undertook without pay during the first decade of the series, which saw the publication of 100 titles. His editorial skills and discretion helped shape the character of AWS, and his success and reputation acted as a magnet that drew writers such as Ngugi wa Thiong'o and Wole Soyinka to the series. In 1967 James Currey became the director of AWS, and he promoted the publication of a wide range of writing, including drama and poetry, that was affordable to its intended African audience of limited economic means. The books were sold and distributed through the existing textbook distribution system, and sales were boosted by the inclusion of some of its titles in the school curriculums of countries such as **Nigeria**. While not all titles were successful, the earnings from Achebe's works alone provided an economic backbone that allowed the series to continue and to subsidize the publishing of lesser-known writers. With a new design and a much heralded relaunch in 1993, as well as the subsequent development of the Caribbean Writers Series and the Asian Writers Series, the African Writers Series remains a significant force in the development of Anglophone literatures throughout the world.

FURTHER READING

Alan Hill, *In Pursuit of Publishing*; Graham Huggan, *The Postcolonial Exotic*; Camille Lizarríbar Buxó, "Something Else Will Stand beside It."

Camille Lizarríbar Buxó

AGATHA, the housegirl who works for **Beatrice Okoh** in *Anthills of the Savannah*. Efficient and rather spunky, Agatha is a member of one of the evangelical churches that have recently sprung up in **Bassa**.

M. Keith Booker

AGBALA. In *Things Fall Apart*, the mysterious and powerful Oracle of the Hills and Caves, seen only by the priestess of the Oracle. Achebe's depiction of the oracle is based on the historical Agbala oracle at **Awka**, which exerted great influence on **Igbo** culture. This oracle was consequently destroyed by the British colonial government as part of the **Bende-Onitsha punitive expedition** because they felt that its power interfered with their rule. The term is also used either for a woman or for a man who has taken no title. The young **Okonkwo** is mortified to realize that his father, **Unoka**, is *agbala*.

M. Keith Booker

AGBASIOSO, Ilo Agbasioso, name of a large hamlet or possibly a town from which the medicine man Aniegboka comes (*Arrow of God*, chapter 11). The Ilo Agbasioso is mentioned only once briefly; Achebe's works are so rich with proper noun references that occasionally a person, place, spirit or other noun may get mentioned in passing never to be referred to again. The effusion of proper names endows a sense of verisimilitude in Achebe's novels, and for Igbo-speaking readers, the names have rich and multifarious connotations.

Rachel R. Reynolds

AGE-GROUPS. See **Otakagu** for an extended discussion on Achebe's presentation of **Igbo** age-groups.

Rachel R. Reynolds

AGHADIKE, alias Anyanafummo, healer of great repute throughout Igboland (*Arrow of God*, chapter 11).

Rachel R. Reynolds

AGWU. In *Anthills of the Savannah* (chapters 8 and 9), the god of diviners, artists, and healers. He is described as "capricious," and possession by Agwu is described as akin to madness, though it also bestows creativity, vision, and inspiration.

M. Keith Booker

AGWU, a minor god of **Umuaro** in *Arrow of God*, chapter 18.

Rachel R. Reynolds

AGWUEGBO, master carver in the region of **Umuaro** in *Arrow of God*, chapter 9.

Rachel R. Reynolds

AHIARA, Igbo town decimated by British-led troops in the **Bende-Onitsha punitive expedition** of 1905 after the people of Ahiara had killed **J. F. Stewart,** an Englishman traveling by bicycle in the area. The story is fictionalized in the account of the fate of the village of **Abame** in *Things Fall Apart*.
FURTHER READING
    Robert M. Wren, "*Things Fall Apart* in Its Time and Place."

M. Keith Booker

AIDOO, AMA ATA. Ghanaian poet, dramatist, and novelist, born 1942. See *Our Sister Killjoy*.

AINA, the wife of **Braimoh** in *Anthills of the Savannah*. A Muslim, she is a native of southern **Abazon**. When she joins the Christian celebration of the birth of the girl **Amaechina** in chapter 18, it serves as an emblem of solidarity among different religious and ethnic groups in postcolonial **Kangan**.

M. Keith Booker

AJOFIA. In *Things Fall Apart*, the leading *egwugwu* of **Umuofia**. In chapter 22, he is identified as the head of and spokesmen for the nine ancestors who administer justice in the clan.

M. Keith Booker

AKAKANMA, the name of **Moses Unachukwu**'s **age-group** in *Arrow of God*.

Rachel R. Reynolds

AKILO, MRS. AGNES, a beautiful woman barrister who practices law in a firm owned jointly by herself and her husband in a town eighty miles from the capital city of **Bori** in the fictional African postcolonial nation featured in *A Man of the People*. In chapter 5, she comes to the capital and arranges to have dinner with **Chief Nanga,** who, with his wife away visiting their home village of **Anata,** rearranges his schedule to attend the dinner. Narrator **Odili Samalu** assumes that Nanga and Mrs. Akilo are sleeping together. Indeed, we later learn that Nanga confided in Samaluthe next morning that Mrs. Akilo regularly came to sleep with him for twenty-five pounds each time, a literalization of the theme of symbolic prostitution that runs through the entire novel.

M. Keith Booker

AKUEBUE is a principal character in *Arrow of God*, and he is one of the only remaining men in **Ezeulu**'s **age-group.** Akuebue frequently provides counsel to both **Ezeulu** and **Edogo.** Note also that the aged Akuebue is the only man left alive with whom Ezeulu can have joking conversations, where both are equals and friends. Akuebue frequently brings the distant Ezeulu "back to the people around him" (chapter 9), and the reader is given entrée to Akuebue's thoughts frequently as a means to discern what motivates Ezeulu: "Akuebue knew the man better than his children or his wives" (chapter 14). In a similar manner, **Obierika** from *Things Fall Apart* also serves this sort of plot device, in which trusted age-mates know the minds of others and explain character motivations. Akuebue has a daughter named **Udenkwo.**

Rachel R. Reynolds

AKUEKE, daughter of **Obierika** in *Things Fall Apart*. In chapter 8, she is described as about sixteen and ripe for marriage. In that chapter, her suitor, **Ibe,** and his relatives call on Obierika to negotiate a **bride-price**, which is settled at twenty bags of cowries. The wedding itself is celebrated in chapter 12. In *No Longer at Ease*, we learn that the British colonial authorities subsequently banned the practice of the bride-price, though it is argued there that the tradition continues as a clandestine one and that the British ban has merely driven the price upward.

M. Keith Booker

AKUEKE, Ezeulu's and **Okuata**'s second oldest daughter, who in the early chapters of *Arrow of God* separates from her abusive husband, **Ibe**. Akueke's half brother **Obika** eventually works to restore the marriage. Obika does so by terrorizing and beating Ibe, although it takes some careful diplomacy by Ezeulu to restore the marriage once Ibe's publicly shamed family begins negotiations to take Akueke back. The passages having to do with this marriage are often alluded to as an ethnographically accurate example of how the abuse of women was dealt with by families in pre-colonial Nigeria. Akueke has a daughter named **Nkechi**.

Rachel R. Reynolds

AKUENI, one of the daughters of **Uchendu** in *Things Fall Apart*. She has given birth to and thrown away many twin babies because they are regarded as taboo by the customs of the clan.

M. Keith Booker

AKUKALIA OKEKE appears in *Arrow of God* as a character whose actions set off the course of events in the novel. He is the man of title from **Umuaro** who is elected to go on a diplomatic mission to discuss a land dispute with the people of **Okperi** village. A hothead, Akukalia is cautioned by an elder of his village, Ogbuefi **Egonwanne**, to use diplomacy and to "put your fearlessness in a bag" (chapter 2). Akukalia does not heed this advice and commits an abomination during his visit to Okperi by deliberately destroying a man's personal god, embodied in an *ikenga* statue. He is subsequently killed by **Ebo**, the man whose *ikenga* has been broken. Thus begins the war between Okperi and Umuaro.

Rachel R. Reynolds

AKUNNA, a great man of **Umuofia** in *Things Fall Apart*. It is a sign of the great progress made by Christian missionaries in the region that he sends his son to learn the white man's knowledge in the school run by the missionary, **Mr. Brown**, in chapter 21. Akunna discusses theology with Mr. Brown in that same chapter, comparing the **Igbo** gods with the Christian one.

M. Keith Booker

AKWU NRO, a festival specific to the village of **Umuachala** in which widows honor their husbands (*Arrow of God*, chapter 17).

Rachel R. Reynolds

AKWUBA, playmate of **Ezeulu**'s youngest children who teaches them the saying: "*Eke nekwo onye uka!*" or "**Python** run, there's a Christian here!" This charm against the python—which also indicates the usurpation of traditional power by impending Christian conversions—begins to haunt Ezeulu, echoing deeply in his mind near the end of *Arrow of God*.

Rachel R. Reynolds

ALI, MOHAMMED (also Muhammad Ali, Mehemet Ali) (1769–1849), referred to in chapter 11 of *No Longer at Ease*. Born in present-day Greece, Ali was an Ottoman soldier of Albanian ancestry who ascended the ranks to become governor and pasha of Egypt from 1805 until his death. During his long rule Ali inhibited potentially progressive forces within Egypt for the sake of enhancing his own power. Nevertheless, he instituted various military, governmental, agricultural, and educational reforms, contributing to the future establishment of an independent, modern Egyptian state. His descendants ruled Egypt until 1952. **Obi Okonkwo**, protagonist of *No Longer at Ease*, once read that "in his old age [Ali] worked in frenzy to modernize his country before his death." This is called to Obi's mind by the work habits and apparent sense of mission to improve Africa displayed by his boss, **William Green**.

Thomas J. Lynn

ALLEN, GEORGE, District Commissioner, is the author of the fictional book *The Pacification of the Primitive Tribes of the Lower Niger*, which is itself loosely based on the story of **Okonkwo** from *Things Fall Apart*. In *Arrow of God*, Achebe provides us with a selection from Allen's work entitled "the Call," which ironically espouses the nobility of spirit of those who become soldiers of the empire. The passage (in chapter 3) is a classic demonstration of Achebe's skill at satirizing language, in this case, the language of those anthropologists in service to colonial governments. Furthermore, the character reading the fictional passage, Tony Clarke, reads for inspiration and self-definition only *after* having answered "the Call." In passages like these, we see Achebe's inordinate sensitivity to the richly ironic ways that colonialists themselves were brought into the process of "**pacification**," creating their own rhetoric about the nobility of their endeavors and developing complex ways of believing it while bringing it into practice. When *Arrow of God* deals with the inner psychological state of colonizers, Achebe outlines an aspect of the deployment of **indirect rule** that often goes unexplored in other fictional sources.

Rachel R. Reynolds

ALOYSIUS, an African servant of **Tony Clarke** in *Arrow of God*. Through the name

alone, Achebe alludes to the position in the colonial establishment of those who were early converts to Christianity. The name is also typical of twentieth-century Nigerian Christian names, which are commonly derived from lists of saints in the Anglican and Catholic Churches.

Rachel R. Reynolds

ALUSI, a spirit, often of the kind also called "mammy water." The term refers to the Nigerian name for the water spirits that are an important traditional deity, especially for **Igbo** women. At the inception of *Arrow of God*, we find out that the (female) oracle of **Umuaro** has given the women of the town a warning: the boulder over **Ota**, the closest water source, is about to topple into the stream, reflecting the displeasure of the spirits. This little passage foreshadows that the total cosmological universe around Umuaro is in upheaval.

Rachel R. Reynolds

AMADI. In *Things Fall Apart*, a leper who sometimes passes near the villages of **Umuofia**. Among the clan, a polite name for leprosy is "the white skin," and Amadi is jokingly compared to the white Europeans who have recently arrived in the area at the end of chapter 8.

M. Keith Booker

AMADI, a prosperous farmer of **Mbanta**, described as the husband of **Nneka** in chapter 17 of *Things Fall Apart*.

M. Keith Booker

AMADIORA. In *Things Fall Apart*, the god of the sky and of thunder and lightning.

M. Keith Booker

AMAECHINA, the infant girl born to **Elewa** (and fathered by the now-deceased **Ikem Osodi**) at the end of *Anthills of the Savan-*

nah. The name, normally given to boys, means "may the path never close." That the girl is given a male name (and that she is named by women rather than men, as would be the tradition) serves as one of the novel's numerous challenges to conventional gender boundaries. Her birth at the end of the novel (after the deaths of Osodi and **Chris Oriko**) symbolizes the continuity of life and hope for the future.

M. Keith Booker

AMALINZE THE CAT, a champion Igbo wrestler. At the beginning of *Things Fall Apart*, we learn that Amalinze had been unbeaten for seventeen years until he was thrown by **Okonkwo**, an achievement that helped Okonkwo rise to fame in the nine villages of **Umuofia** and beyond.

M. Keith Booker

AMALU. An **Ogbuefi** of the village **Umuachala** who is very ill and then dies despite various ministrations. Amalu's death provides Achebe with reason to provide an ethnographic-like description of the passing of an elder; he also describes a few medicine rituals and how they might have been regarded (*Arrow of God*, chapter 11.) Near the end of the novel, it is Amalu's family who must break the fast before the **Feast of the New Yam** in order to properly bury their father, whose funeral has been delayed (chapter 19). Son is Aneto.

Rachel R. Reynolds

AMECHI, sickly baby son of **Amoge** and **Edogo** in *Arrow of God*.

Rachel R. Reynolds

AMIKWU, the youngest of the five sons of **Uchendu** (and thus a cousin of **Okonkwo**) in *Things Fall Apart*.

M. Keith Booker

AMOGE, wife of **Edogo** and mother of **Amechi** in *Arrow of God*.

Rachel R. Reynolds

AMONG THE IBOS OF NIGERIA (1921, full title *Among the Ibos of Nigeria: An account of the Curious & Interesting Habits, Customs & Beliefs of a little known African People by one who has for many years lived amongst them on close & intimate terms*), an anthropological work on the Igbo by the missionary G. T. Basden. Despite the datedness of its methodology and its blatantly colonial perspective, Basden's work is an important source for **Igbo** institutions in the early twentieth century, and Achebe revisits and corrects many of Basden's themes in *Things Fall Apart* and *Arrow of God*.
FURTHER READING
  G. T. Basden, *Niger Ibos*.

Nicholas Brown

AMUMEGBU, of **Umuogwugwu**, is a man of **Obika**'s age who comes to **Umuachala** in order to perform a special masquerade in a new mask for the festival of **Akwu Nro** (*Arrow of God*, chapter 17).

Rachel R. Reynolds

ANASI, the first wife of the wealthy **Nwakibie** in *Things Fall Apart*. A tall, middle-aged woman of impressive bearing, she seems well suited for the role of the leader of the women of Nwakibie's large and prosperous family. When **Okonkwo** takes palm-wine to Nwakibie in chapter 3, the other wives, out of respect, must wait for the arrival of Anasi before they can partake of the wine.

M. Keith Booker

ANATA, the home village of **Chief Nanga** in *A Man of the People*. It is also the site of the **Anata Grammar School**, where **Odili Samalu**, the narrator of that novel, teaches as the book begins and where Nanga had taught sixteen years earlier, when Samalu was a student there.

M. Keith Booker

ANATA GRAMMAR SCHOOL, a grammar school in the village of **Anata** in *A Man of the People*. Now presided over by **Jonathan Nwege**, the principal, it is the site of a visit by prominent politician and Minister of Culture **Chief Nanga** at the beginning of the novel. Nanga's visit, for which Nwege makes elaborate preparations, is particularly significant because Nanga had taught at the school many years earlier. Indeed, we learn that narrator **Odili Samalu**, who teaches at the school as the book begins, had been a student at the school when Nanga taught there. Late in the book, Samalu is sacked by Nwege because he undertakes an electoral campaign to unseat Nanga as the member of parliament from Anata and the surrounding region.

M. Keith Booker

ANENE, the first husband of **Ekwefi** in *Things Fall Apart*. Though in love with Okonkwo, Ekwefi married Anene because **Okonkwo** was at that time too poor to marry. Ekwefi runs away from Anene after two years of marriage so that she can marry the newly prominent Okonkwo.

M. Keith Booker

ANENE, one of the sons of **Obierika** in *Things Fall Apart*. Anene is a friend of **Nwoye** and sends his greetings to him via Obierika, who visits **Okonkwo** and family in exile in **Mbanta** in chapter 15.

M. Keith Booker

ANENE, MR. In chapter 4 of *No Longer at Ease*, a primary school teacher of **Obi Okonkwo's** who correctly predicted that Obi would go to England for more advanced education. In the passage in which Mr. Anene

is recalled by **Joseph Okeke**, the unnamed headmaster of the same school is recalled by **Obi Okonkwo**. The two friends attended the school during World War II, during which time the headmaster told the young children "every morning that for every palm-kernel they picked they were buying a nail for Hitler's coffin." The adult Obi considers this to have been "quite immoral" on the part of the headmaster and implies that his writing a letter at that time to Hitler, for whom he may have "felt sorry," was a reaction against the headmaster's urgings. (It may be noted that the headmaster of the primary school that Achebe attended, also during World War II, called another student there "an offspring of Satan and flogged him before the whole school" for writing a letter to Hitler [Ezenwa-Ohaeto 13, with quotation from Achebe "The Education" 55].)

FURTHER READING

Chinua Achebe, "The Education of a 'British Protected Child' "; Ezenwa-Ohaeto, *Chinua Achebe: A Biography*.

Thomas J. Lynn

ANETO, an **Igbo** man hanged by the British colonial government in **Umuofia** in *Things Fall Apart* because he killed another man, **Oduche**, in a fight over the ownership of a piece of land. In chapter 20, the colonial government grants the disputed piece of land to the family of **Nnama**, who has given much money to the white man's messengers and interpreter.

M. Keith Booker

ANETO. Eldest son of **Amalu** in *Arrow of God* (chapter 19).

Rachel R. Reynolds

ANI, the **Igbo** earth goddess, regarded by the clan in *Things Fall Apart* as the owner of all land and the source of all fertility. Considered the ultimate judge of morality and conduct, Ani plays a bigger role in the daily lives of the people of **Umuofia** than any other diety. In chapter 4, **Okonkwo** must pay penance to Ani after he disrupts the **Week of Peace** prior to planting by beating his youngest wife, **Ojiugo**.

M. Keith Booker

ANI MO, afterworld for the souls of the dead. Some rest here before they are reincarnated as newborns while others stay in *ani mo*. Mentioned in *Arrow of God*.

Rachel R. Reynolds

ANICHEBE UDEOZO is a man of **Umuaro** of high title who pleads with **Ezeulu** to begin the **Feast of the New Yam** in *Arrow of God* (chapter 18).

Rachel R. Reynolds

ANIEGBOKA, medicine man–diviner who performs the rite of marriage for **Obika** and **Okuata**. Aniegboka slightly changes the marriage sacrifice ritual by keeping a sacrificial chicken for his own supper. He does so all the while boasting that he assiduously maintains tradition. Aniegboka's minor change in ritual practice, commented upon by **Edogo** and Okuata, is a means by which Achebe depicts the incremental ways that social change is manifested in ritual practice (*Arrow of God*, chapter 11).

Rachel R. Reynolds

ANIETITI, a plot of land partially owned by Akuebue, mentioned in the opening of chapter 11 of *Arrow of God*. In this passage, Achebe glosses agricultural management, **Igbo**-style. Akuebue is expertly preparing for hired day laborers to plant seed yams on the faraway family plot, which has particularly rich soil. It may be that Achebe is indicating that Anietiti is land obtained at the outskirts of Umuaro in exchange for debts or repara-

tions following a war, a common practice in pre-colonial Igboland.

Rachel R. Reynolds

ANINTA, the village in which **Isaac Okonkwo** served as catechist during the second year of his marriage to **Hannah Okonkwo**. As described in chapter 19 of *No Longer at Ease*, Hannah provoked the wrath of the villagers when she killed the he-goat dedicated to **Udo**, a "great god of Aninta." However, the furor over the goat's death soon abated, and the narrator declares that this signified how "successful had been the emasculation of the clan by the white man's religion and government." This emasculation was the outcome of an incident identical to one referred to repeatedly in *Arrow of God*: Captain **Thomas K. Winterbottom**'s order that the firearms used in the feud between the people of **Umuaro** and **Okperi** be destroyed. The version of the event in *No Longer at Ease* discloses that, fifteen years prior to Isaac and Hannah's arrival in Aninta, "the white man's government" had ordered the destruction of all the firearms there after the village had "reduced" the neighboring village "to submission." This occurrence apparently robbed Aninta of its vitality.

Thomas J. Lynn

ANINTA, a town in the general area of **Umuaro** in *Arrow of God*.

Rachel R. Reynolds

ANOSI, Ezeulu's gossipy neighbor from *Arrow of God*.

Rachel R. Reynolds

ANTHILLS OF THE SAVANNAH (1987), Achebe's latest and most complex novel, was short-listed for the **Booker Prize**. The book combines important elements of African oral narrative traditions with sophisticated literary devices (such as the use of multiple narrators) that are often associated with Western modernism. This formal and stylistic complexity, meanwhile, is motivated by the complex issues addressed in the book. The most overtly political of all of Achebe's novels, *Anthills* is, among other things, a sort of political thriller that explores the dangers and difficulties of postcolonial politics. However, it addresses these public issues through an intense and effective focus on the stories of a number of individual characters, including **Christopher Oriko**, the Minister of Information in the postcolonial nation of **Kangan, Ikem Osodi**, a poet and the editor of the Kangan *National Gazette*, and **Beatrice Okoh**, an educated woman who serves as Senior Assistant Secretary to the Minister of Finance in the Kangan government.

Anthills is a novel that grapples primarily with Nigeria's political problems. The novel begins with a cabinet session of the military government, which is full of sycophants and cowed political personalities and dominated by an authoritarian figure. The book is presented by different characters and often also by an omniscient narrator, who is privy to the inner thoughts and ideological perspectives of each of the characters and other members of the nation as a whole. The main issues concern the manner in which the nation is run, the way it affects the majority of the people (including those in power), and the ways in which statesmen, leaders, and politicians are either complicit with or resistant to the undemocratic administration of the nation. The military dictator of the novel ruthlessly alienates any opposition to him, and a state of terror is created within the society. Eventually, he is overthrown by some of his own close allies. In the meantime, progressive individuals seeking an alternative means of existence bond together in solidarity as a means of overcoming the intimidating atmosphere created within the nation. There is the question of how the positive-minded among the elite can combine forces with the dispossessed masses to ensure the creation of a more just and fair society. In the end, there is a change of government and several casualties, including the dictator himself. Integrated within the critique of post-independence political practice and the engagement with deep political problems such as neocolonialism is a consistent evaluation of the nature of interpersonal relationships and how these affect the idea of the nation as an imagined community. The novel suggests in the final analysis that there is hope for the nation if the right forces can come together and have the power to direct national policy and the political culture of the people.

As Neil Ten Kortenaar notes, *Anthills of the Savannah* explores the possibilities for shaping a more positive future for the nation after the general disappointments of nationalism and nation-statism in Africa, bringing new perceptions to bear on the question of leadership in post-independence Nigeria. Achebe's bleak portrait of political developments in Nigeria echoes the problem he identified in his 1983 ideological blueprint and political manifesto, ***The Trouble with Nigeria***, as a "litany" of "national deficiencies" (2). Unlike in *The Trouble with Nigeria*, however, Achebe does not propose solutions to his country's problems in *Anthills*. Twice during his lecture at the University of Bassa, Ikem Osodi, editor of the *National Gazette* and an exemplary artist-revolutionary figure within the nation, challenges the notion that a writer must provide solutions. "A writer wants to ask questions," he asserts. "These damn fellows want him to give answers" (157–58, 145). At the same forum, he points out, "Writers don't give prescriptions. . . . They give headaches" (161, 148). Ikem is obviously speaking for Achebe because the fictional **Kangan** is closely identifiable with Achebe's own **Nigeria**. The term "nation" is polemically deployed several times in a narrative that is written against the background of a general loss of faith by members of the educated elite and the majority of the dispossessed masses of Africa in the idea of a nation-state. Among other things, an "explanation" is sought for how "His Excellency" **Sam**, the military leader of the troubled West African state of Kangan, "came to power without any preparation for political leadership" (12, 11).

The spotlight of Achebe's critique is the dictatorial Sam, whose rule his Minister of Information, **Christopher Oriko**, describes as "a game that began innocently enough and then suddenly went strange and poisonous" (1, 2). In the course of the novel, Nigeria's latter-day dictator is compared to previous African despots such as Idi Amin of Uganda and Jean-Bedel Bokassa of the Central African Republic. Collectively, these megalomaniacal dictators are described as "virulent misshapen freaks . . . sired on Africa by Europe" (52, 47). The atrocities and "transactions of soldiers-turned politicians" and their "cohorts in business and bureaucracy" (141, 130) are presented as part of the general tradition of misrule and authoritarianism in post-independence Africa. Thus, the "civilian politicians" from whom Sam takes over power are said to have "finally got what they had coming to them" because of their corrupt and incompetent attitudes (12). Reviewing nationalism in Nigeria in the years after the **Nigerian Civil War**, Achebe strategically reminds his readers about the attempted secession of the **Igbo** from Federal Nigeria without directly discussing the tragic details of that experience. Achebe is keen to prevent a national amnesia, yet the civil war is referred to occasionally in the story of Kangan simply as "The Rebellion" (18). *Anthills* undertakes a specific investigation of the political culture of post-independence Nigeria, but the deepening crisis in the country reflects the general manner in which the state in Africa has become a repressive ideological apparatus and instrument of domination. Significantly, the Westernized members of Sam's government who fail miserably in duty to their community are described as "the cream of our society and the hope of *all* the black race" (2; emphasis added). Achebe's reference to notions of African identity at the same time as he prosecutes a critique of retrogressive and counter-productive policies by African politicians is a deliberate statement. His concern with Africa's plight is evident as Sam's tyrannical rule is linked to the visible change in his behavior after his first Organization of African Unity (OAU) meeting (52), a particularly memorable occasion for him during which he met and began to hold in the highest regard President-for-Life **Ngongo** (53). The novel's discussion of postcolonial politics is obviously shaped as much by Achebe's specific concern with the Nigerian situation as by his continued interest in the wider socioeconomic, cultural, and political problems that have bedeviled Africa.

Bad leadership is not limited to the politicians and the nation's elite leaders. Though students often constitute the revolutionary vanguard, they are criticized for their selfishness and shortsightedness. Like nationalist politicians, students have failed to put Kangan-Nigeria "on the road to self-redemption" (160). In Ikem's lecture at the University of Bassa, he questions their moral authority to lead the nation because of their failure to purge themselves of detrimental attitudes (160). The awful example is cited of their razing to the ground "a new maternity block built by peasants" for the simple reason that they had been "posted to a rural station without electricity and running water" (160). The attitudes of ordinary Nigerians toward power are also examined because disenchantment derives from a multiplicity of sources within the nation.

Achebe's analysis of the postcolonial political situation in *Anthills* has not been without its critics. Emmanuel Ngara, for example, questions the legitimacy of Achebe's critique on the basis of the fact that Achebe's "analysis of African society is presented from the point of view of one class—the *petite bourgeoisie*, or, to be more precise the intelligentsia"(Ngara, 122). David Maughan-Brown argues similarly, concluding that "nowhere in the novel . . . is the possibility ever entertained that 'rule' by an elite leadership might be replaced by genuinely democratic structures, whereby the people become responsible for the government of the world that is said to belong to them" (Maughan-Brown, 147). However, one could also argue that both critics too easily accept the problematic assumption that "the people" are more progressive custodians of power than the elite. As Chris, **Braimoh**, and **Emmanuel Obete** flee the turbulent environment of **Bassa**, bad leadership is shown not to be of the making of the elite alone. The following passage is instructive:

The bus pulled on one side. Some of the crowd were rushing towards it like a tipsy welcoming party. But the pulling of the bus and the sudden explosion inside it, like a hand-grenade thrown from the crowd, of the word COUP! came on top of each other. The bus was evacuated like a vessel on fire. The driver, *unlike a good and honourable captain*, shoved people aside to get to the ground first. (212; emphasis added)

The driver is an ordinary Nigerian who abdicates responsible behavior in a manner detrimental to all. The lesson is clear. Ordinary people have contributed in their own different ways to the chaos in Nigeria. Achebe is more concerned with changes in leadership and less with wholesale revolution. The problem not only is with elite leadership but derives from the general nature of human relationships. **Beatrice Okoh**'s housemaid **Agatha**, over whom it can be said that Beatrice wields a power relationship, provides a different example. Given a chance, Agatha proves to be no better when she occupies a position of power. Represented as a devout, even a fanatical Christian, Agatha forsakes the image of true Christian charity in her dealings with **Elewa**. Mean to Elewa with food, she abnegates any sense of exemplary Christianity. She thus fails to observe even the most basic of Christian tenets: humility and sympathy. Resentful at having to serve Elewa, whom she considered "judging from the contempt in her eyes and the way she curled her lips, was no better than a servant herself," Agatha is presented as cruel in her own way as she internalizes traits of domination. Agatha's conceit, self-indulgence, and her individualism call into question Ifi Amadiume's description of *Anthills* as being only "about the elite classes and their individualism" (Amadiume 9).

Speaking to an audience at the **University of Nigeria** in 1986, a year before the publication of *Anthills*, Achebe reformulated the question of elite leadership along lines similar to those of Ikem's in the novel. The "real point about an elite," Achebe argued, "is not whether it is necessary or not but whether it is genuine or counterfeit" (Achebe, *The University*, 15). This argument compares directly with Ikem's that "[t]he most we can hope to do with a problematic individual psyche is to *re-form* it" (99, Achebe's emphasis). It is therefore part of Achebe's visionary and programmatic agenda for his country that the novel brings together a disparate group of intellectuals, elites, and largely dispossessed people.

Anthills historicizes the gap between the rich and the poor and consistently uncovers the huge difference between the privileged and the underprivileged in Nigerian society. For example, it is only in his personal moment of crisis, as he travels up North with Braimoh the taxi driver that Chris becomes exposed to the differences between the rich and poor. He himself is forced to adopt the way of life of the less privileged locals of Bassa. However, while the novel shows the gap between the elite, on the one hand, and the peasants and other ordinary people, on the other, it allows for the possibility of bridging this gap. At the point in the story when Chris is searching unsuccessfully for the abducted Ikem, he decides to modify his strategy by appealing to the power inherent in the institutions of ordinary Nigerians:

He knew he could count on some of the representatives in Bassa of foreign news agencies, their press and radio. On the home front there was no comparable resource to lean on but there was the enormous potential of that great network nicknamed VOR, the Voice of Rumour, the despair of tyrants and shady dealers in high places. Before evening both systems, foreign and local seemed set to start buzzing in the interest of the abducted man. (68)

The real power of the people is codified as the "Voice of Rumour." Achebe seems to be suggesting that drawing together the progressive elements within both elite and popular culture can forge a true sense of resistance. Despite their palpable marginalization from the institutions of the nation, the people are powerful. As citizens of the nation, they are at the mercy of state power as embodied in Sam. On the other hand, the "Voice of the People" is still a potent cultural institution for being able to work in the interest of one of their own. Ikem's acknowledgment of the communication gap between himself and the masses and the peasants is such that he has a "yearning" to "connect his essence with earth and earth's people" (140–41). Although he has no clear idea of how to go about this, the narrative provides openings for better communication between elite intellectuals like Ikem and less privileged people.

Another striking feature of the novel is Achebe's self-conscious foregrounding of the extent to which the culture and language of ordinary Nigerians form part of the public discourse of the wider society. **Pidgin English** is the lingua franca of the majority or the masses, but it fosters unity when spoken with progressive elites resisting domination. Ikem is a member of the elite whose relationship with Elewa may be problematic; yet the power of his writing is disseminated in the consciousness of the ordinary people, as this story from Braimoh, the taxi driver, demonstrates:

The thing wey oga [Ikem] write too plenty. But na for we small people he de write every time. I no sabi book but I sabi say na for we this oga de fight, not for himself. He na big man. Nobody fit do fuckall to him. So he fit stay for him house, chop him oyibo chop, drink him cold beer, put him air conditioner and forget we. But he no do like that. So we come salute am. (135–36)

This acknowledgment of Ikem's contribution by a member of one of the underprivileged makes Ikem a public intellectual. Further evidence of language as a sign of solidarity is provided after Ikem's abduction by the brutal agents of Sam's military force. Bemoaning the increasingly repressive situation in the country as a whole, Ikem's neighbor asserts in conversation with Chris and Beatrice: " 'This our country na waa. Na only God go save person' " (166).

The novel engages with other forms of malaise within Nigerian society such as the generally sycophantic attitudes of political officeholders toward their leaders and benefactors. **Professor Reginald Okong** is presented as an embodiment of the farcical and obsequious attitudes of the politicians who constitute Sam's government. At one stage

Okong declares typically, " 'Your Excellency is not only our leader but also our Teacher. We are always ready to learn. We are like children washing only their bellies, as our elders say when they pray' " (18). Achebe's nationalist politicians are cast in an ironic role as they themselves—rather than their critics—give us a vivid insight into the reasons that the post-independence nation-state in Africa has become such a loathsome institution.

Anthills demonstrates that those who, unlike Professor Okong, resist manipulation and subordination by standing up to Africa's dictatorial regimes are fated to either lose their lives or succumb one way or the other. Consequently, the activities of individuals and ethno-national communities seeking social justice and a generally better form of government are highly delimited and circumscribed. There is the example of Ikem, who is presented as a champion of the cause of both his own **Abazon**ian community and those of other ordinary people in Nigerian society as a whole. However, he is abducted and murdered for being critical of the retrogressive policies of Kangan's military government. Chris, whom Ikem accuses of complicity with Sam, is not murdered by Sam's agents. However, he too suffers what is almost a predetermined fate when he is murdered by a policeman of the Kangan government as he attempts to save a girl from being raped. Annihilation one way or the other at the hands of the brutal and repressive agents of Sam's government is a fate that awaits not only his political rivals and opponents but all those seeking different kinds of social justice, freedom, and liberation. The example of the disaffected Abazonians who refuse to be coerced into voting for Sam to assume the title of president-for-life is further instructive. Punished and denied the basic necessities of life such as water and electricity, they suffer poverty and material hardship. Achebe's portrait of the tyrannical Sam—and by impli-

cation other like-minded rulers—illustrates Achille Mbembe's argument that by "exercising an unlimited hold over every individual" the postcolonial African nation-state has "been conceived on the basis of . . . making it the organizer of public happiness" (Mbembe 31).

Anthills also engages further with the tribalism and ethnic politics within Nigerian society that contributed to the civil war. The community of Abazon, described as "Ikem's native province" and "the distant sustainer of all his best aspirations," is also "a province of unspecified and generalized disaffection to the regime" (195). To the extent that Achebe is himself an Igbo whose situation in Nigeria is similar to that of Ikem in Kangan, the Abazon of the novel is also a signifier for Igboland and other parts of Eastern Nigeria that were in conflict with Federal Nigeria. If the deprived Abazon can be taken as a signifier for Igboland, it is because Achebe is concerned with the question of sub-nationalism. *Anthills* intimates that dissident communities like Abazon will identify themselves as part of the imagined community of the nation only if they can be guaranteed equal access to the nation's resources. It is clear that Achebe is drawing attention to the fact that the problems Nigeria faced before and during the war are far from over. This argument is plausible because just as Igboland and Eastern Nigeria sought secession from the rest of Nigeria in 1967, it is the Abazonians' preference for political self-autonomy that informs their refusal to endorse Sam's bid to be made president-for-life in a national referendum. The Abazonians further remind us of an earlier Igbo community, the **Umuofia**ns of *Things Fall Apart*. According to Ikem, who is not only an Abazonian but also an Igbo, just like the Umuofians, the Abazonians believe in the concept of "*Nneka*," the Igbo philosophical viewpoint that means "Mother is Supreme" (98).

There is no sense, however, that Achebe is concerned with a parochial sub-nationalism merely for the sake of it. This is demonstrated by the fact that after his death, the flight to Abazon, Ikem's native province, is a period of anxiety and tension for other characters within the novel. Abazon is a safe haven not only for Chris and Beatrice, who are identified by their Igbo names—Oriko and Nwanyibuife—but also for Braimoh and **Aina**, Braimoh's wife, for Elewa and for Emmanuel, the President of the Student Union of Bassa in Kangan, all of whom are from different parts of Nigeria. The journey to Abazon is also the moment in the narrative when Chris recounts the tale of the bedbug to Beatrice after she asks, "What's the bedbug's excuse, for biting without bothering to sing first?" (199). The anecdote of the bedbug that Chris proceeds to relate is of significance to the narrative and resonates with constructive and referential profundity for all. The personal circumstances of Beatrice and Chris having changed so much with Ikem's murder by Sam's security forces, Chris is himself in danger of being arrested and murdered. Beatrice is also apprehensive about parting with Chris since "she had a powerful premonition that Chris and she had come tonight to a crossroads beyond which a new day would break, *unpredictable*, without precedent" (196; emphasis added). The entire nation of Kangan is in turmoil, and it is within this chaotic atmosphere that Achebe has Chris relate the tale. The exact moment in the narrative is when Beatrice and Chris have just made love in the hideout provided to the endangered Chris by Braimoh and Aina. In response to Beatrice's question, Chris replies that "man once tried to destroy her and her new-hatched brood by pouring a kettle of hot water on them. Her little ones were about to give up the struggle but she said to them: Don't give up, whatever is hot will become cold" (199).

The story of the bedbug speaks eventually not only to the condition of Beatrice, who loses Chris and now has to bear the strenuous state of solitude alone. It speaks to the situation of Emmanuel, who is also fleeing for his life from the terror of Sam's forces of annihilation. It gestures also toward the humane relationship between the Northerner **Captain Abdul Medani**, leader of Bassa's Security Forces (the pack of wolves who arrest and murder Ikem on Sam's instructions), and Beatrice. Abdul Medani is not the stereotypical callous soldier, for it is his sensitivity toward his fellow humans that enables him to strike a productive relationship with Beatrice and the others. For each and every one of these people, the narrative generates multiple spaces for them to renegotiate their identities along a flexible axis of interpretation. As far as the question of humans resisting oppression is concerned, the story of the bedbug resonates with abundant meaning and significance for all. Thus, although Elewa's life is marked by the devastation she experiences over Ikem's death, both she and Beatrice are sustained by the memory of his spirit.

Ruminating on the state of affairs in her country after independence, Beatrice, the leader of the multi-ethnic group of individuals brought together as a result of the chaos and the violence within the nation, comments that the deaths of Chris and Ikem did not occur by chance or as the result of unique events. Instead, she sees both as the victims of a troubled history that promises to bring death to many more unless something is done to change it (220).

Beatrice is, herself, a particularly important character in the text, and much critical discussion has focused on Achebe's characterization of her as a commentary on the politics of gender in Nigerian society. While many consider *Anthills* to be Achebe's most emphatic statement to date on the power of women within Nigerian society, there is critical consensus among some African feminist critics that he presents a distorted image of women even in this novel. In "Class and Gender in *Anthills of the Savannah*," Ifi Amadiume accuses Achebe of demonstrating a "lack of understanding of female issues" (Amadiume 9). In a similar vein, Chikwenye Okonjo Ogunyemi argues that "Achebe's macho spirit with his disdain for women robs him of the symbolic insight into the nurturant possibilities of woman's vital role" (Ogunyemi 66). By far the most provocative thesis, however, comes from Patricia Alden, who contends that "Achebe's portrait of Beatrice Okoh betrays a significant failure of imagination—a failure to take seriously, as part of contemporary, political struggle, the feminist challenge to patriarchal authority" (Alden 67–68). Further, Alden argues, "the novel achieves its closure in an uncritically examined connection between the fertility of women and the rebirth of the nation" (Alden 68).

It is important to note, however, that as an elite middle-class African stateswoman in a military government of late 1980s Nigerian society, who comes across as a well-educated and knowledgeable woman, Beatrice inhabits a subversive position within the narrative. While critics like Amadiume, Alden, and Ogunyemi have taken serious issue with Achebe's portrait of Beatrice, not all the critics interested in the novel's gender politics have reacted negatively to the portrait of Beatrice as symbolic of the importance of women in society. Full of praise for Achebe, M.E.M. Kolawole notes that, while Achebe's early novels present "naive images of women who did not make remarkable socio-political contributions" to society, *Anthills* marks "a radical shift" in his ideology. For Kolawole, Achebe's depiction of a strong woman character in Beatrice is a sign that women are "actively involved in opposing the forces of social degeneracy" (Kolawole 195). The South African writer and Nobel Prize winner Nadine Gordimer has described *Anthills* as "a work in which 22 years of harsh experience, intellectual growth and self-criticism" mark the "deepening understanding" of politics by Achebe (Gordimer 26). Otherwise critical of Achebe, Chioma Opara also contends that "the lull of about a quarter of a century in the author's creative production has proved to be the gestation of Achebe's new women infused with dynamism and selfhood" (Opara 113).

In *Anthills*, Achebe engages in an elaborate transposition of oral forms into the written in a detailed manner of representation that connects the overriding themes of the story: power, tyranny and their consequences. Justifying his insistence on the use of mythological forms, Achebe has argued that the myths derived from traditional Igbo society's traditions of storytelling are of supreme relevance to his discussion of the crises in his community. Achebe returns to the traditions of his ancestors because myths wield significant possibilities for illuminating the contradictions of the contemporary age. Speaking in an interview in 1990, Achebe pointed out that his familiarity with Igbo traditions made the integration of myths into his narratives essential. Achebe's interviewer, Raoul Granqvist, asks: "Could I ask you how you conceived your new book? How did you fit its three dimensions, history, mythology and politics, into a whole?" Achebe answers:

[t]he bringing together of the threads of story telling and of my tradition, is of course something that I have given much thought to. And my tradition is very rich on this [myth] . . . power is not something new in the world. And I found that my ancestors had thought about this, and had put their thoughts in the form of . . . very powerful myth[s]. (Granqvist 32)

Myths sustain for Achebe's texts a critical narratological ambience that derives from their heuristic value. To adequately describe the contradictions and uncertainties of the contemporary era, Achebe cannot find a more appropriate means of narration. His recourse to myth is therefore engendered by the fact that he is compelled to link together the diverse strains of his narratives as a means of engaging the representation of reality.

The myth of **Idemili**, "the divinity that controls . . . the transactions of the market place that is their world" (102) is a myth about secular power in which man's excessive misappropriation of the power entrusted to him necessitates divine intervention. The Almighty thus sends Idemili, his daughter, to moderate man's power. Through this myth Achebe suggests another means of appreciating the realities of cultural power through storytelling. As a way of broadening the locus of meaning in the novel, Idemilli's sending down of his daughter is proffered as a general critique of the egotism of masculine power in which even Chris and Ikem implicitly participate. In the myth of Idemili, Sam's authority is figured at an abstract level as "Power" (102); however, Achebe's critique also illustrates the legitimacy of this figuration through the extent to which the structures of power and authority within the community are revealed as masculine. For example, in her encounter with Sam, Beatrice informs us that Sam "stir[s] in" but later abandons "the shrubbery of my shrine" (81). As the priestess of Idemili, Beatrice's message is to caution Sam against the dangerous alliance, sexual and political, that he seeks with agents of neo-colonialism such as the American journalist **Lou Cranford**. Achebe's richly textured myths enable a further insight into his mode of narration in their explicit prefiguration of the dramatic confrontation between Sam and Beatrice when the latter is invited to Sam's palatial retreat. In

Ikem's **"Hymn to the Sun,"** we learn "[b]y way of comment [and] the voice of legend" that "*a man who deserts his town and shrine-house*, who turns his face resolutely away . . . must carry death in his eyes" (32–33; emphasis added). The myth creates a space for Beatrice, also known as "Nwayibuife" and priestess of the goddess Idemili, to execute the mission of "the Almighty," who sends his daughter Idemili to wrap "around Power's rude waist a loincloth of peace and modesty" (102).

In establishing an association between the character of Beatrice and her symbolic role as priestess of Idemili, the narrative locates an enclave of societal consciousness through which Achebe reproduces a critique of Sam and his dictatorial powers. Achebe's characterization of Beatrice brings the important historical roles of Nigerian women into focus. The narrative represents the tangibility of the consciousness of deified female figures within Nigerian history, a facet of Nigerian culture that scholars such as Nina Emma Mba have seen as crucially important. Indeed, Achebe's confident characterization of Beatrice as a deified woman is substantiated at an intertextual level by the prominence of other deified women in Nigerian history. As Nina Mba argues, "hero deities" in Nigerian society "were mythical or semi-mythical figures of the past, some of whom were women" (Mba 19).

In *Anthills*, myth facilitates the appropriation of an alternative conceptual framework within which to locate the social, cultural, and political dilemmas that Achebe communicates. The text also suggests a further correlation between storytelling and resistance. Explaining the value of storytelling and the ideological effect of the story itself as a viable mode of cultural production, the **old man of Abazon** asserts that the telling of the stories of wars may be an even more important undertaking than the wars themselves, because it allows future generations to learn crucial lessons from making some of the same mistakes that might have led to the original conflicts (123–24, 114). If self-rehabilitation derives from the ability to recount and re-possess the story, it is largely because genuine storytelling is inevitably awake to the dangers of modern society. Speaking tongue-in-cheek, the elder of Abazon asserts on behalf of his people that "we are ready to learn new things and mend our old, useless ways" (127). The real object of the old man's criticism is not Abazon. It is Sam and his dangerous ways. As a subversive narrative, *Anthills* cautions against untruths. To compromise truth within story telling is to undergo a process of self-fragmentation. It is clear that not all of Achebe's protagonists are aware of this. When Beatrice accuses Chris, Ikem, and Sam of egocentrism, Chris confesses her criticism may be apt and that he and the others may have forgotten that their stories are only a few among millions (66–67).

FURTHER READING

Simi Afonja and Bisi Aina, eds., *Nigerian Women in Social Change*; Patricia Alden, "New Women and Old Myths"; Ifi Amadiume, "Class and Gender in *Anthills of the Savannah*"; Holger G. Ehling, ed., *Critical Approaches to Anthills of the Savannah*; Nadine Gordimer, "A Tyranny of Clowns"; M.E.M. Kolawole, "Gender and Changing Social Vision in the Nigerian Novel"; David A. Maughan-Brown, "*Anthills of the Savannah* and the Ideology of Leadership"; Nina Emma Mba, *Nigerian Women Mobilized*; Achille Mbembe, *On the Postcolony*; Emmanuel Ngara, "Achebe as Artist"; Chikwenye Okonjo Ogunyemi, "Women and Nigerian Literature"; Chioma Opara, "From Stereotype to Individuality"; Neil Ten Kortenaar, "Only Connect."

Kwadwo Osei-Nyame Jr.

ANYANAFUMMO. See Aghadike.

APAPA, a mainland section of **Lagos**, its quay is the major outlet for Nigerian exports. In chapter 12 of *No Longer at Ease* Apapa is the location of the Roman Catholic convent where **Nora** and **Pat** teach and where they are visited by **Obi Okonkwo** and his friend, **Christopher**.

Thomas J. Lynn

APPROACHES TO TEACHING ACHEBE'S **THINGS FALL APART,** edited by **Bernth Lindfors** (1991), offers essential resources and diverse approaches for teaching "Africa's most famous novel" (ix). Lindfors's preface and introductions emphasize the interdisciplinary appeal and complex richness of *Things Fall Apart*, as well as special challenges for North American and European teachers and students unfamiliar with the novel's African contexts. Lindfors's bibliographical essays in "Part One: Materials" survey available editions of *Things Fall Apart*; key biographical sources and **Igbo** studies; background studies from multidisciplinary perspectives (anthropology, history, politics, religion); selective literary criticism; and audiovisual aids (films, videotapes, and audiotapes). Recommended materials remain foundational for students of Achebe and his first novel, but more recent bibliographies must be consulted for primary and secondary sources published since 1991.

"Part Two: Approaches" opens with a statement by Achebe, followed by sixteen essays of classroom teachers describing their varied approaches to teaching *Things Fall Apart*. The essays are grouped by subheadings, beginning with "The Author as Teacher." In "Teaching *Things Fall Apart*," Achebe explains that he has chosen not to teach the novel because he wrote it. Drawing instead upon diverse responses of readers and critics over three decades, Achebe reflects upon **Okonkwo**, the novel's protagonist; the meaning and impact of his story; and the narrative intention of the novel's ending. How authorial perspectives should be used in teaching and interpreting the novel is considered in the next section, "Teaching the Author," featuring "Chinua Achebe and Signs of the Times" by **Simon Gikandi** and "Following the Author in *Things Fall Apart*" by Emmanuel Obiechina. Another key pedagogical issue is addressed in "Teaching the Context," offering the recommendations of **Robert M. Wren** and Dan Izevbaye. Essays on point of view by Ashton Nichols and Okonkwo's characterization by Arlene A. Elder make up the fourth section, "Teaching Texture." "Traditional Paradigms and Modern Intertextuality" presents comparative literary approaches, coupling study of *Things Fall Apart* with Igbo epic and mythic paradigms (Ousseymou B. Traore), African folktale (Barbara Harlow), the literature of empire by Western authors (Hunt Hawkins), and the Latin American novel *Men of Maize* (Edna Aizenberg).

The sixth grouping, "Challenging Approaches," offers "essays that challenge conventional notions of *Things Fall Apart*" (Lindfors 18). Rhonda Cobham complicates charges that *Things Fall Apart* is "sexist" in depicting the role of women, after examining how Achebe's intellectual milieu and Judeo-Christian education shaped his selective, gendered representation of Igbo traditional culture. Zohreh T. Sullivan uses Mikhail Bakhtin's theories to challenge the view that *Things Fall Apart* is a "traditional realistic novel" (101) in "The Postcolonial Novel and the Dialogic Imagination." Wahneema Lubiano insists that *Things Fall Apart* offers much more than simple ethnographic evidence about African culture in "Narrative, Metacommentary, and Politics." Like Sullivan and Lubiano, Biodun Jeyifo challenges simplistic notions of the novel's verisimilar "truth value." In "The Problem of Realism in *Things Fall Apart*: A Marxist Exegesis," Je-

yifo reminds us that any novel, realistic or otherwise, depicts not *the* truth, but a particularized and partisan version of truth. The last section, "Specific Courses," offers descriptive syllabi for using *Things Fall Apart* in a humanities core course (Eric Sellin) and in an applied literary criticism class (Richard K. Priebe). "Works Cited" at the end of Part Two provides an extensive bibliography for further reading.

FURTHER READING

Simon Gikandi, *Reading Chinua Achebe*; C. L. Innes and Bernth Lindfors, eds., *Critical Perspectives on Chinua Achebe*; Robert M. Wren, *Achebe's World*.

Cora Agatucci

ARMAH, AYI KWEI. Ghanaian novelist and essayist, born 1939. See *The Beautyful Ones Are Not Yet Born*.

ARROW OF GOD (1964), Achebe's third novel, was published in a revised edition in 1974. If *Things Fall Apart* is Achebe's best-known book, *Arrow of God* may be his masterpiece. **Robert M. Wren**, for example, regards the novel as "the most complex, richly-textured novel to come out of Africa" ("*Mister Johnson*" 207). In his enigmatic preface to the revised edition, Achebe refuses to name directly a favorite among his own novels, but he admits of *Arrow of God* that it is "the novel which I am most likely to be caught sitting down to read again." Like *Things Fall Apart*, the narrative substance of *Arrow of God* is the coming of colonialism and the consequent collapse of autonomous **Igbo** village life and the sometimes violent integration of African cultural pathways into larger, globalizing political, ideological, and economic systems. But *Arrow of God*, while preserving the clarity and apparent simplicity of Achebe's earlier novels, is structurally a much more complex affair than *Things Fall Apart*. Indeed, the fact that the tremendous allegorical armature of the novel does not interfere in the slightest with the representational immediacy of the action as it unfolds places *Arrow of God* solidly in the first rank of realist fiction.

The basic structure of the novel is laid out in the second chapter in a flashback to an event that predates the action of the novel itself. **Umuaro**, a polity of six villages and the setting for the novel, is engaged in a land dispute with the neighboring community of **Okperi**. The priest of **Ulu** (**Ezeulu**, the novel's protagonist), Chief Priest of the six villages, claims that the land originally belonged to Okperi along with the rest of the area occupied by Umuaro and so opposes going to war over the parcel. **Nwaka**, a rabble-rouser who we later discover is the agent of **Ezidemili**, the priest of a rival god, stirs up Umuaro against Okperi, and the village sends the firebrand **Akukalia** to lead a delegation to Okperi. The nearly imperceptible slowness of the rise in tension throughout the rest of the chapter to its final explosion into violence is one of the novel's marvels. In their impatience the delegation commits a diplomatic *faux pas*, arriving on Okperi's **market day**. A difference in custom provokes laughter at the men from Umuaro. A man from Okperi inadvertently insults Akukalia; in the resulting melee, Akukalia splits the man's *ikenga*, his personal god. The man, who has "been made a corpse before his own eyes" (24), shoots Akukalia and kills him. But the episode does not end there; rather than exploding into war, tensions ease momentarily as nobody seems to know quite what to do in the face of this unprecedented situation. But another difference in custom reignites tensions, and war is waged for four days.

What happens next is world-historical. The next day sees the war brought to a sudden close as the white man, Wintabota (**Captain T. K. Winterbottom**), brings soldiers to Umuaro to force a stop to the fighting. The story of what these soldiers had earlier done in **Abame** is still told with fear, and so the men of Umuaro make no effort to resist but lay down their arms. However, "the white man, not satisfied that he had stopped the war, had gathered all the guns in Umuaro and asked the soldiers to break them in the face of all, except for three or four which he carried away. Afterwards he sat in judgement over Umuaro and Okperi and gave the disputed land to Okperi" (28).

The importance of this episode to the rest of the book lies in the fact that not a single element in this story (e.g., the rivalry between the two priests, the accidental insult, the diplomatic *faux pas*) was inevitable. None of these events were necessary in themselves, and had any one of them failed to take place, Umuaro would have been saved the necessity of going to war. Yet one thing was inevitable in the story: the outcome, which was quite different from anything the actors intended. Everything could be imagined differently, except that Umuaro might remain forever independent of the colonial authority on Government Hill. This structure is what Achebe has called, in a discussion of *Arrow of God*, the "powers of event": "The '*powers of event*' achieve their own logic. . . . I don't think we should ignore this force or phenomenon, whatever it is, maybe providence. If you are religious, you will call it God." (in Lindfors, *Conversations* 117; see also Achebe, *Hopes and Impediments* 57).

The title *Arrow of God* points to a conception of history whereby the passions of individuals accomplish only an end that was somehow determined in advance—by God, by the "Powers of Event," or by history itself. Achebe encapsulates this apparently paradoxical structure narratively in a saying that Ezeulu uses when speaking to his friend Akuebue about the war with Okperi: "We went to war against Okperi who are our blood brothers over a piece of land which did not belong to us and you blame the white man for stepping in. Have you not heard that when two brothers fight a stranger reaps the harvest?" (131).

This proverb plainly sums up the narrative that unfolds in the second chapter. But we find the same proverb expressed somewhat differently in the last pages of the book in another context: this time it is **Akuebue** who uses it as an argument against Ezeulu. " 'It troubles me,' he said, 'because it looks like the saying of our ancestors that when brothers fight to death a stranger inherits their father's estate' " (220). The difference between Akuebue's and Ezeulu's version of the proverb is palpable and in the context of the novel speaks volumes about the characters themselves. This sort of subtle modulation of language between characters and situations, so fine as to be almost subliminal, accounts for much of the restrained brilliance, quite without stylistic fireworks, of Achebe's style. What is important here, though, is that this proverbial theme, central to the second chapter, turns out to characterize the shape of the novel as a whole. The historical event of the stranger inheriting the estate provides the principal content of *Arrow of God*.

This is the first allegorical axis of *Arrow of God*, for "Umuaro" cannot be seen only as a single fictional entity; as Achebe put it in an interview, the "pacification" and ultimate defection of Umuaro "is not something which one should see in terms of Umuaro alone; it is something one ought to see in terms of the whole movement of world history" (Lindfors 138). In this first, synchronic dimension, the narrative of Umuaro dramatizes the long moment of the coming of colonialism on three planes that can be analyzed separately but that in the narrative are thoroughly intertwined with one another: we might think of these planes conveniently as the political, the religious or ethical, and the material.

The central conflict of the novel is that between Ezeulu and Ezidemili, a conflict that leads to a disruption in the agricultural cycle and ultimately to Umuaro's defection to Christianity and the destruction of its political and economic autonomy. Captain Winterbottom (also known as Wintabota), impressed with Ezeulu's integrity over the land dispute with Okperi, calls him to Government Hill to offer him a position in the colonial bureaucracy of British **indirect rule**: the "warrant chieftancy" for Umuaro. A tradition prohibits the chief priest from leaving the village, but at the insistence of Ezidemili's camp (who gain the support of the village) and not knowing what Winterbottom wants with him, Ezeulu accepts the invitation to Government Hill. Once there he declines what for him is an absurd proposition, but he is imprisoned for his obstinacy. During his imprisonment he realizes that his captivity is a weapon he can use against Ezidemili and Umuaro. While he is away, he cannot eat two sacred yams; when he returns, he refuses to call the harvest until the yams have been eaten, which delays the harvest by two months. Umuaro faces famine. Finally the Christian mission steps in, offering immunity from Ulu's wrath to anyone who harvests his yams and brings offerings to Christ. Ezeulu cracks, living the rest of his days in the "haughty splendor of a demented high priest" (*Arrow* 229).

The rivalry between the two priests goes much deeper than a mere personal antagonism; it reveals a deep rift at the heart of Umuaro, a fracture that marks a crisis in the unfolding of Umuaro's political history. This crisis is unexpectedly subsumed by another history altogether, one whose presence on the horizon both widens the rift and, after a fashion, resolves it.

In the key second chapter we learn that Ezeulu's god, Ulu, is relatively new. Indeed, Achebe's narrator relates that the six villages of Umuaro were once independent political entities and that they banded together only as a matter of survival in order to defend themselves against continual raids by the hired soldiers of Abam. In order to accomplish this defense, the people of Umuaro hired a team of powerful medicine men, who in turn installed Ulu as a common deity to oversee the new confederation of villages. From that day onward, we learn, the men of Umuaro had never been defeated in battle by any enemy (15).

Ezeulu's god thus has a definite origin within historical memory. The origins of Ezidemili's god, on the other hand, are not given so explicitly. Ezidemili claims that "**Idemili** was there at the beginning of things. Nobody made it" (42). Of course, there is no reason to take Ezidemili's word for this. But his account is finally confirmed by Ulu himself, who appears to Ezeulu late in the novel, telling him, "Go home and sleep and leave me to settle my quarrel with Idemili, whose envy seeks to destroy me that his **python** may *again* come to power" (191; emphasis added; the word "again," emphasizing Idemili's former supremacy, was inserted by Achebe in the 1974 revision). Idemili predates Ulu, from the time when the six villages "lived as separate peoples."

The surface conflict between Ezeulu and Ezidemili reveals some of its depth when we consider that it is the conflict between the priest of a presumably autochthonous god and the priest of a synthetic god created for a specific purpose. That is, in the light of the passage above, the central conflict is actually between the village structure, older than historical memory, and the new, larger political structure that has supplanted it. But this new alliance has weakened: in the years after Winterbottom's intervention in the Okperi dispute, Ezeulu's and Ezidemili's villages reach "the point which Umuaro people called *kill and take the head*" (39). The embodiment of this new political arrangement, the priest-

hood of Ulu, is also weakened. Ezeulu's grandfather and father had had the power to change the law single-handedly, outlawing facial scarification and the practice of enslaving children born to widows, respectively (132, 133). Already, in the flashback to the conflict with Okperi, Ezeulu is unable to stop the war and asks, "How could such a people disregard the god who founded their town and protected it? Ezeulu saw it as the ruin of the world" (15). Praise of the deity itself approaches a conditional tone: "[Ulu] is still our protector, *even though* we no longer fear Abam warriors at night" (27; emphasis added).

This last phrase deserves closer attention. The danger that had integrated the six villages—the threat of the Abam raiders—has disappeared. The reason for the end of this threat is given with admirable economy a paragraph later, in a passage we saw above: the Abam have been "pacified" by a British military expedition. (The story of the "pacification" of Abame is told in greater detail in *Things Fall Apart* [119–22]. Historically, raids by the Abam, mercenary warriors under the Aro, a group who traded in Igbo slaves, were indeed halted by the British "Aro Expedition" of 1901–1902.) Winterbottom's troops, not Ulu or the alliance of the six villages, now protect Umuaro from the Abam. The conflict between the two priests comes about because the integrative function of Ulu is no longer necessary, and a submerged power structure based around an older political organization is struggling to reassert itself.

Throughout the novel, Ezidemili claims that Ezeulu wants to be king: "He is a man of ambition; he wants to be king, priest, diviner, all. His father, they said, was like that too. But Umuaro showed him that Igbo people knew no kings" (27). Indeed, critics such as Umelo Ojinmah, in *Chinua Achebe: New Perspectives*, have argued that Achebe presents Ezeulu as a figure of excessive ambition and abuse of power. On the other hand, some of the changes made by Achebe in the revised edition of *Arrow of God* make Ezeulu appear to be a more positive figure, and indeed Achbed refers to Ezelueu in the preface to that edition as a "magnificent man." In any case, one could dispute Ezidemili's charge on two fronts. First, Ezeulu, whose basis of power is religious, turns down a chance to be secular chief of Umuaro. Second, the democratic traditions in Igbo society as portrayed by Achebe (democratic in an older sense, since slaves and women have no official voice) prevent authority from accumulating *de jure* in the figure of the chief priest. But as we saw above, Ezeulu's precursors wielded *de facto* executive power over the six villages. Indeed, it has been suggested that "impure" forms of stateless society where age-grades, priestly offices, and masked societies exist (as they do in the fictional Umuaro) tended to become centralized states when faced simultaneously with a fracturing of internal politics and a substantial threat from outside. Whether or not this is the case in the fictional Umuaro, it is clear that, with the "pacification" of the Abam, the integrative power of the office of Ezeulu is no longer needed, and a rift that had no doubt existed since the new god was installed suddenly emerges as a crisis. But this crisis is quickly subsumed by another history that had, unbeknownst to anybody, caused the crisis to emerge in the first place. Ulu owes its obsolescence not to a return to village autononomy that would re-empower Ezidemili, but to a new and powerful integrative force on the horizon: the Christian mission and the colonial government.

This political allegory can be formulated quite differently in religious and ethical terms. Indeed, these categories are not separable from the political in the context of *Arrow of God*, since competing modes of political organization are represented by gods. Behind the scenes, a battle takes place of which we only catch the briefest glimpse, when Ulu descends to berate Ezeulu: "As for me and Idemili we shall fight to the finish, and whoever throws the other down will strip him of his anklet!" (191). On this level the conflict is between gods rather than men: the first god, Idemili, remains from a time when each god integrated a village. The second, Ulu, which integrates the six villages in their alliance against the Abam, leaves the old gods in place while relegating them to secondary importance. With the coming of colonialism, the second god has outlived its utility. But this is also because, unbeknownst to either of the first two gods, a third god has appeared on the horizon, a god that also represents a new and exponentially larger political configuration. In a moving scene, Ezeulu returns to Ulu's shrine to ask, for the last time, if the harvest can take place after all. Unfortunately, his consultation with the god produces no result, leaving the villages locked in their current situation and causing widespread alarm in Umuaro (209–10). Of course, Ezeulu's consultation provokes no response from his deity because Ulu is dead. Superseding the battle between the god of the village and the god of the alliance, it is the new Christian god who takes Umuaro. Henceforth, yams will be "harvested in the name of the son" (230): in the name of both the sons who have converted to the new religion and, of course, the Son, Christ.

This central narrative of the "stranger inheriting the estate" plays out on yet a third plane. It is far from accidental that the engine of Umuaro's dissolution is a land dispute. The situation that led to the dispute is implicit throughout the novel, but it could be clarified most efficiently by turning to the background against which the novel is set. The "stateless society" of the Igbo lineage required large amounts of land. The system of titles that has such a prominent place in *Things Fall Apart* and *Arrow of God* prevented any one person from accumulating a great deal of capital, tending to prevent significant division of labor among freemen: every freeborn male was a subsistence farmer. But the poor forest soil, when cleared, could sustain a yam crop only for three or four years before the thin topsoil is eroded away, so that for each plot of arable land there had to be many more recovering from earlier farming. Although "subsistence" is not an accurate term for this form of agriculture, since it did produce surpluses, it did not, even when the environment was cooperative and the social order stable, result in a particularly rich and stable source of nutrition. Throughout *Arrow of God*, the response to polite inquiries after family is: " 'We have no trouble except hunger' " (e.g., 62). However, such an economy was able to sustain a growing population—as long as available land was effectively infinite. But at the time in which the novel is set, population pressure had long ago begun to feed the slave trade and to drive some groups—such as the Abam, against whom Umuaro was integrated—to organize into marauding bands. This had been to a great extent stopped, as we saw earlier, not so much by the abolition of the slave trade in 1807 as by punitive expeditions against kidnappers like the Abam. In the crucial second chapter of *Arrow of God*, it can be seen that territorial expansion has run up against its limit: previously unclaimed land has suddenly become a matter of dispute between Umuaro and Okperi.

The defection of Umuaro ultimately originates in a very material crisis: the famine nearly caused by Ezeulu's obstinacy is only an instance of a more general feature of Umuaro's life—and also the harbinger of an inevitability. Umuaro could not feed itself without acquiring more land, and the aversion of this particular food crisis is only the

allegory of an eventual crisis forestalled by Umuaro's integration into a world economy that would pay cash for the palm-oil—a sustainable crop indigenous to the region—that was used as a lubricant in English factories. As Achbe puts it in *Things Fall Apart*, "The white man had indeed brought a lunatic religion, but he had also built a trading store and for the first time palm-oil and kernel became things of great price" (153).

This new economy is a cash economy that can be taxed for roads and other public works, that can buy European and particularly British commodities, that would eventually produce groundnuts and cotton—and, later, of course, fossil oil—as well as palm products. But this integration cannot be thought of as a solution; the new economic system is virtually synonymous with colonialism, which Achebe has elsewhere characterized, in a neat play upon Hobbesian characterizations of pre-colonial life, as "nasty, British, and short" (*Hopes and Impediments* 146).

This brings us back to the strangely lyrical preface to the second edition of *Arrow of God*, in which Achebe characterizes Ezeulu as a victim with a "high historic destiny" whose agony helps to raise the defection of the people of Umuaro to the "stature of a ritual passage." But surely this is a strange introduction to a tragic novel: suddenly the most tragic of plots—the decisive end of village autonomy, figured as the destruction of a personality, with the coming of colonialism—is given a strangely positive valence. This contradiction originates in the assumption that "destiny" ends with the present, that henceforth the entire world is to be "Western" as we know it. But the epochal change that takes place in the fictional Umuaro allegorizes quite another possibility that emerges with the movement toward independence in Africa. When Achebe titled his first novel *Things Fall Apart*, he added a new allegorical level to Yeats's **"The Second Coming,"** which, in representing the *going* of Christianity, is suddenly able to represent its *coming*. This structure is inverted in *Arrow of God*, which, in narrating the *coming* of colonialism, secretly anticipates its *going*.

If the first allegorical axis of *Arrow of God* was synchronic, narrating a single moment in its most universal significance, the second axis is diachronic. Paradoxically, this novel, set in the past (a Reuter's telegram and an administrative report in chapter 15 both establish that the action takes place in 1921), represents a future moment that has not yet emerged. To understand this second axis, we need to turn to the level of the image. In his famous essay on **Conrad, "An Image of Africa: Racism in Conrad's *Heart of Darkness*,"** it was plain that Achebe's main focus of ideological critique was the image of Africa in the objectifying gaze of the colonial observer. The relationship between the "image of Africa" in Achebe's village novels and the colonial image is best exemplified by the road-building scene in *Arrow of God*, which rewrites a similar scene from Joyce Cary's ***Mister Johnson***.

Both Achebe's and Cary's scenes take place toward the end of a dry season. It appears, however, as though the road cannot be finished before the rains. The road builder—Rudbeck in *Mister Johnson*, **John Wright** in *Arrow of God*—resorts to unpaid, "volunteer" labor to supplement the paid laborers. But it is the festival season, and none of the young men sent to work on the road are particularly interested in this unpaid work; in fact, most of them are hung over. The seasoned laborers chaff the listless, latecoming "volunteers." In *Mister Johnson*, the tension of this scene is quickly defused: the new laborers are fused with the old (and with the foremen and boss as well) by the magic of a work song in a collective project that, of course, only Rudbeck understands—and he

only intuitively and incompletely. In *Arrow of God*, however, the initial tension explodes into violence at several different levels. Wright, Rudbeck's analogue, whips one of the insolent latecomers, who leaps at him in a fury before being subdued and further whipped; the tension between the latecomers and the others plays into the feud between the two villages, resulting in a skirmish; the workers organize a meeting about how to resist the road work, a meeting that itself dissipates in acrimony. The difference between this and the relatively idealized scene in *Mister Johnson* is, of course, significant and restores a dialectic of repression and resistance that is absent in Cary's representation of the colonial project.

But the primary rewriting takes place at the level of the image and is centered around the analogous pair of Johnson and Moses Unachukwu. Now is not the time to enter into a detailed discussion of *Mister Johnson*, whose representation of colonial society itself, without reference to the colonized, is not so different from that of *Arrow of God*, which is remarkable for its complex portrayal of Wright, Winterbottom, and the other residents of Government Hill. But if *Arrow of God* is able to represent these characters without reducing them to one-dimensionality, *Mister Johnson* is not able to do so with its eponymous central character, who is not so much a character as a pidgin-speaking exuberance.

In *Arrow of God*, Wright, after the skirmish among the two groups, commands the laborers through **Moses Unachukwu**, who translates:

"Tell them this bloody work must be finished by June."
"The white man says that unless you finish this work on time you will know the kind of man he is."
"No more lateness."
"Pardin?"

"Pardon what? Can't you understand plain, simple English? I said there will be no more late-coming."

"Oho. He says everybody must work hard and stop all this shit-eating." (83)

Here one of Achebe's most achieved effects comes to the fore: the translation of English into "Igbo," an instance of the modulation into different registers of English (which reaches its apotheosis in his technically masterful political drama *Anthills of the Savannah*). At the very least these two registers—Wright's cursory English and the more elegant Igbo into which Unachukwu translates it—mark an incommensurability between Wright's understanding of the situation and that of the laborers'.

But there is yet a third register, as Unachukwu at one point speaks, with a clownlike scratch of his head, to Rudbeck in a comic pidgin reminiscent of that spoken by Cary's Johnson. It would be wrong to say that the point of view here is Wright's; but suddenly—and only—in speaking to Wright, Unachukwu becomes that which Wright estimates him to be: a "native." The single sentence of pidgin English reveals Unachukwu as Johnson, reveals the poverty as well as the inescapability of Wright's interpretation of Unachukwu: Wright could not conceive of Unachukwu other than as Johnson. This is the moment of the colonial image as objectification. But rather than reduce Wright in turn to a crude exploitative intention—Wright is, like Ezeulu, a tangle of conflicting motivations that are no more clear than are the priest's or, for that matter, Rudbeck's in *Mister Johnson*—the narrative steps back to reveal this interpretive poverty in relation to a totality of which Wright has no conception. The image in *Arrow of God* is no longer the product of a reductive gaze but a snapshot of the totality. Wright's gaze is not returned, but narrated. It has become history.

The significance of a historical period, the synthesis of all the partial truths and the meaning *for us* of all the contingent events that populate it can be constructed only as a totality from a perspective for whom that period is past. Achebe's village novels, in narrating the coming of colonialism, bring into being at its end a genuinely postcolonial space from which the colonial period could be completely understood. But that moment has not yet come. Few would now deny that independence was not simply the "end" of colonialism but a much more complex mutation of First World domination. *Arrow of God*, written after independence in 1960, still embodies the anticipation of a decisive end to the colonial situation, and the narrative voice of *Arrow of God* is, even now, the voice of a possible future.

This, then, is the "optimistic" or utopian content to be found in novels whose themes have sometimes been denounced as "pessimistic." As Achebe has said in response to such criticisms, the work of art exists to give us "something that is not already given, something which is not flying around the life of the community, the life of the individual. . . . I think this is what happens when there is *optimism*" (in Lindfors 116).

Optimism is not something given as content, as though all we need to help us imagine a truly postcolonial future are books with happy endings. Rather, "optimism" is a precondition for conceiving anything beyond the current state of affairs. It cannot be forgotten how heroic independence was for the new African states: "We were going to take the initiative again in history. . . . And there was this feeling that at long last all this was coming to an end and one was intoxicated" (in Lindfors 116). The sense in the years just before and just after the moment of national independence that a radically different social formation was just around the corner may seem in retrospect to have been naive, but this can only be an index of what separates us from the euphoria of that time. The future of the relationship between the First and Third Worlds, the very engine of world history since the end of World War II, is still open to question. The meaning of the possibility projected by *Arrow of God* is not yet decidable. On the long view, it may ultimately be prophetic.

FURTHER READING

Adeleke Adeeko, "Contests of Text and Context in Chinua Achebe's *Arrow of God*"; Simon Gikandi, *Reading Chinua Achebe*; Robin Horton, "Stateless Societies in the History of West Africa"; Bernth Lindfors, ed., *Conversations with Chinua Achebe*; Umelo Ojinmah, *Chinua Achebe*; Neil Ten Kortenaar, "Beyond Authenticity and Creolization"; Robert M. Wren, *Achebe's World* and "*Mister Johnson* and the Complexity of *Arrow of God*."

Nicholas Brown

ARU-MMO, sickness that kills **Amalu** in *Arrow of God*.

Rachel R. Reynolds

ATLANTIC TERMINAL, briefly depicted at the outset of chapter 4 of *No Longer at Ease*, a building on the **Lagos** wharf that accommodates arriving and departing boat passengers and their parties. The point of return to **Nigeria** for **Obi Okonkwo, Clara Okeke**, and other passengers on the **MV** *Sasa*, the Atlantic Terminal boasts a "beautiful and airy waiting room" that on bustling "mail boat days . . . would be full of gaily dressed friends and relations [of arriving passengers] . . . drinking iced beer and Coca-Cola or eating buns." However, the MV *Sasa* is a cargo boat, and due to the unpredictability of such boats nobody is there to greet its passengers. See also **Ogbonna, Matthew**.

Thomas J. Lynn

ATTORNEY-GENERAL, a member of the cabinet of **Sam, the President**, in *Anthills of the Savannah*. Identified only by the title of his cabinet position, the Attorney-General is something of a sycophant who expresses unmitigated worship for the President. He is nevertheless ambitious, and his protestations of humility (supposedly derived from his humble "bush" beginnings) mask an effort to advance his own position at every opportunity. He is described by **Ikem Osodi** in his narration of chapter 4 as a "shyster."

M. Keith Booker

AUDEN, W(YSTAN) H(UGH) (1907–1973). Eminent Anglo-American poet whose poetry is cited by **Obi Okonkwo** as he propounds his own theory of tragedy in chapter 5 of *No Longer at Ease*. Obi declares that "a real tragedy takes place in a corner, in an untidy spot, to quote W. H. Auden. The rest of the world is unaware of it." The reference is to Auden's poem, "Musée des Beaux Arts."

Thomas J. Lynn

L'AVENTURE AMBIGUË, by Cheikh Hamidou Kane (1961), is an important early Francophone postcolonial African novel that addresses many of the key issues involved in the attempt to construct viable postcolonial cultural identities in Africa. In particular, the semi-autobiographical novel enacts a dialogue between Western and African philosophical traditions and modes of thought that puts into clear perspective some of the differences that have made the encounter between the two civilizations so perplexing to the former and so damaging to the latter.

Published in English translation (as *Ambiguous Adventure*) in 1963, the novel focuses on Samba Diallo, an aristocratic member of the Diallobé people. Once a promising student of the Koran, Samba changes his educational direction and travels to France to be educated in the ways of the French conquerors who have ended nearly

1,000 years of Islamic rule in the West African savannah country where the Diallobé live. The leaders of the Diallobé see their decision (made after much anguished consideration) to send their children to French schools not as a capitulation or admission of French superiority but merely as an attempt to gain a tactical advantage by learning to understand their conquerors. Unfortunately, Samba finds that the adventure he undergoes in Paris is far more complex than expected, thus the title of the book.

Fascinated by Western philosophy, Samba immerses himself in the study of it. He finds, however, that he is unable merely to observe Western ways from an objective distance. Instead, he is profoundly changed by his encounter with Western thought, and his studies in this new individualistic way of viewing the world hopelessly shatter his once firm sense of his place in the Diallobé community. At the same time, he finds that, as a black African Muslim, he can never be accepted as an equal among the French. He sinks into a profound state of alienation, a man adrift, cut off from his African roots but unable to sink new roots in Europe, where the individualism that has so seduced him combines with a materialistic, scientistic outlook that offers him no spiritual nourishment. By the time he returns to Africa, supposedly to provide leadership to his people, Samba feels that he has little in common with them and is thus incapable of providing that leadership. He is, in fact, able to overcome his alienation only in death, after which he experiences a sense of reintegration with the cosmos as the novel comes to a close.

Achebe discusses *L'Aventure ambiguë* in the essay "The Writer and His Community" (published in **Hopes and Impediments**), where he regards the novel as an impressive achievement and as an important statement of the dilemmas it explores. Achebe particularly relates Samba's predicament to that of the African writer, who, for Achebe, must avoid being drawn in by the individualistic influences of Western literature and maintain a vital and organic sense of connection to his or her African community.

FURTHER READING

Chinua Achebe, *Hopes and Impediments*; Abiola Irele, *The African Experience in Literature and Ideology*; J. P. Little, "Autofiction and Cheikh Hamidou Kane's *L'Aventure ambiguë*."

M. Keith Booker

AWKA, a town that now serves as the capital of Anambra State in Eastern **Nigeria**. Its population was estimated in 1995 at a little over 100,000. Historically, Awka was important as the site of a major **Igbo** oracle, which was destroyed in 1905 by the British colonial government as part of the **Bende-Onitsha punitive expedition**. Achebe's father, **Isaiah Okafor Achebe**, was trained as a Christian missionary at St. Paul's Teachers' College in Awka beginning in 1904. Awka was the birthplace and ancestral home of Achebe's mother, **Janet Anaenechi Achebe**, and wife, **Dr. Christie Chinwe Achebe**. Awka is now the site of the Nnamdi-Azikiwe University. It was near Awka that Achebe suffered serious injuries in an automobile accident in March 1990.

M. Keith Booker

AWOONOR, KOFI (1935–   ), Ghanaian poet, dramatist, novelist, and critic. See *This Earth, My Brother*.

AZIKIWE, NNAMDI (1904–1996), one of the key intellectual and political leaders of **Nigeria** of the twentieth century, affectionately known as "Zik of Africa." Though of **Igbo** ancestry, Azikiwe was born in Zunguru, Northern Nigeria, and grew up speaking the Hausa language. At the age of eight, he moved to **Onitsha** to live with his paternal grandparents. There, he learned Igbo, as well as Yoruba and English. Azikiwe was a great admirer of the African American thinkers Marcus Garvey and W.E.B. Du Bois. In the 1920s, he studied in America at Storer College, Howard University, Lincoln University, and Columbia University. In 1930, he worked to complete his M.A. in political science at Lincoln, at the same time writing the first of his many books, *Liberia in World Politics* (1931). After a stint as the editor of the *African Morning Post* in Accra, Azikiwe returned to Nigeria in 1937, soon becoming a key leader in the movement to found a viable printing and publishing industry in Nigeria. He entered politics in 1947, winning a seat in the Lagos Legislative Council. Subsequently, he became a key leader in the drive for Nigerian independence. In January 1960, he was sworn in as president of the Nigerian Senate, and in 1963 he became the first president of the Republic of Nigeria, a post he held until he was removed by the military coup of January 1963. At that time, he retreated to his country home in Nsukka but again became a public figure as he worked first to encourage international support for secessionist Biafra, then to bring an end to the **Nigerian Civil War** in the late 1960s. He also remained active in politics, again standing for election to the presidency as the leader of the National People's Party in 1983, though still another military coup prevented the establishment of an elected government at that time. Azikiwe then lived in retirement at Nsukka until his death in 1996.

Among other things, Azikiwe was a key figure in the founding of the **University of Nigeria, Nsukka**, in 1960. From 1972 to 1975, he served as the chancellor of the University of Lagos. His contributions to Nigerian education have been recognized in the naming of the Nnamdi Azikiwe University at **Awka**. Though greatly beloved in Nigeria and widely recognized as one of the founding fathers of Nigerian nationalism, Azikiwe was sometimes criticized for his excessive willingness to compromise and for his Igbo nationalism. In *The Trouble with Nigeria* Achebe criticizes Azikiwe as an example of the baleful political leadership that has plagued postcolonial Nigeria, opposing both Azikiwe and Chief Obafemi Awolowo to **Aminu Kano**, whom Achebe regards as an exemplary figure of Nigerian political leadership.

FURTHER READING

Nnamdi Azikiwe, *My Odyssey*; K.A.B. Jones-Quartey, *A Life of Azikiwe*.

M. Keith Booker

AZOGE, a blind man who is called to the shop of **Josiah** in the **Waya** market of *A Man of the People*. As described in chapter 9, Josiah then attempts to substitute a new walking stick for Azoge's old one, which the shop proprietor hopes to use in the making of a juju medicine to sell for considerable profit. Azoge detects the substitution, leading to a scandal and public outrage that drives Josiah out of business. Note that narrator **Odili Samalu**, never one to be in touch with the traditional culture of his people, admits that he does not understand the nature of this medicine or how a blind man's stick would be used in making it (86).

M. Keith Booker

B

BALDWIN, JAMES (1924–1987), born in Harlem, was an important African American playwright, essayist, poet, and intellectual. However, his main cultural importance was as a novelist, and books such as *Go Tell It on the Mountain* (1953), *Giovanni's Room* (1956), *If Beale Street Could Talk* (1974), and *Just Above My Head* (1979) helped to establish him as perhaps the most important African American novelist since Richard Wright, of whom Baldwin's view was harshly critical. In his fiction, his nonfiction, and his life, Baldwin, a gay black man, was an outspoken critic of discrimination based on race, gender, or other categories of social difference. Frustrated with the state of race and gender relations in his native country, he spent much of his life abroad, especially in France.

Shortly after Baldwin's death in 1987, Achebe wrote a tribute to him, which he delivered at a memorial service for Baldwin on December 16, 1987, at the **University of Massachusetts at Amherst**, where Baldwin had been a visiting professor. The tribute was published in ***Hopes and Impediments*** as "Postscript: James Baldwin (1924–1987)." In it, Achebe relates the inspirational impact of his first encounter, in **Nigeria**, with *Go Tell It on the Mountain* and of his first meeting with Baldwin himself, in 1980, at a conference in Gainesville, Florida, where the two writers reaffirmed the affinities between African and African American writers. Achebe sees Baldwin not only as a brilliant novelist but also as an important crusader for human rights and justice. As long as discrimination of any kind persists, suggests Achebe, "the words of James Baldwin will be there to bear witness and to inspire and elevate the struggle for human freedom" (176).

FURTHER READING

Chinua Achebe, *Hopes and Impediments*; Keneth Kinnamon, ed., *James Baldwin*; David Leeming, *James Baldwin*; Horace A. Porter, *Stealing the Fire*.

M. Keith Booker

BARD COLLEGE, a small, private, progressive, co-educational liberal arts college in Annandale-on-Hudson, New York, ninety miles north of New York City. Founded in 1860 as St. Stephen's College for men in affiliation with the Episcopal Church, the school was initially oriented toward preparing its students to enter the seminary. Beginning in 1919, the school broadened and secularized its curriculum, and it became an undergraduate college of Columbia University in 1928. The school was rechartered as

Bard College in 1935, and it began to admit women in 1944, at which time it severed its ties with Columbia and became an independent institution.

Bard College is known for its flexible curriculum and emphasis on independent study, as well as for its faculty, which has included a number of renowned figures, especially in the arts. Such faculty members have included Mary McCarthy, Ralph Ellison, Anthony Hecht, Franco Modigliani, and Saul Bellow. Achebe accepted a position as Charles P. Stevenson Professor of Literature at the school in 1990 and remains there at this writing. His wife, **Christie Achebe**, also teaches at Bard College.

FURTHER READING

Reamer Kline, *Education for the Common Good*.

M. Keith Booker

BASDEN, G(EORGE) T. (1873–1944), missionary anthropologist who published two works on **Igbo** life, *Among the Ibos of Nigeria* (1921) and *Niger Ibos* (1938). Basden's mission in the Onitsha-Ogidi-Awka area, which began in 1900, brought him into contact with Achebe's father, **Isaiah Okafor Achebe**, to whom he was a teacher and friend. Although its approach and clearly colonialist perspective make Basden's work maddening to contemporary readers, his two books are still valuable sources for understanding Igbo life at the beginning of the twentieth century. What is most interesting in the context of Achebe's writing is how extensively his village novels, particularly *Things Fall Apart*, revisit and rewrite many of the elements that Basden found to be important: the existence of love, the fate of twins, the meaning of titles, the nature of the masked spirits, the functioning of the oracles, the etiquette of kola, the social function of eloquence, the relationship of the living to the dead, the extremity of human sacrifice, and the significance of the *osu*, among others. In every case Basden's account, an extreme objectification of Igbo practice, a frozen instance of pure behavior, mute and incomprehensible, is supplanted in Achebe's work by a more supple, narrative representation that not only gives these practices a logic and meaning but translates them into the medium of the novel.

For example, the throwing away of twins is given a definitive explanation by Basden (animals have multiple births, making twins less than human), while in *Things Fall Apart* the reason is never fully given. The hospitality ritual is much the same in Basden as it is in *Things Fall Apart*; however, in the latter the ritual is subtly different each time, so that the social meanings of a particular instance are never finally available to the reader. In **Arrow of God**, the social meanings of the ritual are finally, as a careful rereading reveals, determinate. But, on a first reading, these meanings do not seem determined in advance—as indeed they are not for the fictional participants—and the outcome of the ritual is always in question until after it has taken place. In fact, on a first reading, the breaking of the kola nut in Achebe does not appear as "ritual" at all: subtle and never entirely determinate social meanings are suggested without the narratorial interpretation that characterizes the ethnographic voice. Achebe rewrites Basden's ethnographic image by introducing a certain reticence in the narrative, a refusal to collapse possible interpretations of human activity into a unitary *thing*. What had been objectified in the ethnographic "image of Africa," Achebe gives the right of subjectivity.

FURTHER READING

G. T. Basden, *Among the Ibos of Nigeria* and *Niger Ibos*.

Nicholas Brown

BASSA, the capital city of the fictional African state of **Kangan** in *Anthills of the Savannah*. It is also the principal setting for the action of the novel.

M. Keith Booker

THE BEAUTYFUL ONES ARE NOT YET BORN, by Ayi Kwei Armah (1969), opens with an unforgettable scene in which an unnamed man sleeps on a bus that has just reached its destination. The conductor, thinking he is alone, recounts the ways in which he cheats passengers as he holds the money made on the latest trip to his nose. Becoming aware of the presence of the passenger, the conductor is overwhelmed by shame and embarrassment and proceeds to chastise the passenger. The refuse that litters the city and the angry dispositions of other people are detailed as the man makes his solitary way through urban desolation to his workplace. Images of offal and decay introduced in the opening scene recur throughout the novel and are symbolic of the social and political landscape in which the unnamed protagonist dwells.

The man avoids his home and the material demands of his wife and mother-in-law. When he refuses to take bribes at work, his wife becomes angry and mocks his Christian piety. For most members of the bureaucracy, work consists of finding ways to look busy, and socialism is regarded as a sham. The man feels like a criminal because he will not be driven by greed. His isolation is alleviated only by his relationship with the vegetarian "Teacher" and with Sister Manaan and Kofi Billy. Teacher explains that the "gleam" of money and material goods is replacing religion as an object of veneration in this new postcolonial society, yet it is this awareness— this unwillingness to partake in consumer culture—that leads to the suffering and isolation of both the Teacher and the protag-

onist. They criticize the nation's leaders for mimicking whites and wish for a new movement to end the corrupt system. The man's relationship with these friends and possibilities for resistance, however, are marginalized in a story that focuses on revealing the corruption of the new nation, most notably through the figure of the politician Koomson. An acquaintance of the man from their school days, Koomson provides the man funds to start a business, but the man's wife and mother-in-law soon realize that the arrangement will benefit the politician more than it will them. When a coup seemingly sends the nation into chaos, Koomson seeks out the man, who helps him escape the country. The novel concludes with the man returning home, having realized that, despite the coup, nothing has changed.

In **"Africa and Her Writers"** Achebe characterizes the novel as "a striking parable of the corruption in Ghanaian society and of one man who refused to be contaminated by this filth" (*Morning Yet on Creation Day* 25). However, Achebe is also critical of the novel, arguing that Ghana is not a modern existentialist space but simply an African state struggling to become a nation (26). "The aura of cosmic sorrow and despair," Achebe argues, "is as foreign and unusable as those monstrous machines Nkrumah was said to have imported from Eastern Europe" (25).

FURTHER READING

M. Keith Booker, *The African Novel in English*; Terry Goldie, "A Connection of Images"; Neil Lazarus, "Pessimism of the Intellect"; Kwadwo Osei-Nyame Jr., "Love and Nation."

David Jefferess

BEKEDEREMO. See *Clark, John Pepper*.

A BEND IN THE RIVER (1979) is one of the most controversial novels by Nobel

Prize–winner **V. S. Naipaul**. A horrifying portrait of violence, chaos, and corruption in postcolonial Africa, the novel chronicles the journey of its protagonist from the east coast of Africa to a remote town in the interior and his subsequent rise and fall in fortune as a trader there. Its Conradian nature has led to comparisons between it and Achebe's *Things Fall Apart*. In particular, while both *Things Fall Apart* and *A Bend in the River* engage in clear dialogues with the work of **Joseph Conrad**, Naipaul appears to corroborate the sinister vision of Africa presented in *Heart of Darkness*, while Achebe radically departs from and challenges it. Naipaul's validation of Conrad's colonialist representation of Africa certainly seems reactionary when compared with Achebe's virulent contestation of this representation in fiction and criticism, and Achebe himself has criticized Naipaul's seemingly colonialist positions.

Perhaps what most divides *A Bend in the River* from *Things Fall Apart* is its conception of how, indeed whether, the past should be recovered in the present as a form of resistance to the colonialist repression of native traditions. For Achebe, the recovery of lost histories is an act of restitution that reverses the silencing of **Igbo** voices with which *Things Fall Apart* concludes. For Naipaul, however, romanticizing the past is a dangerous habit for two reasons: first, because it ultimately paralyzes Africans rather than enabling them to confront a modernized present, and second, because it results in claims to the effect that some Africans are more "truly African" than others.

Naipaul's conviction that a nostalgic longing for the splendors of the past can only encumber the modern African is echoed by some of his characters in *A Bend in the River*. For example, Salim, his narrator and central character, eschews African art in favor of European modernist aesthetics. This rejection of indigenous culture is what Christopher Wise sees as the fundamental flaw of *A Bend in the River*, a flaw that the earlier *Things Fall Apart* anticipates and corrects. Wise is well aware that Naipaul and Achebe offer competing accounts of postcolonial Africa. However, rather than declare one view "the truth," he recognizes that their two novels together illustrate the complexity of African history.

Reed Way Dasenbrock is less conciliatory. He sides with Naipaul, whose refusal to resuscitate the past is far preferable, he believes, to Achebe's reconstruction of it. The latter's project, Dasenbrock contends, problematically overlooks its effects on such marginal people as Salim, a member of the Arab-Indian community, and Metty, a mixed tribal. Certainly *A Bend in the River* reveals that the attempt to recuperate in the present a holistic community of the past—an attempt represented in the book by the process of "Africanization" spearheaded by the African chief, "Big Man"—is premised upon the creation and marginalization of cultural and racial outsiders. The novel reminds its readers of the readiness with which a celebration of the past such as *Things Fall Apart* performs can become a politics of intolerance, if not genocide, aimed at annihilating those Africans deemed impure. In all fairness to Achebe, however, later novels such as *Anthills of the Savannah* recognize that while the nation claims to be based on inclusion, it is in fact predicated on exclusion, a paradox these works attempt to resolve.

FURTHER READING

Reed Way Dasenbrock, "Creating a Past: Achebe, Naipaul, Soyinka, Farah"; V. S. Naipaul, *A Bend in the River*; Christopher Wise, "The Garden Trampled."

Julie McGonegal

BENDE-ONITSHA PUNITIVE EXPEDITION, a 1905 military action in which British-led troops, using the killing of Englishman **J. F. Stewart** as a pretext, marched into the **Igbo** hinterlands on a mission of "**pacification**," wreaking considerable havoc, including the decimation of the village of **Ahiara** and the destruction of the **Agbala** oracle at **Awka**. This expedition did a great deal to open the way for increased British control of the Igbo lands.

M. Keith Booker

BEWARE, SOUL BROTHER AND OTHER POEMS (1971), a collection of twenty-three poems by Achebe. The collection, revised and enlarged to include thirty-one poems, was published in London by Heinemann and in Nigeria by Nwamife in 1972 and republished as *Christmas in Biafra and Other Poems* in the United States in 1973 by Anchor-Doubleday. *Christmas in Biafra*, which was co-winner of the first Commonwealth Poetry Prize, has five sections—a Prologue (with four poems); "Poems about War" (with seven poems, one of which gives the volume its title); "Poems Not about War" (with twelve poems); "Gods, Men and Others" (with four poems); and an Epilogue (with the remaining three poems). There is also a section of Notes on thirteen of the poems.

The note to "Misunderstanding" is particularly helpful in guiding readers to an idea that gives the volume an overriding unity. Achebe writes: "The Igbo people have a firm belief in the duality of things. . . . Take any proverb which puts forward a point of view or a 'truth' and you can always find another which contradicts it or at least puts a limitation on the absoluteness of its validity" (90). Whatever the mood or tone of the poems, ranging from the wit of "Misunderstanding," to speculation on the relationship between humans and their deities in "Gods, Men and Others," to the dark and bitter irony about the **Nigerian Civil War** in, for example, "An If of History," Achebe's poems exploit the in-

tuitive Igbo sense of duality that informs all aspects of Igbo life.

"Misunderstanding" turns on the duplicity practiced by a husband who thinks he is successful in deceiving his wife with a mistress. In the end the wife knows about the mistress, knows in fact where something stands alongside her. In "Lazarus" an unfortunate villager is killed when struck by the automobile of a barrister passing through the village. The kinsmen of the "dead" man club the barrister to death only to find that their kinsman has not in fact been killed. Blaming him for the horror they have vented on the barrister, they then kill the kinsman in order to justify their taking the life of the agent of his first "death." "Refugee Mother and Child" makes a mockery of the Christian Christmas scene of the "Madonna and Child" as expectations of grace and deliverance are contrasted with the utter horror of war in which the innocent child of the title suffers starvation. "An If of History" questions the legitimacy of succession and identifies the series of paradoxes of recent history in assigning right and wrong, guilt and innocence, and the conduct of war. "Remembrance Day" turns on the irony that any ceremony on behalf of the dead, however well managed, is faint retribution for those who have died. The poem says that the living must not be complacent in their attitudes toward the dead: the dead have their own vitality, and the living had better be aware. Death is tolerable only when it leads again to life.

The section "Poems Not about War" is about how the aftermath of war shapes the lives of those who grope toward reality; it particularly conveys the confusion and uncertainty that inform their subsequent lives. The image of a vulture is used to suggest the predatory nature of life, the difficulty of survival, and the constant fear of reprisal.

"Beware Soul Brother" is a meditation on the duality of life and death and reflects on the difficulty of reconciling traditional and Christian beliefs and especially on how the Igbo sensibility is threatened by "the Cross" and the "lures of ascension day." Other poems in the volume—"Bull and Egret," "Benin Road," and the companion pieces "Mango Seedling" and "The Explorer"—are meditations on youth, aging and dying, instinct, emotion, and reason.

The poems range in style and tone from the comic and the colloquial to the rhetorical. The imagery is derived from both African and European sources. The volume possesses an overall unity through speculation in individual poems on the relationship of human and extra-human existence as this is determined and described in the consequences of personal encounters, political action, or religious beliefs. The complexity of Achebe's poetics, belied by simplicity of language, is particularly well represented by the poem that gives the volume its name, "Beware, Soul Brother."

Christmas in Biafra is Achebe's only collection of poems. He has published poems from time to time in *Okike*, the literary journal he founded at the **University of Nigeria** in 1971, including "Non-Comitment"in *Okike* No. 1, 1971; "The Old Man and the Census," *Okike* No. 6, 1974; "The American Youngster in Rags," *Okike* No. 12, 1978; "Agostinho Neto," *Okike*, No. 18, 1981. Achebe's poems from *Okike* have also been reprinted in the collection *Rhythms of Creation*, edited by D. I. Nwoga.

FURTHER READING

David Carroll, *Chinua Achebe*; C. L. Innes, *Chinua Achebe*; Umelo Ojinmah, *Chinua Achebe*.

Douglas Killam

BIAFRA, REPUBLIC OF, an **Igbo**-dominated secessionist state in southeastern **Nigeria**, named for the Bight of Biafra. Biafra, with a population of approximately fifteen million, declared its independence under the leadership of Lieutenant Colonel Chukumeka Odumegwu Ojukwu in May 1967 in order to provide a haven for Igbo who felt that they were being persecuted in federal Nigeria, especially in the northern region, where anti-Igbo violence had escalated to alarming levels. The federal government responded to the secession with economic sanctions, then with a military assault, leading to the **Nigerian Civil War**, beginning in July 1967.

The Biafran economy depended heavily on oil, and when the oil fields were captured by federal forces early in the civil war, Biafra was left with insufficient resources either to carry on the war effectively or to survive independently, especially when severe food shortages led to widespread famine in the region. The Biafran capital of Enugu fell to federal forces in October 1967, forcing the removal of the capital to Umuahia. While several prominent Igbo, including Achebe, campaigned for international support and aid for the Biafran cause, little of this aid was forthcoming. In the face of famine and continuing military reversals, the Biafran state struggled to survive, eventually collapsing in January 1970. By that time, upward of one million Biafrans had died either in combat or of disease and starvation.

After the civil war, the area of Biafra was reintegrated into federal Nigeria, though the memory of the Biafran experience continued to play a role in the ethnic tensions that Achebe has identified as a crucial social problem in *The Trouble with Nigeria*. Biafra and the civil war have provided material for a great deal of subsequent Nigerian literature. In Achebe's writings, Biafra is echoed in the depiction of the failed secessionist state of Abazon in *Anthills of the Savannah*. Biafra and the Nigerian Civil War are also central to many of Achebe's poems and short stories.

FURTHER READING

Herbert Ekwe-Ekwe, *The Biafra War*; Frederick Forsyth, *The Biafra Story*; Arthur Ravenscroft, "The Nigerian Civil War in Nigerian Literature"; Ken Saro-Wiwa, *On a Darkling Plain*.

M. Keith Booker

BIAFRA WAR. See **Nigerian Civil War**.

BISI, one of the young women with whom **Obi Okonkwo**'s economist friend, **Christopher**, has a liaison in *No Longer at Ease*. In chapter 11 Bisi and Christopher go dancing on a Saturday night with **Clara Okeke** and Obi at **the Imperial**, a nightclub in **Lagos**. Although Bisi clearly enjoys the music at the Imperial, starts dancing almost as soon as she arrives, and leaves only reluctantly at two in the morning, her wish earlier in the evening is to go to a movie rather than go dancing, which is Christopher's preference. To Bisi's wish Christopher responds, "Look here, Bisi, we are not interested in what you want to do. It's for Obi and me to decide. This na [is] Africa, you know." Whether Christopher's words are spoken in jest or in earnest or whether they arise from an ambivalent impulse is left to the reader to determine.

Thomas J. Lynn

BLACKETT, MR. Mr. Blackett is a West Indian **missionary** who serves as a teacher at **Umuaro** in *Arrow of God*. **Oduche** is inspired to learn by Blackett, whom Oduche thinks "has more knowledge than the white man" (chapter 4).

Rachel R. Reynolds

BLACKIE'S *ARITHMETIC*, mentioned in chapter 13 of *No Longer at Ease*, is a mathematics text that **Isaac Okonkwo** "used in 1908," which corresponds approximately to the later events of *Things Fall Apart* (see Wren, *Achebe's World* 23, 68). The text is still in Isaac's personal library during the time frame of *No Longer at Ease*. His long possession of it helps illustrate his "mystic regard for the written word," and due to this he "never destroyed a piece of paper."

FURTHER READING

Robert M. Wren, *Achebe's World*.

Thomas J. Lynn

BONIFACE, houseboy or "small boy" at "Government Hill" house in **Okperi**, where **Winterbottom** resides in *Arrow of God*.

Rachel R. Reynolds

BONIFACE, a somewhat unsavory local thug (though he is not originally from the region) in **Urua** whom **Odili Samalu** hires as his chief bodyguard during his bid for election to parliament in *A Man of the People*. The bodyguards turn out to be necessary, given the considerable attempts of the supporters of Samalu's opponent, **Chief Nanga**, to disrupt Samalu's campaign. Boniface is an effective bodyguard, though his willingness to employ violent measures goes beyond what Samalu is willing to endorse. Samalu clearly wonders if he himself might be in danger from his violent employee, who seems willing to sell his services to the highest bidder, despite his expressed contempt for Nanga.

M. Keith Booker

BOOKER PRIZE, prestigious literary award given annually for the best full-length novel written in English by a citizen of the United Kingdom, Ireland, Pakistan, South Africa, or the British Commonwealth. The award is administered by the Book Trust in the United Kingdom and was long financed by the Booker McConnell Corporation, an international conglomerate. Until 2002, in fact, its full name was the Booker McConnell Prize for Fiction, though it is typically known by the shorter name. In 2002, the Man Group (another international conglomerate) was named the new sponsor of the award, the official name of which then changed to the Man Booker Prize.

The Booker Prize has been awarded to such writers as India's Arundhati Roy (for *The God of Small Things*, 1997) and Nigeria's Ben Okri (for *The Famished Road*, 1991). *Midnight's Children* by India's Salman Rushdie not only won the award in 1981, but that book also won a special award in 1994 for the best novel eligible for the prize to have been published in the first twenty-five years of the award. Achebe was short-listed for the Booker Prize in 1987 for *Anthills of the Savannah*, the only one of his novels to have been published since the inception of the award.

The Booker Prize has drawn valuable attention to the works of a number of postcolonial writers. However, the award has also been criticized as a form of cultural imperialism, partly because of the international operations of the Booker McConnell conglomerate and partly because it tends to identify literature from all of the eligible areas as subsets of British literature.

FURTHER READING

Graham Huggan, "Prizing 'Otherness': A Short History of the Booker"; Richard Todd, *Consuming Fictions*.

M. Keith Booker

BORI, the capital city of the fictional postcolonial African nation of *A Man of the People*. Clearly modeled on **Lagos** (just as the nation is rather transparently modeled on **Nigeria**), Bori is also the principal site of the urban portion of the novel's action, much of which revolves around the corrupt political climate in the capital, depicted as a city of stark contrasts between the lives of the rich,

who live in impressive luxury, and the poor, who live in abject squalor.

M. Keith Booker

BRADDELEY, MR. In *No Longer at Ease*, chapter 14, the teacher at the then-new Christian teacher training college in **Umuru** who criticized young **Isaac Okonkwo**'s response to his father, **Okonkwo**'s, death. This is recounted decades later by Isaac to his son, **Obi**. Upon hearing the news of Okonkwo's suicide Isaac commented, "those who live by the sword must perish by the sword," a veiled reference to Okonkwo's killing of **Ikeme-funa**. Mr. Braddeley told Isaac that "it was not the right thing to say" and that he should return home for the burial. Isaac, however, refused to go. (See also chapter 21 of *Things Fall Apart*.)

Thomas J. Lynn

BRAIMOH, an honest and virtuous taxi driver in *Anthills of the Savannah*. In the course of the novel, he befriends **Chris Oriko** and accompanies him on his flight from **Bassa** late in the novel. After the killing of Oriko, Braimoh remains a member of the circle of the survivors and friends of Oriko and **Ikem Osodi**. He is the husband of **Aina**, who also joins this circle.

M. Keith Booker

BRIDE-PRICE. In traditional **Igbo** culture, the gifts that a suitor and his family present to a woman and her parents in order that the suitor may be accepted as the woman's husband and that their children will be legitimate. In chapter 8 of *Things Fall Apart*, **Ibe**, **Ukegbu**'s son, wishes to marry **Akueke**, **Obierika**'s daughter. The initial portion of bride-price, settled at twenty bags of cowries, is negotiated between Ukegbu and Obierika in the latter's hut. In chapter 12 Ibe and Ukegbu arrive again at Obierika's compound, this time with numerous relatives, for the *uri*, a ceremony that involves additional bride-price payment. *Uri* is "really a woman's ceremony," according to the narrator, "and the central figures were the bride and her mother." In the novel the groom and his family bring fifty pots of palm-wine to the *uri*, which is marked by a feast and dancing, and at the end of the ceremony they bring Akueke back to their village for seven market weeks. But betrothal also involves significant expenditure on the part of Akueke's family, which not only prepares the lavish feast but also presents a large goat to the groom's family.

Bride-price is mentioned as well in chapters 10 and 14 of *Things Fall Apart*. In chapter 10 bride-price is associated with the marital dispute between **Mgbafo** and her abusive husband, **Uzowulu**, a dispute brought before the *egwugwu* to determine in part whether "the law of **Umuofia** . . . that if a woman runs away from her husband her bride-price is returned" applies in the case. **Robert M. Wren** observes the important, positive role of bride-price in this case and in traditional Igbo society in general:

The settlement made by the groom's family upon the family of the bride became a mutual guarantee of a stable marriage. That is to say, if the man should prove to be a bad husband, his wife could return to her kin and they could deny him restitution of the wealth. If she, on the other hand, abandoned him without good reason, he could claim full recovery. Usually—as in the case that comes before the *egwugwu* in Chapter X—the marriage dispute is arbitrated and the marriage restabilized; the wealth has assured that the effort would be made. (49)

In chapter 14 bride-price has already been paid for **Amikwu**'s marriage to an unnamed young woman, so that "all but the last ceremony had been performed." This last ceremony, which seals the marriage, is that of the *isa-ifi*, the "confession" by the bride that she has been faithful to the groom since the marriage negotiations commenced.

In chapter 5 of Achebe's second novel, *No Longer at Ease*, reference is made to the fact that the British have outlawed bride-price, yet according to **Joseph Okeke**, the friend of the novel's protagonist, **Obi Okonkwo**, the effect of the law has been to "push[] up the price, that's all." This information and the indications in *Things Fall Apart* that women have a vital and honored role in relation to the betrothal observances suggest that one function of bride-price is to confer dignity and status on the bride. It may be noted, too, that the reverse impact of the bride-price law is one of the varied forms of resistance by traditional African culture to British domination in *No Longer at Ease*.

The survival of bride-price in post-independence Nigeria among Western-influenced characters is illustrated in the final chapter of *A Man of the People*. The novel's protagonist and narrator, **Odili Samalu**, wishes to marry **Edna**. Consequently his father, **Hezekiah Samalu**, some of Hezekiah's close relatives, and Odili himself bring a "big pot of palm-wine to Edna's father" to begin negotiations for his consent and to agree on how much bride-price he will receive. Odili insists on paying not only the bride-price that Edna's former suitor, **Chief Nanga**, previously paid—and that Edna's father must now presumably return—but also the 100 pounds that Nanga had paid for her formal education and "other incidentals." This aspect of the negotiations provides a glimpse of the increasing emphasis placed on academic opportunities for women.

Yet the most recent reference to bride-price in Achebe's fiction—in the final chapter of *Anthills of the Savannah*—tellingly suggests that in the contemporary urban environment such a tradition is honored at least sometimes in the breach. This reference is part of a proverb-laced commentary by **Elewa**'s unnamed, elderly uncle, who participates in the naming ceremony for the infant of **Ikem Osodi** and Elewa (whose plans to marry end with Ikem's murder by security forces): "Something is amiss. We did not hear *kpom* to tell us that the palm branch has been cut before we heard *waa* when it crashed through the bush. I did not hear of bride-price and you are telling me about naming a child" (chapter 18). Thus, bride-price in Achebe's novels is one kind of prism through which African tradition and its multifaceted reaction to Western pressures may be viewed.

FURTHER READING

Robert M. Wren, *Achebe's World*.

Thomas J. Lynn

BRITISH AMALGAMATED, a large fictional British corporation that still has considerable business dealings in the former British colony (now a new nation) featured in *A Man of the People*. The continuing operations of British Amalgamated suggest the ongoing neocolonial influence (especially economic) of the British in their former colony, while there are numerous hints that the African operations of British Amalgamated are greatly enhanced by the paying of bribes to local officials. In addition, British Amalgamated (along with "the Americans") makes large contributions to the campaign funds of the ruling **People's Organization Party (POP)**, hoping to keep the current government in power and further enhance the opportunities offered to the British corporation. Thus, Achebe suggests a strong Western contribution to the African corruption and greed that he satirizes in the novel.

M. Keith Booker

BROWN, MR., white Christian missionary in *Things Fall Apart*. Based in **Umuofia**, he pays regular visits to the congregation in **Mbanta** during **Okonkwo**'s exile there. He is depicted as a moderate man, respected by the **Igbo** because of his insistence on restraint and on showing respect for the traditional faith and customs of the local people, even as he works to convert them to Christianity. He has great success until he is forced to return home due to ill health.

M. Keith Booker

BUCHAN, JOHN (1875–1940), British writer of adventure stories and "thrillers," colonial administrator. Buchan's adventure narratives, like those of **H. Rider Haggard**, a short generation before him, were to be found on the shelves of Chinua Achebe's secondary school library, components of the "tradition of British writing about Africa," samples of which had been compiled by Dorothy Hammond and Alta Jablow in their anthology *The Africa That Never Was* (1992). According to Achebe, that collection, which includes selections from over four centuries, is a categorical exhibit on behalf of the argument that such a tradition "does not begin and thrive . . . unless it serves a certain need" (*Home and Exile*). While the specificities of such needs might have developed across the turns of centuries—from the slave trade to territorial aggrandizement to resource extraction—the general aims of British imperialism remained the determining factor. Important for Achebe then is the examination of the "content, style and timing of this literature."

Like those of H. Rider Haggard, John Buchan's stories became part of the library of imperial adventure—and adventurism. *Prester John* (1910), for example, follows in the tradition of legendary gem hunters and prescriptions for white rule so paradigmatic in Haggard's *King Solomon's Mines*. Buchan's hero, the young Scotsman David Crawfurd, not unlike Haggard's Allan Quatermain, sets out in search of a precious stone concealed in a secret cave in the Rooirand. But along the way, rather than restore an African chief to his position of leadership, Crawfurd, just as much a mercenary as Quatermain, must assist instead in the subduing of a native uprising, led by the redoubtable Laputa, and both recover the sacred ruby necklace of Solomonic legend and discover the diamonds alleged to have been pilfered by the African workers from the mines and said to have been collected in a hidden ceremonial cave secreted well beyond the mountain passes of the region.

Again like Haggard, John Buchan began his political career in South Africa, where he had gone out in secretarial service to Lord Milner in 1901, to assist in the reconstruction of the country following the devastation of the Anglo-Boer War (1899–1901). Buchan remained politically and ideologically affiliated with the young Oxonians that Milner collected around him in those South African years, the group, known as "Milner's kindergarten," that eventually went on to establish the Round Table movement and its journal of the same name, advocating the ideal of empire not as a collection of colonies but as a federation of dominions. His tetralogy of "thrillers," featuring the South African-born Richard Hannay and written between 1915 and 1924, follows the fate of British imperialism from the African continent across the Levant and home to England as World War I alters the parameters and possibilities of maintaining the cohesion of the imperial agenda. When Buchan died in 1940, at the beginning of the World War II, he was serving as governor-general of Canada. See also **Haggard, H. Rider**.

FURTHER READING

John Buchan, *The Four Adventures of Richard Hannay*; Janet Adam Smith, *John Buchan*.

Barbara Harlow

BULLFROG IN THE SUN, a 1971 film directed by the West German Hans Jürgen Pohland and based on both ***Things Fall Apart*** and ***No Longer at Ease***. A joint Nigerian, West German, and American production, the film was also later distributed under the title *Things Fall Apart* to make more clear its status as an adaptation of Achebe's best-known novel. However, the film is constructed around a continual shift in context from one novel to the other and really relies almost equally on *Things Fall Apart* and *No Longer at Ease*. Indeed, the postcolonial context of the latter novel is presented as the baseline time frame of the novel, with scenes based on *Things Fall Apart* presented essentially as flashbacks that provide background to the political and economic woes of postcolonial **Nigeria**. The film was not widely distributed in the United States and has been seen by American viewers largely on public television.

As Frank Ukadike summarizes it, "following a sociohistorical path, indicative of Nigeria's emancipation, this film constitutes a tapestry of caustic vignettes of contemporary life amongst pervasive scenes of squalor and corruption" (146). *Bullfrog in the Sun* is, in fact, extremely negative in its depiction of conditions in Nigeria in the present-day segments of the film. It stars Johnny Sekka, who plays the role of **Obi Okonkwo**, the protagonist in the present-day frame of the story, as well as Obi's grandfather, **Okonkwo**, the protagonist of the past-time segments. The plot of the film is reasonably consistent with the plots of the novels on which it is based, though the formal dual-time-frame construction of the film did force some modifications, while the overall tone of the film is far more pessimistic than the tone of Achebe's novels, which consistently allow for the possibility of better conditions in the future, however baleful conditions in the present might be.

This difference in tone no doubt partly accounts for Achebe's reportedly negative reception of the film.

Charles Larson (who provides a useful sequence-by-sequence plot summary of the film) praises it as a well-made film about Africa but also notes the film's lack of commercial and critical success, suggesting that, in an attempt to appeal to both African and Western viewers, the makers of the film succeeded in appealing to neither (108). Ultimately, however, Larson finds that the film adheres more to a Western than an African perspective, arguing that it is informed by a rather Kafkaesque sense of the futility of modern life. Further, Larson argues that the film's strongly negative and pessimistic depiction of the conditions of life in modern Africa is reminiscent of works such as **V. S. Naipaul**'s *A Bend in the River*: "Things have indeed fallen apart in this film—so far that there is no sense of their ever being mended again, which is not the feeling one derives from living within the society itself" (110).

FURTHER READING

Charles R. Larson, "The Film Version of Achebe's *Things Fall Apart*"; Nwachukwu Frank Ukadike, *Black African Cinema*.

M. Keith Booker

C

CARROLL, DAVID (1932–   ), an important scholar, teacher, and literary critic whose book-length study *Chinua Achebe: Novelist, Poet, Critic* was a crucial work in the growth of Achebe's critical reputation in the West. Born in Yorkshire, Carroll received his B.A. from Durham in 1953, his M.A. from the London University in 1957, and his Ph.D. from Durham in 1962. He has held a number of teaching posts at African, Canadian, and British universities. From 1957 to 1963, he taught at Fourah Bay College in Freetown, Sierra Leone; from 1963 to 1972, he taught at the University of Toronto; from 1972 to 1989, he taught at Lancaster University, where he also served a term as the head of the Department of English. He formally retired in 1989 but continued to work with the Lancaster Department of English until disabled by a serious stroke in 1998.

Carroll's study of Achebe and his writing was first published in 1970, then followed by expanded versions in 1980 and 1990, updated to reflect Achebe's ongoing literary production. In 1980, Carroll also published *Chinua Achebe, Arrow of God: Notes*. In addition to his important work on Achebe, Carroll has worked and published in a number of other areas. He was, for example, joint editor of the Longon Literature in English series, of which about thirty volumes were published. He is especially well known for his work as a scholar of George Eliot, in which role he published a book-length study, *George Eliot and the Conflict of Interpretations* (1992), while also compiling and editing *George Eliot: The Critical Tradition* (1971). He was also the editor of the much-respected 1986 Clarendon Press edition of Eliot's *Middlemarch*.

FURTHER READING

David Carroll, *Chinua Achebe, George Eliot and the Conflict of Interpretations* and *George Eliot: The Critical Heritage*.

M. Keith Booker

CARY, JOYCE (Arthur Joyce Lunel Cary, 1888–1957), British novelist, born in Londonderry, Northern Ireland. After taking part in the Balkan War (1912–1913), Cary joined the British political service in colonial **Nigeria** in 1913. He subsequently served in the Nigeria Regiment during the Cameroons campaign of 1915–1916. After being wounded in the Cameroons, he served for a time in the civil capacity of district officer in colonial Nigeria.

Having returned to England to devote himself to writing, Cary's career as a novelist began in 1932 with the publication of *Aissa*

Saved, concerning a West African girl's relationship to Christianity. His next three novels—*An American Visitor* (1933), *The African Witch* (1936), and **Mister Johnson** (1939)—are all set in Africa. The last of these provided an important impetus for Achebe himself to begin writing. Calling *Mister Johnson* "appalling," and "superficial" in its portrayal of Nigeria and Nigerians, Achebe was inspired to write his early novels *Things Fall Apart, No Longer at Ease*, and *Arrow of God* partly as a corrective response. On the other hand, Achebe's ironic but sympathetic approach to the lives of British colonists in some of his works may owe something to Cary's portrayals. Whatever the case, certain characters and scenes in *Mister Johnson* identifiably make their way, though completely transformed, into *Arrow of God*, where the introduction of perspectives entirely lacking in the earlier work reveals its blindnesses with regard to the reality of the colonial venture.

FURTHER READING

Alan Bishop, *Joyce Cary*; Michael T. Harris, *Outsiders and Insiders*; C. L. Innes, *Chinua Achebe*; Abdul R. JanMohamed, *Manichean Aesthetics*.

Nicholas Brown

CENTRAL INTELLIGENCE AGENCY (U.S.). See **Foundations**.

CHI. In **Igbo** tradition, the personal god that helps to determine the fortune of each individual. The concept figures prominently in **Things Fall Apart**, with reference to the fate of **Unoka** and that of his son, **Okonkwo** (refer to chapters 3, 4, and 14 of *Things Fall Apart*). It is also mentioned in chapters 5 and 18 of **No Longer at Ease**. Kalu Ogbaa concludes that the concept of chi "is at the root of individualism in Igbo tradition." However, he points out that, while *chi* provides a link to the ancestors and grants individuals a cer-

tain amount of guidance and protection in life, "*chi* does not help an individual who fails to help himself" (15).

The notion of chi has been illustrated in Achebe's *Things Fall Apart*. To the Igbo, chi is a person's guardian spirit or personal god, a person's other self in the spirit realm, his "complementary spirit being." A person's chi is believed to wield enormous power over him or her in ways that no other forces can. Thus, the Igbo believe that chi solely controls one's destiny and actually determines the extent to which one can prosper. This peculiar power of the spirit being makes its human counterpart particularly vulnerable to it. The Igbo also believe that a person receives his or her life's portion in the spirit realm before he or she comes into the world; there are options open to the person at this point, and he or she can make choices in the presence of his or her chi regarding his or her ultimate destiny. Once this covenant is made, it cannot possibly be altered when the person comes into the world. On the other hand, there are countless numbers of Igbo proper names, proverbs, folktales, rituals, and so on that suggest that if a person perseveres, the chi will concur; in other words, if a person says yes, his or her chi will agree. The people believe that no evil plotted against a person to bring about his or her destruction will come to fruition unless his or her chi is in accord.

Chi is so central to Igbo spirituality and thought that it can be said to form the core of their existence. Thus, the Igbo acknowledge the supremacy of chi by the names they give to their children. One can take a peek into a man's life though his children's names; his joys, hopes, sorrows, fears, and anxieties are all embodied in these names. Through the names of his children, an Igbo man directly pays homage to his chi for favors received or implores it to create a desired equilibrium in any aspect of his life. Consequently, there are few names in Igbo that have no direct connection with chi.

Not only is chi personal to an individual, but the individual is also created by it. Again, names, rituals proverbs, and expressions abound in Igbo that refer to the creative role of chi, that is, chi that creates. One might ask at this point, and rightly so, what the role of the Supreme Being is in the creation process. Chi as perceived by the Igbo is clearly distinct from Chi Ukwu "Great Chi" or **Chukwu**, the Supreme Being and the creator of everything, but both are believed to have a very close relationship; both are believed to be in close communion with the sun from which the earth receives daylight, also known as "chi" in Igbo. Thus, *chi ofufo* means daybreak. Chi is perceived as a manifestation of Chukwu, a delegate of sorts to Chukwu, and is not far removed from Him.

If the original covenant taken with one's chi at the beginning is taken into account, then the question of a good or bad chi may not strictly arise. Besides, a human being has been given the option to transcend his or her originally agreed upon limitations provided he or she has the proper recourse to his or her chi. In *Things Fall Apart*, Okonkwo's father, Unoka, a pathologically lazy individual, sits around, plays his flute, drinks palm-wine, and habitually owes his friends and neighbors; he is a man with no ambition whatsoever. He makes no attempt to say yes, and so his chi lets him be. Could his chi then be blamed for his fate? The Igbo believe that there is a universal equity and fair play; most often, when a person reaps misfortune while persistently working hard, they attribute it to several factors, one of the factors being the method of seeking his or her desired goal in life. If this method is unethical, then the person cannot succeed. That is, although it has been stated that when a person says yes, the chi will concur, it is not always so, as the case of Okonkwo in *Things Fall Apart*

clearly demonstrates. Okonkwo's inflexibility, a trait abhorrent to the Igbo, is largely responsible for his fate; his one-dimensional quest for power and greatness blinds him to the repercussions of some of his actions. His hubris leads him to see himself as the center of everything. Hence, he perceives everything masculine as powerful and everything feminine as weak. In fact, he challenges both his chi and **Ani**, the earth goddess, by his rashness and impulsiveness. It is no wonder then that his chi looks the other way as he plunges headlong to his destruction—first by his ignoble participation in the execution of his "son," **Ikemefuna** and later by the other atrocities perpetrated by him in *Things Fall Apart*. As a suicide and abomination, Okonkwo could not be accorded a proper burial and will not join the community of ancestors and, like his father, will be cast into the **Evil Forest**. He lives true to the Igbo saying that no man can rise above the destiny of his chi.

For Achebe's comments on the concept of chi, see the essay "Chi in Igbo Cosmology," included in *Morning Yet on Creation Day*.

FURTHER READING

Chinua Achebe, "Chi in Igbo Cosmology" (*Morning Yet on Creation Day*); Mazi Elechukwu Nnadibuagha Njaka, *Igbo Political Culture*; Kalu Ogbaa, *Gods, Oracles, and Divination*.

Christine Nwakego Ohale

"CHI IN IGBO COSMOLOGY." Achebe essay. See *Morning Yet on Creation Day*.

CHIELO, the priestess of **Agbala**, the Oracle of the Hills and Caves, in *Things Fall Apart*. In daily life she is a widow with two children. She is a friend of **Ekwefi**, with whom she shares a common shed in the market. She is also very fond of **Ezinma**, the daughter of **Okonkwo** and Ekwefi, whom she takes to the oracle in chapter 11.

M. Keith Booker

CHIKA. In *Things Fall Apart*, the priestess of **Agbala** the Oracle of the Hills and Caves in the days of **Okonkwo**'s boyhood. In chapter 3 she chides **Unoka** for his weakness with his machete and hoe, to which she attributes his poor yam crops. Chika is the predecessor of **Chielo**.

M. Keith Booker

CHIKE AND THE RIVER, one of several children's books by Achebe, was first published in 1966 by Cambridge University Press, indicating the cultural prestige that Achebe had already accumulated by that time. Featuring drawings by Prue Theobalds, *Chike and the River* is the longest and most complex of Achebe's books for children. In it, the title character is a boy who leaves his home village to live with his uncle in **Onitsha**. This new environment leads him to meet new friends from a different cultural background, leading to numerous comparisons between various aspects of Chike's village culture and the urban culture of Onitsha. The book thus reflects Achebe's own stated feeling of growing up at the crossroads of two different cultures. In the course of these comparisons, the book attempts to teach a number of lessons, as in its satire of the foolishness and laziness of some of the Onitsha schoolboys who seek to succeed in school by taking "brain pills" rather than through hard work.

Chike and the River, along with his other children's books, including *How the Leopard Got His Claws* (1972), *The Drum* (1977), and *The Flute* (1977), thus enacts Achebe's own expressed belief that the African novelist must also serve as a teacher. He describes this notion in the essay "The Novelist as Teacher," which appears in *Morning Yet on Creation Day*. Still, despite this didactic intent, *Chike and the River* is also a spirited adventure designed to hold the attention of young readers. In the story, Chike becomes fascinated with the River Niger and dreams of riding a ferry across the river from Onitsha to Asaba. After some initial setbacks, his hard work and determination allow him to earn enough money to pay the fare and to ride the ferry across. Unfortunately, he misses the last boat home and spends a night of harrowing adventure with a gang of robbers, whom the police eventually identify and arrest, largely thanks to Chike's testimony. As a reward for his courage and honesty, Chike's picture appears in a local newspaper and his name is mentioned on the radio, while he himself is given a scholarship that will fund his education through secondary school. Children who read the book are thus encouraged to behave with similar virtue, though the story can also be taken, at another level, as an admonition to Nigeria's political leaders to show greater courage and responsibility in carrying out their duties.

Chike and the River reveals its kinship with Achebe's major fiction in several ways. For example, the protagonist is from **Umuofia**, the same rural **Igbo** village in southeastern **Nigeria** as **Okonkwo** and **Obi Okonkwo**, the protagonists of Achebe's first two novels. Like Achebe's novels, moreover, *Chike and the River* presents a wealth of Nigerian cultural images and details involving, for example, food specialties, sleeping conditions, songs, and the varied use of **pidgin English**, as well as certain Igbo proverbs (including, appropriately enough, "Why should we live by the River Niger and then wash our hands with spittle?" (28), a proverb that appears twice in *No Longer at Ease*). The perspective and emphasis in the story are consistent with the concerns of an active and intelligent boy, yet they reach beyond those concerns and hold interest for mature readers.

FURTHER READING

Miriam Dow, "A Postcolonial Child"; James Miller, "The Novelist as Teacher."

M. Keith Booker and Thomas J. Lynn

CHINUA ACHEBE (1990), by **C. L. Innes**, was published in the Cambridge Studies in

African and Caribbean Literature series. It covers most of Achebe's writing and provides a fairly broad introduction to Achebe's work. However, *Chinua Achebe* is a sophisticated critical study that goes beyond introductory surveys of various works to provide insightful critical analysis of the writings of Achebe within the context of the work of such theorists as Mikhail Bakhtin and **Frantz Fanon**. In particular, Innes is concerned with the literary nature of Achebe's writing and with the way in which that writing, as literature, not only confronts the legacy of Western literature but also makes important contributions to the development of an African literary tradition. Though Innes also discusses Achebe's essays, short stories, and poems, her principal focus is on his novels and on the way in which they contribute to the "Africanization" of the novel as a genre, rendering this most Western and bourgeois of genres useful and appropriate for the expression of African postcolonial cultural sensibilities.

Innes begins with a brief introductory chapter in which she describes her project of reading Achebe within a literary context and especially in opposition to the novels of **Joyce Cary**. She then follows with a chapter entitled "Origins" that provides some useful biographical information on Achebe, a brief introduction to **Igbo** culture, and a survey of Nigerian history as background to Achebe's life and career. Chapter 2 then discusses *Things Fall Apart*, providing a detailed reading of Achebe's first novel that focuses on Achebe's response in this novel to the Western literary tradition, particularly to Cary's *Mister Johnson*. Innes notes the way in which Cary's novel is structured around a polar opposition between logical, thinking Europeans and emotional, feeling Africans; she then demonstrates the ways in which Achebe undermines this opposition, particularly by representing African characters who themselves embody both poles of this duality. She

also provides a discussion of the obvious parallels between Achebe's **Unoka** and Cary's Mister Johnson but points out that Unoka is a much more positive figure because he is a conscious artist, while Johnson is an unthinking primitive who acts strictly on the basis of feeling and instinct.

In chapter 3, Innes turns to a discussion of *No Longer at Ease*, again concentrating on its status as literature. Here, she notes the important thematic focus on Western literature and on the ways in which **Obi Okonkwo**'s consciousness has been crucially informed by his study of Western literature and Western modes of critical thought. When Obi finds himself caught between European and African cultural forces, he is unable to reflect a resolution between them, thus failing in the project that is Achebe's own: to take Western literary forms (such as the novel) and to make them his own as an African writer, thus effectively combining Western and African cultural traditions.

Chapter 4 discusses *Arrow of God*, which, in comparison to *Things Fall Apart*, Innes sees as providing "a much more convincing and complex portrayal of a traditional community and the tensions and rivalries which make it active and vital" (72). In this case, Achebe also uses his representation of traditional Igbo culture to address a number of fundamental political and philosophical issues, including the question of leadership and "the problem of 'knowing,'" which Innes sees as the "central theme" of the novel (72). Innes also again formulates her reading of Achebe in opposition to the work of Cary, though here she concentrates on Cary's *The African Witch* as an important forerunner of *Arrow of God*. For example, she notes the way in which Achebe's representation of traditional Igbo religion as a legitimate and coherent theological and philosophical system can be taken as a response to Cary's treatment of African religion as a form of primitive superstition.

In chapter 5, Innes explores Achebe's treatment of postcolonial politics in *A Man of the People*. She again identifies *The African Witch* as an important predecessor, arguing that Achebe here enters into a dialogue with Cary's novel in terms of the themes of "interlinked political and sexual jealousy, of the young westernized idealist and would-be leader of his people, of political demagoguery, and of political abuse" (83). However, maintaining her literary focus, Innes also discusses the way in which language itself functions as a crucial theme of the novel.

In chapter 6, Innes discusses Achebe's role as critic and political activist during the period 1960–1988, noting his emergence as an important international spokesman for African literature and culture. Chapter 7 then treats the stories of *Girls at War and Other Stories*, arguing that they continue many of the same themes as the earlier novels but tend to focus on more marginal characters, while the novels tend to focus on characters who aspire to leadership in their communities. Chapter 8 discusses Achebe's treatment of the **Nigerian Civil War** in the poems of *Beware, Soul Brother*.

In chapter 9, Innes discusses *Anthills of the Savannah*, which she sees as differing in fundamental ways from the earlier novels. In particular, while the earlier novels are set against the backdrop of the Western literary tradition, *Anthills of the Savannah* is late enough that it needs to be read with the developing African literary tradition as an important part of the intertextual background. Innes also finds that Achebe's exploration of language in his latest and most complex and sophisticated novel tends to move toward an emphasis on writing and away from the emphasis on speaking in the earlier novels.

In her conclusion, Innes sums up her findings, noting that Achebe's novels often resemble Georg Lukács's description of the best European realist novels, especially in their portrayal of characters as organically connected to the social and historical context in which they live. However, Innes also argues that it would be a mistake to regard Achebe's fiction simply as realist. In particular, she argues that he challenges and modifies the realist tradition by insisting that his readers take a much more active role in the generation of meaning. In this sense, Innes concludes, Achebe's reformulation of the genre of the novel is reminiscent, for Innes, of Bertolt Brecht's important challenge to the realist tradition of European drama in his development of the technique of epic theater (168–69).

FURTHER READING

David Carroll, *Chinua Achebe*; Simon Gikandi, *Reading Chinua Achebe*; G. D. Killam, *The Writings of Chinua Achebe*.

M. Keith Booker

CHINUA ACHEBE: A BIOGRAPHY, by Ezenwa-Ohaeto (1997), is a full-length critical biography of Achebe that usefully employs details from Achebe's life to illuminate his writing. Authored by a student and later colleague of Achebe himself, *Chinua Achebe: A Biography* reveals its purpose in a preface, which makes clear that Ezenwa-Ohaeto's project is not merely to recount the life and work of the distinctive African author but also to explore "the social, historical, and cultural milieu that influenced and inspired him." For Achebe, Ezenwa-Ohaeto observes, is a remarkably gifted author whose influence on African literature, especially on young African writers, has been phenomenal. Achebe deserves such broad and penetrating treatment for these reasons. Ezenwa-Ohaeto's claims are well borne out in his biography; it portrays Achebe as that rare personality who has given an entire continent a voice.

Ezenwa-Ohaeto provides a detailed account of Achebe's life, beginning with his birth in 1930 as Albert Chinualumogu Achebe, the son of **Isaiah Okafor Achebe**, a zealous Christian convert who was working for the Church Missionary Society as a catechist. In addition to such central facts, Ezenwa-Ohaeto includes a great deal of interesting anecdotal material. For example, when World War II began, Achebe (always an exemplary student) was still at St. Philip's Central School. Run by English **missionaries**, the school initiated a program of supporting the war effort by requiring young children to gather palm-kernel, a chore they didn't particularly like. One boy wrote a letter to Hitler, presumably evincing admiration for him. When the act was discovered, the boy was pronounced "an offspring of Satan" by the headmaster and was flogged before the entire school (13).

It was a measure of Isaiah Achebe's tolerance and interest in his son's education that he didn't send Achebe to a secondary school run by English missionaries, though he was one of them and despite their entreaties to have him as their student. Instead, Achebe went to the **Government College at Umuahia** (the term "college" here being roughly equivalent to an American high school), which was free from missionary management. Achebe performed well in the Government College, earning impressive grades in the final exams at the end of the program. These years, on the other hand, were unremarkable in other respects. Achebe read profusely as well as indiscriminately. When reading literature dealing with colonial encounters, he began to share some of the same colonial prejudices as Nigeria's white rulers (27). From the Government College at Umuahia, Achebe went to the **University College, Ibadan**, originally to study medicine on a scholarship. Soon he changed his mind and switched to English—though the decision caused him to lose the scholarship. Later he was awarded a bursary, though a major source of support during these years was the

help he received from his brothers. The University College provided Achebe with opportunities to try his hand at creative writing. He contributed several stories and essays to the university magazine, the *University Herald*.

In 1958, Achebe published ***Things Fall Apart***, a masterpiece of African literature that has sold more than three million copies and been translated into forty-five languages (246). At that time, he was working as the head of the talks department of the **Nigerian Broadcasting Service** (NBS, later changed to **Nigerian Broadcasting Corporation**, or NBC) at **Lagos**. He accepted this position after a short stint as a teacher at a local school in Oba, his first job after graduation from the University College. Ezenwa-Oahaeto describes how the manuscript of *Things Fall Apart* finally reached **Alan Hill**'s desk at Heinemann. Since typing was a facility not available in **Nigeria** at that time, Achebe sent the only handwritten copy to a typing service in London via regular post. Even after he paid the fee, he didn't receive the typed manuscript for months. Finally, Achebe had to rely on a friend and colleague who went to London during a vacation to pursue the matter at the office of the business. The manuscript was found after an intense search, and Achebe received only one copy of its typed version later. He later admitted that if the manuscript got lost in either transit, he would have been too grief-stricken to pursue a writing career and that even if he rewrote the novel, it would have been a different work (63).

It was also during his employment at NBC that Achebe wrote and published several of his other novels: ***No Longer at Ease***, ***Arrow of God***, and ***A Man of the People***. The last work, a political **satire** on contemporary Nigeria, treats the corruption and incompetence of politicians running the country. Prophetically, the novel anticipates the **Nigerian Civil War** surrounding the **Biafra** movement. Achebe's ending, a military coup, according to Ezenwa-Ohaeto, suggests "a creative purge of the rotten political system" (109). In reality, the sought-after purge didn't occur, however. Events proceeded in such a manner that tribal and regional affiliations eventually threatened Nigeria's national unity. Military coup followed military coup, and Achebe, working for NBC at Lagos at the time, had to send his family east for safety; he himself joined them later. He had reasons to be concerned. He was an **Igbo**, and *A Man of the People*, his recently published work, dealt with corruption in high places of the government and recommended military intervention as a solution to the problem. The proposed remedy rendered Achebe vulnerable to the accusation that he possessed an insider's knowledge of military plans.

Ezenwa-Ohaeto treats the civil war with great care and patience, explaining the complex issues and acquainting the people involved in the struggle to the reader. Achebe lent his full support to the Biafra movement, writing papers to defend the new statehood and reading them on diplomatic missions abroad. However, he and the leaders of the movement quickly found that the world was not willing to listen to the plight of his people. While some African nations recognized Biafra, it received no support in the West. Harold Wilson, the prime minister of Britain, still the most influential international player in Nigerian affairs, was hostile to it. This was one of the reasons that Biafra became a lost cause.

Loss of a political vision is not easy to deal with. Adding to that huge loss were the painful personal losses Achebe endured. His pregnant wife, **Christie Achebe**, suffered a miscarriage. Achebe himself narrowly escaped death twice during the time, losing books and manuscripts. The most grievous blow to him was the death of **Christopher Okigbo**, a gifted poet and close family friend. Ezenwa-Ohaeto's powerful depiction of the Biafra episode demonstrates that this was the most traumatic experience for Achebe. Yet he wrote several poems and children's stories during the civil war. The poems he wrote then poignantly captured the miseries of war. When the Biafra struggle ended in defeat because of the overwhelming superiority of the Nigerian military, Achebe rejoined the African Studies department at **University of Nigeria, Nsukka** (the University of Biafra during the civil war) and became as productive as ever, writing poems and stories, attending seminars and conferences worldwide, inspiring young writers, and teaching in Nigeria as well as abroad.

In Ezenwa-Ohaeto's detailed account of Achebe's career, what emerges is the portrait of a man whose manifold contributions to African literature are outstanding and perhaps unrivaled. A distinctive feature of the biography is that it makes us aware of aspects of Achebe's personality that his identity as a novelist somewhat obscures. An author of children's literature, a dedicated teacher, a political thinker and commentator, a literary and cultural critic, Achebe exerts far-reaching influences on the arts and letters of Africa and beyond. Particularly significant is his ability to blow away stale misconceptions about Africa. Take, for example, his essay on **Joseph Conrad**'s *Heart of Darkness,* **"An Image of Africa."** This pathbreaking study of a canonical text—which has been a pet text in college English courses for many decades—has revolutionized Conrad criticism. Achebe delivered it as a paper at the **University of Massachusetts at Amherst** when he was teaching there and received considerable flak from several English professors for his refusal to see Conrad's text as anti-racist (189). Also crucial are Achebe's contributions to Heineman's **African Writers Series** and *Okiki*—a journal that moved back and forth with Achebe between the University of Nigeria, Nsukka, and the University of Massachusetts at Amherst. He edited both, and his efforts there became a shaping influence on the growth of modern African literature. Certainly, the honorifics "the Father of African Literature" or "a pace-setter" that people have bestowed upon him are well deserved (247, 253).

Achebe has received many honors for his accomplishments, and it would be difficult to find his parallel anywhere in the world. The prestigious Nobel Prize, however, has eluded him so far. Ezenwa-Ohaeto suggests a possible reason: Achebe once refused to attend a conference on African literature in Stockholm, Sweden. With his characteristic humility, he explained that he "consider[ed] it [in]appropriate for African writers to assemble in Europe in 1986 to discuss the future of their literature (qtd. in Ezenwa-Ohaeto 241). Ezenwa-Ohaeto implies that in all likelihood the act was perceived as a snub by the Nobel Prize committee, who assumed that this refusal was an indication Achebe would refuse the prize itself if awarded (242).

Well researched and well written, *Chinua Achebe: A Biography* is admirable in scope and adequate in performance. Ezenwa-Ohaeto's book provides abundant information on Achebe's life and work. It is the only conventional biography of the foremost African novelist of the time, though it has now been supplemented by Phanuel Akubueze Egejuru's ***Chinua Achebe: Pure and Simple***, an oral biography that is even richer in anecdotal material. While it goes without saying that other biographies of Achebe will be written later, Ezenwa-Ohaeto's book will remain the starting point of many. Undoubtedly, the mass of information that Ezenwa-Ohaeto has collected on Achebe is the product of painstaking effort. The book includes a bibliography on Achebe as well as an index, though this sort of supplemental apparatus could be usefully extended to include a list of important events and dates in Achebe's life, such as publications, appointments, travels, and honors. Crucial dates in Nigeria's stormy political history, which are hard for non-Nigerians to follow but are important in understanding the context of many of Achebe's writings, could be incorporated in such a list.

FURTHER READING

Phanuel A. Egejuru, *Chinua Achebe: Pure and Simple*.

Farhad B. Idris

CHINUA ACHEBE: A CELEBRATION, (1990). This collection of essays on Achebe's work, edited by Kirsten Holst Petersen and Anna Rutherford, was compiled and published as a tribute to Achebe on the occasion of his sixtieth birthday and in recognition of his influence on modern African literature. The first essay, "African Literature as Restoration of Celebration," is by Achebe himself and touches briefly on topics such as the celebration of art (*mbari*) of the **Igbo** in Nigeria, Western images of Africa and Africans, and, on a more personal note, what Achebe terms his own colonial inheritance and his views on the use of English by African writers. Essays by both African and Western scholars offer critical perspectives on Achebe's texts, particularly on ***Things Fall Apart*** and ***Anthills of the Savannah***, and on broader themes within African literature in relationship to Achebe's literary work. In addition, there are three poems written for Achebe by the Ghanaian writer Ama Ata Aidoo. The collection includes an interview by Kirsten Holst Petersen with James Currey, Alan Hill, and Keith Sambrook on the **African Writers Series** that provides an insight into Achebe's pivotal role in establishing and shaping the series as both its first writer and editor.

Compare *Eagle on Iroko*, another sixtieth-birthday-celebration volume.

FURTHER READING

Chinua Achebe, *Hopes and Impediments*; Bernth Lindfors, ed., *Conversations with Chinua Achebe*.

Camille Lizarríbar Buxó

CHINUA ACHEBE: NEW PERSPEC-TIVES, by Umelo Ojinmah (1991), is a good example of the way in which Achebe's work has spurred not only the development of African literature but also the development of African literary criticism, for which Achebe's work has been a crucial focus. Written by an African critic and published by an African publishing house, *Chinua Achebe: New Perspectives* is a solid critical overview of all of Achebe's major fiction, concentrating on the engagement of that fiction with social and historical reality in **Nigeria**. Drawing important inspiration from some of **Ngugi wa Thiong'o**'s comments on Achebe, Ojinmah emphasizes the realism of Achebe's fiction, which he sees as a vivid and accurate depiction of Nigerian society in both the colonial past and the postcolonial present. For Ojinmah, Achebe's fiction is an enactment of Achebe's own beliefs that the artist has a responsibility to educate his or her audience about both the past and the present so that they can reclaim the positive legacy of their past heritage, while also seeking to overcome the weaknesses of that heritage and of the society of the present. In particular, Ojinmah sees Achebe's most important theme to be the abuse of power by Nigerian social and political leaders in both the traditaional societies of the past and the postcolonial society of the present.

The first chapter of *Chinua Achebe: New Perspectives* outlines Achebe's views on the social responsibility of the artist as educator and social critic. The second chapter then addresses Achebe's treatment of traditional Igbo society in *Things Fall Apart* and *Arrow of God*. Ojinmah argues that figures such as **Okonkwo** and **Ezeulu** in these early novels serve as forerunners of contemporary Nigerian leaders, showing that abuses of power and privilege in postcolonial Nigeria arise not just from the legacy of colonialism but also from certain tendencies that date back to precolonial times. Thus, for Ojinmah, Okonkwo, in *Things Fall Apart*, is an embodiment of excess who violates the traditional Igbo emphasis on balance and moderation with his extreme behavior. Similarly, Ezeulu, in *Arrow of God*, is a man of excessive pride who abuses the considerable power accorded to the Chief Priest of **Ulu** in the interest of his own ambitions.

In his third chapter, Ojinmah addresses Achebe's treatment of postcolonial Nigerian society in *No Longer at Ease* and *A Man of the People*. For Ojinmah, a major theme of these texts is the repudiation of traditional values by postcolonial leaders, who are thereby alienated from both the past traditions and the current lives of the general population of Nigeria. In addition, these leaders often assume power due to their educational achievements, though they have had little real preparation for power and have few genuine qualities of leadership. On the other hand, Ojinmah argues that Achebe locates at least some of the roots of these problems in the pre-colonial past rather than simply attributing all of them to the negative consequences of the colonial encounter. As a result of the legacy of both colonialism and the abuses inherent in the societies of the pre-colonial past, Nigeria was a nation tragically born with the germs of decay already present at birth—much in the mode of the prematurely decadent postcolonial societies described in the work of **Frantz Fanon**, though Ojinmah does not mention the work of Fanon in this regard.

In his fourth and final chapter, Ojinmah

discusses **Anthills of the Savannah** and Achebe's short stories, emphasizing the impact of the **Nigerian Civil War** on these later works. Ojinmah sees the stories as an effective representation of the tragedy of the civil war. He also finds *Anthills of the Savannah* particularly effective as a work of social critique because of the way in which it begins to propound remedies for Nigeria's political troubles while at the same time effectively dramatizing Achebe's vision of the role of the artist in helping to solve these problems. In particular, for Ojinmah, Achebe's alternative to the current situation is not a simple rejection of Western values but a combination of the positive values of Western society and traditional Igbo and other African societies. Ultimately, then, Achebe's criticism of the corruption and abuse of power in both traditional Igbo society and postcolonial Nigerian society is not purely negative but also offers a hopeful vision for Nigeria's future by challenging Nigerians and other Africans "to salvage what is useful from their past, graft those to what is useful from European culture, and re-form the colonial political and social heritage around their existing cultural world-view" (109).

FURTHER READING

Chinua Achebe, *Morning Yet on Creation Day*; Frantz Fanon, *The Wretched of the Earth*; Ngugi wa Thiong'o, *Homecoming*.

M. Keith Booker

CHINUA ACHEBE: NOVELIST, POET, CRITIC, by David Carroll, is a solid study of Achebe's body of work, focusing on the novels but also including coverage of some of the stories and poems, as well as brief commentary on Achebe's gradual evolution into an important social critic. First published in 1970, the book was reissued in 1980 and 1990, the latter primarily in order to add coverage of **Anthills of the Savannah**, which had been published in the meantime. Espe-

cially in the introduction, Carroll also seeks to contextualize Achebe's writing within the history of **Nigeria** and as a response to the legacy of Western colonialist stereotyping of Africa and Africans. Thus, the book serves as an extremely useful introduction to Achebe's work and as an excellent source for scholars and students who are just beginning their study of Achebe and his work.

Carroll's first chapter is a broad introduction that uses **Joseph Conrad**'s **Heart of Darkness** as a starting point for a discussion of the colonialist stereotyping of Africa as a timeless and primitive land and of Africans as exotic beings who are not fully human. Carroll also provides a good deal of historical background on colonialism and its aftermath. He situates the works of African writers within this background and notes the ways in which such writers challenge the legacy of colonialism. Finally, he provides some good, if somewhat brief, information on the traditional **Igbo** society and culture that provide such crucial background to Achebe's work.

Carroll's second chapter is a discussion of **Things Fall Apart**, focusing on Achebe's achievement in presenting a vivid and credible picture of the traditional way of Igbo life before the coming of colonialism at the end of the nineteenth century. At the same time, Carroll also notes the status of the novel as an impressive work of art, noting, for example, the "sensitive control of narrative voice" that allows Achebe to add special nuance and power to his narrative (33). This chapter includes an extensive treatment of Achebe's characterization of **Okonkwo** and of his treatment of **missionaries** and their impact on traditional Igbo society.

Like many critics, Carroll appears to regard **No Longer at Ease** as one of Achebe's lesser achievements. For example, he characterizes Achebe's second novel as a "tragicomic postscript" to *Things Fall Apart* (62). Carroll notes that *No Longer at Ease* revolves around the unsuccessful attempts of Obi Okonkwo to reconcile the values of African and Western cultures. Ultimately, however, he feels that the novel lacks the broad resonances of its predecessor and remains relevant only to its West African setting.

Arrow of God is, for Carroll, another major achievement in Achebe's career. His discussion of that novel focuses on Achebe's depiction of the antagonism between the traditional and modern worlds (and worldviews) of Umuaro and the British colonial administration, respectively. For Carroll, this exploration of a conflict between competing value systems is more successful here than in *No Longer at Ease*. In particular, Carroll notes that this depiction gains special force from its location in the 1920s, at a time of rapid and fundamental change in Africa. It also gains complexity from the depiction of missionaries as a sort of intermediate group that embodies largely Western values but gains power in Africa through its flexible negotiation with the African system of myth and religion. *Arrow of God* is, for Carroll, a highly successful "political novel in which different systems of power are examined and their dependence upon myth and ritual compared" (118).

A Man of the People, for Carroll, continues Achebe's technique of exploring the competition between competing value systems for power in Africa. Here, however, the opposition is primarily dramatized in the confrontation between the two main characters, **Odili Samalu** and **Chief Nanga**, who occupy positions at opposite ends of the political spectrum. Odili's view of the world is thoroughly determined by his European education. On the other hand, Chief Nanga, the "man of the people" of the title, at first glance seems to be the embodiment of the traditional African values of his people. Ultimately, however, Nanga is revealed to be a scheming and opportunistic politician whose situation

reveals the corruption of traditional values in contemporary Nigerian society. His political success, then, is tied not to his genuine connection to the people and their values but to his hypocritical ability to manipulate those values for his own purposes.

In chapter 6, Carroll discusses the stories of *Girls at War and Other Stories* and the poems of *Beware, Soul Brother*. The stories, for Carroll, are particularly impressive in the way they manage to "embody several different kinds of fictional reality, ranging from traditional life in the clan to a modern society engaged in civil war" (158). He also notes the way in which the poems represent the **Nigerian Civil War** and its aftermath, effectively portraying the uncertainties of life in a world that has "become impersonal, unpredictable and finally hostile to poetry" (166).

Chapter 7, added for the revised edition, discusses *Anthills of the Savannah*, which Carroll reads as another of Achebe's fictional meditations on the workings of power in Nigeria, though the novel is ostensibly set in a fictional African country. Carroll is much impressed by the "scope and ambition" of Achebe's latest novel and by the way in which Achebe presents a realistic depiction of postcolonial power struggles while at the same time combining its treatment of contemporary politics with elements from myth and legend in an attempt to explain the bitter turn taken by the history of the fictitious country of the book and thus of Nigeria (183–84). Carroll argues that the novel well illustrates "the central strength of Achebe's art," which "lies in his belief in story and its various expressions in myth, legend, parable, and folktale" (184).

In the conclusion, Carroll sums up the previous chapters and reiterates his belief that Achebe's principal strength as an artist lies in his abilities as a storyteller. He emphasizes the coherence and continuity of Achebe's body of work and notes the way in which the various works together represent a cumulative history of modern Nigeria. Carroll ends by contrasting the ongoing vitality of storytelling in Achebe's work with Walter Benjamin's argument, in the essay "The Storyteller," that the art of storytelling has radically declined in modern Western culture.

FURTHER READING

Simon Gikandi, *Reading Chinua Achebe*; C. L. Innes, *Chinua Achebe*; G. D. Killam, *The Writings of Chinua Achebe*.

M. Keith Booker

CHINUA ACHEBE: PURE AND SIMPLE, AN ORAL BIOGRAPHY, by Phanuel Akubueze Egejuru, usefully supplements other scholarly work on Achebe (including the more traditional biography by Ezenwa-Ohaeto) by including insights gleaned from interviews with Achebe and with a number of individuals who have been intimately acquainted with Achebe throughout large portions of his life and career. Egejuru herself is a professor of English at Loyola University in New Orleans. She has a Ph.D. in comparative literature from the University of California, Los Angeles (UCLA), but she also shares much of Achebe's cultural background, having been born in what is now Nigeria's Imo State and having, for example, attended the same girls' school (St. Monica's) as Achebe's mother and sisters. As Egejuru states in her preface, a total of seventy-one people were interviewed in the course of compiling the biography, allowing her to construct a picture of "Chinua the son, the brother, the uncle, the son-in-law, the husband, and the father. Chinua, the student is revealed by his teachers, his classmates and his friends. And we learn of Chinua the professional from his employers, his colleagues, his students and his own employees such as his secretary, his house-boy and his driver."

Among other things, the oral nature of this biography places it more in keeping with **Igbo** traditions of oral culture than a more conventional, Western-style scholarly biography could be. Perhaps because so many of the sources are friends and family members of Achebe, the book is something of a celebration. Not only does it present Achebe as a human being, rather than merely a writer, but it presents him as a remarkable human being indeed, greatly admired and respected by all of those who have known him. However, as Egejuru also notes in her preface, it was impossible to produce anything but such a glowing picture, because she felt obligated to report accurately the information gleaned in the interviews, all of which was admiringly positive. As one interviewee puts it, the only regrettable thing about Achebe's character is that it is so flawless that there are no "juicy tales to tell about him."

FURTHER READING

Ezenwa-Ohaeto, *Chinua Achebe: A Biography*.

M. Keith Booker

CHRISTMAS IN BIAFRA. See *Beware, Soul Brother*.

CHRISTOPHER. In *No Longer at Ease*, a graduate of the **London School of Economics**, an economist by profession and (see chapter 2), and the close friend of **Obi Okonkwo**. Christopher is not portrayed in great depth at any single point, but he has a recurring, if somewhat enigmatic, role in the novel. He is not given a surname, unlike less prominent characters, and although he is one of Obi's best friends, he tends to oppose all of Obi's political opinions (chapter 2). Christopher also adopts an evidently flexible stance in regard to both bribery (chapter 12) and dating: "He seemed to enjoy going around with four or five [women] at once" (chapter 11). His use of language is flexible as well since, depending on circumstance, he skillfully alternates between formal English and **pidgin English** (and presumably **Igbo**). It is with reference to this talent that Christopher is described as doing an excellent job of "coming to terms with a double heritage" (chapter 11). Yet either the apparent freedom of Christopher's thinking and speech does not extend to traditional gender roles, or he is being at least partly ironic in chapter 11 when, with Obi and **Clara Okeke** present, he declares to his female companion, **Bisi**, his lack of interest in her preferences. No trace of irony on Christopher's part is discernible, however, when he says to Obi rather late in the novel, "You may say that I am not broad-minded, but I don't think we have reached the stage where we can ignore all our customs. You may talk about education and so on, but I am not going to marry an *osu*" (chapter 15). It is a measure of the strength of the *osu* prohibition that the often supple-minded Christopher does not conceptualize Obi's wish to marry the *osu*-descended Clara much differently than do **Joseph Okeke**, members of the **Umuofia Progressive Union**, or Obi's parents.

Thomas J. Lynn

CHUKWU, supreme god of the **Igbo**, described in *Things Fall Apart* as the creator of all things. In chapter 21, **Akunna** describes Chukwu to the missionary **Brown**, who relates him to the Christian God. Chukwu is referred to as the "high god" in chapter 2 of *Arrow of God*.

M. Keith Booker

CHUKWULOBE, a ritual assistant to **Ezeulu** in *Arrow of God*, chapter 18.

Rachel R. Reynolds

CHURCH MISSIONARY SOCIETY (CMS) BOOKSHOP, the store in **Lagos** at which the newly engaged **Obi Okonkwo** buys a Bible to go with the engagement ring

he has just purchased for his fiancée, **Clara Okeke**, in chapter 7 of *No Longer at Ease*.

Thomas J. Lynn

CITADEL PRESS, publishing company founded at **Enugu**, **Nigeria**, by Achebe and **Christopher Okigbo** in 1967. After an initial (successful) solitication of manuscripts, the operation of the press had to be terminated after the outbreak of the **Nigerian Civil War** and the subsequent death of Okigbo.

M. Keith Booker

CLARK, JOHN PEPPER (1935–), Nigerian poet, essayist, journalist, and dramatist, also widely known as "Bekederemo," a name he adopted in the 1980s, deriving from the family name of his father, Chief Clark Fuludu Bekederemo, of Kiagbodo village near Warri in the Delta State of **Nigeria**. A graduate (in English) of **University College, Ibadan** in 1960, Clark has held academic posts at universities in both Nigeria and the United States. In 1991, he was awarded the Nigerian National Merit Award for Excellence in the Arts and Sciences.

Clark worked as a journalist in **Lagos** in the early 1960s, at which time he became personally aquainted with Achebe. The two established a friendship, though an antagonism later grew between them when Achebe backed Biafra in the **Nigerian Civil War**, while Clark sided with Nigeria. The friendship was gradually restored in the late 1970s. In the 1980s, Clark and Achebe joined with Wole Soyinka as important writers who served as voices for social justice in Nigeria.

Clark's poetry has gained widespread critical recognition for its complex combination of elements from indigenous African culture and modern international culture. The poetry addresses a wide variety of themes, but much of it directly engages topical issues in Nigerian politics, in which Clark has long been an active and important voice. His poetry as a whole has made crucial contributions to the development of a postcolonial Nigerian cultural identity. His drama is also important, evolving through his career from works heavily influenced by classical Greek drama to ones inspired primarily by indigenous African forms. He has also actively worked to promote theater in Nigeria, long serving as the artistic director of the PEC Repertory Theatre in Lagos, which Clark and his wife, Ebun Odutola, founded in 1982.

FURTHER READING

Isaac I. Elimimian, *The Poetry of J. P. Clark Bekederemo*; Robert M. Wren, *J. P. Clark*.

M. Keith Booker

CLARKE, TONY. Captain Tony Clarke is a member of the British colonial government who arrives in **Okperi** at the inception of the time span of *Arrow of God*. He is assistant district officer to **Captain Winterbottom**. Clarke is the Cambridge-educated son of a bank clerk whose naiveté is used by Achebe as a foil between Winterbottom and **John Wright**, both of whom gossip about each other with Clarke. Clarke is also an important character study for how a young officer might cope with the moral dilemmas of being a colonizer. In chapter 14, for example, Clarke has a brief, almost semi-conscious mental breakdown over Wade's desecration of an **Igbo** shrine, coming to the conclusion that "it would fall on him (Clarke) to defend his natives if need be from the thoughtless acts of white people like Wade." Clarke's interior monologue here evokes complex tropes of paternalism and self-examination. (See also entry for **George Allen**.) The mental and moral dividedness that happens to Clarke on account of his contact with Africans—and its effect on his consciousness—is also contrasted to the ways that **Ezeulu**'s consciousness is divided when he comes into contact with the British (chapter 14). For more about

class relationships among colonists, see entry for Wright.

Rachel R. Reynolds

THE COLONIAL CHURCH. The church in **Lagos**, mentioned in chapter 11 of *No Longer at Ease*, at which a sidesman (assistant to a parish churchwarden) is **William Green**, whom **Marie Tomlinson** describes at this point in the novel as "a very devout Christian."

Thomas J. Lynn

COLONIALIST CRITICISM. A general term for literary and cultural criticism that fails to break free of the ideology of colonialism. It is especially used to designate such criticism of works by postcolonial writers, criticism that is particularly invidious because these writers are struggling to overcome the legacy of colonialism. This kind of criticism sometimes involves crude declarations of Western cultural superiority. However, it is often written by well-intentioned critics who legitimately believe that they are in sympathy with the postcolonial writers they are criticizing but fail (out of their ignorance of non-Western cultures) to see the ways in which they continue to read these writers using standards and perceptions that are themselves thoroughly saturated with colonialist ideas.

Colonialist criticism tends to fall into one of two basic categories. "Universalist" criticism tends to view all cultural products through values derived from the premises of the Western Enlightenment. Such approaches regard Western aesthetics as transcultural and transhistorical, applying to works from all cultures in all time periods. In reality these "universal" aesthetics largely involved in the eighteenth and nineteenth centuries, reflecting the values and worldview of the bourgeois class that rose to power in Europe during those centuries. For colonialist critics, works of postcolonial culture are valuable only to the extent that they adhere to the criteria and values of Western aesthetics. Alternatively, colonialist critics sometimes adopt the attitude that the works of writers from non-Western cultures are strange, exotic artifacts that have nothing whatsoever in common with Western works of art. This attitude is often referred to as "Orientalism" after the book by that title in which **Edward Said** demonstrates the way in which Western writers from the eighteenth century forward have tended to view the people and cultures of the Middle East as embodying values that are diametrically opposed (and hopelessly inferior) to those of Europe and the West.

Both of these extremes obviously fail to apprehend the complexity of the dialogue between postcolonial cultures and the cultures of their former colonial rulers. The African novel is a classic case of this complexity, with novelists such as Achebe entering into clear (but often antagonistic) relationships with Western literary traditions, while at the same time drawing in important ways upon African cultural traditions in an attempt to contribute to the development of genuinely new modes of cultural expression that move beyond the legacies of both colonialism and African traditionalism. Achebe himself has commented on the pitfalls of colonialist criticism in an essay of that title, included in the collection *Morning Yet on Creation Day*. Here Achebe complains of arrogant Western critics who base their readings of African literature on the idea that Africa was a timeless continent steeped in savagery and primitivism until Europeans brought the blessings of civilization, only to have Africans respond with ingratitude. But he also complains of the more subtle colonialist attitudes of critics such as Charles Larson, who seem to want to promote African literature, but only by arguing for its universalism (which really amounts to an argument that it follows the rules of Western literature).

Indeed, Achebe muses that he would like to see the word "universal" completely banned from critical discussions of African literature at least as long as the word continues to be used as a synonym for "European." He also notes that colonialist criticism is particularly harmful when it begins to be practiced unwittingly by African critics or even to influence African writers to attempt to meet its standards. For Achebe, Western critics are highly unlikely to have the kind of organic understanding of African cultures that allows them to conduct a truly informed critique of African literature. He does not, however, suggest that Western critics should not comment on African literature. Rather, he simply counsels that such critics approach African literature with caution and humility, granting that works of African culture might be constructed according to premises and values that are fundamentally different from (but not necessarily any better or any worse than) those according to which works of Western art are produced. Such criticism is, of course, one of the central goals of the emergent field of postcolonial studies, though it is certainly the case that scholars and critics in this field must remain ever vigilant lest they lapse into the old bad habits of colonialist criticism.

FURTHER READING

Chinua Achebe, "Colonialist Criticism" and "Where Angels Fear to Tread," both included in *Morning Yet on Creation Day*; Bill Ashcroft, Gareth Griffiths, and Helen Tiffin, *The Empire Writes Back*; Elleke Boehmer, *Colonial and Postcolonial Literature*; M. Keith Booker, *The African Novel in English*; W.J.T. Mitchell, "Postcolonial Culture, Postimperial Criticism"; Edward Said, *Culture and Imperialism* and *Orientalism*.

M. Keith Booker

"COLONIALIST CRITICISM." Achebe essay. See *Morning Yet on Creation Day*.

COLONIALIST HISTORIOGRAPHY. Mode of historical analysis based on the tradition of Eurocentric thinking in which the West is envisioned as the locus of true history, while the rest of the world lags behind in primitivity and underdevelopment. This mode of thinking is clearly a form of the phenomenon of Orientalism as described by **Edward Said**. It dates back particularly to the historicist vision of the German philosopher **G.W.F. Hegel**, who essentially envisioned the process of history as the gradual realization of God's plan for the ultimate development of humanity, with Western Europe having well advanced along this path, while other parts of the world (especially Africa) remained lands without history, still mired in primeval savagery. This notion was used in the nineteenth century as a justification for colonialism, the argument being that the colonization of Africa and other parts of the world by Western powers could help to bring the colonies into history and onto the path of human development intended by God.

Catherine Coquery-Vidrovitch describes the impact of this phenomenon, noting that

colonialist histories have long perpetuated the myth of a sub-Saharan Africa conquered fairly easily and profiting from pacification. . . . The local populations, according to these histories, were finally delivered by the "colonial peace" from the internal struggles of little local rulers forever raiding their neighbors' territories in search of slaves or livestock. (66)

As V. Y. Mudimbe notes, such histories "speak neither about Africa nor Africans, but rather justify the process of inventing and conquering a continent and naming its 'primitiveness' or 'disorder,' as well as the subsequent means of its exploitation and methods for its 'regeneration' " (20). Western historians such as Basil Davidson, in works

such as *The Black Man's Burden, Let Freedom Come*, and *The Search for Africa*, have attempted to correct the misrepresentation of the African past in colonialist historiographies. Meanwhile, Mudimbe and other African scholars and historians have worked to counter this tendency with histories written from an African perspective. One version of this effort involves what Anthony Appiah calls "nativist" discourses of African history—discourses that espouse a return to the precolonial past and a rejection of the entire colonial period as an aberration and a break in the flow of history. Such discourses typically seek to emphasize the positive aspects of precolonial African culture and attempt to draw upon this culture as a model for the present. For Appiah, these discourses are best represented by the work of Chinweizu et al., particularly in *Toward the Decolonization of African Literature*. On the other hand, Chinweizu and his fellow *bolekaja* critics do not simply romanticize the African past. Indeed, they warn against a tendency toward such romanticization in the writers of the Négritude movement in French African literature, noting that such romanticization might "imprison the contemporary imagination in a bygone era" (258). Nevertheless, such critics do tend to emphasize the supposed cultural superiority of the pre-colonial past, which is presented as a positive alternative to the present degraded by the colonial encounter with European civilization. Supporters of this attitude recommend that African writers should return for their inspiration to the pre-colonial cultures and traditions of their societies if they are to overcome the problems that colonialism imposed on Africans.

Given the material impact of colonialism on African history and the symbolic impact of colonialist historiography on the African imagination, it is obvious that history is a crucial area of contestation for African writers who seek to wrest control of their cultural identities from the metropolitan center of Europe. It is thus not surprising that African writers have also quite often employed the historical novel as part of their program to generate new postcolonial African cultural identities that transcend this inherited tradition of European bourgeois historiography and that escape definition by the colonial past. For example, each of the novels of **Ngugi wa Thiong'o** focuses on a particular moment in the history of Kenya, and together his novels, ranging from *The River Between* to *Matigari*, constitute a sweeping historical narrative that tells the story of Kenya from the early days of British colonization to the contemporary postcolonial period, focusing on the strong Kenyan tradition of resistance to oppression. Indeed, Ngugi has openly proclaimed that Kenyan history provides the principal inspiration for his fiction, especially in the sense that "the Kenyan peoples' struggle against foreign domination" is the "one consistent theme" of this history over the past 400 years (*Moving the Centre* 97). In a similar (if less politically specific) manner, Achebe, in works such as ***Things Fall Apart***, seeks to provide his African readers with a realistic depiction of their pre-colonial past, free of the distortions and stereotypes imposed upon that past in European accounts. Meanwhile, Achebe's novels, from *Things Fall Apart* to ***Anthills of the Savannah***, collectively trace the colonial and neocolonial history of **Nigeria**. Thus, Chinwe Christiana Okechukwu notes that Achebe's five novels together "encompass the entire sociohistorical and political experience of Nigeria, from precolonial times to the present" (2).

Other representative examples of African historical novels include Nadine Gordimer's intense engagement with the history of apartheid in South Africa in works such as *Burger's Daughter* and *A Sport of Nature*, Sem-

bène's dramatization of a 1947–1948 railway strike in French colonial Africa in *God's Bits of Woods*, M. G. Vassanji's imaginative retelling of the history of Tanzania in *The Gunny Sack*, Ben Okri's attempt to capture the spirit of modern Nigerian history through an Africanized magical realism in *The Famished Road*, Yambo Ouologuem's somewhat notorious depiction of African history as a never-ending cycle of abject violence in *Bound to Violence*, and Ayi Kwei Armah's *Two Thousand Seasons*, a more positive and mythic version of African history (written partially in response to Ouologuem).

FURTHER READING

Kwame Anthony Appiah, *In My Father's House*; Chinweizu et al., *Toward the Decolonization of African Literature*; Catherine Coquery-Vidrovitch, *Africa*; Basil Davidson, *The Black Man's Burden*, *Let Freedom Come*, and *The Search for Africa*; V. Y. Mudimbe, *The Invention of Africa*; Ngugi wa Thiong'o, *Moving the Centre*; Edward Said, *Orientalism*.

M. Keith Booker

COMIC STRIP ADAPTATIONS. See *A Man of the People* (comic strip).

COMMON PEOPLE'S CONVENTION (CPC), a newly organized political party that seeks to offer an alternative to the virtually interchangeable major parties that dominate the postcolonial African nation featured in ***A Man of the People***. Given that the ruling **People's Organization Party (POP)** and the opposition **People's Alliance Party (PAP)** seem to be informed by the same sorts of self-serving greed and corruption, this new party is envisioned as a legitimate alternative that has the interests of the common people of the country at heart. It is clearly informed by leftist ideas, as indicated by the fact that, in chapter 8, one of its inner circle is identified as being from an "Eastern Bloc" (i.e., communist) country and by the fact that Eunice, a beautiful woman lawyer (engaged to **Maxwell Kulamo**) who is one of the party founders, cites **Karl Marx** as one of the party's important predecessors. The party, however, comes in for satire in the novel, largely because, despite its name and declared intention of representing the common people, its leadership is composed entirely of professional people and intellectuals whose connection to the common people is tenuous and indirect at best. Further, there is some hint that the party might be compromised by the fact that one of the central figures behind it is a junior minister in the POP government. Nevertheless, Kulamo, Eunice, and the other leaders of the CPC are depicted as well-meaning idealists who certainly lack the overt greed and corruption of the leaders of the other parties, even if they are sometimes a bit out of touch with the daily lives of the common people they hope to represent. Narrator **Odili Samalu** runs (unsuccessfully) for parliament on the CPC ticket late in the novel. Meanwhile, Kulamo withdraws from this same parliamentary election when he is offered a 1,000-pound bribe by **Chief Simon Koko**, the POP candidate he opposes. Kulamo uses the money to help support CPC campaigns in other parts of the country, but Samalu is nevertheless shocked by the bribe-taking, which indicates the potential for corruption that exists in even the most idealistic of political activities, given the climate that reigns in the country.

M. Keith Booker

COMMONWEALTH POETRY PRIZE. Annual prize established by the Commonwealth Institute in 1972 to award the year's finest achievement by a poet from Britain and the British Commonwealth. Achebe was the co-winner of the first award for his volume *Beware, Soul Brother*. The award was dis-

continued in 1988 and has not been given since that time.

M. Keith Booker

CONGRESS FOR CULTURAL FREEDOM. See **Foundations**.

CONRAD, JOSEPH (1857–1924). Josef Teodor Konrad Korzeniowski was born in Berdyczow in a part of Poland that had been part of the Russian Empire since the 1793 partition of the country by Russia, Prussia, and Austria. In 1861 Conrad's father, Apollo, was arrested for planning a failed revolt against Russian rule. Conrad and his parents were exiled to northern Russia where his mother, Ewa, died of tuberculosis in 1865. Conrad and his father were then allowed to return to Poland, but Apollo, heartbroken, died in 1869. Orphaned, Conrad was raised by an uncle until he left Poland to become a sailor in 1874.

These experiences made Conrad strongly opposed to Russian rule in Poland and to imperialism generally while leaving him melancholy and wary of political activism. He spent the next twenty years working first on French, then British ships, sailing primarily to the Far East. He published his first novel, *Almayer's Folly* (1895), using the pen name "Joseph Conrad." After that, he settled into a career as a British author living in Kent. Over the next thirty years he produced thirty volumes, including many that have become literary classics, including ***Heart of Darkness*** (1899), *Lord Jim* (1900), *Nostromo* (1904), *The Secret Agent* (1907), *Under Western Eyes* (1911), and *Victory* (1915).

Although Conrad became a British subject in 1886, married an Englishwoman (Jessie George) in 1896, and wrote fiction exclusively in English, his attitude toward the British was ambivalent. While he envied their self-confidence and purposefulness, he suspected their tendencies toward self-absorption and domination. He himself remained an outsider to British society, speaking English with a heavy Polish accent to the end of his life. His visitors described his appearance and gestures as "Oriental." In 1924, the year of his death, he refused a British knighthood.

Conrad set much of his fiction, especially during his first decade as a writer, in the colonies he had visited as a sailor. His plots were based on his own experiences or those of people he met. His depictions of imperialism are negative overall, though complicated by a more favorable view of British colonialism. Whereas his Belgian, Dutch, French, and German imperialists tend to be selfishly exploitative, his British characters are more benevolent. Conrad shows, however, that the paternalism of Tom Lingard, Lord Jim, and Charles Gould is ultimately as destructive as the villainy of Kurtz. This complexity has made some critics, such as Edward Said, hesitate to call him anti-imperialist, but Chinua Achebe has clearly stated in **"An Image of Africa"** that "Conrad saw and condemned the evil of imperial exploitation." Conrad is referenced elsewhere in Achebe's work as well. In chapter 11 of *No Longer at Ease*, the protagonist, **Obi Okonkwo**, recalls his study of Conrad for his university degree in England. In **"The African Writer and the English Language,"** Achebe refers to Conrad's ability to write effectively in English, even though, as with Achebe, it was not his first language. In this context Achebe gives several examples of African writers past and present of whom the same may be said: Olauda Equiano (Gustavus Vassa), Casely Hayford, **Amos Tutuola**, **Christopher Okigbo**, and **J. P. Clark** (*Morning Yet on Creation Day* 98–101).

Achebe is, in general, bitterly critical of Conrad's representations of Africans, especially in *Heart of Darkness*. He goes on in the "Image of Africa" essay to say that Conrad was "strangely unaware of the racism on which it [imperialism] sharpened its iron tooth." Achebe is certainly correct that Conrad's portrayal of Africans in *Heart of Darkness* is minimal and derogatory. This is especially problematic given that, in his works set in Asia, where he spent much more time, Conrad's portraits of non-Europeans are detailed and generally sympathetic. Dain Maroola, Karain, Dain Waris, Lakamba, Babalatchi, Doramin, Hassim, and Immada are all characters with names, language, thoughts, and intentions. They hope to shake off European rule, a goal Conrad supports. Conrad in these works does condemn the white racism that accompanied imperialism. The Dutch Almayer, forced into marriage with a Malay woman, rejects Mrs. Almayer due to her ethnicity and refuses to recognize the Malay half of the heritage of their daughter, Nina. Caught between two worlds, Nina rebels against her father's wish that she pass as European. She runs off with Dain Maroola, who is amassing gunpowder to blow up the Dutch. Similarly, in *An Outcast of the Islands* (1896), the Dutch Peter Willems sees white skin as conferring special privilege. He reacts against the half-Arab, half-Malay Aissa staring at him by protesting, "I am white! All white!" Conrad clearly had no patience with the racial vanity of these whites just as he clearly condemned the more extreme and murderous racism of Kurtz, who ended wanting to "Exterminate all the brutes!" Among European writers of his time, Conrad was unusual in his criticism of both imperialism and white racism.

FURTHER READING

Jocelyn Baines, *Joseph Conrad*; Frederick R. Karl, *Joseph Conrad*; Zdzislaw Najder, *Joseph Conrad*.

Hunt Hawkins

CONVERSATIONS WITH CHINUA ACHEBE. See **Interviews**.

COOL MAX. See **Kulamo, Maxwell**.

"COUPLE," the nickname of a former corporal in the colonial police, now a local politician in **Anata** in *A Man of the People*. Though he claims to have been framed for expressing opposition to his British bosses, he had been jailed for bribe-taking during the colonial era. He now works as a lackey for the **People's Organization Party (POP)**, in which capacity he pressures **Hezekiah Samalu**, the father of **Odili Samalu**, to disown his son for his opposition to that party. Couple also leads the heckling that disrupts a speech being made in **Urua** by **Maxwell Kulamo** in support of the efforts of Samalu to unseat **Chief Nanga** as the local member of parliament.

M. Keith Booker

CRANFORD, LOU, American woman reporter representing the American United Press in **Bassa** in *Anthills of the Savannah*. Beatrice Okoh meets Cranford in chapter 6 when she attends a dinner being hosted by **Sam**, **the President** of **Kangan**, at his remote lakeside retreat. The two women do not get on well. Cranford is described as looking like a dark-haired Italian beauty.

M. Keith Booker

CRITICAL PERSPECTIVES ON CHINUA ACHEBE (1979) is a collection of critical essays edited by **C. L. Innes** and **Bernth Lindfors**, themselves two of the most important critics of Achebe's work. The existence of this collection of essays can be taken as a sign of the growing maturity of Achebe criticism and of the growing reputation of Achebe as a literary artist by the late 1970s. The essays all appear to have in common a commitment to assessing Achebe's artistic achievement as a writer of literature that takes its well-deserved place in the very forefront of African literature but also within the canon of world literature in English. As the editors' introduction to the essays makes clear, Achebe's work transcends the notions of simple plots and anthropological detail. Not only are his writings (especially his novels) aesthetically complex, but they go beyond their own boundaries to engage important social and political issues. They also engage in extensive intertextual dialogues, sometimes quite contentious, with the works of other writers, especially Achebe's predecessors among British writers, including **Joseph Conrad, T. S. Eliot, William Butler Yeats**, and **Joyce Cary**. Together, these essays make a convincing argument that Achebe's literary and critical work forever changed the face of literature written in English.

The essays in the volume are divided into five major sections. The first section, "General Essays," includes a discussion by Abiola Irele of the tragic aspects of Achebe's fiction, focusing especially on the fate of **Okonkwo** in *Things Fall Apart*. Essays in this section also include ones by Lloyd W. Brown and by Lindfors that discuss the historical and cultural context of Achebe's work, plus an essay by Kolawole Ogungbesan that takes issue with Achebe's insistence that the African writer should be politically engaged, arguing (in a mode that echoes the ideas of the American New Critics) instead that African literature might be aesthetically improved by a disengagement from politics.

This first section is then followed by sections that include groups of essays devoted to each of the four novels that Achebe had published at that time. The approaches in these essays vary considerably. Solomon Iyasere discusses Achebe's narrative technique in *Things Fall Apart*, while **David Carroll** focuses on the narrative structure of *A Man of the People*. Bu-Buakei Jabbi looks at the importance of fire as an image in *Things Fall Apart*, while Donald J. Weinstock and Cathy Ramadan discuss the overall symbolic structure of that novel. Roderick Wilson's essay explores the intertextual connection between *No Longer at Ease* and the poetry of Eliot, while A. G. Stock looks at the relationship between *Things Fall Apart* and the poetry of Eliot. Emmanuel Obiechina discusses the historical background of *Arrow of God*, and **Robert M. Wren** explores the relevance of Cary's *Mister Johnson* to that novel. Finally, a sixth section of the collection includes only one essay, in which Philip Rogers discusses Achebe's poetry but also makes a strong argument in favor of Achebe's view of the necessary social and political commitment of the African writer.

This collection of essays is particularly remarkable because it includes contributions by many scholars and writers who in 1979 were themselves establishing their own international credentials as contributors to the wealth of African literature and its burgeoning tradition. Innes, Lindfors, Carroll, and Wren are certainly at the forefront of critics who helped to make the Western academic world aware of Achebe and of African literature as a whole. Irele and Obiechina would go on to become leaders among African critics of African literature, while another contributor, Molly Mahood, taught Irele and **Wole Soyinka**, among others, at the **University of Ibadan**. Particularly notable in this regard is the inclusion of an essay by the eminent Kenyan novelist **Ngugi wa Thiong'o**, who has sometimes had his disagreements with Achebe (especially over the **language question**) but who makes clear his great admiration for Achebe's work and especially for his attempt to make a genuine political contribution in *A Man of the People*.

Susan Williams

D

DAILY CHRONICLE, a daily newspaper that serves as the official propaganda organ of the **People's Organization Party** in *A Man of the People*.

M. Keith Booker

"DEAR TAI SOLARIN." Achebe essay. See *Morning Yet on Creation Day*.

DESTROYER OF COMPOUNDS. African-born civil engineer in collusion with **James Ikedi**, the first warrant chief of **Okperi** in *Arrow of God* (chapter 5). Destroyer of Compounds is accused of extorting money from villages whose compounds supposedly lay on a planned roadway. By briefly mentioning characters of this ilk, Achebe invokes the early roots of Nigerian corruption, born of the warrant chief system (or certainly exacerbated by it).

Rachel R. Reynolds

DICK, an Englishman visiting **John Kent** in **Kangan** in *Anthills of the Savannah*. He is the founding editor of *Reject*, a thriving poetry journal that publishes only poems already rejected by more mainstream literary journals. In chapter 13, we learn of an aerogram he sent to John Kent extolling the virtues of **Ikem Osodi**, whom he had just met during his visit to **Kangan**.

M. Keith Booker

DISTRICT COMMISSIONER, pompous British colonial officer in *Things Fall Apart*, identified only by his official title. Responsible for overseeing the British system of **indirect rule** in the area of **Umuofia**, he is greatly disliked by the local people due to his heavy-handed approach in dealing with them and their customs. He is responsible for the treacherous imprisonment of **Okonkwo** and five other **Igbo** leaders who have been called to a meeting with him, presumably to air their grievances. At the end of *Things Fall Apart*, after the death of Okonkwo, he concludes that Okonkwo's story might make an interesting anecdote in the book he is writing, to be entitled *The Pacification of the Primitive Tribes of the Lower Niger*. Not named in *Things Fall Apart*, the District Commissioner is identified in *Arrow of God* as **George Allen**. *Arrow of God* also includes a segment of Allen's book. See also **Pacification**.

M. Keith Booker

DOGO, the thuggish, one-eyed bodyguard and henchman of **Chief Nanga** in *A Man of the People*.

M. Keith Booker

"DON'T LET HIM DIE: A TRIBUTE TO CHRISTOPHER OKIGBO." Achebe essay. See *Hopes and Impediments*.

DON'T LET HIM DIE: AN ANTHOLOGY OF MEMORIAL POEMS FOR CHRISTOPHER OKIGBO (1932–1967). Published in 1978, this volume of poems, edited by Achebe and Dubem Okafor, commemorates the life and poetry of **Christopher Okigbo**, seeking to keep alive the memory of his art and the example set by his life. The thirty-four poems in the collection were written by poets from Nigeria, other parts of Africa, the West Indies, Great Britain, Canada, and the United States. In addition to Achebe, authors represented in the collection include such well-known figures as Andrew Salkey, **Kofi Awoonor**, **J. P. Clark**, and **Wole Soyinka**. Thirty-two of the poems are in English, while two poems in **Igbo** (by Achebe and Obiora Udechukwu) are also included. The collection is introduced by Achebe's preface, which briefly details Achebe's friendship with Okigbo and the circumstances under which Okigbo died fighting for **Biafra** in the **Nigerian Civil War** in August 1967. As Achebe notes in this preface, the wide variety of the poets and poems contained in this tribute to Okigbo "bears witness to the power of his personality, his poetry, his life and death" (viii).

M. Keith Booker

THE DRUM, one of several children's books by Achebe, was first published in 1977 through Fourth Dimension Publishing in **Enugu**, **Nigeria**. Featuring illustrations by Anne Nwokoye, the book draws upon African traditions of oral storytelling, particularly of fables involving the **tortoise**. In this particular story, the cunning tortoise searches desperately for food in a time of great famine. In the course of this search, he accidentally stumbles into the world of the spirits, where he acquires a magical drum that produces food when it is beaten. The tortoise takes the drum home to the real world, where he beats it and generously produces food for the other animals.

Though a delightful and entertaining children's tale, *The Drum* also has other dimensions. In particular, Achebe embellishes the traditional story to make it into a political fable with obvious connotations for postcolonial Nigeria. After dispensing food to the other animals, the tortoise decides to use his newfound power and prestige to become king of the animals, but, in the course of his elaborate preparations for coronation, the drum is broken. The tortoise is forced to return to the land of the spirits to seek a second drum. However, whereas his first quest for food was an honorable one, this time his quest is merely for power. As a result, this time he is rewarded with a drum that produces not food but various torments, such as stinging bees, which he in turn decides to share with the other animals, just as he had earlier shared his magical food. He thus becomes the emblem of the postcolonial political leader who may begin with good intentions of helping his people but results in distributing only misery due to his corruption by power.

Achebe describes his project in *The Drum* in the interview "Achebe on Editing," contained in the volume *Conversations with Chinua Achebe* and also including the text of a talk that Achebe gave on the educational and literary uses of folk orature at a workshop on Education for Self Reliance at the University of Guelph in 1984. Achebe's writing of children's books, which also include *Chike and the River* (1966), *How the Leopard Got His Claws* (1972), and *The Flute* (1977), indicates the seriousness with which he approaches his own declared notion of the writer as teacher. He describes this notion in the essay "The Novelist as Teacher," which appears in *Morning Yet on Creation Day*.

FURTHER READING

Michael Scott Joseph, "A Pre-Modernist Reading of 'The Drum' "; Bernth Lindfors, ed., *Conversations with Chinua Achebe.*

M. Keith Booker and Thomas J. Lynn

DURRELL, LAWRENCE GEORGE (1912–1990). British poet and novelist, he was born in India of Irish parents and lived away from England most of his life. His most famous work is *The Alexandria Quartet,* which consists of four intertwined novels, *Justine* (1957), *Balthazar* (1958), *Mountolive* (1956), and *Clea* (1960). Durrell's books, on the evidence of chapter 13 of *No Longer at Ease*, were a part of **Obi Okonkwo's** youthful reading, then became a part of the personal library of **Isaac Okonkwo**, whose "mystic regard for the written word" is the reason he "never destroyed a piece of paper."

Thomas J. Lynn

E

EAGLE ON IROKO: SELECTED PAPERS FROM THE CHINUA ACHEBE INTERNATIONAL SYMPOSIUM. Edited by Edith Ihekweazu, this large collection (published in 1996) represents papers presented at a symposium held in February 1990 at the **University of Nigeria, Nsukka**, to honor Achebe on the occasion of his upcoming sixtieth birthday. The collection includes thirty-nine different essays from a variety of international contributors, though it is dominated by a solid core of Nigerian scholars. Most are simply scholarly essays on various aspects of Achebe's work, though the collection begins with a section, entitled "Tributes," that is less scholarly and more in the way of celebrations of Achebe's achievements. Contributors in this section include **Michael Thelwell** and **Emmanuel Obiechina**. Thelwell's opening sentence perhaps best sums up the theme of the entire book: "I know of no contemporary writer, in any language and out of any culture, whose *oeuvre*—in sustained excellence of craft; meaningful literary innovation; clarity of vision and purpose; cultural importance and international acceptance; as well as in universal popular affection and respect—approaches that of Chinua Achebe's" (1).

The collection ends with personal reminiscences by John Munonye and **Alan Hill**, detailing their long and extensive personal associations with Achebe. In between these opening and closing sections is a variety of more conventional scholarly sections on such topics as "History and Worldview," "Social Commitment," "The Image of Women," "Narrative Art," and "Comparative Perspectives." A separate section of essays devoted to *Anthills of the Savannah* (which, at the time of the symposium, was still a rather recent work) is also included. These scholarly essays include contributions by such scholars as Emmanuel Ngara, Dan Izevbaye, **Phanuel Egejuru**, and **Bernth Lindfors**. Together, they represent an important body of criticism and scholarship on Achebe and his work.

Compare *Chinua Achebe: A Celebration*, another sixtieth-birthday celebration volume.

M. Keith Booker

"EASTER HYMN," a two-stanza, twelve-line poem by **A. E. Housman**, published in the posthumous *More Poems* (1936) and again in *Collected Poems* (1939). The latter volume is owned by **Obi Okonkwo**, who, at the end of chapter 10 of *No Longer at Ease*, reads "Easter Hymn," which is "his favorite poem." The poem's somber tone (moderated somewhat by a hopeful note in the second stanza) accords with Obi's mood when he reads it—he has just had a disagreement with **Clara Okeke**. In addition the poem's lament over "The hate you [Christ] died to quench and could but fan" (line 5) anticipates Obi and Clara's future troubles. Their wedding plans and relationship dissolve after Obi's parents, **Isaac** and **Hannah Okonkwo**, in spite of their deep Christian convictions, vigorously oppose their son's marriage to an *osu* (see chapter 14).

Thomas J. Lynn

EBO, man of **Okperi** whom **Akukalia** provokes in *Arrow of God*. Akukalia is eventually shot by Ebo.

Rachel R. Reynolds

EDNA, a beautiful young woman who is being groomed as the second wife of **Chief Nanga** in *A Man of the People*. Though Nanga himself explains that the planned second marriage is designed to provide help for his first wife, **Margaret**, rumor has it that the ruthless Nanga has concluded that Margaret is too "bush," given his lofty political ambitions, and that he needs a better-looking and more sophisticated wife to accompany him at official functions as a more presentable "parlour wife."

Narrator **Odili Samalu** is clearly fascinated with Edna from the first time he sees her during Nanga's visit to the **Anata Grammar School** at the beginning of the novel. Later, after Nanga seduces Samalu's girlfriend **Elsie**, Samalu vows that he will seduce Edna in revenge. When Salamu gets to know Edna, however, he finds that she is really just a simple village girl caught up in forces beyond her control. In fact, he falls in love with her and begins to pursue her for herself rather than as a plot against Nanga. Edna herself clearly has no emotional attachment to Nanga but feels obligated to him because he has helped to pay for her education through the "college" level (roughly the equivalent of an American high school) and because he has already paid the **bride-price** to her abusive father, **Odo**. She thus initially spurns Salamu's advances, especially after she hears (and believes) rumors of his bad behavior. Ultimately, however, she comes to Salamu's side in the hospital after he is badly beaten by Nanga's supporters during an election campaign in which Salamu opposes Nanga for parliament. By the end of the book, Salamu and Edna are engaged to be married, Salamu having paid back Nanga the money he had invested in preparing Edna to be his second wife.

M. Keith Booker

EDOGO, Ezeulu's eldest son in *Arrow of God*. Edogo has two sisters, **Adeze** and **Akueke**; his mother is **Okuata**, and his wife is **Amoge**. In the first half of *Arrow of God*, Edogo is the constant personality around which the high tempers and civil inconsistencies of the other male members of Ezeulu's family are contrasted. For example, the even-tempered Edogo is frequently the target of unjustified verbal attacks by his father, even while Ezeulu goes all out to support **Obika**, his impetuous, irresponsible, drunken younger son. Edogo's position in the novel is also that of unfavored eldest son—somewhat of an anomalous position in **Igbo** traditional society. Furthermore, Edogo seeks approbation from the other men of **Umuaro** for his work as a carver, but he never really receives it and seems to remain socially insecure. As one who carves **masks** for all the masqueraders of Umuaro, Edogo is ironically the single member of the family whose works may simply help to unite the uneasy alliance of Umuaro villages.

Rachel R. Reynolds

EGONWANNE, a great orator of **Umuofia** in *Things Fall Apart*, regarded by **Okonkwo** as a coward because he typically uses his rhetorical talents to argue for peace, as opposed to the great war-singers of the past, such as **Okudo**.

M. Keith Booker

EGONWANNE, an elder of **Umuaro** in *Arrow of God*. His speech in chapter 2, cautioning the younger men of Umuaro to "put your fearlessness in your bag," is a good example of how Achebe represents the measured speeches of wise elder councillors (the speech nonetheless goes unheeded). Egonwanne is also the father of **Nwodika**'s wife, **Nwego**.

Rachel R. Reynolds

EGWUGWU, an ancestral spirit of the clan, represented in masquerade by village elders during important official and ceremonial occasions. The unmasking of an *egwugwu* by the zealous Christian convert **Enoch** in *Things Fall Apart* triggers a crucial confrontation between the clan of **Umuofia** and the local British colonial administration.

M. Keith Booker

EKE, the principal market day of **Okperi**. To attack a village on its big market day would be an abomination, but Akukalia does so anyway by attacking men of Okperi on Eke. See also **Market days**.

Rachel R. Reynolds

EKE-IDEMILI, the royal **python** who serves as the messenger of **Idemili**, Daughter of the Almighty, in the Kanganese legendary structure of *Anthills of the Savannah*. Though carrying no venom, he is described in chapter 8 as being held in greater awe than even the deadliest of poisonous serpents.

M. Keith Booker

EKEMEZIE, from **Okperi**, *Arrow of God*, chapter 14, is a man in the colonial service

who persuades **John Nwodika** also to join the white man.

Rachel R. Reynolds

EKWEFI, the much-suffering second wife of **Okonkwo** in *Things Fall Apart*, given a sound beating by her husband in chapter 5 for cutting a few leaves off of a banana tree, though he is really just taking out his frustrations from his inability to enjoy the **New Yam Festival** as much as he feels he should. Ezinma ran away from her first husband, **Anene**, in order to marry Okonkwo, with whom she had fallen in love largely due to his prowess in wrestling matches, of which she is a great fan. She is the friend of **Chielo**, priestess of **Agbala**, the Oracle of the Hills and Caves. She is also the mother of **Ezinma**, having given birth to nine earlier children who died in infancy or early childhood. In chapter 11, Ekwefi tells the important parable of **"The Tortoise and the Birds."**

M. Keith Booker

EKWENSU, mischievous deity known as "bringer of Evil" (*Arrow of God*, chapter 2).

Rachel R. Reynolds

EKWUEME, a leader of the people of **Umuofia** in *Things Fall Apart*. He serves as a spokesman for the group of six men who answer the **District Commissioner**'s invitation in chapter 23 to call on him to air their grievances after the zealous Christian convert **Enoch** unmasks an *egwugwu*.

M. Keith Booker

ELEWA, the earthy, sensible (but somewhat volatile) working-class girlfriend of **Ikem Osodi** in *Anthills of the Savannah*. The daughter of a simple market-woman in the **Gelegele Market**, Elewa herself is a salesgirl at a Lebanese shop in **Bassa**. Osodi sometimes envies her ability to communicate easily with the common people, with whom he feels solidarity but from whom he is separated by his education and class position. Elewa's own class position is indicated in the novel by the fact that she speaks almost entirely in **pidgin English**. At the end of the novel, she becomes something of a fertility figure by giving birth to the girl **Amaechina**, after the father, Osodi, has been killed.

M. Keith Booker

ELIOT, T(HOMAS) S(TEARNS), highly influential twentieth-century Anglo-American poet, playwright, and critic, a quatrain from whose poem, **"The Second Coming,"** forms the epigraph to *No Longer at Ease*. Eliot is referred to in this novel, moreover, in a placating if pretentious remark by **Obi Okonkwo** at the end of the second chapter. To **Clara Okeke**'s complaint, "I don't know why you should want me to meet people that I don't want to meet," Obi responds, "that's pure T. S. Eliot." In his essay on Eliot and Achebe, Roderick Wilson argues that Eliot's poetry and critical prose in some respects influenced *No Longer at Ease* and in some respects share a certain outlook with that novel. The poems by Eliot that Wilson points to are "The Second Coming," "The Waste Land," "The Hollow Men," and "Burnt Norton" (from *Four Quartets*), while the critical essay is "Tradition and the Individual Talent."
FURTHER READING
   Lloyd W. Brown, "Cultural Norms and Modes of Perception in Achebe's Fiction" and "The Historical Sense"; Roderick Wilson, "Eliot and Achebe."

Thomas J. Lynn

ELSIE, the sometime girlfriend of narrator **Odili Samalu** in *A Man of the People*. Elsie first became sexually involved with Samalu when they were in college together and while her fiancé, **Ralph**, was away at medical school at the University of Edinburgh. When Samalu returns from his teaching job at **Anata Grammar School** to the capital city of **Bori**, near which Elsie still lives and works (at a hospital twelve miles outside the city), he eagerly hopes to resume their liaison. To that end, Samalu arranges for her to join him as houseguests of **Chief Nanga** in his luxurious residence. Unfortunately, when she does so, she is quickly seduced by the charismatic (and sexually insatiable) Nanga, leading to an angry confrontation between Samalu and Nanga, after which the former moves out of the house. Elsie is a superficial woman who uses her sexuality for pleasure and profit, and it is clear that her attraction to Nanga has largely to do with the lure of his considerable wealth. Thus, she serves as an emblem of the negative effect of a Western-inspired materialism on the values of the African society of the novel, an effect that leads to an alienation between individuals and converts virtually everyone in the novel into a sort of prostitute.

M. Keith Booker

ELUMELU, another town in the region of **Umuaro** in *Arrow of God*.

Rachel R. Reynolds

ENEKE NTULUKPA, the bird who challenges the whole world to a fight. Birds appear as central figures in **Igbo trickster** legends, and there is more than one story about Ntulukpa in *Arrow of God*. The most extensive folk story of the whole novel appears in chapter 15, in which **Obiageli**'s mother tells a lengthy legend about a greedy boy who tries to dupe the beings in the land of the spirits but is himself duped into bringing disease to the world.

Rachel R. Reynolds

ENEKE-NTI-OBA, the bird who has learned to fly without perching, a reference to a story and a proverb about the importance of adapting to changing times. In this story, the bird learns to fly without perching because men have learned to shoot without missing (*Arrow of God*, chapter 4).

Rachel R. Reynolds

ENOCH, a zealous **Igbo** convert to Christianity in *Things Fall Apart*. He is reportedly cursed by his father, the snake-priest, after he kills and eats the sacred **python** in an excess of religious zeal. The event causes great tension in **Umuofia** between the new church and the traditional clan. These tensions grow even stronger when Enoch unmasks an *egwugwu* (a deed tantamount to killing the ancestral spirit represented by the masquerader) in public in an attempt to demonstrate the falseness of the traditional religion. This extremely serious transgression draws a violent response on the part of the clan and leads to the crisis that ultimately ends in **Okonkwo**'s death.

M. Keith Booker

ENUGU, a city (population 593,300 in 2002) in southeastern **Nigeria** in which **Obi Okonkwo's** friend, **Christopher**, is employed before being transferred to **Lagos**, as indicated in chapter 2 of *No Longer at Ease*. A center of **Igbo** culture and commerce, Enugu was established as the capital of the Republic of **Biafra** upon its formation in May 1967. However, the city fell to federal forces in October of that year.

Thomas J. Lynn

ERU. The eldest of the nine sons of the first father of the clan of **Umuofia** in *Things Fall Apart*. See **Umueru**.

ERU, the **Igbo** deity associated with wealth. In *Arrow of God*, he is represented as light-skinned, well-dressed, wearing an eagle feather in a red cap and carrying an elephant tusk. He is also the deity associated with the town of **Umunneora**. It is Eru who visits in a dream to terrorize a young **Obika** in *Arrow of God*. Whether Eru and his followers can stand as subordinate to **Ulu** is a central debate between competing interests in the **Umuaro** village complex.

Rachel R. Reynolds

EUNICE, a beautiful young woman lawyer, the fiancée of **Maxwell Kulamo** in *A Man of the People*. Like Kulamo, Eunice is a political idealist, strongly inspired by the thought of **Karl Marx**. With Kulamo and others of her circle, she helps to found the **Common People's Convention (CPC)**, a new political party that hopes to offer a genuine alternative to the ruling **People's Organization Party (POP)** and its principal (equally corrupt) opposition, the **People's Alliance Party (PAP)**. Eunice campaigns actively at the side of her fiancé during the parliamentary elections that are held late in the book and narrowly misses being killed when Kulamo is assassinated by POP thugs on election night. She then pulls out a gun and shoots **Chief Simon Koko**, the POP functionary for whom the killers are working. She is then arrested for the shooting but is subsequently released after a military coup removes the POP from power.

M. Keith Booker

EVIL FOREST, a place to which dangerous, despised, and abject things are consigned in traditional **Igbo** culture. In chapter 3 of *Things Fall Apart*, we learn that **Unoka**, father of **Okonkwo**, had been taken to the Evil Forest to die of a swelling disease (dropsy) considered an abomination to the earth goddess **Ani**. According to chapter 17, every traditional Igbo "clan and village had its 'evil forest,' " which is described as the burial ground of "all those who died of the really evil diseases, like leprosy and smallpox" and "the dumping ground for the potent fetishes of great medicine men when they died." This chapter, which is one that treats Okonkwo's stay in **Mbanta**, narrates the granting of the Evil Forest by the rulers of Mbanta for the church to be built by recently arrived Christian **missionaries**. The rulers assume, wrongly, as it turns out, that the efforts of the Christians (led by **Mr. Kiaga**) in Mbanta will come to naught if the church is built in the Evil Forest.

FURTHER READING

Kalu Ogbaa, *Gods, Oracles, and Divination*; Robert M. Wren, *Achebe's World*.

Thomas J. Lynn

EVIL FOREST, the name given to the leader of the *egwugwu* who gather to adjudicate the case of **Mgbafo** and **Uzowulu** in chapter 10 of *Things Fall Apart*. Evil Forest represents **Umueru**, one of the nine villages of **Umuofia**. He ordains that Mgbafo be returned to her husband, Uzowulu, but only after he pays a penance of wine to her family for repeatedly beating her.

M. Keith Booker

EZEANI, priest of the earth goddess, **Ani**, in *Things Fall Apart*. In chapter 4 he excoriates **Okonkwo** for beating his youngest wife, **Ojiugo**, during the **Week of Peace** prior to planting time, a week consecrated to Ani.

M. Keith Booker

EZEKWESILI EZUKANMA, a man of **Umuaro** with high title who pleads with **Ezeulu** to begin the **Feast of the New Yam** in *Arrow of God*, chapter 18).

Rachel R. Reynolds

EZEUDU, the oldest man in **Iguedo**, one of the nine villages of **Umuofia** in *Things Fall Apart* and the home of the protagonist, **Okonkwo**. In chapter 7, the wise and much-respected old man warns Okonkwo not to have a hand in the killing of **Ikemefuna** because the boy regards Okonkwo as his father.

A great man, Ezeudu dies in chapter 13, leading to an elaborate funeral ceremony attended by the entire clan. During the ceremony, Okonkwo's rusty old gun explodes and kills the dead man's sixteen-year-old son. The laws of the clan require that Okonkwo be exiled to the neighboring village of **Mbanta** for this offense. Ezeudu also is cited by **Ogbuefi Odogwu** in chapter 5 of *No Longer at Ease* as one of the great men of Iguedo in former times.

M. Keith Booker

EZEUGO. In *Things Fall Apart*, a powerful orator of **Umuofia**, typically chosen to speak on important public occasions. In chapter 2, he announces to the people of Umuofia that one of their daughters has been murdered in **Mbaino**.

M. Keith Booker

EZEULU. Ezeulu is the principal character in Achebe's *Arrow of God*. He is a priest of the deity **Ulu**, a spirit associated with the sun and moon who unites the ritual interests of the cluster of villages called **Umuaro**. He is the direct descendant of a man who has been priest of the chief deity of the village cluster in the past, and his power and his hubris are derived from this position. Ezeulu's name is "Eze" (priest) of "Ulu" (the god). His youthful nickname was Nwa-anyanwu, or son of the sun (chapter 12).

Ezeulu is a figure whose tragic flaw is a complex combination of mental dividedness and pride, which eventually leads to his madness. As for his dividedness, we see in Ezeulu's life a repeated theme of division between him and his brother, **Okeke Onenyi**, and between Ezeulu and his sons, particularly his eldest, **Edogo**. There is also a division between Ezeulu and his people. These human divisions ultimately also lead him to division from his god, who betrays him by allowing favorite son **Obika** to die (chapter 19) and driving Ezeulu into madness.

Ezeulu's mind is also frequently divided and therefore changeable and subject to his pride. Indeed, the entire novel can be seen as a study of the repercussions for the villages of the chief priest being a divided man. After returning from briefly being held at **Okperi** by the colonial government, Ezeulu returns to Umuaro and examines the long-term divisions that colonization is already putting on the people of Igboland: "As long as he was in exile it was easy for Ezeulu to think of Umuaro as one hostile enemy. . . . Again, at the end of the day, Ezeulu continued his division of Umuaro into ordinary people who had nothing but goodwill for him and those others whose ambitions sought to destroy the central unity of the six villages. From the moment he made this division, thoughts of reconciliation began, albeit timidly, to visit him" (chapter 16). However, this reconciliation does not happen. The remainder of the novel involves the slow and irreversible dissolution of unity in the village. In the quotation, we also see how Ezeulu's pride works, in that he considers those hostile to him personally to be those against Umuaro in general.

Ultimately, in Ezeulu, we also see a representation of the divided interests of the village in the face of encroaching colonization, embodied in conflict between traditional religion and Christianity, wage-employment in colonial service and yam farming, and so forth. Just as Ezeulu's spirit is conquered by divisions, so will Umuaro be.

For other approaches to interpreting Ezeulu's role in the novel, see Ogede, who examines the problem of Ezeulu's ego in disrupting the democratic forms of village governance; Okechukwu develops an argument based on how Ezeulu's miscommunications with those around him was a failure at community leadership; Wren discusses in depth the notion of how the course of the novel leads up to Ezeulu's betrayal by his own deity; and finally, Achebe's own opinions about his character Ezeulu are discussed in an interview with Fabre, where Achebe highlights the fact that, although Ezeulu has tragic flaws, he also finds the right way in the face of extreme duress.

FURTHER READING

Michel Fabre, "Chinua Achebe on *Arrow of God*"; Ode Ogede, *Achebe and the Politics of Representation*; Chinwe Christiana Okechukwu, *Achebe the Orator*; Robert M. Wren, *Achebe's World*.

Rachel R. Reynolds

EZIDEMILI, priest of **Idemili**, the protector deity of the town **Umunneora**. Ezidemili is also the praise-singer and drummer for Nwaka.

Rachel R. Reynolds

EZIGBO, "the good one." The name given to **Ezinma** by the mother of **Nwoye** in *Things Fall Apart*, chapter 5.

M. Keith Booker

EZINMA, daughter of **Okonkwo** and **Ekwefi** in *Things Fall Apart*, their tenth child and the first to live beyond early childhood. Though she is sickly, Ezinma's parents have great hopes that she will survive and break the cycle of *ogbanje* children that has plagued the couple. Okonkwo is especially fond of Ezinma, though he wishes she had been a boy.

M. Keith Booker

EZINMA, wife of **Onwuzuligbo** in chapter 6 of *Arrow of God*.

Rachel R. Reynolds

F

FAGUNWA, D(ANIEL) O(LORUN-FEMI) (1903–1963), Yoruba chief, teacher, and pioneer of Nigerian imaginative prose, born in Oke-Igbo, Nigeria, and educated at St. Luke's School, Oke-Igbo, and St. Andrew's College, Oyo. His highly popular books influenced the work of **Amos Tutuola** and made him an important forerunner of the development of the Nigerian novel. Fagunwa's picaresque, Yoruba-language narratives include elements—rhetoric, fantasy, magic, and wordplay, among others—derived from Yoruba oral tradition, while blending Christian and Yoruba teachings as well as original and traditional proverbs. The first of his book-length narratives, whose title, literally translated, is *The Brave Hunter in the Forest of Four Hundred Spirits*, was published in 1938 and represents an important milestone in Yoruba fiction, in part due to its scope, and in the history of the African novel. Achebe praises Fagunwa in the essay **"The African Writer and the English Language,"** declaring that while he himself uses English, "I hope . . . that there always will be men, like the late Chief Fagunwa, who will choose to write in their native tongue and insure that our ethnic literature will flourish side by side with the national ones" (103).

FURTHER READING

Ayo Bamgbose, *The Novels of D. O. Fagunwa*; Ulli Beier, "Fagunwa, a Yoruba Novelist"; Viktor Beilis, "Ghosts, People, and Books of Yorubaland"; Abiola Irele, *The African Experience in Literature and Ideology* and "Tradition and the Yoruba Writer"; Bernth Lindfors, "Amos Tutuola"; Emmanuel Obiechina, *Language and Theme*.

Thomas J. Lynn

FANON, FRANTZ OMAR (1925–1961) was a leading Third World intellectual whose work provided important inspiration to the struggle against colonialism and theoretical support to the subsequent growth of postcolonial culture. Indeed, Fanon was one of the most influential thinkers of the twentieth century. Though born in the French Antilles, he was particularly influential in Africa, where his writings provided a background for the works of a number of important anticolonial writers, especially Kenya's **Ngugi wa Thiong'o** and Senegal's Ousmane Sembène. During the 1950s and early 1960s, just as modern African literature was coming into being, Fanon's various writings, especially *Les damnés de la terre* (1961, English translation *The Wretched of the Earth*, 1963), presented an impassioned elaboration of the historical conditions of anticolonial struggle. Significantly, Fanon articulated the role to be played by intellectuals in this struggle, offering stern (and prescient, as it turned out) warnings of the difficulties that would face emerging African nations once independence had been won.

Born to a middle-class black family on the French colonial island of Martinique, Fanon grew up amid descendants of former African slaves brought to the Caribbean in earlier centuries to provide labor for the island's sugar plantations. As a teenager, he became intellectually attuned to the problems of colonialism and racism. He was politically active, participating on Martinique in the Free French guerrilla struggle against the supporters of the pro-Nazi French Vichy government. After the Free French forces gained control of Martinique in 1943, Fanon volunteered to go to Europe to fight with the Free French forces there. He emerged a decorated war hero, thereafter settling in France to complete his education and training as a psychiatrist in Paris and Lyons. Despite his background of service in the interest of the French state, he found that the white population of France regarded black French subjects like himself as *the Other*, as alien and inferior, yet frightening and dangerous. He came to understand that, in spite of his intelligence, high level of education, and mastery of the French language, he was regarded not as a human being, but as a specimen of an exotic and savage race, viewed through stereotypes developed over centuries of racial prejudice.

While in France, Fanon began his writing career, publishing his first book in 1952, *Peau Noire, Masques Blancs* (English translation *Black Skin, White Masks*, 1967) which describes Fanon's growing awareness of racism in France. The work, personal and lyrical, shows the strong influence of Fanon's

psychiatric training, concentrating primarily on the impact of racism and colonialism on the black psyche. It also engages in a critical dialogue with French existentialism and exhibits the influence of the **négritude** movement, which, in the 1940s and 1950s, asserted a distinctive black cultural identity in opposition to complete assimilation into French culture. Indeed, one of the leaders of that movement, Aimé Césaire, had been Fanon's teacher and mentor back in Martinique and remained an important influence on Fanon throughout his life. What is perhaps most moving about this chapter is Fanon's anguished and angry account of the various stages of accommodation and alienation that characterize black life in white societies. In particular, Fanon tells of his own struggle to make sense of the white world and to address it on its own rationalist terms, only to be rejected on the basis of his race and driven back to an antirational, primitivist stance by white prejudice. Then, realizing that such primitivism was taken by whites merely as a verification of their own stereotypical attitudes toward blacks, Fanon moved toward an exploration of the cultural achievements of African civilization, finally achieving a dialectical resolution between his original Western rationalism and his subsequent Africanist primitivism.

After completing his medical training, Fanon was appointed, in 1953, head of the psychiatric department of the Blida-Jonville Hospital in Algeria, a French colony in North Africa. Much of Fanon's work there involved explorations of the negative psychological impact of colonialism on colonial subjects, work that Achebe has described as "profoundly important" (*Hopes* 14). In 1954, the Algerians, led by the National Liberation Front (FLN), revolted against French colonial rule, initiating a period of violent revolutionary struggle that would last until the attainment of full Algerian independence in 1962.

Sympathetic to the revolution from its inception, Fanon resigned his medical post in 1956 in order to become the editor of the FLN newspaper. He remained involved in the revolution until his death, due to leukemia, in 1961, at the age of thirty-six.

During his involvement with the Algerian revolution, much of Fanon's writing concentrated on that event, including the essays published in *L'An Cinq, de la Révolution Algérienne* (1959, English translation *A Dying Colonialism*, 1965). Other essays he wrote during this period were posthumously collected and published in 1964 as *Pour la révolution Africaine* (English translation *Toward the African Revolution*, 1967). The culmination of his work, however, was the 1961 publication of his most important work, *The Wretched of the Earth*, just weeks before his death. This volume, featuring an impassioned introduction by Sartre, gained widespread recognition and solidified Fanon's reputation as a leading revolutionary thinker of the twentieth century.

Fanon's works are marked by a distinctive political vision, centrally informed by the European tradition of **Marxism**, but heavily modified to reflect Third World, anticolonial perspectives. For example, in his conviction that colonialism would be ended only through violent anticolonial struggle, Fanon was very much in accord with the Marxist belief that capitalism would come to an end only through violent revolution. However, Fanon elaborated specific reasons that this violence would be necessary in the anticolonial struggle; primarily, it would effect a cleansing of the long-term psychological impact of the violence of colonialism itself. In addition, whereas **Karl Marx** envisioned the European working class, or proletariat, as the crux of the revolution, Fanon felt that, in Africa and other colonial regions, revolution would have to be led by a coalition of peasants and social outcasts, the so-called lumpenproletariat, in whom Marx saw little revolutionary potential in Europe.

Perhaps the most important aspect of Fanon's political thought was his insight into the complex interaction between class and race in the colonial situation. Intensely aware of the centrality of racism to European colonialism, Fanon, as a Marxist, argued that social, economic, and political oppression in the Third World was ultimately a matter more of class than of race. This perspective informs most of Fanon's work but can be seen most clearly in his influential discussion in *The Wretched of the Earth* of the potential for disaster in postcolonial African nations if those nations simply replace their white colonial bourgeois leaders with a black African postcolonial bourgeoisie, while leaving the basic class structure of the societies still in place.

In 1971, Achebe became the first director of the short-lived Frantz Fanon Research Centre at the **University of Nigeria, Nsukka**. The center was intended to coordinate the work of a number of intellectuals and artists, most with socialist inclinations.

FURTHER READING

Chinua Achebe, *Hopes and Impediments*; Anthony Alessandrini, ed., *Frantz Fanon: Critical Perspectives*; M. Keith Booker, "Writing for the Wretched of the Earth"; David Caute, *Frantz Fanon*; Frantz Fanon, *Black Skin, White Masks* and *The Wretched of the Earth*; David Macey, *Frantz Fanon: A Biography* (2000).

M. Keith Booker

FARFIELD FOUNDATION. See **Foundations**.

FEAST OF THE NEW YAM, featured prominently in *Things Fall Apart*, a joyous festival dedicated to the earth goddess, **Ani**, in gratitude for her bringing of fertility to the land. Held every year shortly before the harvest, it is an occasion to honor the ancestral spirits of the clan and for giving thanks to Ani for the bounty of the upcoming harvest. This harvest celebration is the counterpart of the **Week of Peace**, a planting celebration. See also **Harvest**.

M. Keith Booker

FILM ADAPTATIONS. See *Bullfrog in the Sun*.

FLORENCE, the new girlfriend of **Christopher** in *No Longer at Ease*. In chapter 12 she is about the depart for England to study nursing, and Christopher wonders if he should attempt to dissuade her from going.

M. Keith Booker

THE FLUTE, one of several children's books by Achebe, was first published in 1977 through Fourth Dimension Publishing in **Enugu, Nigeria**. Like Achebe's other children's books, *The Flute* draws upon African traditions of oral storytelling. Here, Achebe follows a fairly common traditional tale by telling the story of a child who returns home with his family only to discover that he has left his prized flute at the farm where they have been during the day. He wants to go back to the remote farm to retrieve the flute, but his parents refuse to allow him to go, because during the night the farm is reserved for the use of the spirits. The boy disobeys his parents' commands and sneaks away to the farm, only to find that it is indeed now inhabited by spirits. Challenged by the king of the spirits for his disobedience to his parents (after all, couldn't he simply buy another flute?), the boy explains that the flute cannot be replaced so easily and is particularly valuable to him because he made it himself. Achebe thus inserts in the traditional tale his own addition concerning the value of constructive effort, commenting on his own role as an artist but also suggesting the impor-

tance of working to build and create things (such as postcolonial Nigeria) in general. Here, it is clear that the value of the flute to the boy is not in the object itself but in the act of creation that went into its making. The king declares that this reason is not good enough to justify disobedience to one's parents. However, he also expresses admiration for the boy's courage in seeking to recover the flute and for his dedication to the making of the flute and to the making of music with the instrument, which the boy is allowed to recover.

Achebe describes his project in *The Flute* in the interview "Achebe on Editing," contained in the volume ***Conversations with Chinua Achebe*** and also including the text of a talk that Achebe gave on the educational and literary uses of folk orature at a workshop on Education for Self Reliance at the University of Guelph in 1984. Achebe's writing of children's books, which also include ***Chike and the River*** (1966), ***How the Leopard Got His Claws*** (1972), and ***The Drum*** (1977), indicates the seriousness with which he approaches his own declared notion of the writer as teacher. He describes this notion in the essay "The Novelist as Teacher," which appears in ***Morning Yet on Creation Day***.
FURTHER READING
Bernth Lindfors, ed., *Conversations with Chinua Achebe*.

M. Keith Booker and Thomas J. Lynn

FORD FOUNDATION. See **Foundations**.

FOUNDATIONS. Some of Achebe's early opportunities to travel, meet fellow writers, and be published were created by American foundations, or by an organization posing as a foundation but in fact funded by the U.S. Central Intelligence Agency (CIA). There is abundant evidence in Achebe's work that he was aware of the mixture of motives that prompted American involvement with Africa and in some cases their interest in African writers. A brief summary of some of his contacts with American funders suggests that he was prepared to take advantage of American largesse but did not compromise himself by accepting it.

Following World War II, numerous American foundations involved themselves in the educational and cultural life of Africa. Given a knowledge of the history of American philanthropy, the motives for their actions have generally been fairly transparent, and the names of major grant-making trusts, such as Carnegie, Ford, and Rockefeller, are so well known as to make further comment on their "philosophies" redundant. Others involved, including the Merrill Foundation, are less well known. It is worth recording that the Merrill Foundation, set up by the poet James Merrill out of his inheritance from Merrill-Lynch, makes grants to writers. Scholarly writing on the operation of American foundations in Africa has been undertaken from various angles. For example, Robert W. July (1987), the Rockefeller Foundation's assistant director for the humanities in West Africa from the late 1950s, has provided a detailed account of his employers' involvement with West African intellectuals, and Peter Benson (1986) has looked at how two influential publications, *Black Orpheus* and *Transition*, were funded and how they contributed to creative life on the continent.

The situation regarding the operation of foundations became more complicated when the CIA set up and funded a sham grant-making body, the Farfield Foundation, to enable it to provide financial support for selected individuals and projects. Beginning with an exposé in *Ramparts Magazine* (1966), the last thirty-five years have seen extensive unraveling and analysis of the funding patterns of the CIA. A very helpful context for the agency's involvement in the cultural Cold War in Africa is given by Fran-cis Stonor Saunders in *Who Paid the Piper?* (1999). Saunders is among the many, some active on the Internet, who have tried to assess the impact of the CIA in the battle for the hearts and minds of artists and intellectuals. However, much of the material concerning operations is based on assertion and anecdote. Examples of this can be found in the writing of Ezekiel Mphahlele, the South African author who was in charge of the Paris-based Congress for Cultural Freedom to and through which the CIA transferred substantial sums. Another South African writer, Lewis Nkosi, who studied in the United States thanks to the Farfield Foundation, has indicated that he does not think the (ultimate) source of his funding compromised him or other beneficiaries. He has written somewhat controversially: "Since, so far as we know, there was never any ideological attempt on our collective virtue, it is difficult to see what American Intelligence hoped to gain by supporting so diverse a group of writers, intellectuals, journals and cultural clubs." Other African intellectuals, notably Chinweizu, Onwuchekwa Jemie, and Ihechukwu Madubuike, have taken a different line and have alleged that even the Rockefeller Foundation, which actually had money of its own to give away, ran a program that was calculated to benefit American policy by derailing progressive African initiatives.

The interventions of foundations touched Achebe at several points, and there were various issues on which he might have been compromised. In 1961, he co-founded the Mbari Club in Ibadan, a center for writers and artists, which received funding from the Farfield Foundation via the Congress for Cultural Freedom; that is, U.S. tax dollars voted to the CIA for clandestine operations reached a Nigerian organization concerned with cultural development. The Ibadan Mbari Club was initially a very modest enterprise and partly self-financing. Larger costs were incurred when it took over responsibility for publishing a periodical, *Black Orpheus*, the major outlet for local writing and point of contact with work written in Francophone Africa and in the African diaspora. Achebe had "The Voter" published in Number 17 of the periodical.

Concerned about the lack of publishing opportunities for African creative writers, Mbari then embarked on a program that resulted in the publication of seventeen titles in three years. In *Afrika, My Music*, Mphahlele describes the role played by his Congress in obtaining funds for this program from the Merrill Foundation. Those who detect the hand of the CIA in projects "irrigated" by U.S. support might see Mbari's decision to publish J. P. Clark and Wole Soyinka as promoting an alienated, irrelevant "Euromodernism." However, it should be noted that the program also supported the direct, accessible, ferociously committed *A Walk in the Night* by Alex La Guma.

Following the impact made by his first novels and supported by July, Achebe was awarded a grant by the Rockefeller Foundation to travel to Uganda, Kenya, Tanganyika, Zanzibar, and Northern and Southern Rhodesia (Zambia and Zimbabwe). Encounters with racism in Central Africa profoundly affected the Nigerian writer, and the journey gave him a new awareness of issues facing the continent. Accounts of experiences from this period can be found in "Tanganyika—Jottings of a Tourist," in ***Morning Yet on Creation Day***, and the article "The Judge and I Didn't Go to Namibia," published in the journal *Callaloo*. The award was made to Ahebec as part of Rockefeller's policy of supporting "key individuals"—a policy that Chinweizu and others asserted was used to advance American interests. It is, however, impossible to demonstrate that this was so in the case of Achebe.

In 1962, Achebe was a member of the Ni-gerian delegation that attended a major writers' conference organized by the Congress for Cultural Freedom and held at Makerere, Uganda. The conference, made possible by funding from the Farfield Foundation, brought together Anglophone writers from East and West Africa. Critics, looking for a "payoff" for American support, see the gathering as part of a campaign against **négritude**, and it could be argued that the contacts made at Makerere helped to establish the Heinemann **African Writers Series** as a continental force in publishing African creative writing.

Even before the Makerere Conference, Uganda was on the literary map of Africa thanks to the journal *Transition*, which had been established in Kampala in 1961 by Rajat Neogy. Initially the publication was on a very uncertain financial base, but, according to Eugene Benson, after the conference Mphahlele made funding available through the Congress for Cultural Freedom (Benson 115). Such support for literary/ intellectual journals was in line with CIA practice in several continents, with *Encounter* as perhaps the best known. As we have seen, *Black Orpheus* had already been supported in West Africa. The benefit of such publications for Western-educated Africans is manifest; that for the CIA, by no means apparent.

Achebe contributed to the debates in *Transition* through "On Janheinz Jahn and Ezekiel Mphahlele" (1963) and "The African Writer and the English language" (1965). The former shows that the pages of the journal were open to the expression of a range of views about négritude, and the latter was a manifesto prompted by Obi Wali's radical comments on the languages of African literature. Achebe considered this statement sufficiently important to include in *Morning Yet on Creation Day*.

At the beginning of the 1970s, out of the suffering of the **Nigerian Civil War**, in a spirit of defiance, recovery, and rediscovery, Achebe founded *Okike: An African Journal of New Writing*. In 1982, he told "The *Okike* Story" in that journal and included in that account acknowledgment of support from a variety of sources, including from the Ford Foundation, which has had a major program in Africa for many years. It is noteworthy that Chinweizu was involved in the publication from very early on. He was on the masthead as an associate editor, and his essay "Prodigals, Come Home!" appeared in *Okike* in 1973 (number 4, December). Described in the Contributors Notes as "currently [hanging] out in Harvard Square, U.S.A.," Chinweizu, with Onwuchekwa Jemie and Ihechukwu Madubuike, subsequently published a two-part essay entitled "Towards the Decolonisation of African Literature" in *Okike* 6 and 7. This material, later used in the book with the same title as the essay, shows the authors' deep suspicions of American policy in Africa and their cynicism about the use made of foundations by those responsible for protecting the interests of the United States. The fact that the Ford Foundation supported *Okike* was just one of the contradictions in which the publication found itself—another was its association with the **University of Massachusetts at Amherst**.

During the late 1980s and in the 1990s, major American foundations linked up with Scandinavian aid agencies to make major contributions to the literary scene in Africa through support for indigenous publishing. This found expression in the establishment of the African Books Collective (ABC, founded 1989) and the African Publishers' Network (APNET, 1992). They are part of an evolving situation that is extremely complex, with suspicions, fueled by experiences of the cultural Cold War, making it particularly difficult to sort fact from fiction.

Achebe has employed a proverb about those who take ant-infested faggots into their homes having to be prepared to expect visits from lizards. A somewhat similar inevitability in relationships is indicated in the saying alluded to in the title of Saunders' book about the CIA: *Who Paid the Piper?* However, the inevitable success of conspiracies and the effectiveness of links between funding and outcome are both doubtful. In any case, despite benefiting from "infected" or "infested" funding, Achebe remained unvisited by "lizards"—or able to show them the door. Irrespective of sources of finance, he did not dance to any tune but his own.

FURTHER READING

Chinua Achebe, "The *Okike* Story"; Peter Benson, *"Black Orpheus"*; Chinweizu et al., *Toward the Decolonization of African Literature*; Rhodri Jeffries-Jones, *The C.I.A. and American Democracy*; Robert W. July, *An African Voice*; Ezekiel Mphahlele, *Afrika My Music*; Lewis Nkosi, "Ezekiel Mphahlele at 70"; Frances Stonor Saunders, *The Cultural Cold War*.

James Gibbs

FREETOWN, referred to in chapter 3 of *No Longer at Ease*, the capital, most populous city, and economic hub of the nation of Sierra Leone. Beginning in the late eighteenth century Freetown became a refuge for former African slaves who arrived from England, Nova Scotia, Jamaica, and elsewhere, and during the mid-nineteenth century it was the administrative center for Britain's colonial territories in West Africa. Sierra Leone's busiest port, Freetown boasts a natural harbor on the Atlantic Ocean. In *No Longer at Ease* Freetown is, along with **Funchal** in the **Madeiras**, one of the **MV Sasa**'s ports of call on its voyage from **Liverpool** to **Lagos**, as well as the destination of one of the boat's passengers, **Mrs. Wright**.

Thomas J. Lynn

FUNCHAL, a port of call for the **MV Sasa** that is lyrically evoked in chapter 3 of *No Longer at Ease*. It is the capital of the **Ma-**

deiras as well as the region's most populous city (102,800 inhabitants in 2002), located at the southern tip of Madeira Island. Along with **Freetown** in Sierra Leone, Funchal is one of the MV *Sasa*'s intermediate stops on its **Liverpool** to **Lagos** voyage, recounted in chapters 3 and 4 of the novel. While the boat is docked at Funchal **Obi Okonkwo**, **Clara Okeke**, and **John Macmillan** enjoy a walk together "on cobbled streets" and in "little gardens and parks."

Thomas J. Lynn

G

GALLOWAY, MR. JUSTICE WILLIAM, the judge (of the High Court of Lagos and the Southern Cameroons) who presides over the bribery trial of **Obi Okonkwo**, as noted in chapter 1 of *No Longer at Ease*.

M. Keith Booker

GELEGELE MARKET, a bustling market in the capital city of **Bassa** in the postcolonial nation of **Kangan** in *Anthills of the Savannah*. Clearly based on the example of such African markets as the one at **Onitsha** in **Nigeria**. The heteroglossic Gelegele Market functions as both an economic and a cultural center, where people of various ethnic and class backgrounds intermingle, sharing goods, customs, and ideas.

M. Keith Booker

THE GENERAL HOSPITAL. In *No Longer at Ease*, the hospital in **Lagos** at which **Clara Okeke** is employed as a nurse (see chapters 11 and 18).

Thomas J. Lynn

"GENTLEMAN BOBBY." In chapter 11 of *No Longer at Ease*, a suggestive song performed by an unnamed vocalist for the **highlife** dancers at the **Imperial** nightclub.

Thomas J. Lynn

GEORGE, SAINT (died A.D. 303?), patron saint of England, considered a Christian martyr whose death occurred shortly before the Roman Empire's official toleration of Christianity (promulgated in the Edict of Milan). Saint George is referred to in chapter 11 of *No Longer at Ease*. Reliable evidence about George's life is scarce, although two early Syrian church inscriptions indicate that he was martyred at Lydda, Palestine (now also called Lod, Israel). Traditional guardian of soldiers, George was also designated protector of numerous medieval states, including Genoa, Venice, and Portugal (as well as England). George is, moreover, an important saint of Eastern Orthodox Christianity. In legend and art he embodies the attributes of courage and honor, the most prominent story and image of him being his vanquishing of a dragon on behalf of a Libyan princess, a deed that results in the embrace of Christianity by her people. In *No Longer at Ease* **Obi Okonkwo** reflects on the career and motives of his supervisor in the civil service, **William Green**, associating him both with Saint

George and, up to a point, with **Kurtz** in **Joseph Conrad**'s *Heart of Darkness*. Surmising that Green, like Kurtz, arrived in Africa with noble but misguided intentions, Obi imagines his boss as a duped Saint George.

Thomas J. Lynn

GIKANDI, SIMON (1956–   ), important African literary critic, born in Nyeri, Kenya, and educated at the University of Nairobi, the University of Edinburgh, and Northwestern University, where he received a Ph.D. in English literature in 1986. Gikandi has taught at California State University, Harvard University, and the University of Massachesetts. Since 1991, he has taught at the University of Michigan, where he is now Robert Hayden Collegiate Professor of English Language and Literature.

Gikandi is a sensitive and theoretically sophisticated literary critic whose work is marked by a detailed understanding of both postcolonial and Western literatures and of the sometimes complex interrelationships between the two. In addition to numerous articles on various aspects of Western and postcolonial literatures, he is the author of *Reading Chinua Achebe* (1991), which did much to further the critical appreciation of Achebe in the West. His other books include *Reading the African Novel* (1987), *Writing in Limbo: Modernism and Caribbean Literature* (1992), *Maps of Englishness: Writing Identity in the Culture of Colonialism* (1996), and *Ngugi wa Thiong'o* (2000). Most recently, he edited the *Encyclopedia of African Literature* (2002).

FURTHER READING

Simon Gikandi, *Maps of Englishness*, *Ngugi wa Thiong'o*, *Reading the African Novel*, *Reading Chinua Achebe*, and *Writing in Limbo*.

M. Keith Booker

GIRLS AT WAR AND OTHER STORIES. See ***The Sacrificial Egg and Other Stories***.

GODS. As David Carroll notes, the traditional religion can be seen to consist of three major "categories of belief" that correspond to different categories of gods (15). The first of these is a belief in a supreme creator god, or **Chukwu**, who remains aloof and unapproachable by human beings. At the opposite extreme, the **Igbo** also believe in the existence of a personal god, or **chi**, which is a sort of spiritual double of each individual human and thus the god with whom each individual has the closest contact and communication. In between are a variety of other gods with whom humans can communicate and who can sometimes serve as intermediaries between humans and Chukwu. Among the most important of these is the earth goddess, **Ani**.

FURTHER READING

David Carroll, *Chinua Achebe*; Kalu Ogbaa, *Gods, Oracles, and Divination*; Victor Uchendu, *The Igbo of Southeast Nigeria*; Robert M. Wren, *Achebe's World*.

M. Keith Booker

GODS, ORACLES, AND DIVINATION: FOLKWAYS IN CHINUA ACHEBE'S NOVELS, by Kalu Ogbaa (1992), is an extremely useful study of Achebe's use of **Igbo** folk culture in his novels. The book serves two basic purposes. First, it provides a great deal of background information on Igbo religion, cosmology, and folk culture, from the point of view of an African scholar well versed in the tradition. Second, it comments extensively on Achebe's use of this material in his fiction, thereby illuminating specific aspects of the fiction and general aspects of Achbe's artistic goals and practice. In addition, the book usefully places all of these discussions within the context of Achebe's participation in the project of constructing a viable postcolonial national identity for modern **Nigeria**. At the same time, Ogbaa rightly emphasizes that Achebe's African novels are not unique in their reliance on elements of folk culture to enhance their presentation of experience. For example, Ogbaa argues that **Things Fall Apart** is quite reminiscent of Thomas Hardy's *The Mayor of Casterbridge* in the way it uses local folk culture to enhance its representation of traditional ways of rural life (5).

After an introductory chapter that helps to place Achebe's writing in its postcolonial context, Ogbaa devotes two very informative chapters to some of the basic aspects of Igbo religion and cosmology, helping to clarify the worldview that lies behind the traditional societies represented in Achebe's novels, while also indicating some of the ways in which this worldview retains importance in modern Nigeria. Making frequent references to Achebe's fiction, Ogbaa discusses **Chukwu**, the supreme Igbo god and creator; *chi*, the personal god or sustaining essence of each individual; nature gods; and man-made gods. He also distinguishes among the different attitudes shown by the Igbo toward each god or group of gods, while also distinguishing between the worship of gods and the honoring of ancestors. Finally, he discusses the crucial role played by oracles and divination in both traditional Igbo society and Achebe's fiction.

The next chapter discusses the importance and significance of names and naming in Igbo folk culture, followed by a very useful chapter on rituals and ceremonies. In particular, Ogbaa notes the extent to which, in traditional Igbo culture, various public rituals and ceremonies not only have religious significance but also function as a form of folk drama and communal entertainment. Indeed, he concludes that "most of the Igbo rituals and ceremonies Achebe includes in his novels embody dramatic elements which qualify them as folk drama, folk opera, or simply folk entertainment" (110). Moreover, Ogbaa argues that Achebe's treatment of these rituals as entertainment is very much in accord with the way these rituals are viewed in Igbo culture itself.

The following four chapters all focus, in one way or another, on stylistic elements of Achebe's writing that can be traced to the influence of Igbo folk culture and of Achebe's desire to invest the English language of his texts with an authentic African spirit. For example, in chapter 6, Ogbaa outlines the importance of proverbs as an element of the Igbo art of conversation, noting that Achebe similarly employs proverbs to reinforce the thematic content of his novels. He reinforces this point with a detailed analysis of specific proverbs used in Achebe's first four novels. The next two chapters detail the importance of folk stories, folk songs, and chants in Igbo culture, again indicating that Achebe uses the same devices in his fiction in a manner that is not only effective in a literary sense but also consistent with the ways in which these devices function in Igbo folk culture. Again, this discussion is enhanced by an analysis of specific examples of Achebe's use of folk stories and songs, as in the story of **"The Tortoise and the Birds"** in *Things Fall Apart*. Chapter 9 then addresses the important **language question** in Achebe's fiction, arguing that Achebe's use of elements from both Igbo folk culture and the Igbo language itself helps him to remake the colonialist language of English into one that is able to convey well an African experience and point of view.

Ogbaa closes with a concluding chapter in which he praises Achebe's achievement in writing novels that manage to fit so well into the European conventions of the genre yet at the same time faithfully portray so many elements of African linguistic and cultural practice. Indeed, Ogbaa concludes that Achebe's success as a novelist can largely be attributed to the way in which he has been able to present the African material of his fiction via the vehicle of the European genre of the novel, modifying that genre as needed "through the structural manipulation of Igbo folkways to explore his themes and explain his culture to his audience" (252).

Though Ogbaa himself is sometimes (understandably) impatient with the ignorance of Western readers and critics with regard to Igbo "folkways," it is probably for such a Western audience that *Gods, Oracles, and Divination* is most useful. Though not an in-depth scholarly account of Igbo folk culture and religion, the book provides a wealth of details for the uninitiated, linking these details to Achebe's fiction in ways that make their application to the interpretation of his work quite obvious. Ogbaa effectively demonstrates that Achebe has drawn upon Igbo folk culture in a way that is even richer and more profound than is immediately obvious. He also demonstrates that no one without at least some appreciation and understanding of this aspect of Achebe's fiction will be able to read that fiction well.

FURTHER READING

Emmanuel Obiechina, *Culture, Tradition, and Society in the West African Novel*; Robert M. Wren, *Achebe's World*.

M. Keith Booker

GOODCOUNTRY, JOHN, or Jaja, missionary and teacher at **Umuaro** in chapter 4 of *Arrow of God*. He preaches tales of how his brother, Joshua Hart, was "martyred" at Bonny. This passage refers to those early **missionaries** in British West Africa who sometimes proselytized by rhetorically linking themselves to the early Christian martyrs. We find out in chapter 18 that Goodcountry comes from Niger Delta country and that he is the catechist for the church in Umuaro, which is named St. Marks CMS Church. Achebe also lampoons the self-serving style

by which catechists would claim credit for success in converting people in chapter 18.

Rachel R. Reynolds

GRAMMAR-PHONE, humorous nickname of the loud-voiced "soloist" of the "Ego Women's Party," who noisily sings the praises of **Chief Nanga** amid the general din of the ceremonies surrounding his visit to the **Anata Grammar School** at the beginning of *A Man of the People*.

M. Keith Booker

GREEN, WILLIAM. In *No Longer at Ease*, the arrogant British supervisor of senior civil servant **Obi Okonkwo** and one of the novel's important, if only occasionally invoked, characters. A colonial administrator in the waning days of British rule in **Nigeria**, Green's chauvinism toward Africans is evident in his crude remarks about the corruption and inferiority of Africans. Yet in contrast to **Mr. Brown, Mr. Smith**, and the **District Commissioner**—the generically labeled British characters of Achebe's preceding novel, *Things Fall Apart*—Mr. Green is a multidimensional figure, one not dismissed by the novel.

While Green issues several repugnant statements, there may be hints of a limited narrative sympathy with his charge (which recurs in chapter 17) that the Nigerian educated elite do not sufficiently identify their interests with those of the nation at large. In any event, a still later echo of Green's charge may lend it the most support. In the final chapter of *Anthills of the Savannah*, **Elewa's** elderly, unnamed uncle, who participates in the naming ceremony for **Ikem Osodi** and Elewa's infant, declares, "We have seen too much trouble in Kangan since the white man left because those who make plans make plans for themselves only and their families" (chapter 18).

Meanwhile, Obi's silent contemplation of Green's motives in chapter 11 contributes to the novel's textured portrayal of the veteran British administrator. Obi believes that his boss arrived in Africa with noble intentions but, like so many European colonialists, became a victim of his own prejudices. As he imagines Green's intense but misguided drive "to bring light to" an Africa that he did not comprehend, Obi conjures up the varied figures of **Mohammed Ali**, **Saint George**, and **Joseph Conrad**'s **Kurtz**. Obi's attempt to understand Green in all his complexity is notable for the way it casts an ironic backward glance at the District Commissioner of *Things Fall Apart* who first drives Obi's grandfather, **Okonkwo**, to suicide and then considers writing a paragraph about him in his prospective book. By contrast Obi determines to write a much more nuanced novel on the tragedy of men like Green.

Thomas J. Lynn

GREENE, (HENRY) GRAHAM (1904–1991), important English writer whose novel *The Heart of the Matter* (set in Africa) is discussed by **Obi Okonkwo** in chapter 5 of *No Longer at Ease*.

Thomas J. Lynn

GUY, Beatrice Okoh's boyfriend during the earlier time she had spent as a student in London before the main action of *Anthills of the Savannah*.

M. Keith Booker

GWEN, an English girl whom **John Kent** arranged for **Sam, the President**, to have sex with while in London during his younger days in *Anthills of the Savannah*. The novel vaguely suggests London as a locus of sexual decadence, thus reversing colonialist stereotypes concerning the sexual promiscuity of Africans and other non-Europeans.

M. Keith Booker

H

HAGGARD, H. RIDER (1856–1925), British writer of boys' adventure stories, historian, and agriculturalist. Achebe remembers reading Haggard's novels, along with those of **John Buchan**, as a boy in 1952, the year that Joyce Cary published *Mister Johnson*. Recalling that there were in the "fine library" of his secondary school a "few 'African' novels by such writers as Rider Haggard and John Buchan," Achebe nonetheless notes that at the time he "did not connect the Africa of these riveting adventure stories among savages even remotely with myself or my homeland" (*Home and Exile*). In *A Man of the People*, the uncultured **Chief Nanga** has only a few books in his library. Two of these are Haggard's novels *She* (1887) and its sequel, *Ayesha: The Return of She* (1904–1905), indicating the questionable quality of Nanga's taste in literature.

The hero of several of Haggard's novels, Allan Quatermain, makes his first appearance in the still popular *King Solomon's Mines* (1885), published in the same year as the Berlin Conference, which divided continental Africa among European contenders, and nearly two decades after diamonds were discovered in the Orange Free State of South Africa. In the company of two other Englishmen, Sir Henry Curtis and Captain John Good, whom he has met on board a ship lingering in Durban harbor, Quatermain, who had until then "made his living as a trader in the old Colony," sets out to follow an ancient map in order to recover Curtis's brother George, to quest for gold and diamonds and, in the process, to liberate a tribe of African natives from their despotic rulers and restore their chief Umbopa/Ignosi, to his rightful place at the head of his people.

H. Rider Haggard began his own public career in South Africa as well, when, in 1871 at the age of nineteen, he became secretary to the governor of Natal, Sir Theophilus Shepstone. In 1877, while still on Shepstone's staff, he assisted in hoisting the British flag over the newly annexed territory of the Transvaal. Meanwhile, in exploring the Natal province, Haggard interested himself in Zulu customs and traditions, publishing several articles on such topics as a "Zulu war dance" in London magazines. Haggard returned to Britain in 1881, where he began writing his adventure stories, took up a life of "farming and gardening," and became known as something of an authority on agriculture. In 1912, Haggard was appointed to the Dominions Royal Commission, charged by Joseph Chamberlain with investigating the "burdens of empire" and how they were to be borne. As a member of the commission, he visited South Africa in 1914, on the eve of World War I. His diary of that trip describes sights and scenes from the vineyards and fruit farms of the Cape to cattle dipping in southern Rhodesia. His final stop, however, was in Zululand, where his own career of adventures and their telling had begun. H. Rider Haggard died in 1925 and was buried in Saint Mary's Church at Ditchingham, but the adventure stories of a man who, as his self-composed epitaph concluded, "with a Humble Heart Strove to Serve his Country," were still being read in 1952 by Nigerian schoolboys such as Chinua Achebe.

FURTHER READING

H. Rider Haggard, *Diary of an African Journey*; Lindy Stiebel, *Imagining Africa*.

Barbara Harlow

HAMMOND, DOROTHY. See *The Africa That Never Was*.

A HANDFUL OF DUST, a novel by **Evelyn Waugh** (1934). **Obi Okonkwo** briefly analyzes the ending of this novel in chapter 5 of *No Longer at Ease* in order to illustrate his view of tragedy.

Thomas J. Lynn

HARGREAVES, J. P., the carpenter/missionary in *Arrow of God* who begins the Onitsha Industrial Mission, where **Moses Unachukwu** learns carpentry.

Rachel R. Reynolds

HARRINGTON DOCK. In chapter 3 of *No Longer at Ease*, the point of departure in **Liverpool** of the **MV** *Sasa*, which carries **Obi Okonkwo**, **Clara Okeke**, and other passengers on its voyage to **Lagos** via **Funchal** and **Freetown**.

Thomas J. Lynn

HART, JOSHUA. "Martyred" missionary invoked by **John Goodcountry** in *Arrow of God*.

Rachel R. Reynolds

HARVEST, the occasion of ritual observance and celebration in *Things Fall Apart*, *No Longer at Ease*, and *Arrow of God*. The treatment of the harvest in *No Longer at Ease* suggests how both Christians and non-Christians in rural Igbo districts adopted elements of each other's rituals in rural districts by the end of the colonial period. (This process is already under way in the earlier time frame of *Arrow of God* insofar as non-Christian villagers undertake Christian observances to meet their agricultural needs.) In chapter 5 of *No Longer at Ease* the narrator observes that the non-Christian elder, **Ogbuefi Odogwu**, "like many others in Umuofia . . . went to church once a year at harvest," and chapter 14 mentions that Carpenter **Moses** "offered . . . to the church at harvest" a table that he made and that was put up for auction after the "Harvest Service." See also **Feast of the New Yam**.

Thomas J. Lynn

HEART OF DARKNESS (1899). Joseph Conrad wrote *Heart of Darkness* in the fall of 1898 and published it in three installments in *Blackwood's Edinburgh Magazine* in the spring of 1899. It was published in book form in 1902. It was based fairly closely on Conrad's own trip to the Congo in June to December 1890. Although it might be a mistake to identify Conrad too closely with Marlow, he preceded his narrator in interviewing in Brussels for a job as riverboat captain, traveling to the Congo, seeing the railway being built at Matadi (the Company Station), meeting Camille Delcommune (the Manager) at Kinchassa (the Central Station), making a single trip upriver to Stanley Falls (the Inner Station), picking up a sick agent Georges Antoine Klein, who died on the way downriver, getting sick himself, and returning to Europe. Although Klein apparently did not commit any of the atrocities of **Kurtz**, other Europeans in the Congo had, such as Captain Leon Rom, who surrounded his hut with human skulls.

Chinua Achebe has pointed out the racism of *Heart of Darkness* in a series of four articles: **"An Image of Africa"** (1977), "Viewpoint" (1980), **"African Literature as Restoration of Celebration"** (1990), and "Africa's Tarnished Name" (1998). For example, Conrad's story shows very little of African culture or people. None of the African characters has a name. Except for Kurtz's mistress, none appear for more than a paragraph. We do not enter their thoughts or perspective. Africans speak a total of four **pidgin English** sentences. Conrad thereby treats Africans primarily as backdrop for the moral struggles of his white characters. He employs the journey upriver as a trope for a journey back in time to humanity's primitive beginnings. Marlow describes Africans as the "prehistoric man" and repeatedly calls them "savages" and "niggers." Those few Africans who have picked up some European skills, such as the helmsman and fireman, are mocked for their ineptitude. In general, Conrad presents Africa as a void, a place without civilization or law where Europeans can run amok. A manuscript passage cut from the final version makes clear that the atheist Conrad was using Africa as a trope for a Godless universe: "And the earth suddenly seemed shrunk to the size of a pea spinning in the heart of an immense darkness." Conrad thereby fell, as Achebe notes, into a long European tradition that posited a dark Africa as foil to an enlightened Europe. In Conrad's case, though, he saw Europe beneath a thin veneer of civilization as also dark and primitive.

Achebe grants in "An Image of Africa" that "Conrad saw and condemned the evil of imperial exploitation." Indeed, the story is probably the strongest attack on imperialism in British literature before the twentieth century. Conrad clearly condemned the carelessness and cruelty of Belgian exploitation by showing the African chain gang and starving workers at the Company Station, the empty villages and the corpse with a bullet in the head on the caravan trail, the scapegoat beaten for the fire at the Central Station, and the company agents on the steamer planning to shoot Kurtz's followers for sport until Marlow frightens them off with his whistle. Conrad extends his condemnation to other European countries by describing the French warship shelling the bush, mentioning that Kurtz was "educated partly in England," and making the general declaration: "The conquest of the earth, which mostly means the taking it away from those who have a different complexion or slightly flatter noses than ourselves is not a pretty thing."

Achebe also alludes to *Heart of Darkness* in chapter 11 of **No Longer at Ease**, in which the protagonist, **Obi Okonkwo**, likens the misplaced civilizing ideals of his boss, **William Green**, before he arrived in Africa, to those that seem to have initially motivated Conrad's Kurtz "before the heart of darkness got him." In his thoughts Obi mocks Conrad's language in *Heart of Darkness* as he reflects that Green "must have come originally . . . to bring light to the heart of darkness, to tribal headhunters performing weird ceremonies and unspeakable rites." However, Obi surmises that "when [Green] arrived, Africa played him false. Where was his beloved bush full of human sacrifice? There was St. George horsed and caparisoned, but where was the dragon?" Still, Obi concedes that the analogy to Kurtz is not a close one, because "Kurtz had succumbed to the darkness, Green to the incipient dawn. But their beginning and their end were alike."

While *Heart of Darkness*, despite its anti-imperialism, does serve to reinforce negative European stereotypes of Africans, it is worth noting that the story also attacks white racism. A key intellectual underpinning of European racism in the late nineteenth century was a misinterpreted version of Darwin's theory of evolution. This theory, as erroneously elaborated by the social Darwinists, posited a unilinear model of "progress" from animals to primitive people to civilized humans. The more "benign" proponents of this model argued that Europeans had a duty to raise "backward" people to their own level or as close as possible. The more malign proponents argued that backward people should be left to die or even be actively exterminated. Darwin himself in his second book, *The Descent of Man* (1871), said, "At some future period . . . the civilized races of man will almost certainly exterminate and replace throughout the world the savage races." The chief social Darwinist, Herbert Spencer, wrote: "The forces which are working out the great scheme of perfect happiness . . . exterminate such sections of mankind as stand in their way." Among European authors of the period, Conrad was unusually aware of and hostile to such genocidal theories. His native Poland had been partitioned in 1793 by Russia, Prussia, and Austria. He warned that as Europeans were wrongly assuming the "white man's burden" with respect to the rest of the world, the Germans were assuming the "perfect man's burden." Conrad had witnessed at firsthand the beginnings of King Leopold's forced labor system in the Congo, which would reduce its population by three million over the next fifteen years. A mere five years after the publication of *Heart of Darkness*, the Germans in Southwest Africa established their first *konzentrationslager* (concentration camps) in their nearly complete effort to wipe out the Herero tribe. Conrad clearly warned against such nihilistic

hubris when he had Kurtz scrawl, "Exterminate all the brutes!" in *Heart of Darkness*. In the original version of "An Image of Africa," Achebe compared Conrad to "all those men in Nazi Germany who lent their talent to the service of virulent racism." However, when Achebe republished this essay in 1988 in his collection ***Hopes and Impediments***, he omitted this comparison.

FURTHER READING

Hunt Hawkins, "Conrad's Critique of Imperialism in 'Heart of Darkness' " and "The Issue of Racism in *Heart of Darkness*"; Sven Lindqvist, *Exterminate All the Brutes*; Ian Watt, *Conrad in the Nineteenth Century*.

Hunt Hawkins

THE HEART OF THE MATTER (1948), one of **Graham Greene's** most famous novels, set in a British-controlled part of West Africa during World War II. **Obi Okonkwo** discusses the novel during a job interview in chapter 5 of ***No Longer at Ease*** and calls it, "The only sensible novel any European has written on West Africa and one of the best novels I have read," though he has reservations about the ending, in which the protagonist, the police officer Scobie, commits suicide. As part of his discussion of the ending Obi articulates his own theory of tragedy in which he rejects the Aristotelian notion that tragedy consists in a clear-cut resolution, such as suicide, and a cathartic purging of the emotions. Rather, according to Obi, "real tragedy is never resolved. It goes on hopelessly forever." In order to illustrate this point Obi makes literary references, citing **W. H. Auden** and **Evelyn Waugh**, but he also cites an elderly **Igbo** man, a Christian convert whom Obi knew in **Iguedo** who had suffered a string of calamities: "He said life was like a bowl of wormwood which one sips a little at a time world without end. He understood the nature of tragedy." This concept of tragedy ironically applies to the fate of Obi himself in *No Longer at Ease*, as opposed to the tragedy of his grandfather, **Okonkwo**, in *Things Fall Apart*, whose life ends in suicide. In any event, it is at least partly on the merit of his literary and philosophical disquisition during the interview that Obi earns the position of secretary to the Scholarship Board.

Thomas J. Lynn

HEGEL, GEORG WILHELM FRIEDRICH (1770–1831). German philosopher and one of the great systematic thinkers of the Western philosophical tradition. His use of the dialectical method represents one of the great advances in philosophical methodology in modern history, among other things providing inspiration for **Karl Marx**, even though Hegel's fundamental reliance on idealistic, metaphysical concepts differs so dramatically from that of the materialist Marx. In works such as *Phenomenology of Spirit* (1807), Hegel attempts to construct nothing less than a total system that attempts to explain rationally virtually every aspect of humanity's situation in the world. However, despite the universalizing tendencies of his philosophical work, Hegel remained firmly trapped within a Eurocentric perspective that led him to view European civilization as a universal model for the world and to regard non-Western societies and peoples (especially in Africa) as primitive and inferior.

Much of Hegel's importance lies in his construction of a philosophical basis for the modern project of scientific historiography. The grand historical narratives characteristic of European thought in the nineteenth century drew heavily upon Hegel's thought, while serving as one of the crucial ideological props for colonialism, teleological models of history as progress quite consistently portraying Europe as more historically advanced than the rest of the world. This phenomenon was most obvious in the case of Africa, which was portrayed in African discourse as a primitive land outside the flow of history. Hegel, whose philosophy is the quintessential expression of nineteenth-century European bourgeois historicist thought, is thus quite typical when he describes Africa as

the land of childhood, which lying beyond the day of self-conscious history, is enveloped in the dark mantle of Night. . . . For it is no historical part of the World; it has no movement or development to exhibit. . . . What we properly understand by Africa, is the Unhistorical, Undeveloped Spirit, still involved in the conditions of mere nature. (*Philosophy of History* 91, 99)

Hegel's attitude here is not unusual: European colonialist historians almost unanimously contributed to the consistent description of Africa as primitive by envisioning it as a timeless place without history, mired in the primeval past and unable to move forward until the European colonizers brought new energies and new knowledge to the continent.

Hegel is thus a crucial figure in the tradition of **colonialist historiography** that provides an important background to the project of African postcolonial writers, who often seek to challenge the legacy of this historiography. Such writers have often been quite overt in their rejection of Hegel, as when **Ngugi wa Thiong'o** refers to Hegel's thought as a forerunner of Nazism, calling Hegel the "nineteenth-century Hitler of the intellect" (*Decolonising* 32 n.15). Achebe, in novels such as *Things Fall Apart*, clearly seeks to present a counter-narrative that demonstrates the inaccuracy of Hegel's view of Africa as a land without history or civilization before the coming of colonialism. On the other hand, Michael Valdez Moses has argued that, however tragic the consequences of European colonization for **Igbo** culture and however sharp Achebe's critique of colonialism may be, Achebe ultimately accepts the historical inevitability of modernization in a mode that shows a fundamental agreement with "the historicist legacy of Hegel's thinking" (108).

FURTHER READING

G.W.F. Hegel, *Phenomenology of Spirit* and *The Philosophy of History*; Michael Valdez Moses, *The Novel and the Globalization of Culture*; Ngugi wa Thiong'o, *Decolonising the Mind*; Charles Taylor, *Hegel*.

M. Keith Booker

HEINEMANN AFRICAN WRITERS SERIES. See **African Writers Series**.

THE HEINEMANN BOOK OF CONTEMPORARY AFRICAN SHORT STORIES, (1992), edited by Chinua Achebe and **C. L. Innes**, contains twenty stories from five general geographic areas. There are five stories from Southern Africa—by Njabulo S. Ndebele, Nadine Gordimer, Lindiwe Mabuza, Daniel Mandishona, and Mia Couto; two stories from Central Africa—by Steve Chimomb and E. B. Dongala; five stories from East Africa—by Abdulrazak Gurnah, Saidi Hagi-Dirie Herzi, Tololwa Marti Mollel, Kyalo Mativo, and M. G. Vassanji; from Northern Africa stories by Assia Djebar and Jamal Mahjoub; from West Africa stories by Ben Okri, Adewala Maja-Pearce, Okey Chigbo, Ba'bila Mutia, Tijan M. Salah, and Kojo Lang. Altogether, fifteen African countries are represented. The volume contains stories written and published since 1980 and thus takes up where an earlier collection edited by Achebe and Innes, *African Short Stories*, left off. Taken together, the two volumes show that the short story continues to attract the attention of writers and that there is an ever-increasing number being produced.

Contemporary African Short Stories begins with a long introduction by Innes that describes the basis of the selection of stories. Of the twenty authors represented here only one, Gordimer, was well known when the book was published. Other writers were at the beginnings of their careers or had not yet established their reputations. Within a few years after publication of the volume, at least Gurnah, Vassanji, Laing, Okri, and Adewale-Pearce would become well known to readers interested in African writing. Innes goes on to characterize each of the stories, their writers, and their locales and suggests how the variety of content in the stories derives from the variety in the cultures of their countries of origin. She notes the continuing interest of writers in political matters and notes as well that there are a greater number of women writers and therefore a greater interest in women's issues as compared to the earlier collection. The varieties of styles—from the realistic narrative of Vassanji to the magical realism of Okri—adopted by authors are also drawn to our attention in the introduction.

The volume includes brief biographical notes on the writers of the stories.

Douglas Killam

HIGH-LIFE, a twentieth-century musical genre popular in western Africa, sometimes defined as a style of African jazz." In its varied formats high-life blends Afro-Caribbean and European musical elements with traditional African ones. Emmanuel Obiechina explains:

The rhythm [of "high-life"] is largely traditional, but the instrumentation is largely Western (traditional drums with Western brass instruments). . . . "High life" is essentially a democratically oriented music. Urban West Africans are "high lifers" all. In a crowded "high life" dance hall, one is likely to find the entire spectrum of the urban population, from ministers of state (in the old civilian political days) down to the office messenger and the artisan. . . . The lack of a rigid formal dance tempo reinforces this general, popular appeal of "high life." (79)

High-life dancing is referred to in some of the modern scenes in Achebe's fiction. **Obi Okonkwo**, the protagonist of *No Longer at Ease*, recalls in chapter 10 his student days in England and specifically his verbal exchange with a woman prior to their sexual encounter: " 'I'll teach you how to dance the high-life when you come' [that is, to Obi's flat], he had said. 'That would be grand,' she replied eagerly, 'and perhaps a little low life too.' " In chapter 11 of the same novel Achebe provides lyrics from two high-life songs performed at the **Imperial** nightclub, including **"Gentleman Bobby,"** and he describes "three patterns" of high-life dancing: angular European, erotic couple, and ecstatic individual. In the next chapter **Obi Okonkwo**'s friend, **Christopher**, teaches two young Irish women, **Nora** and **Pat**, "how to dance the high-life" at his apartment, with Obi joining in once he arrives. In chapter 2 of *A Man of the People* the narrator and protagonist, **Odili Samalu**, recalls that he and **Elsie** began their relationship by dancing at a student party to the music of a "noisy highlife band." Then, in chapter 5 of that novel, Odili dances the high-life with **Jean**, a married white American woman, as a prelude to sex. Jean's exaggerated sexual movements during the dance may announce her eventual intentions, but they also suggest a somewhat arrogant ignorance of African culture.

FURTHER READING

Emmanuel Obiechina, *Culture, Tradition, and Society in the West African Novel*.

Thomas J. Lynn

HILL, ALAN (1912–1995). A publisher of great zeal and vision, Hill was instrumental in publishing Achebe's first novel and in the subsequent creation and promotion of Heinemann's **African Writers Series**. Hill be-gan to work at William Heinemann Ltd. in the 1930s and in 1946 became the director of the Heinemann Educational Books (HEB) department. He was determined to publish not only schoolbooks but "the whole range of writing intended for enlightenment." Through his efforts HEB developed into its own company. A key factor in his success was his emphasis on expanding into the vast overseas markets of Africa, Asia, and America, which he promoted with great passion and dedication.

In 1958 Heinemann published *Things Fall Apart*, a novel by an unknown Nigerian writer, and the instant acceptance of this book in Britain and North America fueled Hill to find and publish other African writers. In 1962, HEB launched the African Writers Series with four titles and Achebe as its first editorial advisor. In the next forty years, the series evolved into a list of over 300 titles and spawned similar ventures through the Caribbean Writers Series and the Asian Writers Series. Hill and Achebe developed a relationship of mutual respect and admiration, evident in Achebe's praise of Hill's work and character in the foreword to Hill's memoir.

FURTHER READING

Alan Hill, *In Pursuit of Publishing*; Kirsten Holst Petersen and Anna Rutherford, "Working with Chinua Achebe."

Camille Lizarríbar Buxó

HISTORY. See **Colonialist historiography**.

HOLT, MR., a missionary who serves a brief tenure at **Umuaro** in chapter 4 of *Arrow of God*.

Rachel R. Reynolds

HOME AND EXILE (2000) contains the text of the three McMillan-Stewart Lectures delivered by Achebe at Harvard University in December 1998. The first lecture, "My

Home under Imperial Fire," relates Achebe's memories of his first trip to his ancestral village of Ogidi, to which his parents, in 1935, were retiring after three decades of missionary work for the Anglican Church. In the process, Achebe discourses on the special nature of **Igbo** individualism and on why the Igbo should be considered a nation, rather than a tribe. He also notes that, while his parents were strong in their Christian beliefs, they also tolerated the traditional religious practices of other members of the family, in this sense showing attitudes more representative of Igbo tradition than of European "religious imperialism." In the second half of the lecture, Achebe relates his discovery of the baleful legacy of racist-colonialist depictions of Africa in European literature, a legacy whose source he locates in attempts to justify the practice of slavery. Drawing upon the scholarly work *The Africa That Never Was*, by Dorothy Hammond and Alta Jablow, Achebe cites several examples of these depictions. Achebe pays special attention to his 1952 encounter, while a student at the **University College, Ibadan**, with **Joyce Cary**'s *Mister Johnson*, a work much admired by Western critics and by Achebe's British professor at the time but one that Achebe and his African classmates found racist, insulting, and dishonest in its depiction of the Nigerian protagonist. From this experience, Achebe learned "to call into question my childhood assumption of the innocence of stories" (33).

The second lecture, "The Empire Fights Back," is a direct continuation of the first. Here, Achebe acknowledges the often-repeated story that his reaction to *Mister Johnson* impelled him to write *Things Fall Apart* but suggests that writing was always in his blood and that he would have become a writer, Joyce Cary or no. Most of this essay is taken up with a continuing discussion of the legacy of European representations of Africa and Africans, with a special focus on the work of Elspeth Huxley, whose years living in Kenya led to the writing of numerous books that were well received in the West but that now seem rather transparent in their racist depiction of Africans. However, Achebe argues that the problem is not so much Huxley's individual racist attitudes as the fact that colonial writing is, by definition, designed to justify the European exploitation of Africa. Thus, for Achebe, the attempt of African writers to seize control of their own representation is of crucial importance. Acknowledging the central importance of Heinemann's **African Writers Series**, Achebe details the rise of the African novel, beginning in the 1950s. He pays special attention to the pioneering work of Amos Tutuola and to the reception of works such as *The Palm-Wine Drinkard* in the West. Achebe approvingly notes the positive response to Tutuola's book by the Irish poet Dylan Thomas but notes how Huxley and others saw the book simply as an example of African primitivism. Further, Achebe notes how some Africans living in the West were embarrassed by the book's failure to adhere to the principles of Western aesthetics as well. Somewhat obliquely singling out his fellow Nigerian, Buchi Emecheta, for criticism, Achebe thus notes that Africans themselves have often had difficulty overcoming the legacy of colonialist stereotypes about the innate inferiority of Africans and African culture. As he puts it, closing the essay, "The psychology of the dispossessed can be truly frightening" (72).

In the third and final lecture, "Today, the Balance of Stories," Achebe continues his insistence on the importance of the attempts of postcolonial writers to tell the stories of their homelands in order to counter the negative legacy of colonialist discourse. However, Achebe warns, postcolonial writers must seek this balance of stories, not through learning to mimic Western literature but by remaining rooted in the cultures and traditions of their homelands, thus calling global attention to "hitherto untold stories, along with new ways of telling" (83). Achebe reminds his audience not only that the Western arrogance that made colonialism possible is still alive and well but that peoples (and writers) from formerly colonized nations must still struggle against the psychological consequences of colonialism. Achebe singles out the Trinidadian writer **V. S. Naipaul** for special criticism, due to Naipaul's advocacy of Western culture as a "universal" culture that should be adopted around the globe, and advocacy that, for Achebe, shows a thorough contempt for the cultures of the postcolonial world. Achebe also expresses a strong skepticism toward the fashionable cosmopolitanism of writers such as Salman Rushdie, who have contributed to the "advertisement of expatriation and exile as intrinsically desirable goals" (96). Finally, he praises African writers such as Ghana's **Ama Ata Aidoo** and Senegal's **Cheikh Hamidou Kane** for their depictions of the problematic status of African expatriates living in Europe.

M. Keith Booker

HOPES AND IMPEDIMENTS: SELECTED ESSAYS (Heinemann, 1988; Anchor-Doubleday, 1990) represents Achebe's "abiding concerns in literature and the arts as well as . . . wider social issues" (Author's Preface, xiii). The collection, written over the period 1965–1987, includes five important essays reprinted from *Morning Yet on Creation Day* (1975; now out of print). To nurture visionary "Hopes"—for full recognition of African humanity and diversity, for free expression and just appreciation of African creative traditions and achievements—"Impediments" must first be challenged and cleared away. Looming foremost among these for Achebe is "the monster of racist habit" (xiv). The collection opens with **"An**

Image of Africa: Racism in Conrad's *Heart of Darkness"* (1974) and closes with a tribute to **James Baldwin** (1987), "one of the most intrepid fighters against racism" (xiii). **"Impediments to Dialogue between North and South"** (1980) contends that *"cultural exchange in a spirit of partnership"* between Europe and Africa remains impossible while Europeans continue to evade the question of African equality (22, 23). When Europe is "[r]eady to concede total African humanity" (28), then "dialogue may have a chance to begin" (29).

Achebe (re)evaluates the achievements of African literature in terms of African purposes, cultural traditions, and social realities—rather than of Eurocentric values and aesthetics. In **"The Writer and His Community"** (1984), Achebe examines individual authorship's privileged position in Western literature (47) and offers the alternative African tradition of Mbari, which attributes cocreative agency to gods and community (48). Achebe praises "voices of doubt," such as **Cheikh Hamidou Kane**'s, that challenge the dominance of Western values (50) and attend to the insights "non-Western values might . . . contribute to the process of modernization around the world" (54). However, Achebe's critical stance does not lead him to reject Western genres and languages; he resists "either/or" dichotomies that limit African writers' choices (61). The novel appropriated for African purposes can transcend the Western "mould of its origins" (55). Yet Achebe does not evade the tough questions and new challenges that accompany such artistic choices. The ancient dialectic between individual and community must continually be worked out anew by particular peoples addressing the changes and problems of their particular times. Thus, African writers must forge a new relationship between themselves and their community (61). In **"The Igbo World and Its Art,"** Achebe maintains that responsiveness to tradition and change create the restless and powerful dynamism of Mbari dance and masquerade (1984). Achebe unveils the sophisticated moral universe and thematic interplay of **"Work and Play in Tutuola's** *The Palm-Wine Drinkard"* (1977) to correct condescending attitudes toward his fellow Nigerian novelist. **"Don't Let Him Die: A Tribute to Christopher Okigbo"** (1978) combines personal and critical praise for "the power of the man's personality, his poetry, his life and death" (117). **"Kofi Awoonor as a Novelist"** (1971) elucidates central themes and allusions of *This Earth, My Brother*, Awoonor's "allegory of contemporary Africa" (121).

"The Truth of Fiction" (1978) presents Achebe's theory of the nature, functions, and persuasive powers of fiction. For Achebe, the best fiction produces a "self-encounter" called "imaginative identification" (144). Never asking us to forget that it is fiction, such "beneficent" fiction consciously engages our capacity for direct and vicarious imaginative experience and gives us a heightened sense of reality. From it we gain important insights that help us to make "our way in the real world" (151). In contrast, "malignant" fictions, such as racism, assert themselves as fact, trespassing the bounds of imagination to "ravage the real world" (148, 149). Bad fictions pervert our imaginative powers by deadening consciousness of evil and suffering (150, 151). Achebe argues for the relevance of fiction to the modernization of Nigeria in **"What Has Literature Got to Do with It?"** (1986). Achieving economic growth and universal health care requires more than money and experts; creating "a new place and a new people" must be guided by a parallel "search for abiding values," sustained by the creative energy of stories (168). Literature offers a constructive means to cope with threats and effect reform and change.

See *Morning Yet on Creation Day* for

"The Novelist as Teacher" (1965), **"Language and the Destiny of Man"** (1972), **"Named for Victoria, Queen of England"** (1973), **"Thoughts on the African Novel"** (1973), and **"Colonialist Criticism"** (1974). See also **"An Image of Africa: Racism in Conrad's** *Heart of Darkness*."

FURTHER READING

Ezenwa-Ohaeto, *Chinua Achebe: A Biography*; Simon Gikandi, *Reading Chinua Achebe: Language and Ideology in Fiction*; Bernth Lindfors, ed., *Conversations with Chinua Achebe*.

Cora Agatucci

HOUSMAN, A(LFRED) E(DWARD) (1859–1936), popular and distinguished English lyric poet who was also a classical scholar and professor of Latin at both University College London and Cambridge University. Housman is best known for his volume of poems *A Shropshire Lad* (1896), but "the favorite poem" of **Obi Okonkwo**, protagonist of *No Longer at Ease*, is Housman's **"Easter Hymn,"** which was not published in a volume of Housman's poetry until shortly after the poet's death. At the end of chapter 10 of *No Longer at Ease* Obi reads the poem in his copy of Housman's *Collected Poems* (1939), and in chapter 16, "when the pessimism of A. E. Housman once again proved irresistible," Obi reaches a second time for *Collected Poems*. In both instances his bitterness is occasioned by strained relations with **Clara Okeke**, although the circumstances are far weightier the second time.

Thomas J. Lynn

HOW THE LEOPARD GOT HIS CLAWS, a children's book co-authored by Achebe and **John Iroaganachi**, also including a contribution by noted Nigerian poet **Christopher Okigbo** and illustrations by Per Christiansen. The book began when Iroaganachi sent to the newly founded **Citadel Press** a manuscript for a children's book entitled "How the Dog Was Domesticated." Achebe, one of the founders of the press, accepted the story for publication, then worked with Iroaganachi in revising the text to its final, substantially altered form.

In its published form, the book is an allegorical tale that depicts a community of animals initially living happily and peacefully together under the leadership of a wise and kindly leopard. Except for the dog, none of the animals have sharp teeth or claws, because none are needed under these tranquil conditions. At the request of the deer, the animals construct a home to shelter them from the rain, though the dog, something of a malcontent, does not participate in the construction. Still, when a heavy rain comes, the dog decides to seek refuge in the shelter, where he chases away the other animals in the absence of their defender, the leopard, who is away on a visit. The deer then sings a lament (written by Okigbo), which brings the leopard back to the scene. However, when the leopard asks the other animals to help him overcome the dog, they instead side with the dog, because they fear his teeth and claws. The dog, despite his selfishness and greed, thus becomes the new king of the animals through force and intimidation.

Dispirited but not defeated, the leopard travels to the home of a blacksmith, who makes him some strong teeth and deadly claws. Then the newly armed leopard visits the Thunder, who gives him a powerful and frightening roar. Thus armed, the leopard returns and easily defeats the dog, who flees to the home of a hunter, retiring to a life of domestication. In retribution for their lack of loyalty, the leopard orders the animals to tear down the community shelter. From that point on, he rules the forest with terror, and the animals no longer live in harmony but battle one another, the strong preying upon the weak.

As with Achebe's other children's books, *How the Leopard Got His Claws* tells a compelling story but also teaches an important lesson. In this case, the battles among the animals can be taken as an allegory of the divisions that led to the **Nigerian Civil War**, while the actions of the dog and, eventually, the leopard, can be taken as a commentary on the postcolonial political leadership of Nigeria. The book thus has a clear didactic intent. Indeed, together with his own children's books, ***Chike and the River*** (1966), ***The Drum*** (1977), and ***The Flute*** (1977), *How the Leopard Got His Claws* indicates the seriousness with which Achebe approaches his declared notion that the postcolonial African writer should also serve as a teacher for his people. He describes this notion in the essay "The Novelist as Teacher," which appears in ***Morning Yet on Creation Day***.

In several respects, *How the Leopard Got His Claws* reads like a fable. In animal fables of folklore the events often explain how animals acquired this or that trait in primordial times. The present story does this, of course, in regard to the leopard's teeth, claws, and roar. Similarly it accounts for the disunity of the animals of the forest and the servility of dogs to human beings at the expense of those animals. Writers create animal fables as well to comment on political folly, as is the case, to cite a famous twentieth-century example, in George Orwell's *Animal Farm*, a book to which *How the Leopard Got His Claws*, though much shorter, bears some resemblance. A significant feature of the latter tale is that the animals incur progressively worse lives by their lack of ability to maintain unity for the common good. Partly what is suggested is the timeless message that when any group is subject to internal division it weakens its potential success.

However, in elements such as the call for unity that concludes the story, one discerns a more topical message, including, as mentioned previously, the violence of the Nigerian Civil War and of the events that led to it. But important features of *How the Leopard Got His Claws* are relevant as well to the more general problem of neocolonialism. The tale suggests that the disunity in and between contemporary African nations leaves them vulnerable to the ravages of foreign power. It might be tempting, moreover, to see the ascendancy of the dog, with his superior weapons, as an allegory of the European domination of many African lands in previous centuries and of division among Africans themselves. But in the story the dog lived at peace with or near his fellow animals for a period of time prior to ascendancy, so the closer analogy may be to the well-armed military rulers of postcolonial Africa who oppress their own people and serve as middlemen for non-African, neocolonial interests—just as the dog serves the hunter at the expense of the other animals. Certtainly the aggrandizement of a charismatic but unprincipled leader (the kind of leader represented, incidentally, by the folkloric Tortoise in *Things Fall Apart* and *The Drum*) has led to the oppression of countless people around the world and in many eras. Nevertheless, oppression at the hands of such a leader has been the fate of many in modern Africa, as Achebe has dramatized in his two novels set in a postcolonial environment, *A Man of the People* and *Anthills of the Savannah*.

FURTHER READING

Ernest N. Emenyonu, "(Re)Inventing the Past for the Present."

M. Keith Booker and Thomas J. Lynn

HUXLEY, ELSPETH (1907–1997), British novelist, biographer, and commentator on Anglo-African affairs. Achebe has described Elspeth Huxley as the "griot for white settlers" (*Home and Exile*). Born in Kenya to English parents, Huxley remained in East Africa until 1925, when she returned to Britain at the age of eighteen. Although she never again lived in Africa, she continued to make frequent visits to the continent. Indeed, her career and her reputation are based on her claims to firsthand experience of life in Africa. Published between 1959 and 1968, four decades after her departure from Kenya, Huxley's three-volume autobiography, *The Flame Trees of Thika* (1959), *The Mottled Lizard* (1962), *Love among the Daughters* (1968), not only tells her personal story of growing up English in Kenya but comments as well on what are identified as the differences, both historical and racial, between British settlers and African natives. The subtitle to a fourth autobiographical narrative, *Out in the Midday Sun: My Kenya*, is indicative of the proprietary relationship assumed by Huxley toward the African country of her birth.

Huxley's public apologia for white settlerdom in Kenya, however, began with her two-volume biography of Lord Delamere, *White Man's Country: Lord Delamere and the Making of Kenya* (1935), the title of which suggests the righteousness of the territorial claims made by white settlers on African lands, claims that Huxley upholds vehemently in an extended and argumentative correspondence with historian Margery Perham in which the two women discussed the "tangled problem of Kenya and its future" (*Race and Politics in Kenya*, 1944, with an introduction by **Lord Frederick Lugard**). According to Achebe, however, commenting on the imperial attitude of ownership that underwrote Huxley's readings of Africa, "I like to think that the title of her next book [after *White Man's Country*], *On the Edge of the Rift*, was either a conscious admission of the precariousness of her proprietorial perch; or, more interestingly still, a piece of—shall we say—unconscious Freudian irony! But I may be underrating altogether the power of tribal advocacy" (*Home and Exile*). Huxley's belief in the superiority of the "white settlers" over their African subjects was extended to African immigrants to Britain in the 1960s, on which she elaborated in *Back Street New Worlds: A Look at Immigrants in Britain* (1964).

In addition to her biographical and autobiographical contributions to the story of British imperialism in Africa, Huxley also wrote a series of mystery novels, set again in Africa. One of these, *The Incident at the Merry Hippo* (1963), describes murder and mayhem in the midst of a commission sent to Kenya charged with the "tricky job of hatching colonies into independent states." As "griot for white settlers"—or "spokesperson for the white settler community," as Achebe also designated her—Elspeth Huxley continued to discharge her own "tricky job" until her death in 1997.

FURTHER READING

Wendy Webster, "Elspeth Huxley."

Barbara Harlow

"HYMN TO THE SUN," a prose poem composed by **Ikem Osodi** and included in chapter 3 of ***Anthills of the Savannah***. The poem acknowledges the life-giving (and life-taking) power of the African sun. The poem is especially relevant in light of the devastating heat and drought that are plaguing Osodi's native Abazon during the action of the novel.

M. Keith Booker

I

IBA, the **Igbo** word for fever. Generally in Achebe it is an all-purpose referent, but when a recurring fever is implied, it is quite possibly a reference to malaria.

Rachel R. Reynolds

IBADAN, city in southwestern **Nigeria**, capital of Oyo State. Ibadan has a population (1995 estimate) of over 1.3 million. Inhabited mainly by the Yoruba, Ibadan, which has an airport and is on the railroad line linking **Lagos** with Kano, is a major transit point between the coast and areas to the north. It is also the center of trade for a surrounding agricultural area that produces cacao, cotton, timber, rubber, and palm-oil. Industries include the processing of agricultural products, tire retreading, and the manufacture of cigarettes. The **University of Ibadan** (founded as a college of the University of London in 1948 and as an autonomous university in 1962) and several libraries and research institutes are located in the city, making it an important cultural and intellectual center. Achebe attended **University College, Ibadan**, from 1948 to 1953.

M. Keith Booker

IBE, son of **Ukegbu** and the suitor and eventual husband of **Akueke** in *Things Fall Apart*. He is identified by **Okonkwo** in chapter 8 as a good palm-wine tapper.

M. Keith Booker

IBE, Akueke's abusive husband in *Arrow of God*. He has a daughter named **Nkechi**.

Rachel R. Reynolds

IBE, CHARLES. In *No Longer at Ease*, a messenger in the same department of the civil service as **Obi Okonkwo**. As revealed in chapter 10, Charles is nervous about a thirty-shilling loan that he has failed to repay Obi and so no longer stops by Obi's office for an exchange of **Igbo** greetings. The reason Charles gave Obi for requesting the loan was that his wife had just had their fifth baby, but now the pressure of Obi's own growing financial predicament prompts him to confront Charles. Among other things, their exchange, conducted in Igbo, English, and **pidgin English**, underscores the fluidity of language boundaries in modern **Lagos**.

Thomas J. Lynn

ICHELE, a fearsome mask spirit used to threaten unruly children in chapter 14 of *Arrow of God*.

Rachel R. Reynolds

IDEMILI, deity and protector of the village of **Umunneora**. Idemili means "pillar of water," and he holds up the clouds. As Achebe explains in *Arrow of God* (chapter 3), the priest **Ezidemili** cannot sit on the ground or be buried in it; rather, he is associated with the air and the sky. Idemili is also associated with the Royal **Python**.

Rachel R. Reynolds

IDEMILI, a legendary daughter of the Almighty, as described in chapter 8 of *Anthills of the Savannah*. A figure of feminine power, she is in a sense the precursor of strong modern women such as **Beatrice Okoh**. However, in this particular case, Beatrice's lack of a sense of real connection to Idemili functions as an emblem of her alienation, due to her Western education and modern way of life, from the traditional culture of her people. Still, Idemili serves as an important inspiration to Beatrice in her attempt to reestablish a connection to the myths of the past.

M. Keith Booker

IFEME, Akuebue's neighbor in *Arrow of God* (chapter 16).

Rachel R. Reynolds

IGBO, one of the principal ethnic groups of **Nigeria**, with its own language (see **Igbo language**) and traditional religion (see **Gods**). Though sometimes referred to as a "tribe," Igbo culture was never tribal in the anthropological sense. Indeed, few African cultures were tribal. As Terence Ranger notes, the notion of African "tribes" was largely invented by Europeans. In the opening essay of his book *Home and Exile*, Achebe objects to the designation of the Igbo as a tribe and suggests that, instead, they be regarded as a "nation."

Achebe is an Igbo, as are most of his major characters. Population estimates vary, but the number of Igbo in modern Nigeria is perhaps over thirty million, or over one-fourth of the total population. The Igbo traditionally lived in what is currently southeastern Nigeria, which remains their central homeland. This area occupies a very considerable portion of southeastern Nigeria, including the west bank of the River Niger. The following are the Igbo states of Nigeria: Abia, Anambra, Ebonyi, Enugu, Imo, and a good part of the Delta and Rivers States. Traditional Igbo society was made up of largely autonomous villages or groups of villages, though a sense of cultural unity made it possible for the Igbo to unite in larger groups when necessary. Nevertheless, the Igbo were very susceptible to colonization by the British and to conversion to Christianity, a phenomenon that Achebe explores at length in *Things Fall Apart* and *Arrow of God*, where he also provides some of the most vivid available descriptions of traditional Igbo culture. Today, most Igbo are of Christian belief, though elements of the traditional religion and culture still survive.

As with most traditional African cultures, Igbo culture was built on a strong sense of devotion to community, though Igbo culture was perhaps more individualistic than most traditional African cultures. This emphasis on individual achievement may account for the fact that the Igbo have been remarkably successful in a variety of professions (including government and military) throughout Nigeria, leading to some resentment on the part of other ethnic groups. Tensions between the Igbo and other ethnic groups (including the massacre of Igbo in northern Nigeria) led to the secession of the Igbolands of southeastern Nigeria as the **Republic of Biafra** in 1967. Biafra was defeated in the subsequent **Nigerian Civil War**, then reabsorbed into Nigeria in 1970.

FURTHER READING

Chinua Achebe, *Home and Exile*; Elizabeth Is-ichei, *A History of the Igbo People*; Mazi Ele-chukwu Nnadibuagha Njaka, *Igbo Political Culture*; Terence Ranger, "The Invention of Tradition in Colonial Africa"; Victor C. Uchendu, *The Igbo of Southeast Nigeria.*

M. Keith Booker

IGBO LANGUAGE. In his novels Achebe has been most successful in conveying the oral tradition of the **Igbo** without impairing its authenticity. His spectacular success in this sense stems from his mastery of the English language and his deliberate extension of its frontiers to accommodate his African experience. Achebe consciously allows the flow of idiom of Igbo, his mother tongue, to filter through in his writings and craftily employs a wealth of sayings, proverbs, and turns of phrase from his own people, which the characters use to express their experiences, justify their actions, and rhetorically enrich their discussions. As African literature in English reached full bloom, some early commentators, concerned with the **language question**, wondered whether it might stifle creativity and that true African literature must be written in African languages. Achebe's reaction to this debate is expressed most clearly in his essay "The African Writer and the English Language," included in *Morning Yet on Creation Day*. Here, he concludes that, yes, the English language can successfully carry the full weight of his African experience, "but it will have to be a new English, still in full communion with its ancestral home but altered to suit its new African surroundings."

The Igbo language, like the people, is quite diverse, consisting of numerous dialects. Achebe most frequently uses a dialect specific to his area around the village of **Ogidi**. The Igbo language is distinctive and rich with inexhaustible linguistic features such as proverbs, idioms, riddles, folktales, anecdotes, aphorisms, folklore, and sayings. Achebe uses Igbo in his works to feature words with conceptual meanings, identify specific ancestors and deities, and indicate the meanings of specific rituals. Achebe has been acclaimed to be spectacularly successful in performing the feat of expressing his African experience in English, punctuated by the use of Igbo words to help preserve the African flavor of his writing.

In the following passage from *Arrow of God*, for instance, the chief priest is telling his son why he is sending him to join the Christians, a decision everyone is surprised that he has taken by virtue of his high position in the traditional culture:

I want one of my sons to join these people and be my eye there. If there is nothing in it you will come back. But if there is something there you will bring home my share. The world is like a Mask dancing. If you want to see it well you do not stand in one place. My spirit tells me that those who do not befriend the white man today will be saying *had we known* tomorrow.

In the above passage the language is English, but the nuances and imagery are clearly Igbo; the thoughts, feelings, and ideas embedded in the expression easily resonate with every Igbo person. To buttress this point, Achebe in "The African Writer and the English Language" singles out this very passage and actually rewrites it in the Queen's English. In the rewritten version, he makes the point that the content is the same but the form and feel are not. This gives us an idea of how Achebe approaches the creative process by consciously choosing his words in order to stay close to the original experience in language. The language of the above passage not only preserves the speech of the Igbo but translates back into it quite effortlessly. When the chief priest says that he would send one of his sons to become his eyes within the Christian community, he is employing a figure of speech that is familiar to every Igbo. The chief priest's conclusion of the passage with a proverb lends credence to Achebe's statement in **Things Fall Apart** that among the Igbo "proverbs are the palm-oil with which words are eaten."

Although Achebe's novels have clearly proven his success in the handling of the problems of writing in a second language, there are situations when the problem becomes truly complicated, such as when a word that cannot be adequately translated has to be translated into English. In *Things Fall Apart* such a word is **chi**, a word that has a complex conceptual meaning. The concept of *chi*—central to Igbo spirituality—has no single English word that can satisfactorily translate it. Achebe sensibly solves the dilemma by not attempting a translation of the word but by leaving it as *chi* in his delineation of the characters. Without proper explanation to a non-Igbo reader, the word may not register its full import in his or her imagination. In the same vein, Achebe provides an unobtrusive contextual explanation for **ogbanje**, another Igbo word that is difficult to translate. This device is inevitable for Achebe because he is writing in a language in which the concepts of *chi* and *ogbanje* are foreign and so must be explained to the reader to be fully understood. These difficulties of translation have necessitated that Achebe retain some words in Igbo so as not to lose their essence in erroneous translations.

In the introductory chapters of *Things Fall Apart* and *Arrow of God*, Achebe introduces to the reader a whole string of Igbo words— *ekwe, udu, ogene, egwugwu, obi, alusi, okposi, ofo*, and so on—occasionally helping the reader with an explanation and at other times deferring his explanation so as not to interfere with the flow of his narrative. These occasional explanations are very useful for the reader, while some editions of the novels also include glossaries of Igbo words. In *Things Fall Apart*, Achebe does some explaining of some of the Igbo words in this way: "His own hut, or *obi*, stood immediately behind the only gate in the red walls"; "The elders, or *ndichie*, met to hear a report of Okonkwo's mission"; "That was how Okonkwo first came to know that *agbala* was not only another name for a woman, it could also mean a man who had taken no title." These sentences contain brief explanations that are insightful for the reader without getting in the way of the narrative.

What emerges from these examples is that in his novels Achebe consciously and skillfully keeps as close as possible to Igbo words and expressions, turns of phrase, nuances, and imagery in order to portray the social norms, attitudes, and values of the Igbo. His innovative prowess in this endeavor has proven beyond doubt that the African experience can effectively be rendered in a second language, even if slightly altered for that purpose. Achebe has stated that "the price a world language must be prepared to pay is submission to many different kinds of use" but cautions that the foreign writer must have mastery of English first and foremost and should strive to use it judiciously so as not to alter "the language to the extent that its value as a medium of international exchange will be lost." Having passed this test himself, Ahebec has been acclaimed as a major contributor in bringing African literature to great glory, and his success has nailed the views of those early critics who predicted no future for African literature; little did they realize that it was "morning yet on creation day."

FURTHER READING

Chinua Achebe, "The African Writer and the English Language," included in *Morning Yet on Creation Day*; Michael J. C. Echeruo, *Igbo-*

English Dictionary; Emmanuel Obiechina, *Language and Theme*; F. C. Ogbalu and E. N. Emenanjo, *Igbo Language and Culture*.

Christine Nwakego Ohale

"THE IGBO WORLD AND ITS ART." Achebe essay. See *Hopes and Impediments*.

IGBONEME, who appears in chapter 7 of **Arrow of God**, is an important man of **Umuaro**.

Rachel R. Reynolds

IGUEDO, one of the nine villages of **Umuofia** in *Things Fall Apart*, in which it is referred to (in chapter 13) as the village of the yellow grinding-stone. Iguedo is the village of the protagonist **Okonkwo**. In *No Longer at Ease* Iguedo remains the focal point of family life for at least one of Okonkwo's children, **Isaac Okonkwo** (**Nwoye** in *Things Fall Apart*), and his family. Three scenes in *No Longer at Ease* are set in Iguedo. The first, in chapter 1, depicts the celebration of **Obi Okonkwo**'s departure for university studies in England hosted by his parents, Isaac and **Hannah Okonkwo**; the second, in chapters 5 and 6, shows Obi's first visit to the village and reunion with his family after he completes his studies in England; and the third, in chapters 13 and 14, dramatizes his second visit there and his confrontation with his parents over his intention to marry **Clara Okeke**. Worthy of special note is the speech in Hannah and Isaac's home in chapter 5 by **Ogbuefi Odogwu**, who valorizes Iguedo and in the process brings Okonkwo and other prominent figures of traditional Iguedo into the context of Obi's homecoming and the present-day village: " 'Iguedo breeds great men. . . . When I was young I knew of them— Okonkwo, **Ezeudu**, **Obierika**, **Okolo**, **Nwosu**. . . . Greatness has belonged to Iguedo from ancient times.' " Finally, although **Kangan**, the fictional nation in which *Ant-*

hills of the Savannah is set, cannot be wholly identified with **Nigeria**, Iguedo is mentioned in chapter 8: "**Idemili's** devotees increased in all the country between Omambala and Iguedo." The references here both to Idemili and Iguedo are among the elements that indicate a partial link of Kangan to the Nigeria that Achebe explicitly represents in previous novels.

Thomas J. Lynn and M. Keith Booker

IJELE, a **mask** that appears in a masquerade enacted in chapter 7 of *Arrow of God*. This mask/masquerade has a very delicate pantomine of steps of his performance.

FURTHER READING

   John McCall, *Dancing Histories*.

Rachel R. Reynolds

IKEDI, a man whom **Ogbuefi Odogwu** praises in chapter 5 of *No Longer at Ease* as one of the "giants" of **Iguedo** prior to **Okonkwo**'s generation.

Thomas J. Lynn

IKEDI, JAMES, appointed first warrant chief or "first Obi" of **Okperi** in *Arrow of God*. In an investigation of Ikedi, **Winterbottom** concludes that Ikedi has become corrupt and with his colonial projects foreman, **Destroyer of Compounds**, has extorted money from the people of **Okperi**. It is through this experience—the senior officers keep reinstating Ikedi in an attempt to get the **indirect rule** policy up and running—that Winterbottom ends up at odds with senior administration (chapter 5).

Rachel R. Reynolds

IKEDI, SAMUEL, the pastor of **St. Mark's Anglican Church**, **Umuofia** who, in chapter 1 of *No Longer at Ease*, presides at the prayer meeting and feast hosted by **Hannah** and **Isaac Okonkwo** at their home in **Iguedo**

to mark the departure of **Obi Okonwko** for England. Reverend Ikedi gives two long speeches, once before and once after the meal, and in doing so reveals a missionary viewpoint with a decidedly colonialist tilt. During the first speech he declares that Obi's scholarship to England is "the fulfillment of the prophecy." In his second speech Ikedi asserts that pre-colonial times in Umuofia "were days of darkness from which we have been delivered by the blood of the Lamb of God." Significant if subtle irony may lie in the fact that, in chapter 5, the non-Christian, **Ogbuefi Odogwu**, as part of his own testimony to Obi, acclaims a man named **Ikedi** as one of the "giants" of pre-colonial Iguedo.

Thomas J. Lynn

IKEMEFUNA. In *Things Fall Apart*, a boy from **Mbaina**, sent at age fifteen to **Umuofia** as partial retribution for the killing of a woman from Umofia in the market at Mbaina, thus helping to avoid a war. He lives with **Okonkwo**'s family for three years and comes to regard Okonkwo as his father. When **Agbala**, the Oracle of the Hills and Caves, finally orders the boy killed, Okonkwo insists on participating in the ceremonial killing in order to avoid being thought weak, even though he has been assured that no one would blame him for abstaining, given his relationship with the boy. The story of Ikemefuna serves as a central example of the lack of restraint that arises from Okonkwo's determination to overcome the legacy of his weak father, **Unoka**.

M. Keith Booker

IKENGA. In traditional **Igbo** culture, a carved spirit or god, usually of wood. An ikenga serves not merely as a representation in the Western sense but also as a literal embodiment.

M. Keith Booker

IKENGA, one of the villages of **Ogidi, Nigeria**. Ikenga was the home of the important priest of Udo and also the birthplace and ancestral home of Achebe's father, **Isaac Okafor Achebe**. After an active career as a Christian evangelist, Isaac Achebe settled in Ikenga in semi-retirement, and it was there that Chinua Achebe was born.

M. Keith Booker

IKEZUE, a champion wrestler of **Umuofia**. In chapter 6 of *Things Fall Apart*, he leads a wrestling team but is defeated by his rival **Okafo**, leader of the opposing team, because of a strategic miscalculation.

M. Keith Booker

IKOLO, very large drum carved out of a tree trunk that rests in the *ilo* or central public area of a given Igbo village. There is an Ikolo performance described in chapter 7 of *Arrow of God*.

Rachel R. Reynolds

IKOT EKPENE, a southern **Nigerian** city (population 209,400 in 2002) mentioned in chapter 2 of *No Longer at Ease*. **Obi Okonkwo** finds that the appearance of **Joseph Okeke's** new, unnamed, female companion, whose dress and makeup heighten certain of her physical attributes, resemble a type of **mask** carved at Ikot Ekpene.

Thomas J. Lynn

IKOYI, the upscale district of **Lagos** to which **Obi Okonkwo** moves in *No Longer at Ease* shortly after he secures the senior government post of Secretary to the Scholarship Board (see chapters 2, 7, and 19). Ikoyi's "luxurious bungalows and flats and its extensive greenery" had once been the site of swamps that later accommodated a cemetery area, but it, like other parts of Lagos, was reclaimed from the sea and became a sizable "reserve" for Europeans. But in the

1950s, as Nigeria neared independence, some Africans in senior civil service posts were given residences there. Nevertheless, Obi sees Ikoyi as essentially sterile, a kind of "graveyard" for the Africans who live there compared to the culturally vibrant poorer districts of Lagos (chapter 2).

FURTHER READING

Robert M. Wren, *Achebe's World*.

Thomas J. Lynn

IKPEZE, MRS. ZINOBIA UZOMA, the third child and first daughter of **Isaiah** and **Janet Achebe**. Like her mother, she attended St. Monica's School, Ogbunike, where she read standard six and passed. When she became a teacher at St. Monica's, she was "picked" to become the wife of Rev. Ikpeze of Ajilija Ugwu, Ogidi. Zinobia played a very important role in Chinua's upbringing. Next to their mother, Zinobia played the role of caregiver to her youngest brother. According to her, she "Carried him, watched over him, saw him crawl, stand and walk" (oral interview with Egejuru, December 1995). When Chinua was old enough to listen to fairy tales, Zinobia told him several. She encouraged him to retell the stories to her, "and he would repeat them exactly as I told them to him," she said. It was then that she noted Chinua's great interest in storytelling as well as his prodigious memory. In his pre-school years, Chinua used to follow Zinobia to school and would stay in class with her. When it was time for him to start real school, he was too afraid to leave his sister's side. It was with much coaxing from Zinobia that Chinua agreed days later, to join his mates at play in the infants' section of the school.

Phanuel Akubueze Egejuru

ILO, means both village center and compound. When Achebe uses the term, it usually indicates the open, public area for meeting and community festivals, adjacent to the marketplace. Chapter 17 of *Arrow of God* provides a description of how the *ilo* of the village **Umuachala** would have been utilized during a village festival.

Rachel R. Reynolds

"AN IMAGE OF AFRICA: RACISM IN CONRAD'S *HEART OF DARKNESS*" (1977) is perhaps Achebe's best-known work with the exception of his novel *Things Fall Apart*. It is certainly the most controversial essay Achebe has ever written. Originally delivered as a Chancellor's Lecture at the **University of Massachusetts at Amherst**, this attack on **Joseph Conrad** first appeared in print in *The Massachusetts Review* in 1977 and was later reprinted in *Hopes and Impediments* (1988). More than twenty years later, speaking from his wheelchair but with little change in sentiment, Achebe renewed his assault on Conrad during his keynote address at the African Literature Association conference in Austin, Texas, in 1998. At century's turn, Achebe's ongoing polemic against one of England's most revered literary figures has lost little of its controversial character, as critics from across the globe have continued to debate the question of Conrad's racism since Achebe's essay first appeared, with no clear consensus emerging. (Ngugi wa Thiong'o, for instance, has taken a far less aggressive position with respect to *Heart of Darkness* while remaining more critical of Isak Dinesen's *Out of Africa*.) Whether or not one agrees with Achebe that Conrad was "a thorough-going racist," few would dispute the merit of his intervention, which arrived like a bombshell upon the landscape of North American literary studies. It is nonetheless important to historicize Achebe's critique within the North American academic context of the late 1970s, before the development of most courses in Third World, postcolonial, "non-Western," and/or African literature, which have now become a standard feature of literary programs in Western universities. In an era when Jungian, myth-critical, and pre-Lacanian psychoanalytic theories of literature enjoyed enormous prestige in English departments across the United States, especially as a remedy to the waning influence of the American New Criticism, Achebe's essay implicitly called such approaches into question, as well as many of the most basic tenets of "Great Books," liberal arts, and canonical English studies programs. Ironically, as the prestige of *Things Fall Apart* increased, Achebe himself came to be canonized in the years following his essay's appearance. (It must be remembered that, at the time of the publication of "An Image of Africa," *Things Fall Apart* was taught more often in anthropology programs than literary ones.) If one of Africa's premier literary authorities had such strong reservations about Conrad, his views on Conrad's racism could not simply be ignored, as often happens when lesser-known African writers raise similar concerns. Focusing upon bestial and other forms of savage imagery from the text of *Heart of Darkness*, Achebe lets Conrad's derogatory descriptions speak for themselves. His essay also carries within it an attack on white liberalism, which he identifies as a particularly poisonous form of patronage, one that has "touched all the best minds in England, Europe, and America." When Achebe states bluntly that "Conrad had a problem with niggers," the effect upon the liberal white reader remains electrifying. He also refuses to let Conrad off the hook because of differences in respective historical eras, contrasting Conrad's views with those of contemporaries like Vlaminck, Picasso, and Matisse. Instead, Achebe insists that Conrad's convenient use of Africa as a mere backdrop for the tale of a petty European ego-in-crisis effectively dehumanizes Africa and Africans, who are, in fact, *less* than props for the "jaundiced-eyed" narrator Marlowe—for Achebe (and numer-

ous other critics, for that matter), a thinly veiled self-portrait of Conrad. If Conrad's racism is made explicit in this essay, Achebe also seeks to undermine modernist ideology, especially as a belief system that will "save" Africa at the expense of its most cherished traditional values. In fact, "An Image of Africa" is an attack on Western Man, the "universal" subject who violently converts the Other into a lesser or defective version of himself, ostensibly out of "concern" for his less advantaged brother. What Achebe shows is not simply that Conrad was racist, which should be obvious to any sensitive reader, but that Conrad's celebrated "critique" of European imperialism is fundamentally flawed, a species of liberal humanism at its worst. In the end, Achebe's target is much bigger than Joseph Conrad, which may be the main reason that so many have found his essay "too extreme." Achebe demands nothing less than a full-scale dismantling of Western epistemology, or ways of knowing other peoples and cultures. See also **Conrad, Joseph**.

FURTHER READING

M. Keith Booker, "Multicultural Approaches to *Heart of Darkness*"; Wilson Harris, "The Frontier on which *Heart of Darkness* Stands"; Hunt Hawkins, "The Issue of Racism in *Heart of Darkness*"; Frances Singh, "The Colonialist Bias of *Heart of Darkness*"; Cedric Watts, " 'A Blood Racist.' "

Christopher Wise

"IMPEDIMENTS TO DIALOGUE BE-TWEEN NORTH AND SOUTH." Achebe essay. See *Hopes and Impediments*.

THE IMPERIAL, a **Lagos** nightclub at which **Obi Okonkwo, Clara Okeke, Christopher**, and **Bisi** go dancing on a Saturday night in chapter 11 of *No Longer at Ease*. Notable at the Imperial is the **high-life** dancing, "but occasionally a waltz or a blues was played so that the dancers could relax and drink their beer, or smoke." The scene in the

Imperial vividly evokes the Lagos nightclub scene with its sexually charged atmosphere, while outside the Imperial Lagos's poverty is also evident in the form of "half-clad little urchins" attending to his car, children whom Obi thinks of as "delinquents." When he and Clara depart from the Imperial late at night, they discover that fifty pounds have been stolen from his car, deepening his financial woes.

Thomas J. Lynn

INDIRECT RULE. See **Pacification**.

INNES,   C(ATHERINE)   L(YNETTE) (1940–   ), an important literary critic whose work has done much to further the appreciation of Achebe as a literary artist. Innes was also a colleague of Achebe at the **University of Massachusetts at Amherst**, and has collaborated with him on such projects as the volumes *African Short Stories* and *Contemporary African Short Stories*, which they co-edited, and the journal *Okike*, of which she served as an assistant editor from 1974 to 1990.

Born in Australia, Innes received her B.A. from the University of Sydney, her M.A. from the University of Oregon, and her Ph.D. from Cornell University. She taught at several American universities before her term at Massachusetts (1973–1975). She has taught at the University of Kent in Canterbury, UK, since 1975. Beginning with her Cornell doctoral dissertation ("Cultural Nationalism with Reference to African, Irish, Caribbean and Afro-American Authors Writing in English, French and Spanish"), Innes has published widely on African, Irish, and other postcolonial literatures. In addition to numerous articles and reviews in books and journals, her book-length publications include Arrow of God: *A Critical View* (1985); *The Devil's Own Mirror: The Irishman and the African in Modern Literature* (1990); *Chinua Ache-*

be: A Critical Study (1990); *Woman and Nation in Irish Literature and Society, 1880– 1935* (1993); and *A History of Black and Asian Writing in Britain, 1700–2000* (2002). In addition to the two collections of short stories she edited with Achebe, she co-edited the volume *Critical Perspectives on Chinua Achebe* with **Bernth Olof Lindfors**. She has also edited special volumes of *Okike*, the *Journal of Gender Studies*, and *Interventions: A Journal of Postcolonial Studies*.

FURTHER READING

C. L. Innes, *Chinua Achebe*; C. L. Innes and Bernth Lindfors, eds., *Critical Perspectives on Chinua Achebe*.

M. Keith Booker

INTERVIEWS. Achebe is easily among the most often taught and critically discussed African writers. He is also among the most often interviewed, and the body of interviews with Achebe himself constitutes an important aspect of existing commentary on his work. Indeed, Achebe's willingness to grant interviews has made a significant contribution to his continuing domination of critical discussions of African writing in the twenty-first century. It is clear that interviews seem to Achebe an important opportunity to explain himself and offer even greater insights about his writings and his world. Achebe is certainly among the easiest and most rewarding African writers to interview. Not only is he highly accessible to interviewers, but in Achebe's interviews it is clear that he aims at getting at the root of the matter in all of his responses. His vision comes through in his interviews very much as it does in his writings. For example, describing an interview on Achebe's essays, *Home and Exile* (2000), Gayle Feldman presents Achebe's idealistic response to some of the questions. "Achebe agrees when it's suggested that the essays convey a fundamental message to any writer: know yourself; be yourself; explore your own stories; share them with the world and we'll learn something. Does that mean that someone who is white cannot or should not tell the story of someone who is black?" "No, not at all," Achebe replies. "What it means is to ask anybody who's dealing with someone else's story to walk softly, as Yeats said, because you walk on my dreams. People dream their world into being. If you're a visitor, remember that, and you can write as strong a story as anybody else" (Feldman 2000). Listening to Achebe's voice on tape and hearing the careful, soft-spoken, and comprehensive ways he makes his points, one understands why Achebe continues to be the central figure in African literature and scholarship. Although it is not practical to list all the interviews that Achebe has given so far in his career, a representative sample of interviews and publications containing interviews is given below.

1. *Africa Report* 9 (1964): 19–21. "Conversation with Chinua Achebe" discussing views on war and humanitarian efforts. Also discussed were unfair laws and the purpose of his books.

2. *Spectrum Magazine: A Magazine of Peace Corps* (1967): 4–7. Interview took place in Nigeria. Interviewer M. Felton. Interview was based on the subject of African philosophical views. Also questioned were the philosophical characteristics of characters in his books.

3. *McGill Reporter* (February 23, 1970): 1–2. Interviewers Michael Smith and Harry Cowen, "A Man of the People." In this interview Achebe answers questions concerning his book **Things Fall Apart** and its relation to today's people.

4. *Africa Report* (1972). Interviewers Ernest and Pat Emenyou. "Achebe Accountable to Our Society," pp. 17 and 25–27. Interview covers Achebe's humanitarian efforts, along with his philosophical debates on our society.

5. University of Washington. Class discussion in person. Achebe addresses African Studies program in lecture style. Institute for Comparative and Foreign Area Studies, 1975, pp. 33–58, at University of Washington, April 6, 1973.

6. *Critics on Chinua Achebe* (1976). Author John Agetua. Interview took place August 16, 1976. Questions were asked about Achebe's success with *Things Fall Apart* and the motivation used to complete such a book.

7. *African Writers Talking: A Collection of Radio Interviews*. This collection begins with a series of four interviews with Achebe, conducted, respectively, by Lewis Nkosi (Lagos, 1962), Donatus Nwoga (Leeds University, 1964), Dennis Duerden (Lagos, 1965), and Robert Serugama (London, 1967).

8. *Research in African Literatures* 12.1 (Spring 1981): 1–13. Interviewer Kalu Ogbaa. This interview took place on April 11, 1980, at the University of Florida at Gainesville, where Achebe was participating in the 5th annual conference of the African Literature Association (ALA). Achebe discusses the roles and responsibilities of the African author, including his own activities as a public intellectual. Reprinted in *Conversations with Chinua Achebe*.

9. *America* 164.24 (1991): 684–85. "An Interview with Chinua Achebe." Interviewer Patrick H. Samway.

10. *Parabola* 17.3 (1992): 19–27. "If One Thing Stands, Another Will Stand beside It: An Interview with Chinua Achebe."

11. *The Paris Review* 35.133 (Winter 1994): 142. "The Art of Fiction." Interviewer Jerome Brooks. Achebe explains why he became a writer. He covers various fields of interest: English, science, history, and religion.

12. *The Chronicle of Higher Education* 40.19 (January 12, 1994): A9. "An African Writer at a Cross Roads." Interviewer Karen J. Winkler. This interview covers some of Achebe's accomplishments including being elected professorial chair at **Bard College**.

13. *America Magazine* 175.11 (October 19, 1996): 2. "Achebe Wins Campion Award." Interviewer Patrick H. Samway. Achebe accepted the 1996 Campion Award at Bard College. The award honors Christian people of letters and is named after a Jesuit priest.

14. *Neohelicon* 26.1 (1999): 185–92. "Postcolonial Nigeria, African Literature and the Twenty-First Century: An Interview with Chinua Achebe." Interviewer Abdul-Rasheed Na'Allah. This interview covers Achebe's vision in his writings, the role of African writers in society, political and ethnic situations in Nigeria, and the killing of Ken Saro-Wiwa by the Abacha military regime.

15. *Publishers Weekly* 247.27 (2000): 40. "Interview with Chinua Achebe." Achebe, confined to a wheelchair and teaching in America, talks about his memoir, in which he documents the difficult birth of African literature.

Perhaps the best collection of interviews with Achebe appears in the volume *Conversations with Chinua Achebe*, published by the University of Mississippi Press in 2000, which collects numerous interviews conducted with Achebe from 1962 to 1995. The collection was compiled and edited by noted Achebe scholar **Bernth Olof Lindfors**, who also wrote an introduction. Together, these interviews help to emphasize the importance of interviews to the body of published commentary on Achebe and his work. Interviews in the collection include the following.

1. From *African Writers Talking*. Interviewer Lewis Nkosi, 1962. Achebe explains why he became a writer and discusses his many accomplishments, including his books and career choices.

2. "An Interview with Achebe." From *Afrique* 27 (1963): 41–42 and translated by Judith McDowell. In this interview Achebe discusses his writing influences and his writing style.

3. "Conversation with Chinua Achebe." Filmed interview retranscribed by Lindfors and published by permission of *Africa Report*. Interviewers Lewis Nkosi and **Wole Soyinka**, 1963. Achebe discusses Igbo society and its relevance to his first two novels.

4. "I Had to Write on the Chaos I Foresaw." From *Sunday Nation* (Nairobi, January 15, 1967): 15–16. Interviewer Tony Hall, 1967. Achebe explains the environment in which he lived in Nigeria. He is questioned about his tolerance of critics and his success on the international library scene.

5. From *Palaver: Interviews with Five African Writers in Texas*. Interviewers Bernth Lindfors, Ian Munro, Richard Priebe, and Reinhard Sander, 1969. Conducted at the University of Texas at Austin. Achebe remarks on the African writer and answers questions posed by students of the University of Texas.

6. "Achebe: Accountable to Our Society." From *African Report* (May 1972): 21+. Interviewers Ernest and Pat Emenyonu, 1972. Achebe discusses his art and its role in society, arguing that the responsible artist should also be a teacher.

7. "Chinua Achebe on *Arrow of God*." From *Echos du Commonwealth* 5 (Pau, France, 1979–1980). Interviewer Michel Fabre, 1973. Achebe discusses *Arrow of God* and answers questions on the importance of women in Ibo society.

8. Interview from *Okike* 30 (1990): 129–33. Interviewer Onuora Ossie Enekwe, 1976. Achebe discusses his reasons for returning to Nigeria. He also remarks on his plans for teaching at **University of Nigeria, Nsukka**.

9. "The Critical Generation." From *Ash Magazine* 5 (Adelaide, Australia, Winter 1980): 5–7. Interviewer Rosemary Colmer, 1980. Achebe addresses the roles of myth, symbol, and fable in African literature. He also answers questions about his children's books.

10. Interview from *Research in African Literatures* 12 (1981): 1–13. Interviewer Kalu Ogbaa, 1980. Achebe discusses the roles and responsibilities of the African author, including his own activities as a public intellectual.

11. "Chinua Achebe: At the Crossroads." From *Parabola: The Magazine of Myth and Tradition* (Spring 1981) 30–39. Interviewer Jonathan Cott, 1980. Achebe addresses the roles of myths, ancestors, community, and networking in **Igbo** society.

12. "Achebe Interviewed." From "The Novels of Chinua Achebe: A Study," an unpublished dissertation of Nagarjuna University, India. Interviewers D.V.K. Raghavacharyulu, K. I. Madhusudana Rao, and B. V. Harajagannadh, 1981. Achebe answers questions on Igbo society. He also remarks on his impact on Indian writers.

13. "Giving Writers a Voice." From *West Africa* (June 22, 1981): 1405–7. Interviewer Lindsay Barret, 1981. Achebe discusses the history of SONA, the Society of Nigerian Authors, of which he had been president when the **Nigerian Civil War** broke out in 1967. He also discusses his role in organizing the first national convention of Nigerian writers at the University of Nigeria, Nsukka, in 1981.

14. "Those Magical Years." From *Those Magical Years*, by Robert M. Wren. Interviewer Wren, 1983. Achebe recalls the beginning of his career while discussing his work as a student.

15. "Literature and Conscientization." From *Contemporary Nigerian Literature: A Retrospective and Prospective Exploration*, ed. Biodun Jeyifo. Interviewer Biodun Jeyifo, 1983. Achebe reminisces on the past when asked about the beginning of his career. Topics discussed include *Things Fall Apart* and Christianity.

16. "Achebe on Editing." From *World Literature Written in English* 27 (1987): 1–5. Interviewer G. D. Killam, 1984. Contains the text of a talk that Achebe gave on the educational and literary uses of folk orature at a workshop on Education for Self Reliance at the University of Guelph.

17. "An Interview with Chinua Achebe." From *Massachusetts Review* 28 (1987): 273–85. Interviewer J.O.J. Nwachukwu-Agbada, 1985. Achebe discusses a variety of topics, including trends in the criticism of African literature.

18. "Interview with Chinua Achebe." From *Africa America Asia Australia* (1988): 69–82. Interviewer Jane Wilkinson, 1987. This interview was carried out in London shortly after the publication of **Anthills of the Savannah**. Achebe discusses the new novel, his relationship with his readers, his teaching experience, and how he presents African literature in his teaching.

19. "Achebe and the Bruised Heart of Africa." From *Wasafiri* 14 (1991): 12–16. Interviewer Chris Searle, 1987. Achebe discusses all of his novels. He also remarks on his change of environment from a village to universities and international libraries.

20. "An Interview with Chinua Achebe." From *Callaloo* 13 (1990): 86–101. Interviewer Charles H. Rowell, 1989. Achebe remarks on his conceptualization of a true artist and on various critical issues concerning his novels.

21. "Interview with Chinua Achebe." Interviewer Gordon Lewis, 1995. Achebe discusses his family, his religion, and why he dropped his Christian name.

FURTHER READING

Gayle Feldman, "Chinua Achebe."

Abdul-Rasheed Na'Allah

IROAGANACHI, JOHN ONYEKWERE. Co-author, with Achebe, of **How the Leopard Got His Claws** (1972). Originally from Amachara, Umuahia, Iroaganachi was a graduate of the University of London who, in 1967, sent to the newly founded **Citadel Press** a manuscript for a children's book entitled "How the Dog Was Domesticated." Achebe, one of the founders of the press, accepted the story for publication, then worked with Iroaganachi in revising the text to its final, substantially altered form.

M. Keith Booker

"IRRE," the nickname (short for "Irresponsible") of a university classmate of narrator **Odili Samalu** in *A Man of the People*. He is a notorious seducer of women, whom he regards merely as sexual prey. Samalu refers to him as a "monster," but clearly envies his "prowess" and seems to aspire to the same sort of superficial sexual success.

M. Keith Booker

ISA-IFI. In chapter 14 of ***Things Fall Apart***, the final stage of the process that unites bride and groom in marriage. As is depicted in that chapter, **bride-price** has already been paid so that the youngest of **Uchendu's** five sons, **Amikwu**, may marry an unnamed young woman. Thus, "the final ceremony of confession," *isa-ifi*, was all that remained to confirm the marital union. This ceremony requires the bride to declare her fidelity to the groom since the outset of the marriage negotiations. The glossary for *Things Fall Apart* elaborates on *isa-ifi* in this manner: "If a wife had been separated from her husband for some time and were then to be re-united with him, this ceremony would be held to ascertain that she had not been unfaithful to him during the time of their separation."

FURTHER READING
Robert M. Wren, *Achebe's World*.

Thomas J. Lynn

IWEKA, python-eating heretic whose actions lead to the demise of the village of **Umuama** (*Arrow of God*, chapter 4).

Rachel R. Reynolds

IWEKA, the father of **Obierika** in *Things Fall Apart*. He is recalled as a great man of **Umuofia** by **Uchendu** in chapter 15, indicating that he was well known in **Mbanta**. He is also recalled as one of the "giants" of **Iguedo** by **Ogbuefi Odogwu** in chapter 5 of *No Longer at Ease*.

M. Keith Booker and Thomas J. Lynn

IYI-UWA, a special kind of stone that provides a link between *ogbanje* children and the spirit world, making it impossible for them to break free of that world and live to adulthood in the material world unless the *iyi-uwa* is found and destroyed. In *Things Fall Apart*, the *iyi-uwa* of **Ezinma** is found and destroyed, allowing her to become the first child of **Okonkwo** and **Ekwefi** to live beyond early childhood.

M. Keith Booker

J

JABLOW, ALTA. See *The Africa That Never Was*.

JALIO. In *A Man of the People*, an important national writer of the fictional postcolonial African country featured in the book. Jalio is the author of *The Song of the Blackbird*, identified in Achebe's book as the country's most famous novel. He is also the President of the Writers' Society. The fame of Jalio and his book is lost on the uncultured **Chief Nanga**, however. When Nanga, as Minister of Culture, attends a book exhibition along with **Odili Samalu** and **Elsie**, he meets Jalio there but clearly has no idea who he is. Jalio himself comes in for a certain amount of satire in this same scene, however. He is described as such a nonconformist that he even insists on designing his own clothing so that it will be unique; it also appears that he designs it rather badly, making him something of a ridiculous (and pretentious) figure, his head having been turned by the success of his novel. Indeed, Nanga chides him on his odd dress and admonishes him that, when he attends such official functions in the future, he should wear either a business suit or the traditional national dress. Jalio, insulted, nevertheless treats Nanga with deference, indicating his appreciation of Nanga's power.

M. Keith Booker

JAMES, Christian name of an **Igbo** who serves as the interpreter for the **District Commissioner** in chapter 23 of *Things Fall Apart*.

M. Keith Booker

JEAN, a somewhat overbearing white American woman who accompanies her husband, **John,** when he comes to Africa as part of a team of experts advising the government of the postcolonial nation featured in *A Man of the People*. In chapter 5 of the novel, Jean drives narrator **Odili Samalu** back to the home of **Chief Nanga** from a party. Alone in the house, Jean and Samalu dance the **high-life** as a prelude to sex while John is away in the town of Abaka attending the opening of a new cement factory built with American capital there. Her exaggerated sexual movements during the dance, learned perhaps from watching an anthropological film, suggest an ignorance of African culture, as does the familiar way in which both she and her husband address Chief Nanga by his first name. Samalu is somewhat taken aback by her rather cavalier attitude toward sex and also becomes irritated by her arrogant attitude toward African culture.

M. Keith Booker

JEKOPU, from **Umuru**, is the Court Messenger for the District Office at **Okperi** (*Arrow of God*, chapter 12).

Rachel R. Reynolds

JOE, an orderly at the **General Hospital** of **Lagos** who serves as an informal courier for **Clara Okeke**, a nurse at the same hospital, in chapter 11 of *No Longer at Ease*. Clara decides to help her fiancé, **Obi Okonkwo**, in his financial straits by giving him fifty pounds to cover his car insurance and asks Joe to carry the money to Obi at his office. While Obi thinks Joe is "sly-looking," Clara describes him as "a great friend."

Thomas J. Lynn

JOE, a trade-unionist who serves as one of the leaders of the newly formed political party, the **Common People's Convention**, in *A Man of the People*. He is a close associate of both **Maxwell Kulamo** and Kulamo's fiancée, **Eunice**. It is Joe who informs narrator **Odili Samalu** of the events surrounding the election-night assassination of Kulamo by thugs working for **Chief Simon Koko** of the ruling **People's Organization Party**.

M. Keith Booker

JOHN, one of **Winterbottom**'s servants at Government Hill in **Okperi** (*Arrow of God*, chapter 3). See **Nwodika, John** for a profile.

Rachel R. Reynolds

JOHN, a white American who is in Africa as part of a team of experts advising the government of the postcolonial nation featured in *A Man of the People* on how to improve their image in America. Described as being about the same age as the narrator, **Odili Samalu**, John shows considerable ignorance in his arguments for the greatness of America, as when he attempts to claim, in chapter 4, that lynching has no racial basis. Both John and Jean show an ignorance of (or obliviousness to) African customs when they speak familiarly to **Chief Nanga**, calling him by his first name of Micah. The joke, however, is on John when his "beautiful and bumptious" wife, **Jean**, sleeps with Samalu while John is away from **Bori** attending the opening of a new cement factory built with American capital in the town of Abaka. The very presence of this plant is one of several hints in this novel that at least part of the corruption of postcolonial Africa can be attributed to the machinations of the American government and the operations of American corporations. Indeed, we learn in chapter 12 that American interests, along with the **British Amalgamated** corporation, have made large contributions to the campaign funds of the ruling **People's Organization Party**, in an attempt to keep the current government (over which they have considerable influence) in power.

M. Keith Booker

JOHN, MRS. ELEANOR, an influential party woman of the **People's Organization Party** in *A Man of the People*. A member of the Library Commission, one of the various organizations over which **Chief Nanga** has authority as Minister of Culture, Mrs. John has traveled from her home in the coastal city of Pokoma to attend the festivities surrounding Nanga's visit to the **Anata Grammar School** at the beginning of the novel. She is described as a rich and powerful woman who has risen from humble beginnings as a street hawker, now presiding over a lucrative trade in imported secondhand clothing. Of course, the fact that this clothing is both imported and secondhand suggests the somewhat degraded economic conditions in the postcolonial country of the novel.

M. Keith Booker

JONES, MR. Mr. Jones works for the United Africa Company and is a fairly heavy eater on the **MV** *Sasa* as it sails from England to **Nigeria** in chapter 3 of *No Longer at Ease*. After the boat has been at sea for several days and nears the Madeiras, Jones (mis)quotes Coleridge, " 'Water, water everywhere but not a drop to drink.' " Jones adds, "What a waste of water." **Obi Okonkwo** silently concurs and thinks of Voltaire: "A microscopic fraction of the Atlantic would turn the Sahara into a flourishing grassland. So much for the best of all possible worlds."

Thomas J. Lynn

JONES, MR., the second white man that seven-year-old **Obi Okonkwo** ever saw (the first having been "the Bishop on the Niger"). Obi is reminded of Jones during his first day in his position as Secretary to the Scholarship Board in chapter 7 of *No Longer at Ease*. What at least partly seems to remind him of Mr. Jones is Obi's new boss, **William Green**. Both Jones and Green are characterized as overbearing in relation to Africans. Jones was the Inspector of Schools when Obi was a child. On the first day that Obi attended school, Mr. Jones became enraged at the headmaster, **Simeon Nduka**, shouting at him, " 'Shut up!' " and slapping him. In an instant Simeon threw Jones to the floor. Such handling of a white man by an African at the time was an extraordinary event.

Thomas J. Lynn

JOSIAH, the proprietor of a "shop-and-bar" in the **Waya** market in *A Man of the People*. Josiah is driven out of business by the public outrage (and subsequent boycott) that arises from his attempt, described in chapter 9, to steal the walking stick of the blind man **Azoge** so that he can use it (in some unspecified way that narrator **Odili Samalu** does not understand) in the making of a traditional juju medicine, which Josiah can then sell for profit. Importantly, Josiah's greed is interpreted by the locals as an outgrowth of the colonial legacy and of the corrupting effect of the "white man's money" (86). Later, Josiah offers to help Samalu in his bid for election to parliament, but Samalu declines the offer, knowing of Josiah's bad reputation. Josiah later seeks retribution by pointing out Samalu, who has come under cover of disguise to a political meeting being held by his opponent in the election, **Chief Nanga**. Nanga's supporters then set on Samalu and beat him so badly that he must be hospitalized.

M. Keith Booker

"THE JOURNEY OF THE MAGI," a 1927 poem by the American-British poet **T. S. Eliot** that provides the epigraph for Achebe's *No Longer at Ease*:

> We returned to our places, these Kingdoms,
> But no longer at ease here, in the old dispensation,
> With an alien people clutching their gods.
> I should be glad of another death.

These lines conclude this first of Eliot's "Ariel" poems, the first poems he wrote after his official conversion to Anglo-Catholicism; indeed, the poem is generally read as a commentary on that conversion. It chronicles the arduous journey and return of the biblical Magi, a journey fraught with self-doubt and regret, with material discomfort and public ridicule. The speaker recalls the former ease of the times before he felt it necessary to make this spiritual pilgrimage: "There were times we regretted / The summer places on slopes, the terraces / And the silken girls bringing sherbet." Here Eliot's flood of Orientalist imagery clearly delineates the journey toward conversion as an ascetic movement away from a decadent East. Indeed, Eliot's Eurocentrism is evident throughout his work, from his image of "Mr. Eugenides, the Smyrna merchant" in *The Waste Land* to his overtly racist representation of savage African cannibals in his 1950 play *The Cocktail Party*.

Yet the magus in Eliot's poem has come far enough only to recognize his conversion as necessary—far enough to attest to the truth of the birth of Christ but not to understand the final meaning of his sacrifice. Proleptic images of Christ's life and sacrifice—three trees against the sky foreshadowing the Crucifixion, men "dicing for silver," recalling both Judas's coin and the moneychangers in the temple—go remarked by the speaker, but not understood. The speaker returns, different and yet empty, after bearing witness to a birth, a birth he calls "Hard and bitter agony for us, like Death, our death." The Magi's quest and revelation have served only—and here is the poem's significance for Achebe—to sever their relationship with their own past. Caught between two worlds—accepting the truth of the new revelation but still a child of the old order—the speaker is a stranger among his own people, who now seem diminished, fetishistic, "an alien people clutching their gods."

Recast in the context of Achebe's novel, this line refers not only to the animist religion of **Obi Okonkwo**'s ancestors but to the deeply felt Christianity of his own father (the convert **Nwoye/Isaac** of *Things Fall Apart*).

The word "grasping" in particular, harking back to the moneychanger imagery used earlier in the poem, suggests in the context of *No Longer at Ease* the materialist corruption of the colonial civil service. Obi Okonkwo, like the weary magus of Eliot's poem, is suspended between cultures, unable to "grasp" the new European "dispensation" he has been taught to prefer, but cut off irretrievably from any connection to an authentic past.

FURTHER READING

Lloyd W. Brown, "Cultural Norms and Modes of Perception in Achebe's Fiction" and "The Historical Sense"; Roderick Wilson, "Eliot and Achebe."

Debra Rae Cohen

JOY was for five months the girlfriend of **Joseph Okeke** in chapter 2 of *No Longer at Ease*. Before their relationship ended, Joy made pillowcases for Joseph, including one on which she had sewn the word "*osculate*" in multicolored letters. This word on the pillowcase and the appearance of Joseph's current but unnamed female companion (who accentuates several of her physical attributes) leave "a nasty taste in **Obi Okonkwo's** mouth," although they bespeak the candid sexuality of the "sinful new world" that fascinates Obi during his first visit to Lagos.

Thomas J. Lynn

JOY is, along with **Mercy**, a distant relative of **Hannah Okonkwo**, mother of **Obi Okonkwo** in *No Longer at Ease*, chapter 14. Joy has been sent by her parents to live with the Okonkwo family so that she can receive training from Hannah in the art of keeping a home.

Thomas J. Lynn

K

KANE, CHEIKH HAMIDOU. Senegalese novelist and government administrator, author of *L'Aventure ambiguë*.

M. Keith Booker

KANGAN, the fictional African nation in which the action of *Anthills of the Savannah* takes place. While Achebe clearly intends Kangan as a sort of allegorical representation of the postcolonial predicament of many African nations, it is clearly related most directly to **Nigeria**.

M. Keith Booker

KANO, AMINU (1920–1983), important Nigerian political leader, often referred to by the title of "Mallam," an honorific indicating achievement as an Islamic scholar. Kanu was educated at Katsina College, gaining his diploma in education in 1942 before going to Bauchi Training College to study to be a teacher. In 1946 he took a one-year course at the Institute of Education in London, then returned to colonial **Nigeria** to teach at Bauchi. There, he became a founder of the Bauchi General Improvement Union. In 1949, he was made president of the Maru Branch of Jam'iyyar Mutanen Arewa, a cultural organization that later developed into the Northern Peoples' Congress Party (NPC).

Throughout the 1950s, Kano was an important leader in the Nigerian quest for independence. After independence, he was initially active in the new government but became important largely for his energetic and courageous opposition to the ruling NPC. In this role, Kanu became the leader of the People's Redemption Party, an organization with which Achebe himself was affiliated and of which Achebe was elected deputy national president in 1983. Kanu established a reputation as a voice of independence and integrity in postcolonial Nigerian politics and is still widely regarded as the founding father of grassroots politics in Nigeria. In *The Trouble with Nigeria*, Achebe singles out Kanu as a paradigm of the kind of political leader that postcolonial Nigeria needs in order to fulfill its potential as a nation.

FURTHER READING

Chinua Achebe, *The Trouble with Nigeria*; Alan Feinstein, *African Revolutionary*.

M. Keith Booker

KATIBE, ANDREW, a friend and colleague of narrator **Odili Samalu** in *A Man of the People*. Both Katibe and Samalu teach at the **Anata Grammar School** as the book begins, and **Anata** is identified in the first chapter as Katibe's home village, which causes him to show a certain loyalty to **Chief Nanga**, who is from the same village. However, in the course of the elaborate ceremonies surrounding the visit of Nanga to the grammar school in the novel's opening chapter, Katibe manages to insult and infuriate the visiting dignitary by referring to him as "M.A. Minus Opportunity," a nickname he had borne quite happily while a teacher at the grammar school sixteen years earlier. Apparently, Nanga is particularly angered because he now presents himself as an opponent of intellectualism (and thus someone who would never aspire to a postgraduate degree of any kind), an attitude he perceives as politically expedient under current conditions, even though he is also so enamored of honors and recognition that he has agreed to accept an honorary doctorate from an American university.

M. Keith Booker

KENT, JOHN (also referred to as the Mad Medico), a white English hospital administrator living and working in **Bassa** in *Anthills of the Savannah*. He is the Director of Administration at Bassa General Hospital, but his unconventional protests against inefficiency and poor care in the hospital have earned him his nickname as well as considerable trouble. We learn, for example, that he had earlier carried on a graffiti campaign to protest the unethical behavior of **Dr. Ofe**, a surgeon in the hospital. At that time (a year before the main action of the novel), Kent escaped firing and deportation only through the intervention of **Chris Oriko** and **Sam, the President**. During the course of the novel, however, Kent is ultimately arrested and deported anyway (chapter 13).

M. Keith Booker

KIAGA, MR., an **Igbo** convert to Christianity who serves as the interpreter for the white **missionaries** in **Mbanta** in *Things Fall Apart*. In chapter 17, he runs the church at Mbanta when the missionary is back at his headquarters in **Umuofia**. He also serves as a teacher for the congregation there, though the main missionary school remains in Umuofia.

M. Keith Booker

KILLAM, GORDON DOUGLAS (1930–), an important early Western scholar of African literature and culture whose work on Achebe and other African writers made important contributions to the growth of the international critical reputations of these writers and of African literature as a whole. Born in New Westminster, British Columbia, Killam was educated at the University of British Columbia and London University, where he received his Ph.D. in 1964. His academic appointments have included terms teaching at several African universities, including Fourah Bay College in Freetown, Sierra Leone (1963–1965), the **University of Ibadan** (1966–1967), the University of Lagos (1967–1968), and the University of Dar Es Salaam in Tanzania, where he was a professor and chairman of the Department of Literature (1970–1971). Killam has also held academic appointments at several Canadian universities, including a professorship at York University (1971–1973), a term as professor and head of the Department of English at Acadia University (1973–1976), and a stint as professor and chairman of the Department of English at the University of Guelph from 1977 to 1988.

Killam's numerous scholarly publications include such books as *Africa in English Fiction* (1968), a useful historical survey of representations of Africa and Africans by English fiction writers; **The Writings of Chinua Achebe** (1977), an important early critical study of Achebe's writing; and *An Introduction to the Writings of Ngugi* (1980), a similar study of the work of the Kenyan writer Ngugi wa Thiong'o. His more recent work includes the co-editing, with Ruth Rowe, of a reference volume, *The Companion to African Literatures* (2000).

FURTHER READING

Douglas Killam and Ruth Rowe, eds., *The Companion to African Literatures*; G. D. Killam, *Africa in English Fiction, 1874–1939, An Introduction to the Writings of Ngugi*, and *The Writings of Chinua Achebe*.

M. Keith Booker

KINGSWAY, a street in **Lagos** having the jewelry shop at which **Obi Okonkwo** purchases a twenty-pound engagement ring for **Clara Okeke**, as described in chapter 11 of *No Longer at Ease*.

Thomas J. Lynn

KOBINO, THE HONOURABLE T. C., the Minister of Public Construction in the government of the fictional African postcolonial nation featured in *A Man of the People*. **Chief Nanga** impatiently describes Kobino as a "very stupid man" because he is slow to go along with a Nanga-sponsored project to tar a road between the towns of Giligili and **Anata**. In particular, Nanga complains that Kobino is delaying the project only because it does not directly benefit his own constituency. Nanga, of course, supports the expensive pork-barrel project precisely it benefits his own constituency quite directly.

M. Keith Booker

"KOFI AWOONOR AS A NOVELIST." Achebe essay. See *Hopes and Impediments*.

KOKO, CHIEF SIMON, the Minister for Overseas Training in the fictional postcolonial African nation featured in *A Man of the People*. When narrator **Odili Samalu** travels to **Bori**, the capital city, **Chief Nanga** takes him to see Koko about the possibility of procuring a scholarship for postgraduate study abroad. Unfortunately, the meeting is abruptly interrupted when the somewhat paranoid and buffoonish Koko (who has a bodyguard dressed as a cowboy) frantically concludes that his coffee has been poisoned by his servant, working in league with his political enemies. It turns out, however, that the cook has simply run out of Koko's usual brand of imported coffee (Nescafé) and has instead substituted a local brand, the irony of which is that the ruling **People's Organization Party (POP)**, of which Koko is a member, has recently been promoting the use of such local products.

Late in the book, Koko stands for re-election to parliament, opposed by **Maxwell Kulamo**, a leader of the new leftist party, the **Common People's Convention (CPC)**. Koko bribes Kulamo to withdraw from the election, but, when Kulamo continues to campaign actively for other CPC candidates, Koko has him killed on election night. Koko himself is then shot and killed by **Eunice**, Kulamo's fiancée and fellow CPC member. After the POP retains power in the elections (which disintegrate into mob violence), Koko's widow is made Minister for Women's Affairs in the new cabinet in an attempt to placate the increasingly restless guild of Bori market women.

M. Keith Booker

KULAMO, MAXWELL, a friend and former schoolmate of narrator **Odili Samalu** in *A Man of the People*. Kulamo had earlier attended **Anata Grammar School** with Samalu, establishing a reputation there as something of an amateur poet. In the present time of the novel he is a lawyer in the capital city of **Bori**. A former student at the prestigious **London School of Economics**, he is also an intellectual and has helped to found, along with some of his intellectual friends and his fiancée, **Eunice**, a new political party, the

Common People's Convention (CPC). Samalu flees to the home of Kulamo after his angry confrontation with **Chief Nanga** due to the latter's seduction of **Elsie**, Samalu's girlfriend. There, Samalu meets the inner circle of the CPC and expresses a certain skepticism that they can really represent the common people, given that they are all professionals and intellectuals—an ironic observation, given that Samalu is in very much the same position.

Kulamo is typically referred to by his friends as "Kulmax" or "Cool Max," a nickname that echoes the name of **Karl Marx**, whose philosophy clearly provides an important inspiration for the CPC. Through most of his narration, Samalu refers to Kulamo simply as "Max." Samalu looks up to his friend and admires his idealistic dedication to improving the political situation in their country. Samalu thus joins the CPC and stands for parliament in the national elections that are held late in *A Man of the People*. Kulamo himself leads the CPC in these elections, campaigning nationwide while also standing for parliament in his own constituency in opposition to **Chief Simon Koko**. Salamu (who has just turned down a bribe to withdraw from the elections) is then horrified when Kulamo agrees to withdraw from the election in return for a bribe of 1,000 pounds, even though Kulamo assures him that his agreement had no legal force and that, in any case, it was a necessary move in the interests of the larger goals of the CPC, which is badly in need of the funds. Indeed, Kulamo continues to campaign actively on behalf of the party's other candidates, so much so that he is eventually attacked and killed by Koko's thugs on election night. After a subsequent military coup topples the **People's Organization Party (POP)** government, Kulamo is posthumously declared a "Hero of the Revolution," a designation that Salamu endorses, despite his severe criticism of Kulamo's bribe-taking.

M. Keith Booker

KURTZ, referred to in chapter 11 of *No Longer at Ease*, is a key figure in **Joseph Conrad**'s novella *Heart of Darkness*. In that work Kurtz had arrived in the Congo region as an idealistic reformer during the height of nineteenth-century European colonization of Africa, but later he indulged various personal appetites at the expense of the Africans over whom he gains power. A powerful Belgian firm in the Congo sends a steamboat up the Congo River to retrieve Kurtz, appointing Marlow, narrator of *Heart of Darkness*, as captain. Although Marlow does succeed in finding Kurtz and getting him on the boat, Kurtz dies from an unspecified illness on the return journey down the Congo River. In *No Longer at Ease*, chapter 11, Kurtz enters **Obi Okonkwo's** thoughts as he contemplates his overbearing supervisor, **William Green**. Obi recognizes that Green came to Africa with exceptional ability and admirable intentions (and thus Obi ironically links Green to **Saint George**), but, as in the case of Kurtz, those intentions were built on European prejudices toward Africans and so could not be fulfilled. An apparent consequence of this frustration is Green's cynicism and bitterness, feelings that ultimately afflicted Kurtz as well and that caused him to write, as Obi recalls, "Exterminate all the brutes," a phrase that reveals Kurtz's altered and deranged vision of European relations with Africans. Yet if "Kurtz had succumbed to the darkness" (a phrase that occurs to Obi), Green retains his devotion to duty, to helping in Africa. Toward the end of his reverie Obi acknowledges that "it was not a close analogy, of course" between Kurtz and Green.

Thomas J. Lynn

L

LAGOS, former capital and still the most populous city of **Nigeria**, located on the Bight of Benin in Lagos State in southwestern Nigeria. The site of the city, then the Yoruba settlement of Eko, was visited by Portuguese traders as early as the fifteenth century. The population of Lagos proper was estimated at around 1.3 million in 1992, though the population of the metropolitan area of Lagos was estimated at over 10 million in 1996. This population has been projected by the United Nations to grow to more than 20 million by 2010, potentially making Lagos one of the world's five largest cities. This large population is quite diverse, though the Yoruba constitute the principal ethnic group in the city. Lagos became the capital of the new nation of Nigeria upon independence in 1960. Though the capital was moved to **Abuja** at the end of 1991, Lagos is still the country's chief port and an important administrative, economic, and cultural center.

By the time period that corresponds to the final events of *Things Fall Apart*, that is, around 1910, Lagos had been colonized by Britain for nearly half a century, with an expanding population that had reached 50,000 (Wren 68). Lagos, however, does not figure in that novel. Instead, the conditions of rural Igboland are juxtaposed by Achebe to the more modern Lagos depicted in *Things Fall Apart*'s sequel, *No Longer at Ease*, set in the late 1950s. In the words of **Robert M. Wren**, "[*No Longer at Ease*] shows a society radically changed from that in *Things Fall Apart*. . . . It is in the city, Lagos, that most of the changes are manifest. The city, in its complexity, is symbolic of the aspiration and corruption of the new society" (68). Of course, it is not the author's second novel alone in which Lagos has a part. Fictional African capital cities that have associations with Lagos play significant roles in *A Man of the People*, in which the political center is **Bori**, and *Anthills of the Savannah*, in which it is Bassa. Also, modern Lagos is one of the two settings of Achebe's short story "Marriage Is a Private Affair," included in *Girls at War and Other Stories*, and his short children's novel, *Chike and the River*.

All the same, *No Longer at Ease* is the fictional work by Achebe that brings Lagos to life, and the better part of the novel is set there. Its protagonist, **Obi Okonkwo**, fresh from his rural home in **Umuofia**, spends an eye-opening few days in Lagos with his school friend, **Joseph Okeke**, before leaving Nigeria for four years of study in England. Lagos is the last stop of the **MV *Sasa***'s voyage, which brings Obi back from England to a civil service career in the capital. Obi's new life in Lagos gives Achebe the opportunity to survey the city in many varied aspects: the commodious **Atlantic Terminal** at which the MV *Sasa* arrives (chapter 4); a slum area with its squalor and festivity, which is compared favorably to the elite but dreary **Ikoyi** district (originally reserved for Europeans), which was built, significantly, on a swamp area and near a vast cemetery (chapter 2); the downtown nightclub scene embodied by the **Imperial**, with its **high-life** music and dancing inside and the danger associated with urban poverty lurking outside (chapter 11); the Roman Catholic convent at **Apapa** at which Obi and **Christopher** visit **Nora** and **Pat**; the congested, one-way streets that heighten Obi's desperation as he futilely searches for **Clara Okeke** in his car (chapter 16).

Lagos represents one pole of *No Longer at Ease*'s dualistic structure and of the related conflict that ultimately tears Obi apart. Obi is split between, on the one hand, the urban economic opportunities and sensual attractions associated with Lagos and, on the other hand, the traditional **Igbo** values and close-knit rural community of Umuofia. Nor can he escape Umuofia in Lagos, for many of the forces derived from the former are at work on him in the latter. This is indicated in the normative judgments of the **Umuofia Progressive Union** and in the various **Igbo-language** conversations in which Obi participates. Indeed, the language picture itself is emblematic of the complex culture that Obi tries to navigate in Lagos, for the city demands that one be sensitive to and, ideally, conversant in a variety of languages and language registers. Roderick Wilson speaks to this aspect of the novel: "There is . . . a particular formal device which Achebe uses in order to enforce the sense of a divided society in *No Longer at Ease* . . . and that is the varieties of language: characters of different kinds or in different contexts speak in 'nor-

mal' English, stilted 'impressive' English, Ibo or **pidgin**" (165). The variety and subtlety of language use in Lagos are evoked in connection with Obi's friend, Christopher, in chapter 11, and in Obi's chapter 10 conversation with **Charles Ibe**, which is conducted in Igbo, English, and pidgin, dramatizing the fluidity of language boundaries in the modern city.

FURTHER READING

David Carroll, *Chinua Achebe*; Emmanuel Obiechina, *Culture, Tradition, and Society in the West African Novel*; Roderick Wilson, "Eliot and Achebe"; Robert M. Wren, *Achebe's World*.

Thomas J. Lynn

LAGOS MOTOR PARK. In chapter 2 of *No Longer at Ease*, the site appointed for **Joseph Okeke** to meet his friend, **Obi Okonkwo**, when Obi arrives in **Lagos** from **Umuofia** on his way to study in England.

Thomas J. Lynn

LANGO, MAJOR-GENERAL AHMED, the Army Chief of Staff under **Sam, the President**, during most of the duration of *Anthills of the Savannah*. Late in the novel, after Sam is kidnapped and murdered, Lango becomes the leader of the new government. The text suggests that Lango was, in fact, complicit in the killing of Sam, though he utters a tearful pledge to the nation to bring his predecessor's killers to justice.

M. Keith Booker

"LANGUAGE AND THE DESTINY OF MAN." See *Morning Yet on Creation Day*.

LANGUAGE QUESTION. Most postcolonial literature from sub-Saharan Africa has been written in English or French, the languages of the former colonial rulers. However, as Abdul JanMohamed appropriately observes, "the African writer's very decision to use English as his medium is engulfed by ironies, paradoxes, and contradictions" ("Sophisticated Primitivism" 20). It is clear that African writers who continue to work in the languages of their former colonial rulers risk the perpetuation of colonialist ideas (especially ideas involving the cultural and linguistic superiority of Europe). But the factors involved in the use of European languages by African writers are quite complicated. As a whole, fewer Africans are literate in any given African language than in English or French. African writers can thus reach a larger African reading audience in European languages and can meanwhile reach a Western audience as well. The economics of the publishing industry thus creates great pressures for the use of European languages. At the same time, most Africans are not literate in these languages either, so that the primary African audience for African novelists who write in European languages is often precisely that educated elite most thoroughly educated in the kinds of Western cultural traditions that the novelists are often seeking to challenge or overcome.

Further, JanMohamed notes that European and African languages quite often operate on fundamentally different premises. In particular, European culture from the Renaissance forward is primarily of a written nature, and European languages reflect this fact. Most traditional African culture, however, is oral in nature, and most African languages did not have written forms before the arrival of colonialism. The very act of writing is to a certain extent a European activity, though it is certainly not the case that there are not traditions of written culture in Africa. Nevertheless a clash between written and oral cultural forms is one of the central defining characteristics of African postcolonial literature, which is itself written but which often seeks to draw upon the traditions of African oral culture. It is important to recognize that the differences between oral and written cul-

ture go far beyond superficial questions of medium, extending to the fact that oral and written cultures tend to conceptualize the world in fundamentally different ways.

African writers have attempted to deal with the conflict between oral and written cultural forms in a number of ways, most obviously through the incorporation of materials from African oral culture into their written texts. **Amos Tutuola** is a good case in point; his texts are marked first and foremost by the "ability to assimilate elements peculiar to the oral tradition with elements peculiar to the literary tradition: in other words, to impose a literary organization upon essentially oral narrative material" (Obiechina, *Language and Theme* 50). Achebe's novels are much more conventional from a Western perspective, but they still derive much of their energy from the enrichment of the written texts with elements derived from traditional **Igbo** oral culture.

In this manner, Achebe, though he writes in English, writes in an English that he has attempted to make his own. Not only does he supplement his written narrative with songs, proverbs, and stories that derive from oral traditions, but he also augments the basic English matrix of his text with words and expressions from the **Igbo language** and from **pidgin English**. As he explains in the essay "The African Writer and the English Language," he feels that the English language is by now part of his African cultural heritage: "I have been given the English language," he writes, "and I intend to use it" (***Morning Yet on Creation Day*** 102). However, for Achebe, "using" English involves far more than a mere acceptance of the linguistic heritage of colonialism. He goes on to argue that "the English language will be able to carry the weight of my African experience. But it will have to be a new English, still in full communion with its ancestral home but altered to suit new African surroundings" (103).

In this sense, Achebe's attitude resembles that expressed by the Indian postcolonial novelist **Salman Rushdie** in his influential article "The Empire Writes Back." Rushdie is very clearly a great lover of the English language, noting in this article that "I don't think there's another language large or flexible enough to include so many different realities." However, in this same article he also shows a profound appreciation for the historicity and political embeddedness of language, arguing that the vestiges of empire are still to be found in the "cadences" of the English language itself. On the other hand, he sees the political charge that inheres in language to be potentially energizing. Citing the Irish writers Joyce, Beckett, and O'Brien as predecessors, Rushdie argues that much "vitality and excitement" can be derived from attempts to "decolonize" the English language. In this vein, Rushdie acknowledges the work of African writers such as Achebe and **Ngugi** who are resisting the history of imperialism that inheres within the language not only by "busily forging English into new shapes" but by placing politics at the very centre of their art" (Rushdie 8).

Many African writers have been less confident than Achebe or Rushdie that English can adequately express the realities of African life. Both **Wole Soyinka** and **Ayi Kwei Armah**, who themselves write in English, have suggested that African writers should begin to work toward the eventual development of a Pan-African literary language, perhaps Swahili. **Ousmane Sembène**, meanwhile, writes his novels in French but has devoted much of his energy in the last two decades or so to the making of films rather than novels, thus extending the accessibility of his work to a wider African audience, especially given that many of his films primarily employ his native Wolof language. Similarly, Ngugi, having made a worldwide reputation as an English-language novelist, has written a number of plays in Gikuyu, thus making his work available to Gikuyu peasants and workers who do not know English or cannot read. Indeed, though identified by Rushdie as a leading "decolonizer" of English, Ngugi has since eschewed the use of English in his writing, preferring to write his later original texts in his native Gikuyu. Ngugi is quite adamant in texts like *Decolonising the Mind* about his belief in the responsibility of African writers to reject the languages inherited from their former imperial oppressors. Language, he argues, is central to one's cultural identity, and Africans will never be able to establish a strong sense of self as long as they continue to express their deepest thoughts in European languages (*Decolonising* 4).

FURTHER READING

Chinua Achebe, *Morning Yet on Creation Day*; Abiola Irele, *The African Experience in Literature and Ideology*; Abdul R. JanMohamed, "Sophisticated Primitivism"; Ngugi wa Thiong'o, *Decolonising the Mind*; Emmanuel Obiechina, *Language and Theme*; Salman Rushdie, "The Empire Writes Back."

M. Keith Booker

LEWIS STREET. In chapter 2 of *No Longer at Ease*, a street in **Lagos** that **Obi Okonkwo** walks along on his first visit to the city while his friend, **Joseph Okeke**, entertains a new, though unnamed, female acquaintance.

Thomas J. Lynn

LINDFORS, BERNTH OLOF (1938–). A pioneer in the criticism of African literature and culture, Lindfors was one of the first Western scholars to pay serious critical attention to the works of African novelists, including a significant focus on the work of Achebe. A native of Sweden, Lindfors was educated at Oberlin College, Harvard University, Northwestern University, and the

University of California at Los Angeles, where he received his doctorate in English in 1969 for a dissertation entitled "Nigerian Fiction in English, 1952–1967." From 1961 to 1963, Lindfors taught English and history at Kisii School in Kisii, Kenya. He has spent the bulk of his academic career as a professor of English and African literatures at the University of Texas at Austin, where he has taught since 1969, helping to make that university an important center of scholarly research in African literature and culture.

Lindfors has published well over 100 scholarly articles on African literature and culture. He is also the author of numerous books on the subject, including *Folklore in Nigerian Literature* (1973), *Early Nigerian Literature* (1982), *"The Blind Men and the Elephant," and Other Essays in Biographical Criticism* (1987), *Popular Literatures in Africa* (1991), *Long Drums and Canons: Teaching and Researching African Literatures* (1995), *Loaded Vehicles: Studies in African Literary Media* (1996), and *African Textualities* (1997). As a leading figure in the institutionalization of studies of African literature in the American academy, Lindfors has also made numerous contributions as an editor and compiler. For example, he is the editor of **Approaches to Teaching Achebe's Things Fall Apart** (1991), *Conversations with Chinua Achebe* (1997), and (with **C. L. Innes**) *Critical Perspectives on Chinua Achebe* (1978).

FURTHER READING

Bernth Lindfors, *African Textualities*, *"The Blind Men and the Elephant,"* *Early Nigerian Literature*, *Folklore in Nigerian Literature*, *Loaded Vehicles*, *Long Drums and Canons*, and *Popular Literatures in Africa*; Bernth Lindfors, ed., *Approaches to Teaching Achebe's* Things Fall Apart, *Conversations with Chinua Achebe*, and *Critical Perspectives on Chinua Achebe* (with C. L. Innes).

M. Keith Booker

LIVERPOOL, a city (population 466,600 in 2002) in northwestern England whose **Harrington Dock** is the **MV** *Sasa*'s point of departure on its voyage to **Lagos** via **Funchal** and **Freetown** in chapters 3 and 4 of *No Longer at Ease*. While the MV *Sasa* is still docked at Liverpool, two of its passengers, **Obi Okonkwo** and **Clara Okeke**, encounter each other for a second time.

Thomas J. Lynn

THE LONDON SCHOOL OF ECONOMICS (formal name The London School of Economics and Political Science, but acronym LSE), distinguished English university founded in 1895. Chapter 2 of *No Longer at Ease* specifies that **Christopher**, the close friend of **Obi Okonkwo** and an economist, studied at The London School of Economics. In *A Man of the People* we learn that **Maxwell Kulamo** and **Eunice** met at The London School of Economics, presumably while they were studying there.

Thomas J. Lynn

LONG LIFE MIXTURE. In chapter 5 of *No Longer at Ease*, a bottled potion promoted by two amplified salesmen in "the great **Onitsha** market" as a remedy for numerous ailments.

Thomas J. Lynn

LORD LUGARD COLLEGE, a British-run colonial college (roughly equivalent to an American high school) attended together by **Ikem Osodi**, **Chris Oriko**, and **Sam, the President**, in *Anthills of the Savannah*. It is named after the somewhat notorious **Lord Frederick Lugard**, a prominent British colonial administrator widely regarded as one of the central architects of the British system of **indirect rule** in Africa.

M. Keith Booker

LOUISE, ex-wife of Chris Oriko in *Anthills of the Savannah*. They were married for six months while he was in London.

M. Keith Booker

LUGARD, LORD FREDERICK JOHN DEALTRY (1858–1945), a prominent British colonial administrator. Born in India the year after the Mutiny, Lugard served in the Afghan Wars (1879), the Suakin (Sudan) Campaign (1885), the Burma Wars (1886), and the Nyasa Campaign against Arab slave-traders (1888–1889). After this campaign he entered the service of the British East Africa Company in Uganda, where, between 1890 and 1892, he secured British control of the area. He then returned to England and successfully worked to convince the British government officially to declare Uganda a British protectorate. After being appointed the British commissioner for Northern Nigeria in 1897, he organized the West African Frontier Force, which worked for the next six years to secure British control of Northern Nigeria, often by the strategy of the "punitive expedition," in which areas of resistance to British control were punished with severe military action in order to make examples of them.

Lugard served as the colonial governor of all of **Nigeria** from 1912 to 1919, and his attempts to establish a unified administration over the large and diverse region helped to set the tone for British colonial rule in much of Africa. In particular, Lugard was a central architect of the British system of **pacification** and **indirect rule**, which is described at some length in *The Dual Mandate in British Tropical Africa* (1922). Lugard's *Political Memoranda*, compiled during his years (1912–1919) as governor-general of Nigeria, began with a description of the "duties of political officers," which also indicates the idea behind indirect rule: "The British rule here is to bring to the country all the gains of civilisation by applied science (whether in development of material resources, or the eradication of disease, &c), with as little interference as possible with Native customs and modes of thought." On conclusion of his service in Nigeria, Lugard returned to England in 1919, where he was eventually appointed as a member of the Permanent Mandates Commission of the League of Nations (1922). Lugard was raised to the peerage as a baron in 1928. He remained active in political debate until his death in 1945 at the end of World War II, and his policy of indirect rule remained ascendant in British imperial practice in Africa through the subsequent era of decolonization. In the late twentieth/early twenty-first centuries, African historians, such as Mahmood Mamdani, identified "indirect rule" as having laid the grounds not only for the "pacification of primitive tribes" but for "genocide" as well.

FURTHER READING

A. E. Afigbo, *The Warrant Chiefs*; Lord Frederick John Dealtry Lugard, *The Dual Mandate in Tropical Africa* and *Political Memoranda*; Mahmood Mamdani, *When Victims Become Killers*; Margery Perham, *Lugard*.

M. Keith Booker

M

MACDERMOTT, SIR HUGH, the pseudonym for the Governor of British West Africa in *Arrow of God*. In the 1920s, British West Africa consisted of the countries that are today **Nigeria**, Ghana, Sierra Leone, and Gambia. The governor to whom Achebe is probably referring is Graeme Thompson, whose lieutenant governor, H. C. Moorhouse, developed early grants for the road-building project that occurs at the beginning of *Arrow of God*. This makes the early timing of the novel 1922 or 1923.

FURTHER READING

A. E. Afigbo, *The Warrant Chiefs*.

Rachel R. Reynolds

MACDONALD, alias for the real life **J. F. Stewart**, missionary killed at **Ahiara (Abame** in Achebe.) His name is first given as MacDonald in *Arrow of God* (chapter 10). Note that Achebe maintains the Scottishness of the character in accordance with the real historical figure.

Rachel R. Reynolds

MACHI, the eldest brother of **Obierika** in *Things Fall Apart*. In chapter 8, he jokes about the leper **Amadi**, comparing him to the newly arrived white Europeans. Among the clan of **Umuofia**, the disease of leprosy is politely referred to as "the white skin."

M. Keith Booker

MACMILLAN, JOHN, a young Englishman whom **Obi Okonkwo** meets on the **MV Sasa** on his journey from England back to Africa in chapter 3 of *No Longer at Ease*. Macmillan, an administrative officer in Northern Nigeria, and Obi become friends during the voyage, and the two of them and **Clara Okeke** enjoy walking together in **Funchal** in the **Madeiras** when their boat stops there on its way to **Lagos**.

Thomas J. Lynn

MACMILLAN, JOHN, Assistant District Officer whom **Tony Clarke** replaces. MacMillan is mentioned as having died of cerebral malaria only four weeks after his arrival at **Okperi**. The mortality rate of British officers from disease throughout tropical locations in the empire was extraordinarily high, while others were brought in to work for a few years until they were severely debilitated and then shipped back home. A large number of these young officers were also young, lower-echelon officers from social classes far below the ranks of nobility; often they were recruited from among Welsh, Scottish, or loyalist Irish regions of the United Kingdom.

Rachel R. Reynolds

THE MAD MEDICO. See **Kent, John**.

MADEIRAS (in Portuguese, Arquipélago Da Madeira), a volcanic archipelago in the North Atlantic Ocean, between 350 and 400 miles west of Morocco. Two of the islands, Madeira, the largest, and Porto Santo, have human populations, while two island groups, the Selvagens and the Desertas, are uninhabited. The greater part of the population descends from Moors, Portuguese, and African slaves. The islands were known to the Romans as the Purple Islands and were rediscovered in the early fifteenth century by Portuguese sailors. Slavery was outlawed in 1775. For a brief time in the early nineteenth century the Madeira Islands were ruled by the British, while today they are an autonomous overseas territory of Portugal, with sugar and wine as the main products as well as exports. The largest town, located on Madeira, is **Funchal**, which in chapter 3 of *No Longer at Ease* serves as the port of call for the small cargo boat, **MV** *Sasa*, that carries fifty crew members and twelve passengers, including **Obi Okonkwo** and **Clara Okeke**, from **Liverpool**, England to **Lagos**, **Nigeria**.

Thomas J. Lynn

MADU, JOSIAH, was a young Christian from **Umuagu** (a village of **Umuaro** cluster) who killed and ate a sacred **python** (*Arrow of God*, chapter 4).

Rachel R. Reynolds

MADUKA, the dutiful son of **Obierika** in *Things Fall Apart*. In chapter 6, he participates in a wrestling contest for boys of fifteen or sixteen and impresses the crowd with his great quickness and skill in winning his

match. In chapter 8, **Okonkwo** congratulates the sixteen-year-old Maduka on his victory.

M. Keith Booker

MADUKA, age-group mate and drinking buddy of **Obika** and **Ofoedu** in *Arrow of God*. In chapter 8, Maduka baits the two in drinking contests and is responsible for challenging the two to drink from the wine of the palm-tree **Okposalebo**.

Rachel R. Reynolds

MAHMOUD, ALHAJI ABDUL, the chairman of the Kangan/American Chamber of Commerce in *Anthills of the Savannah*. He is in attendance at the dinner hosted by **Sam, the President**, at his lakeside retreat in chapter 6. He is described as being the only person at the dinner with whom **Beatrice Okoh** does not exchange a single word beyond a "lukewarm" hello upon introduction. He is a powerful man and has apparently built a large fortune through his shady and ruthless business dealings, including smuggling. He thus serves as a figure of postcolonial selfishness, corruption, and opportunism.

M. Keith Booker

MAKINDE, DR., the former Minister of Finance in the fictional African postcolonial nation of *A Man of the People*. Makinde had been deposed by the Prime Minister, leader of the ruling **People's Organization Party (POP)**, for fear that his honest and intelligent plan for economic reform in the midst of a crisis might prove unpopular with the voters. His removal (and subsequent public vilification as an enemy of the state and the people and a member of the "Miscreant Gang") serves as an example of the dishonest, self-serving, and ruthless practices with which the POP rules while paying little heed to the good of the nation. The attack on Makinde is spearheaded by **Chief Nanga**, who uses the opportunity as an occasion for his own political advancement.

M. Keith Booker

MAMI WOTA. Mami Wota, the Lady of the River Niger, figures prominently in Achebe's story "Uncle Ben's Choice," included in the collection *The Sacrificial Egg and Other Stories*. In this story, the seductive Mami Wota offers herself to the title character, but he flees her embraces, knowing that if he stays with her, she will bring him wealth but he will be denied children. Instead, she becomes the lover of a trader on the River Niger, who indeed achieves great wealth but remains childless. See also **Alusi**.

M. Keith Booker

MAMMY WATER. See **Alusi**; **Mami Wota**.

A MAN OF THE PEOPLE, Achebe's fourth novel, was originally published in 1966 by Heinemann Publishers in London, just before the political upheavals in **Nigeria** that led to the **Nigerian Civil War** and to a substantial interruption in Achebe's career as a writer. Though nominally set in an unnamed fictional African postcolonial nation, *A Man of the People* is a political satire that obviously comments on the postcolonial political situation in Nigeria, thus joining the earlier *No Longer at Ease* to become the second of Achebe's novels to address the postcolonial era in Nigeria. *A Man of the People* is a serious novel that deals with the abuses of power by postcolonial political leaders, a concern that would be central to all of Achebe's writings from that point forward. At the same time, it treats these weighty issues in a mode of satire that is often quite comic. Indeed, *A Man of the People* is probably Achebe's funniest novel, even as it is ultimately his darkest. It is, along with **Ayi Kwei Armah**'s *The Beautyful Ones Are Not Yet Born*, to which it is often compared, one of the bitterest and most insightful denunciations of postcolonial corruption in all of African literature. Its relevance to Nigerian political life might be indicated by the fact that it appeared in serial comic strip form in the *New Nigeria* daily newspaper from September 1974 to October 1975. See *A Man of the People* (comic strip).

The "man of the people" in the book's title is ostensibly **Chief the Honourable Micah A. Nanga, M.P.**, an unscrupulous, uncultured, ruthless, and ambitious politician who has maneuvered himself, by the beginning of the present time of the book in 1964, into the position of Minister of Culture in the cabinet of the national government. Achebe's satirical depiction of Nanga as a man interested only in his own personal advancement makes it quite clear that the title of the book is entirely ironic: Nanga, though a charismatic politician who has a natural ability to make the people believe that he has their interests at heart, is clearly interested in no one's welfare but his own. In addition, the book's narrator, **Odili Samalu**, enters politics late in the novel, challenging Nanga for his seat in parliament. Samalu thus aspires to be a man of the people as well, making the title doubly ironic while at the same time projecting warnings that the idealistic Samalu might be in danger, given the political climate in this country, of eventually becoming as corrupt as Nanga.

The opposition between the young, idealistic Samalu and the middle-aged, cynical Nanga, perhaps the central structural device in the book, is hardly a simple one. While a superficial list of their characteristics might make them appear to be polar opposites, such oppositions tend not to hold up in this novel. Nanga is not all bad, by any means, exhibiting an intense personal charm and a strong understanding of the common people of his country. Samalu, on the other hand, is far from perfect, displaying, through his alienation from the traditions and common people of his country, weaknesses precisely where Nanga shows strengths. Thus, while Samalu may be an idealist, his ideals are almost entirely modern and Western, leaving him as a figure of the young African intellectual whose education has left him out of touch with his country's indigenous traditions and common people. As **C. L. Innes** puts it, Samalu seems to have "nothing but contempt for the traditions of his nation" (83).

Indeed, the complexity of the opposition between Nanga and Samalu typifies the way in which, in this chaotic postcolonial African nation, there are no simple choices or easy answers. Crucial to the book, in fact, is the way in which Samalu clearly desires such answers and almost desperately yearns for simple choices but cannot find them. Meanwhile, readers who make such simple choices are in danger of badly misunderstanding the book. As critics such as **Simon Gikandi** have emphasized, the narrative voice in this book is so ironic that virtually nothing Samalu says can be taken at face value: "Achebe uses a first person narrator to tell the story from within so that he can show how postcolonial subjects are caught up in a great ironic moment which also calls attention to their historical belatedness—independence was expected to be a break with the colonial past, but has become, instead, the apotheosis of colonialist ideology and rhetoric" (**Reading Chinua Achebe**, 110).

One of the chief ironies of *A Man of the People* involves the apparent ignorance of Samalu to the perilous road that lies ahead of him, and one can surmise that one of the most important goals of the novel is to provide a warning to other young, idealistic, African intellectuals that they, too, are in danger of being seduced by Western materialism, especially if they lose touch with the traditions and culture of their own people. What is particularly striking about Samalu is that he is very capable of seeing the tendency of other young idealists to become corrupt yet retains confidence that he himself will be able to avoid corruption. At the same time, he is blind to the fact that Nanga's corruption is largely Western-inspired, regarding Nanga as an unsophisticated "bush man" who lacks the education to behave properly in modern society.

As *A Man of the People* begins, Nanga is visiting the **Anata Grammar School**, in his home village, where he had served as a teacher many years earlier, before his rise to political power. Samalu, through his narration, makes clear from the very beginning that Nanga is a self-absorbed egomaniac who glories in the attention paid to him during the ceremonies surrounding his visit. This characteristic, meanwhile, is exacerbated by the fact that the locals, led by school principal **Jonathan Nwege**, are all to happy to feed Nanga's ego with their elaborate preparations for his visit—not because of their great admiration for the politician but because they hope to win his favor and thus gain advancement for themselves. Samalu, who now teaches at the grammar school and who had been a student there when Nanga was a member of the faculty, suggests very quickly that power has corrupted Nanga and that he is now a far less likable figure than he had been during his earlier days as a mere provincial teacher. Samalu also shows contempt for the fawning efforts of Nwege and others to impress Nanga, yet he himself is quick to accept Nanga's offer of helping him to procure a scholarship for postgraduate study abroad. Moreover, in light of events narrated later in the book, it is quite possible that some of Samalu's distaste for the elaborate ceremonies held in honor of Nanga's visit arises from sheer envy, from a desire to receive such attentions himself. Indeed, Samalu consistently demonstrates a tendency toward precisely the behavior that he decries in others.

Samalu very deftly informs us of a number of Nanga's central characteristics (most of them negative) in the initial chapter. For example, in the midst of describing the ceremonies at the school, Samalu inserts an anecdote describing Nanga's self-serving political opportunism, depicting him as a somewhat buffoonish lout who furthered his own ambitions by swooping down like a vulture to lead the criticism of one **Dr. Makinde**, the former Minister of Finance, who had fallen out of favor with the Prime Minister after proposing an economic program that might have proved politically unpopular, even if it was technically sound. Meanwhile, we learn that Nanga is accompanied on his visit to **Anata** by a beautiful young woman (eventually identified as **Edna Odo**) rumored to be in line to be his second wife because his first wife, **Margaret Nanga**, is too "bush" to serve as a suitable partner in his new position of political power. Thus, we are alerted very early on to expect Nanga to be a womanizer and that he is a pretentious figure with little loyalty to anyone who cannot help him move still farther up the political ladder.

Samalu, in fact, seems to go out of his way to depict Nanga in a negative light in this initial scene, though we will not learn until somewhat later in the book the most important reason (sexual jealousy) for Samalu's antagonism toward the politician. Nevertheless, Samalu quickly accepts Nanga's invitation to come see him in the capital city of **Bori** (obviously based on Lagos), where he hopes that Nanga can use his influence to help him procure the scholarship. In Bori, Samalu is invited to stay at Nanga's luxurious home, which he does gladly, especially as he plans to use his room there to host his old college girlfriend **Elsie**, who still lives and works in the Bori area, and to renew his sexual relationship with her. In short, though Samalu presents his position as entirely honorable (as opposed to the reprehensible Nanga), it is clear to the careful reader that Samalu is drawn to the capital by some of the same ambition and sexual appetite for which he criticizes Nanga.

Meanwhile, the characterization of Nanga is especially furthered in one scene in chapter 6 in which Samalu, Elsie, and the politician all attend an important book exhibition being held in the city. This exhibition is being chaired by one Jalio, an important national writer and the author of *The Song of the Blackbird*, identified as the country's most famous novel. He is also the President of the Writers' Society. However, the fame of Jalio and his book are lost on the uncultured Nanga, who has clearly never heard of either, despite his position as Minister of Culture. Nanga is not entirely illiterate, but his own reading habits, we have already learned in chapter 4, tend toward how-to books and the works of such problematic British colonial writers as **H. Rider Haggard**. The latter motif thus becomes one of the many ways in which Nanga's corruption is at least in part derived from the legacy of colonialism, and Samalu reminds us several times during the book of Nanga's expressed preference for dealing with imported white experts rather than educated Africans.

At the same time, we must also consider the source, recognizing that Samalu narrates this event from a later perspective in which he has become a bitter opponent of Nanga. Thus, his description of the book exhibition can be taken as a calculated effort to make Nanga look ignorant and uneducated relative to Samalu himself. In fact, there is clearly a certain arrogance in Samalu's attitude toward Nanga, an arrogance derived from his own Western-inspired education, an education that has left him out of touch with the traditional culture of his people and has made him prone to the kind of radical alienation that is typical in the capitalist West. As **David Carroll** puts it, Samalu's "detachment from his fellow human beings is virtually complete," a fact that seriously compromises his description of all of the other characters in the novel, none of whom he truly understands (124). That Samalu also does not understand himself merely adds further layers of irony to his narration.

Perhaps, then, it should come as no surprise that virtually no one in this novel comes off completely well when described by Samalu. For example, Jalio himself comes in for a certain amount of satire in the book exhibition scene, perhaps because Samalu is jealous of the famous writer. Jalio is described as such a nonconformist that he even insists on designing his own clothing so that it will be unique; it also appears that he designs it rather badly, making him something of a ridiculous (and pretentious) figure, his head having been turned by the success of his novel. Indeed, Nanga chides him on his odd dress and admonishes him that, when he attends such official functions in the future, he should wear either a business suit or the traditional national dress. Yet, despite this rude treatment, Jalio nevertheless treats the minister with deference, suggesting the way in which artists such as Jalio are, in this postcolonial nation, intimidated by the power of such politicians. At the same time, the obvious gap between Nanga and Jalio indicates the way in which writers and politicians, both presumably engaged in the crucial task of building a viable postcolonial cultural identity for their new nation, have fallen out of phase with one another, while both are in danger of losing touch with the needs of the common people.

Meanwhile, Samalu has arranged to have Elsie come stay at Nanga's house, and Nanga even invites her to sleep in the bedroom of his wife, Margaret, who is away in Anata taking their children to visit their family in their home village. However, as Samalu eagerly creeps up the stairs on Elsie's first night there so that he can fetch her back to his own room for a night of wild sexual fun, he realizes that she is already in the throes of intercourse with Nanga. That she cries out Samalu's name in the height of passion is little consolation to him, because he remembers that she had called out the name of her then-fiancé, **Ralph** (away in Edinburgh attending medical school), during her first sexual encounter with Samalu back during their university days. Nor does Samalu show any awareness that Nanga is essentially doing to him what he himself had earlier done to Ralph.

Shocked and infuriated, Samalu storms out of the house to wander about the city in anger and confusion. What he fails to see is that Elsie has been seduced by the trappings of power and wealth that surround Nanga, trappings that had, until this point, nearly succeeded in seducing Samalu himself. Nor does he seem to recognize that Elsie's lack of loyalty to him is matched by his lack of commitment to her, whom he regards largely as a sexual conquest, bragging to the reader that he slept with her within an hour of first meeting her. When he returns to the house, he angrily confronts Nanga, who defends his action simply by pointing out that Samalu had already assured him that his relationship with Elsie was not an important one. He offers, in return, to furnish Samalu with a whole bevy of girls, but Samalu, his pride wounded, is unplacated. He moves out of Nanga's house and goes to the home of his old friend **Maxwell Kulamo**, a former grammar school classmate and now a prominent lawyer in Bori. There, Samalu meets **Eunice**, Kulamo's beautiful fiancée, who is also a lawyer. He also meets other members of their circle, who are involved in the founding of the **Common People's Convention (CPC)**, a new leftist political party heavily informed by the ideas of **Marxism**.

Both Kulamo and Eunice are clearly idealists, genuinely dedicated to improving the lives of the common people of their country by offering them a real political alternative to the ruling **People's Organization Party (POP)**, of which Nanga is a member, and the **People's Alliance Party (PAP)**, the chief opposition party. As the names POP and PAP satirically suggest, these two parties are virtually interchangeable, each offering the same empty promises while dedicating their true energies to furthering the ambitions of the party politicians who run them. In this sense, the CPC is clearly a step forward, though Kulamo immediately expresses a certain skepticism that a party led exclusively by professionals and intellectuals can effectively represent the interests of the common people, especially after he learns that a junior minister in the POP government is behind the new party.

Soon afterward, it is discovered that **Alhaji Chief Senator Suleiman Wagada**, the POP Minister of Foreign Trade, has been involved in shady dealings with **British Amalgamated**, the British conglomerate that serves as one of the central emblems of the ongoing neocolonial exploitation of Africa. The resultant scandal forces the Prime Minister to resign and call new parliamentary elections, at which time Salamu decides to run on the CPC ticket in opposition to Nanga. Clearly, some of Samalu's motivation in this campaign is genuine political idealism. Just as clearly, however, he is also driven by motives of jealousy and sexual revenge. Having earlier declared his intention to seduce Edna in retribution for Nanga's seduction of Elsie, Samalu has by this time developed a genuine affection for Edna, even though she repeatedly rejects his efforts to lure her away from Nanga. Still, it is also clear that Samalu hopes to impress Edna with his newfound importance as a parliamentary candidate—and perhaps even ultimately as a member of parliament. Even Samalu admits that he is unable to separate out his various motivations: "How important was my political activity in its own right? It was difficult to say; things seemed so mixed up; my revenge, my new political ambition and the girl" (109–10).

Such jumbled and confused motivations on the part of the protagonist represent some of the central images of confusion in a book that seeks, among other things, to portray the air of chaos that reigns in the postcolonial society it depicts. This chaos particularly pertains to the political process, and it should come as no surprise that the subsequent electoral campaign is an unruly one. Samalu is probably not a serious threat to the master politician Nanga, and the narrator admits that most in the region seem to find his challenge to Nanga a joke. However, Samalu himself seems to take his candidacy quite seriously, slogging onward with the support of the CPC to the point where he at least becomes a genuine nuisance to Nanga. In response, Nanga tries threats, intimidation, and bribery but is unable to convince Samalu to withdraw from the election. Meanwhile, Nanga exercises his political influence to put further pressure on his opponent. Samalu is fired from his job at the grammar school, and even Samalu's father, **Hezekiah Samalu**, though the leader of the POP in his home village of **Urua**, suddenly receives word that his taxes have been increased in an obvious bid to coerce him into trying to convince his son to withdraw.

Samalu hires bodyguards for protection and resists Nanga's other efforts as well, rejecting with particular vehemence Nanga's offer of a foreign scholarship and 250 pounds in cash in return for withdrawing from the election. He is even more angered when

Nanga triumphantly informs him that Kulamo has already accepted such a bribe and has agreed to drop his opposition to the parliamentary re-election bid of **Chief Simon Koko**, another POP leader, currently the Minister for Overseas Training. Hearing this news, Samalu attempts to retaliate by calling Nanga a "bush man," apparently the worst insult he can muster but one that also reflects poorly on Samalu and his attitude of superiority to the common and uneducated people of his own country.

Later, when Samalu confronts Kulamo about the bribe, his friend assures him that his agreement with Koko has no legal force and that, in any case, it was a necessary move in the interests of the larger goals of the CPC, which is badly in need of the 1,000 pounds that Koko agreed to pay him in exchange for his withdrawal. Indeed, Kulamo continues to campaign actively on behalf of the party's other candidates, including Salamu. Still, Samalu refuses to endorse Kulamo's act of realpolitik and declares that the moral position of the CPC has thereby been compromised. That Samalu is also insulted because Kulamo was offered 1,000 pounds, while he himself was offered only 250, is merely another hint of his tendency toward egocentrism and inconsistency in his attitudes.

Ultimately, Samalu destroys his own electoral hopes when he decides to disguise himself and sneak into Nanga's inaugural campaign meeting. Pointed out in the crowd, Samalu is set upon and beaten so badly that he winds up hospitalized with a cracked skull, broken arm, and multiple bruises. He remains hospitalized (and officially under arrest) for four weeks, missing the election itself and learning only on election day that he had never even really been a candidate because Nanga and his minions had succeeded in preventing the official filing of the paperwork that would have made his candidacy official.

If Samalu's electoral hopes are thereby short-circuited, the same goes for the entire election. On the very night of the voting, Kulamo is attacked and killed by Koko's thugs, while Koko himself is shot and killed in turn by Eunice. The subsequent fighting between Koko's thugs and Kulamo's bodyguards sparks similar violence all over the country, leading the Prime Minister to declare the elections moot and to reappoint the existing government. Soon afterward, a military coup topples this government. The country's new military leaders then release Eunice (arrested for the shooting of Koko) from jail, declaring Kulamo a "Hero of the Revolution," a designation that Salamu endorses, despite his severe criticism of Kulamo's bribe-taking.

Salamu, however, takes little comfort in the coup, feeling that it represents not a cleansing but simply another step toward cynicism. In fact, he bitterly rejects the notion that the coup resulted from popular disgust with the corruption of the POP government. Instead, he simply suggests that the people feel nothing but cynicism and apathy toward politics and that military rule was a natural result of the violent forces unleashed by the political parties themselves. Indeed, far from being elated, Salamu is revolted by the change of heart that leads the people roundly to denounce figures such as Nanga, whom they had so recently fawned over.

Of course, Salamu's disgust at the cynicism of his people is again ironic, given that it indicates, among other things, his own cynicism and inability to believe that the situation is improving. Indeed, critics such as Umelo Ojinmah have seen *A Man of the People* as a profoundly pessimistic book that shows Achebe's own despair at the worsening political situation in postcolonial Nigeria. It is certainly true that there are few indications in the book of any impending solution to the political morass that it depicts. On the other hand, there are some signs of hope in the final pages of the book, even if these signs themselves cannot be entirely trusted given that they come to us from Salamu, whose narration is never entirely objective. This is especially true given that these signs of hope have to do with certain potentially positive changes in Salamu's personal life. For one thing, he has at least begun to move toward a better relationship with his father, who has surprised him with the extent to which he has supported, however grudgingly, Salamu's right to contest the parliamentary election. To an extent, this suggestion that Salamu might, in the future, establish better relations with his father indicates a possibility that Salamu might eventually be able to overcome some of his other alienation from the traditions of his people. It might also lead to further self-recognition, given that Salamu's rejection of his father has largely to do with the fact that the elder Salamu worked as an interpreter for the British during the colonial era.

Salamu's relationship with his father is, in fact, a more important part of the book than might first appear. Hezekiah had apparently been much despised in Urua during Odili's childhood in the colonial era because he prospered as an interpreter for the British. He was thus (as such interpreters often were in British colonial Africa) regarded as a turn-coat who had colluded with the country's co-lonial rulers. Odili, in fact, has grown up with a certain sense of shame regarding his father, echoing the attitude of **Okonkwo** toward his father, **Unoka**, in *Things Fall Apart*. What the younger Salamu does not recognize, how-ever, is that his own thorough immersion in Western values represents a collaboration with foreign forces that is similar to, if more subtle than, his father's work for the British. In any case, by the present time of the book, Hezekiah seems to have been largely reha-bilitated, however, leading to his current po-

sition with the POP. That position, of course, suggests the additional possibility that some of Samalu's complex and contradictory atti-tude toward the older Nanga is influenced by an association in his unconscious mind be-tween Nanga and Hezekiah.

The fact that Salamu begins to doubt his earlier judgment of his father as a corrupt schemer can be taken as a sign that the nar-rator might be moving toward overcoming the radical alienation that has separated him from all of those around him during the novel. An even more promising suggestion that this alienation might be overcome re-sides in Salamu's growing relationship with Edna, who comes to his side in the hospital, having now been won over by his predica-ment and appalled by the violence that Nanga had called down upon him at the meeting. By the end of the book, in fact, Salamu and Edna are engaged to be married and have even managed to gain the blessing of her greedy father, **Odo**, who had so looked forward to having such a rich and powerful man as Nanga for a son-in-law.

Still, even this positive turn in Salamu's life is complicated by certain ironies. For one thing, in order to secure the blessing of Edna's father, Salamu has had to pay back to Nanga the 250 pounds he had invested in grooming Edna to be his wife. To an extent, then, Salamu might be seen as purchasing Edna's favors, a possible interpretation that gains force from the way in which prostitu-tion, at least in a figurative sense, functions throughout the novel as a metaphor for the way in which so many individuals in this postcolonial country seem willing to sell themselves for money. In the book, for ex-ample, Nanga seduces Elsie largely with the help of his shiny new Cadillac and literally pays a woman lawyer to have sex with him. Yet he himself is also a prostitute of sorts, seemingly willing to sell his favors to the highest bidder. Indeed, money, power, and sex, the three great goals of Nanga, seem almost inextricably intertwined not only in his mind but in the society at large, as can be seen in Salamu's own confusion regarding his motives with regard to Elsie. Meanwhile, Salamu's refund of Nanga's investment takes on an even greater irony from the fact that Salamu comes up with the money by "borrowing" it from official CPC funds, a questionable procedure at best. To top things off, the amount that he pays Nanga is 250 pounds—precisely the amount that Nanga had earlier offered him as a bribe. Thus, he offers Nanga the same bribe to withdraw from the contest for Edna that Nanga had earlier offered him to withdraw from the electoral contest.

A Man of the People was written shortly before postcolonial Nigeria's first military coup, in which (in January 1966) a group of **Igbo** military officers took control of the government, placing Major General Johnson T. U. Aguiyi-Ironsi in charge of the new military regime. This fact has led many critics to see the novel as prophetic and even led some, during the political confusion surrounding the coup, to charge that Achebe himself might have known about the impending Igbo-led coup or even been involved in planning it. Achebe vehemently denied such charges, which seem silly. As Gikandi points out, conditions in Nigeria when Achebe was writing the novel were such that virtually any observer could have seen that a crisis was approaching and that this crisis might lead to a coup (*Reading Chinua Achebe* 103–4). In any case, *A Man of the People* does show an acute understanding of the contemporary situation in Nigerian politics, engaging that situation in a profound and direct way, even though this engagement, as Gikandi also notes, tends to make the politics of the novel (which reflect the confusion of the time in Nigeria) seem a bit incoherent (105).

Nevertheless, much of the satire of *A Man*

of the People* is quite clear and very much on the mark, even if Achebe is not necessarily able to offer hopeful alternatives to the baleful practices he skewers in the novel. For example, Achebe's rejection of political corruption and of the popular apathy that makes it possible is unambiguous, and his suggestion that the best hope for the future lies in combining respect for indigenous traditions with a well-informed understanding of modern practices seems clear. Meanwhile, though Achebe's chief satirical targets in the book are corrupt African postcolonial politicians, he also suggests that the legacy of colonialism and the ongoing machinations of neocolonialism must bear part of the responsibility for this corruption. Thus, near the end of the book, we find that the cynicism that Samalu attributes to the general population arises largely from their inability to imagine a system that is not corrupt, given their past experience with colonialism. Samalu informs us that the popular attitude toward corrupt politicians is simply, "Let them eat." After all, during the colonial era, the country's foreign rulers did exactly such eating, yet "where is the all-powerful white man today? He came, he ate and he went. But we are still around" (145).

Of course, given the neocolonial situation described in the book, one place to find the white man is still in Africa, where Western forces continue to exert a considerable corrosive influence. The principal white characters in *A Man of the People* are **John** and **Jean**, an American couple who have come to Africa because he is serving as part of a team of foreign experts who have come to offer advice to the government on how to improve their public image in America, presumably to encourage further American investment in their country. However, it is also clear that such investment comes with considerable strings attached. Both the Americans and the British (largely through the corporate operations of British Amalgamated) continue to reap huge profits at the expense of the local populations, while at the same time offering tantalizing visions of wealth and glamour that are among the central enticements that lure local politicians into corruption. Indeed, the American and British interests in the book routinely further their own ends by securing the cooperation of the local government through bribery and flattery. For example, when the new parliamentary elections are called late in the book, both British Amalgmated and American interests make huge donations to the POP to help ensure that the cooperative ruling party will stay in power.

In this sense, both the British and the Americans appear in the book as looming powers, pulling strings behind the stage while offering dazzling and seductive public visions of capitalist wealth. However, Achebe makes it quite clear that the British and Americans who are exercising such influence in Africa are hardly godlike figures. Indeed, they are almost ludicrous in their arrogant assumption of their own superiority and in their ignorance of African culture. John and Jean, in particular, are comic figures who come in for some of the book's funniest satire. Samalu, for example, is quite shocked in chapter 4 when he hears the Americans address Chief Nanga by his first name, despite their young age and the minister's lofty position. Then again, what is even more shocking is that Nanga, who sometimes seems to fawn on foreigners almost as much as his own constituency fawns on him, seems to be pleased and honored to be on such familiar terms with the two Americans.

In this and other ways, Nanga is the prototypical postcolonial bourgeois leader described in the important work of **Frantz Fanon**, especially in *The Wretched of the Earth*, where Fanon issues stern warnings that the coming of independence will not lead easily and naturally to freedom in Africa be-

cause the new black African leaders will have been trained to behave very much in the same way as their white European forebears. In fact, this change of leadership might in many ways make the situation even worse. At least the European colonial rulers were members of a genuine bourgeoisie, descendants of the class that had swept into power in Europe in probably the most dynamic historical struggle in all of world history. The new African bourgeoisie, on the other hand, are merely mimic men, attempting to behave like their European predecessors but lacking their historical background in historical struggle and assuming power not as an energetic revolutionary class but as already decadent lackeys of foreign powers.

John, meanwhile, comes off as the prototypical ugly American, bragging loudly of his country's greatness and assuring his African hosts of America's benevolence and lack of racism. Thus, in his first conversation with Samalu (carried on while Jean flirts shamelessly with Nanga in the background), John proudly brags that lynching in America is on the wane and was never really racially motivated in the first place. Thus, he displays his arrogant confidence in American superiority by offering up some of the ugliest and most reprehensible racial crimes in world history as evidence of the virtues of America. John then goes on to offer, as another bit of evidence of American generosity, the fact that his country did not drop an atomic bomb on Moscow after World War II, ignoring the fact that the Americans and Soviets had been allies during the war and that the Soviets had actually been principally responsible for the defeat of fascism in that war (45–46). Indeed, John expresses surprise (and perhaps even regret) that no such bombing occurred, suggesting that Americans are probably just too naive in their desire to avoid interfering in the affairs of others—even as he sits in an Africa where Americans like himself are busily involved in manipulating local affairs for their own gain.

Meanwhile, John's obliviousness to politics extends into his personal life as well. As he talks with Samalu, he seems entirely unaware of Jean's flirtation with Nanga. For her own part, Jean seems to have no conception of marital infidelity, and it is no particular surprise that she later seduces Samalu the first chance she gets. That she carries out this seduction while dancing an exaggerated version of the **high-life**, while clearly regarding her dancing as authentically African in style, suggests her own arrogant ignorance of African culture. Meanwhile, Samalu is somewhat taken aback by her very cavalier attitude toward sex, as when she calmly carries on a telephone conversation with a friend while Samalu still lies atop her. Yet Jean then promptly claims that sex means much more to a woman than to a man, showing a complete lack of awareness of the contradiction between this statement and her own attitude, a lack, of course, that echoes the one Samalu repeatedly demonstrates in the book.

On the other hand, Samalu does, at times, seem on the verge of moving toward self-recognition. One of the most telling moments in *A Man of the People* occurs during a scene in chapter 11 in which Samalu, having declared his candidacy for parliament in opposition to Nanga, speeds across the countryside in an automobile (a brand-new Volkswagen—a car of the people for a budding man of the people) supplied to him by the CPC for his use during the campaign. Realizing the irony that he had very recently traversed this same territory on a bicycle, Samalu experiences a revelatory moment that provides one of the crucial indications that, late in the book, he is beginning to learn and mature in ways that might prevent him from traveling down the slippery slope into becoming another Nanga. In particular, the car reminds him of a time during his days as a

university student when he had become completely enamored of the notion of owning a car, that ultimate symbol of postcolonial privilege (and, not entirely coincidentally, perhaps the central symbol of American wealth and prestige worldwide). Meanwhile, his dream of owing a car had been informed by his typical alertness to sexual opportunities: the model he picked out had seats that fully reclined into a bed, a feature that he identifies in his later narration as a central selling point.

At the time of his earlier fascination with the automobile, a bout of idealism, triggered partly by his radical Irish lecturer in history, had interrupted Samalu's dreams of car ownership, causing him to realize that he was in danger of suffering the same fate as a former radical student leader (once a "fire-eating" president of the Student Union) who had by then joined the government, becoming an "ice-cream eating Permanent Secretary in the Ministry of Labour and Production." The man had also become a wealthy and corrupt landlord and a bitter opponent of trade unions, completely betraying his earlier principles and leading Samalu and his fellow students to demonstrate against him and burn him in effigy. Now, as Samalu drives his Volkswagen several years later, he wonders if he is really immune to the lures of wealth, power, and shiny cars, musing proverbially to himself that "a man who avoids danger for years and then gets killed in the end has wasted his care" (110–11).

However, Samalu quickly puts these thoughts out his mind when he receives what he interprets as an encouraging letter from Edna. He then proceeds in his campaign against Nanga, leading to the events of the remainder of the book. Those events are themselves inconclusive. As the book ends, we are not sure what the future holds for the country under its new military regime. Nor are we entirely sure what is in store for Samalu and Edna. What we do know is that the country is in deep trouble that only strong, courageous, and selfless leadership will have any chance to overcome. Ultimately, then, *A Man of the People* can be taken as a plea for such leadership, which can itself be taken as a sign that Achebe, even in the dark times in which he was writing, had not given up on the future of the Nigerian nation.

FURTHER READING

David Carroll, *Chinua Achebe*; Frantz Fanon, *The Wretched of the Earth*; Simon Gikandi, *Reading Chinua Achebe*; C. L. Innes, *Chinua Achebe*; G. D. Killam, *The Writings of Chinua Achebe*; Wolfgang Klooss, "Chinua Achebe: A Chronicler of Historical Change in Africa"; Bernth Lindfors, "Achebe's African Parable"; Umelo Ojinmah, *Chinua Achebe: New Perspectives*; Chinwe Christiana Okechukwu, *Achebe the Orator*; Kwadwo Osei-Nyame Jr., "Gender, Nationalism and the Fictions of Identity in Chinua Achebe's *A Man of the People*"; Onyemaechi Udumukwu, "Ideology and the Dialectics of Action."

M. Keith Booker

A MAN OF THE PEOPLE (COMIC STRIP). In terms of critical reception, Achebe's *A Man of the People* has stood in the shadow of his other novels, such as *Things Fall Apart* and *Arrow of God*. It is as if the enthusiastic reception of Achebe's brilliant accounts of traditional **Igbo** society and the colonial encounter had left no room for a proper appreciation of his trenchant description and penetrating analysis of postcolonial **Nigeria**. But without doubt *A Man of the People* continues, more than three decades after its publication, to offer one of the finest fictional analyses of electoral politics in Africa. *A Man of the People* is also virtually unique in having been translated into a comic strip. That strip appeared in *New Nigerian*, a major national daily newspaper in Nigeria in the 1970s as the country prepared for a return to democratic rule, testimony to the pertinence of Achebe's creation for an apprecia-

tion of the difficulties faced by parliamentary democracy in the new African nations. With the emergence of a wide array of democracy movements across the continent following Benin's "Velvet Revolution" in 1990, *A Man of the People* has taken on renewed relevance.

A Man of the People, though nominally set in a fictional African country, poignantly describes the grassroots level politics of Nigeria's short-lived First Republic, serves as an excellent analysis of the failure of representative electoral regimes in newly independent Africa, and stands as a prophetic tale that predicted developments in Nigeria with uncanny accuracy. As we come to know the novel's protagonists—the government minister **Chief Nanga** defending his privileged position, the opportunistic teacher (and narrator) **Odili Samalu**, and a population cynical and complicit—we begin to understand the sources of corruption and violence. Achebe focuses on human foibles, and he makes us see them as part of the human condition. We sympathize with the immediate concerns of poor villagers, we smile at the teacher's self-deprecating account of his opportunism, and we appreciate that the minister is loath to relinquish his newfound position and riches. Achebe shows us furthermore that the new state, unlike the village community, has no effective institutional mechanisms to control human greed and the lust for power.

A reading that claims that the aims and principles of the democratic system hurriedly installed by the colonial regime as it got ready to leave are not understood by the electorate, or if understood not supported (Booth 106), misses the point. The voters understand perfectly well that politicians allocate resources and seek to maximize their share. Of course, electorates everywhere are swayed by their perceived self-interest. But in a largely peasant society self-interest tends to be community-focused in terms of the government providing infrastructure and services. Achebe's peasants compete for the allocation of resources to their local communities, and they are backed up by many of their sons who work in the cities but remain deeply involved in rural affairs. Conflicts over the allocation of resources thus opposed the representatives of villages, of village groups, of states in the Federation of Nigeria. Such politics may be characterized as "ethnic" if it is understood that the identities of many of the competing groups bear little relationship to pre-colonial social or cultural entities.

A Man of the People is Achebe's most Nigerian novel, at least prior to the publication of *Anthills of the Savannah* two decades later, in that it is most clearly addressed to his fellow Nigerians—not least in the irritation expressed about the deference shown arrogant foreigners. To Nigerians, Achebe emphasizes the degradation of the Nigerian polity but does not dwell on countervailing forces. Thus, his account of a new radical party, the **Common People's Convention (CPC)**, remains sketchy. He seeks to shock his Nigerian readers out of cynicism and apathy with an account of the dismal reality, rather than offering a guide to a better future. This strategy entailed the risk of contributing to a negative image of Africa overseas at a time when many well-wishers were still optimistic about the continent's future.

The persuasive power of this, as of Achebe's earlier novels, resides in the fact that he presents us with differentiated characters, humans with their strengths and weaknesses—more weaknesses than strengths in the free-for-all of newly independent Nigeria. Even the roguish Nanga is a rather likable rogue. These characters come alive in a rich dialogue whose very language is finely attuned to the circumstances: ranging from an African language, presumably Igbo, to **pidgin English**, to formal English. The novel's appeal is heightened by the irony that pervades

it and by numerous finely wrought incidents of comedy.

A Man of the People also stands as the classic example of a novel describing and analyzing a political situation so accurately as to correctly anticipate its outcome. It depicts a military coup only months before the first actual military takeover of Nigeria's government. Indeed, Achebe even has Samalu reflect that a coup might be followed by a counter-coup, while Nigeria had its second military coup within six months, the first consecutive army coup anywhere in Africa.

A Man of the People was serialized as a comic strip in the *New Nigerian*. Beginning on September 30, 1974, the strip was published three times a week, the 150th and last strip appearing in October 1975. Two days before the strip began, the paper's front page carried a statement by Achebe. It is a rare occasion when a man of letters makes it to the front page of a daily, and in this case the author provided an excellent assessment of his own novel. Achebe stated that

> *A Man of the People* has often been described as a story of the corruption of politicians. I prefer to see it as a novel of political corruption. I featured politicians in it because they were handy in 1964–65 when the book was written. If I wrote today the dramatis personae in all likelihood would be in uniform.

The comic strip of *A Man of the People* was designed by Oke Hortons. It is best characterized as a serialized graphic novel rather than the conventional and less cumbersome "comic strip" I use here. Hortons created an accomplished work. The various characters come alive, the dialogue is well integrated with the design, and brief statements preceding many of the strips effectively contextualize them. Hortons reproduced the entire novel, not just the principal elements of the story but also most of the incidental events.

He packed a lot of text into many of his strips, Still, he reduced the novel's approximate 65,000 words to about 10,000 words. While he reproduced verbatim much of the dialogue, some was lost. More importantly, the shift in medium entailed major changes. Pictures, of course, can speak volumes, but the voice of the narrator does not readily lend itself to such transformation. Occasionally, Samalu's account is translated into speech, but we miss his recollections of the past and his reflections on the present. Paradoxically, the presumably less educated reader of the comic gets less guidance than the reader of the novel.

The greatest loss in the move to the comic strip is the absence of the narrator's reflection on the new rulers, a key element in Achebe's analysis of post-independence politics. However, Hortons does present the complementary element in Achebe's analysis, a population that goes along with corrupt politicians to get a share of the spoils. (His verbatim rendering of most of two speeches—the leader of Odili's party introducing him as the local candidate for parliament and the response of a local representative—can be found on the fifth page of the photo essay following page 160 of this work.)

The publication of a comic strip based on Achebe's novel in the *New Nigerian* was a remarkable event. The paper is one of the major national daily newspapers, government-owned and published in Kaduna in northern Nigeria. The publication began less than five years after the end of the bitter **Nigerian Civil War**. Achebe had been identified with the cause of **Biafra**, the secessionist republic that had defied the federal government in which northern Nigeria held a powerful place. Eventually, he had become an active ambassador for the Biafran cause.

If the very publication of the comic strip could thus be seen as testimony to an effective policy of reconciliation, its political thrust appeared well timed. The first comic strip and Achebe's statement preceding the publication of the strip, appeared while Nigeria prepared for elections and civilian rule. The military government had led the country to expect that it would hand over power to an elected government in 1976. In this context the strip could be seen as a salutary tale of the consequences of corruption and violence, as a warning against repeating the sort of politics that had characterized the First Republic and led to its demise. However, on October 1, one day after the first strip, the Head of State, General Yakubu Gowon, announced that the return to civilian rule would be delayed. Now the strip was likely to be read as a justification that extended military rule was required until the country could be entrusted to politicians again. Such a reading was fostered by the last frame, which highlights what the novel mentions only in passing: it has an army officer concluding the announcement of the coup with the statement: "All public servants who defrauded the state will be tried." Gowon's October 1 statement had not been altogether unexpected, and we are left to speculate about the motives that prompted the publication of the comic strip: to prepare for better civilian rule? Or to discourage the return to civilian rule?

FURTHER READING

James Booth, *Writers and Politics in Nigeria*; Larry Diamond, *Class, Ethnicity and Democracy in Nigeria*; Wolfgang Klooss, "Chinua Achebe: A Chronicler of Historical Change in Africa"; Bernth Lindfors, "Achebe's African Parable"; Gerald Moore, *Twelve African Writers*.

Josef Gugler

MARK. In chapter 5 of *No Longer at Ease*, the "houseboy" of **Obi Okonkwo**'s friend **Joseph Okeke**. Joseph did not go to secondary school partly because "his parents were poor" (chapter 2), and he is not a wealthy man, but he is a government clerk and so wealthy enough by Nigerian standards to be able to afford a houseboy. As with other houseboys referred to in the novel, Achebe hints at the harshness of Mark's subservient position and duties. Prior to Obi's departure for England, when he visits Joseph in **Lagos**, Joseph's houseboy (not identified here as Mark) is understood to sleep on a mat on the floor in Joseph's single-room apartment whereas Joseph sleeps on a bed (chapter 2). Once Obi returns from England and has a meal with Joseph in his room, Mark goes to the store to obtain two bottles of ice water for them and "carr[ied] all the way and back a smudge of soot at the tip of his nose. His eyes were a little red and watery from blowing the fire with his breath" (chapter 5).

Thomas J. Lynn

MARK, ELSIE, a young **Igbo** woman in *No Longer at Ease* who is desperate for a university scholarship. In chapter 9, not long after Obi is appointed Secretary to the Scholarship Board, Elsie's brother, **Mr. Mark**, attempts to offer **Obi Okonkwo** a bribe on her behalf in Obi's office. Later the same day Miss Mark appears at Obi's apartment intending to offer herself to him, also as a bribe. **Christopher**, who is Obi's friend as well as a philanderer, later calls Obi "the biggest ass in Nigeria" (137) for not obliging Miss Mark. The incident with her is the first but not the last time that Obi will be offered a sexual bribe—and later in the novel he succumbs. By depicting this form of bribery Achebe suggests that the practice of bribery is a moral failing, not merely a type of business transaction.

Thomas J. Lynn

MARK, MR., an **Igbo** character in *No Longer at Ease*, used up his family's money for a protracted but unsuccessful education in England. He goes to **Obi Okonkwo's** office in chapter 9 in order to bribe Obi on behalf of his sister, **Elsie Mark**. This first attempt

to bribe Obi takes place a fairly short time after Obi is appointed Secretary to the Scholarship Board, a governmental administrative position in **Lagos**.

Thomas J. Lynn

MARKET DAYS. In the **Igbo** traditional calendar, there are four market days that constitute the Igbo week. They are used to reckon time and to label dates. There is always a principal market day that varies by village. The names are uniform across most of Igboland: **Afo**, **Nkwo**, **Eke**, and **Oye**.

Rachel R. Reynolds

MARX, KARL (1818–1883), German thinker whose philosophies of history and economics have made him one of the most important and influential intellectual figures in world history. Marx was principally concerned with developing a detailed theoretical understanding of the driving forces behind history, which he found to be primarily economic. Much of Marx's work was aimed at explaining the historical foundations of the system of capitalism, during his lifetime still solidifying its dominance in Europe. Employing a dialectical methodology influenced by the work of the German idealist philosopher **G.W.F. Hegel** (but otherwise rejecting most of Hegel's ideas), Marx developed a model of history as driven by economic antagonism between competing social classes, an antagonism that could end only with the establishment of a classless socialist society in which all individuals had equal status.

Having been expelled from his native Germany because of what was perceived as the dangerous nature of his work, Marx settled in London in 1849 and spent his subsequent career in an England in which the Industrial Revolution was at its height. Working in this environment, Marx conducted extensive critiques of what he saw as the shortcomings and injustices of capitalism, concluding that certain inherent flaws in the capitalist system would inevitably lead to its downfall. Marx also elaborated a scenario through which this downfall might occur as a result of a revolutionary uprising of the working class, or proletariat, a unique new historical class produced by capitalism itself. After this revolution, Marx hoped for the establishment of a new socialist system based on just and equitable treatment of all individuals.

Marx had already become an important thinker by his mid-twenties with the writing of the *Economic and Philosophical Manuscripts of 1844*, in which he detailed a number of aspects of the emergent capitalist system, including the important phenomenon of alienation. For Marx, capitalism by its nature alienated workers from the products of their labor, contributing to a general system through which individuals are estranged from the world around them, other individuals, and even themselves. In 1848, in response to the revolutions that were then sweeping Europe, Marx and his frequent collaborator, Friedrich Engels, published the most concise and accessible statement of their vision of history as driven by the conflict between social classes. In *The Communist Manifesto*, Marx and Engels outlined their respect for the historical triumphs of the European bourgeoisie, as well as their contempt for the growing decadence and hypocrisy of that class, whose rule they felt would be ended by the inevitable collapse of capitalism, which carried within it the seeds of its own destruction. During his decades working in London, Marx wrote and published indefatigably, producing a large number of texts, the most important of which is *Das Kapital*, a massive and magisterial exposition of the economic basis of capitalism, published in three volumes in 1867, 1885, and 1894, the latter two volumes appearing posthumously under the supervision of Engels.

Marx, in his own writing, often referred to literature to illustrate points he was making. Indeed, despite the political, historical, and economic emphasis of their work, Marx and Engels are also among the central figures in the history of literary theory and criticism because their work suggests that literature and culture are integral parts of the totality of society, closely connected to broader social, political, and historical phenomena. Marxism is particularly relevant to the study of African literature, partly because Marxist theory (which includes detailed explorations of imperialism and colonialism as natural consequences of capitalism) has been crucial to the development of **postcolonial studies**, and partly because Marxist ideas have been so important in the evolution of African thought during the late colonial and postcolonial periods.

Critics such as Emmanuel Ngara and Georg Gugelberger have rightly called attention to the important influence of Marxism on African literature. Meanwhile, the African philosopher V. Y. Mudimbe notes that, while African thought from the 1930s to the 1950s was informed by a number of important influences, Marxism was clearly the most important of these (90). Further, Mudimbe notes that (while he himself works from a somewhat Foucauldian perspective) Marxism, along with a more general critique of imperialism, remains the most vital force in African philosophy to this day. Figures such as Aimé Césaire, Leopold Senghor, Kwame Nkrumah, Julius Nyerere, Patrice Lumumba, Amilcar Cabral, Chris Hani, and Agostinho Neto all made important contributions in the attempt to adapt socialist ideas to an African context, working and fighting from Marxist-inspired positions in their attempts to build a modern, independent Africa.

African novelists have drawn considerable energy from the work of all of these important thinkers and leaders. Marx himself was a forward-looking critic of colonialism, arguing consistently that no one in Europe could be considered free until the European empires had also freed their colonial subjects. African thinkers have also significantly contributed to the expansion of the Marxist tradition to include the special perspectives of the colonial and postcolonial worlds. For example, the single figure who probably looms largest as a theoretical inspiration for radical African novelists is the Martinique-born psychoanalyst, political theorist, and anticolonial activist **Frantz Fanon**. Fanon's various writings, especially *The Wretched of the Earth*, present an impassioned elaboration, during the last decade of European colonial rule in Africa, of the historical conditions of anticolonial struggle. Fanon also effectively articulates the role to be played by intellectuals in this struggle, while providing stern (and prescient, as it turned out) warnings of the difficulties that would face emerging African nations once independence had been won. Fanon's work is situated firmly within the Marxist tradition. However, while that tradition itself resides largely within the framework of the European Enlightenment, Fanon considerably expands that framework to include African and Caribbean perspectives.

Achebe has not been as heavily influenced by Marxist ideas as many other prominent African writers, such as Kenya's **Ngugi wa Thiong'o**, Senegal's Ousmane Sembène, and South Africa's Alex La Guma. However, though Achebe, in *A Man of the People* and (to a lesser extent) *Anthills of the Savannah*, satirizes African intellectuals who have been influenced by Marxism, his hostility to Marxism certainly does not rival the anticommunist hysteria that informed the mind-set of many in the West during the Cold War. Indeed, the work of Fanon, as critics such as **Simon Gikandi** have pointed out, provides an extremely valuable framework within which to read *A Man of the People*, which explores many of the same ideas.

FURTHER READING

M. Keith Booker, "Writing for the Wretched of the Earth"; Terry Eagleton and Drew Milne, eds., *Marxist Literary Theory: A Reader*; Frantz Fanon, *The Wretched of the Earth*; Simon Gikandi, *Reading Chinua Achebe*; Georg M. Gugelberger, ed., *Marxism and African Literature*; David McLellan, *Karl Marx*; V. Y. Mudimbe, *The Invention of Africa*; Emmanuel Ngara, *Art and Ideology in the African Novel*; Robert C. Tucker, ed., *The Marx-Engels Reader*.

M. Keith Booker

MARXISM. See Marx, Karl.

MARXIST CRITICISM. One of the major branches of literary and cultural criticism, fundamentally inspired by the writings of **Karl Marx** and Friedrich Engels but having, by the late twentieth century, established an extremely rich and diverse tradition that draws upon numerous sources in its attempt to elaborate the social, political, and historical significance of literature and culture. Because postcolonial literature, arising from colonization and subsequent decolonization, is inherently engaged with the historical process, Marxist approaches have proved especially useful to a critical understanding of that literature. Meanwhile, Marxist theory has provided one of the central underpinnings to the emergent field of postcolonial studies.

FURTHER READING

M. Keith Booker, "Marxist Literary Criticism"; Terry Eagleton, *Marxism and Literary Criticism*; Terry Eagleton and Drew Milne, eds., *Marxist Literary Theory: A Reader*; Georg M. Gugelberger, ed., *Marxism and African Literature*; Emmanuel Ngara, *Art and Ideology in the African Novel*.

M. Keith Booker

MARY, a highly devout Christian friend of **Hannah Okonkwo** and a leading participant at the prayer meeting and feast marking **Obi Okonkwo**'s departure from **Umuofia** in the first chapter of *No Longer at Ease*. Mary leads the entire company in prayer, reflecting the Umuofia Christian community's observance of egalitarian principles, as does the singing of a devotional song, "Leave me not behind Jesus," by the women. This song, which at its conclusion improvises a petition for Obi when he is in "the White Man's Country," is commenced at the gathering by Mary and was rehearsed by the women at their own prayer meeting. Although she lives miles away and must walk in every kind of weather, Mary never misses the early morning prayer at **St. Mark's Anglican Church**.

Thomas J. Lynn

MASK. Rituals involving masked dancers (usually representing departed ancestors of the clan) are an important part of traditional **Igbo** culture, and the often highly colorful masks (which may be facial coverings or entire costumes) that these (male) dancers wear can themselves be important works of art. The word "mask" may refer to this costume, to the dancer, or to the entire ritual. Achebe discusses the centrality of the mask, or masquerade, to Igbo culture in his essay "The Igbo World and Its Art," contained in *Hopes and Impediments*.

FURTHER READING

Kalu Ogbaa, *Gods, Oracles, and Divination*; Keith Ray and Rosalind Shaw, "The Structure of Spirit Embodiment in Nsukka Igbo Masquerading Traditions"; Robert M. Wren, *Achebe's World*.

M. Keith Booker

MASQUERADE. See **Mask**.

MATEFI, Ezeulu's senior surviving wife and the mother of **Obika** (son) and **Ojiugo** (daughter). Matefi doesn't show the gener-

osity to children of the compound that is normally expected, and she is jealous of her husband's other wife and their children.

Rachel R. Reynolds

MBAINO. In *Things Fall Apart*, a neighboring village that is sometimes at odds with the villages of **Umuofia**. In chapter 1, war looms between Mbaino and Umuofia, much to the chagrin of the cowardly **Unoka**. In chapter 3, another war threatens when the wife of Ogbuefi **Udo**, from Umuofia, is killed in the market at Mbaino. This war is averted when the people of Mbaino send to Udo a young virgin to replace the murdered wife. They also send a fifteen-year-old boy, **Ikemefuna**, who is to bear the brunt of the punishment for the crime, in which his father has taken a hand.

Mbaino is also alluded to in chapters 5, 8, and 14 of *No Longer at Ease*. In chapter 5 it becomes a point of reference in a vivid dialogue between **Isaac Okonkwo** and two other men of Umuofia. Isaac argues that certain supernatural powers instigated by men following traditional cultural beliefs are illusions inspired by Satan. One of Isaac's interlocutors, an old man, observes that Umuofia "elders say that thunder cannot kill a son or daughter of Umuofia," and they also observe that nobody in Umuofia, past or present, can be recalled who was so killed. All of this he attributes not, as Isaac opines, to "the work of God," but to "the work of our forefathers [who] built a powerful medicine. . . ." The third man gives the example of **Nwokeke**, an Umuofia man who survived being "hit by thunder last year. All his skin peeled off like snake slough, but he was not killed." To Isaac's remark that if the "medicine" really worked, Nwokeke "should not have been hit at all," the third man replies not only that this "is a matter between him and his *chi*," but that Nwokeke "was hit in Mbaino and not at home. Perhaps the thunder, seeing him at Mbaino, called him an Mbaino man at first."

In chapter 8 of the novel a member of the **Umuofia Progressive Union** refers to "that bad bush between Umuofia and Mbaino," while in chapter 14 **Obi Okonkwo** tells **Isaac** that Okeke of Mbaino is the father of the woman (**Clara Okeke**) whom Obi wishes to marry. Isaac replies that he " 'know[s] about three' " men named Okeke, but it is not clear whether he means that all are from Mbaino. Isaac refers in particular to a retired teacher named Okeke, and Obi responds that he is, indeed, the man in question, namely, **Josiah Okeke**.

M. Keith Booker

MBANTA, a neighboring village to **Umuofia**, lying just beyond the borders of **Mbaino** in *Things Fall Apart*. Mbanta is the traditional home of the family of the mother of **Okonkwo**, and it is to Mbanta that he and his family are exiled for seven years after Okonkwo's gun is responsible for the accidental death of the son of **Ezeudu** during the funeral ceremonies for the latter in chapter 13.

M. Keith Booker

MBARI, a traditional institution peculiar to Owerri people of **Nigeria**, linked to the veneration of the Earth Deity. Every once in a while, the Earth Goddess ordains the creation of an mbari—a collection of statues and other artistically forged figures, all in kneaded special clay. This special clay is actually taken from anthills that the young men and women who make up the select group of mbari "inmates" collect from the farmlands. The inmates are picked by the priest or priestess of the Earth Goddess, following specific directions from the Earth Goddess herself. The chosen youth are secluded in an enclosure with dwelling places constructed for their particular use during their twelve or more months in seclusion. Their assignment is to "document" the events, past and present, of the town or village. This "documentation" takes the form of molding statues and other figures in clay. The finishing touch is painting the figures in multiple colors of white, black, red, and yellow. The entire mbari is housed in a large, half-walled hall, in which the steps holding the figures are arranged as in a stadium. When the mbari is ready to be seen by the public, the inmates stage a dance to which everybody in the town and neighboring towns is invited. The exhibition goes on for months or until people get tired of going to see it. Some mbari houses still stand in parts of Owerri region, but the construction of mbari at the dictates of the Earth Goddess is no longer in practice.

Chinua came to know of mbari when he was spending his last year of primary school at Nekede Central School in Owerri. The way he described an mbari "museum" shows that he must have visited an mbari exhibit in the area. In 1961, a group of writers and fine artists in Nigeria launched an "Artists" Club. Chinua suggested Mbari as the name of their club, and the group adopted it. The reason behind the choice was that mbari embodied both the functional and aesthetic dimensions of African art. Mbari Club ceased to exist with the outbreak of the **Nigerian Civil War** in 1967. Later in his literary career, Chinua would fall back on his experience to create out of the mbari tradition a powerful metaphor of inclusion and acknowledgment of every presence in human society. He uses the mbari analogy to demonstrate how the African acknowledges and celebrates every presence in his world. He equally uses mbari as a counterfoil to the Western concept of art.

FURTHER READING

Chinua Achebe, "The Igbo World and Its Art," in *Hopes and Impediments*; "African Literature as Celebration," *African Commentary*, November

1989; Phanuel A. Egejuru, *Chinua Achebe Pure and Simple*.

Phanuel Akubueze Egejuru

MBARI CLUB. Cultural organization cofounded by Achebe at **Ibadan** in 1961 to further the work of writers and artists in the area. See also **Foundations**.

MEDANI, CAPTAIN ABDUL, a military officer who brings **Beatrice Okoh** the news of **Chris Oriko**'s death in chapter 18 of *Anthills of the Savannah*. When he does so, she recognizes him as the officer who earlier (chapter 13) led a group of soldiers in conducting a search of her flat. He begins to spend time with Beatrice and her friends, and, though later admitting that he has been officially assigned to watch them, he also develops a certain sense of solidarity with them.

M. Keith Booker

MEMBOLU'S WIDOW is a character in *Arrow of God* who lives on the road between **Umuachala** and **Umuezeani**.

Rachel R. Reynolds

MERCY, like **Joy**, is one of the distant relatives of Obi Okonkwo's mother, **Hannah Okonkwo**, in *No Longer at Ease*, chapter 14. Joy has been sent by her parents to live with the Okonkwo family so that Hannah can provide her with the training she needs to keep a home.

Thomas J. Lynn

MGBA AGBOGHO, a feast (also called the "Wrestling of the Maidens") held by the people of **Umuaro** (*Arrow of God*, chapter 17).

Rachel R. Reynolds

MGBAFO, the wife of **Uzowulu** in *Things Fall Apart*. In chapter 10, she and her two children are taken from her husband's home by her brothers because the husband frequently beats her. **Evil Forest**, the leader of the *egwugwu* who gather to adjudicate the case, ordains that Mgbafo be returned to her husband after he pays a penance of wine to the in-laws.

M. Keith Booker

MGBOGO. Along with **Udenkwo**, one of two women in chapter 12 of *Things Fall Apart* who fail to heed a call for help when a cow has accidentally been let loose on a neighbor's crops. Mgbogo does not appear because she is ill.

M. Keith Booker

MISSIONARIES. It was some years into **Okwonko**'s banishment from his village of **Umuofia**, in Achebe's first novel *Things Fall Apart*, that his friend **Obierika** visited him with the news that the "missionaries had come to Umuofia." What is more, they had "built their church there, won a handful of converts and were already sending evangelists to the surrounding towns and villages." But these first missionaries, although they succeeded in attracting into their midst Okonkwo's first son, **Nwoye**, were not considered as immediately threatening by the villagers. Soon, however, there were stories that the "white man had not only brought a religion but also a government." But even these innovations were not totally rejected by the people, for although the "white man had indeed brought a lunatic religion, . . . he had also built a trading store and for the first time palm-oil and kernel become things of great price, and much money flowed into Umuofia" (*Things Fall Apart*). Christianity, civilization, commerce, in other words: the "three Cs" of British imperialism heralded by one of the most famous missionaries of all—David Livingstone.

So famous would Livingstone become as exemplary of the missionary zeal of empire that well into the twentieth century a book on the life of the evangelist-explorer was the standard prize for nearly every student at a Protestant missionary school throughout the English-speaking world. Livingstone spent his early years as a child factory worker, was ordained in 1840 by the London Missionary Society (LMS), and arrived the following year in South Africa, where he joined Robert Moffat's LMS mission in Kuruman, just south of the Kalahari, and married Moffat's daughter Mary, who accompanied her husband on several of his African expeditions but returned to England in 1852 with their children. As Livingstone described to an audience at Cambridge University in 1857, the missionary's work in Africa required of him a zeal for exploration as well as evangelism, and, thus, after a number of years in southern Africa, he told his rapt listeners: "I resolved to go into the country beyond, and soon found that, for the purposes of commerce, it was necessary to have a path to the sea. I might have gone on instructing the natives in religion, but as civilization and Christianity must go on together, I was obliged to find a path to the sea, in order that I should not sink to the level of the natives." And so it happened that Livingstone became the first European to cross the African continent from coast to coast. He also became a national hero and on his death in 1873 was buried in Westminster Cathedral.

Missionaries, however, continued—and continue—to ply their trade across Africa and to make recurrent appearances in Achebe's novels after their arrival in Umuofia during Okonkwo's exile. They directly influence events in *Arrow of God*, set in a Nigeria of the 1920s, and they are still influential on the new rulers of independent Nigeria who had passed through missionary schools on their way to worldly power in *A Man of the People, No Longer at Ease*, and *Anthills of the Savannah*. As Achebe described their work in an August 2000 interview with Katie Bacon of *The Atlantic Monthly*, "The society of Umuofia, the village in *Things Fall Apart*, was totally disrupted by the coming of the European government, missionary Christianity, and so on. That was not a temporary disturbance; it was a once and for all alteration of their society."

FURTHER READING

Katie Bacon, "An African Voice"; National Portrait Gallery, *David Livingstone and the Victorian Encounter with Africa*.

Barbara Harlow

MISTER JOHNSON (1939), the fourth and last of the Anglo-Irishman **Joyce Cary**'s novels set in Africa, made into a film in 1991. Because the title character and presumed protagonist of the novel is an African, many saw the novel, on its initial publication, as a significant step forward in the sympathetic fictional portrayal of Africans in European fiction. However, Achebe has made clear (as in a 1964 interview with Lewis Nkosi and in his own essay, "Named for Victoria, Queen of England") his own negative reaction to *Mister Johnson*, which he has called "appalling." Indeed, Cary's caricatured and one-dimensional portrayal of his eponymous protagonist is precisely the kind of racist image—even though Cary drew it with liberal intentions—that spurred Achebe to write. On the other hand, in reading *Arrow of God* one realizes that Achebe may have learned something from Cary even as he despised his novels in the main, since Achebe's nuanced depiction of the life of the colonial administrators on Government Hill is quite congruent with Cary's. Be that as it may, the relationship between *Arrow of God* and *Mister Johnson* is never one of imitation or, surprisingly, of outright negation. The relationship between the two novels comes out most clearly in the road-building scene in *Arrow of God*, which rewrites a similar scene in Mister Johnson. In the earlier work, Johnson plays the role of overseer, translator, and intermediary between Rudbeck and the laborers, while in *Arrow of God* these roles are occupied by **Moses Unachukwu** and **Mr. Wright**. In *Mister Johnson* we are given one perspective on the scene, a perspective that is all the more problematic in that it presents itself as omniscient, despite its limited view. In *Arrow of God*, however, Achebe presents us with a kaleidoscope of perspectives, all communicated in the third person by a masterful manipulation of the various linguistic registers in which the various characters speak to each other or past each other. In this scene the utter poverty of Cary's version becomes apparent. Still, in Wright, Achebe preserves Cary's Rudbeck with surprising sympathy. We are made to see that from Wright's limited perspective he has no choice but to look at Moses Unachukwu and see Mister Johnson. For a more detailed reading of the relationship between *Mister Johnson* and *Arrow of God*, see *Arrow of God*.

FURTHER READING

Stephen Criswell, "Colonialism, Corruption, and Culture"; Michael T. Harris, *Outsiders and Insiders*; C. L. Innes, *Chinua Achebe*; Abdul R. JanMohamed, *Manichean Aesthetics*; Lewis Nkosi, "Conversation with Chinua Achebe."

Nicholas Brown

MOLOKWU. Molokwu is the missionary teacher at **Umuaro** who is transferred to **Okperi** in *Arrow of God*, chapter 4. He also serves as catechist in Umuaro at a point when there are no priests available, and he is part of a group of **missionaries** who are the first of three to successfully convert some of the people of Umuaro.

Rachel R. Reynolds

MORNING YET ON CREATION DAY: ESSAYS (1975) captures Achebe's major contributions to critical debates on postcolonial African literature and its aesthetics between 1961 and 1974. That African literature, particularly the novel, is still in the formative stages of becoming, is suggested by the collection's title. That its future will be shaped by those critical debates charges Achebe's fifteen essays with urgency and conviction. Part I opens with **"Colonialist Criticism"** (1974), presenting key tenets of Achebe's aesthetics. Achebe attacks the racist arrogance and ignorance of "colonialist" criticism and challenges Eurocentric notions of universality and art for art's sake misdirecting many African writers and critics. Any literature should "speak of a particular place, evolve out of the necessities of its history . . . and the aspirations and destiny of its people" (11). Critics should apply distinctly African aesthetics, appropriate to African contexts and worldviews, to understand and appreciate the "unheard of things" that African writers do with colonizers' languages and genres (10) and the literary "earnestness" derived from African traditions of communal responsibility (21). Achebe advises Western critics with "limited experience of the African world" to "cultivate the habit of humility" and discard racist stereotypes (8)—a message elaborated in **"Where Angels Fear to Tread"** (1962). At the same time, African critics must take "control of our literary criticism" (27), and Achebe, an astute literary critic, would lead by example.

In **"Africa and Her Writers"** (1973), Achebe proposes that African writers look for inspiration to indigenous traditions such as **mbari** that affirm the "indivisibility of art and society" (33), rather than cater to Western "capitalist and communist aesthetics" irrelevant and false to African situations and values. Of those values, reverence for the power of the Word lies in the ancient roots of many cultures, as demonstrated in **"Language and the Destiny of Man"** (1972). However, Achebe warns that, unyoked from truth, language is abused and perverts the pathways of human destiny. **"What Do African Intellectuals Read?"** (1972) examines the influence of colonialist education, library holdings, reading habits, and direct contact in shaping African attitudes toward literature and the West. **"The Novelist as Teacher"** (1965) avows African writers' responsibility to re-educate and regenerate their readers. Achebe declares himself satisfied if his novels "teach my readers that their past—with all its imperfections—was not one long night of savagery from which the first Europeans acting on God's behalf had delivered them" (72). In **"Thoughts on the African Novel"** (1973), Achebe resists premature and narrow definitions of the genre and challenges the prescriptions of African critics still obsessed with Europe. "Don't fence me in," pleads the African novelist (89): writers must be free to use their imaginations according to their sensibilities and visions "without seeking anyone's permission" (90). Achebe articulated these positions a decade earlier in **"The African Writer and the English Language"** (1964), wherein he defends African writers' freedom to exploit genres and world languages inherited from Africa's colonized past. Good can be made of this legacy, Achebe argues, if transformed to express African purposes. New voices, "speaking of African experience in a world-wide language" (100), are creating exciting "national" literatures that may flourish side by side with "ethnic" literatures. The African publisher's crucial intermediary role in supporting new writers and shaping a desirably dynamic relationship with their readers is addressed in **"Publishing in Africa: A Writer's View"** (1973).

The first two selections of Part II are explicitly autobiographical. In **"Named for Victoria, Queen of England"** (1973) Achebe reflects on growing up in Ogidi, Eastern Nigeria. "We lived at the crossroads of cultures" (119): young Albert Chinualumogu was born into colonist missionary culture but

became increasingly fascinated by traditional **Igbo** language, story, and ritual. Creative ferment at this cross-cultural intersection and a "mental revolution" at university forged the young writer Chinua Achebe. *Things Fall Apart* was "an act of atonement with my past, the ritual return and homage of a prodigal son" (123). Achebe's critical insights from a first opportunity to travel in East Africa produced **"Tanganyika—Jottings of a Tourist"** (1961). Written amid the crisis of the **Nigerian Civil War**, **"The African Writer and the Biafran Cause"** (1968) calls upon African writers, with heightened sensitivities to human injustice, to create literature relevant to contemporary sociopolitical issues. **"Dear Tai Solarin"** (1966), a corrective response to the Nigerian *Daily Times* columnist's "unwarranted attack" (149), clarifies Achebe's positions on language debates earlier advanced in "The African Writer and the English Language." Achebe again considers the remarkable creativity generated at occult, oppositional cultural "crossroads" in **"Onitsha, Gift of the Niger"** (1973). Finally, Achebe's commitment to infusing his novels with Igbo oral traditions may be gauged by **"Chi in Igbo Cosmology"** (1974). A careful examination of the denotations and connotations of *chi*, this essay elucidates even as it complicates this enigmatic concept central to Igbo psychology and worldview. See also *Hopes and Impediments*.

FURTHER READING

Ezenwa-Ohaeto, *Chinua Achebe: A Biography*; Simon Gikandi, *Reading Chinua Achebe*; Bernth Lindfors, ed., *Conversations with Chinua Achebe*.

Cora Agatucci

MOSES, referred to in chapter 14 of *No Longer at Ease* as "Carpenter Moses," built a table years before the main time period of the novel and offered it to the Christian church in **Umuofia** for a fund-raising auction at **harvest**. When **Obi Okonkwo** sees

Moses's table in the middle of his father's room, he recalls that **Isaac Okonkwo** bought it at the auction for approximately eleven pounds.

Thomas J. Lynn

MV *SASA*. In chapters 3 and 4 of ***No Longer Ease***, the small cargo boat with fifty crew members that carries twelve passengers, including **Obi Okonkwo** and **Clara Okeke**, from the **Harrington Dock** in **Liverpool**, England, to the wharf in **Lagos**, **Nigeria**, via **Funchal** in the **Madeiras** and **Freetown**, Sierra Leone. It is on the MV *Sasa* that Obi and Clara accidentally meet for the second time, and during the voyage they fall in love.

Thomas J. Lynn

THE MYTH OF AFRICA. See ***The Africa That Never Was***.

Chinua Achebe receives an honorary Doctorate of Literature from the University of Guelph, Canada, in 1984. Photo courtesy of Doug Killam. Used with permission.

Doug Killam with Chinua Achebe at the University of Guelph, Canada, in 1984. Photo courtesy of Doug Killam. Used with permission.

Chinua Achebe during the festivities celebrating his seventieth birthday at Bard College in 2000. Photo courtesy of Doug Killam. Used with permission.

Christie Achebe seated beside her husband during festivities celebrating his seventieth birthday at Bard College. Dr. Ali Mazrui is seated in the background. Photo courtesy of Doug Killam. Used with permission.

The bustle of a modern Nigerian market, in this case the Dugbe market in Ibadan, circa 1982. Photo courtesy of Joe Butler. Used with permission.

The urban sprawl of modern Ibadan. Photo courtesy of Joe Butler. Used with permission.

FRANCIS OLADELE
PROUDLY
PRESENTS
CHINUA ACHEBE'S

"THINGS FALL APART"
&
"NO LONGER AT EASE"

THE MOST PROVOCATIVE LOVE STORY EVER FILMED IN BLACK AFRICA

STARRING

ORLANDO MARTINS   JOHNNY SEKA   SONNY OTI AND
UGANDA'S PRINCESS ELIZABETH OF TORO
Femi Marquis, Gab Fagbure Boniface Afoko Carey-Jaja, Iyabo Aboaba,
And Princess Cecil Akenzua.

TIME: _____

PLACE: _____

_____

FILMED IN TECHNICOLOUR CINEMASCOPE   CERT 'U'

Poster distributed for use in promoting showings of the combined film adaptation of *Things Fall Apart* and *No Longer at Ease*, also distributed under the title *Bullfrog in the Sun*. Supplied by Josef Gugler.

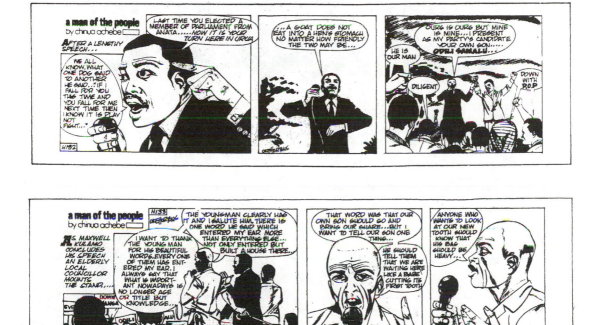

Panels 132 and 133 from the comic strip version of Chinua Achebe's novel *A Man of the People*. These panels respectively appeared in the *New Nigerian* newspaper on August 8 and 11, 1975. Provided by Josef Gugler.

Traditional masks in modern Nigeria. Photo courtesy of Joe Butler. Used with permission.

A Nigerian royal python. Photo courtesy of Joe Butler. Used with permission.

Traditional culture meets modern Nigeria as a tapster climbs a palm tree with a modern street light nearby. Photo courtesy of Joe Butler. Used with permission.

Chinua Achebe has maintained an awareness of the power of the media throughout his career. Here he reads a "Letter of Nigeria" over the Canadian Broadcasting System in 1984. Photo courtesy of Doug Killam. Used with permission.

N

NAIPAUL, SIR V(IDIADHAR) S(URAJ-PRASAD). Born in Trinidad in 1932 to Brahmin Hindu parents, V. S. Naipaul went to school in Trinidad, then later received his bachelor's degree in English literature from University College, Oxford. He began his writing career while working for the Caribbean service of the British Broadcasting Corporation and soon received recognition as a major literary voice in Britain and abroad. In addition to fiction, Naipaul has produced a substantial amount of nonfiction prose, primarily travel writing. He is a prolific writer; to date, he has authored more than two dozen books. He won the Nobel Prize in literature in 2001, in particular for his *The Enigma of Arrival*, a "novel" that intricately combines a number of genres, such as the autobiography, travelogue, and fiction. *Enigma* is also indicative of Naipaul's later work in the way it suggests a mellowing of Naipaul's notoriously harsh attitude toward developing Third World societies. This attitude has been distasteful to many, provoking Derek Walcott, another Caribbean author and a Nobel winner himself, to call him "V. S. Nightfall" in one of his poems.

Africa, however, receives the worst score in Naipaul's writing on postcolonial Third World societies; African writing and writers don't fare well either. He refers somewhat positively to Achebe in a 1971 interview where he discusses a variety of issues. He says, "there are good writers who are African. Chinua Achebe is a grand writer by most people's standards" (Jussawalla 27). Then he adds, "but he [Achebe] is not published in his own country. His work needs the blessing of a foreign market . . . the local society doesn't have any body of judgment as yet" (27). Next Naipaul goes on to attack the whole enterprise of "African writing," and what begins as something of a tribute becomes a veiled denigration of Achebe and his like—though Achebe is not mentioned again in the interview. African writers won't help themselves by writing "the sort of self-conscious 'African Writing' which is obsessed with tribal *mores*," Naipaul declares (28). One wonders who he has in mind when he says, "[T]o encourage a young man merely to write nostalgically about tribal life is really slightly ridiculous" (29). The following statement reveals his undisguised loathing of Africa and its people: "I began my recent book about Africa with a great hatred of everyone, of the entire continent; and that had to be refined away, giving place to comprehension" (30). Naipaul probably refers to *In a Free State*; it was published the same year the interview was held. It is also possible that he has *A Bend in the River* in mind if he is talking about a book that he has just started to write; *A Bend in the River* was published in 1979, and Naipaul is known to work on a book for years. Whichever book he means in the interview, the "comprehension" he claims to have applied while writing it is not easy to find.

Achebe dislikes Naipaul, and the reason is obvious. Naipaul's depiction of Africa in the two books mentioned above is relentlessly disparaging. Africa, to him, is a dark continent given to witchcraft and consumed by wild vegetation. It is a land without hope, rendering all human endeavors futile and regressing humanity itself into an earlier state of bestiality and lawlessness. It is this Naipaul that Achebe finds extremely disturbing. He takes Naipaul to task on a few occasions. In **"Impediments to Dialogue between North and South,"** Achebe remarks that Naipaul resembles **Joseph Conrad** in denying Africa humanity (*Hopes and Impediments* 27–28); Achebe's views on Conrad appear in **"An Image of Africa: Racism in Conrad's *Heart of Darkness*,"** a well-known essay. In **"Colonialist Criticism,"** Achebe warns writers and readers of the danger that Naipaul's non-English background is deceptive because it has a tendency to lead people to think he is on the side of the victims in the colonial divide (*Hopes and Impediments* 82).

A sustained critique of Naipaul appears in "Today, a Balance of Stories," a paper Achebe delivered at Harvard University and later published in *Home and Exile*. Here Achebe indicates that Naipaul has promoted the concept of "universal civilization" to emphasize the curious claim that Europe has spread civilization everywhere in the world and has made an " 'extraordinary attempt to accommodate the rest of the world, and all the currents of the world's thought' " (85). Pointing at Naipaul's writing about India, Achebe argues that Naipaul misrepresents India and was ill received by Indians themselves; they found Naipaul "too insensitive, arrogant, and plain ignorant" (86). Then Achebe turns to *A Bend in the River* and illustrates that it employs Naipaul's notion of "universal civilization" in a very constrictive manner. In it Naipaul presents a civilization that excludes Africans, trivializes their efforts, and rejects their history. So, Achebe asks, how can Naipaul claim that this universal civilization exists? Achebe's short but in-depth analysis of some of the disturbing aspects of Naipaul's novel leaves little room for doubt about its prejudice concerning Africa. That *A Bend in the River* is reminiscent of *Heart of Darkness* Achebe demonstrates convincingly, the difference being "while Conrad gives us an Africa of malignant mystery and incomprehensibility, Naipaul's method is to ridicule claims to any human achievements in Africa" (87–88). Indeed, in Achebe's comparison, Conrad fares better than Naipaul: "Conrad's 'great wall of vegetation,' which has, at least, a kind of ambiguous grandeur, is now cut down to Naipaul's mere 'bush'; Conrad's 'black incomprehensible frenzy' of the Africans to a rather black pitiful rage that will try to set fire to concrete" (88–89).

It is curious that Achebe is able to divine Naipaul's real feelings about Africa: "He held Africans in deep contempt himself and made no secret of it. Although he was writing about Africa, he was not writing about Africans" (88); whether Achebe is aware of Naipaul's interview in 1971 is not possible to determine, though he does refer to another interview by Naipaul for *Forbes* magazine. Naipaul's disdain for Africa seems to derive at least in part from his conviction that Africa leads nowhere; it is a dead end, and its people amount to nothing. The Africans whom "Naipaul would love to hammer into the ground with his well-crafted mallet of deadly prose," are, on the other hand, important to Achebe

(95). These are people using the "dusty little road"—the unloved road Naipaul's character in *A Bend in the River* turns away from but is treasured by Achebe, for whom this road is a "link to all the other destinations" (91).

FURTHER READING

Feroza Jussawala, *Conversations with V. S. Naipaul*; V.S. Naipaul, *A Bend in the River* and *The Enigma of Arrival*; Rob Nixon, *London Calling*.

Farhad B. Idris

"NAMED FOR VICTORIA, QUEEN OF ENGLAND." Achebe essay. See *Morning Yet on Creation Day*.

NANGA, CHIEF THE HONOURABLE MICAH A., M.P., the ostensible title character of *A Man of the People*. A leading figure in the **People's Organization Party (POP)**, Nanga has risen to prominence through sheer force of ambition and is now the Minister of Culture in the fictional postcolonial African nation in which the novel is set. Despite this position and despite his former job as a teacher, Nanga is a man of little learning and almost no culture. He is, however, a crafty politician who has the ability to charm everyone with whom he comes into contact into believing that he has only their best interests at heart. Nanga is also deeply corrupt and clearly uses his political power for his own financial gain. He is also ruthless, willing to do anything to advance his own power. In addition, though a man of about fifty, Nanga is a man of nearly insatiable sexual appetites, a characteristic that leads him into conflict with narrator **Odilu Samalu** when Nanga seduces Samalu's girlfriend **Elsie** under Samalu's very nose.

Achebe's depiction of Nanga makes a number of important points, including the fact that he and the other corrupt postcolonial politicians in the book seem to have learned many of their unscrupulous practices from their colonial predecessors. However, Achebe makes it clear that the colonial past is no excuse for the continuation of such practices into the postcolonial present, and he is unsparing (if sometimes surprisingly good-humored) in his satirical condemnation of the kind of political behavior for which Nanga stands as the book's chief emblem.

M. Keith Booker

NANGA, MRS. MARGARET, the longtime wife of **Chief Nanga** in *A Man of the People*. When Nanga courts **Edna**, a beautiful young woman, toward the end of making her his second wife, rumor has it that he does so because he finds Margaret too "bush" to serve as a suitable partner for someone in his now lofty political position. However, Margaret is, in fact, a very intelligent (if largely uneducated) woman who sees through most of her husband's charades and is very much aware of his philandering. She puts up with him largely because of her devotion to their children. In chapter 9, narrator **Odili Samalu** has a conversation with Margaret in which he is surprised by the bitterness and vehemence with which she denounces her powerful husband.

M. Keith Booker

NARAYAN, R(ASIPURAM) K(RISHNASWAMI). A teller of deceptively simple but exquisitely crafted tales, the Indian author R. K. Narayan was born in 1906 in South India. He lived in that region his entire life, initially in Madras and the remainder in Mysore. Until his death in 2001, Narayan, in his sixty-five-year-long writing career, had authored nearly three dozen novels, collections of stories, translations of epics, and memoirs. His fiction is set in Malgudi, an imaginary town in South India. Narayan describes the curious doings of the people of Malgudi and treats them with humorous irony. Malgudi, though identifiable as a twentieth-century Indian town, remains for the most part cut off from the major political upheavals India has witnessed before and after independence. Narayan's admirers are many. Graham Greene, also a friend, regarded him as a great writer of the twentieth century. Narayan's seeming lack of interest in the decisive affairs of his nation, on the other hand, has been a matter of concern for some.

In a brief but perceptive discussion, Achebe reveals deep esteem for Narayan in "Today, a Balance of Stories," a paper he read at Harvard University and published in *Home and Exile*. In this essay, Achebe appears critical of expatriate writers glorifying exile. He also notes that in today's world, many go through forced expatriation because of economic reasons, a consequence of unequal developments of the world's wealth among nations. Achebe, however, makes a distinction between writers who identify themselves with the victims of the disparity, writers such as **Ama Ata Aidoo** and **Salman Rushdie**, and writers who collude with the other side, for example, **V. S. Naipaul**. Achebe's essay, it is useful to note, denounces Naipaul and scathingly censures his attitude to Indians and Africans, people whom modernity has seemingly passed by, people who believe in tradition. Such people, however, are of great interest to an author who feels for and lives among them. Narayan is a prime example of such an author because he is deeply intrigued by the people of Malgudi and is content to be with them all the time (Narayan rarely traveled abroad).

It is pertinent to observe here that in several books about India Naipaul has discussed Narayan. Naipaul points with admiration to the fact that Narayan wrote in English at a time when very few authors ventured to do so. But Narayan's indifference toward issues shaping India's politics and modernity troubles him. In *Area of Darkness*, Naipaul says, "There is a contradiction in Narayan, between his form, which implies concern, and tween his form, which implies concern, and his attitude, which denies it. . . . He is inimitable, and it cannot be supposed that his is the synthesis at which Indian writing will arrive" (206). Naipaul, in various places, typically praises Narayan, but the praise soon becomes an enumeration of his flaws. Achebe's regard for Narayan, on the other hand, is unqualified. He implies that Narayan is an author after his own heart, an author he himself draws inspiration from, which also serves as a subtle hint that Narayan is an effective and exemplary antithesis to Naipaul.

FURTHER READING

V. S. Naipaul, *An Area of Darkness*.

Farhad B. Idris

NATHANIEL joins others who, like him, are from **Umuofia** but who live in **Lagos**, for a gathering at the apartment of **Obi Okonkwo** in chapter 18 of *No Longer at Ease*. Obi's mother, **Hannah Okonkwo**, has recently died, and the gathering is intended to comfort Obi. The **Tortoise** tale that Nathaniel narrates on this occasion is not meant for all in the room to hear, but everyone including Obi ends up hearing it. It is an unflattering comment on Obi's decision not to return to Umuofia for his mother's funeral.

Thomas J. Lynn

NATIONAL COUNCIL OF NIGERIA AND THE CAMEROONS. Referred to at the beginning of chapter 3 of *No Longer at Ease*, an organization whose London branch holds, at St. Pancras Town Hall, a dance at which **Obi Okonkwo** and **Clara Okeke** meet for the first time. Obi is "immediately struck by her beauty" at this function and succeeds in getting a dance with her, but his nerves betray him. Neither his speech nor his dancing reveal any distinction, and Clara is clearly not interested at this point.

Thomas J. Lynn

NATIONAL GAZETTE, the official newspaper of the postcolonial regime of **Kangan**

in *Anthills of the Savannah*. Though it is ostensibly semi-independent of government editorial control, the paper is clearly expected to promote the policies and goals of the current regime. Thus, when editor **Ikem Osodi** refuses to adhere to the party line, he is summarily suspended—and ultimately murdered. **Chris Oriko**, the government's Commissioner for Information during most of the action of the novel, had preceded Osodi as the editor of the *Gazette*.

M. Keith Booker

NDU, extolled by **Ogbuefi Odogwu** in chapter 5 of *No Longer at Ease* as among the "giants" of **Iguedo** prior to **Okonkwo**'s generation.

Thomas J. Lynn

NDUKA, SIMEON, the headmaster of the mission school in **Umuofia** when **Obi Okonkwo** first attended it as a child. Simeon, who had come to follow British customs later in life, had learned the art of wrestling when he was young. His skill in this area reemerged on Obi's first day at the school, when Simeon threw to the floor **Mr. Jones**, the white Inspector of Schools, who had just slapped him. The teachers and the pupils at the school ran away at that point since such handling of a white man by an African was unheard of at that time. The narrator compares this action by Simeon to "unmasking an ancestral spirit," recalling the actual provocation by **Enoch**, the zealous Christian convert, toward the non-Christian community in Umuofia that prompts their burning of the first missionary church there in part 3 of *Things Fall Apart*.

Thomas J. Lynn

NDULUE. In *Things Fall Apart*, the oldest man in the village of Ire, one of the nine villages of **Umuofia**. His death, in chapter 8, is followed by the death of **Ozoemena**, his senior wife, on the same day. In accordance with local custom, the funeral of Ndulue is postponed until after the burial of Ozoemena.

M. Keith Booker

NDULUE, a character mentioned in passing in *Arrow of God*, chapter 18.

Rachel R. Reynolds

NÉGRITUDE. A mid-twentieth-century political and cultural movement, dominated by writers and thinkers from Francophone Africa, in which a variety of black intellectuals sought to express their distinctive racial and cultural identities apart from the identities formerly imposed upon them by their European colonial rulers. The term négritude first appeared in 1939 in the long poem *Cahier d'un retour au pays natal*, by Aimé Césaire, who would go on to become one of the key figures in the movement. In the 1940s, the movement gained force among African and Caribbean intellectuals living in Paris, though it had important precedents dating back to the 1920s. Perhaps the single most influential figure in the movement was the Senegalese poet Leopold Senghor, partly because ideas associated with négritude strongly informed the political program that eventually brought Senghor to the presidency of Senegal from 1960 to 1980. The movement also featured numerous other important figures, as well as a variety of perspectives, though individuals associated with the movement were united in their attempts to further a sense of black racial pride, thereby revising colonialist histories and overcoming the historical experience of the racial denigration and discrimination.

Because of its emphasis on distinctively black modes of expression, négritude was an important force in the rise of African literature in the 1950s and 1960s, though many felt that the movement relied far too heavily on European precedents such as surrealism in its quest for alternative aesthetic models.

Indeed, the négritude movement has had numerous critics among postcolonial intellectuals, who have variously charged it with merely replicating ideas derived from French intellectuals, with failing to break free of the colonial past, and with relying on simplistic and essentialist notions of racial identity. Anglophone African writers and intellectuals have been among the strongest critics of négritude, as when **Wole Soyinka** famously remarked (at an important congress of African writers held at Kampala's Makerere University in 1962) that a tiger does not need to proclaim its tigritude. Achebe, however, has generally been more conciliatory, as when he notes in *Hopes and Impediments* that Senghor's reply to Soyinka (that a tiger cannot proclaim its tigritude because it cannot talk) was "adequate" and powerful in its "breathtaking simplicity" and in its reminder that black Africans can talk and should be allowed to speak for themselves (24).

FURTHER READING

Abiola Irele, *The African Experience in Literature and Ideology*; Lilyan Kesteloot, *Black Writers in French*.

M. Keith Booker

NEKEDE, a town very close to the city of Owerri, the capital of Imo State, **Nigeria**. Up until the late 1930s, Nekede had one of the few Central Schools established by the British Church Missionary Society (CMS) in Nigeria. While feeder-schools in surrounding towns had classes ranging from the Infant Division or Junior Primary Division or Senior Primary up to standard five, only the Central Schools had all divisions including standard six, the final class of the primary school in Nigeria. Chinua's brother, the late Rev. John Achebe, was the Agriculture Master at Nekede Central School in the early 1940s, and it was he who took Chinua (then known as Albert) to Nekede. It was there that Chinua did

standard six. Chinua established himself as a star pupil when he scored 100 percent at an impromptu dictation administered to him by an unannounced white Education Officer, who didn't believe that such a feat was possible. It was from Nekede that Chinua took the entrance exam to **Government College, Umuahia**. A couple of weeks after he started classes at Umuahia he was awarded a government scholarship. It happened that scholarships were awarded by provinces; thus, the student from Nekede Central School (with appropriate qualifying marks) merited the scholarship for Owerri Province. Although Chinua's home province was **Onitsha**, he received the scholarship because his brother was teaching at Nekede and paying taxes there.

Phanuel Akubueze Egejuru

NEW YAM FESTIVAL. See Feast of the New Yam.

NGENE, is a minor god of **Umuaro** (*Arrow of God*, chapter 18).

Rachel R. Reynolds

NGONGO, PRESIDENT, a prominent African leader mentioned in *Anthills of the Savannah*, perhaps based to some extent on such important African statesmen as Ghana's Kwame Nkrumah, Tanzania's Julius Nyerere, and (especially) Kenya's Jomo Kenyatta. Ngongo serves in the novel as a role model for **Sam, the President** of postcolonial **Kangan**. Having encountered the aging Ngongo at a meeting of the Organization of African Unity (OAU), Sam returns to **Kangan** much changed, talking much of the old man and mimicking his mannerisms and speech patterns. In particular, inspired by Ngongo, Sam becomes much cooler toward his former friends and much more ambitious in his quest to become president for life (though he claims to disavow the role). Ngongo thus becomes an emblem of the way in which, for Achebe, even the greatest postcolonial African leaders have sometimes played a negative political role by encouraging worship rather than democracy.

M. Keith Booker

NGUGI WA THIONG'O (1938–), important Kenyan novelist, dramatist, critic, teacher, and activist, one of the major figures of modern African literature and culture. Known especially for his novels, Ngugi has been an extremely influential figure in the development of postcolonial African literature. The critical recognition he has received worldwide has helped to gain international respect for African literature, while Ngugi's own intense political commitments have helped to call attention to a number of crucial social, historical, and political issues surrounding the postcolonial predicament of Kenya and other modern African nations. Ngugi has also had an important academic career; he was the first African to chair the English Department at the University of Nairobi, and he has taught at several American universities, including Northwestern, Yale, and New York University. He has sometimes disagreed with Achebe on issues such as the question of African writers writing in English, but he has also acknowledged Achebe as one of the central inspirations in his own decision to become a writer.

Ngugi was born the son of Gikuyu subsistence farmers in 1938 in Limuru in Highland Kenya. His parents separated about 1946; Ngugi and his five siblings were then cared for by their mother, whose hard work has remained an example to Ngugi throughout his career. His childhood in colonial Kenya made him intensely aware of the social and economic distance between native Kenyans and European settlers. He was educated in both mission and independent Gikuyu schools, and his political commitments grew at least in part from personal experience. In 1954 his brother, Wallace Mwangi wa Thiong'o, joined the Mau Mau movement and remained in the forests as a guerrilla until 1956. In 1955 Ngugi's mother was detained by the British and underwent three months of torture and interrogation. In that same year, Ngugi himself won a place at the prestigious Alliance High School, where he received secondary education, doing especially well in English and becoming fascinated with literature. That same year he returned home on a school vacation to find his mother incarcerated, his family home and village razed as part of the British project of resettlement during the Emergency.

In 1959, Ngugi entered Makerere University College in Uganda, at that time the most prestigious institution of higher learning in East Africa. There he began writing, and by graduation in 1964 he had completed initial versions of what would become his first two novels and had a play, *The Black Hermit*, produced at the Ugandan National Theatre in Kampala. In 1964 Ngugi began postgraduate study at Leeds University in England. That same year his novel *Weep Not, Child* (written in 1962) was published. *Weep Not, Child* reflects the political reality of Kenya during the late 1940s and throughout the 1950s, a period of intense resistance to the British colonial presence in Kenya, especially among the Gikuyu. In particular, the partly autobiographical novel focuses on the tribulations of an impoverished Gikuyu family that is struggling to survive amid political turmoil and harsh material conditions. *The River Between* (written in 1961) was published in 1965. This novel reaches back to the 1920s to depict the impact of British colonialism on traditional Gikuyu culture, somewhat in the way Achebe's ***Things Fall Apart*** had shown the impact of colonialism on **Igbo** society. Ngugi's book revolves around the attempts (largely unsuccessful) of the protagonist, Waiyaki, to overcome the rifts in Gikuyu society brought about by colonialism.

A Grain of Wheat, published in 1967, marked an important departure in Ngugi's career. Dealing with events surrounding the moment of Kenyan independence, it announced the end of Ngugi's focus on the colonial period and the beginning of his increasing concern with the ills of Kenyan society in the era of independence and neocolonialism. During his graduate studies at Leeds, Ngugi (partially due to the influence of his teacher, the Marxist literary scholar Arnold Kettle, and partly due to his fellow students) was also exposed for the first time to the thought of **Marx**, Engels, Lenin, and other Marxist thinkers. *A Grain of Wheat* clearly exhibits the impact of this experience, showing the influence of Marxist ideas, especially as filtered through the work of **Frantz Fanon**, though Lenin's *Imperialism: The Highest Stage of Capitalism* was also important in forming Ngugi's new understanding of the complicity between capitalism and imperialism. In *A Grain of Wheat* Ngugi abandons his earlier focus on the individual and begins to turn his attention to the Kenyan people as a collective protagonist. His treatment of individual characters shifts from a concern with their private trials and tribulations to a concern with their relation to "politics—more precisely, characters in the process of creating their own history" (Nkosi 45).

A Grain of Wheat is to some extent a transitional novel that still shows remnants of the more conventional bourgeois ideology that informs Ngugi's early work. But *Petals of Blood* (1977) shows the full emergence of Ngugi's Marxist consciousness; it also represents the first unequivocal endorsement in Ngugi's work of violent resistance to oppression. In its depiction of postcolonial life in the fictional Kenyan town of Ilmorog, the novel focuses on the discrepancy between the reality of postcolonial Kenya and the ideals for which so many (especially in the Mau Mau movement) fought and died in the struggle for independence. *Petals of Blood* is Ngugi's most formally complex novel, mixing modernist techniques with a detective-story plot and a basic mode of social realism to condemn the evils of neocolonialism in Kenya.

By 1977 Ngugi had been active for a number of years in various editorial activities and as a member of the English Department of the University of Nairobi, which he was instrumental in changing to the Department of Literature, with an increased emphasis on African literature and a de-emphasis of the British tradition. In addition, he had been active for some time in organizing adult education and other cultural activities among the Gikuyu villagers at the Kamiriithu Community Educational and Cultural Centre. His satirical play *Ngaahika Ndeenda* (written in Gikuyu with Ngugi wa Mirii, English translation *I Will Marry When I Want*) was produced by the center's amateur community theater group in October 1977, causing the Kenyatta government almost immediately to ban the play as a danger to "public security," then later to raze the center itself and to detain Ngugi, leading to the writing of *Devil on the Cross* in prison. Ngugi was released from detention in December 1978, only to find that he had been stripped of his post at the University of Nairobi, that he was still subject to continual government harassment, and that he and his family were receiving frequent death threats. Ngugi continued to work diligently for freedom in Kenya and to promote his ideas through amateur theatrical productions. In 1982, he was forced into exile to avoid a further detention in Kenya. He has lived in exile ever since and now lives in the United States and teaches at New York University.

A central figure in debates over the post-colonial **language question**, Ngugi believes that African writers who write in European colonial languages are only furthering the continuation of European cultural imperialism in Africa. Thus, since the late 1970s, he has worked to promote writing in Gikuyu and other African languages, through both his own writing and editing the Gikuyu-language cultural journal *Mutiiri*. His Gikuyu novel *Matigari* (1986, English translation by Wangui wa Goro in 1987) draws heavily upon traditions of Gikuyu oral narrative to tell the story of its title character, a seasoned Mau Mau warrior who emerges from the forests of Mount Kenya several decades after Kenyan independence only to discover that very few of the goals of the Mau Mau anticolonial struggle have actually been accomplished. Enraged, Matigari vows to renew the fight for freedom in Kenya. Matigari is probably modeled upon a real-life Mau Mau hero, the famous general Stanley Mathenge, who disappeared with 200 fighters at the end of the Mau Mau rebellion. On the other hand, Matigari is clearly an allegorical figure who represents the Kenyan people and their spirit of resistance, reemerging after a period of neocolonial slumber.

Ngugi's impressive body of novels, plays, and short stories (see the volume *Secret Lives and Other Stories*) has made him widely regarded as one of the giants of African literature. His numerous essays and speeches (collected in volumes like *Homecoming*, *Writers in Politics*, *Barrel of a Pen*, *Decolonising the Mind*, and *Moving the Centre*) have made him an important figure in politics and literary criticism as well. Taken together, his novels in particular comprise an alterna-tive history of Kenya that emphasizes the strong Kenyan tradition of resistance and thus serves as a counter to distorted colonialist histories that view Kenya as a timeless land without history apart from the history of British activities there. For Ngugi it is crucial for Kenyans to develop a positive sense of their own history as they attempt to overcome current oppression to build a positive future. As he puts it in his essay "Mau Mau Is Coming Back," "How we look at our yesterday has important bearings on how we look at today and on how we see possibilities for tomorrow. The sort of past we look back to for inspiration in our struggles affects the vision of the future we want to build" (*Barrel* 8).

Ngugi's work has received extensive critical attention. In addition to hundreds of articles in scholarly journals and numerous chapters in books on African literature, there have been a number of book-length studies of Ngugi's work. These include early studies like those of Robson and Killam, which are limited because they were written before either *Devil on the Cross* or *Matigari*. The slightly later study by Cook and Okenimkpe includes *Devil on the Cross* and is particularly useful as a general introduction to Ngugi, though it is also too early to cover *Matigari*. More recent studies include those by Jeyifo, Nwankwo, and Gikandi. Particularly useful as a background source is Carol Sicherman's *Ngugi wa Thiong'o: The Making of a Rebel*, which includes extensive historical and biographical documentation of Ngugi's work.

FURTHER READING

David Cook and Michael Okenimkpe, *Ngugi wa Thiong'o*; Simon Gikandi, *Ngugi wa Thiong'o*; Biodun Jeyifo, *Ngugi wa Thiong'o*; G. D. Killam, *An Introduction to the Writings of Ngugi*; Ngugi wa Thiong'o, *Homecoming*, *Writers in Politics*, *Barrel of a Pen*, *Decolonising the Mind*, and *Mov-*

ing the Centre; Lewis Nkosi, *Tasks and Masks*; Chimalum Moses Nwankwo, *The Works of Ngugi wa Thiong'o*; Clifford Robson, *Ngugi wa Thiong'o*; Carol M. Sicherman, *Ngugi wa Thiong'o*.

M. Keith Booker

NIGER IBOS (1938, full title *Niger Ibos: A description of the primitive life, customs and animistic beliefs, &c., of the Ibo people of Nigeria by one who, for thirty-five years, enjoyed the privilege of their intimate confidence and friendship*). An anthropological work on the **Igbo** by the missionary **G. T. Basden**. Despite the datedness of its methodology and its blatantly colonial perspective, Basden's work is an important source for understanding Igbo institutions in the early twentieth century, and Achebe revisits and corrects many of Basden's themes in *Things Fall Apart* and *Arrow of God*.

FURTHER READING

G. T. Basden, *Among the Ibos of Nigeria*.

Nicholas Brown

NIGERIA, with a population of over 110,000,000 (1999 estimate), is easily the most populous nation in Africa. It is also one of the largest, covering an area of approximately 357,000 square miles—somewhat larger than France and Great Britain combined. The Niger-Benue river system divides the country into three physically diverse sections. The hot, dry north is a heavily cultivated area of rolling savannahs located roughly 1,500 feet above sea level. Lake Chad, in the northeast, is one of the few large, permanent, standing bodies of water in the country, though its size varies with changes in seasonal levels of rainfall. The southwest region contains both low-lying coastal plains and upland areas. The southeast region, consisting primarily of the delta of the Niger River, is largely covered by dense tropical forest. Nigeria's rich petro-leum reserves are also located principally in this region. The new city of **Abuja** (designed and built beginning in the mid-1970s and located almost exactly in the middle of the country) became the capital in late 1991. The population of Abuja in 1997 was about 440,000, though it was growing rapidly. The largest city in Nigeria is the southwestern coastal city of **Lagos**, the former capital. The nearby city of **Ibadan** is also a major commercial and intellectual center, the site of the University of Ibadan (formerly **University College, Ibadan**).

English is widely used in Nigeria in government, commerce, and education. In their everyday activities many of the inhabitants speak a form of **pidgin English** that preserves most of the basic grammatical features of English but incorporates a number of changes in syntax and vocabulary arising from the influence of local cultures. The more than 250 ethnic groups have their own languages as well. The largest of these groups are the Hausa and Fulani in the north, the Yoruba in the southwest, and the **Igbo** in the southeast. About half the total population, mostly in the north, are Muslim; about one-third of the population, almost all in the south, are Christian. Just over fifty percent of the adult population are literate, mostly in English. The economy of Nigeria is mostly agricultural. More than half the workforce is engaged in farming (much of it of a subsistence variety), and a variety of crops (including sorghum, millet, cassava, soybeans, groundnuts, cotton, maize, yams, rice, palm products, rice, and cacao) are produced. Goats, sheep, and cattle are raised as well. Nevertheless, periodic droughts frequently reduce agricultural production to the point that food must be imported. Hardwoods such as mahogany and ebony are produced in the forest regions, and there is some industry in the urban regions, though most manufactured products are imported. Nigeria is rich in mineral resources, producing iron, magnesium, niobium, tin, lead, and zinc. The major mineral resource, however, is petroleum, of which Nigeria is Africa's largest producer. Most of the petroleum reserves (estimated at about 20 billion barrels) are controlled by the government.

What is now southern Nigeria had extensive contact with Europeans as long ago as the late fifteenth century, and the region has a rich history that goes back hundreds of years before that. The first centralized state in the region was Kanem-Bornu, probably founded in the eighth century A.D. Important states such as Oyo and Benin had arisen in the area by the fourteenth century, establishing a rich artistic tradition, especially in the production of bronze artifacts. By the seventeenth and eighteenth centuries, the area was one of the centers of a brutal slave trade in which millions of Nigerians were forcibly removed by European slave traders and brought to America to work as slaves. Arab slave traders had earlier operated in the region as well. The slave trade was abolished in the early nineteenth century, but European traders continued to visit the region, exchanging manufactured goods for local agricultural products. The area occupied by modern Nigeria eventually became one of the most important regions of British colonial power in Africa. Ceded to British control in the Berlin Conference of 1884–1885, the area was the object of extensive missionary activity in the late nineteenth century. British colonial rule was solidified through a massive program of "pacification" that lasted from 1900 to 1920, with the region now occupied by Nigeria being officially amalgamated as a single colony in 1914, under the leadership of **Lord Frederick Lugard**. This program included the planned destruction of important cultural sites and artifacts such as the great oracle of the Aro, an Igbo people. It also included the military conquest of peoples such

as the Aro, who resisted British rule. Villages that resisted this rule were often subject to so-called punitive expeditions that amounted to massacres of the local population. For example, British-led troops slaughtered much of the population of the village of **Ahiara** in late 1905, a historical event that forms the basis for the destruction of the fictional village of **Abame** in Achebe's *Things Fall Apart*. This slaughter was precipitated by the killing of one **J. F. Stewart**, an Englishman traveling by bicycle in the area. This same killing was also the pretext for the massive **Bende-Onitsha punitive expedition** into the interior of Nigeria, an expedition that included the destruction of an important oracle at **Awka** and that opened the way for more thorough British penetration of the region.

Under the direction of Lugard, the British established an elaborate system of "**indirect rule**" that relied largely on African agents of the colonial government and on cooperative local rulers (often installed as puppets by the British themselves) for its everyday operation, though all important decisions were made by the British governor. British rule led to some development such as the building of roads and railways, but the system of indirect rule was an open invitation to corruption and abuse. Moreover, it often came into conflict with long-established local traditions. For example, the culture of the Igbo was based on discussion and decentered collective rule by groups of elders, no one of whom could be identified as the local ruler. When the British, bent on being able to deal with a single individual as the leading power in any given village, sought to establish such rulers, conflicts necessarily arose. Indeed, well-established social customs and traditions among the Igbo and other peoples in the region were so foreign to the customs and traditions of modern Britain that the British typically concluded that the indigenous peoples were mere savages without any legitimate culture or social structure. This belief was used to justify the various atrocities committed by the British during the period of pacification and to legitimate the continuation of British rule in the ensuing decades.

Nigeria finally gained nominal independence from British rule on October 1, 1960. The new nation was divided into northern, western, and eastern administrative regions along the lines of the natural geographic division of the country. Nigeria became a republic in 1963, with Nnamdi Azikiwe as its first president. The early years of independence were marked by considerable political conflict and unrest, leading eventually to a January 1966 coup in which a group of Igbo military officers took control of the government, placing Major General Johnson T. U. Aguiyi-Ironsi in charge of the new military regime. By July 1966 Ironsi was ousted (and killed) in another coup, this time led by Hausa officers. The new regime, headed by Lieutenant Colonel Yakubu Gowon, attempted to move toward civilian government, but internal troubles (especially the massacre of a number of Igbo living in the Hausa-dominated north) led to continuing instability. The dissatisfaction of the Igbo with their position in Nigeria led to the secession of the eastern region, led by Lieutenant Colonel Chukwuemeka O. Ojukwu, from the nation. Ojukwu proclaimed the region the Republic of Biafra on May 30, 1967. The bloody **Nigerian Civil War** ensued, leading eventually to Biafra's surrender on January 15, 1970, and to the restoration of the original boundaries of Nigeria. In addition to massive casualties from the actual fighting, it is estimated that more than a million Igbo starved to death as a result of the war.

A worldwide boom in oil prices in the early 1970s led to an era of rising prosperity in Nigeria, marked by a massive government program of construction and industrialization, including the founding of the new capital of Abuja. On the other hand, the rapid influx of wealth was unevenly distributed and led to considerable corruption. By 1975, Gowon had still not restored civilian rule, and his regime was toppled in a coup led by General Murtala Muhammad and a group of officers who pledged to return the country to civilian rule as soon as possible. Muhammad was assassinated in an unsuccessful coup attempt a year later and replaced by General Olusegun Obasanjo. By the late 1970s the government had established increasingly close ties with the United States, and a new civilian government, headed by President Alhaji Shehu Shagari and modeled on the American system, was installed. The new federal system was plagued by corruption and social disturbances. Shagari was re-elected in 1983 but overthrown in a violent military coup only a few months later. Another coup in 1985 instituted a military regime that held power until 1993, when a joint civilian-military government was installed and elections held. However, on November 17, 1993, General Sani Abacha seized control of the government in a bloodless coup and declared the recent elections, apparently won by Moshood K. O. Abiola, void. Abiola was jailed a year later when he declared himself president of Nigeria.

Abacha developed a growing reputation for corruption during his reign and also drew considerable international criticism for the harsh quelling of dissent among the Ogoni people on Nigeria's oil-rich delta region, which led to the execution of the internationally known writer Ken Saro-Wiwa in 1995. Abacha died in 1998 at the age of fifty-four, reportedly of a heart attack, though rumors of possible poisoning by political rivals abounded. In 1999, general elections at last brought a fully civilian government to power, though that government was headed by Obasanjo, the former military ruler, who had been jailed by Abacha from 1995 to 1998.

Obasanjo was elected on a promise of working against corruption and for democratic reform, but his subsequent record, especially in the latter area, has been widely criticized. At this writing, Obasanjo plans to run for re-election in 2003.

FURTHER READING

Chinua Achebe, *The Trouble with Nigeria*; Johnson U. J. Asiegbu, *Nigeria and Its British Invaders, 1851–1920*; Paula Ben-Amos, *The Art of Benin*; Michael Crowder, *Nigeria: An Introduction to Its History* and *The Story of Nigeria*; Larry Jay Diamond, *Class, Ethnicity, and Democracy in Nigeria*; Herbert Ekwe-Ekwe, *The Biafra War*; Elizabeth Isichei, *A History of the Igbo People* and *A History of Nigeria*; Heather Millar, *The Kingdom of Benin in West Africa*; Chidozie Ogbalu and E. Nolue Emenanjo, eds., *Igbo Language and Culture*; Richard Olaniyan, ed., *Nigerian History and Culture*; Ken Saro-Wiwa, *On a Darkling Plain: An Account of the Nigerian Civil War*; V. C. Uchendu, *The Igbo of Southeast Nigeria*.

M. Keith Booker

NIGERIA–BIAFRA WAR. See **Nigerian Civil War**.

NIGERIAN BROADCASTING CORPORATION (NBC), a radio and television broadcasting corporation that, beginning in 1957, succeeded the **Nigerian Broadcasting Service (NBS)** as the principal broadcasting agency in Nigeria. By the 1980s, NBC had developed into the Federal Radio Corporation of Nigeria, under which title, at this writing, it still operates.

M. Keith Booker

NIGERIAN BROADCASTING SERVICE (NBS), a radio broadcasting company founded in the early 1950s as part of the development of colonial Nigeria toward eventual independence. Modeled after the British Broadcasting Company, NBS employed Achebe beginning in mid-1954. As head of the Talks Department, Achebe developed and produced a variety of programming. He remained with the service until it became the **Nigerian Broadcasting Corporation (NBC)** in 1957. He then went on to become the Director of External Broadcasting for NBC, founding the **Voice of Nigeria** radio service in 1961. Achebe continued his affiliation with NBC until 1966, when events leading to the **Nigerian Civil War** caused him to leave **Lagos** and return to the Igbolands of Eastern Nigeria.

M. Keith Booker

NIGERIAN CIVIL WAR. Conflict between the secessionist state of Biafra and federal Nigeria, also known as the Biafra War and the Nigeria-Biafra War. The war lasted from July 1967 until January 1970, when the original boundaries of **Nigeria** were restored. When widespread violence and other forms of persecution against **Igbo** led to the formation of the Igbo-dominated **Republic of Biafra** in May 1967, the Nigerian federal government responded with sanctions designed to force Biafra to rejoin federal Nigeria. By July 1967, the tensions between Nigeria and Biafra led to an all-out war. Though Biafra scored some initial military successes, it was clear early on that the conflict was one-sided, as federal Nigeria had large advantages in terms of men, weapons, money, and other resources. This was especially true after the oil fields, which supplied a crucial source of income to Biafra, fell to federal forces.

Nevertheless, the Biafrans put up a fierce military resistance, while also waging a campaign for popular and official support around the world. Achebe himself contributed to this effort, which gained considerable public sympathy but garnered relatively little in the way of official aid and support. By the time Biafra finally collapsed in January 1970, more than one million Biafrans had died in combat or of disease and famine. Widespread destruction wrecked the economic productivity of the Biafran region for years to come, while photographs depicting slaughter, starvation, and other forms of suffering in Biafra became some of the indelible images of world history in the twentieth century.

The Nigerian Civil War exerted a profound effect on the subsequent development of Nigerian literature, and, as such, the event is widely regarded as a watershed in Nigerian literary, as well as political, history. Numerous important works of poetry, drama, fiction, and nonfiction were directly inspired by the events of the war, though this inspiration is often so direct that the line between fiction and nonfiction is extremely unclear. Thus, "novels" such as Chukwuemeka Ike's *Sunset at Dawn* (1976) and Isidore Okpewho's *The Last Duty* (1976) derive largely from actual personal experience in the war. Nigerian Civil War literature has been dominated by writers from Biafra, much of it sympathetic to the Biafran cause. However, some of the most powerful depictions of the chaos and devastation of the war see the entire event as an outbreak of historical absurdity and insanity. Some of the most horrifying accounts in this vein appear in the works of the non-Biafran **Wole Soyinka**, such as the novel *Season of Anomy* (1973). Soyinka presents the war as a confusing and chaotic event in which there are no clear heroes and villains. An even stronger denunciation of the war appears in Festus Iyayi's *Heroes* (winner of the Commonwealth Writers' Prize in 1986)), which rejects the ethnic terms of the conflict as misguided, seeing instead class inequality as the crucial social phenomenon dividing Nigerian society. The central point made by Iyayi in the book is a simple one: the intertribal warfare that informed the civil war was instigated by a few powerful leaders on both sides who stood to gain both power and wealth from the war. Meanwhile, the common soldiers who fought on both sides were being manipulated by these leaders into slaughtering one another when in fact their real enemies were not the soldiers on the other side but the generals and politicians instigating the war from both sides.

The prominent Nigerian poet **Christopher Okigbo** was killed while fighting for the Biafran side in the war. Achebe and his family themselves had several close calls. Achebe strongly supported the Biafran cause during the civil war, though he, too, came to question the ethnic terms of the conflict. In terms of his writing, he reacted most directly to the civil war in his stories and poems; indeed, he stated that the turmoil of the war made it impossible for him to construct something as extensive as a novel at the time and for some time afterward. However, his later depiction of the postcolonial state of **Kangan**, which has recently won a civil war against the secessionist region of **Abazon** in *Anthills of the Savannah*, obviously owes a great deal to the events of the Nigerian Civil War.

FURTHER READING

Elechi Amadi, *Sunset in Biafra*; Herbert Ekwe-Ekwe, *The Biafra War*; Frederick Forsyth, *The Biafra Story*; Alexander Madiebo, *The Nigerian Revolution and the Biafran War*; Arthur Ravenscroft, "The Nigerian Civil War in Nigerian Literature"; Ken Saro-Wiwa, *On a Darkling Plain*.

M. Keith Booker

NKECHI, daughter of **Okonkwo** and his third wife in *Things Fall Apart*. She is mentioned only briefly, at the end of chapter 5.

M. Keith Booker

NKECHI, daughter of Ibe and Akueke in *Arrow of God*.

Rachel R. Reynolds

NKISA, a spring in which women of **Umuaro** (*Arrow of God*) do their washing and bathing. See also **Alusi**.

Rachel R. Reynolds

NKISA, a town in the region of **Umuaro** in *Arrow of God* where the mission doctor lives.

Rachel R. Reynolds

NKWO. See **Market days**.

NNABENYI, NWOKEKE, an elder of **Umuaro** in *Arrow of God* (chapter 12).

Rachel R. Reynolds

NNADI, the mythical protagonist of a rhyme chanted by the children of **Umuofia** in *Things Fall Apart* whenever it rains. He is mentioned at the end of chapter 4, where we learn that he traditionally lives alone, cooking and eating.

M. Keith Booker

NNAMA. In chapter 20 of *Things Fall Apart*, the colonial government grants a disputed piece of land to the family of Nnama, which has given much money to the white man's messengers and interpreter.

M. Keith Booker

NNEKA, the wife of the prosperous farmer **Amadi** of **Mbanta** in chapter 17 of *Things Fall Apart*. Having previously borne (and thrown away) four sets of twins, Nneka is beginning to be regarded as an outcast, so that no one (including her family) seems particularly concerned when she runs away to join the Christians as a convert. "Nneka" is identified in chapter 14 as a common **Igbo** name meaning "mother is supreme." Out of politeness to his mother's family, **Okonkwo** gives the name to his firstborn child while in exile in Mbanta (chapter 19).

M. Keith Booker

NO LONGER AT EASE, Achebe's second novel, was initially envisioned by the author as forming only the final section of a single book, but that section and the projected pre-liminary one evolved into two separate volumes. The preliminary section became Achebe's first novel, *Things Fall Apart*, while the final section became *No Longer at Ease*, published in 1960, the year of Nigerian Independence. *No Longer at Ease* forms a kind of sequel to *Things Fall Apart* but is set during the few years just prior to independence—that is, not one but two generations after the period treated in *Things Fall Apart*. Although the second novel has not gained as large an audience as its predecessor, despite the invaluable cumulative effect of reading both, it merits high regard as an influential, finely wrought, and engaging work in its own right. *No Longer at Ease* traces the long-term impact of British colonialism in West Africa, dramatizes social and economic dilemmas still facing modern Africa, and has helped lay a vital part of the stylistic as well as thematic groundwork for important works of African literature that have followed.

As in much **postcolonial literature**, the tension of a dual legacy permeates *No Longer at Ease*. This tension is signified by the novel's very title and epigraph—drawn from **T. S. Eliot**'s poem **"The Journey of the Magi"**—a tension signified in the content of the poem as well as in the fact that this Anglo-American verse is made to serve the purposes of an African novel. Achebe exploits this dual legacy to dramatize how fundamentally the world embodied by the Okonkwo family has altered over two short generations and how formidable a challenge such a legacy poses to a coherent postcolonial national identity.

Fairly modest in length, *No Longer at Ease* depicts the rise and fall of a young Nigerian of **Igbo** heritage, **Obi Okonkwo (Michael Obiajulu Okonkwo)**, who is the grandson of **Okonkwo**, the protagonist of *Things Fall Apart*. Obi is talented, well-meaning, and idealistic, and he wins the first scholarship to study in England offered by the **Lagos** branch of the **Umuofia Progressive Union (UPU)**, an Igbo support club whose membership comes from Obi's home district. In order that there may be subsequent Umuofian beneficiaries of the scholarship, its funds must be paid back by Obi to the UPU once he returns from England, where, notwithstanding the UPU intention that he study law, he takes a degree in English. Obi completes his studies in England in 1956, at age twenty-five or twenty-six, and returns to Nigeria. Shortly thereafter, he secures a position in the senior civil service in Lagos as Secretary to the Scholarship Board, a position that by its nature tends to attract bribes from favor seekers. Even before his appointment, Obi staunchly opposes the widespread practice of bribe-taking in official circles, believing that the hopes of his beloved, soon-to-be independent homeland depend on the integrity of its leaders. Due to these principles, he resists participating in all forms of corruption when first at his post, but in this and other respects he later becomes irresolute.

Although Obi's transformation from unwavering idealist to indecisive and venal bureaucrat occurs rather more swiftly than one might expect, the transformation is not unmotivated. Over a period of months, he goes deeply into debt, partly due to his own mismanagement of his salary and partly due to circumstances that are beyond his control. When he first returns to his rural village, he finds that his beloved mother and father, **Hannah** and **Isaac Okonkwo**, are underfed and diminished in physical capacity, so he decides that he must assist them financially. Before long he has a host of other monetary obligations, including the payment of his brother's school fees and the reimbursement of his own scholarship. During Obi's second visit to the village, moreover, Hannah and Isaac sternly oppose his decision to marry **Clara Okeke**, a young Igbo woman with whom he is deeply in love, because she de-

scends from the forbidden *osu* caste. Hannah goes so far as to tell Obi that she will kill herself if he marries Clara. Upon returning to Lagos, Obi finds that Clara is pregnant with their child, but they agree on an abortion, though Obi has a change of heart moments too late. Clara leaves him, and as a final blow he learns shortly afterward that Hannah has died. Obi's subsequent grief combines with his financial desperation to lead him to accept one of the bribes that are readily available to him. Although Obi's bribe-taking recurs (in both monetary and sexual forms) and occasions his arrest and conviction, he grows more rather than less tormented as time passes and appears close to renouncing the activity just prior to his arrest.

The narrative of *No Longer at Ease* is a skillfully woven story with subtle and effective attention to detail, image, symbol, and structure, and it is narrated in Achebe's characteristically lucid prose. But, with respect to literary merit, it is not merely the novel's Western-influenced formal features and elegant English style that merit critical attention. No evaluation of the formal features of *No Longer at Ease* can neglect the fact that it advances Achebe's project, begun with *Things Fall Apart*, of creating a distinctively African fiction in English. Achebe continues to render Igbo speech patterns and proverbs in an English that is "*in character*," as he puts it in **"The African Writer and the English Language"** (*Morning* 102), appropriate, in other words, to the manner of a given character. But in *No Longer at Ease* many of the Igbo characters speak, in addition to Igbo, either **pidgin English** or formal English or both. While this complicates the language picture, Achebe still manages to seamlessly interweave Igbo and English verbal patterns.

Notwithstanding the widespread use of English by modern Nigerians, Igbo-language usage is rendered eloquently in *No Longer at*

Ease. A similar practice in *Things Fall Apart* began the process of correcting the notion of Africans as semi-articulate and uncivilized that had been propagated by generations of European writers, and in *No Longer at Ease* the pride in Igbo usage, whether in the city or country, remains ardent. When Obi returns for the first time to his home district of **Umuofia** and hears Igbo speech in all its richness, his pride swells. He wishes that those English who are uncomprehending with respect to African language "were here today to see. Let them come to Umuofia now and listen to the talk of men who made a great art of conversation. Let them come and see men and women and children who knew how to live, whose joy of life had not yet been killed by those who claimed to teach other nations how to live" (57). Obi is an advocate not only of Igbo culture but of **Nigeria,** and it is one of the tenets of his idealism that the people of his nation will prosper through a strong sense of unity and common purpose. This outlook is reflected in the poem "Nigeria," which he wrote in England in 1955 and which is quoted twice in the novel. Even after Obi's idealism fades, one may detect a lingering belief in the idea of a unified Nigeria, as may be discerned in a conversation he has late in the novel with **Marie Tomlinson**, the secretary of Obi's boss, **William Green**:

"I suppose so," said Marie, "but surely it's time someone stopped all the Moslem holidays."
"Nigeria is a Moslem country, you know."
"No, it isn't. You mean the North."
They argued for a little while longer. (175)

No Longer at Ease's many allusions to imminent Nigerian self-rule contribute to a sense that the novel itself is relevant to the building of a nation. In the manner of a cautionary tale, the novel traces the course by which Obi fails to fulfill his own vision of personal and governmental integrity. In so doing it identifies a number of forces arrayed

against the success of the nation-to-be. In particular these forces act to undermine a sense of unity, as in the narrow factionalism to which one pompous speaker pays tribute at a UPU meeting: "Every town and village struggles at this momentous epoch in our political evolution to possess that of which it can say: 'This is mine' " (36). Later in the same scene the narrator almost explicitly condemns the self-centeredness of the national outlook: "In Nigeria the government was 'they.' It had nothing to do with you or me. It was an alien institution and people's business was to get as much from it as they could without getting into trouble" (37).

This selfish outlook clearly overlaps with the acceptance and practice of official corruption that the novel explores. In the opening scene alone (which is sequentially the end of the plot) we are told that civil servants frequently pay bribes to obtain a doctor's certificate of illness for the day so that they might leave work and hear the verdict in Obi's bribery trial. Achebe shows that the problem lies not merely in corrupt practices but in the wide social acceptance of corruption. This attitude is countered in the recurring attention the novel gives to the issue of sexual bribery. This motif reminds us that graft is not merely one style of transaction among many in the modern world, but is rather a moral failing, one that ultimately damages society as a whole by tearing down the bonds of common purpose.

In *No Longer at Ease* official corruption is only one manifestation of the decadence that is tied to the modern urban environment. Meanwhile, counterpoised with the idea of urban decadence and volatility is the idea of rural piety and stability. The novel expresses apprehension that, without the moral grounding of traditionally tight-knit community structures, conditions in the larger state are in jeopardy. Yet, as there are signs that even these resilient communal structures are eroding, the outlook for the nation seems all the more doubtful. The critical point in the tension between city and country dramatized in *No Longer at Ease* is Obi himself, whose British education and social and professional ties to Lagos, the former capital city of Nigeria, cause him to drift from family members in his home village, **Iguedo** (the village of his grandfather, Okonkwo). Yet the ties to family prove to be more deeply rooted than he has recognized and help to weaken his resolve to wed Clara. In short, Obi finds himself simultaneously drawn to and alienated from both the city and the countryside, and it is out of this equivocal geographic orientation, which is both an image of and a source of his moral indecision, that much of *No Longer at Ease*'s drama is generated. In fact it may be remarked that the pull on Obi by the city and the country and the social forces they embody are what pulls him apart.

Among the attractions of the city depicted in *No Longer at Ease* are cultural sophistication and variety, sexual freedom, and the availability of glamorous consumer items. The musical and erotic allure of the Lagos nightclub scene is vividly evoked in the novel, as it is also a vital element in *People of the City* (1954) and *Jagua Nana* (1961), by another Igbo pioneer of the Anglophone African novel, **Cyprian Ekwensi**). *No Longer at Ease* also considers the seductiveness and the psychological and moral effects of desiring and acquiring expensive consumer items (a theme explored at length in Ghanaian novelist **Ayi Kwei Armah**'s ***The Beautyful Ones Are Not Yet Born*** [1969]). Achebe, characteristically, views these matters from multiple angles. Obi's evening with Clara and friends at a Lagos nightclub, **the Imperial**, abounds with sexual insinuation and longing, and the author evokes a vital beauty in the atmosphere, especially in the **high-life** music and dancing; this scene of real and potential erotic license, in which

dance partners are interchangeable, is then followed shortly by Obi's nearly sexual encounter with **Nora**, a young teacher from Ireland. This is the first token of his fragile loyalty to Clara.

Prior to these events and almost immediately after he is appointed to his government post, Obi acquires a new Morris Oxford automobile, which becomes a focal point of Achebe's questioning of the materialism and uneven economic development that are identified with an urban, capitalist economy. Obi really cannot afford this car and its many related expenses (he even hires, for a time, a chauffeur), but he considers neither delaying its acquisition nor selling it when his debt takes on alarming proportions. In this and other respects he finds himself in the position of so many in consumer cultures: unable to extricate himself from debt while earning more than ever—in his case far more than the vast majority of his compatriots. Certainly this disparity between the income of people like Obi and the income of most others, even the relatively well educated, is a prominent feature of what amounts to Achebe's critique of capitalist development in Nigeria. Such disparity, symbolized by Obi's car, is regarded from one angle as unhealthy for the soon-to-be independent nation, which requires unity rather than a cadre of leaders that uses its wealth and formal education only to set itself apart from the rest of the people. All this is suggested when someone waiting in a long line to see a doctor levels at Obi a telling rebuke in pidgin for forcing himself ahead of the others: " 'You tink because Government give you car you fit do what you like? You see all of we de wait here and you just go in. . . . Foolish man. He tink say because him get car so derefore he can do as he like. Beast of no nation!' " (173).

No Longer at Ease reminds us here and elsewhere of the immense gulf separating the few well-off from the multitude of the poor, a gulf given striking dimensions in the second chapter's juxtaposition of a slum area in Lagos, where there is poverty but also a rich social mosaic, with the city's luxurious Ikoyi district. The building in which Obi lives, though rather nondescript, is in that district, and to further emphasize the dubious quality of the urban hierarchy, it is later revealed that whereas he, a highly successful African in the senior civil service, lives in this building, all its other occupants are only "unimportant Europeans on the lower rungs of the service" (190). Achebe further questions the social exclusiveness signified by Ikoyi by likening it to "a graveyard," while characterizing the Lagos mainland, which includes the slums, as "a bazaar" and as a palm-nut kernel, "shiny black and alive" (20).

Still the author cannot be charged with unduly glamorizing the lives of the poor in the city, as is evident in his description of the slum, with its "wide-open storm drain from which came a very strong smell of rotting flesh [from] the remains of a dog which had no doubt been run over by a taxi" (17) and its "night-soilman . . . trailing clouds of putrefaction" (18). (The link between urban filth and corrupt materialism is also exploited by Armah in *The Beautyful Ones*.) Further, at the end of the scene set in a Lagos nightclub, Achebe exposes the realities of urban blight and again of social division in relation to Obi's car. Upon returning to it after dancing, Obi and Clara find that the fifty pounds in cash that was temporarily in the glove box has been stolen by the "half-clad little urchins" (126) whom they encountered when they parked the car earlier in the evening. One child sought, perhaps on behalf of his group, a threepence tip for looking after the car, but "in principle Obi never gave anything to these juvenile delinquents" (127). The connection between Obi's car and the poverty of the children who prey on it is not arbitrary. Rather, it may be read as one of the novel's cautionary notes concerning freedom and prosperity: these cannot be enjoyed for long, either by the individual or the nation, if the dispossessed are ignored.

Nonetheless, the novel does suggest that the modern city is a source of legitimate opportunities and progress. It is through the work the city offers to migrants from Obi's home district of Umuofia that they are able to collect enough money to establish the scholarship that provides him with an education in England—an education that they justifiably believe will benefit them (especially if Obi becomes a lawyer) as well as Obi. The city is the source of other, government-sponsored university scholarships (including ones to England), and the benefits of such an education and of university education in general are undeniable: "It was rather sheer hypocrisy to ask if a scholarship was as important as all that or if university education was worth it. Every Nigerian knew the answer. It was yes. A university degree was the philosopher's stone" (105).

However, there are so few university scholarships relative to the demand that men and women are willing to resort to monetary bribery, and some women offer their bodies, to obtain them. From this angle one problem with urban modernity in Africa is not the economic and educational opportunities themselves, but rather the scarcity of such opportunities. Such scarcity makes it rather likely that a person in Obi's position will fall into debt. Despite having found a relatively well-paying job in Lagos, he is still bound by strong kinship affiliations, so the fewer the number of well-paying positions, the greater the portion of his income will go to family members.

The novel's descriptions of women seeking a better chance at a scholarship by offering themselves to Obi due to his influential position as Secretary to the Scholarship

Board are also part of the novel's pattern of representing the city as a site of immorality and decadence. The rural countryside, on the other hand, is generally viewed as a site of simple virtue. This pattern is underscored by the varied images of music-making. The only music in the city that the author depicts is that of the Imperial nightclub. The licentious nature of that music is reflected in its suggestive lyrics and in the rather lewd dancing it inspires.

By contrast, in the village of Iguedo, which is the only rural community portrayed in the novel, the adult singing described is entirely pious in nature. In the first instance, which occurs when Obi is given a send-off to England by Christian community members at Isaac's home, both of the songs performed are sacred. In the second instance, which occurs during Obi's second return visit, the singing is done by a band of non-Christian young women. Their song teaches a moral lesson that underscores the traditional importance placed on kinship ties, namely, that the need to cherish the members of one's family is far greater than the need for material wealth. Importantly, the simple virtue that is associated in the novel with people of the countryside is given emphasis by the singing of pious songs in *both* Christian and non-Christian contexts.

The emblem of the contrasting moral tones of city and country in *No Longer at Ease* unexpectedly consists of two pillowcases. When he is about twenty-one, Obi visits Lagos for the first time, traveling the 500 miles from Iguedo, his rural Igbo village in Umuofia, to the city in order to take a plane to England for nearly four years of study. In Lagos he stays for a few days in the one-room lodgings of his friend from school in Umuofia, **Joseph Okeke**. Obi is fascinated by the frank sexuality in "this strange and sinful new world" (16), and when Joseph tells him about a former girlfriend, **Joy**, he

mentions that she made the pillowcases in his apartment. On one of these Joy sewed the word "*osculate*" in multicolored letters. This word on the pillowcase as well as the appearance of Joseph's current, unnamed female companion, whose dress and makeup heighten the effect of some of her physical attributes, leave "a nasty taste in Obi's mouth" (17). On the other hand, when Obi is back in his room at his parents' home in Iguedo four years later, he notices the brand-new white sheet and "pillow-slips with their delicate floral designs," which are "no doubt **Esther**'s work." He thinks, " 'Good old Esther!' " (69) and remembers that she, his sister and eldest sibling, became a schoolteacher when Obi was a young child. Then people in the community, including her siblings, began calling her Miss as a sign of respect, though Obi sometimes forgot and called her Esther. These wholesome details and the devoutly Christian home that provide their setting make the second allusion to a pillowcase stand in relief to the previous, mildly lewd one, a relief image that reinforces the novel's moral distinction between the urban and rural spheres.

Apart from a glimpse of Obi's erotic thoughts about Clara while he is lying in bed at his family's home, sexuality, let alone lewd sexuality, plays no role in the Iguedo scenes. Yet the overall treatment of sexuality is considerably more frank and extensive in *No Longer at Ease* than in *Things Fall Apart*. This treatment includes varied moments of sexual humor, as illustrated in one of Obi's debates about bribery with his economist friend, **Christopher**. Obi tells him the story of **Elsie Mark**, a young woman who, desperate for a university scholarship, offered herself to Obi not long after he was appointed Secretary to the Scholarship Board. Christopher, an unrepentant libertine, calls Obi "the biggest ass in Nigeria" for not obliging Miss Mark (137). Denying that accepting sexual favors from a woman for official considerations is the same as bribery (and ignoring the fact that Obi was already engaged to Clara at the time), Christopher says to Obi, "You are being sentimental. A girl who comes the way she did is not an innocent little girl. It's like the story of the girl who was given a form to fill in. She put down her name and her age. But when she came to sex she wrote: 'Twice a week' " (137). Nearly all the novel's many moments of humor, sexual and otherwise, have such an ironic edge to them, but in general the humor, the sexuality, the music, the varied language styles, the sights and sounds of urban and rural Nigeria contribute to the vitality and vividly realized atmosphere of *No Longer at Ease.*

Still, for all its vitality and despite its intricate relationship with *Things Fall Apart,* *No Longer at Ease* is not a novel of action the way its predecessor often is. Rather, it is a novel of moral reflection and political anticipation. To a considerable degree, this distinction is traceable to essential qualities in the protagonists of the two novels, Okonkwo, courageous warrior and wrestler, filled with pride in his village and clan, and Obi, intelligent student and administrator, filled with pride in his new nation. There is yet another important figure that contributes to the distinction between the two novels in their orientation to action, namely, Isaac Okonkwo, the former catechist who directly links the two novels and their protagonists. In *Things Fall Apart* Okonkwo frowned on his son, **Nwoye**, precisely because he was not becoming a man of action in Okonkwo's image and was thus reminding him of his own indolent father, **Unoka**. Nwoye's rejection of his father, conversion to Christianity, and assumption of the name Isaac expressed his feeling that he somehow did not fit in the traditional Igbo world of his father. Isaac's essential nature is captured in a reflection of Obi's: "His father, although uncompromising in conflicts between church and clan, was not really a man of action but of thought" (188). With regard to education, religion, and morality, the village world in which Obi was raised and that still has a deep influence on him is a world that is an extension of Isaac himself. So it is fair to say that Isaac's qualities and convictions influence the spirit of *No Longer at Ease* in a way that they cannot in *Things Fall Apart.*

Much of the relative lack of action in *No Longer at Ease* can be attributed to the ambivalence and indecision that increasingly beset Obi. He is caught between the claims of powerful competing forces, especially those associated with his Western tendencies and Clara, on the one hand, and his traditional African orientation and family, on the other. It may also be added that Obi is clearly a sensitive young man, as suggested by the tears he sheds at various times; so the conflicts that accrue from his dual inheritance are certain to take a greater toll on him than on his brazen friend, Christopher, who "was rather outstanding in . . . coming to terms with a double heritage" (126).

Obi's career in the novel is notable for its missed opportunities, wasted effort, poor judgment, and indecision. The vital gestures he does make and the admirable principles he does possess are consistently thwarted in one way or another. He becomes engaged to Clara but cannot marry her and even has tentative relations with the teacher, Nora; he gets Clara pregnant but agrees with her on an abortion; he changes his mind about the abortion but does so too late; he loves his mother but does not return to Iguedo for her funeral (replicating in a passive way the young Isaac's active refusal, which we learn of in *No Longer at Ease,* to return home for Okonkwo's burial); he condemns bribery in its monetary and sexual forms but ends up indulging in both. The culmination of this downward spiral is, indeed, the monetary bribe for which he is arrested at the end of the novel. When it is first brought to him, he can neither touch it, due to his growing moral revulsion, nor refuse it. Rather, "he just sat looking at it, paralyzed by his thoughts" (103). Implicit in this remark is the essential difference between the original Okonkwo and his grandson Obi and hence between the manner of the narratives about them. Okonkwo actively destroys himself when he determines, in spite of his people's strict prohibition against suicide, that self-destruction is the only action by which he may uphold his own sense of honor. Obi passively destroys himself in the social realm when he fails to act in accord with his own sense of honor and accepts bribes.

There is, however, a character in *No Longer at Ease* "who got things done," a phrase applied not to a man at all but rather to a woman, Hannah Okonkwo, Obi's mother (188). As we shall see below, Hannah is a capable person in numerous ways, from farming to traditional storytelling to child raising, and upon her death Obi realizes that Isaac "would be completely lost without her" (184). Hannah has a devoted, monogamous marriage and eight children with Isaac, but the novel asks whether conditions for her and other women have dramatically improved between the culture depicted in *Things Fall Apart* and that in *No Longer at Ease*. In the former Okonkwo has three wives, so they must share him, but they also have the support of each other and, presumably, many of their children, as well as that of Okonkwo, whereas, in the latter, when Hannah and Isaac grow too old to farm (and thereby supplement his pension), there is no one to farm for them. In *Things Fall Apart*, all of Okonkwo's wives tell folk stories, as do the children, while in *No Longer at Ease* Hannah "could read, but she never took part in the family reading. She merely listened to her husband and children" (66). In the traditional culture,

mothers of twins had to endure the exposure of the babies in the forest, but in the modern one some mothers-to-be, like Clara, must endure abortions.

In the modern environment, moreover, paying jobs can be obtained by women, such as Clara, who is a nurse, but there is social resistance and ridicule in store for such women. On the bus that Obi takes for his first visit home, traders sing "gay and bawdy songs addressed mostly to young women who had become nurses or teachers instead of mothers" (48). This attitude may appear to be at odds with the lesson of "Lady first" that, according to **Sam Okoli**, a popular politician who is Obi's acquaintance, the white man has brought to Nigeria (77). Sam is an Anglophile, and from his perspective the fact that the British have outlawed **bride-price**, may be all to the good, though the effect of the ban, according to Joseph, has been to "push up the price, that's all" (47). Still, it would appear from the references to bride-price here and in *Things Fall Apart* that a partial function of the custom is to confer dignity and status on the bride. In light of this and other information in *No Longer at Ease* it is clear that not everyone is as biased as Sam. Obi thinks of the British in a disapproving moment as a people "who claimed to teach other nations how to live" (57). It may be noted, too, that the reverse impact of the bride-price law is one of numerous signs in *No Longer at Ease* that African tradition is a resilient adversary of British legislation and influence.

It is not only with respect to women that Achebe, through his subtle juxtaposition of elements in the two novels, urges us to reflect on just how much, if at all, the European-influenced culture is an improvement over the traditional Igbo one. Absent from *No Longer at Ease* is an **Evil Forest**, which in the world of *Things Fall Apart* was "the dumping ground for the potent fetishes of great medicine men when they died" (148). But in *No Longer at Ease* one finds the open storm drain with a rotting carcass of a dog, which may be one of the "many dogs killed by drivers in Lagos" for "good luck" (17–18). In *No Longer at Ease* there are no tales of British massacres of Africans like the massacre at **Abame** described in *Things Fall Apart* (based on the massacre at **Ahiara**). Yet in *No Longer at Ease* Africans are shown to be the objects of British ignorance and chauvinism. Some humor is derived from the woman in England who, after sexual relations with Obi, "said she thought she had been attacked by a tiger" (100). The possible misconception concerning African fauna may serve as a commentary on the stereotype concerning African sexuality. (On the other hand, in **Anthills of the Savannah**, chapter 5, **Christopher Oriko** observes, "Not for her [i.e., **Beatrice Okoh**] the lover as tiger that some women crave.") There is not much humor, however, in Obi's British boss, William Green, a complex figure who, just the same, repeatedly expresses virulent prejudice against Africans, as when he observes to Obi, " 'In a country where even the educated have not reached the level of thinking about tomorrow, one has a clear duty.' He made the word 'educated' taste like vomit" (109).

Now prejudice is not the same as mass killing (though, of course, the former can give rise to the latter). But prejudice can be destructive to the spirit of countless people, as Achebe makes clear in his essay **"An Image of Africa"** (on *Heart of Darkness*) and also in his essay **"The Novelist as Teacher"**: "Here then is an adequate revolution for me to espouse—to help my society regain belief in itself and put away the complexes of the years of denigration and self-abasement. . . . For no thinking African can escape the pain of the wound in our soul" (*Morning* 71). (This essay also includes a valuable discussion of one reader's response to *No Longer*

at Ease.) Such a wound seems to account for, in *No Longer at Ease*, Sam Okoli's identification with the British and for his denigration, first in mocking pidgin, of other Nigerians: " 'White man don go far. We just de shout for nothing,' he said. Then he seemed to realize his position. . . . 'I used to have a Nigerian as my [Assistant Secretary]. . . . Now I have a white man who went to Oxford and he says 'sir' to me. Our people have a long way to go' " (78–79). Such internalized prejudice and cynicism on the part of a rising Nigerian politician is one of the signs in *No Longer at Ease* of potential political troubles for the nation.

If Obi is not an Anglophile in the manner of Sam Okoli, neither does he hate everything about England or about modern technological culture. Achebe himself has resisted, in various statements, unqualified condemnation of the West. In "The Novelist as Teacher," for example, he remarks, "I am for choosing my cause very carefully. Why should I start waging war as a Nigerian newspaper editor was doing the other day on the 'soulless efficiency' of Europe's industrial and technological civilization when the very thing my society needs may well be a little technical efficiency?" (69–70). While the technologically oriented urban environment in *No Longer at Ease* has its problems, such as a scarcity of really desirable opportunities, it is not utterly rejected by the novel. Neither, on the other hand, is the traditional rural village, which is subject to its own forms of scarcity.

When Obi returns to his family's village, Iguedo, for the first time after studying in England, he perceives not only how seriously ill his mother is but also that "his father too [is] all bones" and that they do not "have enough good food to eat" (63). The limited or unreliable supply of essential resources associated with the rural village and, in this case, with Hannah and Isaac's malnutrition, is partly what impels large-scale migrations to urban centers with their cash economies. Yet the case for urban migration is hardly unqualified. Often it exacerbates the ills of overcrowded cities and erodes family and community coherence in the countryside. This erosion and the rural exodus in general deprive those who do stay in the countryside of the abundance that was formerly enjoyed in such areas, including the presence of family members. As *No Longer at Ease* illustrates, this is not merely a matter of lifestyle preference, for such migration is likely a source of Hannah and Isaac's malnutrition (another being the meagerness of Isaac's pension from the church that he served for nearly thirty years). They are now unable, due to advanced age, to supplement Isaac's income with their own farming, as they had previously done. Yet it is revealed during Obi's second visit that they have eight dispersed children who, in a somewhat earlier era, may well have provided the compensatory labor. Hannah's own perception of this dilemma is given eloquent emphasis by an Igbo proverb: "Children left their old parents at home and scattered in all directions in search of money. It was hard on an old woman with eight children. It was like having a river and yet washing one's hands with spittle" (153).

The fundamental tension in *Things Fall Apart* between Africa and Europe and in particular between the Igbo and the British may appear to have shifted in *No Longer at Ease* to the tension between British-imposed modernity (associated with the city) and African tradition (associated with the countryside). But while Achebe does juxtapose the two in pronounced ways, as has been suggested, the situation dramatized in *No Longer at Ease* is more complex than that, partly due to the legacy of Christian evangelism in Igboland. Whereas in the first novel Christian missionaries are closely allied with British administrators in the colonial effort to undermine

Igbo traditions, Igbo Christians in the second novel both suppress and sustain those traditions in *No Longer at Ease*. The multifaceted role of these Christians attests in part to the long-term success of missionary efforts, but also in part to the hardiness of Igbo culture.

As a pillar of the Christian community in the district of Umuofia, Isaac Okonkwo has asserted the priority of the new faith over and against Igbo religion through much of his life. In his own family he has done so with the support of Hannah, who converted as an adult and who "sometimes show[ed] more zeal than even her husband" (67). Obi remembers that at four years old he refused, like his older sisters, to partake of a neighbor's gift, a result of their mother's teaching, but embarrassed the sisters by adding aloud that they never eat "heathen food" (67). Isaac does not rigidly dismiss all aspects of the culture that he was born into as Nwoye, thus permitting the traditional presentation of the kola nut to guests, as long as it is not sacrificed to idols. The adult Obi's faith, however, has weakened, and he wonders about the consequences of saying to Isaac, " 'Father, I no longer believe in your God' " (65).

In addition Obi "used to wonder whether . . . [his mother] would not have preferred telling her children the folk stories that her mother had told her" (66). Hannah had done so with her daughters before Obi was born, but eventually Isaac forbade the practice because such tales were for "heathens . . . not for the people of the Church" (66). But Achebe is quick to show that the oral tradition is not so easily proscribed. The prohibition against folk stories by Isaac—who himself uses Igbo proverbs—was eventually breached by Hannah when she taught the young Obi a tale about the wicked leopardess in order that he could tell it to his class at school. The teacher encouraged the students to do so, and when Obi narrated the story, he embellished it with his own final twist. The entire passage casts a backward glance at *Things Fall Apart*. There Nwoye, the future Isaac, ironically prefers his mother's folktales to his father's "masculine stories of violence and bloodshed" (53); and there, Okonkwo's second wife, **Ekwefi**, tells their daughter, **Ezinma**, the splendid story of **"Tortoise and the Birds."**

In different ways, moreover, these passages resonate with one near the end of *No Longer at Ease*. **Nathaniel**, an Umuofia man in modern Lagos, narrates for a group of people at the bereaved Obi's apartment a Tortoise tale that is meant to comment on Obi's decision not to return to Iguedo for Hannah's funeral. The tale, perhaps improvised, describes Tortoise's attempt to avoid the burden of burying his mother. What this narration has in common with the young Obi's narration (besides possibly the improvisatory element), and what it has in common with Isaac's selective use of Igbo ritual and oral tradition, is an affirmation of the power of African tradition in a modern environment. The tenacity of that tradition is evident not only in the alliance it sometimes forges with European culture, but also, alliance or not, in its multiform survival of the European onslaught. (One may add here that the resilience of African tradition is embodied in the fact that its resources, as well as Achebe's confidence in them, permitted the author's deft reconfiguration of aspects of the English novel.)

Clearly, the potential for irony, self-contradiction, and hypocrisy is great where two traditions—here Igbo and Christian—that have stood in violent opposition to each other within a community's living memory both have elements that are accepted and even honored by the community at present. During each of the two scenes in which Obi visits Iguedo the currents of such irony culminate in relation to Obi's grandfather, Okonkwo. As part of a gathering to celebrate

Obi's first visit back to Iguedo, a village elder and non-Christian, **Ogbuefi Odogwu**, presides at the Okonkwo family home over the kola nut ceremony in a way that will not offend Isaac, who countenances Odogwu's role, or any of the other Christians. Odogwu has a benign attitude toward Christianity, and his first good-natured remarks concerning the faith recall those of **Akunna** in his discussions with **Mr. Brown** in *Things Fall Apart*. But in a little while Odogwu pays tribute to Okonkwo—presumably an uncomfortable topic for Isaac, who, as mentioned in an early scene, "rejected everything about his father except . . . one proverb" (11). One of the questions that *Things Fall Apart* raises is whether Okonkwo died heroically or shamefully, but at Isaac's house Odogwu leaves no doubt where he (and possibly numerous other villagers) stands on the issue. In praising Obi, he shapes the historical record in a way that exalts Okonkwo's resistance to the British incursion in Umuofia: " '[Obi] is the grandson of Ogbuefi Okonkwo who faced the white man single-handed and died in the fight. Stand up!' Obi stood up obediently. 'Remark him,' said Odogwu. 'He is Ogbuefi Okonkwo come back. He is Okonkwo *kpom-kwem*, exact, perfect' " (61–62). Odogwu goes on to extol other renowned, non-Christians of Iguedo of previous generations, and the entire speech indirectly honors the traditional culture. Such praise in Isaac's Christian home for the father and way of life he rejected so long before is sharply ironic since it draws together many of the tensions left unresolved in *Things Fall Apart*.

The irony springing from these tensions culminates in Obi's visit to Iguedo. His parents take the opportunity to express strong opposition to his intention to marry Clara due to her status as an *osu*. In particular, when Isaac pressures his son to abandon these plans, he reprises the role of his own father, Okonkwo, who pressured him to conform to

Igbo customs. That pressure and some of the customs themselves, including one in particular that dismayed Nwoye (the exposure of twins), paved the way for his becoming the Christian, Isaac. What Isaac pressures Obi to accept in this scene is precisely an Igbo custom that dismays Obi (the *osu* prohibition). Obi uses Isaac's own Christian teaching to suggest his hypocrisy in supporting for the moment the belief system that for so long he has staunchly rejected: " 'We are Christians. . . . The Bible says that in Christ there are no bond or free. . . . Have we not seen the light of the Gospel?' " The narrator here tells us that Obi uses "the very words that his father might have used in talking to his heathen kinsmen" (151). But in so doing, Obi is being hypocritical himself, or at least disingenuous, since it is clear from other passages that his Christian convictions have almost or entirely vanished. At this point the cultural struggle that Achebe dramatizes is no longer one of binary, but rather multidimensional, opposition. The fact that Obi is caught amid all these complex forces helps account for his failure to take a firm grip on his circumstances.

When Obi first returns to Nigeria, his remarks to the UPU reflect his own, still vital belief in the possibilities of the future nation, possibilities that, if they are to be realized, will demand integrity, hard work, and sacrifice on behalf of not a single faction but the nation as a whole: "With our great country on the threshold of independence, we need men who are prepared to serve her well and truly" (37). He certainly is referring here to his expectations for himself among others. But before much time passes, he yields the contribution he wished to make to the self-seeking, and the compromises that he understood all along were poised to strike those like him who had gained extended formal education. The novel's sobering message is that the self-interest and moral disorientation that

succeed in fragmenting Obi as an individual threaten to splinter the larger political entity. In painting this rather bleak portrait of the nation on the verge of self-rule, Achebe may be accused of a certain pessimism but not of the cynicism that overtakes Obi. The author is issuing, after all, a warning for the sake of the nation rather than simply condemning it in order to vent his fury. In issuing that warning, in dramatizing so trenchantly where the danger lies, he carries out his own part in the task of nation building—of serving his country well and truly.

FURTHER READING

Chinua Achebe, *Morning Yet on Creation Day*; C. A. Babalola, "A Reconsideration of Achebe's *No Longer at Ease*"; David Carroll, *Chinua Achebe*; Rosemary Colmer, "The Start of Weeping Is Always Hard: The Ironic Structure of *No Longer at Ease*"; J. Michael Dash, "The Outsider in West African Fiction: An Approach to Three Novels"; Richard S. Davis, "In Search of Agency among Colonized Africans"; Ernest Emenyonu, *The Rise of the Igbo Novel*; Ezenwa-Ohaeto, *Chinua Achebe: A Biography*; Annie Gagiano, *Achebe, Head, Marechera*; Simon Gikandi, "Chinua Achebe and the Poetics of Location" and *Reading Chinua Achebe*; C. L. Innes, *Chinua Achebe*; Nnadozie F. Inyama, "Genetic Discontinuity in Achebe's *No Longer at Ease*"; Emmanuel Obiechina, "Chinua Achebe's *No Longer at Ease*" and *Culture, Tradition, and Society in the West African Novel*; Umelo Ojinmah, *Chinua Achebe: New Perspectives*; Chinwe Christiana Okechukwa, *Achebe the Orator*; Andrew Peek, "Betrayal and the Question of Affirmation in Chinua Achebe's *No Longer at Ease*"; Felicity Riddy, "Language as a Theme in *No Longer at Ease*"; Philip Rogers, "*No Longer at Ease*"; Roderick Wilson, "Eliot and Achebe."

Thomas J. Lynn

NORA, one of the two young Irish women, newly arrived in **Nigeria**, who teach at a Roman Catholic convent near **Lagos** in chapter 12 of *No Longer at Ease*. **Obi Okonkwo's** friend, **Christopher**, is the first to meet Nora and her compatriot, **Pat**, and introduces them to Obi. The four dance the **high-life**, have supper, and, on two later occasions, play tennis. During their first encounter Obi and Nora kiss, revealing the tenuous quality of Obi's commitment to **Clara Okeke**, to whom he is engaged at the time. Nora does not allow him to advance further, however, and after the tennis dates she and Pat discourage future visits to the convent by the two young men because of the warning to them by the convent's Mother "about going around with African men." One of the novel's themes sounded by this brief and rather odd episode with the two women is Obi's ambivalent feelings toward the English. When he first meets the two women, he finds that "they [are] rather more anti-English" than he is, which makes "him somewhat uneasy." Indeed Obi's lack of ease in the novel may be traced in large measure to his divided affiliation with both African and English cultures.

Thomas J. Lynn

"THE NOVELIST AS TEACHER." See *Morning Yet on Creation Day*.

THE NOVELS OF CHINUA ACHEBE. See *The Writings of Chinua Achebe*.

NSUGBE. A town mentioned in *Arrow of God*, famous for its coconuts.

Rachel R. Reynolds

NSUKKA, a town in the Udi Hills of Enugu State, southern **Nigeria**. A traditional center of agricultural trade and of **Igbo** crafts such as weaving, Nsukka has, since 1960, been the site of the main campus of the **University of Nigeria**.

M. Keith Booker

NSUKKASCOPE, a magazine established by Achebe in 1971 to provide a forum for protest against the policies of the administration of the **University of Nigeria, Nsukka**, which Achebe saw as overbearing and insensitive to the concerns of faculty. The magazine's motto was "Devastating, Fearless, Brutal and True," and Achebe sought, as editor, to carry out that motto in the contents of the publication.

FURTHER READING
Ezenwa-Ohaeto, *Chinua Achebe: A Biography*.

M. Keith Booker

NWAFO, the youngest son of **Ezeulu** and **Ugoye** in *Arrow of God*. In the first half of the novel, Nwafo is a focal figure in Achebe's portrait of Ezeulu. Although only the divine can appoint successors to the priesthood of any given god, Ezeulu has half-consciously chosen his son Nwafo to succeed him as chief priest of **Ulu**. For example, Ezeulu focuses on the possibility that Nwafo may have had seizures as a child as evidence of the boy's connection to the divine. He puts the boy at a central position in the family compound, and it is obvious to all that he is being groomed to take over as chief priest. Nonetheless, it is the jealous **Edogo**, the eldest brother of Nwafo, who begins to realize that the shaping of the divine may have more to do with Ezeulu's self-importance than with any plan by the divine. This web of male jealousy and pride—something that also occurred a generation earlier between Ezeulu and his brother Okeke—is one of the ways that the priesthood of Ulu loses its power and the entire family is made tragic.

Rachel R. Reynolds

NWAGENE, a spring in which women of **Umuaro** (*Arrow of God*) do their washing and bathing. See also **Alusi**.

Rachel R. Reynolds

NWAKA, a man of title from **Umunneora** who calls himself the Eru of **Umuaro**, a title taken after the god of wealth, **Eru**. Nwaka is one of the wealthiest men in Umuaro with the highest possible title as well as a local reputation for being a great talker or "Owner of Words" (chapter 4). Throughout *Arrow of God*, Nwaka jockeys to gain even more power by challenging the status of **Ulu** as the chief deity of Umuaro and replacing that chief deity with Eru. To do so, he must discredit Ulu's priest **Ezeulu**.

Rachel R. Reynolds

NWAKA DIMKPOLO, a character in a traditional **Igbo** story who is killed when he is hit by falling *ukwa* fruit. **Obiageli** sings this story in chapter 6 of *Arrow of God*.

Rachel R. Reynolds

NWAKIBIE, a wealthy man in **Okonkwo**'s village of **Iguedo** in *Things Fall Apart*. Renowned for his wealth and success (he has three huge barns, nine wives, and thirty children), he serves as a sort of role model for Okonkwo, standing in the stead of the father Okonkwo does not admire. In chapter 3, we learn that Okonkwo worked for Nwakibie to earn his first seed yams, thus beginning his own road toward prosperity.

M. Keith Booker

NWANKU, the dog who lives by **Edogo**'s home in *Arrow of God*.

Rachel R. Reynolds

NWANKWO, a relative of **Obierika**, who sends him to the busy but notoriously treacherous market at **Umuike** to buy goats for use in the celebration of the *uri* of Obierika's daughter, **Akueke**, in chapter 12 of *Things Fall Apart*.

M. Keith Booker

NWANYIEKE, literally "woman of Eke," the deity of **Okperi**'s special **market day**, **Eke**. Nwanyieke is a elderly woman-spirit who sweeps the market grounds each Eke morning and assures the prosperity of the market.

Rachel R. Reynolds

NWANYIEKE, Ezeulu's mother in *Arrow of God*. She is also called Nwanyi Okperi since she was born in **Okperi**. Like Ezeulu's daughter, **Obiageli**, Nwanyieke is a gifted singer of songs. But Nwanyieke goes mad, and "these old songs and others she might have made forced themselves out in eccentric spurts through the cracks in her mind. Ezeulu in his childhood lived in fear of these moments when his mother's feet were put in stocks, at the new moon" (chapter 19). We see here a complementary set of contrasts between Ezeulu's failing grip on the priesthood, his descent into madness, and his mother's own insanity.

Rachel R. Reynolds

NWANYIEKE, a widow of **Umuachala** who informs a neighbor woman that her child **Obielue** has shown the colonial police how to get to **Ezeulu**'s compound. The passage is an example of how Achebe conveys ethnographic information through story reportage. In chapter 12 of *Arrow of God*, we are treated to a stranger's walk through Umuachala, where no one is willing to point out the location of Ezeulu's home. There were in fact a complex set of prohibitions and formal rules in various places in Igboland for calling strangers and familiars by names, as well as introducing strangers formally to the geography of the village. The colonial officer **Matthew Nweke** violates these rules, and the unlearned child Obielue is the only one he can dupe into giving directions. Nwanyieke and the child's mother then must come together as women to ensure that Obielue is watched and corrected (*Arrow of God*, chapter 12).

Rachel R. Reynolds

NWANYINMA, the widowed girlfriend of **Edogo**, before his marriage (*Arrow of God*, chapter 4).

Rachel R. Reynolds

NWEGE, JONATHAN, the thin and wiry proprietor and principal of the **Anata Grammar School** when **Chief Nanga** returns there to give a speech in 1964 at the beginning of *A Man of the People*. The fawning Nwege makes elaborate preparations for Nanga's visit, hoping he will be rewarded with the advancement within the **People's Organization Party** (**POP**) that his political efforts at the local level have thus far failed to win. He also fires narrator **Odili Samalu** from his position as a teacher at the grammar school when Samalu undertakes an electoral campaign to unseat Nanga as the member of parliament representing **Anata** and the surrounding region.

M. Keith Booker

NWEGO, outstanding cook and wife of **John Nwodika**. She is also a daughter of **Umuagu**; her father is **Egonwanne** (*Arrow of God*, chapter 13).

Rachel R. Reynolds

NWEKE, identified in chapter 15 of *Things Fall Apart* as the husband of the second daughter of **Okadigbo**. He accompanies **Obierika** when the latter visits Okonkwo in **Mbanta**.

M. Keith Booker

NWEKE, CORPORAL MATTHEW, a colonial policeman working under **Clarke** and **Winterbottom** in *Arrow of God*. He is not from the **Umuaro–Okperi** region and hence is easily misled by local people when traveling through the area. The villages in **Umuaro** intentionally mislead him when he tries

to find **Ezeulu**'s compound in chapter 12. See also **Nwanyieke**, widow of **Umuachala**.

Rachel R. Reynolds

NWEKE UKPAKA, malicious and funny satirical singer whose songs are transcribed in *Arrow of God*. These songs are examples of "*oke ikpe*" or men's **satire**, which is a form of extempore satirical song.

FURTHER READING

Nnabuenyi Ugonna, "Igbo Satiric Art."

Rachel R. Reynolds

NWODIKA, medicine man from **Umuofia** who fails to revive the ailing **Amalu** (*Arrow of God*, chapter 11). No relation to **John Nwodika**.

Rachel R. Reynolds

NWODIKA, JOHN (whose **Igbo** first name is Nwabueze). Second steward to **Winterbottom** who figures largely in the weeks of **Ezeulu**'s captivity at **Okperi** in *Arrow of God*. Nwodika is a son of Ezeulu's rival village of **Umunneora**, but he becomes a blood brother to **Edogo** during Ezeulu's captivity. In chapter 14, Nwodika explains that he was talked into joining the colonial service by a friend, **Ekemezie**, who said John should join "in the race for the white man's money" and that people "we all used to despise—they were all now in high favour." This little passage glosses why so many disaffected young men joined the colonial service. Nwodika's wife's name is **Nwego**.

Rachel R. Reynolds

NWOFIA, name given to the son born to **Okonkwo** while in exile in **Mbanta**. The name means "begotten in the wilderness."

M. Keith Booker

NWOKAFO, a minor character and drinking buddy of **Obika** in *Arrow of God*. Nwokafo lives in the compound in which the famous palm-tree **Okposalebo** stands.

Rachel R. Reynolds

NWOKEKE. In chapter 5 of *No Longer at Ease*, a man of **Umuofia** who survived being hit by lightning a year before the main action of the novel. An unnamed Umuofia man vividly characterizes the event: Nwokeke's "skin peeled off like snake slough, but he was not killed." See also **Mbaino**.

Thomas J. Lynn

NWOKONKWO, a neighbor of **Nwokafo** and **Amalu** in *Arrow of God*.

Rachel R. Reynolds

NWOSISI. In chapter 5 of *No Longer at Ease*, he is honored by **Ogbuefi Odogwu** as one of the "giants" of **Iguedo** who preceded **Okonkwo**'s generation.

Thomas J. Lynn

NWOSISI, an important man of **Umuaro** who comes from **Umuogwugwu**. Nwosisi is also a ritual helper to **Ezeulu** and one of his supporters (*Arrow of God*, chapters 7 and 18).

Rachel R. Reynolds

NWOSU, a man celebrated by **Ogbuefi Odogwu** in chapter 5 of *No Longer at Ease* as a great man of **Iguedo** in **Okonkwo's** lifetime.

Thomas J. Lynn

NWOYE (see also **Isaac Okonkwo**), first son of **Okonkwo** in *Things Fall Apart*. He causes his father great consternation because of his early apparent inclination toward laziness and other attributes that Okonkwo associates with his own father, **Unoka**. He becomes deeply attached to **Ikemefuna** while the latter is staying with the family and during that time seems to be developing in directions of which Okonkwo approves. Ultimately, however, Nwoye becomes an especially great disappointment to Okonkwo when he converts to Christianity and changes his name to Isaac, after which his father disowns and curses him. Isaac Okonkwo is the father of **Obi Okonkwo**, the protagonist of *No Longer at Ease*.

M. Keith Booker

NWOYE UDORA, minor character in *Arrow of God*, and a member of the Otakagu **age-group**.

Rachel R. Reynolds

NWOYE'S MOTHER, never identified by name, is the first wife of **Okonkwo** in *Things Fall Apart*. A prominent figure in the text, she is especially skilled at singing and the telling of stories. She has three other children in addition to **Nwoye**, and she also takes responsibility for the care of **Ikemefuna** while the latter is staying with the family. In the 1986 Nigerian Television Authority miniseries adaptation of the novel, Nwoye's mother is given the name Mgbeke.

M. Keith Booker

O

OBALENDE, the district of **Lagos** in which **Joseph Okeke, Obi Okonkwo's** friend, lives in a one-room apartment in *No Longer at Ease* (see chapters 2 and 7).

Thomas J. Lynn

OBETE, EMMANUEL, the president of the Students Union at the University of Bassa in *Anthills of the Savannah*. He becomes acquainted with **Ikem Osodi** when the latter gives a talk at the university. Later, he joins **Chris Oriko** and the taxi driver, **Braimoh**, in their attempted flight from **Bassa** to **Abazon**. He also attempts to aid the flight by planting a story in the *National Gazette* that Oriko has escaped to London. After Oriko's death, he remains a member of the circle of survivors and friends who habitually hang out in the flat of **Beatrice Okoh**.

M. Keith Booker

OBIAGELI, sister of **Nwoye** in *Things Fall Apart* and thus the daughter of **Okonkwo** and **Nwoye's mother**. She figures prominently in chapter 5, where she breaks her water pot on the day of the **New Yam Festival**, after which she initially laughs, then later cries.

M. Keith Booker

OBIAGELI, the youngest daughter of **Ezeulu** and the daughter of **Ugoye**. She is a consummate singer of songs, the cheery optimist of *Arrow of God*. She sings several songs throughout the novel, including one in chapter 6 about **Nwaka Dimkpolo**, a lullaby in chapter 12, and another song in chapter 16.

Rachel R. Reynolds

OBIAKO. In *Things Fall Apart* a skilled palm-wine tapper who decides to give up his trade, reportedly because the Oracle warned him that he would fall off a palm-tree and be killed as punishment for his refusal to sacrifice a goat to his dead father, a man apparently of little accomplishment, much like **Unoka**, the father of **Okonkwo**.

M. Keith Booker

OBIAKO, master carver of **Umuaro** in *Arrow of God*.

Rachel R. Reynolds

OBIELUE, son of **Akuebue** in *Arrow of God* who sings a song in chapter 18 to taunt the troubled **Nwafo**. See also **Nwanyieke**, a widow of **Umuachala**.

Rachel R. Reynolds

OBIERIKA, the closest friend of **Okonkwo** in *Things Fall Apart*. He refuses to participate in the killing of **Ikemefuna**. Indeed, in chapter 8 he criticizes Okonkwo for his own participation in that act. Obierika is the father of **Akueke** and **Maduka**. He visits Okonkwo in exile in **Mbanta** in chapter 15, bringing news of the destruction of the village of Abame after the killing of a white man by the people of the village. He visits Okonkwo again in chapter 16, bringing news of the great success of the Christian **missionaries** in **Umuofia**, including the news that Okonkwo's son, **Nwoye**, has joined the Christian converts. In chapter 25, Obierika castigates the **District Commissioner** for the role played by the white men in the destruction of Okonkwo. Obierieka is also mentioned by **Ogbuefi Odogwu** in chapter 5 of *No Longer at Ease* when he enumerates **Iguedo**'s leading men of the past.

M. Keith Booker and Thomas J. Lynn

OBIESILI, a ritual assistant to **Ezeulu** in *Arrow of God*, chapter 18.

Rachel R. Reynolds

OBIKA, accorded praise by **Ogbuefi Odogwu** in chapter 5 of *No Longer at Ease* as one of the "giants" of **Iguedo** prior to **Okonkwo**'s generation.

Thomas J. Lynn

OBIKA, the handsome, quick-tempered favorite son of **Ezeulu**. In a sense, the first half of *Arrow of God* can be seen as Obika's coming-of-age story. He begins as an impetuous cad with a deep penchant for palm-wine, then develops into a defender of the women of his lineage (his sister **Akueke**). Later he becomes a good husband to **Okuata**, a masquerade performer of great skill, and the leader of the **Otakagu age-group**. All of these characteristics—including his high-spiritedness as a youth and his always grow-ing strength in maturity—are prototypes of exemplary **Igbo** manhood. This makes the tragedy of his sudden and peculiar death that much greater. Obika's nickname is Ugona-chomma, in direct translation "Eagle-beauty," but commonly meaning "Extremely Handsome."

Rachel R. Reynolds

OBIKWELU, a member of the **Otakagu** age grade in *Arrow of God* who makes two gross errors during a masquerade performance: failure to catch a machete during a dance move and misstriking the sacrificial lamb. These fiascos may symbolize the ritual missteps that are being taken in **Umuaro** through the course of the novel. It may also portend the disastrous diminution of ritual power among leaders of the traditional religion.

Rachel R. Reynolds

OBIORA, childhood boyfriend of **Okuata** (*Arrow of God*, chapter 12).

Rachel R. Reynolds

OBIOZO EZIKOLO, old drum master of **Umuaro** who plays the **Ikolo** in chapter 7 of *Arrow of God*.

Rachel R. Reynolds

ODO, the fat, oafish, and abusive father of **Edna** in *A Man of the People*. Always one to be on the lookout for profit, Odo has essentially prostituted his own daughter by agreeing to marry her to **Chief Nanga** in return for certain financial payments (which turn out to have been relatively meager). A lowly farmer, Odo's venality serves as a reminder that greed and corruption in the post-colonial African society of the novel are not limited to high-placed politicians but filter down to the common people, who have also been infected by a lust for the "white man's money."

M. Keith Booker

ODUCHE. In *Things Fall Apart*, a man killed by **Aneto** in a fight over land, leading to the hanging of Aneto by the British colonial authorities in chapter 20.

M. Keith Booker

ODUCHE, a middle child of **Ezeulu** who is sent to the Christian church and school. Oduche, whose Christian name is Peter, is symbolic of the practice common in colonial Nigeria in which **Igbo** men would send one of their offspring to Christian school. There are many reasons that children would be sent, and Achebe addresses several of them through his portrayal of Oduche in *Arrow of God*. For one thing, his education is seen as appeasing the local **missionaries** and therefore keeping them at bay; in this sense it is also a sacrifice in service of the times—a major theme of *Arrow of God* addressed in detail in chapter 12. Also, some children would have been a family's "eyes and ears among the white man," implying that these children were both to help satisfy curiosity about the new religion as well as to keep options open for what the white man might bring in the future. Finally, as we find out with **Nwaka**'s son, frequently Igbo families would send their least promising sons to the mission school, while the best sons stayed home to increase family wealth through farming. Generally speaking, the earlier converts and their families were to become the clerical class of government workers or merchants trading internationally or as in the case of Achebe's own father, the well-educated mission teachers working throughout large areas of Nigerian territory.

Rachel R. Reynolds

ODUKWE. In *Things Fall Apart*, one of the brothers of **Mgbafo** who take her and her children from the home of her husband, **Uzowulu**, because of his repeated beatings of her.

M. Keith Booker

OFE, DR. In *Anthills of the Savannah*, an unethical **Bassa** surgeon against whom **John Kent** had carried on a graffiti campaign after one of Ofe's patients died because Ofe refused to operate unless he was paid in advance.

M. Keith Booker

OFODILE, a young man of **Okperi** who joins the colonial service in *Arrow of God*, chapter 14.

Rachel R. Reynolds

OFOEDU. In chapter 8 of *Things Fall Apart*, the man who brings **Okonkwo** and **Obierika** the news that both **Ndulue** and his wife **Ozoemena** have died.

M. Keith Booker

OFOEDU, pugnacious age-mate and drinking buddy of **Obika** in *Arrow of God*.

Rachel R. Reynolds

OFOKA, an elder of **Umuaro** who is known as a straight talker (*Arrow of God*, chapters 16 and 18).

Rachel R. Reynolds

OGANLANYA, a "Man of Riches" **mask** (*Arrow of God*, chapter 4)

Rachel R. Reynolds

OGBA, a traitor of **Aninta** whose historical betrayal and subsequent deportation from Aninta appear symbolically in **Ezeulu**'s nightmares about losing power in **Umuaro** (*Arrow of God*, chapter 14).

Rachel R. Reynolds

OGBANJE (often spelled *ogbaanje*), a changeling or "spirit" child who repeatedly dies and returns to its mother to be reborn. It is almost impossible for an *ogbanje* child to survive to adulthood unless its ties with the spirit world of the *ogbanje* are broken by finding and destroying its *iyi-uwa*. In *Things Fall Apart,* **Okonkwo**'s second wife, **Ek-wefi**, is plagued by a series of *ogbanje* children until the cycle is broken when the *iyi-uwa* of their daughter **Ezinma** is found and destroyed.

FURTHER READING

Misty Bastian, "Irregular Visitors."

M. Keith Booker

OGBAZULOBODO, another town in the region of **Umuaro** in *Arrow of God*. Ogbazulobodo is also mentioned as a night spirit who walks by Ezeulu's hut in the final chapter of *Arrow of God*.

Rachel R. Reynolds

OGBONNA, MATTHEW, a guest at the celebration of the **Umuofia** homecoming of **Obi Okonkwo**, hosted by **Hannah** and **Isaac Okonkwo**, in chapter 5 of *No Longer at Ease*. Matthew has been a carpenter in the market town of **Onitsha**, some miles distant from Umuofia. He tells those at the gathering that they should be thankful that Obi had not returned "home with a white wife," an outcome that at least one guest finds "rather farfetched." But Obi confirms that "many black men who go to the white man's country marry their women." Matthew further attests that a man in Onitsha married and had two children with a white woman. As he tells what he knows about the marriage—the woman left it and the two children and returned to Europe—his strong disapproval of such alliances becomes clear. He finds it inevitable that a white woman in such a situation will depart. To this view another guest adds that such a woman's departure is not the problem but, rather, " 'her turning the man's face away from his kinsmen while she stays.' " Matthew concludes the exchange on this subject by telling Obi, " 'I am happy that you returned home safe.' " It may be noted that a key element of this exchange—oppo-sition among Nigerians to interracial unions—appears even earlier in the novel. The first paragraph of chapter 4 includes a reference to the **Atlantic Terminal**, the docking site for boats (including the **MV** *Sasa*) arriving at the **Lagos** wharf. On days designated for the arrival of mail boats at the terminal, one sometimes would find among the cheerfully expectant crowd "a little group waiting sadly and silently. In such cases you could bet that their son had married a white woman in England."

Thomas J. Lynn

OGBUEFI. In *Things Fall Apart* and *Arrow of God*, an epithet of distinction that, according to Kalu Ogbaa, is conferred upon **Igbo** men who have taken the *ozo* title. "Ogbuefi" literally means "Killer of Cows," because the ceremony for initiation into the rank of *ozo* involves the sacrifice of a cow.

FURTHER READING

Kalu Ogbaa, *Gods, Oracles, and Divination*.

M. Keith Booker

OGBUEFI EGONWANNE. See **Egonwanne**.

OGBUEFI EZEUDU. See **Ezeudu**.

OBGUEFI EZEUGO. See **Ezeugo**.

OGBUEFI NDULUE. See **Ndulue**.

OGBUEFI ODOGWU. In chapter 5 of *No Longer at Ease* a non-Christian elder of **Iguedo** who attends the celebration of **Obi Okonkwo**'s first return visit there. Odogwu expresses respect for Christianity during this celebration, which is held at the home of **Isaac** and **Hannah Okonkwo**, and he presides over the kola nut ceremony in a way that does not offend the Christians there. In so doing he even explicitly honors " 'Jesu Kristi.' " His well-intentioned remarks concerning Christianity recall those of **Akunna** in his discussions with **Mr. Brown** in *Things Fall Apart*. Nevertheless, when Odogwu speaks again at the celebration, it is neither "the things of the white man" that he most honors nor Iguedo of the present day, though he attempts to praise both. Rather, it is Iguedo's past to which he emphatically pays tribute, naming illustrious Iguedo men of an earlier era, all or most of whom were non-Christians. These include **Okonkwo, Obierika**, and **Ezeudu** of *Things Fall Apart*.

FURTHER READING

David Carroll, *Chinua Achebe*.

Thomas J. Lynn

OGBUEFI OKONKWO. See **Okonkwo**.

OGBUEFI UDO. See **Udo**.

OGEDE, ODE. See *Achebe and the Politics of Representation*.

OGENE, a type of small drum that each man will have in his compound. *Arrow of God* opens with **Ezeulu** beating the Ogene drum at the new moon in a private priestly ritual.

Rachel R. Reynolds

OGULU ARO, a type of fever (*Arrow of God*, chapter 19).

Rachel R. Reynolds

OGWUGWU, one of the twin principal deities of the town of **Okperi** in *Arrow of God*.

Rachel R. Reynolds

OJINIKA, gossipy older woman involved in the women's fracas about rumors that Oduche has injured a royal **python** (*Arrow of God*, chapter 12). Wife of Ndulue.

Rachel R. Reynolds

OJINMAH, UMELO. See *Chinua Achebe: New Perspectives*.

OJIUGO, the youngest wife of **Okonkwo** in *Things Fall Apart*. In chapter 4 she goes to plait her hair and is thus late in cooking the afternoon meal. Infuriated, Okonkwo beats her, even though it is during the **Week of Peace**. He is then punished as a result, forced to pay one she-goat, one hen, a length of cloth, and a 100 cowries to the earth goddess **Ani** in retribution.

M. Keith Booker

OKAFO. In *Things Fall Apart*, a champion wrestler who, in chapter 6, leads a team in the wrestling matches in **Umuofia**. In those matches, he defeats his rival, **Ikezue**, after the latter makes a strategic miscalculation. Okafo is carried away on the shoulders of the crowd as they sing his praises.

M. Keith Booker

OKAGBUE UYANWA. In *Things Fall Apart*, a medicine man consulted by **Okonkwo** after the death of **Onwumbiko**. He is described as a striking figure, with a full beard and bald head. A man with great knowledge of *ogbanje* children, he mutilates and disposes of the body of the dead child in an attempt to prevent it from returning and continuing the cycle of deaths that has marked the progeny of Okonkwo and **Ekwefi**. The procedure is not successful.

M. Keith Booker

OKECHUKWU, CHINWE CHRISTIANA. See *Achebe the Orator*.

OKEKE, a man of **Umuofia** from whom **Okonkwo** buys snuff in *Things Fall Apart*. In chapter 11, we learn that Okeke's snuff tends to go damp because there is too much saltpeter in it.

M. Keith Booker

OKEKE, a man from **Mbanta** who incurs the wrath of **Okonkwo** in chapter 18 of

Things Fall Apart because he urges the villagers not to take action against the Christians because one of them (apparently **Okoli**) killed the sacred **python**.

M. Keith Booker

OKEKE, a man from the distant village of Umuru who serves as the interpreter for the missionary Rev. **James Smith** in chapter 22 of *Things Fall Apart*. Okeke stands by Smith when the irate band of *egwugwu* spirits from **Umuofia** confronts him and then destroys his church because of the sacrilege earlier committed by Smith's follower **Enoch** in unmasking an *egwugwu*. Earlier, Okeke had fallen out of favor with Smith because he strongly condemned Enoch's behavior and argued that the congregation should not attempt to shield him from the wrath of the people of Umuofia.

M. Keith Booker

OKEKE, CLARA. In *No Longer at Ease*, a beautiful, English-educated **Igbo** nurse and the daughter of **Josiah Okeke**. The novel's protagonist, **Obi Okonkwo**, meets Clara in London, falls in love with her on a voyage to **Lagos**, and becomes engaged to her in that city. However, the secret Clara discloses to Obi immediately prior to their engagement fundamentally alters the course of their relationship and, indeed, the plot of the novel. Clara reveals that she is a member of the Igbo *osu* caste. She is descended, that is, from an ancestor who had been dedicated to the service of a god, a circumstance that rigidly set the ancestor and all of her or his descendants apart from the entire freeborn community, making marriage to any freeborn individual forbidden. In *No Longer at Ease* the disclosure of Clara's family background exposes the fault lines that have been present for some time in Obi's life, fault lines created by the disjunction between the claims of his modern sensibility and the claims of his traditional background. These claims are em-

bodied by his parents, **Isaac and Hannah Okonkwo**, who sharply reject Obi's wish to marry Clara. **Simon Gikandi** remarks aptly on the conflicts to which Clara's relationship with Obi give rise: "In quite unexpected ways, Clara confronts Obi with the problem of abomination that had plagued his ancestors. As an *osu* . . . she inhabits a place that is part of Igbo culture, but outside its norms" (10–11).

Despite his stated determination to wed Clara regardless of difficulties, Obi falters when his parents weigh in regarding the proposed union. Indeed Clara is a victim of Obi's vacillation in several respects. He becomes engaged to her but cannot follow through to actual marriage after his parents' disapproval; he has tentative relations with the Irish teacher, **Nora**, even before they disapprove; he gets Clara pregnant but collaborates with her on an abortion; he changes his mind about the abortion but does so too late. After the abortion, which severely impairs her health, she refuses to see him. Here it may be noted that in the traditional Igbo culture portrayed in *Things Fall Apart* mothers of twins had to endure the exposure of their infants in the forest, while in the modern culture portrayed in that novel's sequel some mothers-to-be, like Clara, must endure abortions. In this and other ways *No Longer at Ease* asks the reader to consider whether "modern" inevitably means progress.

It is not only as an *osu* that Clara is set apart. Her education in England, which may have come about partly through her *osu* status, gives her, ironically, an elevated status in modern Lagos, which she sometimes uses in problematic ways. Her behavior is questionable in other ways as well. When angry, she appears quite ready to break off communication with Obi—even before the final break—including when they discuss saving their engagement (see chapters 10, 15). Her reaction to **Joseph Okeke**'s disclosure to the President of the **Umuofia Progressive Union**

(UPU) that Obi plans to wed an *osu* is acrimonious: "Obi was sometimes amazed and terrified at the intensity of her hate, know how much she had liked [Joseph] before." On the other hand, Clara may be at least partly excused for this, given how much she and her family have suffered for being *osu*. Concerning this stigmatization, Emmanuel Obiechina argues that Clara "has suffered so much psychological cruelty that she has no more illusions and would not have attached any serious importance to Obi's marriage intentions had the latter not argued so strenuously that he would win over all those concerned, including his parents" (136). Also, Clara is quite kind and generous to Obi after their quarrel in chapter 10, lending him the fifty pounds sterling he needs to help him pay off his debts.

Ill-humor on Clara's part may be the reason that **Zacchaeus** quits as Obi's steward (see chapters 2, 10), but it simply may be that Zacchaeus resents being given orders by a woman. This suggests another way in which Clara is set apart: she is a professional woman, a nurse, in a society that seems to be adjusting to a shift in women's roles. This is reflected in the fact that professional women are abstractly the object of ridicule in popular music. Traders traveling by bus to **Umuofia** with Obi sing "gay and bawdy songs addressed mostly to young women who had become nurses or teachers instead of mothers" (chapter 5).

FURTHER READING

Rosemary Colmer, "The Start of Weeping Is Always Hard"; Simon Gikandi, "Chinua Achebe and the Poetics of Location"; Emmanuel Obiechina, "Chinua Achebe's *No Longer at Ease*."

Thomas J. Lynn

OKEKE, JOSEPH. In *No Longer at Ease*, one of protagonist **Obi Okonkwo's** two close male friends. Joseph and Obi attended primary school together at the **Umuofia CMS Central School** and remained friends, although, unlike Obi, Joseph did not attend secondary school. The reason for this is that "his parents were poor" (chapter 2), and while he does not become fabulously wealthy as an adult, he is a "second-class [government] clerk," earning enough to afford his own flat, a "houseboy," and, ultimately, "a hundred and thirty pounds **bride-price**" to marry (chapters 2, 5). This expensive adherence to **Igbo** custom, of which Joseph informs Obi shortly after Obi returns to **Lagos** from his studies in England, contrasts ironically with the fact that Joseph introduced Obi to the "strange and sinful" erotic world of Lagos when Obi stayed with him before departing for England four years earlier (chapter 2).

Indeed, like Obi's other friend, **Christopher**, and like Obi himself, Joseph is somewhat divided in words and behavior. In the interest of tradition he strongly urges Obi not to marry **Clara Okeke** because she is an *osu*, yet he believes that tradition hinders civilization and will necessarily be outmoded: "In the future, when we are all civilized, anybody may marry anybody. But that time has not come. We of this generation are only pioneers" (chapter 7). The intensity of Joseph's opposition to Obi and Clara's engagement prompts him to inform the President of the **Umuofia Progressive Union (UPU)** of Obi's intentions, and although Joseph tells the President in confidence, the latter openly begins to urge Obi against the marriage at a UPU meeting, infuriating him immediately (chapter 8). Joseph's action understandably alienates Obi from him (chapter 9), yet it is Joseph at the end of the novel who organizes another UPU meeting—in this case so that members may comfort Obi on the death of his mother (chapter 18). Obi is deeply touched by Joseph's gesture and the support of "so many of his people."

Thomas J. Lynn

OKEKE, JOSIAH, a retired teacher and the father of **Clara Okeke**, who is **Obi Okon-**

kwo's fiancée in *No Longer at Ease*. Josiah does not appear in the novel, but in chapter 14 he is an important point of reference in a pivotal dialogue in which Obi and his father, **Isaac Okonwo**, discuss Obi's intention to marry Clara, even though she is an *osu*. Isaac acknowledges that Josiah "is a good man and great Christian," yet "he is *osu*," and on this basis Isaac, though a Christian himself, urges Obi to understand why "he cannot marry" Josiah's daughter.

Thomas J. Lynn

OKEKE ONENYI, Ezeulu's younger brother in *Arrow of God*, which includes a passage in which Ezeulu contemplates how his brother received the skills of a medicine man from their father, while Ezeulu received the spiritual link with **Ulu**. This sort of binary is then contrasted to the brothers' mutual envy of each other, effectively demonstrating how Ezeulu's pride and self-involvement separate him from both his sons and his brother (*Arrow of God*, chapter 13). See also **Nwafo**.

Rachel R. Reynolds

OKIGBO, IFEANYICHUKWU CHRISTOPHER (1932–1967), Nigerian poet and political activist. Okigbo was born to Catholic parents in Ojoto village, near **Onitsha** in Anambra State, **Nigeria**. A graduate (in classics) of **University College, Ibadan**, in 1956, Okigbo was tragically killed in the **Nigerian Civil War** while serving as a major in the army of **Biafra**. Thus, his career as an active poet spanned only a decade or so. Indeed, his most important publications during his lifetime appeared in the brief period from 1961 to 1964, including *Heavensgate* (1961), *Limits* (1962), *Silences* (1963), *Lament of the Drums* (1964), and *Distances* (1964). Important posthumous volumes of Okigbo's poetry include *Labyrinths, with Path of Thunder* (1971) and *Collected Poems* (1986). Thomas

Knipp believes that the interlinked poems of *Labyrinths* represent "arguably the most important single volume of poetry to emerge from Anglophone Africa," and it is certainly the case that Okigbo is one of the major figures of postcolonial African poetry (116). For example, he, Achebe, and **Wole Soyinka** are often referred to as the "Big Three" of Nigerian literature. Okigbo has, meanwhile, himself become the stuff of literature, his life and death having inspired such works as Ali Mazrui's novel *The Trial of Christopher Okigbo*.

Despite the brevity of his life and career, Okigbo is one of the major figures of modern African poetry. His poetry addresses a wide variety of themes, ranging from fundamental philosophical topics such as the nature of life and death, to explorations of religious topics (including the relationship between Christianity and traditional **Igbo** religion, to which Okigbo returned despite being born into a Christian family), to self-conscious meditations on art and the role of the artist in society. This role, for Okigbo, was intensely political, and his most important poems are political in nature, many of them standing as specific cries of protest against social and political abuses in postcolonial Nigeria and postcolonial Africa as a whole.

Stylistically, Okigbo's poems are often complex and difficult in ways that are reminiscent of Western modernism. However, they employ a variety of voices and forms. They clearly reflect Okigbo's familiarity with the Western tradition, ranging from the ancient Greeks to modern poets such as Gerard Manley Hopkins, T. S. Eliot, and Ezra Pound. However, they also draw in crucial ways upon indigenous Igbo and other African cultural traditions, enacting a complex dialogic encounter between European and African modes. Nevertheless, despite the diversity of his themes and styles, his various poems are intricately interrelated and can, in a sense, be read as a single long meditation on the struggle for political justice and human dignity in colonial and postcolonial Africa.

Though the flamboyant Okigbo differed dramatically from Achebe in temperament and lifestyle, the two writers became close associates. Achebe would ultimately acknowledge his respect for Okigbo by basing **Chris Oriko**, the tragic hero of *Anthills of the Savannah*, rather transparently on Okigbo. A schoolmate of Achebe at **Umuahia Government College** and later at Ibadan, Okigbo remained a close friend of Achebe from their university days until Okigbo's death. It was Okigbo who introduced Achebe to **John Pepper Clark**, and it was Achebe who wrote one of the first published critical responses to Okigbo's poetry. In the mid-1960s, Okigbo became a representative of Cambridge University Press, and his interest in publishing led him to join Achebe in making plans to open their own publishing house, **Citadel Press**, in Enugu, Nigeria. Those plans, however, were interrupted by the civil war, when Enugu was bombed and Okigbo volunteered to join the Biafran army, never to return. Achebe's tribute to Okigbo, entitled **"Don't Let Him Die,"** can be found in *Hopes and Impediments*.

FURTHER READING

Uzoma Esonwanne, ed., *Critical Essays on Christopher Okigbo*; D. S. Izevbaye, "Death and the Artist"; Thomas Knipp, "English-Language Poetry"; Ali A. Mazrui, *The Trial of Christopher Okigbo*; Donatius Ibe Nwoga, ed., *Critical Perspectives on Christopher Okigbo*.

M. Keith Booker

OKIKA, a great man of **Umuofia** in *Things Fall Apart*. Though he does not have a booming voice, he is known as an orator. In chapter 24, he is identified as one of the delegation of six clan leaders who are invited to air their grievances before the **District Commissioner**, only to be treacherously imprisoned and held as hostages until a fine is paid.

M. Keith Booker

OKIKE. Subtitled "A Nigerian Journal of New Writing" and edited by Chinua Achebe, the first issue of *Okike* (meaning "creation") appeared in April 1971. Its distinctive cover design by Obiora Udechukwu, a black-and-white image of Ala the **Igbo** goddess of creativity, was to remain a feature throughout its more than twenty years of existence. The contents, including poems and short stories by Dennis Brutus, **Wole Soyinka**, Gabriel Okara, Cyprian Ekwensi, and Achebe himself, together with a review by Emmanuel Obiechina of **Ayi Kwei Armah**'s first novel, indicate the quality of writing that *Okike* would continue to attract and sustain.

Begun amid the ruins of the **Nigerian Civil War** and the end of hopes to achieve an independent state of **Biafra** and its political ideals, *Okike* signaled the determination of Achebe and his editorial team to establish the continuing vitality of the Igbo presence and perspectives within the Nigerian nation, as well as their intention to influence the future of the nation's cultural life. The second issue expanded its title to *Okike: An African Journal of New Writing*, and subsequent issues were to include writers throughout the African diaspora, as well as some poems, stories, and essays by European writers. The journal's aims were to provide a forum for writing by Africans, to establish high standards, and to debate the criteria by which African writing should be judged.

The first three issues were published in magazine format in **Enugu**, with a team of colleagues at the **University of Nigeria, Nsukka**, and funded in part by a gift from Ulli Beier. When Chinua Achebe moved to Amherst, Massachusetts, in 1972, he took the journal with him. The **University of Massachusetts** provided *Okike* with an office, secretarial help, and also a team of academic colleagues who willingly assisted as editors. These included Michael Thelwell and Irma McLaurin in the Africana Studies Department and Assistant Editors Esther Terry in Drama and **C. L. Innes** in English. *Okike* was also given a firmer basis by three substantial grants from the Ford Foundation between 1972 and 1980.

The journal now changed to book format with a back spine, which could be produced more economically and more easily marketed to libraries. To allow room for substantial critical essays, it was produced in a smaller type and increased from the fifty-six pages of the first issue to ninety-eight pages for the fourth, the first to be produced at the University of Massachusetts. This issue published the first section of a three-part study by the South African writer and academic Ezekiel Mphalele of African American writing. Seeking (successfully) to provoke debate on the criteria for African writing, issues 6 and 7 published the first version of what would become the book *Toward the Decolonization of African Literature* by Chinweizu, Onwuchekwa Jemie, and Ihechukwu Madabuike, whom Wole Soyinka was to refer to in his response as "the troika." At 116 pages, with contributions by poets Edward [Kamau] Brathwaite, Dennis Brutus, Sonia Sanchez, and Mari Evans, John A Williams, and Isidore Okpewho, fiction by **Kofi Awoonor**, drawings by Nelson Stevens and Obiora Udechukwu, *Okike* 7 demonstrates well the widening scope and high ambitions of the journal in these years. Later issues would include a special focus on particular writers or areas such as Angostinho Neto and Angola, South Africa, and teaching African literature in Britain. After his return to Nsukka in 1976, Achebe and his editorial team produced special educational supplements to *Okike*, aimed at secondary school students and teachers.

In 1981, *Okike* celebrated its tenth anniversary and twentieth issue with two anthologies culled from contributions to the journal *Rhythms of Creation: A Decade of Okike Poetry*, edited by Donatus Nwoga, himself a fine poet; and *African Creations: Stories from Okike*, edited by Emmanuel Obiechina. At Nsukka, the *Okike* editorial committee formed the Okike Arts Centre, which became the base for a variety of enterprises. These included staging the Okochi Festival, featuring performers and professional poet-singers such as Ekwegbalu Anyanyu and Afam Ogbuotobo. Their poetry was recorded and transcribed to be published, along with other Igbo language compositions, in what was projected as an annual Igbo journal, *Uwa Ndi Igbo*, which sought to document traditional and contemporary oral literature by Igbo bards and minstrels. The Arts Centre also published *Aka Weta*, an anthology of contemporary Igbo poetry.

Achebe relinquished editorship of *Okike* in 1986 to his very capable Assistant Editor, Ossie Onuora Enekwe, a colleague in the Theatre Department at the University of Nigeria, Nsukka. Despite the difficulties of distribution and severe paper shortages in Nigeria's crippled economy, *Okike* continued for another decade.

Speaking at the launch of the tenth anniversary issue, Number 21, Achebe remarked that *Okike* was "born out of a conviction that . . . out of the trauma of the Biafran experience something good and valuable might be recovered for Nigerian and African literary development and civilization." One of a very few African literary journals to survive beyond the first few issues, *Okike* could now be found in a majority of university libraries throughout the world as well as many public libraries. For over twenty years *Okike* succeeded in providing a forum for writers and critics interested in new African writing and brought to readers throughout the world work of the highest standard by writers of African descent.

C. L. Innes

OKOH, BEATRICE, one of the central characters in *Anthills of the Savannah*. The holder of an honor's degree in English from London University, she is the girlfriend of **Chris Oriko** and works as the Senior Assistant Secretary to the Minister of Finance in the **Kangan** government. A strong, intelligent, independent, and well-educated woman, Beatrice clearly represents an effort on the part of Achebe to build positive female characters into his work. Thus, when she chides the otherwise radical **Ikem Osodi** for ignoring the importance of gender in his vision of political liberation, she serves as a rebuke to African intellectuals who have similarly ignored the plight of women. Though herself disturbed by the fact that her education and profession have distanced her from her traditional African culture, she nevertheless attempts, in her own thinking, to effect a reconciliation between that culture and the modern culture into which her training and experience have introduced her. Indeed, she symbolically assumes the role of priestess of the goddess **Idemili** in the text. After the deaths of Osodi and Oriko, Beatrice becomes a leader of the circle of their survivors, becoming an emblem of the crucial role that Achebe sees for women in the political future of Africa.

M. Keith Booker

OKOLI. In *Things Fall Apart* a Christian convert in **Mbanta** who is rumored to have shown his devotion to his new religion by killing the **python** that is held sacred in the traditional religion of the clan. He falls ill and dies soon after the purported act, convincing the clan that he was guilty but that the gods have taken their own revenge, so that the clan need take no further action.

M. Keith Booker

OKOLI, SAM, who is referred to as "the Hon. Sam Okoli," is a popular politician and the fiancé of **Clara Okeke**'s best friend in *No Longer at Ease*. Okoli is an Anglophile, and in his speech, manner, and possessions he emulates the British. Although a rising star in Nigerian politics, he does not seem, in general, to think highly of other Nigerians. Speaking to Clara and **Obi Okonkwo** in chapter 7, he denigrates, first in mocking **pidgin English**, his countrymen: " 'White man don go far. We just de shout for nothing,' he said. Then he seemed to realize his position. . . . 'All the same they must go. . . . I used to have a Nigerian as my [Assistant Secretary]. . . . Now I have a white man who went to Oxford and he says 'sir' to me. Our people have a long way to go.' " Okoli is a fascinating but sparingly used character, and a reader of *No Longer at Ease* may well wish that his role in the novel were more prominent.

Thomas J. Lynn

OKOLO, honored by **Ogbuefi Odogwu** in chapter 5 of *No Longer at Ease* as numbering among the great men of **Iguedo** when **Okonkwo** was alive.

Thomas J. Lynn

OKONG, PROFESSOR REGINALD, a Professor of Political Science in postcolonial **Kangan** and a member of the cabinet of **Sam, the President** in *Anthills of the Savannah*. Depicted quite satirically (and openly called a buffoon), he is described as an intellectual who aspires to the military look, wearing only khakis with epaulettes. Okong is a former Baptist minister, initially trained by American missionaries in Africa but later educated (through his own determination and with no support from his original missionary sponsors) at American universities, where he ultimately received his doctorate. Ambitious and completely without political morality, he nevertheless attempts to use his religious background to present himself as a source of moral authority.

M. Keith Booker

OKONKWO, the protagonist and dominant figure of *Things Fall Apart*. If *Things Fall Apart* is first and foremost a story of the disintegration of traditional African societies under the impact of European colonial intrusions, it is also the personal tragedy of this single individual, whose life falls apart in the midst of that same process. Indeed, Okonkwo as a character unites these communal and individual elements. Obiechina, for example, emphasizes Achebe's achievement in presenting Okonkwo both as an embodiment of certain traditional **Igbo** cultural values and as a distinct "individual with obvious personal weaknesses" (204). In the same vein, Okonkwo is in many ways a distinctively Igbo character, yet he is also often viewed as a tragic figure much in the mold of the heroes of ancient Greek tragedy. Thus, as Arlene Elder puts it, Okonkwo is a "paradoxical" figure who "is a trustworthy representative of the traditions of his clan but whose individualism finally leads to his defeat" (58).

Even as a "representative" Igbo, Okonkwo is a complex figure, because he embodies both the strengths and the weaknesses of traditional Igbo society, often ironically violating the traditions of the clan through his excessive attempts to carry out those traditions. Much of Okonkwo's behavior appears to be motivated by his shame at the fact that his father, **Unoka**, had not worked productively, gaining titles for himself and wealth for his family. As a result, Okonkwo works doggedly to prove that he does not share his father's weakness, becoming a successful man of many titles and a central leader of his village of **Iguedo**, one of the nine allied villages of **Umuofia**.

Okonkwo regards his father's weakness as feminine, and thus he himself attempts to pursue what he regards as a masculine course, making him the central focus of much of the critical commentary concerning the treatment of gender in the novel. While some of this commentary (as in the work of Florence Stratton) is critical of Achebe himself, it is clear that Achebe often intends for his readers to regard Okonkwo's behavior as excessive and wrongheaded in its attempt to avoid any semblance of "feminine" weakness. Thus, we learn in chapter 3 that he rules his household with a "heavy hand" and that his wives and children live in perpetual fear of his fiery temper. In chapter 4, he has to pay a penance to the earth goddess **Ani** because he beats his wife during the **Week of Peace**, which is devoted to the goddess. Finally, in chapter 7, afraid of being thought weak, Okonkwo strikes the key blow in the ritual killing of the boy **Ikemefuna**, even though Ikemefuna had come to regard Okonkwo almost as a father. This act draws the criticism of **Obierika**, Okonkwo's great friend, who grants that it was done in literal accordance with the traditions of the clan but argues that no one would have blamed Okonkwo had he chosen not to participate.

In chapter 13, an old gun belonging to Okonkwo misfires during the celebration of the funeral of **Ezeudu**, killing Ezeudu's son. In retribution, Okonkwo is exiled from Umuofia to the village of **Mbanta**, the traditional home of his mother's family. He and his family live in Mbanta for seven years, during which time the traditional life of the clan erodes considerably, largely due to the inroads made by Christian missionaries in the region. During this time, Okonkwo's first son, **Nwoye**, becomes a Christian convert, changing his name to Isaac. Okonkwo returns to Umuofia in chapter 20, first throwing a great farewell feast for those in Mbanta who had shown him such hospitality there. Back in Umuofia, he finds that the villages have become a Christian stronghold and that the British have established an extensive system of colonial administration there.

Okonkwo subsequently takes a leading role in the efforts of the clan to resist the destruction of their traditional way of life by the twin forces of British colonialism and Christian evangelism. In chapter 24, Okonkwo, in a fit of anger, decapitates a court messenger who has brought a message from the British **District Commissioner** ordering the leaders of Umuofia to break up a meeting that is being held to discuss ways in which they might resist British domination. After this deed, Okonkwo is sure to be condemned to death by the colonial system of justice. Further, he knows that the entire village of **Abame** had earlier been destroyed by the British after the people there killed a white man. Hoping to save Umuofia from a similar fate, Okonkwo hangs himself, committing suicide in a last act of defiance of colonial justice and devotion to the cause of the traditional society of Umuofia. By committing suicide, however, he violates one of the clan's most sacred taboos. He thus becomes an outcast whose body cannot be touched by the people of Umuofia, who must wait for outsiders to cut Okonkwo down and bury him. Seeing the hanged man, the arrogant District Commissioner observes that the story of Okonkwo might make an interesting anecdote in the monograph he is writing, entitled *The Pacification of the Primitive Tribes of the Lower Niger*.

FURTHER READING

Arlene A. Elder, "The Paradoxical Characterization of Okonkwo"; Biodun Jeyifo, "Okonkwo and His Mother"; Michael Valdez Moses, *The Novel and the Globalization of Culture*; Emmanuel Obiechina, *Culture, Tradition, and Society in the West African Novel*; Ode Ogede, *Achebe and the Politics of Representation*; Umelo Ojinmah, *Chinua Achebe*; Damian U. Opata, "Eternal Sacred Order versus Conventional Wisdom"; Florence Stratton, *Contemporary African Literature and the Politics of Gender*.

M. Keith Booker

OKONKWO, AGNES, third eldest child of **Isaac** and **Hannah Okonkwo** in *No Longer at Ease*. In chapter 6 **Obi Okonkwo** feels sympathy for this elder sister concerning the death of her first child, although she does have one child that survived. Agnes probably married at an early age and is considered to behave somewhat immaturely. Also in chapter 6 Obi reflects on an incident that occurred earlier the same night that reveals not only Agnes's purported immaturity but also, perhaps, an **Igbo** childrearing custom. Agnes was asked to carry her and her sisters' children, who are sleeping, to bed, and upon grabbing the first one by the wrist to pull him up, Hannah screamed at her, in part: "How often must I tell you to call a child by name before waking him up?"

Thomas J. Lynn

OKONKWO, CHARITY. In *No Longer at Ease*, the sister and next oldest sibling of **Obi Okonkwo**, whom she was inclined to dominate when they were children. As indicated in chapter 6, her **Igbo** name means, "A girl is also good," but when she and Obi squabbled as youngsters, he would call her, "A girl is not good." In these instances Charity, who "was as strong as iron" and feared by neighboring children of both sexes, would hit Obi until he was in tears—"unless their mother happened to be around, in which case she would postpone the beating." She also would emphasize Obi's rudeness when he forgot to call their eldest sister, **Esther Okonkwo**, "Miss" once she became a teacher.

Thomas J. Lynn

OKONKWO, ESTHER, the sister and eldest sibling of **Obi Okonkwo** in *No Longer at Ease* and the mother of three children. In chapter 6, during his first visit to his family's home in **Iguedo**, Obi recalls that when he was a young child, Esther became a schoolteacher and consequently, as a sign of respect, was called "Miss," even by family members. When Obi recognizes that the pillowcases on his bed, "with their delicate floral designs," were made by Esther, he thinks, " 'Good old Esther!' " (the contrasting associations of these pillowcases and those made in **Lagos** by **Joy** for **Joseph Okeke**, particularly the one with "*osculate*" sewn on it in multicolored letters, are worth examining.) After learning in chapter 18 of the death of his mother, **Hannah Okonkwo**, Obi reflects that all of his married sisters would return home temporarily to be with their father, **Isaac Okonkwo**, but it would be "Esther [who] could be relied on to look after him."

Thomas J. Lynn

OKONKWO, EUNICE. Mentioned briefly in chapter 14 of *No Longer at Ease*, she is the youngest sibling of **Obi Okonkwo** and the only one of **Isaac** and **Hannah Okonkwo**'s children still living with them at home during the novel's time frame.

Thomas J. Lynn

OKONKWO, HANNAH, mother of **Obi Okonkwo** and wife of **Isaac Okonkwo** in *No Longer at Ease*, in which she is an important character in her own right. Obi has always had "a special bond [with] his mother. Of all her eight children Obi was nearest her heart" (chapter 7). This bond heightens the dramatic tension of Hannah's fierce opposition to Obi's plans to wed an *osu* woman, **Clara Okeke**, an opposition so intense that Hannah threatens to kill herself if Obi goes ahead with the marriage (chapter 14). In regard to Hannah's role at this point, **David Carroll**

comments, "This instinctual opposition of his mother is more disturbing even than that of his father because it cannot be explained and discussed. She expresses through her dream the collective horror of the tribe at the proposed act of sacrilege" (80). Hannah's threat and her death shortly afterward (which is not a suicide) are among the decisive factors that discourage Obi from going forward with the marriage.

While her words in this situation may appear to be a misguided and cruel exercise of her influence over son, Hannah's strength and character are presented in a positive light elsewhere in the novel. It may be argued, in fact, that she is the first in a line of strong, positive female characters in Achebe's novels with **Eunice**, the fiancée of **Max Kumalo** in *A Man of the People*, and **Beatrice Okoh** in *Anthills of the Savannah* as Hannah's spiritual successors. (See the remark about Eunice and Beatrice by Jane Wilkinson in her interview with Achebe in Lindfors, *Conversations* 149.) In fact, in her strength and determination Hannah contrasts with the wavering ineffectuality of Obi, who remembers his mother after her death "as the woman who got thing done" (chapter 19). Hannah is certainly a capable person in numerous ways, from farming to traditional storytelling to child raising to mentoring future housewives. In one of his recollections Obi recalls that, during the season that yam was scarce, Hannah beheaded with a machete an ever-unruly male goat dedicated to **Udo** after it entered her kitchen and ate a course of yam she was preparing for a meal (chapter 19). Upon her death Obi realizes that his father, Isaac, "would be completely lost without her" (chapter 18).

But despite the devoted, monogamous marriage between Hannah and Isaac and eight children together the novel asks whether conditions for her and other women have dramatically improved between the culture depicted in *Things Fall Apart* and that in *No Longer at Ease*. In the former **Okonkwo** has three wives, so they must share him, but they also have the support of each other and, presumably, many of their children, as well as that of Okonkwo, whereas, in the latter, when Hannah and Isaac grow too old to farm (and thereby supplement his pension), there is no one to farm for them (discussed below). In *Things Fall Apart* all of Okonkwo's wives tell folk stories, and so do the children, while in *No Longer at Ease* Hannah "could read, but she never took part in the family reading. She merely listened to her husband and children" (66). However, Hannah was the family storyteller until Isaac forbade this activity due to his view of traditional folktales as "heathen." She did, however, make an exception on one occasion for Obi, telling him the story of the "wicked leopardess" (chapter 6).

When Obi returns to **Umuofia** for the first time after completing his studies in England, he realizes that his mother is seriously ill, that she, like his father is all bones," and that they do not "have enough good food to eat" (chapter 6). They are now unable, due to advanced age, to supplement Isaac's income with their own farming, as they had previously done: "he planted yams and his wife planted cassava and coco yams" (chapter 6). Yet it is revealed during Obi's second visit that they have eight dispersed children who, in a somewhat earlier era, may well have helped their aged parents. Hannah's feelings about this situation are eloquently conveyed by the narrator, partly by means of an **Igbo** proverb: "Children left their old parents at home and scattered in all directions in search of money. It was hard on an old woman with eight children. It was like having a river and yet washing one's hands with spittle" (chapter 14).

FURTHER READING

David Carroll, *Chinua Achebe*; Rosemary Colmer, "The Start of Weeping Is Always Hard";

Bernth Lindfors, ed., *Conversations with Chinua Achebe*.

Thomas J. Lynn

OKONKWO, ISAAC. Originally introduced in *Things Fall Apart* as **Nwoye**, the son of Okonko, Isaac Okonkwo figures in *No Longer at Ease* as the husband to **Hannah Okonkwo** and the father of the protagonist, **Obi Okonkwo**, and seven other children. In *Things Fall Apart* Isaac changed his name from Nwoye when he converted to Christianity. While he is neither the protagonist of that novel nor its sequel, the significance of his role should not be underestimated, particularly insofar as he serves as the chief bridge between these two quite different narratives. Arguably, the epigraph to *No Longer at Ease*, the final four lines from **T. S. Eliot**'s **"The Journey of the Magi,"** applies more specifically to Isaac's situation than to that of Obi. In the first novel Nwoye was attracted to the newly arrived faith partly because it seemed to possess a less violent, less rigidly patriarchal orientation than traditional **Igbo** culture. That orientation was epitomized by Nwoye's father, **Okonkwo**, who frowned on him precisely because he was not becoming a man of action in Okonkwo's image and was indeed reminding him of his own indolent father, **Unoka**. So Christianity offered a welcome escape to Nwoye, but just as the Magi of Eliot's poem underwent "hard and bitter agony" when they realized what the Advent meant for their habitual outlook and existence, Nwoye/Isaac "went through fire to become a Christian," as he tells Obi in chapter 14 of *No Longer at Ease*. Just as the Magi returned to "the old dispensation, / With an alien people clutching their gods," so too Isaac's life after his conversion has been spent not only with Christians but also among those whom he would regard as clutching their own gods, that is, adherents to Igbo religious tradition, a tradition he sees as "heathen" (chapters 5, 6).

No Longer at Ease, which takes up the Okonkwo family story several decades after Nwoye's rupture with Okonkwo and conversion to Christianity, presents Isaac as a retired catechist who has remained a devout Christian. A benefit of *No Longer at Ease*'s portrayal of Isaac, especially for readers of *Things Fall Apart*, are the details not given in the earlier novel concerning his conversion, his reaction to his father's suicide, and his missionary perspective. Particularly poignant is Isaac's recollection (in conversation with Obi) of his devastation at both Okonkwo's killing of the beloved **Ikeme-fuma** and cursing of Nwoye (that is, the young Isaac) when he committed himself to the **missionaries**: "When a man curses his own child it is a terrible thing. And I was his first son" (chapter 14).

An aspect of Isaac's nature that spans the decades between *Things Fall Apart* and *No Longer at Ease* is captured in a reflection of Obi's: "His father, although uncompromising in conflicts between church and clan, was not really a man of action but of thought" (188). Notwithstanding that converting to an entirely foreign religion under the circumstances that Nwoye faced *is* a dramatic action, Nwoye was contemplative as a boy and preferred his mother's storytelling to violent action. This same mild aspect of his personality (which contrasts with the portrayal of his wife, Hannah, "the woman who got things done" [chapter 19]) helps shape the content of *No Longer at Ease* in a way that it did not in *Things Fall Apart*, for while Achebe's first novel revolves around action in several respects, not much in the way of dramatic exploit occurs in *No Longer at Ease*, whose characters think and talk. (**Clara Okeke**'s going through with an abortion may be viewed as an exception.) Three of the most dramatic incidents in the novel involve limited or passive, rather than forceful, action: Obi converses with his severely dissenting parents about his prospective marriage to Clara; he declines to marry her; he accepts bribes. Rather than decisive action, dialogues about ethical values, religion, marriage, and duty to family and group fill the novel, reflecting the influence on his family and community of Isaac, who contributed non-violently to the establishment of Christianity in **Umuofia** and who reveals in various conversations his enduring passion for that religion's precepts.

Isaac is a thoughtful and effective conversationalist (including in his climactic discussions with Obi in chapter 14, discussed below), and there are still other indications that the contemplative youth, Nwoye, remains inside the elderly Isaac. He "never destroyed a piece of paper" or got rid of a book (whether "Obi's **Durrell** [or] obsolete cockroach-eaten translations of the Bible into the **Onitsha** dialect") because he has a "mystic regard for the written word," a regard reflected as well in his remarks, made "with deep feeling" to an illiterate relative: " 'books which clerks wrote twenty years ago or more . . . are still as they wrote them. They do not say one thing today and another tomorrow, or one thing this year and another next year" (chapter 13). (This attitude toward the written word also suggests a dedication to the ways of the white man, and we are told that "Mr. Okonkwo believed utterly and completely in the things of the white man" [chapter 13].) Further, when Isaac encounters a dilemma, he tends to "weigh it and measure it and look it up and down, postponing action" (chapter 19).

Perhaps Isaac's ability to see a matter from an unexpected angle helps account for his position during climactic conversations with Obi about the proposed marriage to Clara (chapter 14). In striking contrast to his staunch defense of Christian precepts in all previous questions of belief and practices, Isaac aggressively opposes the proposed marriage because Clara is an *osu*, a hereditary outcast among the Igbo. The culture's deeply rooted aversion to the intermingling of *osu* and freeborn and Isaac's paternal instinct seems to overwhelm his alliance with missionary ideology in this case, which rejected the *osu* prohibitions. Indeed, the early missionary success in Umuofia partly was built on the many conversions among the *osu* (see *Things Fall Apart*, chapter 18). The irony, not to say hypocrisy, of Isaac's position (Obiechina argues that Issac "is not a hypocrite") is compounded by Obi's own appeal to the very Christian teachings he has heard from his father: " 'The Bible says that in Christ there are no bond or free. . . . Our fathers in their darkness and ignorance called an innocent man *osu*' " (14). This argument is somewhat disingenuous, however, and adds a further irony, because the narrative has indicated that Obi "had very little religion nowadays" (chapter 3; see also chapter 6). But Isaac persists, placing intense pressure on his son: "*Osu* is like leprosy in the minds of our people. I beg of you, my son, not to bring the mark of shame and of leprosy into your family. If you do, your children and your children's children unto the third and fourth generations will curse your memory" (chapter 14). Isaac may well be unaware that by playing such an aggressive role here he, in effect, reenacts the role of his own father, Okonkwo, who pressured Nwoye to embrace traditional concepts of manhood. One possible difference between the two situations, however, is that while Nwoye broke away from Okonkwo and his wishes, Obi's discovers the next night "that there was nothing in him to challenge [his parents' position] honestly." This augurs the collapse of his commitment to Clara, which probably occurs, in part, because of his parents' opposition to the alliance.

It may be noted that *Things Fall Apart* was not the only early work of fiction by Achebe to prepare ground for the character of Isaac Okonkwo. An early story, the final version of which is "Marriage Is a Private Affair," portrays a father living in a rural area who so strongly opposes his son's choice of spouse that he cuts off relations with him, his wife, and their child, who live in **Lagos**. The father opens himself up, however, to reconciliation at the close of the story. The tale originally appeared as "The Old Order in Conflict with the New," in the May 1952 issue of *The University Herald*, Ibadan, then as "Beginning of the End," in 1962 in **The Sacrificial Egg and Other Short Stories**, and finally as "Marriage Is a Private Affair" in 1972 in **Girls at War and Other Stories**. Concerning this relatively youthful tale, M.J.C. Echeruo comments how early "Achebe was interested in the subject which matured into his second and better novel, *No Longer at Ease*. Of particular interest is the interview between Nnaemeka in this story with his father, a study virtually for a similar interview between Obi Okonkwo and his father in *No Longer at Ease*" (3).

FURTHER READING

C. A. Babalola, "A Reconsideration of Achebe's *No Longer at Ease*"; David Carroll, *Chinua Achebe*; Rosemary Colmer, "The Start of Weeping Is Always Hard"; M.J.C. Echeruo, Introduction; Nnadozie F. Inyama, "Genetic Discontinuity in Achebe's *No Longer at Ease*"; Emmanuel Obiechina, "Chinua Achebe's *No Longer at Ease*."

Thomas J. Lynn

OKONKWO, JANET, the second oldest sister of **Obi Okonkwo** in **No Longer at Ease** and the mother of two children. She is mentioned in the context of Obi's thoughts about his siblings in chapter 6. As a child Obi got along well with Janet and the two sisters who came before and after her, **Esther** and **Agnes**.

Thomas J. Lynn

OKONKWO, JOHN, younger brother of **Obi Okonkwo** in *No Longer at Ease*. John is never actually depicted, but the payment of his school fees, which are mentioned in chapters 6 and 13, is one of the numerous financial responsibilities that weigh heavily on Obi. In fact, these fees, which are hardly negligible (sixteen pounds ten shillings per term), are taken seriously enough by Obi to elicit from him, in chapter 13, a rare instance of self-awareness and practical resolve concerning his expenditures: "Obi knew that unless he paid [John's] fees now that he had a lump sum in his pocket he might not be able to do so when the time came."

Thomas J. Lynn

OKONKWO, OBI (MICHAEL OBIA-JULU OKONKWO), the **Igbo** protagonist of *No Longer at Ease*, he is the grandson of **Okonkwo**, the son of **Isaac** and **Hannah Okonkwo**, and the brother of **Esther Okonkwo** and seven other siblings. An intelligent young man who wins a financial award sponsored by the **Umuofia Progressive Union (UPU)** to attend university in England for four years, Obi possesses an idealistic devotion to **Nigeria** upon his return there in the late 1950s, that is, shortly before its independence from Britain. Convinced that the well-being of his nation depends on the integrity of its officials, he earnestly advocates the removal of corrupt civil servants. In this context he is soon appointed to a senior government post in **Lagos**, Secretary to the Scholarship Board, a position that by its very nature attracts bribes, which he resists at first.

In a fairly short period of time, however, he goes into alarming debt, due in part to his own naïveté and irresponsibility, in part to the debt awaiting him upon his return to Nigeria (that is, the pre-arranged refund of the scholarship, which is, in effect, a loan), and in part to family obligations. Upon returning

for the first time to **Iguedo**, his rural village in **Umuofia**, he finds that his beloved mother and father, **Hannah** and **Isaac Okonkwo**, are undernourished and in failing health, so he undertakes to assist them financially. But these are only the beginning of his many financial burdens, including his brother **John Okonkwo**'s tuition, his various automobile expenses, and his engagement to **Clara Okeke**, a young Igbo woman with whom he fell in love on his voyage home from England.

During Obi's second visit to Iguedo his parents forcefully oppose his prospective marriage to Clara, despite their deeply held Christian beliefs, because they have discovered that she descends from the forbidden *osu* caste, whose members are forbidden according to traditional norms to mix with freeborn members of the Igbo community. Obi is freeborn, and in this matter his parents adhere to cultural tradition. Hannah goes so far as to tell Obi that she will kill herself if he marries Clara. Obi's resolve to marry Clara, who is pregnant with their child, is shaken, which she discerns when he returns to Lagos. Together they seek an abortion, although moments too late Obi changes his mind. Clara leaves him, and he suffers another devastating blow when he learns shortly afterward that Hannah has died. His grief and financial distress lead Obi to accept for the first time one of the bribes readily available to him. Obi's bribe-taking continues (in both monetary and sexual forms) and results in his arrest and conviction, although he has grown more rather than less troubled as time passes and appears to be close to renouncing the activity just prior to his arrest. The novel frames the story of Obi's rise and fall with a trial scene that shows his conviction on charges of accepting bribes.

Obi's character is built to a remarkable degree on a series of oppositions that create conflicts he cannot escape. He is a Christian-trained, Western-educated Igbo man who finds himself torn between the claims of urban modernity and rural tradition. He is split between, on the one hand, the urban economic opportunities and sensual attractions associated with Lagos and, on the other hand, the traditional Igbo values and close-knit rural community of Umuofia. Nor can he escape Umuofia in Lagos, for many of the forces derived from his birthplace are at work on him in the city where he works, and this is emphasized through the normative judgments about him made by the UPU.

Another reflection of Obi's internal divisions is his ambivalence toward England and the English language. Obi took his degree in English and specialized in English literature. As suggested, the UPU had anticipated that his degree would be in law so that he might work on the members' behalf in land disputes, and it may be suspected that Obi's educational alliance, as it were, with his English rulers instead of his Igbo supporters may partly fuel his pangs of conscience in taking an English degree. In any case his guilty feeling over the degree is closely associated with his feelings of humiliation he experienced in England when forced to speak English with other Nigerians: "It was humiliating to have to speak to one's country man in a foreign language, especially in the presence of the proud owners of that language. They would naturally assume that one had no language of one's own" (chapter 5).

Obi seems to resent any feeling of linguistic condescension that his use of English might have on English soil. So Obi wants to own English himself, through study, but not be owned by it—or, indeed, by the people who conferred it on his people: The divided allegiances symbolized in Obi's ambivalence over language ultimately alienate him from both his ties to Umuofia and a meaningful life in the modern world of Lagos. In this regard, **Robert M. Wren** observes tren-

chantly that "Obi Okonkwo's failure arose from his disassociation from the authority that owned him, from his lineage, from Umuofia. Within the lineage there is a moral certainty that need not be stated because it is the collective awareness of the clan. The great, the terrible difficulty of all nations, all people in the twentieth century, is the loss of that moral center" (141).

Obi is not, however, a mere stick figure representing postcolonial conflicts in Africa. Rather, Achebe skillfully portrays a talented, well-meaning, if immature, man wracked by those conflicts. From the outset of the novel Obi finds it difficult to suppress the tears that accrue from his inability to reconcile the competing forces he faces, and his weeping is reinforced by the proverb that Achebe invokes twice in the novel, "The start of weeping is always hard" (see Colmer). His tears and his irresolution—the latter a trait that ultimately destroys his relationship with Clara and his career in the civil service—are not merely a function of a weak will. They are also symptoms of an authentic impasse between the claims of modernity and tradition, one that has eluded many well-intentioned and intelligent individuals in the postcolonial world.

FURTHER READING

David Carroll, *Chinua Achebe*; Rosemary Colmer, "The Start of Weeping Is Always Hard'; Simon Gikandi, *Reading Chinua Achebe*; Emmanuel Obiechina, "Chinua Achebe's *No Longer at Ease*"; Felicity Riddy, "Language as a Theme in *No Longer at Ease*"; Philip Rogers, "*No Longer at Ease*"; Robert M. Wren, *Achebe's World*.

Thomas J. Lynn

OKOYE, a friend of **Unoka** in *Things Fall Apart*. Like Unoka, Okoye is a musician. However, he serves as a sort of foil to Unoka, achieving wealth and success through hard work and determination of the kind that Unoka consistently fails to display. We learn in chapter 1 that Unoka had been unable to return the 200 cowries he had earlier borrowed from Okoye.

M. Keith Booker

OKOYE. Akukalia Okeke's brother, who is one of the three men from **Umuaro** killed in the short-lived war between Okperi and Umuaro (*Arrow of God*, chapter 2)

Rachel R. Reynolds

OKPERI, next large village cluster down the road from **Umuaro** and the location of the British regional district office in *Arrow of God*. At the beginning of the novel, there is a "war" between Okperi and Umuaro, as well as the colonial construction project of a modern road linking Okperi to Umuaro. **Nwaka** "rewrites" Okperi history in chapter 2 by claiming that the wandering people of Okperi were driven away by **Umuofia**, **Aninta**, and **Abame**, though closer inspection of the 1920s Achebe universe shows that this would not have been possible. If anything, Okperi is larger and older than Umuaro, and Okperi must be at least contemporary with Umuofia. Achebe presents this sort of town-versus-town rhetoric as central to Igbo politics; pre-colonial governance in Igboland involved special affiliations of families, hamlets, and villages and then village clusters. Along the lines of a "colonial" history, Achebe also notes that Okperi is the earliest town in the region to have gotten an established mission, and hence it is also made the seat of government (chapter 3) and the location of the trading store (chapter 11). Achebe often includes two historical points of view with his parallel visions of history from a local **Igbo** perspective and a colonialist history.

FURTHER READING

J.O.J. Nwachukwu-Agbada, "Chinua Achebe."

Rachel R. Reynolds

OKPOSALEBO, the name of a palm-tree in *Arrow of God* that is famous for the potency of its palm-wine. The name means "Dispenser of Kindred," and the name implies that brothers who drink wine from its tap will become so drunk they will fight. The tree stands in the family compound of **Nwokafo.**

Rachel R. Reynolds

OKUATA, deceased first wife of **Ezeulu** and mother of a son, **Edogo,** and two daughters, **Akueke** and **Adeze.** Okuata is portrayed as having been compassionate and dutiful, in direct contrast to Ezeulu's other surviving wives, **Ugoye** and **Matefi,** who have complementary flaws.

Rachel R. Reynolds

OKUATA, alias Oyilidie, the comely bride of **Obika** in *Arrow of God*. She hails from the village of **Umuezeani.** Okuata-Oyilidie's nuptial ritual is described in great detail in chapter 11, and it is frequently cited as an example of Chinua Achebe's detailed portrayal of **Igbo** pre-colonial life.

Rachel R. Reynolds

OKUDO. In *Things Fall Apart*, a former great war-singer of **Umuofia.** Though not a warrior himself, his songs turned ordinary men into lionlike warriors. Okudo's greatness as compared to the orators of the present day (who tend to counsel peace) is regarded by **Okonkwo** in chapter 24 as a sign of the decline of Umuofia.

M. Keith Booker

"OLD CALABAR." In chapter 5 of *No Longer at Ease*, a song played by the brass band of the **Umuofia CMS Central School** to help celebrate **Obi Okonkwo**'s first visit to Umuofia after the completion of his studies in England.

Thomas J. Lynn

OLD COASTER, a cocktail deemed suitable for African climates by the colonial officers in *Arrow of God*. Brandy with ginger ale.

Rachel R. Reynolds

OLD MAN OF ABAZON, a member of the a delegation of five sent from **Abazon** to **Bassa** to see **Sam, the President**, to ask for aid to the region of Abazon, which is currently suffering from a killing drought in *Anthills of the Savannah*. Not named and described only as an old man with a beard, this character has considerable wisdom, which he displays amply in chapter 9, in which he discourses, among other things, on the power and importance of storytelling.

M. Keith Booker

OMENYI, or Ogbanje Omenyi, is a woman of **Umuaro** who is rumored to be sexually loose. "Every girl knew of Ogbanje Omenyi whose husband was said to have sent to her parents for a machete to cut the bush on either side of the highway which she carried between her thighs" (*Arrow of God*, chapter 12). See also **Satire**.

Rachel R. Reynolds

OMO, MR. In chapters 7, 9, and 17 of *No Longer at Ease*, the Administrative Assistant in the government office in which **William Green** serves as supervisor and **Obi Okonkwo** as a senior official. Since he takes and solicits bribes, Mr. Omo personifies Obi's concept of "the old Africans at the top": Obi considers them both venal and undereducated (see chapter 5). Omo has been a civil servant for thirty years and is trying to put his son through a law degree in England. While his age is partly what makes him suspect in Obi's eyes, it is also partly what elicits the reader's sympathy for him when he is demeaned by Green. Still, Omo is content to pass the misery onto a junior employee, rebuking a junior clerk after Green affronts him.

Thomas J. Lynn

OMUMAWA, the **age-group** cohort just younger than **Otakagu** in *Arrow of God*. Omumawa is a shortened form of the **Igbo** proverbial phrase, "Men's loincloth over boy's penises," implying that the younger group underwent initiation, even though their ability to behave as men was in doubt. Otakagu age-group named their younger cohort Omumawa out of contempt, and the name was so humorous that it was adopted permanently by the village for this age-group.

Rachel R. Reynolds

ONE WAY. In chapter 5 of *No Longer at Ease*, a beggar familiar to the market women in "the great **Onitsha** market." One Way, who is "perhaps . . . a little mad," dances to the rhythmic beat of the women's "empty cigarette cups" in exchange for a handful of the traditional dish, *garri* (pounded yams), from them. This yields him enough food for two generous meals.

Thomas J. Lynn

ONENYI NNANYELUGO, a man of **Umuaro** with high title who pleads with Ezeulu to begin the **Feast of the New Yam** in *Arrow of God* (chapter 18).

Rachel R. Reynolds

ONITSHA, port city on the Niger River in southeast **Nigeria**. Located at a crucial geographic nexus that links a number of different areas, the city is known internationally for its important market, where traders from these regions (and people of widely varied backgrounds) have gathered for centuries to do business and exchange ideas. In the seventeenth century, Onitsha became the capital of an **Igbo** kingdom. In the twentieth century, the Onitsha market played an important role in the evolution of African literature through its function as a locus for the printing and distribution of a variety of inexpensive pamphlets and chapbooks, collectively known as "market literature."

Onitsha is a principal setting for Achebe's children's novel **Chike and the River** and is mentioned prominently in chapters 5 and 14 of **No Longer at Ease**, which includes a description of the "great Onitsha market." Achebe acknowledges the importance of Onitsha in his essay "Onitsha, Gift of the Niger," included in **Morning Yet on Creation Day**. Borrowing a phrase from **Frantz Fanon**, Achebe describes Ontisha as a "zone of occult instability," attributing its status as the central seat of the market literature phenomenon to the fact that Onitsha functions as a gathering place where many different cultural forces meet and interact (*Morning* 153). He describes Onitsha's location as "the crossroads of the world" and characterizes it "the marketplace of the world" since ancient days (154–55). He also notes that Onitsha has long been a center of learning and culture, as well as commerce.

FURTHER READING

Donatus Nwoga, "Onitsha Market Literature"; Emmanuel Obiechina, *An African Popular Literature*.

M. Keith Booker

"ONITSHA, GIFT OF THE NIGER." Achebe essay. See **Morning Yet on Creation Day**.

ONWUMA, the daughter of **Okonkwo** and **Ekwefi** in **Things Fall Apart** and the seventh consecutive of their children to die young, apparently confirming their belief that the dying children are *ogbanje*. Out of defiance and frustration, in chapter 9 Ekwefi gives the girl this name, meaning "Death may please himself."

M. Keith Booker

ONWUMBIKO, the son of **Okonkwo** and **Ekwefi** in **Things Fall Apart**, their third child and the third to die young, leading them to conclude that all of the children are the same *ogbanje* child, returning repeatedly. After the death of Onwumbiko in chapter 9, Okonkwo seeks the help of the medicine man **Okagbue Uyanwa** in an unsuccessful attempt to break the cycle. The name means "Death, I impore you," indicating Ekwefi's growing despair.

M. Keith Booker

ONWUZULIGBO, an in-law of **Ezeulu**, is **Akueke**'s husband's relative. Onwuzuligbo lives in **Umuogwugwu**, and he is married to **Ezinma**.

Rachel R. Reynolds

ONYEKA. In **Things Fall Apart**, an orator with a booming voice who is therefore chosen in chapter 24 to salute **Umuofia** and call together the people for a public meeting to discuss the recent outrages committed against their traditions and customs by the newly arrived Europeans and their Christian converts among the **Igbo**.

M. Keith Booker

ONYEKULUM, night spirits that come out from the **egbu** tree to sing and gossip on their post-harvest journey each season. Appears as a metaphor about a hangover in chapter 8 of **Arrow of God**.

Rachel R. Reynolds

ORIKO, CHRISTOPHER, one of the central characters of **Anthills of the Savannah**. A friend since schooldays of both **Ikem Osodi** and **Sam, the President**, Oriko serves during most of the novel as the Commissioner for Information in the postcolonial nation of **Kangan**. Though less idealistic and more willing to compromise than Osodi, Oriko is nevertheless a positive character who serves as a counter to the corruption and ruthless personal ambition that inform much of the postcolonial politics of Kangan. He functions as a voice of reason in Sam's cabinet, providing advice that is not tempered by the calculated quest for personal gain that drives most of the cabinet members. After Osodi is removed as the editor of the *National Gazette* for political reasons, Oriko attempts to resign his cabinet post in protest, but his resignation is not accepted. Then, as conditions deteriorate into the violence that leads to the political murders of both Sam and Osodi, Oriko himself flees the capital and attempts to take refuge in the northern region of **Abazon**. On the way, he is shot and killed while attempting to prevent a police sergeant from raping a young girl along the road. Remembered by his girlfriend, **Beatrice Okoh**, and his other friends, Oriko becomes an inspiration to them to continue to strive for justice. He thus becomes a key indication of the way in which Achebe, despite his unflinching portrayal of violence and corruption in postcolonial Africa in *Anthills of the Savannah*, also indicates hope for a better future.

M. Keith Booker

OSENIGWE, Akuebue's neighbor in *Arrow of God*, chapter 16.

Rachel R. Reynolds

OSO NWANADI, a feast held by the people of the **Umuaro** village group to placate those unsettled spirits dead from past wars (*Arrow of God*, chapter 17).

Rachel R. Reynolds

OSODI, IKEM, one of the central characters of *Anthills of the Savannah*. A talented poet and a native of **Abazon**, he serves during most of the novel as the editor of the *National Gazette*, the central newspaper in **Bassa**, the capital of **Kangan**. A friend since schooldays of both **Chris Oriko** and **Sam,** **the President**, Ikem is something of a radical who espouses revolutionary change in Kangan. However, he is skeptical of **Marxism** and seems to have no truly coherent political philosophy beyond sympathy for the poor and downtrodden and suspicion of the rich and powerful. Meanwhile, his situation is made more difficult and confused by his growing sense of isolation from precisely the groups he seeks to represent. Thus, as Gikandi notes, he is "Achebe's example of an African deeply involved in the intellectual project of postcolonialism . . . gripped by doubts about his own notions of self, community, and social purpose" (*Reading* 131). Ultimately, Osodi's editorial positions against corruption and inequity lead to his arrest and execution, though his shooting is portrayed in the media as an accident that occurs during an attempted escape.

FURTHER READING

Simon Gikandi, *Reading Chinua Achebe.*

M. Keith Booker

OSSAI, JOHNSON, the efficient and tireless young Director of the State Research Council (secret police) in the postcolonial nation of **Kangan** in *Anthills of the Savannah*. Nicknamed "Samsonite" because of his impressive stamina, Major Ossai is promoted to full colonel late in the text. It is Ossai who issues the announcement of **Ikem Osodi**'s "accidental" killing while under arrest, and it is clear that Ossai and his organization are responsible for Osodi's death. Eventually, Ossai himself falls victim to the deteriorating political situation, and it is revealed in chapter 18 that he has disappeared.

M. Keith Booker

OSU. In traditional **Igbo** society, an individual who has been dedicated to the service of a god, an event that rigidly sets the person and all of his or her descendants (who are also *osu*) apart from the entire freeborn community (traditional Igbo culture also includes a non-*osu* slave class [Wren 40]), making marriage to any freeborn individual forbidden). In *Things Fall Apart* the *osu*, who are disfranchised outcasts, join the newly introduced Christian church under **Mr. Kiaga**'s tutelage in getting the church established in **Umuofia** (chapter 18).

In *No Longer at Ease*, **Clara Okeke**, a beautiful nurse educated in England with whom protagonist **Obi Okonkwo** is in love, reveals to him that she is an *osu*, precipitating not only the crisis in their relationship, but the central crisis of the novel. The discovery of Clara's *osu* status by Obi's friends and family divides him between his love for her and his desire to embrace an independent, Westernized life, on the one hand, and his bond to his family (notwithstanding that they are Christians) and his roots in Igbo culture, on the other. The climax of the plot occurs when Obi's parents, despite their devout Christian convictions, explicitly and forcefully reject his plans to wed Clara (chapter 14). The apparent irony that one so abject in traditional culture as Clara gains an education is explained by the fact that, as indicated in *Things Fall Apart*, the *osu* were among the first members of the Igbo community to convert to Christianity. This would lead to their gaining the privileges associated with a missionary and, by extension, colonial education, and with an apt pupil (Clara's father, **Josiah Okeke**, is a teacher) this privilege may go as far as being sent to England for further education (Wren 40)

In Achebe's short story, "Chike's School Days," first published in 1960 and later appearing in *Girls at War and Other Stories*, we are told that "**Chike**'s father [**Amos**] was not originally an *osu*, but had gone and married an *osu* woman in the name of Christianity. It was unheard of for a man to make himself *osu* in that way, with his eyes wide open. But then Amos was nothing if not mad.

The new religion had gone to his head" (38). The story attests, moreover, that European institutions among the Igbo had transformed the conditions for the *osu* so much that an *osu* child could condescend to a freeborn one (38).

FURTHER READING

Simon Gikandi, "Chinua Achebe and the Poetics of Location"; Kalu Ogbaa, *Gods, Oracles, and Divination*; Roderick Wilson, "Eliot and Achebe"; Robert M. Wren, *Achebe's World*.

Thomas J. Lynn

OSUGO, a man who contradicts **Okonkwo** at a kindred meeting in chapter 4 of *Things Fall Apart* that is being held to discuss the next ancestral feast. Okonkwo angrily responds by calling Osugo a woman because he has taken no titles. The others present regard this reaction (partly spurred by Okonkwo's bitterness toward his father, who had taken no titles) as excessive and side with Osugo.

M. Keith Booker

OTA, a spring in *Arrow of God* in which the women of **Umuaro** have been forbidden to do their washing and bathing until the water spirits have been appeased. See also **alusi**.

Rachel R. Reynolds

OTAKAGU, means "Devourer Like Leopard" (*Arrow of God*). It is the name of an **age-group** that is three or so years older than the age-group named **Omumawa**. **Obika** and **Ofoedu** belong to Otakagu. When **Winterbottom** conscripts men from **Umuaro** to help build the **Okperi**–Umuaro road, Otakagu and Omumawa age-group are volunteered to help by village elders. These two age-groups are in conflict, however, because Otakagu members gave Omumawa its humiliating name. The conflict runs so deep that the two age-groups must be scheduled to work on alternating days on the crew building the road.

Achebe examines age-group conflicts from an **Igbo** point of view in detail throughout *Arrow of God*. The effect is that the reader is given intimate knowledge and emotional investment in Igbo age-group politics, while learning that the colonial administrators have no sensitivity to these same issues. For example, in the following passage, Achebe contrasts the Igbo notion of age-group relationships to Winterbottom's persistent colonial gaze. Here Winterbottom is talking to Clarke about an African servant:

"He's a fine specimen, isn't he? He's been with me four years. He was a little boy of about thirteen—they've no ideas of years—when I took him on. He was absolutely raw."

"When you say they've no idea of years. . . ."

"They understand seasons, I don't mean that. But ask a man how old he is and he doesn't begin to have an idea." (Chapter 3)

Besides being a means by which generations and the passage of time could be reckoned and besides their functions in organizing collective labor, age-groups were also commonly cohorts that determined governance and ritual. As these groups grew older together, they would become the elders of the village, gradually conferring titles upon each other and sponsoring new **masks** and masquerade performances like the one described by Achebe in *Arrow of God*, chapter 17. In other words, they also held collective power of governance in the villages.

Rachel R. Reynolds

OTAKEKPEKI, known as an evil medicine man twice accused of foul play, has to swear twice that he is telling truthfully of his innocence and pass the test of an oath. The profile of Otakekpeki and the community reaction to his purportedly malificent presence at a ritual appears in chapter 17 of *Arrow of God*. It is one Achebe's priceless characteri-

zations of a type that might have populated a pre-colonial village in Igboland. The description itself warrants a bit of analysis. In order to echo how rumors about the man might ciruclate, Achebe uses language such as "it could mean" and "people did not believe" and "from what was known of him" and "perhaps the most suspicious thing." By building the character profile this way, Achebe shows us how the aura of mystique surrounding a powerful medicine man—especially an evil one—is sustained through village gossip and speculation.

Rachel R. Reynolds

OTIKPO, town crier of **Okperi,** who was once a famous runner. Otikpo has a daughter, **Ogbanje,** and a son, **Nweke,** who make brief appearances in chapter 2 of *Arrow of God*.

Rachel R. Reynolds

OUR SISTER KILLJOY: OR REFLECTIONS FROM A BLACK-EYED SQUINT, by Ama Ata Aidoo (1977), is characterized by Achebe in **Home and Exile** as a masterpiece. He argues that Aidoo speaks on behalf of the poor and afflicted (95). While the book is classified as a novel, the narrative structure of *Our Sister Killjoy* draws upon a variety of modes, including prose, poetry, and letters; for instance, prose descriptions of the protagonist's experiences in Europe are disrupted by poetic social and political commentaries. The form of the text is just one way in which *Our Sister Killjoy* may be read as a counter-narrative. The text disrupts the formal expectations of the European novel, and in it Aidoo rewrites the dominant European narrative of Africa and Africans in significant ways.

In contrast to canonical works of English literature of Africa, such as **Joseph Conrad**'s **Heart of Darkness** or **Joyce Carey**'s **Mister Johnson**, in which Africa is described through the European gaze, Aidoo turns the tables by describing Europe through the first-person narrative of Sissie, a Ghanaian student during her travels in Europe. As an African in Europe, Sissie describes Europeans or whites in terms of their difference; she condemns Europeans for treating their pets better than other human beings, for instance. Unlike the protagonists of many European novels of Africa, however, Sissie seems conscious of the way in which she understands her surroundings through her own culture, not least because she is ever-conscious of her status as "exotic" in Europe. Sissie's sojourn in Germany and London allows her the opportunity to formulate and solidify her ideas of Africa and her African identity, in racial, political, and cultural terms. This is another way in which *Our Sister Killjoy* may be read as a counter-narrative; it centers the experience of Africans.

A central theme of the narrative is Aidoo's concern for the issues surrounding exile. Sissie's meeting with an Indian doctor in Germany and her love affair with a Ghanaian in England lead to her condemnation of these exiles in Europe, not for taking advantage of educational opportunities but for neglecting their homelands and identity: "They work hard for the / Doctorates— / They work too hard / Giving away / Not only themselves, but / All of us" (87). While she understands the exile's reasons for not returning to Africa, and she herself condemns the corruption and mismanagement of "a dance of the masquerades called independence" (95), she believes that to adopt European ways and manners is to lose oneself: "So we must hurry to lose our identity quickly in order to join the great family of man" (121). While much critical debate surrounds the extent to which Aidoo idealizes African culture and identity in presenting a nationalist novel, the text also provides a critique of dominant male constructions of African nationalism. Sissie's gender is a significant aspect of the novel, in terms of both the way she is sexualized and masculinized by Europeans and the way she understands the cultural and political role of women in Africa.

FURTHER READING

M. Keith Booker, *The African Novel in English*; Ranu Samantrai, "Caught at the Confluence of History"; Gay Wilentz, "The Politics of Exile."

David Jefferess

OYE. See **Market days**.

OYILIDIE, older woman whom **Ojiugo** bites in a women's scuffle over rumors that **Oduche** had injured a royal **python** (*Arrow of God*, chapter 12).

Rachel R. Reynolds

OYILIDIE. See **Okuata**.

OZO. In *Things Fall Apart*, one of the four titles of distinction of the clan of **Umuofia**. In chapter 8 we learn that **Okonkwo** has taken this title. According to Kalu Ogbaa, men who have taken this title also gain the epithet **Ogbuefi** as part of their names.

FURTHER READING

Kalu Ogbaa, *Gods, Oracles, and Divination*.

M. Keith Booker

OZOEMENA. In *Things Fall Apart*, the first wife of **Ndulue**, the oldest man in the village of **Ire**, one of the nine villages of **Umuofia**. She herself is quite old and walks with the help of a stick. His death, in chapter 8, is followed by hers, on the same day. In accordance with local custom, the funeral of Ndulue is postponed until after the burial of Ozoemena.

M. Keith Booker

OZOEMENA, one of the children of **Okonkwo** and **Ekwefi** in *Things Fall Apart*. Seeking to break the cycle of early deaths among her children, in chapter 9 Ekwefi gives the girl this name, which means "May it not happen again." The girl still dies young.

M. Keith Booker

OZUMBA, an old man who is the "keeper of the night spirits" in the men's ritual society of **Umuaro**. He dresses Obika for a masquerade in the last chapter of *Arrow of God*.

Rachel R. Reynolds

P

PACIFICATION, name given to the British policy of subduing resistance in **Nigeria** and other areas of their colonial rule in Africa, essentially another name for the policy of "**indirect rule**," the philosophy and practice of governance elaborated by **Lord Frederick Lugard** during his years as colonial administrator of Nigeria. Under this policy, the British theoretically sought to secure the co-operation of their colonial subjects indirectly through indigenous institutions. However, this practice often involved the destruction of those institutions and the subsequent installation of strong indigenous local rulers, or "warrant chiefs," who would be responsible for day-to-day local administration but who would ultimately answer to the British. This system was particularly incompatible with the political practices of the **Igbo**, who did not traditionally invest power in strong individual rulers but rather relied on the judgments of collective councils.

Achebe comments critically on this system, especially in *Arrow of God*, in which British colonial officer **Tony Clarke**, newly arrived at his new posting in 1920s Nigeria, goes for dinner with his District Officer, **Captain T. K. Winterbottom**, having just come to the final chapter of *The Pacification of the Primitive Tribes of the Lower Niger*, which had been lent to him by Winterbottom. Winterbottom, who had been at his post for well over a decade, did not approve of the current policy of "pacification," and he says as much to his new assistant over dinner: "What do we British do? We flounder from one expedient to its opposite. We do not only promise to secure the old savage tyrants on their thrones—or more likely filthy animal skins—we not only do that, but we now go out of our way to invent chiefs where there were none before. They make me sick" (*Arrow of God*). The book itself was a hand-me-down, from Achebe's first novel *Things Fall Apart*, which concluded with the **District Commissioner** contemplating the composition of a manual of the same title as Winterbottom's and considering the space that might be assigned to the ill-fated Okonkwo—"not a whole chapter but a reasonable paragraph, at any rate." After all, the District Commissioner finally decides, "There was so much else to include, and one must be firm in cutting out details" (*Things Fall Apart*).

FURTHER READING

A. E. Afigbo, *The Warrant Chiefs*; Lord Frederick John Dealtry Lugard, *The Dual Mandate in Tropical Africa*; Mahmood Mamdani, *When Victims Become Killers*.

Barbara Harlow

THE PACIFICATION OF THE PRIMITIVE TRIBES OF THE LOWER NIGER.

A book being written, at the end of *Things Fall Apart*, by the **District Commissioner**, who seeks to describe the British experience in the colonial subjugation of **Nigeria**. Though fictional, the book is representative of accounts written by such British colonial administrators as **Lord Frederick Lugard**, and such books continue to serve as monuments of British arrogance and insensitivity, even if they occasionally suggest presumably good intentions. Thus, Achebe's haughty District Commissioner suggests that the story of **Okonkwo** might make an interesting anecdote for his book, good, perhaps, for a paragraph. The book also makes an appearance in *Arrow of God*. See also **Pacification**.

FURTHER READING

Lord Frederick John Dealtry Lugard, *The Dual Mandate in Tropical Africa*.

M. Keith Booker

THE PALM-WINE DRINKARD AND HIS DEAD PALM-WINE TAPSTER IN THE DEAD'S TOWN,

by Amos Tutuola (1952), draws upon symbolism, cosmology, and other themes from Yoruba folklore and culture to tell the tale of a palm-wine drinker in search of the tapster of his palm-wine, who has died. While the book was internationally recognized due to Dylan Thomas's enthusiastic review, it was harshly criticized by some critics in Tutuola's homeland of **Nigeria**. The novel's language, which largely fails to conform to expectations of English grammar, was characterized as poor English and crude. Similarly, some Nigerian intellectuals argued that the narrative's series of episodes in which the Drinkard uses juju to escape ferocious, supernatural beasts, for instance, promotes stereotypes of Africans as primitive. In contrast, in *Home and Exile*, Achebe characterizes the novel as a "startling literary concoction" (44) and argues that it "led the way for modern West African literature in English" (54). In response to criticism of the novel by his fellow Nigerians, Achebe contends that this criticism reflects "their badly damaged sense of self" (81).

Accustomed to a life of pleasure and ease in which he spends his days drinking palm-wine supplied by his father and tapped by a particular tapster, the Palm-Wine Drinkard's life is disrupted by the deaths of his father and the tapster. Seeking to reestablish his life of leisure, the Drinkard embarks upon a journey in search of the Dead's Town in hopes of finding the tapster and therefore restoring his palm-wine drinking pastime. Traveling from place to place, the Drinkard continually enters into arrangements in which he must conduct some labor or errand in return for directions to the Deads' Town. For instance, having been told that he will learn the whereabouts of the tapster if he rescues and returns a man's daughter, the Drinkard uses his juju to save the girl from her captor, a gentleman who has become only a skull. In other instances, the Drinkard must aid in farming, is tricked into carrying the corpse of a prince, and is asked to adjudicate a court case. While the Drinkard and the wife he marries during his journey are able to travel from place to place, a recurring image in the novel is the inability of those with whom the Drinkard builds relationships or those the Drinkard must defeat or escape to cross these same boundaries. Ultimately, the Drinkard does find the tapster, and they return to their village in a time of famine.

In **"Work and Play in Tutuola's *The Palm-Wine Drinkard*,"** Achebe argues that the novel focuses upon social and ethical questions, namely, "what happens when a man immerses himself in pleasure to the exclusion of all work," and contends that the novel is a "rich and spectacular exploration of this gross perversion, its expiation through appropriate punishment and the offenders final restoration" (*Hopes and Impediments* 69). Further, in "**The Truth of Fiction**," Achebe states: "Without having to undergo personally the ordeals which the drinkard has to suffer in atonement for his idleness and lack of self-control, we become, through an act of our imagination, beneficiaries of his regenerative adventure" (*Hopes and Impediments* 99).

FURTHER READING

Patrick Colm Hogan, "Understanding *The Palm-Wine Drinkard*"; Oyekan Owomoyela, *Amos Tutuola Revisted*.

David Jefferess

PAT. In chapter 12 of *No Longer at Ease*, one of two newly arrived teachers at a Roman Catholic convent near **Lagos** who make the acquaintance of **Obi Okonkwo** and his friend, **Christopher**. The other teacher, **Nora**, is paired with Obi, while Pat is "appropriated" by Christopher. The association between the two women and two men is short-lived due to the disapproval of the Mother of the convent. See also **Nora**.

Thomas J. Lynn

PEDLER, F. J. See *West Africa*.

PEOPLE'S ALLIANCE PARTY (PAP), the leading opposition party in the fictional postcolonial African nation of *A Man of the People*. Clearly, the ideals and morals (or lack thereof) of the members of PAP differ little from those of the members of the ruling party, the **People's Organization Party (POP)**, all of whom seem devoted only to serving their own interests and lining their own pockets.

M. Keith Booker

PEOPLE'S ORGANIZATION PARTY (POP), the ruling party in the fictional postcolonial African nation of *A Man of the People*. It is depicted as a party of corrupt and self-serving power-mongers, interested only in furthering their own ambitions (and fattening their own bank accounts) rather than helping their constituents. In this sense, however, it differs little from its principal opposition party, the **People's Alliance Party (PAP)**. Indeed, POP and PAP are depicted in the novel as a sort of Tweedledee and Tweedledum of postcolonial politics, offering little real choice to the people.

M. Keith Booker

PETER, the houseboy of narrator **Odili Samalu** in *A Man of the People*. Like Samalu, Peter comes from the village of **Urua**, though, as the novel begins, he lives with Samalu in **Anata**.

M. Keith Booker

PIDGIN ENGLISH, a modified and simplified form of English spoken in many parts of the former British Empire. In fact, the term pidgin (apparently derived from Chinese attempts to pronounce the English word "business") applies to any number of such modified languages (not necessarily based on English) spoken in various places around the world. Nigerian pidgin is a particularly rich combination of simplified English with words, inflections, and syntax derived from indigenous Nigerian languages. It originally evolved during the period of British colonial rule but has continued to develop during the postcolonial period and is still widely spoken.

Achebe is renowned for his ability to reproduce a literary form of pidgin English that imparts the flavor of the language to readers of Standard English. He also tends to make a metacommentary about the perceived value of English or pidgin English to local people. This example from *Arrow of God* is exemplary: "The two policeman conferred in the white man's tongue to the great admiration of the villagers. 'Sometine na dat two porson we cross for road.' " The scene goes on for several lines. Indeed, knowledge of English was seen early on as a commodity of great use in Igboland, especially for those who wanted to enter trades or government service.

Achebe makes particularly extensive use of pidgin English in *No Longer at Ease* and *A Man of the People*, while it is also used in *Anthills of the Savannah*. In these novels, pidgin is frequently used in modern urban settings where individuals with different ethnic, cultural, and linguistic backgrounds come together and use pidgin as a *lingua franca* to further their common communication. In these novels, the use of pidgin is often a marker of class position, just as dialect often indicates the class origins of characters in British novels. Thus, pidgin is often used by servants, laborers, and less-educated characters, while the wealthier and more educated characters tend to speak a more standard form of English—except when they use pidgin to communicate with their servants, employees, or other less educated characters. Educated characters may also occasionally use pidgin among themselves to indicate intimacy or conviviality. Often such educated speakers use pidgin poorly or incorrectly, subtly suggesting that their command of language is not necessarily superior to that of less educated or lower-class characters.

In some cases, Achebe uses pidgin as an indicator of illicit linguistic activity, as when characters who usually speak Standard English switch to pidgin while negotiating bribes or conducting other illegal business. In other cases, however, pidgin is used as a supplement and enrichment to Standard English, certain pidgin expressions being more colorful and vivid than the English from which they originally arose. In general, in fact, Achebe's use of pidgin can be taken as part of his response to the **language question** that confronts all postcolonial writers. By his use of pidgin, as with his use of the **Igbo lan-guage**, Achebe signals his desire to make the English language serve his own African cultural purposes rather than simply to accept Standard English as a literary language superior to indigenous African languages.

FURTHER READING

Edmund O. Bamiro, "The Social and Functional Power of Nigerian English"; Ben Ohiomamhe Elugbe and Augusta Phil Omamor, *Nigerian Pidgin*; Nicholas Faraclas, *Nigerian Pidgin*; Robert A. Hall Jr., *Pidgin and Creole Languages*; Tony Obilade, "The Stylistic Function of Pidgin English in African Literature"; Kalu Ogbaa, *Gods, Oracles, and Divination*; Kofi Yankson, "Use of Pidgin in *No Longer at Ease* and *A Man of the People*."

M. Keith Booker and Rachel R. Reynolds

PILATE, PONTIUS, a reputedly ruthless Roman prefect of Judaea (A.D. 26–36) under the emperor Tiberius, referred to in the works of Josephus, Eusebius, Tacitus, and Philo. A main source of information on Pilate is Christian scripture, according to which he presided at the trial of Jesus and gave the decree for his Crucifixion. In chapter 13 of *No Longer at Ease* Pilate is invoked somewhat ironically by the devout **Isaac Okonkwo** in his effort to convey to "an illiterate kinsman" the wonder of " 'the writing of the white man' " with its relative permanence. Isaac declares that " 'books which clerks wrote twenty years ago or more . . . are still as they wrote them. They do not say one thing today and another tomorrow. . . . In the Bible Pilate said: 'What is written is written.' "

Thomas J. Lynn

POSTCOLONIAL CRITICISM, the branch of literary criticism dealing with works of **postcolonial literature** and sometimes with works of Western literature from a postcolonial perspective. See also **Postcolonial studies**.

POSTCOLONIAL LITERATURE, the collective term used to indicate the literature produced by writers from nations that were formerly the colonies of European imperial powers. This loose definition encompasses a wide variety of cultures and societies. In the most literal sense, postcolonial literature includes the literature of nations such as Australia, Canada, and even the United States, all of which were formerly British colonies. Indeed, American writers in the nineteenth century, such as Ralph Waldo Emerson, often expressed a conscious desire to contribute to the development of a new postcolonial cultural identity that would move beyond the legacy of the British-dominated past. Thus, one of the pioneering studies of postcolonial literature, *The Empire Writes Back* (1980), by Bill Ashcroft, Gareth Griffiths, and Helen Tiffin, argues that "in many ways the American experience and its attempts to produce a new kind of literature can be seen as the model for all later post-colonial writing" (16). That volume also pays substantial attention to Canadian and Australian literature. However, such cases of postcolonial nations dominated by settlers from Europe after the indigenous peoples have been largely exterminated or displaced clearly represent a different situation from that which obtains in Africa or Asia, where the nations emerging after independence are still dominated by indigenous peoples and where indigenous cultures make a far more important contribution to the postcolonial cultural identities than in nations formed from settler colonies. The literature of Latin America represents a sort of middle case. When Latin American nations emerged (generally in the nineteenth century) from colonization by Spain and Portugal, the descendants of Spanish and Portuguese settlers continued to play crucial roles, while indigenous cultures typically remained strong influences as well. Ireland, meanwhile, represents another case of a postcolonial society

that is dominated by the descendants of people who lived there before colonization but in which the "indigenous" people are themselves Europeans. Finally, Caribbean literature represents still another special situation. Here, the indigenous peoples were essentially exterminated, but the postcolonial societies and cultures tend to be dominated by the descendants not of European settlers but of African slaves (and sometimes East Indian indentured workers) brought to the region to provide labor for sugar plantations and other European colonial enterprises.

In its strictest sense, the term "postcolonial literature" tends to apply to the literature produced by writers from nations that achieved independence from European rule in the major wave of decolonization that occurred after World War II, a designation that would apply primarily to African, Caribbean, and certain Asian literatures, though the latter have tended to receive less attention as objects of academic study in the West, partly because they are written primarily in Asian languages, while African and Caribbean literature has been dominated by works written in English or French, the two dominant colonial languages (see **Language question**). However, as Africa is far larger and more populous and as Caribbean history is a sort of special case in which African culture already plays a crucial role, one might regard African literature as the paradigm of this narrower definition of postcolonial literature. Meanwhile, one might regard the postcolonial novel as the central genre of postcolonial African literature, though it is certainly the case that important works of poetry, drama, and film have been produced by writers and artists from Africa (and other areas of the postcolonial world) as well.

The African novel is a paradigmatic genre of postcolonial literature because of its prominence in the project of construction of viable postcolonial national cultural identities. It is also crucial in that it enacts a direct confrontation with the tradition of Western literature. After all, by the time most of Africa was colonized by European powers in the late nineteenth century, the novel had long been the dominant literary genre in Western Europe. Indeed, scholars and historians have frequently seen the novel as the principal literary form by which the European bourgeoisie, newly emerging as the dominant class in Western Europe in the seventeenth and eighteenth centuries, sought to express their own sense of a new post-medieval cultural identity. The novel is thus the ideal genre for postcolonial literature because of its history of participation in a successful process of cultural transformation in Europe. Yet the novel is also problematic as a postcolonial form in that it is the genre traditionally associated most closely with the ideology and worldview of the ruling class in the very European powers that colonized Africa.

It is partly because of the double and somewhat contradictory status of the novel as a postcolonial genre that the novels of Achebe have been regarded as so central to the evolution of postcolonial literature. After all, Achebe's novels enact this doubleness in a particularly vivid way, making a resource of this potential problem. On the one hand, Achebe actively strives to create, through his novels, a strong sense of African cultural identity that moves beyond the legacy of colonialism. On the other hand, he directly confronts the traditions of colonialist literature, challenging in an especially direct way the representation of Africa and Africans in the European novel.

Of course, Achebe is also crucial to the development of the African novel because his work, especially *Things Fall Apart* (first published in 1958), appeared so early in that development. Indeed, among Anglophone novels by black African writers, only the works of Amos Tutuola had appeared earlier,

and those works (such as *The Palm-Wine Drinkard*, first published in 1952) have typically been regarded only marginally as novels, given their basis in Yoruba folklore. Thus, many critics consider not Tutuola, but Achebe to be the founding figure of the modern African novel and even of modern African literature as a whole. **Simon Gikandi**, in his excellent study of Achebe's novels, discusses at some length the reasons that Achebe has been seen as such a foundational figure in the history of African literature, even though he in fact had a number of important predecessors. Gikandi concludes that Achebe's importance lies in the fact that his work was a genuine breakthrough in its direct confrontation with the cultural traditions of colonialism, in its ability "to evolve narrative procedures through which the colonial language, which was previously intended to designate and reproduce the colonial ideology, now evokes new forms of expression, proffers new oppositional discourse" (4).

In particular, argues Gikandi, Achebe is able to use the colonial language of English and the Western genre of the novel to mount a powerful challenge to the myth of European cultural superiority, thereby recovering elements of African experience that have been effaced by colonialism and producing a viable sense of an alternative African cultural identity. "I want to insist," writes Gikandi, "that Achebe was possibly the first African writer to be self-conscious about his role as an African writer, to confront the linguistic and historical problems of African writing in a colonial situation, and to situate writing within a larger body of regional and global knowledge about Africa" (5–6).

By the beginning of the twenty-first century, writers such as Nigeria's **Wole Soyinka** and Buchi Emecheta, Ghana's **Ayi Kwei Armah** and **Ama Ata Aidoo**, South Africa's Alex La Guma, and Kenya's **Ngugi wa Thiong'o** had joined Achebe as important writers of African novels in English, though Ngugi switched to writing novels in the Gikuyu language midway through his career. Francophone African novelists such as Senegal's Ousmane Sembène, Cheikh Hamidou Kane, and Mariama Bâ had also become major figures in world literature, as had Caribbean writers such as George Lamming, Wilson Harris, Sam Selvon, and Merle Hodge. In the meantime, the global prominence of writers such as the Nobel Prize–winning **V. S. Naipaul** (born of Indian parents in British colonial Trinidad but adopting a resolutely pro-Western stance in many of his novels and other writings) and **Salman Rushdie** (born in India shortly after independence but heavily influenced by Western modernism and postmodernism in his writing) further indicates the complexity of the designation "postcolonial literature."

FURTHER READING

Bill Ashcroft, Gareth Griffiths, and Helen Tiffin, *The Empire Writes Back*; Elleke Boehmer, *Colonial and Postcolonial Literature*; M. Keith Booker, *The African Novel in English*; M. Keith Booker and Dubravka Juraga, *The Caribbean Novel in English*.

M. Keith Booker

POSTCOLONIAL STUDIES. The branch of literary studies dealing primarily with works of postcolonial culture. Beginning especially in the 1990s, postcolonial studies became a major enterprise within the Western academy, though many of the leading scholars in the field came from India, Africa, and other postcolonial locations. The rise of postcolonial studies was facilitated by both the explosion in production of **postcolonial literature** from the 1960s onward and the increased awareness, within the Western academy, of the crucial role played by historical and political context in the production and reception of literature.

Much of the intense critical interest in postcolonial literature has to do with its obvious relevance to real-world problems: postcolonial writers (Achebe is exemplary here) are involved in serious efforts to develop viable cultural identities to replace those that have been thrust upon them by the culture of their former colonial masters, and the stakes in these efforts are clearly high. Thus, the work of postcolonial writers has been an important inspiration for literary theorists seeking to understand literature in ways that escape the mystifications created by the complex cultural forces in which all literature participates.

At the same time, literary theory, no matter how iconoclastic, remains dominated by white male Europeans and North Americans, creating a disjunction between the cultural positions of critics and theorists and those of the subaltern writers to whom they often turn for inspiration. Thus, while the recent increase in critical attention to works by postcolonial writers is undoubtedly a positive development, it also raises a number of vexing issues, including the question of whether such critics and theorists are not themselves enacting a sort of intellectual imperialism by conscripting multicultural texts in the interest of their own professional endeavors. In short, the insights of Western literary theory can provide extremely useful approaches to the criticism of multicultural literature, but critics should remain vigilantly aware that Western theory and multicultural literature arise from fundamentally different cultural positions. Achebe himself has addressed this sort of problem in his well-known call for Western critics to approach African literature with "humility," acknowledging its difference and their necessarily partial access to it.

Postcolonial studies have tended to draw upon a variety of forms of Western theory, modified with insights gained from an array of recent historical, sociological, psychological, and political meditations on subaltern cultures and societies. Indeed, the field has prominently featured a number of thinkers from the colonial and postcolonial world. For example, **Frantz Fanon** (born and raised in French colonial Martinique) was trained in France as a psychoanalyst but also drew extensively upon **Marxism** (in many ways the antithesis of psychoanalytic theory). Fanon died prematurely in 1961, very early in the postcolonial moment. But his work remains powerfully relevant to the postcolonial condition more than thirty years after his death. A fierce advocate of independence, he nevertheless eschewed the utopian rhetoric of African nationalism and warned that, in an era of global capitalism, it was necessary to continue the fight against cultural and economic colonialism even after independence:

We should flatly refuse the situation to which Western countries wish to condemn us. Colonialism and imperialism have not paid their score even when they draw their flags and their police forces from our territories. For centuries the capitalists have behaved in the underdeveloped world like nothing more than criminals. (*Wretched* 101)

In particular, Fanon warned against the possibility of continuing neocolonial oppression in postcolonial nations dominated by a ruling class that attempted to model itself on the European bourgeoisie and by a national consciousness based on the model of European nationalism. He was thus the first major theorist to recognize that the nationalist spirit of independence in the colonial world did not necessarily stand in direct opposition to foreign imperial domination but might in fact extend that domination in more subtle ways. As Said puts it, Fanon "more dramatically and decisively than anyone . . . expresses the immense cultural shift from the terrain of nationalist independence to the theoretical domain of liberation" (*Culture* 268).

Fanon's attempt to delineate a means by which postcolonial peoples could pursue the development of viable personal and cultural identities free of domination by the colonial past, along with his radically adversarial stance toward the traditional domination of white Western culture, has proved inspirational to insurgent political movements around the globe, including American black-power advocates in the 1960s. They have also strongly influenced a number of postcolonial African novelists (see Booker, "Writing"), while his analyses of the negative consequences of the colonialist stereotypes produced by Western discourses have numerous implications for literary criticism and theory. Fanon's body of work, with its distinctively multicultural adaptation of psychoanalytic and **Marx**ist theory and its fiercely dedicated political opposition to continuing domination of the postcolonial world by Western theory and thought, also remains among the founding texts of postcolonial literary theory.

While Fanon's work was crucial to the beginnings of postcolonial theory, many recent postcolonial theorists have drawn upon more recent developments, especially in French poststructuralist theory. For example, the influential work of Homi Bhabha draws upon Fanon but has been particularly marked by sophisticated applications of Lacanian and Derridean theory to the postcolonial situation (especially in India). Abdul JanMohamed, who has been critical of Bhabha's readings of Fanon, makes extensive use of Lacan and of the Marxist theorist Fredric Jameson in his work. Gayatri Chakravorty Spivak regards Fanon as an important precursor to her own project, which involves sophisticated applications of Derridean, Marxist, and feminist theory to the postcolonial situation.

The poststructuralist orientation of postcolonial critics like Bhabha and Spivak often includes an emphasis on language and representation that points to an important focus in postcolonial theory on the possibility that signification may operate according to fundamentally different principles in postcolonial texts than in texts of the Western tradition. Indeed, an entire field of "colonial discourse theory" (usefully reviewed by Benita Parry) has arisen in order to study this possibility. Jameson, for example, has suggested that it would be useful to consider the possibility all "third-world texts"—and particularly the major characters in those texts—might be read as "national allegories" focusing on the historical process of colonialism, decolonization, and independence.

Jameson goes on to remark that postcolonial texts should be read as allegorical "particularly when their forms develop out of predominantly western machineries of representation, such as the novel" ("Third-World" 69). In these cases, Western readers, believing that they are encountering a familiar literary form, might be especially tempted to read postcolonial literature as if it operates according to Western principles of literary signification, one of the most ingrained of which (particularly in the novel) is the tendency to think of characters as representing individual human beings. Jameson's notion certainly applies well to much of the fiction of Achebe. On the other hand, Jameson's sweeping claim for the allegorical functioning of Third World literary texts would seem to come dangerously close to a safe reinscription of the otherness of the Third World within a preexisting Western analytical category. Further, as Aijaz Ahmad has pointed out, Jameson's vision of the Third World tends to cast that world as the passive product of the clash between the active "First" and "Second" Worlds, while his emphasis on national allegory tends to place too much emphasis on the fundamentally Western concept of nationalism as the only available Third World response to the legacy of colonialism and imperialism.

Jameson sees a consistent attempt in Third World texts to contribute to the development of national cultural identities in postcolonial states by creating coherent images of such identities in literary texts. But this process, so seemingly similar to the literarization of colonial reality in the work of British writers from Kipling to Scott, clearly resembles the process of textualization of the Orient that Said describes in *Orientalism* as a crucial strategy of European visions of the East. Said demonstrates that stereotypical Orientalist European depictions of the East are consistently textual in nature. Orientalists, he concludes, do not study and describe the Orient in the direct ways that their Western Enlightenment ideologies would like to claim. Instead, they generate highly stylized textual representations of the Orient, thereby creating Oriental cultural identities via imperial allegories that serve as clear predecessors of the national allegories Jameson identifies in the work of postcolonial writers. Following Said, Christopher Miller has used the term "Africanism" to describe the similar stereotypical treatment of Africa and Africans in Western writing.

Jameson, meanwhile, is perfectly aware of the potential drift toward Orientalist stereotyping embodied in his totalizing analysis of Third World literature. He argues that "*any* articulation of radical difference . . . is susceptible to appropriation by that strategy of otherness which Edward Said, in the context of the Middle East, called 'orientalism' " (77). At the same time, Jameson concludes that the potential pitfalls of such an appeal to cultural otherness are preferable to what he sees as the only alternative: a "liberal and humanistic universalism" that would fail to respect the alterity of Third World cultures.

Whether an Orientalist emphasis on difference and a universalist insistence on similarity are the only two alternative approaches to postcolonial literature is debatable, however.

Indeed, Bhabha, exploring these two alternatives, has suggested what he sees as a preferable third course: to approach postcolonial texts through a mode of ideological analysis in the mode of the Marxist structuralist theorist Louis Althusser. For Bhabha ideological analysis provides an alternative to reading strategies based strictly on interpretation of a text's meaning as the representation of some preexisting reality and allows an interrogation of the historical situation in which that text was produced. This mode of reading thus potentially allows a comprehension of the different signifying practices at work in colonial texts, rather than merely projecting Western modes of representation onto non-Western writing. In the particular case of the colonial situation, this interrogation potentially results in fundamental challenges to the Western notion of the transcendental self and to the aligned concepts of authority and intention. It is for this reason, according to Bhabha, that uncanny scenes of colonial abyss like that in Forster's Marabar Caves or that encompassed by the "horror" of **Joseph Conrad**'s **Kurtz** can be so powerfully unsettling.

One could argue, of course, that in his appeal to Althusser (as in his appeals to various forms of poststructuralist theory elsewhere in his work) Bhabha—like Jameson—is in danger of inscribing Third World literature within First World theoretical categories. Indeed, in their different ways Bhabha and Jameson illustrate the tremendous difficulty faced by any critic who would attempt to approach Third World texts through a critical vocabulary that will make them accessible to a First World audience. Bhabha himself has addressed the charge that the application of Western theory to non-Western literature involves a kind of critical imperialism, arguing that the rejection of theory on the basis of this assumption is "damaging and self-defeating" (19). For Bhabha simply to avoid the use of Western theory deprives the critic

of Third World literature of potentially powerful tools with which to explicate and galvanize the cultural energies of that literature. Moreover, Bhabha concludes that the very notion of a strict separation between First World theory and Third World literature is the "mirror image" of the nineteenth-century Orientalist polarity between East and West.

Indeed, central to Bhabha's critical project is a rather Derridean deconstruction of the opposition between the cultures of the colonizers and the colonized. He thus insists that a complexly ambivalent cultural hybridity—on both sides—is the inevitable consequence of all colonial encounters. Bhabha has in mind a subtle mutual implication of the discourses of colonizer and colonized (especially of England and India), and this colonial hybridity of British culture is especially strong given the overt ambivalence of the British imperial project in India, a project informed by fascination and fear, confidence and insecurity, responsibility and guilt. On the other hand, JanMohamed takes Bhabha to task for what he sees as an overly sanguine deconstruction of the polar opposition between colonizer and colonized. JanMohamed argues that Bhabha's poststructuralist perspective ultimately ignores the real point of Fanon's discussion of binary oppositions, thus effacing politics and the realities of domination in the colonial situation ("Economy" 78–79).

JanMohamed's critique of Bhabha recalls the recent concern of scholars such as Epifanio San Juan Jr. about the potential implications of the turn toward poststructuralist theory in postcolonial studies in the late 1990s (which also represents a turn away from Fanon). In his *Beyond Postcolonial Theory*, San Juan argues that this phenomenon can be attributed largely to the "worldwide hegemony of poststructuralist ideology that valorizes the primacy of exchange, pastiche, fragmentation, textuality, and difference as touchstones of critique and understanding" (259). Aijaz Ahmad, Timothy Brennan, Arif Dirlik, and M. Keith Booker (*Ulysses*) have also complained about the suppression of Marxist thought in favor of poststructuralist "sophistication" in recent postcolonial theory. Moreover, the social and historical engagement of Achebe's work tends to suggest that this sophistication, to the extent that it diverts attention from this engagement, is inappropriate and damaging.

FURTHER READING

Aijaz Ahmad, *In Theory*; Homi K. Bhabha, *The Location of Culture*; M. Keith Booker, *Ulysses, Capitalism, and Colonialism* and "Writing for the Wretched of the Earth"; Timothy Brennan, *At Home in the World*; Arif Dirlik, *The Postcolonial Aura*; Frantz Fanon, *The Wretched of the Earth*; Fredric Jameson, "Third-World Literature in the Era of Multinational Capitalism"; Abdul Jan-Mohamed, "The Economy of Manichean Allegory"; Christopher Miller, *Blank Darkness*; Bart Moore-Gilbert, *Postcolonial Theory*; Benita Parry, "Problems"; Edward Said, *Culture and Imperialism* and *Orientalism*; Epifanio San Juan Jr., *Beyond Postcolonial Theory*.

M. Keith Booker

POSTCOLONIAL THEORY. See **POSTCOLONIAL STUDIES**.

"PUBLISHING IN AFRICA: A WRITER'S VIEW." Achebe essay. See *Morning Yet on Creation Day*.

PYTHON, a large, nonvenomous constrictor snake found in tropical regions of Africa, Asia, Australia, and the South Pacific. A member of the boa family, the python is named for a huge serpent from Greek mythology that was slain by the god Apollo. The python also plays an important role in traditional **Igbo** myth and culture, where the royal python is associated with the god **Idemili** and considered sacred. Given the traditional association of serpents with Satan in Christian tradition, it is perhaps not surprising that the British colonizers of Nigeria worked especially hard to eliminate the python worship. This aspect of the conflict between British and Igbo cultures figures prominently at several points in Achebe's work. For example, in *Things Fall Apart*, the new Christian convert, **Okoli**, kills a sacred python, then soon falls ill and dies. In the same novel, **Enoch**, son of the snake-priest, indicates his devotion to his new religion by killing and eating a sacred python. Christian converts also kill and eat pythons in *Arrow of God*, where the prevalence of attacks of Christians on the cult of python worship are indicated by the fact that Igbo children learn the saying: "*Eke nekwo onye uka!*" or "Python run, there's a Christian here!" However, the convert **Moses Unachukwu** in that novel determines that it is not necessary for Christian converts to kill sacred pythons, therefore easing the terror of new converts who might otherwise have been required to perform such an act to demonstrate their Christian piety.

FURTHER READING

Richard Bryan McDaniel, "The Python Episodes in Achebe's Novels."

M. Keith Booker

R

RALPH, the fiancé of Elsie when she first became sexually involved with Odili Samalu, the narrator of *A Man of the People*, back during his college days. When Samalu and Elsie had first had sex, she had called out the name of Ralph, then away attending medical school at the University of Edinburgh. This event leads Irre, a fellow student and local wag, to dub Samalu "Assistant Ralph." Ironically, when Elsie later has sex with Chief Nanga even as Samalu is approaching her room in the expectation of a sexual liaison, she calls out Samalu's name at the key moment.

M. Keith Booker

READING CHINUA ACHEBE: LANGUAGE AND IDEOLOGY IN FICTION,

by Simon Gikandi (1991), remains one of the more important critical discussions of Achebe's work. Gikandi's book derives its strength from its rigorous contextual analysis, which places Achebe's writings in their proper political, socioeconomic, and cultural perspectives. It is only by situating Achebe's novels in the colonial and postcolonial realities that produced them that we can even begin, Gikandi claims, to understand how they represent those realities in narrative. His study shows how Achebe's novels not only describe Igbo and Nigerian societies but also reinvent them. In so doing, Gikandi uses the ideas of Edward Said, specifically the latter's insight in *Orientalism* that one way of coming to critical terms with the postcolonial condition is to analyze not so much its content as its form. Gikandi's debt to Said's methodology is evident in the scrupulous attention he pays to the narrative structures of Achebe's five novels.

Beginning with *Things Fall Apart* and proceeding chronologically to *Anthills of the Savannah*, Gikandi examines the new set of narrative paradigms that Achebe's gradual shift away from the encounter between Africa and the West and toward more localized conflicts required. With each novel Achebe has written, the oppositional relation between colonizer and colonized has become less secure and more fragmentary, so that the dualities that seemed to configure *Things Fall Apart* have gradually collapsed. Achebe's shift away from binary forms of representation and his subsequent search for different forms of narration coalesced, Gikandi illustrates, with his disillusionment with the Nigerian nation. "Clearly, narration in the postcolonial situation could not be predicated on the evocation of a precolonial past nor a postcolonial future," Gikandi explains in his reading of *A Man of the People*. "Rather the writer had to develop new forms to account for, and represent, a historical period which was still in the making" (103). By the time *Anthills of the Savannah* was published, Achebe had experimented with a full range of narrative forms, all in an attempt to characterize the contradictions of national consciousness.

It is significant that while Achebe has modified and changed his approach to narration dramatically, he still has faith in the novel's ability to suggest alternatives to colonial and postcolonial domination. Gikandi devotes much of his introduction to an exploration of how—despite his anxiety about the translation of his discourse from the realm of the imaginary to the realm of the everyday—Achebe has remained committed to his belief that the novel holds endless possibilities for re-creating the national community. Making the novel his chosen mode of representing reality enables Achebe, Gikandi concludes, to probe the conditions of past and present African societies while creating an ideal future society.

FURTHER READING

Simon Gikandi, *Reading Chinua Achebe*; Lekan Oyegoke, "Misreading Simon Gikandi's *Reading Chinua Achebe*."

Julie McGonegal

ROBERTS, Assistant Superintendent of the Police in **Okperi** in *Arrow of God*, chapter 3.

Rachel R. Reynolds

ROCKEFELLER FOUNDATION. See **Foundations**.

RUSHDIE, SALMAN (1947–   ). Born in India to prosperous Muslims parents in 1947, Salman Rushdie was educated in England, where his writing career began. His *Mid-night's Children*, a novel that deals with the Indian independence and recounts the political histories of India as well as Pakistan, has the won the prestigious **Booker Prize** as well as the "Booker of Bookers" award, given for the outstanding work of the first twenty-five years of the prize. Rushdie's *The Satanic Verses* caused a huge uproar in Islamic nations because it deals with the birth of Islam and casts the Prophet Muhammad in a role that many Muslims find offensive. Such was the outrage perceived by them that, acting on their behalf, Ayatollah Khomeini, then spiritual leader of Iran, sentenced Rushdie to death and offered a reward of $1 million to his murderer, which was later doubled. Rushdie went into hiding under police protection immediately, has remained in police protection since, and has continued to write in that state. According to some reports, he has moved to the United States recently and lives in New York—though the fact cannot be definitively established because of the secrecy he maintains about his whereabouts. Many prominent authors of the world have protested the death threat Rushdie received and the forced incarceration he suffers because of it. Achebe, too, has expressed his solidarity with him, but he also feels that writers should be sensitive to the sentiments of the people they write about (Ezenwa-Ohaeto 273).

Like Achebe, Rushdie writes in English, and the fact that both writers do so, though they are not from English-speaking nations and write about people and societies where the national languages are not English, is a shared concern for them, which they address in their writings. Rushdie, however, seems to be more of an avid proponent of English in non-English speaking nations than Achebe. Rushdie's views on the topic appear in two well-known pieces, among others. In "The Empire Writes Back," written in the early

1980s, Rushdie sees a new English emerging—new because it has rid itself of its former imperial and oppressive baggage. This English will create a fresh cultural identity for Britain as well as for its former colonies. Rushdie mentions Achebe twice in this essay, calling attention to the "new shapes" Achebe and other international authors have given the English language, praising his "public approach to literature"—meaning his awareness of political issues in fiction, like Rushdie himself—and describing Achebe as "the doyen of Nigerian writers" (6). Fifteen years after "The Empire Writes Back," in the introduction to *The Vintage Book of Indian Writing: 1947–1997*, Rushdie goes well beyond the scope laid out in his earlier essay and claims that in India, literature in English is far superior to that in the local languages. He writes,

the prose writing—both fiction and non-fiction—created in this period [the five decades following independence in 1947] by Indian writers *working in English*, is proving to be a stronger and more important body of work than most of what has been produced in the "16 official languages of India," the so-called "vernacular languages." (x) (emphasis added)

Though generally sympathetic to Rushdie due to their admiration for *Midnight's Children* and for the precarious state in which he writes, several Indian authors have sharply reacted to this comment. The primacy that Rushdie assigns to English in India, they indicate, is grossly misplaced. Even those who write in English don't claim such privileged status for English themselves. One writer was so rankled by Rushdie that she saw in the expatriate South Asian writer a sort of reincarnation of the imperialist icon Lord Macaulay (Narayan 246). Lord Macaulay was a nineteenth-century policymaker in England

who recommended English to be the only medium of instruction in Indian education. His was convinced of Europe's cultural superiority over Asian countries and claimed in his notorious "Minute on Indian Education" that he had found in a "single shelf of a good European library" more value than in "the whole native literature of India and Arabia" (qtd. in Narayan 266).

Achebe takes up the issue of writing in English in **"The African Writer and the English Language,"** an essay written in 1963, well before Rushdie's "The Empire Writes Back." In his essay, Achebe deals with some of the same issues that Rushdie does in his. Achebe's focus, on the other hand, is not the cultural reclamation of Britain by writers of non-English origin; rather, it is the usefulness of English in the African literary scene. He points out that in African literature, English offers a much greater potential for wide communication than any African language. Using **Nigeria** as an example, he shows "the national literature . . . is the literature written in English" whereas "the ethnic literatures are in Hausa, Ibo, Efik, Edo, Ijaw," and so forth (93). Like Rushdie, Achebe differentiates between "national" literature and "ethnic" literature. According to Rushdie, the distinction, incidentally, is between "official" or "vernacular" literature and simply "literature written in English" or "Indo-Anglian" literature, which, though a problematic categorization (see Narayan 264), is accurate for the most part. Rushdie knows that even he, with his penchant for controversy and admiration for English, cannot propose literature written in English to be India's "national" literature. It is useful to clarify here that in the Indian context, the term "national" includes a strong sense of cultural legacy, where literature written in various Indian languages has existed for many centuries. Rushdie is aware that it would be ludicrous to suggest

English should replace those. Achebe, on the other hand, uses "national" to mean something that is common and accessible to everybody—a shared identity for all within the nation.

Both Rushdie and Achebe make a distinction between literature written in English and literature written in the local languages of their countries. What sets Achebe apart from Rushdie in this distinction is his absolute refusal to make any value judgment between the two. Achebe prefers the latter to the former merely for convenience. Writing in English, he explains in "The African Writer and the English Language," promises a wider readership than writing in any African language, even such a prominent one as Swahili, and he regrets that he cannot read Shabaan Roberts, the Swahili poet, because he doesn't read Swahili (96). In a later essay, "Today, a Balance of Stories," Achebe discusses Rushdie—as well as several other Asian and African writers—and treats a number of interesting issues. In it, though he doesn't quite examine the subject of writing in English, he addresses a related topic: his concern that in today's postmodern world, stories originating in the West or the metropolis tend to obscure those originating in the non-Western world or the margin. Rushdie is mentioned twice in "A Balance of Stories," originally delivered as a paper at Harvard and later included as the last of the three essays in *Home and Exile*—first, early in the essay when Achebe acknowledges his debt to Rushdie and then, toward the end, when he

disapproves of Rushdie's privileging of the exile motif in his writing. Achebe praises "The Empire Writes Back," paying rich tribute to its author, who was the first to describe "the phenomenon of postcolonial literature in four memorable words" (75). But he rejects Rushdie's notion that literature has no link with the writer's provenance (105). Achebe uses the metaphor of postal correspondence throughout "A Balance of Stories" as the valued conduit that allows literature written in non-Western societies being sent to the West, and this to him is the decolonizing process that postcolonial literature can accomplish. Exile, on the other hand, defeats not only the purpose of equal representation but also valorizes certain kinds of literature at the expense of others—hence, "a balance of stories" in Achebe's title. It is significant to note that Achebe thinks exile is made attractive through publicity and that the phenomenon of exile itself is indicative of the fundamental problem of uneven wealth distribution in the world: "I am concerned only with the advertisement of expatriation and exile as intrinsically desirable goals for the writer or as the answer to the problem of unequal developments in the world" (96).

FURTHER READING

Timothy Brennan, *Salman Rushdie and the Third World*; Ezenwa-Ohaeto, *Chinua Achebe*; Shyamala Narayan, Review of *The Vintage Book of Indian Writing: 1947–1997*; Salman Rushdie, "The Empire Writes Back"; Salman Rushdie and Elizabeth West, eds., *The Vintage Book of Indian Writing: 1947–1997*.

Farhad B. Idris

S

THE SACRIFICIAL EGG AND OTHER STORIES (1962), a collection of thirteen short stories by Achebe. This collection was enlarged and published as *Girls at War* (1972) (reprinted in 1973 and revised and republished in 1977). From the latest edition Achebe removed "Polar Undergraduate" and "In a Village Church" and added "Sugar Baby," first published in *Okike*, No. 3 (1972).

Achebe's short stories fall into three general classes. First are those that dramatize a conflict between traditional and modern values, such as "The Sacrificial Egg," "Dead Man's Path," and "Marriage Is a Private Affair." Second are those stories that display the nature of custom and religious belief without attempting to probe or explain their meaning. A third grouping includes the stories that deal with aspects of the **Nigerian Civil War**, one of which gives the enlarged volume its title.

All of the stories are ironic in tone and reveal different levels of irony. "The Madman" tells the story of Nwibe, a man who through hard work has achieved wealth in the form of a successful farm, several wives, and many children. Proud and ambitious, he aspires to the highest titles in his clan. His ambition is thwarted, however, when, as he bathes in a local river, a madman steals his clothes. In his pursuit of the madman he inadvertently offends the local deity. His quest is ruined, and Nwibe, not the man who has stolen his clothes, is seen as a madman. "Such a man" writes Achebe, "is marked forever" (10). Nwibe is seen, through the eyes of the man who has stolen his clothing, as embodying all those who have oppressed him, who have denied him the right to live his life as he pleases. Ironically, the opposition between sanity and insanity remains ambiguous, as do answers to such questions as what is just behavior and what is fit punishment.

A lighter irony informs "Uncle Ben's Choice." Told retrospectively by the eponymous hero, the story tells of one of the most important events of Ben's life. The time is New Year's Eve, 1919. Ben returns home after a lavish party at the club in Umbra to find his bed occupied by a woman of compelling pulchritude. Ben climbs in but then flees his bed and his home when he finds that he is in bed with Mami Wota, the Lady of the River Niger. If he stays with her, she will give him wealth but deny him children. What is wealth without children, the story asks? It provides an answer: Mami Wota becomes the lover of an English trader on the Niger who achieves great wealth, but when he dies, "all his wealth went to outsiders. Is that good wealth? I ask you? God Forbid" (89).

"The Sacrificial Egg" tells of the conflict between generations and the beliefs held by each. Julius Obi falls in love with Janet. Ma, Janet's mother, informs Obi of the power of local spirits. Obi, an educated man, feels himself above superstitions of this kind. When a smallpox epidemic strikes Janet's village, Obi is told not to see her until the epidemic passes. On his way home Obi steps on and crushes a sacrificial egg, thus taking the sufferers' ill luck on himself. Janet and her mother are carried away by the epidemic. Obi is forced by his encounter with the sacrificial egg and the spirits that witnessed him crush it to re-examine his beliefs and to take on the misfortune of Janet and her mother.

"Vengeful Creditor" tells the story of Veronica, a young girl who goes to work as a baby nurse for Mrs. Eminike when the federal government's experimental policy of free primary education (known as "free primadu") is suspended. As more and more demands are made on her time, Veronica comes to blame the baby as an impediment to getting the education promised by Mrs. Eminike. She abuses the child and is beaten by Mrs. Eminike (a paid government social worker). Confronted by Veronica's mother, Mrs. Eminike retorts with a comment that damns the attitudes of the educated elite, "I have always known that the craze for education will one day ruin us all." "Vengeful Creditor" is a damning and powerfully ironic comment on the hypocrisy of the middle class, whose private beliefs belie their public practices.

The stories that deal with the civil war are "Civil Peace" and "Girls at War." In the latter, through the relationship between Reginald Nwankwo and Gladys, which extends over the period of the civil war, Achebe adroitly traces the ways in which the heady optimism of the early war years gives way,

inevitably, to the point where self-serving attitudes and actions become a "mirror reflecting a society that has gone completely rotten at the center." Moral speculation and right conduct are replaced by the need simply to survive by whatever means.

In "Civil Peace" Jonathon Iwegbu returns to his home in **Enugu** after the civil war has ended. He applies to have his Biafran money converted into twenty Nigerian pounds, given *ex gratia* (and locally called "egg rasher") by the federal government. Unfortunately, in the process Jonathon gives the impression he is a wealthy man, and he and his family are threatened by thieves. To save his family, he gives the twenty pounds to the thieves. He loses in peace what he had previously lost in the war. Consoling himself with the reflection that "Nothing puzzles God," he has to face the truth that there is little to distinguish civil peace from civil war and that the way ahead will be long and hard.

Achebe has said that "a dozen stories in twenty years must be accounted a pretty lean harvest by any reckoning" (ii). The stories nevertheless display the work of an accomplished artist of the genre. They also display the full range of Achebe's gifts as a writer.

FURTHER READING

David Carroll, *Chinua Achebe*; C. L. Innes, *Chinua Achebe*; Umelo Ojinmah, *Chinua Achebe*.

Douglas Killam

SAID, EDWARD (1935–), an important literary critic and theorist, has also been a prominent political activist, especially as an advocate of the rights of Palestinians. A Christian born in Jerusalem of Palestinian heritage, Said and his family moved to Cairo due to political tensions in 1947. In Cairo, Said attended British colonial schools, later continuing his education in an American prep school and finally at Princeton and Harvard, where he completed a doctoral dissertation on the work of **Joseph Conrad**, later published as *Joseph Conrad and the Fiction of Autobiography*. This complex background has no doubt helped to shape Said's later career, which has combined a number of different theoretical influences (especially Marxists such as Raymond Williams and Antonio Gramsci and the French poststructuralist Michel Foucault) to produce a sophisticated and influential body of work marked most importantly by its strong engagement with real-world social and political issues and a passionate concern for the rights of those who have traditionally been excluded from positions of wealth and power in the modern world system.

Said has produced numerous important works, starting with the early *Beginnings: Intention and Method* (1975), which explores the different poststructuralist approaches of Foucault and his fellow French theorist Jacques Derrida, ultimately siding with the former. *The World, the Text, and the Critic* (1983), meanwhile, is an important meditation on the state of contemporary literary theory and criticism that rejects the textualism of deconstructionists such as Derrida and Paul De Man in favor of a more socially engaged literary criticism.

Much of Said's most recent work involved meditations on the role of intellectuals in society and commentary on political issues such as the status of Palestinians. His most important work, however, is probably *Orientalism* (1978), which employs a methodology highly influenced by the work of Foucault to argue that Europeans in the nineteenth century often justified their imperial expansion into the rest of the world through a belief in "Orientalist" stereotypes that envisioned non-Europeans as lazy, irresponsible, irrational, and sexually promiscuous. Importantly, for Said, the major purveyors of these "Orientalist" stereotypes were not politicians, but scholars, the anthropologists and ethnologists charged with generating "knowl-

edge" about the Orient. Said's work suggests, however, that these Orientalist scholars were not a unique phenomenon. He argues that all human knowledge is filtered through ideological discourses and that "all cultures impose corrections upon raw reality, changing it from free-floating objects into units of knowledge" (67). These corrections occur even (and maybe especially) in the most academic of disciplines:

fields of learning, as much as works of even the most eccentric artist, are constrained and acted upon by society, by cultural traditions, by worldly circumstance, and by stabilizing influences like schools, libraries, and governments. (201)

As a result, according to Said, the findings of "a 'science' like Orientalism in its academic form are less objectively true than we often like to think" (202). Said's findings are, of course, highly relevant to literary theory and criticism. Indeed, his work may be especially important for literary scholars, who historically have often regarded their work as particularly free of political and ideological distortion.

Orientalism is a founding work in the field of colonial discourse analysis (which focuses on studies of Western writings about the colonial world) and in **postcolonial studies** as a whole. In the important volume *Culture and Imperialism* (1993), Said extends his coverage in this area, noting the way in which Western literature (especially the novel) has helped to promote the ideology of imperialism but also exploring some of the ways in which colonial and postcolonial writers have responded to the colonialist legacy of Western literature. In this book, Said places particular emphasis on the theoretical work of **Frantz Fanon**, while identifying Achebe as one of the most important non-Western writers to have challenged Western literary stereotypes, producing works in which "the formerly silent native speaks and acts on territory taken back from the empire" (31).

FURTHER READING

John M. Mackenzie, *Orientalism*; Bart Moore-Gilbert, *Postcolonial Theory*; Edward Said, *Beginnings*, *Culture and Imperialism*, *Joseph Conrad and the Fiction of Autobiography*, *Orientalism*, and *The World, the Text, and the Critic*; Michael Sprinker, ed., *Edward Said: A Critical Reader*.

M. Keith Booker

ST. MARK'S ANGLICAN CHURCH. Referred to in chapter 1 of *No Longer at Ease*, the congregation in **Umuofia** where **Reverend Samuel Ikedi** is pastor and with which the **Okonkwo** family is affiliated.

Thomas J. Lynn

ST. PANCRAS TOWN HALL. In chapter 3 of *No Longer at Ease* and chapter 6 of *Anthills of the Savannah*, the London venue of rather ill-fated dances attended by important characters when they were students in England. In *No Longer at Ease* **Obi Okonkwo** and **Clara Okeke** first meet at a dance there sponsored by the **National Council of Nigeria and the Cameroons**, London Branch, but Clara is impressed neither with the nervous Obi's attempt at small talk nor with his dancing, and they don't meet again until they coincidentally return to **Nigeria** on the **MV** *Sasa* at the same time. In the novel he published twenty-seven years later, Achebe revisits the hall by having **Beatrice Okoh** recall that when she was a student in London she danced with her "black" boyfriend, **Guy**, but was then stood up by him in favor of a white girl with a "heavy Cockney" accent. Beatrice's recollection of this "Desdemona" experience is occasioned by another one years later when His Excellency, **Sam, the President,** seeks a liaison with a white

American reporter, **Lou Cranford**, who attends a party at which Beatrice is present.

Thomas J. Lynn

SAM, THE PRESIDENT, a military officer who has recently seized the presidency of **Kangan** in a coup at the opening of *Anthills of the Savannah*. Identified only by his Christian name, he is generally addressed by others as "Your Excellency." He is a long-time associate of **Chris Oriko** and **Ikem Osodi**, the three having attended **Lord Lugard College** together. However, he grows distant from his friends and increasingly distrustful of those around him as his power grows. A dedicated Anglophile, Sam becomes an image of the damaging effects of neocolonial cultural imperialism as well as an emblem of the problematic nature of military regimes in postcolonial Africa. Though he seems to be relatively benevolent upon his initial rise to power, Sam grows increasingly authoritarian and ambitious as he gains more and more power, thus illustrating the way in which the temptation of absolute power corrupts absolutely in the postcolonial political situation. Late in the novel, he is kidnapped and murdered, thus falling prey to the seemingly endless sequence of coups and violence that have plagued Kangan (and many real-world African nations) since independence, a sequence to which he himself had contributed while in power.

M. Keith Booker

SAMALU, HEZEKIAH, the father of **Odili Samalu**, the narrator of *A Man of the People*. Samalu still lives in his home village of **Urua**, though he was apparently much despised there during Odili's childhood in the colonial era because he prospered as an interpreter for the British. He was thus (as such interpreters often were in British colonial Africa) regarded as a turncoat who had colluded with the country's colonial rulers. Odili, in fact, has grown up with a certain sense of shame regarding his father, echoing the attitude of **Okonkwo** toward his father **Unoka** in *Things Fall Apart*. By the present time of the book, Hezekiah seems to have been largely rehabilitated, however, and now serves as the local chairman of the **People's Organization Party (POP)** in Urua. Indeed, his participation in the POP is one of the many ways in which Achebe suggests that the corrupt political practices of the ruling party are at least in part a carryover from colonial days. On the other hand, Hezekiah is not an entirely negative figure. In the last chapter, he refuses to sign a statement dissociating himself from his son and his son's political activities, even though the statement would be to Hezekiah's own financial advantage, leading to a refund of increased taxes that had recently been levied on him as a way of putting pressure on Odili. Odili thus wonders if he has perhaps misjudged his father and admits that he has never really understood him or known him well but decides that now is not the time for an extensive reevaluation.

M. Keith Booker

SAMALU, ODILI, the narrator and central figure in *A Man of the People*. Samalu is a graduate of the **Anata Grammar School**, where **Chief Nanga**, the novel's title character, had been one of his teachers sixteen years before the beginning of the novel. However, whereas **Anata** is Nanga's home village, Odili comes from the nearby village of **Urua**, where his family was much despised during Odili's childhood because Odili's father, **Hezekiah Samalu**, had prospered during colonial times as an interpreter for the British. Samalu's mother died at his birth, and he was largely raised by "Mama," Hezekiah's senior wife. As *A Man of the People* begins, Samalu is now a university graduate who himself teaches at the grammar school. However, Samalu soon leaves the school to travel to the capital city of **Bori**, where he has been given reason to believe that Nanga might be able to help him secure a scholarship for postgraduate study abroad.

Samalu, in his narration, is highly critical of the corruption and ruthless ambition of Chief Nanga, but it is worth remembering that this narration occurs after Samalu has been bitterly insulted by Nanga's seduction of **Elsie**, a girlfriend of Samalu. Indeed, much of the narration of *A Man of the People* subtly criticizes Samalu, even though it is presented by Samalu himself. Indeed, the fact that Samalu's point of view dominates the narration has led some critics, especially early on, to see him as an entirely positive figure and even to identify him with Achebe (see **Okpaku**). Yet Achebe endows Odili's narration with a number of subtle ironies that act to undermine the narrator. For example, Samalu is very much like Nanga in many ways, including his own ambitiousness and tendency toward womanizing. It is no accident, then, that when Samalu enters politics late in the book, he joins the **Common People's Convention (CPC)** party and runs for the parliamentary seat currently occupied by Nanga, literally seeking to follow in Nanga's footsteps. Samalu's political activities add an extra irony to the novel's title, as he, too, seeks to become a man of the people

As his bitter denunciations of Nanga indicate, Samalu tends frequently to be critical of others for faults that he himself displays, though this tendency seems to arise less from hypocrisy than from the fact that he is simply better at seeing faults in others than in himself. This is especially true in his double standards with regard to sexuality. Thus, he considers Elsie a trollop and a whore for engaging in sex with Nanga, even though he himself seems rather promiscuous. Further, he is infuriated that Nanga would behave in this way, even though he himself had earlier had sex in the house with **Jean**, a married American woman who is Nanga's house-guest. Moreover, Samalu does not hesitate to resolve to seduce Nanga's intended second wife, **Edna**, in retribution for Nanga's seduction of Elsie.

Though his understanding of himself seems quite limited, Samalu is nevertheless an idealistic figure. Unfortunately, his ideals are almost entirely modern and Western, leaving him as a figure of the young African intellectual whose education has left him out of touch with his country's indigenous traditions and common people. As **C. L. Innes** puts it, Samalu seems to have "nothing but contempt for the traditions of his nation" (83). For example, in a fit of anger against Nanga in chapter 11, he can think of no worse insult to hurl against him than to call him a "bush man" (120). Samalu does learn certain things in the course of the book, and the genuine affection that he seems to develop for Edna in the course of pursuing her seems to indicate a growing ability to treat women as human beings rather than sexual objects. Still, there is a final irony in the fact that Samalu, in order to become engaged to Edna, repays Nanga the 250 pounds that he has invested in preparing Edna to be his wife, a sum that Samalu "borrows" from CPC funds and one that exactly matches the amount of the bribe that Nanga had earlier offered him in exchange for withdrawing from the parliamentary election.

FURTHER READING

C. L. Innes, *Chinua Achebe*; Joseph Okpaku, "A Novel for the People."

M. Keith Booker

SAMSON. In chapters 7 and 9 of *No Longer at Ease*, the steward of **Sam Okoli**, one notable for his livery of "immaculate white and brass buttons" and attentive utterances in **pidgin English**. The steward's traits, like much

else connected to Okoli, help project the minister as an ambitious Anglophile.

Thomas J. Lynn

SATIRE. A satirical impulse runs through much of Achebe's work, whether it involves contemporary political satire, as in *A Man of the People* and *Anthills of the Savannah*, or representations of traditional forms of **Igbo** satire, as in the depiction of **Nweke Ukpaka**, the satirical singer in *Arrow of God*. In fact, all of the satire in Achebe's work can be related to Igbo satirical traditions. Satire is so prevalent among the Igbo that virtually all Igbo participate in it at least at some point. Igbo satire has a long history, ranging from its beginnings as a tool for the propagation of moral and social control to its present function as an aesthetic tool and form of entertainment. A major factor that helped to change the context in which Igbo satire was practiced was undeniably the colonial encounter—a factor that provided the impetus for the reappraisal of several aspects of the culture. Igbo communities underwent enormous transformations during this period, so it is not surprising that Igbo satire would be transformed as well.

In pre-colonial times, satire was a powerful instrument of social control in Igbo communities, and the satirical singer/poet, perceived as having magical power, was feared and respected. This attitude stems from the Igbo belief in the power of words, and it is generally believed that, at some point in their traditions, the Igbo did believe in the magical power of satire. This is not an exclusively Igbo concept; other African communities share the belief as well. In addition, shame is a powerful motivating force in Igbo culture, and satire serves as a means of punishment and social control. The fear of ridicule forewarns prospective offenders and keeps them in check. The intensity of punishment or societal reaction depends on the crime or offense. Pre-colonial Igbo communities had no formal prisons; consequently, most criminal offenders, particularly those who had committed any of the abominations, were often ostracized or sold into slavery. Such punishments were in addition to the raucous satires and the ritual cleansing of the perpetrator.

Some offenses surpass others in magnitude. In addition, different kinds of offenses warrant different sorts of satirical punishments. As a result, satire was necessarily categorized into male and female. Female satire was used to deride minor offenses such as premarital pregnancy, promiscuity, quarrelsomeness, laziness, and so on. In spite of the gravity of certain offenses, the most persistent subject of satirical expression among the Igbo is misdemeanor against sexual morality. The shame and ridicule associated with premarital pregnancy or premarital sexual experience, for instance, could be enormous (refer to chapters 11 and 12 of *Arrow of God*).

Male satire was used to denounce major offenses or crimes such as stealing and all abominations. Three abominations are murder, especially the killing of a kinsman (refer to chapters 8 and 13 of ***Things Fall Apart***); stealing, especially the stealing of seed yams after they have been planted, that is, before they have germinated from the soil; and incest, the big taboo. These are three of the most abhorrent offenses that violate the laws of man and nature. Among the Igbo, these abominations are abhorred because they offend **Ani**, the earth goddess, the ultimate judge of morality and conduct. Thus, a ritual cleansing must accompany any other punishment prescribed for the offense. Among abominable offenses, some are considered major and others minor, but all abominations require purification ceremonies. In addition to this purifying function, the humiliation brought on the culprit and the cost of the propitiatory rituals can serve as deterrents.

Unlike female satire, which tends to be highly scripted and ritualized, male satire was performed extemporaneously. Upon uncovering an abomination, a gong was beaten to publicize the offense and elicit widespread condemnation from the members of the community. As soon as people arrived at the scene, satirical songs were begun about the culprit, usually from a repertoire of such songs already in existence. The act provided an opportunity for members of the community to hurl invectives at the culprit and register their aversion to the abominable act. At the moment of performance, all the feelings that ideally would be hidden, all the emotions that normally would be suppressed would finally find the occasion where they could be expressed. The forum provided an opportunity for talented people in the crowd spontaneously to compose appropriate satirical songs, which would add to the existing repertoire of such songs. The culprit was subjected to extreme mockery and, in some cases, direct physical abuse. The theft of a yam, for instance, provoked, and still provokes, extreme reactions in many Igbo communities because it is believed to offend the earth goddess from whose bowels the yam was stolen. As recently as the middle of the twentieth century, the villagers would have a field day of satirical performance as the thief endured a shameful parade through the village with a piece of yam hung around his neck.

In the process of time, there occurred a slackening of satire's initial power. The advent of the colonial powers and their subsequent intervention in the existing cultural practices of the Igbo finally helped satire to make a transition to a more "civilized" and "acceptable" form of criticism, the archetypal. Archetypal satires employ type characterization; people who have committed a type of offense are collectively derided. These satires direct the audience's attention away from the satirical culprit and toward the art of criticism itself. As a result, Igbo satire began to shift at this time from a mode of social control to a form of art and public performance.

The intervention of the early colonialists and the establishment of a formalized legal system gradually curtailed the impunity with which people satirized the deviants of their communities; criminal offenders were often duly tried and appropriately punished. These developments significantly weakened the original potency of satire and gradually began to direct its course toward entertainment; that is, the emphasis of the satirical activity shifted from the correction of vice to emphasis on performance, on licensed entertainment for all and sundry. Today, in the act of modern Igbo satirical performance, the performer is motivated more by the aesthetic desire for self-expression and the entertainment of the audience than by the ethical desire for reform or preservation of the social order. Although satire is being performed more frequently for entertainment than for reform, a sense of social function is still perceivable. Particularly in its traditional contexts, the notion of social control is apparent and is an essential component of the Igbo view of satire regardless of whether this notion is the motivation for its continued practice. Achebe clearly draws upon the function of satire as an aesthetic tool. However, it is also obvious that he draws upon earlier traditions in which he seeks to criticize (and, hopefully, correct) social abuses such as postcolonial political corruption.

FURTHER READING

Donatus Ibe Nwoga, "The Concept and Practice of Satire among the Igbo"; Christine Nwakego Ohale, *From Ritual to Art.*

Christine Nwakego Ohale

SAVAGE, DR. MARY, the mission doctor at **Nkisa** who nurses a stricken **Winterbottom** back to health in *Arrow of God*. She is "severe and unfeminine," and it is implied that she has a romantic obsession with Winterbottom. The Africans around the Nkisa mission refer to her as Omesike or "One Who Acts with Power," to imply that her lack of emotional display is like that of a powerful man, rather than the local expectations of womanhood.

Rachel R. Reynolds

SEBASTIAN. In chapters 10, 16, and 18 of *No Longer at Ease*, the second "steward boy" (later referred to as "houseboy") of **Obi Okonkwo**. The replacement for **Zacchaeus**, who did not like his treatment by **Clara Okeke** (chapter 2), Sebastian is treated somewhat harshly by Obi in chapter 10.

Thomas J. Lynn

"THE SECOND COMING," a poem by the Irish poet **William Butler Yeats** that provides the epigraph (and title) for Achebe's *Things Fall Apart*. One of most frequently anthologized and taught poems in the English language, "The Second Coming" is a much-cited poem that has provided titles for many modern works. In Achebe's case the poem provides more than a recognizable catchphrase; indeed, the reference to Yeats's poem and to the apocalyptic theory of history it illustrates serves as the linchpin of Achebe's corrective anticolonialist historical narrative. Based on Yeats's notion of cyclical history, the poem depicts the loosening of the bonds that have formed the Christian Era, giving way to a new age born in violence, a "Second Coming" not of Christ but of a bestial Anti-Christ.

Yeats opens the poem with the image of the "gyre" of history wobbling apart, losing its coherence. The spirit of the age that is ending is evoked as a falcon, once controlled by its falconer—an image of ordered ritual that is quintessentially aristocratic—but now unresponsive to his call. The lapse of religion as a unifying force is thus concatenated with the decline of aristocratic gentility and the rise of a disquieting (for Yeats) democracy: "Mere anarchy is loosed upon the world, / The blood-dimmed tide is loosed, and everywhere / The ceremony of innocence is drowned."

In the second stanza Yeats links this fear of the lower classes to the non-European "waste places" of the world where the new/old Sphinx-like deity will rise from his "twenty centuries of stony sleep." The poem ends with foreboding, heralding the end of the world, the new scientific, "blank and pitiless" barbarism that will emerge to engulf the prevailing order. Though for Yeats such unraveling of each age is a historical inevitability, here it is nevertheless a vision he contemplates with horror.

In *Things Fall Apart*, Achebe at once recapitulates and reverses Yeats's vision of historical process. It is indeed ritual, the crucial daily observances that hold together a vital **Igbo** culture, that the book shows being swept away. Under the overwhelming tide of a violent colonialism, "ceremonies of innocence"—like the villagers' willful suspension of disbelief in order *not* to recognize the village elders animating the masks of the *egwugwu*—can no longer be sustained. The order that has held together the present age is weakened, and the future is unfathomably threatening.

In Achebe's version, however, the "blood-dimmed tide" emanates neither from the lower classes nor from the "dark" parts of the globe, but from the very Europe Yeats saw as custodian of civilization; the flood of barbarism, in his rendition, washes Christianity in, not out. Nor is it an inevitable process, but one set in motion purposefully. By appealing to Yeats's indelible image of the end of order—in a sense, wielding the enemy's weapons against him—Achebe underscores his scathing indictment of colonial discourse and practice. On the other hand, Achebe's ironic reversal of Yeats is not quite as com-

plete as it might first appear. Yeats, after all, is not an English poet but an Irish one. Further, he is an Irish poet with an extensive history of opposition to English colonial rule in Ireland. Therefore, despite his generally retrograde politics, Yeats does, in fact, serve as an important predecessor for a number of later anticolonial and postcolonial writers.

FURTHER READING

Stephen Criswell, "Okonkwo as Yeatsian Hero"; Edward Said, "Yeats and Decolonization"; A. G. Stock, "Yeats and Achebe."

Debra Rae Cohen

SLATER, ADRIAN P. L., was the English-language Master at Government College Umuahia when Achebe was a student there from 1944 to 1948. Mr. Slater made it clear during an interview with Phanuel Egejuru that he could not single out Achebe as the "best" student in English at the time, because the entire student body was "very selective, the peak of the pick." Mr. Slater was also reluctant to take credit for Achebe's mastery of the English language. "If I were responsible for any of Chinua's style of English, I am very proud of it. What I would say is that this class as a whole would be writing this English of the same caliber," he said. On the other hand, Achebe himself gives much credit to Mr. Slater for his success with the English language. In 1982, when Achebe received an honorary degree from the University of Kent at Canterbury, he pointed at Mr. Slater in the audience and said: "I am pleased to see the person who first introduced me to the English language." Mr. Slater showed off his autographed copy of Achebe's **Arrow of God**, which read, "To the man who taught me respect for language."

FURTHER READING

Phanuel A. Egejuru, *Chinua Achebe Pure and Simple*; Ezenwa-Ohaeto, *Chinua Achebe*.

Phanuel Akubueze Egejuru

SMITH, JAMES, the successor to **Mr. Brown** as the chief Christian missionary to

Umuofia. A harsh and zealous man, Rev. Smith does not continue his predecessor's attempts at conciliation but instead openly seeks to destroy the traditional religion of the clan, which he associates with Satanic forces of evil. His attitude is partly responsible for inspiring the convert **Enoch** to unmask an *egwugwu*, triggering an important crisis that ultimately leads to the suicide of **Okonkwo**.

M. Keith Booker

SO THEREFORE, MR., a neighbor of **Ikem Osodi** and an employee of the Posts and Telegraphs Office in *Anthills of the Savannah*. Notorious for beating his beautiful wife, he acquires his sardonic nickname when a concerned neighbor calls the police to report the beatings, only to have the desk sergeant merely respond, "So therefore?" His story suggests not only the prevalence of domestic violence in postcolonial **Kangan** but also the obliviousness of the authorities to that violence.

M. Keith Booker

THE SONG OF THE BLACKBIRD, the most famous novel of the fictional African postcolonial nation featured in *A Man of the People*, authored by one **Jalio**, a much-respected national writer. However, it is clear in the book that **Chief Nanga**, Achebe's title character, is completely unfamiliar with Jalio or his novel. Told that Jalio is the author of *The Song of the Blackbird*, the uncultured Nanga assumes that this title refers to a musical composition.

M. Keith Booker

SOYINKA, WOLE (1934–). Nigerian dramatist, poet, critic, and autobiographer. Soyinka received his early education in Abeokuta, Western **Nigeria**. The winner of the Nobel Prize in literature in 1986, he became the first black African writer to be so honored. He and Achebe are often considered to be the two most prominent Nigerian writers worldwide. Both have received considerable critical attention, and the two are often discussed together. For example, many of the issues raised in this entry are the subject of a book-length study of the two authors by Kole Omotoso. Significantly, however, Omotoso did not entitle his study "Achebe and Soyinka," but instead chose *Achebe or Soyinka?*, suggesting substantial points of disparity between the two.

Best known as a playwright, Soyinka is the author of such plays as *The Lion and the Jewel* (1963), *The Road* (1965), *Kongi's Harvest* (1967), *Death and the King's Horseman* (1975), *Opera Wonyosi* (1981), *Beatification of Area Boy* (1995), and *King Baabu* (2002). He has also published two novels, *The Interpreters* (1965) and *Season of Anomy* (1973), both of which reflect developments in independent Nigeria and incorporate a mythological dimension. Soyinka's volumes of poetry include *Idanre and Other Poems* (1967) and *Mandela's Earth and Other Poems* (1988). His important autobiographical writings include *The Man Died* (1972), based on the writer's detention by the Nigerian government during the **Nigerian Civil War**; *Aké: The Years of Childhood* (1981), an account of his first eleven years; and *Isara: A Voyage around "Essay"* (1989), a re-creation of the world of his father. Soyinka's works of criticism and cultural commentary include *Myth, Literature and the African World* (1976) and *Art, Dialogue and Outrage: Essays on Literature and Culture* (1988). More recent published volumes of collected lectures, including *The Burden of Memory, the Muse of Forgiveness* (2000) and *The Open Sore of a Continent* (2001), comment on a variety of moral, cultural, political, and historical issues.

In 1983, Achebe was asked, Was there "any overt or subtle clash between him and Wole Soyinka?" He replied "No, there is not," and countered with the question, "Why should there be?" When asked whether there was any "literary competition," Achebe replied: "There may well be but again that's not great news. There's competition between people in the same profession everywhere. The purpose of all that is not to say that you discredit the other man or anything like that but that you try to excel."

From a distance, the authors of *Things Fall Apart* and *Kongi's Harvest* may appear as the twin pillars of Nigerian, or indeed black African, literature, constantly bracketed by commentators as "Achebe *and* Soyinka." There are indeed many similarities. Both were born during the 1930s into teaching-preaching, Anglican, Nigerian families. Both were educated at elite, government-funded, British-influenced secondary schools, and both became undergraduates at the fledgling **University College, Ibadan**. Both emerged as short story writers, and both found outlets in broadcasting. Both had educational experiences in the United Kingdom, and, by the end of the 1950s, both had begun to enjoy local and international reputations. As writers and critics, both began to define themselves in relation to similar forces, such as colonialism and **négritude**. The two men became involved in the literary life of their country at about the same time, both were both published in the Heinemann **African Writers Series**, and both were funded for various activities by American foundations. In due course, the Nigerian university system provided employment for both, and both had work filmed by Calpenny Productions. Recently both have been lionized, celebrated, and studied, involved in promoting the work of fellow Nigerians, and drawn into the American academic system. Many more areas of shared experience could be reeled off, but that is enough to suggest common experiences and explain why there are so many references to the two as a pair.

There have been moments when Soyinka and Achebe have not only been close, but have actually been united. For example, during the Nigerian Civil War, Achebe was asked to put himself in the position of a Nigerian. He replied: "I find the Nigerian situation untenable. If I had been a Nigerian, I think I would have been in the same situation as Wole Soyinka is—in prison." In 1978, when the University of Ile-Ife, where Soyinka was working, awarded Achebe an honorary doctorate, it was Soyinka who read the citation. Some eight years later, in March 1986, Achebe and Soyinka were part of a small delegation that spoke to President Ibrahim Babangida about the case of a fellow author, Mamman Vatsa, who was under sentence of death. In 2000, Soyinka was present at the celebrations to mark Achebe's seventieth birthday.

But it is possible to make too much of the similarities and the points at which they were together. For a fuller picture of the relationship between Achebe and Soyinka, it is necessary to spell out some of the differences between the experiences, personalities, and conduct of the two writers. Soyinka, who traces descent from two distinct Yoruba communities, the Egba and the Ijebu, was brought up in a major trading, administrative, and educational center in Western Nigeria. Before entering University College, he had spent time at the Egba nationalist Abeokuta Grammar School, headed by one of his internationally renowned relatives, a man who, incidentally, played an important part in the creation of University College, Ibadan, and had a hall of residence named after him. After leaving school, Soyinka worked for a time in the bustling, cosmopolitan Nigerian capital, **Lagos**. He spent just two years at University College, where he made his mark as an actor and, in the pages of irreverent cyclostyled student publications, as a witty and polemical writer. While at Ibadan, he founded, with friends, the Pyrates fraternity, on whose somewhat rowdy outings, or "sailings," he was known by the swashbuckling soubriquet "Cap'n Blood."

Soyinka spent five impressionable years in the foggy, soggy, grey, grimy United Kingdom, where he did a full undergraduate degree, worked, traveled, gained experience of the professional theatre, married, taught, and fathered a child. Both Achebe and Soyinka had early careers in the radio industry. Achebe began a career in broadcasting, becoming a professional producer. Diligent, talented, he mastered the necessary skills and was made responsible for presenting Nigeria to an international audience. As a precocious school-leaver, Soyinka wrote plays for the **Nigerian Broadcasting Service (NBS)**, and while in England he freelanced for the BBC, reporting, being featured, and presenting. During the early 1960s, while he and Achebe were occasionally contributing to discussion programs, he also wrote scripts for the **pidgin English** comedy series *Broke Time Bar*. In fact, over a forty-year period he went on to compose radio plays for domestic and foreign stations that have ranged from the poetic *Camwood on the Leaves* (1960) to the political *The Detainee* (1965), from the personal *Document of Identity* (1999) to the wide-ranging *Rain of Stones* (2002).

Soyinka has used radio resourcefully to advance his individual and individualistic brand of politics. In 1965, after a disputed Nigerian election and at the time when Achebe was Director of the **Voice of Nigeria**, Soyinka entered the control room of the radio station in Ibadan, pulled out a gun, and had his tape played in place of the victory address recorded by the man who had been declared winner at the polls. In the decades since then Soyinka has made dozens of broadcasts and telecasts and given scores of interviews on political issues. Sometimes these have been on Nigerian broadcasting stations, sometimes on the BBC, the Voice of America (VOA), or Cable News Network (CNN). In 1983, he broke into protest song, joining with Tunji Oyelana in the lyrics he had written for a record, *Unlimited Liability Company*, which was given considerable airtime. Convinced of the power of radio, Soyinka was a prime mover in establishing Radio Kudirat, which challenged the dictator Sani Abacha during the 1990s.

Of course, Achebe has occasionally contributed to political debates in his native land. He has done this through his writing, for example, in *The Trouble with Nigeria* and in his fiction. He has, moreover, recognized the role played by political organizations and for a time held high office in the Peoples Redemption Party. Soyinka, by contrast, has characteristically operated independently, indeed individualistically. At one point, he described himself as a "self-suspended member of the PRP," but Achebe was among those who rejected the possibility of such a status.

It is instructive to consider an exchange that can be found in Lindfors's *Conversations with Chinua Achebe*. The year is 1963, and Lewis Nkosi, host of the African Writers Talking television series, has brought Soyinka and Achebe together in the Museum of Nigeria, Lagos, for a discussion about Achebe's writing. After a few "warm-up" questions, Soyinka, mercurial, abrasive, begins to look for lines of attack. He slips in a reference to Achebe's "precise workmanship" and "almost unrelieved competence" and follows up with a challenge: "How do you react to this?" Stung, Achebe begins: "You don't expect me to accept that!" before adding, somewhat defensively: "I don't particularly spend a lot of time on polishing." Since the tension is palpable, Nkosi steps between the combatants for a moment. Soyinka, after dropping in a soft inquiry about research, is soon opening up a major area of difference. He picks up a reference by Achebe to **Joyce Cary**'s

Mister Johnson as being "merely a caricature" and counters with a probing: "but then a caricature is really something you exaggerate. You exaggerate some factual elements." In this and other exchanges, the two writers emerge as old sparring partners.

The conflict, apparent enough in the transcript, is emphasized in the tape of the program. Soyinka leans forward. Achebe, the heavier, slower man has his weight well back. He is clearly aware that he may have to parry a lightning-quick blow and seek an opening to land solid punches. Eventually respect wins out, as it has at other points in the last fifty years, and the two champions back away from one another with "referee" Nkosi left to dictate the latter part of the program.

FURTHER READING

James Gibbs, *Wole Soyinka*; Biodun Jeyifo, ed., *Perspectives on Wole Soyinka*; Ketu H. Katrak, *Wole Soyinka and Modern Tragedy*; Bernth Lindfors, ed., *Conversations with Chinua Achebe*; Kole Omotoso, *Achebe or Soyinka?*; Derek Wright, *Wole Soyinka Revisited*.

James Gibbs

STEPHEN, Tony Clarke's African steward (not **Igbo** though) in *Arrow of God*.

Rachel R. Reynolds

STEWART, J. F., Englishman killed by villagers of **Ahiara** in November 1905 after he strayed into their area while traveling on bicycle from Owerri. The killing prompted British-led troops to decimate the village of Ahiara and also served as the pretext for the **Bende-Onitsha punitive expedition**, in which British-led troops marched into the hinterlands on a mission of "**pacification**," wreaking considerable havoc, including the destruction of the **Agbala** oracle at **Awka**.

FURTHER READING

Robert M. Wren, "*Things Fall Apart* in Its Time and Place."

M. Keith Booker

SYLVANUS, Chris Oriko's talented and rather proud cook in *Anthills of the Savannah*.

M. Keith Booker

T

"TANGANYIKA—JOTTINGS OF A TOURIST." Achebe essay. See *Morning Yet on Creation Day*.

TELEVISION ADAPTATIONS. See *Things Fall Apart* (television miniseries).

THINGS FALL APART, Achebe's first novel, was published in 1958, becoming the inaugural text in the Heinemann **African Writers Series** and one of the founding texts of modern African literature. It is almost certainly the African novel that is most often read by Western readers and most often taught in British and American classrooms. Not only is it a staple of college courses in African literature, but it is also widely taught in courses in world literature. It is also frequently taught in courses on African culture, society, and history as an introduction to the workings of a pre-colonial African community. As a result, Achebe's book is frequently the first African novel to be encountered by its Western readers, and rightfully so. Not only is the book one of the earliest important African novels, but it exemplifies a great number of the fundamental issues that typically face Western readers of African novels. For most readers the most memorable part of the book is its vivid evocation of **Igbo** soci-ety at the time of the first major incursions of British colonialism into the Igbo lands at the beginning of the twentieth century. Achebe has made it clear that his principal purpose in the book was to provide African readers with a realistic depiction of their pre-colonial past, free of the distortions and stereotypes imposed upon that past in European accounts.

Things Fall Apart can be divided into three basic segments. The initial section, spanning the first thirteen chapters, is largely concerned with providing readers with a vivid picture of the traditional way of life enjoyed by the inhabitants of an Igbo village before the incursion of the British. Focusing on the village of **Iguedo**, one of the nine confederated villages collectively known as **Umuofia**, this section of the book provides an account of the daily social, economic, political, family, and spiritual lives of the villagers, seen largely through an account of the character and activities of the protagonist, **Okonkwo**. As this part of the book ends, Okonkwo's old rusty gun explodes during the funeral ceremonies for **Ezeulu**, a prominent villager, killing the sixteen-year-old son of the deceased man. As a result of this event, Okonkwo and his family are exiled for seven years to the village of **Mbanta**, the traditional home of the family of Okonkwo's mother. The second part of the book concerns this exile, during which both the British colonial administration and Christian **missionaries** make significant headway in displacing the traditional way of life in Umuofia. In chapter 20, Okonkwo returns to Umuofia, beginning the third and final part of the novel, in which he helps to lead a futile and ill-fated attempt to resist this cultural destruction, leading to his death by suicide.

In the first section of *Things Fall Apart*, the villagers of Umuofia live in a well-ordered society, with intricate social customs that are clearly designed to work for the benefit of the community as a whole. In contrast to colonialist notions that Africans lived in primitive savagery before Europeans brought "civilization," the villagers in Achebe's book live in a society "in which life is rounded and intricate and sensitively in correspondence with a range of human impulses. It admits both the aristocratic and the democratic principles. It is a life lived by a dignified clan of equals who meet together in an Athenian way" (Walsh 49). Achebe's reminders that pre-colonial African societies functioned in such sophisticated ways are, of course, valuable to both African and Western readers. On the other hand, the detailed depiction of the workings of Igbo society in *Things Fall Apart* makes the book particularly prone to the kind of Western anthropological readings that have sometimes prevented African novels from receiving serious critical attention as literature rather than simply as documentation of African cultural practices. However, *Things Fall Apart* is a rich and complex novel that provides far more than an anthropological account of life in a traditional Igbo village. Moreover, even the account of Igbo life in the first part of the book is constructed in a highly literary fashion, as Achebe manages to provide an amazing number of details about traditional Igbo life in an extremely subtle and inobtrusive way that never interferes with the ongoing narrative. Indeed, most readers of the book are probably unaware that they have been given as many details about the customs and practices of Umuofia as they actually have.

For example, we learn in the very first paragraph of *Things Fall Apart* that Okonkwo, the protagonist, is a well-known figure in Umuofia because of his many personal achievements, beginning, at age eighteen, when he won a wrestling match against **Amalinze the Cat**, a famous champion. Wrestling matches are mentioned at several other points in the book as well, gradually making it clear that these matches have an important social function in the Igbo society of Umuofia. Yet at no point does Achebe's narrator deliver anything like an extended discourse on wrestling as a social institution. In a similarly subtle way, Achebe provides numerous details regarding Igbo religion and cosmology, the domestic life of Igbo families, and the political culture of Umuofia, all integrated within the narrative and without lengthy discursive passages.

The various details about Igbo village life and culture that we receive in the first part of the book are almost always provided as an integral part of the ongoing narration. For example, chapter 2 begins as the men of Umuofia are summoned to a group meeting by the town crier. We then learn that this meeting has been called in response to the recent killing of a woman from Umuofia in the neighboring village of **Mbaino**. The subsequent response to this crisis—the Umuofians follow the "normal course of action" in such situations—allows Achebe to tell us a great deal about the workings of the society of Umuofia, which turn out to be quite orderly and to proceed in accordance with well-established rules. Moreover, while the infuriated villagers of Umuofia regard the killing as an abomination and as an affront to their entire society, their response is designed to avoid an all-out conflict between Mbaino and Umuofia, seeking not revenge but a restoration of the natural order that has been upset by the killing. As a result of the subsequently negotiated peaceful solution, a young virgin from Mbaino is sent to Umuofia as a replacement wife to the dead woman's husband. Meanwhile, as further retribution for the killing, **Ikemefuna**, a fifteen-year-old boy from Mbaino, is also sent to Umuofia, apparently to bear the brunt of the punishment for the crime. However, even here the clan of Umuofia responds slowly and carefully, waiting for a clear direction from **Agbala**, the Oracle of the Hills and Caves, before deciding the boy's punishment.

In the meantime, Ikemefuna lives with Okonkwo for three years and becomes like a member of the family, growing especially close to Okonkwo's eldest son, **Nwoye**. Ultimately, the oracle decrees that Ikemefuna must be killed as a sacrifice to atone for the crime, thus restoring the natural order of things. Indeed, there is a great deal of emphasis in *Things Fall Apart* on the tendency of the Igbo citizens of Umuofia to seek order and balance in all of their dealings, a characteristic that makes the subsequent destruction of this balance by the impact of British colonialism and Christian evangelism all the more damaging and traumatic. Meanwhile, Achebe uses the story of Ikemefuna not only to provide a number of details about Igbo law and cosmology but also to further the plot of the novel and the characterization of the protagonist. Okonkwo, as a leader of Umuofia, knows that he must abide by this decision that the boy be killed. However, always anxious to demonstrate his strength and courage, Okonkwo does far more than simply accept the fact that Ikemefuna must die. Although warned by the elder Ogbuefi **Ezeudu** not to participate in the killing, Okonkwo, "afraid of being thought weak," himself strikes the fatal blow, cutting the boy down with his machete (43). Ironically, Okonkwo, in seeking strictly to meet his society's standards of admirable conduct, performs a deed that is considered to be reprehensible by many in that society, including his good friend **Obierika**, who is horrified by Okonkwo's participation in Ikemefuna's killing, even though he himself regards that killing to be justified. "If the Oracle said that my son should be killed," Obierika tells Okonkwo, "I would neither dispute it nor be the one to do it" (47).

The episode of the killing of Ikemefuna is a pivotal one in *Things Fall Apart* for a number of reasons. For one thing, this sacrifice dramatizes aspects of Igbo society that seem harsh, cruel, or even savage by modern European standards and thus illustrates Achebe's determination to provide a realistic description of traditional Igbo society and his refusal to romanticize that society in order to impress a Western audience. As Oladele Taiwo puts it, "Besides the strengths in tribal society he gives the weaknesses. We therefore have a true and complete picture in which the whole background is fully realised" (112). It is important to recognize, however, that the killing of Ikemefuna, however startling by Western standards, does not necessarily demonstrate a weakness in Igbo society. This act has, from the Igbo point of view, a genuine justification. Michael Valdez Moses thus notes that the ritualistic killing of Ikemefuna (who had nothing to do with the original crime) "is cruel and violates liberal norms of justice" but points out that this sacrifice "does serve to prevent a war between the two clans and therefore helps to ensure the long-term security of both villages." This action, for Moses, "suggests not the absence of ethical standards among the Igbo people, but the existence of a strict premodern morality that values the welfare of the clan and tribe above that of the individual" (115). In this way, the episode serves not only to provide a striking illustration of Okonkwo's personality, but to make an important point about the differences between Igbo social values (which place the good of the community above that of any single individual) and Western liberal standards of individualism.

On the other hand, *Things Fall Apart* makes it clear that the Igbo society of Umuofia is, in fact, much more individualistic in its own way than are many of the traditional societies of Africa. This individualism is figured in a number of ways, most obviously in the consistent focus on Okonkwo as the book's single central protagonist. Okonkwo himself is a proud and individualistic man, so much so that many in the clan are disturbed by his single-minded determination and by his brusqueness in dealing with others. Indeed, Okonkwo's excessive individualism is no doubt a key to his ultimate downfall in the book, a motif that, by extension, potentially suggests that the individualism of the Igbo made their society more susceptible to Western intrusions and thus contributed to the quick downfall of their traditional ways once the British arrived in the area.

The lengthiest digression from the main narrative of *Things Fall Apart* probably occurs in chapter 11 when Okonkwo's second wife, **Ekwefi**, tells the story of **"The Tortoise and the Birds"** to her daughter, **Ezinma**. This episode combines with other references to storytelling in the text to indicate the importance of oral narrative as an element of daily Igbo life. However, even this story is not really as much of a digression as it first appears, because the implications of this particular story resonate with and reinforce the rest of the narrative. For one thing, the self-centered Tortoise can obviously be read as an allegorization of Okonkwo, the downfall of the Tortoise in the story anticipating the eventual downfall of Okonkwo. At the same time, the allegory of this parable is quite complex, and the Tortoise also functions, among other things, as an emblem of the rapacious European intruders who come to Igboland, destroying the traditional societies there.

Indeed, the formal strategies employed by *Things Fall Apart* are so complex and sophisticated that they sometimes recall the works of Western modernism, though the aesthetics of the novel are basically realistic, supplemented by elements derived from Igbo oral narrative traditions. As a result of this complexity, Western critics are in danger of falling into old habits of formalist reading and thereby of failing to do justice to the important social and political content of Achebe's book. Indeed, such readings, by circumscribing Achebe's book within European aesthetic traditions, are in danger of perpetuating precisely the colonialist gestures that the book is designed to oppose. *Things Fall Apart* thus provides an excellent example of the special problems that must be faced by Western readers in approaching the African novel; it illustrates particularly well Achebe's warning that the European critic of African literature "must cultivate the habit of humility appropriate to his limited experience of the African world and be purged of the superiority and arrogance which history so insidiously makes him heir to" (*Morning Yet on Creation Day* 8).

Readers and critics of Achebe's novel must pay close and careful attention not only to both the style and the content of the book, but also to the intricate relationships between them. The content of the first part of the book is striking for its depiction of the workings of traditional Igbo society. Meanwhile, the style and structure of the entire book are striking for the way in which they incorporate elements of Igbo oral cultural traditions. Any number of critics have remarked on the sophisticated extent to which Achebe has been able to weave traditional oral forms into his written text, as in his deft use of the **trickster** tale of the Tortoise and the Birds. Indeed, Iyasere notes that much of the complexity of Achebe's narrative technique arises from his effective use of strategies derived from Igbo oral culture. Similarly, JanMohamed, while emphasizing the fundamental differences between oral and written, or chirographic, cultures, concludes that *Things Fall Apart* manages to achieve an impressive combination of the two modes and to remain "delicately poised at the transition from the epic (oral) to the novel (chirographic)" ("Sophisticated" 34).

The very existence of Achebe's text as a written, bound book places it in dialogue with the Western novelistic tradition, even as it draws heavily upon Igbo oral traditions for its style and content. Moreover, it is important to note that Achebe wrote the book in direct reaction to the demeaning and objectionable depictions of Africans in European novels such as **Joseph Conrad**'s *Heart of Darkness* and **Joyce Cary**'s *Mister Johnson*. Innes not only extensively discusses the way in which Achebe responds to Cary's stereotypical vision of Africans, but also shows that Cary's "African" figure, Mister Johnson, is a purely European creation, many of whose characteristics (such as his individual isolation and lack of contact with family or relatives) are almost unimaginable from an African point of view (Innes 21–41). In keeping with the book's integration of style with content, of atmosphere with narrative, and of written with oral forms, *Things Fall Apart* is itself a complex cultural hybrid that is a product not simply of the Igbo cultural traditions it so vividly portrays, but of the encounter between those traditions and the culture of the West.

On the other hand, Achebe's book is in some ways a striking demonstration of **Frantz Fanon**'s observation that "the colonial world is a Manichean world" (Fanon 41).

In the book, European and African societies come together in a mode of radical difference. The resulting encounter between the two cultures (in an atmosphere of almost total mutual lack of understanding) leads to cataclysmic results for Africa, which is no match for Europe in terms of military and economic power. Of course, depictions of Africans and African society as strange and incomprehensible to Westerners can be found in any number of examples of European Africanist discourse, including literary works like *Heart of Darkness*. One of the most valuable aspects of *Things Fall Apart*, at least for Western readers, is its presentation of the estrangement between European and African cultural traditions from an African perspective, thus reminding us that there are two sides to this story of encounter between alien cultures. Achebe presents Igbo society in a way that makes its workings seem perfectly natural and comprehensible, carefully weaving not just Igbo customs, but even Igbo words into his narrative in a way that makes them accessible to Western readers. Meanwhile, the Europeans of Achebe's book are depicted as peculiar, incomprehensible, and even vaguely ridiculous—as when a white missionary has his translator speak to the people of the village Mbanta in Igbo, not realizing that the translator speaks a different dialect from the audience, causing his words to seem strange (and sometimes comical). The translator thus continually says "my buttocks" whenever he means to say "myself" (102). Meanwhile, among the people of Umuofia, leprosy is politely referred to as "the white skin," leading one villager jokingly to compare the newly arrived white Europeans to lepers (52). Such reversals from the norm of British literature (in which the British are depicted as normal and Africans or Indians as deviations, comically struggling with the English language or English customs) make a powerful statement about the importance of point of view in confrontations between foreign cultures and thoroughly undermine the Western tendency to think of our values as absolute and universal.

On the other hand, *Things Fall Apart* establishes numerous points of contact between European and African cultures, and Achebe is careful to avoid depicting African society as totally foreign to Western sensibilities. For example, any number of critics have observed the parallels between Achebe's story of Okonkwo and ancient Greek tragedy. Moses notes the "strikingly Homeric quality" of the book and compares Okonkwo to Homer's Achilles (110). Okonkwo also sometimes resembles Oedipus, as when he is banished from Umuofia for the accidental killing of a fellow clansman, thus recalling Oedipus's punishment for the inadvertent murder of his own father. In this vein, Rhonda Cobham argues that Achebe has chosen to present "those aspects of Igbo traditional society that best coincide with Western-Christian social values," thereby establishing a worldview that is not limited to the pre-colonial past but that speaks to the postcolonial present as well (98). As Achebe himself has put it, a point that is "fundamental and essential to the appreciation of African issues by Americans" is that "Africans are people in the same way that Americans, Europeans, Asians, and others are people" ("Teaching" 21).

The crucial issue in this regard is, of course, the book's characterization, and Achebe does an excellent job of presenting characters whose humanity Western readers can recognize, though it is also true, as Florence Stratton points out, that the complex characters of the book tend to be male, while the female characters are depicted in vague and superficial ways (29). Okonkwo's wives have virtually no identities outside their domestic roles. For example, his first wife is not even identified by name in the book, but is simply referred to as "**Nwoye's mother**." His daughter Ezinma is probably the strongest female character, yet she is repeatedly presented as being so because she has a number of masculine characteristics. Moreover, she essentially disappears late in the narrative, having determined to pursue a conventional role as wife and mother.

The ultramasculine Okonkwo, meanwhile, dominates the text, though it is also the case that Achebe clearly presents Okonkwo's rejection of all things that he regards as "feminine" as extreme and destructive. In the initial section of the book, we are introduced not only to a number of general aspects of life in Umuofia, but to the background and characteristics of Okonkwo, whose excessive quest for masculine strength is clearly motivated by his shame at the perceived feminine weakness of his father, **Unoka**, a talented musician whose irresponsibility and aversion to hard work had left him poor and in debt, eventually to die as an outcast. In contrast, Okonkwo has worked extremely hard to overcome this legacy, rising from his humble beginnings to a position of prominence in his village. This section also provides a number of details about Okonkwo's family life. We learn, for example, that he has three wives and eight children. We also learn something of the texture of the everyday life in Okonkwo's household, which consists of a compound that includes Okonkwo's own private hut and separate huts for each wife and her children.

Okonkwo rules this household "with a heavy hand," and the first part of *Things Fall Apart* presents not only fairly extensive descriptions of his sometimes harsh treatment of his wives and children, but also detailed background on the causes behind his rather authoritarian personality (9). Okonkwo's major motivation (and the principal reason for his domineering behavior) is his determination to succeed where his musician father (whom he regards as cowardly and effeminate) failed. Okonkwo thus goes out of his way to behave in what he considers to be a staunchly masculine manner and to demonstrate his strength in every way possible. This strength, however, arises from a kind of weakness. "His whole life," the narrator tells us, "was dominated by fear, the fear of failure and weakness. . . . It was the fear of himself, lest he should be found to resemble his father" (9).

Much of the description of Igbo society in Achebe's book focuses on the presentation of the crucial role played in that society by communal activities such as the **Week of Peace** and the **Feast of the New Yam**, making it clear that Okonkwo's extreme individualism and self-reliance are something of an aberration. Many of the book's more dramatic scenes (such as the killing of Ikemefuna or Okonkwo's exile from Umuofia after the accidental killing of the son of Ezeudu in the midst of the communal ritual of the latter's funeral) are built around confrontations between the good of the community and what Westerners would regard as the "rights" of individuals. But this aspect of Achebe's book is built into the text in more profound ways as well. For example, **C. L. Innes** notes that the narrative voice of the text is itself a sort of amalgam of traditional Igbo voices, in contrast to modern Western expectations that the narrator of a story will be a distinct individual (32).

The characterization of Okonkwo is a crucial part of the book's central focus on the relationship between the individual and the community in Igbo society. Among other things, it is clear that Okonkwo can, to a certain extent, function as an allegorical stand-in for traditional Igbo society as a whole. Any number of critics have noted this aspect of the book, as when Walsh sees Okonkwo's downfall as a marker of the destruction of traditional Igbo society "because of the way

in which the fundamental predicament of the society is lived through his life" (52). JanMohamed, working from a perspective specifically influenced by Jameson's work, follows Walsh in suggesting that Achebe makes "his heroes the embodiments of the fundamental structures and values of their cultures" (*Manichean* 161). On the other hand, the relationship between Okonkwo and his society is complex and problematic. It comes as no surprise, then, that the implications of the relationship between Okonkwo and his society have been the object of considerable critical disagreement. Eustace Palmer, for one, agrees that Okonkwo is "the personification of his society's values." Thus, "if he is plagued by a fear of failure and of weakness it is because his society puts such a premium on success" (Palmer 53). For Palmer, then, Okonkwo's ultimate tragedy results from weaknesses that are the direct result of flaws in Igbo society itself. For other critics, Okonkwo's fall results not from the characteristics of Igbo society, but from the destruction of this society by British colonialism. Killam thus agrees that Okonkwo consolidates "the values most admired by Ibo peoples" but concludes that his fall occurs because colonialism disrupts these values and not from shortcomings in the values themselves (16).

Killam's reading is clearly more consonant with the overall theme of *Things Fall Apart* than is Palmer's. For one thing, Palmer (though himself an African) obviously reads the text from a purely Western, individualistic perspective. From this point of view, which privileges strong individuals who are willing to oppose conventional opinion, it is clearly a flaw for an individual to embody the mainstream values of his culture. On the other hand, Killam's reading does not fully acknowledge the extent to which Okonkwo, through his excessive determination to be strong and "masculine," already seems headed for trouble even before Umuofia is aware of the British presence. Several times he breaks fundamental rules of his society and then must be punished, culminating in his banishment from Umuofia at the end of the first part of the book, though it is also the case that his most common mistakes occur when he follows the rules of his society too literally and too strictly, as when he strikes the fatal blow in the slaying of Ikemefuna. Many critics thus argue that Okonkwo's fall occurs not because he embodies the values of his society, but precisely because he deviates from his society's norms of conduct. Biodun Jeyifo, for example, argues that Okonkwo is "doomed because of his rigid, superficial understanding—really misrecognition—of his culture" (Jeyifo 58). Similarly, Carroll believes that Okonkwo's successes are largely achieved through an inflexible focus on his goals, a focus that eventually sets him at odds with a society "remarkable for its flexibility" (41). Finally, critics such as Ravenscroft and Ojinmah note that the Igbo society depicted by Achebe is characterized by a careful balancing of opposing values (particularly of masculine and feminine principles), while Okonkwo focuses strictly on the masculine side of this personality and thus fails to achieve this balance (Ojinmah 15–16; Ravenscroft 13).

Such gendered readings of Okonkwo's characteristics are central to many critical discussions of *Things Fall Apart*. For example, much of JanMohamed's discussion of Okonkwo's typicality focuses on the way Okonkwo "becomes an emblem of the masculine values of Igbo culture." But JanMohamed emphasizes that the culture itself balances masculine with feminine values. Thus, for JanMohamed, Okonkwo's rejection of the feminine aspects of his culture makes him seem "rigid, harsh, and unfeeling in his pursuit of virility" (*Manichean* 164). Innes, meanwhile, grants that Okonkwo's tendency

to categorize various activities as either masculine or feminine is typical of traditional Igbo society, but again pointing out that Okonkwo has less respect for feminine values than does his society as a whole (25–26). Several feminist critics, however, have pointed out that the society itself, at least as depicted by Achebe, is heavily oriented toward a respect for masculinity. While some value is placed on feminine virtues and activities, the values labeled by the society as masculine are consistently valued more highly than those labeled as feminine. In addition, the power structure of Igbo society, while decentered and in many ways democratic, is entirely dominated by males. Okonkwo's domination of his household thus becomes a sort of microcosm of the domination of the society as a whole by patriarchal figures.

It is certainly the case that the political leaders of Umuofia in *Things Fall Apart* are all male, though it is also true that women such as **Chielo**, the priestess of Agbala, sometimes occupy important ceremonial and social positions. Still, the male political leaders of Umuofia are often shown exercising power directly over women, just as Okonkwo exerts power over his wives. In one of the book's key demonstrations of the workings of justice in Umuofia, the village elders meet to adjudicate a marital dispute in which the woman **Mgbafo** has fled the household of her husband, **Uzowulu**, because he has repeatedly beaten her (sometimes severely) for nine years. The legal proceedings are restricted to males, and no women (including Mgbafo) are allowed inside the hut where they occur. Indeed, we are told that no woman has ever participated in such proceedings and that women know better than even to ask questions about them (63). In the proceedings, Uzowulu presents his case, asking that Mgbafo be ordered to return to him. Then, Mgbafo's brother argues that she should be allowed to remain with him and her other brothers apart from her abusive husband. The elders (some of whom seem to regard the case as too trivial to be worthy of their attention) order Uzowulu to offer a pot of wine to Mgbafo's brothers in restitution. They then order the brothers to return Mgbafo to her husband. They refuse even to cast blame on the abusive husband, though the latter occurs not so much because they regard him as blameless as because they see their role as one of restoring the peace rather than casting blame.

One might also argue that Achebe's masculinization of Igbo society represents an anticolonial gesture that reverses the colonialist tendency to feminize colonial societies and colonial subjects. Stratton acknowledges this possible interpretation, noting that the narratives of colonialist writers such as Cary, Conrad, and **H. Rider Haggard** do indeed tend to feminize Africans in their fictional depictions of them. On the other hand, Stratton believes that Achebe may undermine colonialist racial stereotypes only at the expense of perpetuating gender stereotypes (37). One could, of course, argue that Achebe is simply being realistic in his depiction of Igbo power relations, but Stratton is probably correct that he could have done more to question these relations in terms of gender. After all, Achebe does an excellent job of deconstructing the hierarchical relationship between the races in colonial Africa, and Stratton is probably justified in suggesting that, while Achebe effectively dismantles "racial romances" such as Cary's *Mr. Johnson*, he does little to prevent his book from becoming a sort of "gender romance" (36). Indeed, Achebe's book sometimes suggests that one of the negative effects of colonialism was its disruption of the clear hierarchy of gender relations in Umuofia. For example, when the men of the village discuss the strange customs of some of their neighbors, Okonkwo mentions that some tribes are

so peculiar that they consider children the property of their mothers rather than their fathers, as in any properly patriarchal society. His friend Machi responds that such a practice would be as inconceivable as a situation in which "the woman lies on top of the man when they are making the children." Obierika then directly links this reversal of gender roles to the arrival of Europeans, who have lately been rumored to have been seen in the area. He suggests that such a sexual inversion would be "like the story of white men who, they say, are white like this piece of chalk" (51).

It may also be significant in this regard that Okonkwo, when exiled from Umuofia in Part Two of *Things Fall Apart*, is sent to the home of his mother's family as punishment. It is precisely while he is in this locale, which for Okonkwo has clearly feminine resonances, that European culture makes its first significant intrusions into traditional Igbo life. Indeed, in Okonkwo's absence, Umuofia becomes a stronghold of Christian missionary activity, as well as a focal point of British colonial control. In this part of the book, the inroads made by Christian missionaries into traditional Igbo society increasingly contribute to the breakdown in traditional values that Okonkwo has long defended and cherished. To make matters worse, one of the converts won by the missionaries in this section of the book is Okonkwo's own son Nwoye, whom Okonkwo thus comes to regard as degenerate and effeminate—that is, as a throwback to his grandfather Unoka. Thus, in another potential reversal of colonialist stereotypes, European Christianity is linked to femininity, while traditional Igbo beliefs are figured as masculine.

In one sense, this part of the book, in which Okonkwo must endure seven years of separation from his beloved Umuofia, ends on a high note. As Okonkwo prepares to return home, he hosts an elaborate feast to thank his kinsmen in Mbanta for their kindness during his years of exile there. This communal event presents traditional Igbo society at its best, but it is undermined by the reader's recognition that this way of life is already being eroded by the incursions of Christianity and Western individualism. One of the elders of the clan thus ends the feast on a sad note, thanking Okonkwo for his hospitality, but gloomily acknowledging that the younger generations of Igbos are already losing their appreciation for the traditional bonds of kinship:

You do not know what it is to speak with one voice. And what is the result? An abominable religion has settled among you. A man can now leave his father and his brothers. He can curse the gods of his fathers and his ancestors, like a hunter's dog that suddenly goes mad and turns on his master. I fear for you; I fear for the clan. (118)

The obvious accuracy of this somber prediction adds a tragic irony to Okonkwo's attempts in the final part of the book to rebuild his life in Umuofia and to regain his status as a leader of the community there, for the traditional life of the community itself is already doomed, and in this part of the book the Christian missionaries are joined by soldiers and bureaucrats as British colonial rule begins to be firmly established in Nigeria. This process culminates in Okonkwo's impulsive killing of a messenger sent by the British in order to break up a meeting of the leaders of Umuofia, who are trying to decide upon a response to the recent detention and abuse of several elders of the community, including Okonkwo himself, by the British **District Commissioner**. The Commissioner then arrives with soldiers to arrest Okonkwo, only to find that the latter (in a final, radical violation of Igbo tradition, which forbids suicide) has hanged himself. Okonkwo, in a final example of the breakdown of Igbo

communal life as a result of British colonialism, dies alone—and in a manner so repugnant to his fellow villagers that they are not allowed by tradition to bury him. That task must fall to the British, as does the task of recording Okonkwo's story. The Commissioner concludes that Okonkwo's story should make interesting reading and thus might be worthy of a chapter or at least a paragraph in the book he himself is writing. This book, ***The Pacification of the Primitive Tribes of the Lower Niger***, serves as an emblem of the Africanist discourse Achebe seeks to overcome with *Things Fall Apart*, which itself tells the story of Okonkwo in an alternative African voice.

Achebe's novel stands as a direct refutation of Africanist discourse like the commissioner's *Pacification* book and makes it clear that the coming of European colonialism to Africa brought not civilization, but chaos and destruction. The depiction of the British colonial administration in the third part of *Things Fall Apart* combines with the portrayal of the missionary Smith (far more strident and uncompromising than his predecessor, Brown) to make Achebe's book both a vivid evocation of traditional Igbo life and a sharp critique of the European colonialism that shattered this life. Ernest Emenyonu calls attention to the latter aspect of Achebe's project when he argues that, "no matter how couched in proverbs, images and innuendoes, the intense virulence of Achebe's indictment of colonial diplomatic tactlessness and absurd human high-handedness cannot be lost on the perceptive reader" (83–84). Again, however, this critical side of Achebe's project is achieved through a variety of complex strategies and goes well beyond mere diatribes or simple description of the damage done by British colonialism to Igbo society. By situating itself in opposition to the depiction of relationships between Africa and Europe that appears in European texts such as *Heart of Darkness* or *Mr. John-son, Things Fall Apart* opens a complex literary dialogue that challenges not only the content of such texts, but fundamental rationalist, individualist, and historicist assumptions upon which those texts are constructed. Margaret Turner thus argues that "Chinua Achebe's trilogy, *Things Fall Apart*, **Arrow of God**, and **No Longer at Ease**, refutes Western standards of literature and Western ideology, in this case Hegel's universal and homogeneous state, by showing that both constitute aspects of the new colonialism" (32).

Still, Achebe's treatment of the impact of the twin forces of colonialism and Christianity on Igbo society is far from simplistic. Just as he points out certain negative aspects of traditional Igbo society (such as the killing of twins and the treatment of certain members of the community—the *osu*—as total outcasts), so too does he suggest potentially positive developments related to the cessation of these negative practices due to the coming of Christianity and European civilization. Ultimately, however, *Things Fall Apart* demonstrates that even the negative aspects of Igbo society were part of an organic whole and that the disruptions brought about by the removal of these aspects led to a collapse of the entire social structure. The book thus raises a number of profound questions not only about the nature and function of literature, but about the nature of human societies and human cultural practices and the extent to which different aspects of a given society are interwoven in complex and interdependent ways. In this sense, it not only looks back to the past but points toward the future, making an important contribution to the development of a viable postcolonial Nigerian cultural identity that moves beyond the legacy of the colonial past.

FURTHER READING

Chinua Achebe, *Morning Yet on Creation Day*, "Teaching *Things Fall Apart*," and *Things Fall Apart*; David Carroll, *Chinua Achebe*; Rhonda Cobham, "Making Men and History"; Ernest Emenyonu, "Chinua Achebe's *Things Fall Apart*"; Frantz Fanon, *The Wretched of the Earth*; C. L. Innes, *Chinua Achebe*; Abdul JanMohamed, *Manichean Aesthetics* and "Sophisticated Primitivism"; Biodun Jeyifo, "For Chinua Achebe"; G. D. Killam, *The Writings of Chinua Achebe*; Bernth Lindfors, ed., *Approaches to Teaching Achebe's* Things Fall Apart; Michael Valdez Moses, *The Novel and the Globalization of Culture*; Kalu Ogbaa, *Gods, Oracles, and Divination* and *Understanding* Things Fall Apart; Umelo Ojinmah, *Chinua Achebe*; Eustace Palmer, *An Introduction to the African Novel*; Arthur Ravenscroft, *Chinua Achebe*; Florence Stratton, *Contemporary African Literature and the Politics of Gender*; Oladele Taiwo, *Culture and the Nigerian Novel*; Margaret Turner, "Achebe, Hegel, and the New Colonialism"; William Walsh, *A Manifold Voice*; Robert M. Wren, *Achebe's World*.

M. Keith Booker

***THINGS FALL APART* (TELEVISION MINISERIES),** 1986 television miniseries produced by the Nigerian Television Authority and based on Achebe's novel of the same title. Broadcast in thirteen episodes totaling approximately ten hours in length, this massive English-language production stands as an important testament to the cultural importance of Achebe's work in **Nigeria**. The miniseries was directed by David Orere and scripted for television by Adiela Onyedibia and Emma Eleanya. It stars Pete Edochie in the central role of **Okonkwo**.

The miniseries is a relatively faithful adaptation of Achebe's novel, especially in terms of plot, although Edochie's Okonkwo is a somewhat more likable figure than the stern protagonist of the novel. Indeed, it is quite clear that, following a well-established global convention of television programming, audiences are meant to identify with and root for the central character in the miniseries, whereas the portrayal of the protagonist in the novel is much more ambiguous. The series is reasonably well done, though with a low budget by American and British standards. In addition, certain elements (such as the often repeated jinglelike theme music) become a bit tiresome as the miniseries proceeds. Nevertheless, the miniseries reinforces the novel in important ways. In particular, by dramatizing the traditional **Igbo** culture and its subsequent downfall, the miniseries makes clear the fact that the novel, despite being rather slim, is in fact an important historical epic that narrates a dramatic and sweeping period of transition in the Igbo (and African) world.

The first episode, entitled "Footprints of a Tiger," introduces Okonkwo, his strained relationship with his father, **Unoka**, and his somewhat domineering relationship with his wives. It shows Okonkwo as he defeats the champion wrestler **Amalinze the Cat**, thus rising to prominence in **Umuofia**. In the second episode, "Crown of Battle," Okonkwo gains still more prestige by establishing himself as a great warrior through leading his fellow villagers in a victorious battle against a neighboring village. Episode 3, "Now or Never," is particularly notable for its prominent representation of Igbo rhetoric and speech making, as the elders of Umuofia debate whether the somewhat rash Okonkwo should be invited to join their council. He is, in fact, chosen, then installed in an elaborate celebration that provides a reasonably good vision of the importance of such ceremonies in traditional Igbo culture. The occasion is, however, tempered by the arrival of news that a woman of Umuofia has been killed in the neighboring village of **Mbaino**, to which Okonkwo wants to respond with all-out war, though the elders adopt a more moderate approach.

In Episode 4, "The Choice," Okonkwo leads a delegation from Umuofia to Mbaino, struggling to control his temper as he conducts the negotiations. The people of Mbaino are reluctant to accede to Okonkwo's demands that they send a boy and a young virgin from their village to Mbaino in retribution for the killing. The threat of war thus looms but is averted in Episode 5, "One Boy, One Girl," when the boy, **Ikemefuna**, and the girl, **Ugonna**, are sent to Umuofia. Ikemefuna is assigned, for the time being, to live with Okonkwo until his fate can be determined by **Agbala**, the Oracle of the Hills and Caves. Okonkwo's temper is shown in a bad light in this episode when he beats his wife, **Ekwefi**, for stripping the leaves off a banana tree.

Episode 6, "A Tale of Two Clans," repeats much of the footage from Episode 5 and also narrates the episode from the novel in which Okonkwo is forced to pay a penance to **Ani**, the earth goddess, for beating his youngest wife, **Ojiugo**, during the **Week of Peace**, consecrated to the goddess. As the episode comes to a close, the oracle delivers the ominous news that Ikemefuna must be killed. In Episode 7, "To Love and to Obey," Okonkwo, afraid to show weakness, participates in the killing of Ikemefuna and even strikes the fatal blow. As the episode ends, a group of spirit women surround Okonkwo and berate him for his participation in the killing. A song of mourning, "Ikemefuna's Song," sung by Nelly Uchendu as lead singer, is prominently featured.

In Episode 8, "Relief," a repentant Okonkwo is tortured by memories of Ikemefuna, while his friend **Obierika** tells him that he himself would not have participated in the killing were he in Okonkwo's position. Meanwhile, Okonkwo worries that his son, **Nwoye**, is showing signs of a lack of strength and courage. The wedding of Obierika's daugher, **Akeuke**, is performed as the series enacts an elaborate wedding ritual. "New Times, New Tides," the ninth episode, includes the funeral rites of old **Ezeudu**, during which Okonkwo's gun explodes and kills Ezeudu's son. Okonkwo and his family are subsequently exiled to his mother's home village of **Mbanta**, where they are received by his mother's uncle, **Uchendu**.

Episode 10, "There They Come," focuses on the disruptive arrival of the white man in the Igbolands, noting the way in which the success of Christian **missionaries** among the Igbo begins to shatter the traditional culture. Despite Okonkwo's vehement opposition to the newcomers, Nwoye becomes a Christian convert. In "Gods and Gods," the eleventh episode, tensions between Christianity and the traditional Igbo religion continue to grow. Okonkwo's exile finally comes to an end, and Obierika urges him to return to Umuofia to lead the fight against the white invaders. Okonkwo agrees, thanking his hosts in Mbanta with a farewell feast.

In Episode 12, "Home at Last," Okonkwo arrives back in Umuofia but finds it much changed. It is, in fact, now a Christian stronghold, the home base of a missionary (a composite of the two figures of **Smith** and **Brown** from the novel) who hopes to convert even Okoknwo to Christinaity. Tensions mount when the Christian church is destroyed after the unmasking of an *egwugwu*. In response, the British authorities treacherously attack and imprison a delegation (including Okonkwo) that comes to the **District Commissioner** to air the grievances of the people of Umuofia. The people of Umofia are forced to raise and pay a fine of 250 bags of cowries to secure their release. In the final episode, "Here I Stand," Okonkwo vows to mount a one-man war against the British when the people of Umuofia fail to rise up in arms after the insult to their delegation in Episode 12. He then strikes and kills the leader of a group of soldiers who come to break up a meeting being held in Umuofia to discuss the situation. In the end, the discon-

solate Okonkwo hangs himself, becoming an abomination of the clan, who are thus unable to bury him or even cut him down. The series ends with a sentimental series of flashbacks to Okonkwo's younger and better days.

Though designed for a Nigerian audience, the television adaptation of *Things Fall Apart* has considerable educational value for Western students of Achebe, who can use the series as an opportunity to help them visualize the unfamiliar cultural setting of the novel, especially through its extensive presentation of traditional rituals such as feasts, weddings, and funerals. The entire miniseries is available on VHS (in the British PAL format) from the African Video Centre in London. Picture and sound quality on the tapes is, however, questionable at best. Note also the existence of an Igbo-language television adaptation of the novel and of a feature film based on a combination of *Things Fall Apart* and *No Longer at Ease*, distributed under the title *Bullfrog in the Sun* as well as the alternative title *Things Fall Apart*.

M. Keith Booker

THIS EARTH, MY BROTHER, by Kofi Awoonor (1972), usually described by critics as a novel, has been characterized by the author as a poem. In any case, the book certainly defies the conventions of the Western novel. Beginning with the author's explanation that the text is allegorical and then a poetic preface, the novel is structured in chapters that alternate between prose vignettes from the life of the protagonist Amamu and poetic commentaries on the new nation of Ghana until the two modes merge in the final chapters of the book.

The first chapter is set in colonial Ghana and describes the corruption of those involved in the construction of a road; this dire image of British-controlled Ghana—symbolized throughout the novel by the recurring image of the dunghill—is set against the birth of a potential savior, Amamu. A series of vignettes follows in which the tone of decay and abuse set in the opening chapter is revisited through events from various moments in the life of Amamu. Amamu is isolated from his peers, and his difference is marked throughout the book by his recognition of injustice within Ghanaian society. For instance, as a schoolboy, Amamu watches as his teachers humiliate themselves in the hope of impressing their British overseers, while the effect of racism on African identity is further developed in Amamu's experiences in London. As a British-educated lawyer, however, Amamu must recognize his power and privilege in a new Ghana that is no more egalitarian than the former colonial state: "The logic of protective custody is the reasoning of preventive detention is the argument for colonialism. To those who have, more shall be given, and from those who have not, even the little they have shall be taken away. That is the new dialectics" (93).

As Achebe asserts in **"Kofi Awoonor as Novelist,"** "through this teeming allegory we catch glimpses of the hero Amamu at significant moments in his life—the catch phrase "glimpses" is in fact misleading, since we know that even in those sequences that are most remote from him personally (e.g., in the invocation of the poet killed in battle, Okigbo, or the assassinated freedom fighter Eduardo Mondlane) it is Amamu who is stretched on the rack and also Africa whose story his life parallels in its purposelessness and self-destructiveness" (*Hopes and Impediments* 86). In one episode, Amamu abandons his wife—from whom he becomes ever more isolated—for a prostitute he had defended. Throughout the book sexuality and violence are interrelated, and for the most part women figure as objects of sexual desire, their innocence or purity, like that of the new nation and its cultural ancestry, having been lost. The book concludes with Amamu's memories of childhood and his mother and grandmother singing funeral dirges. His attempt to return to the woman of the sea, a symbol of African wisdom, results in his death. For Achebe, such a conclusion is a disappointment. Having portrayed the decay and corruption of the newly independent nation, "Awoonor gives no answers—a return journey womb-wards to a rendezvous with golden-age innocence is clearly inadequate" (*Hope and Impediments* 86).

FURTHER READING

Richard K. Priebe, "Kofi Awoonor's *This Earth, My Brother* as an African Dirge"; Edward Sackey, "Oral Tradition and the African Novel"; Derek Wright, "Scatology and Eschatology in Kofi Awoonor's *This Earth, My Brother*."

David Jefferess

"THOUGHTS ON THE AFRICAN NOVEL." Achebe essay. See *Morning Yet on Creation Day*.

TIMOTHY, a middle-aged Christian in *A Man of the People*. He is among the first to denounce (via a proverb) the shop proprietor **Josiah** after his attempt to rob the blind man **Azoge** of his walking stick in chapter 9.

M. Keith Booker

TINUBU SQUARE, in chapter 9 of *No Longer at Ease*, a busy site in **Lagos** to which **Obi Okonkwo** and **Clara Okeke** bring **Elsie Mark** so that she can secure a taxicab after her interview with Obi.

Thomas J. Lynn

TODD, MR., a character in **Evelyn Waugh**'s novel *A Handful of Dust*. Todd is mentioned by **Obi Okonkwo** in chapter 5 of *No Longer at Ease* to illustrate Obi's concept of tragedy.

Thomas J. Lynn

TOMLINSON, MARIE, the attractive English secretary of **William Green** in *No Longer at Ease* who shares an office with **Obi Okonkwo**. During Obi's first weeks at his post as Secretary to the Scholarship Board he is somewhat suspicious of Marie, having heard that some of the people in her position spy on African workers (chapter 9). Over time, however, Obi begins to let down his guard, gratified by Marie's apparently uncalculating enthusiasm for Obi's fiancée, **Clara Okeke**. Marie likes to talk with Obi, and they have fairly candid conversations on topics ranging from Mr. Green (chapter 11) to what Marie perceives to be the excessive amount of holiday time, at least for some, in **Nigeria** (chapter 17).

Thomas J. Lynn

TORTOISE, a cunning, self-centered, and somewhat comical **trickster** of **Igbo** oral tradition, also is found in Latin American, African American (as Terrapin), and other African trickster narratives. This particular trickster figure has a distinctive place in Achebe's oeuvre. Most notable is the tale from the oral tradition, "**Tortoise and the Birds**," that **Ekwefi**, second wife of **Okonkwo**, narrates to their daughter, **Ezinma**, in chapter 11 of *Things Fall Apart*.

Also, a brief Tortoise tale is narrated (and possibly improvised) by **Nathaniel** at a gathering at the apartment of **Obi Okonkwo** in chapter 18 of *No Longer at Ease*. The tale is Nathaniel's means of making an unflattering comment on the fact that Obi does not travel from **Lagos** to his family home in **Umuofia** in order to attend the funeral of his mother, **Hannah Okonkwo**. In Nathaniel's tale Tortoise requests that he not be summoned during a long journey "unless something new under the sun" happens. Tortoise hopes to "escape the burden of his mother's funeral" this way.

In *Arrow of God*, moreover, Tortoise is referred to on several occasions in order to illuminate or comment on specific circumstances. For example, in one of the novel's final passages **Ezeulu** tries to make sense of the incomprehensible (that the god, **Ulu**, has lost his power and abandoned the community, **Umuaro**, that has depended on him) by adverting to a proverb: "What could it point to but the collapse and ruin of all things? Then a god, finding himself powerless, might take flight and in one final, backward glance at his abandoned worshippers cry: 'If the rat cannot flee fast enough / Let him make way for the tortoise!' " In Achebe's subsequent novel, *A Man of the People*, **Edna**'s father disparages **Odili Samalu**'s new Volkswagen by calling it "a tortoise" (chapters 10, 13).

In *Anthills of the Savannah*, on the other hand, "tortoise" refers in a flattering way to **President Ngongo**, an African autocrat whom **Kangan**'s ruler, **Sam, the President**, thinks of as "the wise old tortoise" (chapter 2). Furthermore, this novel features a tale quite possibly derived from oral tradition, "**The Tortoise and the Leopard**," in which Tortoise's trick is seen in a decidedly positive light, rendering him a role model for the oppressed (chapters 9 and 12). He is represented, in other words, as a kind of culture hero—a role that trickster figures, in keeping with their paradoxical natures, sometimes assume in folklore. Also, the central character in Achebe's children's book *The Drum* is Tortoise, who tries to become king of the animals by sharing the food he can produce with a drum he has gained from the land of spirits. (It may be noted that the series of books, published in Nigeria, to which this and another children's book by Achebe, *The Flute*, belong is Tortoise Books.)

In *Yoruba Trickster Tales* Oyekan Owomoyela makes a remark about the Yoruba Tortoise that is germane to the Tortoise of Igbo origin in Achebe's work: "Like the tricksters of other cultures, Àjàpá [Tortoise] is a human surrogate, as his anthropomorphic character is meant to attest" (xiv). Similarly, an old wise man in **Ngugi wa Thiong'o**'s *Devil on the Cross* declares, "stories are not about ogres or about animals or about men. All stories are about human beings" (61–62). The primacy of Tortoise in Igbo tradition is disclosed by the narrator of Nkem Nwankwo's *Danda*, which is set in an Igbo village: "The tortoise was always the centre of all fables" (107–8).

FURTHER READING

Chinua Achebe, *The Drum* and *The Flute*; Barbara Harlow, " 'The Tortoise and the Birds' "; Ngugi wa Thiong'o, *Devil on the Cross*; Charles E. Nnolim, "The Form and Function of the Folk Tradition in Achebe's Novels"; Nkem Nwankwo, *Danda*; Emmanuel Obiechina, "Narrative Proverbs in the African Novel"; Oyekan Owomoyela, *Yoruba Trickster Tales*; Richard Priebe, *Myth, Realism, and the West African Writer* and "Teaching *Things Fall Apart* in a Criticism Course."

Thomas J. Lynn

"TORTOISE AND THE BIRDS," the longest "folk story" in *Things Fall Apart*, is a splendid example of the rich narrative resources of **Igbo**—and African—oral tradition. This and other traditional tales embedded in *Things Fall Apart* contribute to the vivid portrait of oral narrative and art that Achebe presents and celebrates in the novel (a tribute found in other of his fictional works). The oral tradition flourished, of course, during the time period in which *Things Fall Apart* is set, but during Achebe's own childhood many elements of this tradition continued to play a role in Igbo culture. The presence of these elements in Achebe's fiction not only gave them a wider audience but also played an essential role in the forging of a new African literature in English.

In *Things Fall Apart* the encounter between **Tortoise**, an Igbo **trickster** figure, with the birds is narrated in chapter 11 by **Ekwefi**, second wife of **Okonkwo**, to their daughter, **Ezinma**. The story begins with a reference to a feast in the sky to which all the birds have been invited. Tortoise, who is extremely hungry and emaciated due to famine ("His body rattled like a piece of dry stick in his empty shell"), wants to partake of the feast, but his reputation for cunning and being ungrateful causes the birds to mistrust him. Nevertheless, Tortoise has "a sweet tongue," and with it he soon convinces the birds of his humility and that "he was a changed man." Each bird "gave him a feather, with which he made two wings." On the feast day Tortoise is "the first to arrive" at the place the birds gather prior to their journey, and then, in his "many-colored plumage," he flies with them to join "the people of the sky," who are the hosts. Tortoise, who "was very happy and voluble as he flew among the birds," is soon selected by them "as the man to speak for the party because he was a great orator." Then, still in flight, Tortoise persuades the birds to "take new names for the occasion," telling them that this is an " 'age-old custom' " for a feast like this. Tortoise adopts for himself the name "*All of you.*" This trick hinges on a verbal ploy similar to the assumption of the name "Nobody" by Odysseus (another Greek trickster) to defeat the Cyclops in the *Odyssey*. After the group joins their hosts, Tortoise gives a speech that is "so eloquent," and due to his role as speaker and to his anomalous appearance the hosts assume that he is "the king of the birds." When Tortoise asks one of the hosts whom the feast is for, the host replies, "For all of you." Inventing another tradition to explain this response to the birds—" 'the custom here is to serve the spokesman first' "—Tortoise is able enjoy "the best part of the food." The hosts do not intervene, thinking that it is the birds' "custom to leave all the food for their king." Later some of the birds share the leftovers, while others are "too angry to eat." Before returning home the birds take back their feathers from Tortoise, and in addition Parrot practices on him the counter-ploy that a trickster's wiles so often incite. Parrot deceives Tortoise and his wife by causing her, in direct opposition to Tortoise's wishes, to spread around Tortoise's compound the hardest items in his house. Falling the immense distance back to earth, Tortoise lands on the compound with a resounding crash, and his shell breaks into pieces. He does not die, however, because "a great medicine man" puts his shell back together, although it is no longer in a smooth condition (*Things Fall Apart* 96–99).

Richard Priebe, commenting on Achebe's use of "Igbo oral art" in *Things Fall Apart*, observes that "versions of . . . the tale about the greedy tortoise named 'All of you' are common throughout West Africa" ("Teaching" 126). Barbara Harlow seems to indicate an even wider distribution of this oral narrative: "The tale of the tortoise and the birds is told in many versions in many regions among the many peoples of Africa" (78). Also, compare the ending of Achebe's version, which explains the seams in tortoise shells (99), to the ending of the Yoruba tale, "Ajapa [the tortoise], Dog, and the Princess," which explains the same phenomenon (Owomoyela 199–202). In both cases, the tortoise drops to an especially harsh portion of earth from a great height as a result of the ire that his treachery has aroused in others. Another parallel to the fall and fragmentation of Tortoise in Achebe's version exists in the form of a brief proverbial remark in the author's fourth novel, *A Man of the People*. At the beginning of chapter 12 **Hezekiah Samalu** says to his son, **Odili Samalu**, the novel's narrator and protagonist, "So you really want to fight **Chief Nanga**! My son, why

don't you fall where your pieces could be gathered?" (121).

As a number of observers have remarked, "Tortoise and the Birds" serves partly as an allegorical comment on a central element of the story in *Things Fall Apart*—the conflict between the Igbo community of Umuofia and the British colonial onslaught. From one perspective Tortoise is an image of the deceit, rapacious appetite, and greed of the white intruders. Thus, like the novel itself, Tortoise's actions in the tale re-envision the nature of the European intrusion from an Igbo perspective. Tortoise's spurious claims to know the customs and intentions of the people of the sky in order to gain the cooperation of the birds in Ekwefi's tale are analogous to the English **missionaries'** presumptuous introduction of the Christian God to Umuofia as part of the colonial pacification of that community in the larger novel. In the tale, the people of the sky notice that Tortoise looks different from the others (92), while in the novel, the strange appearance of the first European to be seen by people in the region is a source of fascination (138). Harlow regards the Tortoise and birds tale as an "allegory of resistance" in which "Tortoise represents colonial power" and "the birds . . . signify the colonized population" (75). Harlow perceives that "the final incidents of Okonkwo's life and the resistant history of the other villagers reenact the fable of the tortoise and the birds" (78). Where Tortoise uses his "sweet tongue" to gain the acceptance of the birds (97), the colonial **District Commisioner** sends "his sweet-tongued messenger to the leaders of Umuofia" late in the novel to draw them into a meeting with him (193). Then, using the particularly dishonorable trick of bringing his henchmen into the meeting on the pretext that they need to be informed of Umuofia's grievances, the District Commisioner has Okonkwo and the other leaders forcibly restrained (193–94). Hence, in the one case, the ruse that Tortoise practices on the birds has the result that "some of them were too angry to eat. They chose to fly home on an empty stomach" (98–99). In the other case, while being handcuffed, jailed, and verbally and physically abused, "the six [leaders] ate nothing throughout that day and the next. They were not even given any water to drink, and they could not go out to urinate or go into the bush when they were pressed . . . Okonkwo was choked with hate" (195).

Priebe, Obiechina, and Nnolim also find this tale functioning allegorically in *Things Fall Apart*, although their interpretations, similar to one another—each viewing Tortoise as an image of Okonkwo (Priebe, *Myth* 55; Obiechina 213–14; Nnolim 37–38)—are different from the one elaborated immediately above. In addition, Obiechina contends that the Tortoise and birds tale and other oral narratives, what he calls "narrative proverbs," embedded in *Things Fall Apart* function—as such narratives do in an array of subsequent African novels—the way that short proverbs do (199–200) and carry a corresponding moral weight. Obiechina observes that "like the use of proverbs proper the embedding of stories in the novels is based upon two main principles of the African oral tradition—authority and association—through which an idea is given validity by being placed side by side with another idea that bears the stamp of communal approval and by its being linked to the storehouse of collective wisdom" (201). Thus, the story of Tortoise and the birds and other elements of the oral heritage in Achebe's work reveal, in addition to considerable aesthetic appeal and entertainment value, a vital rhetorical and moral dimension for his characters, for his culture, and for the author himself. In depicting the moral subtlety, wisdom, and attractiveness of the oral heritage in the lives of his precolonial and colonial Igbo characters, Achebe affirms traditional Igbo and African culture. He renders this affirmation explicit in his essay **"The Role of the Writer in a New Nation"**: "African people did not hear of culture for the first time from Europeans . . . their societies were not mindless but frequently had a philosophy of great depth and value and beauty . . . they had poetry and, above all, they had dignity" (*Morning* 8).

FURTHER READING

Chinua Achebe, *Morning Yet on Creation Day*; Barbara Harlow, " 'The Tortoise and the Birds' "; Bernth Lindfors, ed., *Approaches to Teaching Achebe's* Things Fall Apart; Charles E. Nnolim, "The Form and Function of the Folk Tradition in Achebe's Novels"; Emmanuel Obiechina, "Narrative Proverbs in the African Novel"; Oyekan Owomoyela, *Yoruba Trickster Tales*; Richard Priebe, *Myth, Realism, and the West African Writer* and "Teaching *Things Fall Apart* in a Criticism Course."

Thomas J. Lynn

"THE TORTOISE AND THE LEOPARD." In *Anthills of the Savannah*, a story, perhaps derived from African oral tradition, told by two different characters: the wise, elderly leader of the delegation from **Abazon** (chapter 9) and **Ikem Osodi** (chapter 12), who initially hears it narrated by the older man. In both instances the tale stands as a protest against the oppression being exerted by the authoritarian **Kangan** administration and an acknowledgment that even if ultimate victory against that oppression cannot be gained, honorable struggle against it is imperative. Protest against a range of forces characterizes the discussion with a university audience that Ikem commences with "the story of the Tortoise who was about to die." He calls this discussion, "The Tortoise and the Leopard—a political meditation on the imperative of struggle."

In the story itself the leopard finally has the tortoise in his power and is about to kill him, but the tortoise asks that he be granted a final wish, and the leopard obliges. The tortoise stirs up a wild commotion "on the road, scratching with hands and feet and throwing sand furiously in all directions." The leopard asks why he does this, to which the tortoise replies, " 'Because even after I am dead I would want anyone passing by this spot to say, yes, a fellow and his match struggled here.' " The tortoise in this tale employs the cunning and deception that typify Tortoise's behavior elsewhere in African folklore, including **"The Tortoise and the Birds,"** which Achebe has **Ekwefi** narrate to **Ezinma** in *Things Fall Apart*. But in contrast to Tortoise's betrayal of the community that assists him in that tale, the tortoise's trick in "The Tortoise and the Leopard" has a more respectable purpose. Indeed, when that trick is shaped first by the elderly man and later by Ikem to represent honorable struggle, the tortoise takes on the culture hero identity that **tricksters** sometimes assume in folklore and literature.

Thomas J. Lynn

TRICKSTER, characters of various guises and traits in world folklore and mythology who generally employ guile and sometimes supernatural powers for selfish but sometimes altruistic ends. Trickster figures are occasionally human, but often they are highly anthropomorphized animals such as Ananse the spider (African and Caribbean), Brer Rabbit (African American), and Coyote (Native American). Whether their schemes (designed to enmesh animals, humans, or divine beings) succeed or backfire, these tricksters of oral tradition are frequently iconoclasts, revealing an irreverent attitude toward rigid social norms and oppressive authority.

This is why Brer Rabbit, for example, was so useful as a symbol of resistance to the sub-

jection of African Americans. Similarly, human tricksters play a significant role in the social and political visions expressed in modern African and other postcolonial literatures. The equivocal behaviors—ingratiating, elusive, and defiant—and social marginality of these literary tricksters mirror the gestures of engagement and nonconformity of the so-called periphery toward the metropolitan center in postcolonial societies. Sometimes charming and often nonconformist, modern tricksters dramatize resistance to unjust local authority as well.

The trickster of oral narrative has been described not only as a culture hero but also as a wise fool, a transformer, a "form of mediation" (Lévi-Strauss 441), a god. Yet, by contrast with these more or less positive attributions, oral traditions around the globe portray their tricksters as selfish, reckless, or outrageously libidinous much of the time. Probably related to the preoccupation of tricksters of folklore with their own powerful appetites and bodily functions is the fact that such characters often take the form of animals, albeit, unmistakably anthropomorphic animals. They are also usually male. While tricksters deceive others, they "constantly overreach" what they can realistically attain (Sutherland 3) and, consequently, often become the victims of their own maneuvers, thus disclosing a rich vein of irony and humor.

Achebe, like other contemporary novelists (such as Toni Morrison, Louise Erdrich, Maxine Kingston, Charles Johnson, and N. Scott Momaday), has employed and updated trickster figures of oral tradition in a range of ways in his novels, which is entirely in keeping with his introduction of other **Igbo** folk, cultural, and linguistic elements. In short it is part of his project of giving an African shape to the English novel (Achebe 100, 103; Gikandi xvii). Achebe's most familiar trickster is **Tortoise**, who in some form is present in all of the novels. Worthy of special note are **"The Tortoise and the Birds"** (***Things Fall Apart***), in which Tortoise's treacherous behavior, zest for experience, and mellifluous tongue are at once reprehensible and ingratiating, reminding us of Richard Priebe's observation that "the trickster is often a positive force, however demonic his actions may sometimes seem" (Review 402); **"The Tortoise and the Leopard"** (***Anthills of the Savannah***), whose Tortoise is employed as a culture hero; and the Tortoise tale that **Nathaniel** narrates during a gathering to comfort **Obi Okonkwo** (***No Longer at Ease***), which comments derisively on the fact that Obi does not return to **Umuofia** for his mother's funeral. Nathaniel's tale almost explicitly bridges the gap between a folklore character and a human character and so in a different way does Achebe's portrayal of **Chief Nanga** in *A Man of the People*. He is a rounded human character with certain trickster attributes, ones comparable to those of Tortoise in "Tortoise and the Birds": both sweet-talk their way to leadership positions, but through greed and effrontery they overreach themselves and alienate their friends so that the friends trick them back. The traits that Nanga and Tortoise have in common contribute first to the success then the thwarting of their intentions.

Finally, it should be noted that Achebe alludes to the Yoruba trickster god, Esun (sometimes called "Eshu"), at the end of his short story "Sugar Baby," included in *Girls at War and Other Stories*. Mike, in avoiding acrimony between himself and his friend Cletus, reflects on "our recent desperate days [the **Nigerian Civil War**] when an angry word dropping in unannounced would start a fierce war like the passage of Esun between two peace-loving friends" (107). The reference to a Yoruba god and tale at the end of the Igbo master's wartime story reinforces the wish for peace.

FURTHER READING

Chinua Achebe, *Morning Yet on Creation Day*; Simon Gikandi, *Reading Chinua Achebe*; Lewis Hyde, *Trickster Makes This World*; Claude Lévi-Strauss, "The Structural Study of Myth"; Robert D. Pelton, *The Trickster in West Africa*; Richard Priebe, Review of *The Trickster in West Africa* by Robert D. Pelton; Paul Radin, *The Trickster*; Jeanne Rosier Smith, *Writing Tricksters*; Efua T. Sutherland, *The Marriage of Anansewa and Edufa*.

Thomas J. Lynn

THE TROUBLE WITH NIGERIA (1983), a collection of essays (republished in 1984 in the Heinemann **African Writers Series**) in which Achebe attempts to use his immense prestige in **Nigeria** to make a positive contribution to overcoming the young nation's considerable social and political difficulties. As Achebe notes in the first chapter, discussions of "the trouble with Nigeria" have become almost a national pastime, though he also makes clear early on his belief that the trouble is rather easy to identify. Indeed, he succinctly states the thesis of the entire book in the very first sentence: "The trouble with Nigeria is simply and squarely a failure of leadership" (1). In the remainder of the book, Achebe elaborates on this central premise, addressing a variety of specific problems while always adhering to the central idea that there is nothing fundamentally wrong with the Nigerian nation or people that cannot be cured by courageous, effective, and imaginative leadership of the kind that has been sorely lacking in the country since it achieved independence from British colonial rule in 1960.

In the second chapter, Achebe addresses the vexing question of rivalries among different ethnic groups in postcolonial Nigeria, which have all too often played out as the oppression of weaker groups by stronger ones. This "tribalism"—which Achebe defines simply as "discrimination against a citizen because of his place of birth (7)—is, of course, made all the more complex by the fact that, as Achebe will later insist in *Home and Exile*, the different groups in Nigeria are not tribes in the usual anthropological sense and that the **Igbo**, in particular, should be regarded as a nation rather than a tribe. Indeed, Terence Ranger has noted in a different context that the notion of tribal organization of the ethnic groups of much of Africa was largely the invention of European colonizers. Achebe, however, does not simply attribute the problem of tribalism in modern Nigeria to the legacy of colonialism but instead argues that tribalism has been institutionalized in the official political practices of postcolonial Nigeria and that it is time for Nigeria to move beyond such practices. He ends by offering the model of the United States, which he notes has at least officially banned such discrimination in public institutions, even if individual citizens may continue to harbor prejudice and bigotry.

This second chapter resonates with the ninth chapter, which discusses the "Igbo problem" and the tendency of many groups in Nigeria (especially the powerful Yoruba) to regard the Igbo as "aggressive, arrogant, and clannish" in ways that make them a disruptive influence in Nigeria. Achebe grants that the Igbo are partly to blame for this reputation. However, his central point in this chapter is that this reputation comes about largely because Igbo culture encourages individualism and innovation, giving the Igbo competitive advantages that others in Nigeria have come to resent. Achebe grants that his fellow Igbo have sometimes abused this advantage but concludes that the "competitive individualism and the adventurous spirit of the Igbo are necessary ingredients in the modernization and development of Nigerian society" (49). He thus urges others in Nigeria to treat the Igbo (and all other ethnic groups)

fairly, regarding them as a resource rather than a difficulty.

In the intervening chapters, Achebe focuses primarily on the corruption, greed, and inefficiency that he sees as characteristic of the political leadership of postcolonial Nigeria. He chides Nigeria's leaders for making grandiose (and falsely patriotic) declarations of the greatness of Nigeria, while failing to deal with the problems that have prevented the nation from becoming truly great, despite its considerable human and material resources. Among other things, the system of patronage and cronyism that is central to Nigerian politics has, for Achebe, helped to create a cult of mediocrity, in which individuals are granted positions of power and authority not because they are qualified to function in those positions but because they are of the right ethnic group and have the proper personal connections. In the longest of these chapters, Achebe addresses the problem of "indiscipline" in Nigerian society, which he sees as exemplified by the lack of official regulation on Nigerian roadways and the concomitant refusal of Nigerian drivers to show discipline in their own driving practices. For Achebe, however, this lack of discipline on the part of ordinary Nigerians can be largely attributed to the lack of discipline displayed by their leaders, and he ends by calling for a Presidential Commission on Road Safety to impose appropriate regulations and provide a model of discipline that might improve conditions in other areas of Nigerian society as well. Given that Achebe himself would suffer serious spinal injuries in a automobile accident in Nigeria in March of 1990, his comments on the hazardous conditions on Nigerian roadways now appear chilling and prophetic.

Achebe closes *The Trouble with Nigeria* with a tribute to the then recently deceased Mallam Aminu Kano, one of the few major Nigerian political figures whom Achebe genuinely admires. He hopes that Kano can serve as an inspiration to new generations of Nigerian political leaders. In the meantime, however, Nigeria has, according to Achebe, all too often fallen into repetitive patterns of corruption, indiscipline, and inefficiency among its political leaders. He notes, for example, the aura of hope surrounding the emergence of the Second Republic in the late 1970s after years of civil war and subsequent military dictatorship. Unfortunately, this new regime came to be dominated by aging political figures from the past, including Dr. Nnamdi Azikiwe and Chief Obafemi Awolo, who for Achebe embody the ills of postcolonial Nigerian politics. Worse, the younger politicians who emerged in this era tended to follow in the footsteps of Azikiwe and Awolo, rather than modeling themselves on more admirable figures, such as Kano. Nevertheless, comparing Kano to Mahatma Gandhi, Achebe argues that Kano should serve as an important role model for aspiring politicians in Nigeria in the future and that the very fact of Kano's existence proves that it is possible for Nigeria to produce honest, selfless, and effective leaders. This fact, for Achebe, bodes well for the future of Nigeria. See also *Home and Exile*.

FURTHER READING

Larry Jay Diamond, *Class, Ethnicity, and Democracy in Nigeria*; Richard Olaniyan, ed., *Nigerian History and Culture*; Terence Ranger, "The Invention of Tradition in Colonial Africa."

M. Keith Booker

"THE TRUTH OF FICTION." Achebe essay. See *Hopes and Impediments*.

TUTUOLA, AMOS (1920–1997), Nigerian author of *The Palm-Wine Drinkard and His Dead Palm-Wine Tapster in the Dead's Town* (1952), arguably the first Anglophone novel by a native West African. Partly due to a highly favorable early review of the book by Dylan Thomas, *The Palm-Wine Drinkard* made Tutuola, a Yoruba, the first West African writer to receive international attention. Tutuola wrote a number of other books that feature the imaginatively fashioned elements drawn largely from oral tradition that distinguish *The Palm-Wine Drinkard*. For each such book the author adapted Yoruba (and, more broadly, West African) tales and sequenced them to form an extended, episodic narrative of a hero's adventures. Written in an idiosyncratic, African-influenced English, these adventures invoke fabulous and magical characters and events that interlink the mundane and otherworldly. While drawing liberally on oral narrative sources, Tutuola's work also reveals the influence of **D. O. Fagunwa**'s writing and, likely, of other literature, such as *The Arabian Nights* and John Bunyan's *Pilgrim's Progress* (see Lindfors, "Amos Tutuola" 336, 340–44).

Although discussions may continue as to whether *The Palm-Wine Drinkard* and other extended fictional narratives by Tutuola are appropriately classified as novels, it is clear that these narratives do not incorporate Western novelistic conventions in the multidimensional manner that Achebe's do. It may be noted that in one Achebe novel, ***No Longer at Ease***, the protagonist, **Obi Okonkwo**, specifically addresses Tutuola when discussing modern literature with the Chairman of the Public Service Commission during a job interview (chapter 5), but neither the nature nor the tenor of Obi's remarks about Tutuola is indicated. In his own voice, however, Achebe, has expressed esteem for Tutuola's work on numerous occasions. For example, in a 1983 interview with Biodun Jeyifo, Achebe remarks that he "was completely impressed by Tutuola from the word go" (Lindfors, *Conversations* 112), while in a 1987 interview with Jane Wilkinson he mentions that in the classroom "I always teach [*The Palm-wine Drinkard*]. This is quite a useful peg on which to hang a discussion of the oral tradition" (Lindfors, Conversations 153–54).

Furthermore, in his 1964 essay **"The African Writer and the English Language,"** Achebe suggests that Tutuola, like other African writers for whom English is a second language (Olauda Equiano, Casely Hayford, **Christopher Okigbo**, and **J. P. Clark** are cited), makes an important contribution to creative writing in English. According to Achebe, Tutuola is a "natural" artist whose "good instinct has turned his apparent limitation in [a second] language into a weapon of great strength—a half-strange dialect that serves him perfectly in the evocation of his bizarre world" (101). Achebe goes on to distinguish his own work from Tutuola's by referring to himself as "a conscious artist" (101). In this essay Achebe also addresses the relationship between the type of book that Tutuola writes and the novel, focusing on Tutuola's *Feather Woman of the Jungle* (1962), which Achebe calls the author's "finest" up to that point: "Tutuola's superb storytelling is at last cast in the episodic form which he handles best instead of being painfully stretched on the rack of the novel" (101). (Here it should be indicated that Tutuola "created an *Arabian Nights* structure" in *Feather Woman of the Jungle* "by having a seventy-six-year-old chief entertain villagers every night for ten nights with accounts of his past adventures" [Lindfors, "Amos Tutuola" 340].)

In July 1961 Achebe contributed a brief item, "Amos Tutuola," to *Radio Times* of Lagos, which had been an on-air introduction to a discussion of the writers William Conton, D. O. Fagunwa, and Tutuola by Wole Soyinka, who was participating in a Sunday night radio series, *The African Novel*, that took place that month. Sixteen years later to the month Achebe first presented what became his most extended published reflection on Tutuola's work. **"Work and Play in Tu-**tuola's *The Palm-Wine Drinkard"* (1977) was the inaugural Equiano Memorial Lecture at the **University of Ibadan** and reinforced Achebe's contention in **"Africa and Her Writers"** (1973) that art and literature make important contributions to the well-being of society. In "Work and Play" Achebe praises Tutuola as "the most moralistic of all Nigerian writers. . . . [one whose] two feet [are] firmly planted in the hard soil of an ancient oral, and moral, tradition" (101). Achebe goes on to declare that *"The Palm-Wine Drinkard* is a rich and spectacular exploration of this gross perversion [i.e., devotion only to pleasure and rejection of work], its expiation through appropriate punishment and the offender's final restoration" (102).

Achebe makes it clear that Tutuola's affirmation of the value of honest work is not merely a timeless bit of wisdom. Rather, it is a highly relevant statement in an era when consumer capitalism has bred a generation so addicted to the pleasures of acquisition and consumption that the condition that affords these pleasures—the virtual economic enslavement of other people and nations—is systematically enforced. Early in the essay Achebe quotes "a simple and brief statement" from the opening of *The Palm-Wine Drinkard* that explains how the drinkard's indolence is sustained:

But when my father noticed that I could not do any work more than to drink, he engaged an expert palm-wine tapster for me; he had no other work more than to tap palm-wine every day. (7)

This statement contains, according to Achebe, a huge social and ethical proposition: "A man who will not work can only stay alive if he can somehow commandeer to his own use the labour of other people either by becoming a common thief or a slave-owner. . . . The Drinkard is enabled [by his father] to press [a slave] into a daily round of exploitative and socially useless work" (103). The exploitation of the poor for the meaningless fulfillment of the "outrageous appetite" of the affluent is the point in *The Palm-Wine Drinkard* that Achebe applies at the end of the essay to Western and Western-influenced consumer culture: "[Tutuola] is speaking strongly and directly to our times. For what could be more relevant than a celebration of work today for the benefit of a generation and a people whose heroes are no longer makers of things and ideas but spectacular and insatiable consumers" (112). This and other comments in Achebe's essay help confirm the depth and importance of "Tutuola's art" (101).

FURTHER READING

Chinua Achebe, Interview with Jane Wilkinson; M. Keith Booker, *The African Novel in English*; O. R. Dathorne, "Amos Tutuola;" William R. Ferris Jr., "Folklore and the African Novelist"; Abiola Irele, *The African Experience in Literature and Ideology*; Bernth Lindfors, "Amos Tutuola," *Conversations with Chinua Achebe*, and *Critical Perspectives on Amos Tutuola* (ed.); Gerald Moore, *Seven African Writers*; Emmanuel Obiechina, *Language and Theme*; Eustace Palmer, *The Growth of the African Novel*; Oladele Taiwo, *Culture and the Nigerian Novel*; Michael Thelwell, Introduction to *The Palm-Wine Drinkard*; Amos Tutuola, *Feather Woman of the Jungle* and *The Palm-Wine Drinkard*; Chantal Zabus, "The Ancestor of Relexification."

Thomas J. Lynn

U

UCHENDU, younger brother of the mother of **Okonkwo** in *Things Fall Apart*. He welcomes Okonkwo and his family to **Mbanta** in chapter 14 after they are exiled there when the misfiring of Okonkwo's gun causes the death of **Ezeudu**'s sixteen-year-old son. Thirty years earlier, he had received the body of Okonkwo's mother when she was brought home to Mbanta for burial.

M. Keith Booker

UDENDO, a woman from **Umunneora**, is **Akuebue**'s neighbor in *Arrow of God*, chapter 16.

Rachel R. Reynolds

UDENKWO. Along with **Mgbogo**, one of two women in chapter 12 of *Things Fall Apart* who fail to heed a call for help when a cow has accidentally been let loose on a neighbor's crops. Udenkwo does not appear because she is nursing her infant child.

M. Keith Booker

UDENKWO, Akuebue's daughter in *Arrow of God*. A story about her stubbornness appears in chapter 14, in which we are treated to an extended discussion on **Igbo** family politics. Akuebue tells **Ezeulu** how his adult daughter takes umbrage when one of her chickens is mistakenly commandeered for sacrifice on the part of Akuebue's husband. We find that her anger, although unjustified over such a minor offense, could be best dealt with by a private apology from her (also proud) husband. Besides Achebe's taking the opportunity to tell a story about gender relations in colonial Igboland, the story about Udenkwo's pride could also be interpreted as a subtle warning from Akuebue to Ezeulu to be propitious in his treatment of both white men and the villagers.

Rachel R. Reynolds

UDEOZO, or Anichebe Udeozo, is an elder of **Umuaro** (*Arrow of God*, chapters 12 and 18).

Rachel R. Reynolds

UDO, a man of **Umuofia** and the husband of the woman murdered in the market at **Mbaino** in *Things Fall Apart*. He is given a young virgin from Mbaino to replace his dead wife.

M. Keith Booker

UDO, a principal deity of the village of **Okperi** in *Arrow of God*.

Rachel R. Reynolds

UDO. As indicated in chapter 19 of *No Longer at Ease*, "one of the great gods" of the village of **Aninta**, where **Isaac Okonkwo** served as catechist in the second year of his marriage to **Hannah Okonkwo**. During the season that **yam** was scarce, an unruly male goat dedicated to Udo was beheaded by Hannah with a machete after it entered her kitchen and ate a course of yam she was preparing for a meal. This elicited an angry response from the village elders and from the women who traded with her in the market. Hannah had previously complained to the priest of Udo about the goat, which had become "a menace at the mission," relaxing and leaving droppings in the church and eating the couple's crops. However, the priest of Udo "(no doubt a humorous old man) said that Udo's he-goat was free to go where it pleased and do what it pleased. If it chose to rest in Okonkwo's Christian shrine, it probably showed that their two gods were pals." Although this response did not solve the problems the goat was causing, it is suggestive of both the pride and tolerance of Igbo non-converts in relation to a tenacious Christian community.

In chapter 8 of *Anthills of the Savannah* Udo is again mentioned in connection with the goat sacred to him, and this time the evocation of the goat—in connection with the legend of a libertine found unworthy by the goddess, **Idemili**—is even coarser. The man was "handsome beyond compare but in randiness as unbridled as the odorous he-goat from the shrine of Udo planting his plentitude of seeds from a huge pod swinging between hind legs into she-goats tethered for him in front of numerous homesteads." Intriguingly, the figure of Udo's goat prompts Achebe to blend the spiritual and corporal in striking fashion in novels separated by nearly three decades. In between these two novels Achebe refers to Udo in his essay, **"Chi in Igbo Cosmology"** (1975) with the proverbial-sounding, "for is it not well known that a man may worship Ogwugwu to perfection and yet be killed by Udo?" which helps illustrate the "Igbo . . . notion of duality" (*Morning* 161).

FURTHER READING

Chinua Achebe, "Chi in Igbo Cosmology," in *Morning Yet on Creation Day*; Kalu Ogbaa, *Gods, Oracles, and Divination*; Robert M. Wren, *Achebe's World*.

Thomas J. Lynn

UDO, JOSHUA, a member of the **Umuofia Progressive Union (UPU)** who in chapter 8 of *No Longer at Ease* asks the UPU for assistance since he has been fired from his post as a messenger in the Post Office for sleeping on the job. Joshua claims that he was not sleeping but merely thinking and that his dismissal was really a consequence of the Chief Clerk's desire for retribution against him for his not having completed the payment of a ten pound bribe. Joshua seeks ten pounds from the UPU—not to complete the bribe payment but to seek another job. The members of the UPU agree to do this, to note any job openings where they work, and to recommend Joshua should a position be available.

Thomas J. Lynn

UDOM, STEPHEN, a Nigerian civil servant who in chapter 3 of *No Longer at Ease* is a passenger with **Obi Okonkwo** and ten others on the **MV Sasa**, the boat that takes them from England to **Nigeria**. Stephen throws only a penny for two boys, approximately ten and twelve, who dive for money near the **Funchal** docks when the boat reaches the **Madeiras**. Although the boys dive for and retrieve all the other coins tossed by passengers, they won't dive for pennies, including that which Stephen tosses.

Thomas J. Lynn

UDUEZUE, maternal uncle of **Akukalia Okeke**, who lives in **Okperi** (*Arrow of God*, chapter 2).

Rachel R. Reynolds

UDUEZUE, an important man of **Umuaro** in *Arrow of God*, chapter 7.

Rachel R. Reynolds

UGONNA, a titled man of **Umuofia** who announces his conversion to Christianity in chapter 20 by discarding the anklet of the two titles he has previously taken. Consequently, he becomes one of the first converts to receive the sacrament of Holy Communion.

M. Keith Booker

UGOYE, the youngest (and favorite) wife of **Ezeulu** and the mother of boys **Nwafo** and **Oduche** and the girl **Obiageli**. Ugoye is portrayed as vain and somewhat negligent in serving her husband on time or in her housekeeping affairs. She has, for example, been forbidden to cook food at special occasions because of her "uncleanness" (*Arrow of God*, chapter 6). Ugoye is also the object of fierce jealousy on the part of her co-wife, **Matefi**.

Rachel R. Reynolds

UKEGBU, the father of **Ibe**, in *Things Fall Apart*. He accompanies his son to marry **Akueke** in chapter 8.

M. Keith Booker

ULU. In *Arrow of God*, Ulu is the principal deity of the six-village federation of **Umuaro**, and **Ezeulu** (literally, "Priest of Ulu") is his priest. Mythologically speaking, Ulu is said to have been a son of the gods of **Okperi**. This is Achebe's way of creating a typical **Igbo** village origin story—a kind of mythologized account of the history of founding various towns throughout Igboland. These myths are highly variable from village to village because each village has a special protector deity and its own special origin myth. Ulu also refers to a type of possession of the living by the voice of a dead person (see Ugonna 78–79; f.19). An Ulu masquerade is described in chapter 7 of *Arrow of God*.

FURTHER READING

Nnanubuenyi Ugonna, "Igbo Satiric Art."

Rachel R. Reynolds

UMEZULIKE. In *Things Fall Apart*, the man who taps the tall palm-trees of **Okonkwo**. In chapter 8, we learn that Okonkwo, having taken the *ozo* title, is forbidden by the traditions of the clan from climbing the tall trees himself.

M. Keith Booker

UMUACHALA, where **Ezeulu** lives, is a village within the cluster called **Umuaro**, a central location for *Arrow of God*.

Rachel R. Reynolds

UMUAGU, one of the six villages of the **Umuaro** village group in *Arrow of God*.

Rachel R. Reynolds

UMUAMA, originally a seventh village of the **Umuaro** cluster. We learn in chapter 4 of *Arrow of God* that Umuama is now defunct from an incident of its denizens eating the royal **python**. Since that time, it has been forbidden for all the people of **Umuaro** to harm the royal python. This is an example of how Achebe uses "recent myth" as a form of **Igbo** history. See also **Iweka**.

Rachel R. Reynolds

UMUARO, the name of the cluster of six villages that are the setting for *Arrow of God*. They include **Umuachala**, **Umunneora**, **Umuagu**, **Umuezeani**, **Umuogwugwu**, and **Umuisiuzo**. There was once a seventh village, the now-defunct **Umuama**. In traditional **Igbo** geography, the village is the primary unit of governance, and small groups of proximate villages were often formed as federations to fight wars and share market interests. Feuding factions between **Ezeulu**'s village Umuachala and **Nwaka**'s village, Umunneora, are a typical dramatic background setting in Igbo mythology as well as Igbo literature. The principal deity of Umuaro is **Ulu**, for whom Ezeulu is the chief priest.

Rachel R. Reynolds

UMUERU, one of the nine villages of **Umuofia** in *Things Fall Apart*. The village of Umueru is the home of the descendants of **Eru**, the eldest of the nine sons of the first father of the clan.

M. Keith Booker

UMUEZEANI, one of the six allied villages that make up **Umuaro** in *Arrow of God*.

Rachel R. Reynolds

UMUIKE, an **Igbo** village in *Things Fall Apart*. In chapter 12, **Obierika** sends his relative **Nwankwo** to Umuike to buy goats in the busy market there for use in the celebration of the *uri* of Obierika's daughter, **Akueke**. Obierika warns Nwankwo that the market in Umuike is a treacherous place where thieves often use magic to cheat and rob the honest and unwary.

M. Keith Booker

UMUISIUZO, one of the six villages of the **Umuaro** village group in *Arrow of God*.

Rachel R. Reynolds

UMUNNEORA, one of the six villages of the **Umuaro** village group in *Arrow of God*.

Rachel R. Reynolds

UMUOFIA, a confederation of nine villages that is the central setting of *Things Fall Apart*. In chapter 10, we learn that the nine villages of Umuofia had been founded by the nine sons of the first father of the clan. **Evil Forest** represented the village of Umueru, or

the children of Eru, who was the eldest of the nine sons. In *Arrow of God*, we learn that the villages of Umofia had initially banded together to defend themselves against raids from the village of **Abame**. In *Arrow of God* we learn that Umuofia is a whole day's walk east of **Umuaro**, the setting for that novel.

In *No Longer at Ease* Iguedo-Umuofia is again the center of family life, but in this case the family is that of one of **Okonkwo**'s children, **Isaac Okonkwo** (**Nwoye** in *Things Fall Apart*), and his wife, **Hannah**, and children (although only one of the children, **Eunice Okonkwo**, still lives at home full-time). Three scenes in *No Longer at Ease* are set in Umuofia.

On the evidence of *No Longer at Ease*, Isaac Okonkwo did not reside in Umuofia throughout his life, but he eventually returned to it, and his son, **Obi**, was raised there. To some extent Obi considers it his hometown after returning from England, even though he resides in **Lagos**. (In his thoughts Umuofia is "home" on several occasions, though his apartment in the **Ikoyi** district of Lagos is considered "home" as well.) The three scenes, including two lengthy ones, that depict Obi in Umuofia reveal the depth of his bond to the town. Indeed, the novel clearly indicates that at the heart of Obi's splintering lies, on the one hand, the conflict between the traditional community and rural values associated with Umuofia and, on the other hand, the modern excitement and materialism associated with Lagos.

FURTHER READING

David Carroll, *Chinua Achebe*; Simon Gikandi, "Chinua Achebe and the Poetics of Location"; Emmanuel Obiechina, *Culture, Tradition, and Society in the West African Novel*; Robert M. Wren, *Achebe's World*.

Thomas J. Lynn and M. Keith Booker

UMUOFIA CHURCH MISSIONARY SOCIETY (CMS) CENTRAL SCHOOL, the primary school in **Umuofia** at which **Obi Okonkwo** and **Joseph Okeke** were classmates, as described in chapter 2 of *No Longer at Ease*. In chapter 5 of this novel all the students and staff at the school turn out for the reception honoring Obi's first visit to Umuofia since returning from England, and the school's brass band plays at least two pieces at the event, including **"Old Calabar."**

Thomas J. Lynn

UMUOFIA PROGRESSIVE UNION (UPU). In *No Longer at Ease*, an **Igbo** support club whose membership comes from **Obi Okonkwo**'s home district. In order that there may be subsequent Umuofian beneficiaries of the scholarship, its funds must be paid back by Obi to the UPU once he returns from England, where, notwithstanding the UPU intention that he study law, he takes a degree in English (chapter 1). The **Lagos** branch of the UPU, which Obi refers to as his "town union" (chapter 17), acts like an extension of Obi's family in **Umuofia**, intervening in his personal affairs but supporting him in his crises involving the death of his mother (chapter 18) and his trial for bribery (chapter 1). Obi's obligation of returning his scholarship loan to the UPU places one of the greatest burdens on Obi's finances, and his inability to meet his various debts contributes to his desperation at the end of the novel.

FURTHER READING

David Carroll, *Chinua Achebe*; Simon Gikandi, *Reading Chinua Achebe*; Emmanuel Obiechina, "Chinua Achebe's *No Longer at Ease*"; Felicity Riddy, "Language as a Theme in *No Longer at Ease*"; Robert M. Wren, *Achebe's World*.

Thomas J. Lynn

UMUOGWUGWU, one of the six villages of **Umuaro** and the original home of **Akueke**'s husband in *Arrow of God*.

Rachel R. Reynolds

UMURO, a town in the general area of **Umuaro** in *Arrow of God*, famous for its Nkwo **market day** in which European goods are marketed. Note that Umuro is a good example of how Achebe invents names with special meanings. Umu-uro can be glossed as "people of uro" or people of the deity of wealth.

Rachel R. Reynolds

UNACHUKWU, MOSES. "The first and most famous convert in **Umuaro**" (*Arrow of God*). Moses, from **Umunneora**, is conscripted for labor as a child by **missionaries**, and so he grows up traveling with them. At **Abame**, for example, he learns how brutal the colonists can be. Moses learns carpentry and builds the church at **Umuaro**; he also serves as de facto leader of the local converts and translator/assistant to Mr. **Wright** in the **Umuaro–Okperi** road-building project. Part of Moses' success can be attributed to his having determined that the Bible does not specify that Christians must kill sacred **pythons**, therefore allowing his fellow converts to evade the terror of having to commit such an act as a demonstration of faith in the new god. Moses sees "his sojourn in **Onitsha** as a parallel to that of the Moses of the Old Testament of Egypt" (*Arrow of God*, chapter 4).

FURTHER READING

Annie Gagiano, *Achebe, Head, Marechera*.

Rachel R. Reynolds

UNIVERSITY COLLEGE, IBADAN (UCI, later **University of Ibadan**), a new colonial university in Ibadan, **Nigeria**, in which Achebe enrolled in 1948. The institution had been established following the findings of the Elliot Commission on Higher Education in West Africa (1943–1945) along the lines recommended by the Asquith Commission (1943–1945). In accordance with a pattern used for the expansion of higher education in other parts of the British Empire, UCI was initially affiliated with the University of London; that is, it prepared students for degrees that were regulated, marked, and awarded by that university. UCI has been seen both as part of a neocolonialist exercise in shaping a comprador class and as a genuine effort to meet the manpower needs of a colony being prepared for independence. In the early years, sections of the Nigerian press attacked it on the grounds of appointments (which were all made in London and which favored European candidates), conditions of service (that again favored non-Nigerians), admissions policy (stories abounded of Nigerians who could not get into UCI succeeding in reputable universities), and curriculum (dictated by London, slow to reflect local experience). Achebe has stated in an interview his opinion that it was "in retrospect, a great institution . . . [that] revealed the paradox of the colonial situation."

UCI drew its first students from Yaba Institute of Technology, housing them in what had been the 56th Military General Hospital, at Eleyele. From the beginning, under Kenneth Mellanby (principal 1947–1953), UCI set high standards; indeed, some local critics argued that the standards were impossibly and inappropriately high. Following the commission's recommendations, Mellanby looked to maintain strong links with London while transplanting the traditions of Oxford and Cambridge to West Africa. "Oxbridge" emphasized residential communities with high research expectations, from which followed a commitment to, for example, academic freedom, tutor groups, hall dinners, gowns, college sports, and a rich cultural life. Although a start was made on fostering these qualities in the rough-and-tumble world of Eleyele, they could really find expression only once UCI moved to its own site and its impressive buildings. The formal opening of this new site was held November 17, 1952.

Many of Achebe's experiences as a student at UCI have been documented by the American researcher Robert M. Wren, whose book *Those Magical Years* explores the contribution of Ibadan to the growth of Nigerian literature. When Achebe entered UCI, he embarked on a course that would lead to a medical qualification. He passed the examinations at the end of the first year, though many, to the fury of some articulate Nigerians, did not. However, as he told Wren, he had found that he "didn't want to do the grinding work in physics. Or ultimately in medicine." As a result, he switched to arts, beginning three years of work toward an External University of London general degree in religious studies, history, and English. This shift meant he sacrificed the Major Scholarship that he had been awarded as a science student.

In lecture room and tutorials, Achebe particularly responded to Geoffrey Parrinder (Ibadan 1948–1952), whose teaching and research interests were in West African religions. Parrinder and his colleague, the Reverend James Welch (Ibadan 1948–1954), recognized Achebe's brilliance, and the latter, who had worked with the BBC, subsequently recommended him for a post in broadcasting. Achebe had a high regard for at least two of the lecturers in the History Department: Jean Copeland and the eloquent, iconoclastic, eccentric John Potter, who was also Achebe's moral tutor. Despite the notorious reluctance of certain historians to take pre-Imperial research seriously, Achebe the undergraduate encountered some who were aware of the challenges of writing local history, among them K. O. Dike, one of only six or seven Africans on the academic staff when Achebe was at UCI.

In the English Department, Achebe was taught by Alex Rodger (Ibadan 1952–1955), who lectured on *Far from the Madding Crowd*. Achebe told Wren, "I took to Hardy immediately." Achebe went on to mention

A. E. Housman as another British author he responded to on a syllabus that included Shakespeare and "English Literature 1798 to the present day." The English component of the London University degree also included a course in phonetics and a test of spoken English.

In several interviews, Achebe has described his experience in entering a short story competition organized by Joyce Green (Ibadan 1950–1955) of the English Department that revealed the limitations of some of his teachers. Although Achebe's entry in this competition was thought worthy of "mention" and dubbed an "interesting effort," neither it nor any other entry was considered to have merited a prize. When Achebe asked Green for her opinion of his work, he was told that it "lacked the form of a short story." When he asked, "What is the form of a short story?" Green was evasive.

Outside the English Department, Achebe the young writer had a more encouraging response. He wrote for the *University Herald*, contributing, for example, "An Argument against the Existence of Faculties," "Polar Undergraduate," "In a Village Church," "The Old Order in Conflict with the New," a poem ("There was a young man in our hall"), and editorials. In his final year, 1952–1953, he was on the editorial board with, among others, Chukwuemeka Ike and Mabel Segun, just two of his gifted contemporaries destined to contribute to Nigeria and Nigerian literature.

Achebe also wrote for the sometimes scurrilous, cyclostyled, student-consumed *Bug*, where his work found a place near that of another gifted contemporary, **Wole Soyinka**. However, Achebe was more at home in the pages of the *Herald*, from which he emerges as a serious and sometimes solemn young man who is glad to have moved from the sciences to the arts. His work occasionally hints at the concerns of the later writer, but the style is still stiff with the Latinate and the clichéd; he is sober-suited, and it will be some time before he dresses in a more relaxed, Nigerian style.

Looking back on his experience in the English Department at UCI, Achebe has been characteristically generous, recognizing that "It doesn't matter really what you teach; it is the spirit." His comments show an awareness that his lecturers, for all their limitations about what might become African literature and who might write it, had "a passion" for their subjects and "they shared that." He added, "a good student could take off from there."

In 1953, Achebe graduated with a University of London "B.A. (General) 2nd Division." He was one of nine to be awarded a Second out of a cohort of twenty-six; there were no Firsts. In the years that followed, Achebe remained in touch with UCI, where he had many friends in the small, close-knit community, and he took an interest in the evolution of the English Department. For example, he returned in 1954 to attend the inaugural lecture given by Molly Mahood, who had been brought in partly to establish the honors degree course in English. In 1961, Achebe and his wife chose to be married at one of the churches on campus. By that time, Nigeria had become independent, he had established himself as a novelist, and UCI was moving toward becoming a full-fledged, degree-awarding body in its own right. This status was achieved in 1962, when UCI became UI, the University of Ibadan.

Achebe did not receive formal instruction in creative writing as an undergraduate, but he was, in the company of some of the brightest of his contemporaries, exposed to kindred spirits in the canon of English writers and to heady ideas. Pondering Parrinder's words and engaging with Hardy's novels were invaluable for the young man who was to write *Things Fall Apart* and *Arrow of God*.

Bernth Lindfors has compared the *University Herald* version of "Dead Men's Paths" with that published twenty years later in *Girls at War and Other Stories*. The comparison shows the extent to which Achebe the undergraduate was the father of Achebe the mature novelist. He didn't exactly find a voice at Ibadan, but he discovered that he liked talking and had something to say.

FURTHER READING

Bernth Lindfors, *Early Nigerian Literature*; Kenneth Mellanby, *The Birth of Nigeria's University*; Nduka Okafor, The *Development of Universities in Nigeria*; J. T. Saunders, *University College, Ibadan*; Wole Soyinka, *The Interpreters*; Tekena N. Tamuno, ed., *Ibadan Voices*; Robert M. Wren, *Those Magical Years*.

James Gibbs

UNIVERSITY OF IBADAN. See University College, Ibadan.

UNIVERSITY OF MASSACHUSETTS AT AMHERST. Achebe's first Visiting Professorship at the University of Massachusetts was originally intended to last for one year but was extended for three years, from 1972 to 1975, while his wife, **Christie Achebe**, studied for a Masters Degree and then a Doctorate in Education. The invitation to take up the professorship was extended and encouraged by Professor Harvey Swados, who had visited Achebe in **Biafra** during the **Nigerian Civil War**. Built in the small rural town of Amherst about eighty miles from Boston, the University of Massachusetts had established a strong academic reputation and an innovative curriculum. By 1972, it had over 20,000 undergraduate students and over 3,000 postgraduates. During the late 1960s and early 1970s, the university had built up a team of artists and scholars in African and African-American Studies, including writers such as the Jamaican Michael Thelwell, author of the novel *The Harder They Come*; historians

such as John Bracey; artists such as Nelson Stevens; theater director Esther Terry; and musicians such as Horace Ove and the drummer Max Roach. All of these made the W.E.B. Du Bois Africana Studies Center, where Achebe was given an office and assistance with the editorial work on the journal **Okike**, a lively, stimulating, and friendly place to work. Achebe had a joint appointment with the Du Bois Center and the Department of English, which also included a number of specialists in African American and African literature. Among their number were young scholars such as Bernard Bell, Joseph Skerrett, and **C. L. Innes** and well-established academics such as Sid Kaplan, known for his work on representation and portraiture of black people in Europe and the Americas. In addition, the consortium of five colleges in the area (Amherst College, Smith College, Hampshire College, and Mt. Holyoke College, together with the University of Massachusetts) encouraged a thriving interest in black studies.

In addition to giving readings of his work and adding to the reputation and status of the university's African Studies and English Departments, Chinua Achebe taught an undergraduate course, based in the English Department, on African literature. It was a wide-ranging course, including Francophone as well as Anglophone writers, among them Senghor, Camara Laye, **Christopher Okigbo**, **Wole Soyinka**, **Ngugi wa Thiong'o**, **Kofi Awoonor**, and Alex LaGuma. At the insistence of his students, he also included his own works but sometimes asked colleagues such as Joseph Skerrett or Lyn Innes to lead the discussion. The class was always oversubscribed, and the students came from a range of backgrounds and disciplines— with majors in mathematics, economics, biology, politics, anthropology, and history, as well as English. Given the pervasive ignorance of African geography, history, and culture, all too often Achebe found that he had to spend much time filling in background information and annotations to the texts, and it was not always easy to persuade the students to take a literary rather than an anthropological focus. The course was received enthusiastically, but Achebe commented at one time that he felt it would also be interesting for students to hear African perspectives on European and American writers such as **T. S. Eliot** or **Graham Greene**.

In 1974 Achebe was invited to give the prestigious Chancellor's Lecture at the university, chaired by the then chancellor of the university, Bromley, and intended to honor distinguished members of the university. The Chancellor's Lecture Series sought to reach a varied audience from the university community and beyond and to celebrate scholarship and creativity. Achebe chose as his subject **Joseph Conrad**'s *Heart of Darkness*, a text widely taught (indeed perhaps one of the most widely taught texts) in English departments throughout North America and Britain. The lecture, given in February 1975 and later published as **"An Image of Africa,"** argued that Conrad's novella was based on racist assumptions that, even given the historical context, could not be condoned and that consequently, although Conrad was a talented writer, this particular work could not be regarded as a great work of literature. The lecture upset many academics in the English Department, some of whom walked out, and began a debate that has continued in seminars, conferences, scholarly essays, and books to this day. At the reception that followed the lecture, one professor of English went up to Achebe and shouted, "How dare you!" Others accused him of failing to distinguish between literature and politics, thus missing Achebe's point that the two were inevitably entangled. But others were to reflect more favorably on the lecture and to reread

and reconsider Conrad's work in its light. The lecture was published as a pamphlet in the Chancellor's Lecture Series, and then, despite some heated opposition within the Editorial Board, disseminated more widely in the *Massachusetts Review*.

Achebe left Massachusetts in the summer of 1975 to take up a Visiting Chair at the University of Connecticut, before returning to the **University of Nigeria, Nsukka** in 1976. He maintained strong links with the University of Massachusetts, however. In May 1977, he returned there to be awarded an Honorary Doctorate of Humane Letters. A decade later, he accepted an invitation from the W.E.B. Du Bois Department of Afro-American Studies and Professor Jules Chametzky, director of the University's Institute of Advanced Study in the Humanities, to spend a year at Amherst together with a distinguished group of black writers who were to include **James Baldwin** and John Wideman, as well as existing staff such as Michael Thelwell and Julius Lester. Sadly, James Baldwin died in November 1987, and Achebe presented a moving memorial address at the service held for Baldwin in December 1987. While at Amherst that year, he again taught an undergraduate course on African literature and led a series of interdisciplinary seminars for faculty and peers.

Achebe's seventieth birthday celebrations in November 2000 were attended by a large contingent of colleagues from the University of Massachusetts, including Michael Thelwell, John Wideman, and Esther Terry. In 2001, he was able to revisit Amherst himself to give an enthusiastically received lecture.

C. L. Innes

UNIVERSITY OF NIGERIA, NSUKKA. Originally envisioned as early as 1919, the University of Nigeria was formally conceived in a report of the International Bank Mission on the Economic Development of Nigeria in

1954. The university opened its doors in 1960 in **Nsukka, Nigeria**, coincident with the attainment of Nigerian independence. The university was intended to serve as the national university of Nigeria as a leading center of scholarship and education in Africa. The university now also has a campus at Enugu and continues to grow despite the many tribulations of postcolonial Nigeria. Achebe became a Senior Research Fellow at the Nsukka campus in 1967 and continued working and teaching at the school until 1972. After a term as a visiting professor at the **University of Massachusetts at Amherst**, Achebe returned to Nsukka in 1976 as a professor of English. Since 1984, he has been a professor emeritus at the university. A special symposium was held at the university in 1990 to celebrate Achebe's sixtieth birthday. The proceedings of that symposium are published as *Eagle on Iroko*.

FURTHER READING

Angus Obinna Chukwuka, *To Restore the Dignity of Man*; Emmanuel Obiechina, Chukwuemeka Ike, and John Anenechukwu Umeh, eds., *The University of Nigeria, 1960–1985*.

M. Keith Booker

UNOKA, father of **Okonkwo** in *Things Fall Apart*. Though a talented musician, Unoka (who died ten years before the opening of the novel) had been lazy and irresponsible. He had acquired no wealth or titles and had, in fact, been in debt when he died. In chapter 1, he is described as a coward who cannot stand the sight of blood. His son, Okonkwo, spends much of his life attempting to overcome what he sees as the weak and shameful legacy left by his father. In chapter 3, we learn that Unoka died of a swelling in the stomach and limbs (now known as dropsy), a malady that is considered an abomination to the earth goddess **Ani**. As a result, Unoka was carried away into the **Evil Forest** and allowed to die alone without burial. The memory of this death reinforces Okonkwo's sense of shame.

M. Keith Booker

URI. The day of *uri* is a traditional **Igbo** day of celebration, marking the day when a girl's suitor and his relatives bring palm-wine as an offering to her family in order to help negotiate a **bride-price**. Chapter 12 of *Things Fall Apart* describes the *uri* day of **Akueke**, daughter of **Obierika**.

M. Keith Booker

URUA, the home village of **Odili Samalu**, the narrator of *A Man of the People*. It is located fifteen miles from **Anata**, where Samalu teaches at the **Anata Grammar School** at the beginning of the novel.

M. Keith Booker

UZOWULU, the husband of **Mgbafo** in *Things Fall Apart*. In chapter 10, Mgbafo and her children are taken from her husband's home by her brothers because the husband frequently beats her. **Evil Forest**, the leader of the *egwugwu* who gather to adjudicate the case, ordains that Mgbafo be returned to her husband after Uzowulu pays a penance of wine to the in-laws.

M. Keith Booker

V

VOICE OF NIGERIA, a broadcasting corporation that operates under the auspices of the Nigerian government, charged with disseminating information about **Nigeria** and Africa to the world at large. The administration offices of the corporation are in the national capital of **Abuja**, but programming is produced in both Abuja and **Lagos**. Now an independent organization, the Voice of Nigeria began in 1961 as the external service of the **Nigerian Broadcasting Corporation (NBC)**. Its founding was spearheaded by Achebe, who was then Director of External Broadcasting for NBC.

M. Keith Booker

W

WADE, Assistant Superintendent of the Prison, **Okperi** (*Arrow of God*, chapter 3). Wade is also the only person in the area who has access to an automobile, in which he is frequently called upon to deliver sick officers to the mission hospital at **Nkisa** (*Arrow of God*, chapter 13).

Rachel R. Reynolds

WAGADA, ALHAJI CHIEF SENATOR SULEIMAN, the Minister of Foreign Trade in the government of the fictional African postcolonial nation featured in *A Man of the People*. Wagada's corrupt practices in dealing with foreign corporations such as **British Amalgamated** trigger a national scandal that topples the government and leads to new parliamentary elections in chapter 10 of the novel. There are suggestions, however, that Wagada is no more corrupt than anyone else in the government and that he is merely following a tradition set by his predecessor as Minister of Foreign Trade, **Chief Nanga**.

M. Keith Booker

WARNER, SISTER, the only other European woman in the region of **Umuaro** in *Arrow of God* besides **Mary Savage**. She is a nurse who works in the **Nkisa** mission hospital with Dr. Savage (*Arrow of God*, chapter 13).

Rachel R. Reynolds

WATKINSON, Senior District Officer who was promoted above **Winterbottom**, although Winterbottom was three years his senior (*Arrow of God*, chapter 5).

Rachel R. Reynolds

WAUGH, EVELYN (1903–1966). English writer whose novel *A Handful of Dust* is cited by **Obi Okonkwo** in chapter 5 of *No Longer at Ease* in support of his concept of tragedy.

Thomas J. Lynn

WAYA, a small roadside market that has been established to serve the **Anata Grammar School** in *A Man of the People*.

M. Keith Booker

WEEK OF PEACE, an annual week devoted to the earth goddess **Ani**, held just before the planting of new crops in order to ask the favor of Ani in overseeing the success of the new planting. During the week, no one is allowed to work or to behave in a violent or disruptive manner, a rule that **Okonkwo** breaks in chapter 4 of *Things Fall Apart* by beating his youngest wife, **Ojiugo**, in a fit of anger. This planting celebration is the counterpart of the **Feast of the New Yam**, a harvest celebration.

M. Keith Booker

WEST AFRICA, by F. J. Pedler (1951), is a broad introduction to the land, people, customs, and social systems of West Africa. It begins with a chapter entitled "The Country" that serves as a sort of travelogue introducing readers to general features of the landscape and local environment in the region. It then follows with a rather ethnographic chapter on "The People" and chapters discussing the history, politics, and economics of colonial West Africa. At the time of its publication it was one of the better introductions to the region for general readers, though it is now obviously somewhat dated.

Intended for Western readers, the book is sometimes condescending in its comments on Africa, and it certainly contains its share of colonialist stereotypes. Pedler is also perhaps a bit too generous in his assessment of the benevolence and beneficence of the French and (especially) British colonial rulers of the various regions of West Africa. On the other hand, Pedler clearly intends to be sympathetic in his representation of the people and societies of West Africa. Achebe, in *Home and Exile*, has described the book as "remarkably advanced for its time, and even for today" (42). For example, Pedler sometimes takes pains to correct misleading Western stereotypes about African people and their customs. However, what Achebe finds especially important is the fact that Pedler takes the trouble to cite writings by Africans, thus acknowledging that the most accurate and informative representations of African people and African life are those produced by Africans themselves. Indeed, quoting from two African short stories to help make this point, Pedler concludes that the effectiveness of these stories leaves one "with the hope that more West Africans may enter the field of authorship and give us authentic stories of the lives of their own people" (51). Published in 1951 (one year before the publication of **Amos Tutuola**'s *The Palm-Wine Drinkard*), these words, in restrospect, seem prophetic in their ability to imagine the coming emergence of African fiction as a vital force in world literature.

FURTHER READING

Achebe, *Home and Exile*.

M. Keith Booker

"WHAT DO AFRICAN INTELLECTUALS READ?" Achebe essay. See *Morning Yet on Creation Day*.

"WHAT HAS LITERATURE GOT TO DO WITH IT?" See *Hopes and Impediments*.

"WHERE ANGELS FEAR TO TREAD." See *Morning Yet on Creation Day*.

WINTERBOTTOM, CAPTAIN THOMAS K. "Old Tom," as he is called by **John Wright**, or Wintabota, as he is called by **Igbo** people, or "Otiji-Egbe," meaning "breaker of guns" after an incident in which he stopped the **Okperi–Umuaro** war by confiscating all the guns in the village in *Arrow of God*. Winterbottom is the British District Officer assigned to the **Okperi** region of Igboland. He has been tempered in the war in Cameroon and sees himself as a career officer in Africa, and yet at the same time he is rankled by having been passed over for promotions. He is a dutiful member of the British army and enforces the policy of **indirect rule**, even though he is personally against the idea (see **Ikedi** for the story of how indirect rule has not worked in Winterbottom's district); Winterbottom himself would rather see local people missionized and Anglicized (*Arrow of God*, chapter 5). Most of what we know about Winterbottom is revealed slowly through the gossip of other Europeans. In chapter 8, for example, Wright tells us that Winterbottom grew up in a missionary family and was abandoned by his wife. Using this device, Achebe presents competing interests among the British and their officers and workers.

Rachel R. Reynolds

"WORK AND PLAY IN TUTUOLA'S *THE PALM-WINE DRINKARD*." See *Hopes and Impediments*.

WREN, ROBERT M. (1928–1989), a pioneering Western scholar of African literature and culture who made important contributions to the international critical reputations of Achebe and other African writers. Born in Washington, D.C., Wren was educated at the University of Houston and at Princeton University, where he received his Ph.D. in 1965. Wren's initial research focused on Northern European theater, but in 1968 he shifted his interests to African literature. He held academic appointments as Instructor in English, Douglas College at Rutgers University (1956–1960); Instructor in Drama, State University of New York at Binghamton (1960–1962); Instructor in English, Knox College, Galesburg, Illinois (1964–1965); and at the University of Houston as Assistant Professor (1965–1968); Associate Professor (1968–1979); and Professor (1979–1989).

Wren was twice a Senior Fulbright Lecturer in **Nigeria**, and much of his scholarly work dealt with Nigerian literature and culture. His first appointment, from 1973 to 1975, at the University of Lagos, was at the invitation of writer and English Department Chair, **J. P. Clark**, on whose work Wren later published a book (1984). While at Lagos, Wren became interested in the work of

Achebe, and he went on to make important contributions to Achebe scholarship, including the extremely useful *Achebe's World: The Historical and Cultural Context of the Novels of Chinua Achebe* (1980). Wren spent his second Fulbright fellowship at the **University of Ibadan** from 1982 to 1983, at which time he compiled the notes that eventually evolved into the writing of his survey of the historical genesis of modern Nigerian literature, *Those Magical Years: The Making of Nigerian Literature: 1948–1966* (published posthumously in 1991).

In addition to his books on African literature, Wren published numerous articles on American and African literature, European Renaissance, seventeenth-century theater, and religion. He also wrote fiction under the pen name Robert Campbell. He was killed June 11, 1989, when a Scenic Air Tours plane crashed in Hawaii. At the time, he was visiting Hawaii prior to taking a Fulbright fellowship in Indonesia. A collection of Wren's papers resides at the Harry Ransom Humanities Research Center at the University of Texas at Austin, from whose Web site (http://www.hrc.utexas.edu/research/fa/wren.html) much of the information in this entry was derived.

FURTHER READING

Robert M. Wren, *Achebe's World*, *J. P. Clark*, and *Those Magical Years*.

M. Keith Booker

WRIGHT, JOHN, a Britisher who works for the Public Works Department (PWD) and is responsible for building the road between **Okperi** and **Umuaro** in *Arrow of God*. Wright, like **Tony Clarke**, is a member of a social class below **Winterbottom**, whom Wright sees as both a symbol of administrative red tape (chapter 8) and a rigid symbol of Anglican propriety (chapter 10). Likewise, Winterbottom sees Wright as having lowered himself through his "behavior" with African women (chapter 3), and Winterbottom has banned Wright from the colonial officers mess club (chapter 3). In this sense, Achebe is using Wright as both a symbol and a plot device for showing how Europeans of various class affiliations relate to each other and relate to the Africans around them. For example, in a flash of uncontrolled anger, Wright lashes **Obika** in front of his age-mates for arriving late to work on the road—both a loss of emotional control and an act of physical engagement with Africans that Winterbottom would utterly avoid; indeed, Clarke selectively protects Wright from punishment by Winterbottom for the transgression by leaving the whipping incident out of Clarke's official report to the Captain. Nonetheless, Wright occasionally has sympathetic thoughts about the foremen of his road crew—even if they are based on miscommunications—that ironically make this cruel man emotionally closer to the inhabitants of Umuaro than any other of the Europeans. However, as K.W.J. Post points out, Wright and the other Europeans are only skeletal character profiles. Instead, Achebe concentrates on the portrayal of **Igbo** villagers' states of mind, and he usually develops his portrayal of colonists only as foils to the states of mind of Igbo folks. See the entries on **Otakagu** and on Clarke for an analysis of how this principle works in Achebe.

FURTHER READING

Abdul R. JanMohamed, *Manichean Aesthetics*; K.W.J. Post, Introduction *to Arrow of God*.

Rachel R. Reynolds

WRIGHT, MRS. In chapter 3 of *No Longer at Ease*, an elderly woman returning to **Freetown**, Sierra Leone, from **Liverpool**, England, on the **MV *Sasa***. At the beginning of the voyage **Obi Okonkwo** and **Clara Okeke** meet for a second time shortly after he sees her holding a conversation with Mrs. Wright and **John Macmillan**.

Thomas J. Lynn

"THE WRITER AND HIS COMMUNITY." See *Hopes and Impediments*.

THE WRITINGS OF CHINUA ACHEBE, by **G. D. Killam** was published in 1977, revising and expanding Killam's earlier *The Novels of Chinua Achebe* (1969) to include discussion of Achebe's poetry and short stories. Killam's book was one of the first major critical studies of Achebe's work and remains indispensable, especially in its expanded form. Even though Killam's book obviously does not discuss **Anthills of the Savannah**, its discussion of Achebe's first four novels, short stories, and poetry provides an excellent background to all of Achebe's work, even including that late novel. For example, Killam's study, including his introduction to the 1977 revision, greatly facilitates the interpretive work required for understanding **Ikem Osodi**'s aesthetic statement to **Beatrice Okoh** in *Anthills of the Savannah*.

In the introduction, Killam makes good use of informative quotations from Achebe's essays to bolster his claim that Achebe's "prose writing reflects three essential and related concerns": (1) "the legacy of colonialism at both the individual and societal level," (2) "the *fact* of English as a language of national and international exchange," and (3) "the obligations and responsibilities of the writer both to the society in which he lives and to his art" (3). Killam reminds his reader that Achebe refers to the yoking of Africa and Europe during "the imperial-colonial period" as the "chance encounter" (2). Addressing the **language question** in African literature, Killam notes that the legacy of this chance encounter, in its unavoidable alterations of African cultures, has resulted in the ironies and ambiguities that have conditioned the ethical and moral choices of both individual and society while providing African cultures with European languages that supervene over the great multiplicity of African languages. Thus, disparate African cultures were unified in voices of undeniable international significance. In short, paraphrasing Killam and Achebe, colonialism may not have provided the African a "song," but it provided "a tongue at least for singing" (5). So Achebe, in Killam's discussion, is committed to the use of English for purposes of mutual communication among disparate peoples and for the reclamation of African dignity; the African writer who writes in English, for example, is to aim, as Achebe urges, "at fashioning out an English which is at once universal and able to carry his peculiar experience" (8, 6).

This is not to say, however, that Achebe is a writer concerned only to explain a Nigerian experience of the world, anymore than Joyce can be said to have concerned himself with an explanation of an Irish experience of the world. Certainly Achebe's work demonstrates "a pre-occupation with certain basic themes, of which the legacy of colonial rule is the central core"; however, "the destructive consequences of the rule of the colonial period. . . . are not displayed for their own sake. They are there because they arise out of and reflect to a sensitive mind a manifest indifference and caprice which mirrors life itself" (11)—hence, the manifestations of ironies and ambiguities in Achebe's novels and stories that sometimes make for inconclusive or open endings that are arguably the hallmark of the postmodern.

These ironies and ambiguities—the failures of **Okonkwo** in light of his success at avoiding his father's failures; **Obi Okonkwo**'s failures as civil servant despite his best efforts to come to grips with a traditional world on the cusp of the more modern; **Ezeulu**'s faithful service gone awry—are not endemic to racial or ethnic differences. As Killam quotes Achebe, they are instead the result of "differences between the established and emerging traditions," stemming "from a group past with its ambiguous and generally bitter experience of colonialism, and from a group present which seeks to define the relevance of the colonial past to the present" (3). They are then the universally modern experience peculiar to Africa. Killam's work, attentive to theme and plot detail, makes this point very clearly. Killam thus helps further the liberation of African literature from the singular confines of ethnic or postcolonial literature.

Of special note in Killam's work is his discussion of female and male principles and of the failure of the male principle in Achebe's stories when this principle is insufficiently informed by the female. Killam's elaboration that the centrality of that which is female is not limited to procreation or merely to biological creativity in Achebe's fictional depictions of women puts the reader better in mind of the timelessness of Achebe's work and prepares the reader for Beatrice's supreme importance in *Anthills of the Savannah.*

Killam's work measures well against more current postcolonial criticism that takes the reader into the literary and critical issues of the postmodern through which he or she is to re-value previous generations' readings and interpretations of Achebe's work. This then is the sense in which Killam's work is classic to the study of Achebe's. The reader is given a chapter each for the first four novels, a chapter on the stories, a chapter on the poetry, as well as a framing introduction and a brief conclusion iterating certain of Abiola Irele's claims for Achebe's work, which Killam quotes:

The importance of Chinua Achebe's novels derives not simply from his theme, but also from his complete presentation of men in action, in living reaction to their fate, as well as from his own perception that underlies his imaginative world and confers upon it relevance and truth. (129)

FURTHER READING
Abiola Irele, "The Tragic Conflict in Achebe's Novels."

Susan Williams

Y

YABA, a mainland section of **Lagos** in which **Clara Okeke**, prior to her appointment as an Assistant Nursing Sister, lives with a cousin, as indicated in chapters 7 and 11 of *No Longer at Ease*.

Thomas J. Lynn

YAM, "King of Crops" as Achebe calls it in *Things Fall Apart*, is a tuberous plant with a vinelike stem covered with thorns like those of a rosebush. It is not to be confused with sweet potato, which Americans call yam. African yam comes in various sizes, shapes, and colors. There are yams that can measure up to ten or more inches in diameter and upward of two feet in length. The outer skin is brown and is covered with coarse or fine stringy "hairs." When peeled, the true color could be pure white, pale pink, or pale or deep yellow. The yam mentioned in Achebe's novels is a staple food in most parts of Igboland. Before the era of money currency and bank accounts, one's wealth was measured by the extent of one's yam barn. Anyone who could feed his or her family on yam from one harvest to another was considered wealthy. The primary purpose for yam farming is to provide food for the family. There are multiple ways of preparing yam as a meal: it can be boiled and pounded into foo-foo and eaten with a rich sauce; it can be boiled and eaten with all kinds of sauces or dips; it can be roasted on an open fire or under wood ash; it can be fried; it can be dried and turned into flour. The secondary purpose for the yam farmer is to raise money for the family by selling yams. In parts of Igboland like Owerri, yam forms part of the dowry that a bride takes with her to start her own yam barn at her new home.

FURTHER READING

G. E. Igwe, *Igbo-English Dictionary* (entry under "Ji"—the Igbo word for yam).

Phanuel Akubueze Egejuru

YEATS, W(ILLIAM) B(UTLER) (1865–1939). Important Anglo-Irish poet and dramatist, the son of prominent portrait painter John Butler Yeats. Born in Dublin, Yeats studied at the School of Art there before deciding to devote himself to poetry rather than following his father into painting. One of the most important Anglophone poets of the twentieth century, Yeats had a long and productive career that stretched from the late 1880s to the late 1930s and saw him go through various stages as a poet, including an early stage heavily influenced by Romanticism and later stages that reflect the emergence of modernism. Yeats's poetry also shows his interest in spiritualism and the occult, especially in theosophy. His writing was importantly influenced by his participation in the anticolonial activities of the Irish Nationalist movement, making him a predecessor of later anticolonial writers. Yeats's poem **"The Second Coming"** provides the epigraph and title for Achebe's *Things Fall Apart*.

FURTHER READING

Richard Ellmann, *Yeats: The Man and the Masks*; Edward Said, "Yeats and Decolonization."

M. Keith Booker

Z

ZACCHAEUS, the first of **Obi Okonkwo**'s two stewards in *No Longer at Ease* (the second being **Sebastian**). Zacchaeus quits his position with Obi possibly because he resents **Clara Okeke**'s insensitive treatment of him, or perhaps because he does not like taking orders from a woman (chapter 2).

Thomas J. Lynn

Bibliography

Achebe, Chinua. "Achebe on Editing." *World Literature Written in English* 27 (1987): 1–5.

———. "African Literature as Restoration of Celebration." Petersen and Rutherford, *Chinua Achebe* 1–10.

———. "Amos Tutuola." *Radio Times* (Lagos) (23–29 July 1961): 15.

———. *Arrow of God*. 1964. Rev. ed. 1974. New York: Anchor-Doubleday, 1989.

———. *Beware, Soul Brother and Other Poems*. Enugu: Nwankwo-Ifejika, 1971. Revised and expanded edition, London: Heinemann Educational Books, 1972. Reprinted as *Christmas in Biafra and Other Poems*. Garden City, NY: Anchor-Doubleday, 1973.

———. *Chike and the River*. Cambridge: Cambridge UP, 1966.

———. *The Drum*. Enugu, Nigeria: Fourth Dimension, 1979.

———. "The Education of a 'British Protected Child.' " *Cambridge Review* 114 (June 1993): 51–57.

———. *The Flute*. Enugu, Nigeria: Fourth Dimension, 1979.

———. *Home and Exile*. New York: Oxford UP, 2000.

———. *Hopes and Impediments: Selected Essays*. London: Heinemann, 1988.

———. *How the Leopard Got His Claws*. 1972. New York: Third P, 1973.

———. "An Image of Africa: Racism in Conrad's *Heart of Darkness*." *Massachusetts Review* 18.4 (Winter 1977): 782–94.

———. Interview with Jane Wilkinson. *Talking with African Writers*. Ed. Wilkinson. Portsmouth, NH: Heinemann, 1992. 46–57.

———. "The Judge and I Didn't Go to Namibia." *Callaloo* 3.1 (1990): 82–84.

———. *A Man of the People*. 1966. New York: Anchor-Doubleday, 1989.

———. *Morning Yet on Creation Day: Essays*. London: Heinemann, 1975.

———. *No Longer at Ease*. 1960. New York: Anchor-Doubleday, 1994.

———. "The *Okike* Story." *Okike* 21 (1982): 1–5.

———. "On Janheinz Jahn and Ezekiel Mphahlele." *Transition* 8 (1963): 9.

———. *The Sacrificial Egg and Other Stories*. Onitsha, Nigeria: Etudo, 1962. Expanded as *Girls at War and Other Stories*. London: Heinemann Educational Books, 1972, and Garden City, NY: Anchor-Doubleday, 1973.

———. "Teaching *Things Fall Apart*." Lindfors, *Approaches to Teaching Achebe's* Things Fall Apart 20–24.

———. *Things Fall Apart*. 1958. Expanded edition with notes. Portsmouth, NH: Heinemann, 1996.

———. *The Trouble with Nigeria*. 1983. Oxford: Heinemann, 1984.

———. *The University and the Leadership Fac-*

tor in Nigerian Politics. Lagos: Abik Books, 1988.

———, and C. L. Innes, eds. *African Short Stories: Twenty Stories from Across the Continent*. 1985. Portsmouth, NH: Heinemann, 1987.

———, and C. L. Innes, eds. *The Heinemann Book of Contemporary African Short Stories*. Portsmouth, NH: Heinemann, 1992.

———, and Dubem Okafor, eds. *Don't Let Him Die: An Anthology of Memorial Poems for Christopher Okigbo (1932–1967)*. Enugu, Nigeria: Fourth Dimension Publishers, 1978.

Adeeko, Adeleke. "Contests of Text and Context in Chinua Achebe's *Arrow of God*." *Ariel: A Review of International English Literature* 23.3 (1992): 7–22.

Afigbo, A. E. *The Warrant Chiefs: Indirect Rule in Southeastern Nigeria, 1891–1929*. London: Longman, 1972.

Afonja, Simi, and Bisi Aina, eds. *Nigerian Women in Social Change*. Ile-Ife: Obafemi Awolowo UP, 1995.

Ahmad, Aijaz. *In Theory: Classes, Nations, Literatures*. London: Verso, 1992.

Aidoo, Ama Ata. *Our Sister Killjoy, or Reflections from a Black-Eyed Squint*. 1977. White Plains, NY: Longman, 1994.

Akwanya, Amechi. "Ambiguous Signs: Disruption in Achebe's *Things Fall Apart* and *Arrow of God*." *Okike: An African Journal of New Writing* 33 (June 1996): 60–74.

Alden, Patricia. "New Women and Old Myths: Chinua Achebe's *Anthills of the Savannah* and Nuruddin Farah's *Sardines*." Ehling, *Critical Approaches to* Anthills of the Savannah 67–80.

Alessandrini, Anthony, ed. *Frantz Fanon: Critical Perspectives*. London: Routledge, 1999.

Amadi, Elechi. *Sunset in Biafra: A Civil War Diary*. London: Heinemann, 1973.

Amadiume, Ifi. "Class and Gender in *Anthills of the Savannah*." *PAL Platform* 1.1 (March 1989): 8–9.

Appiah, Kwame Anthony. *In My Father's House: Africa in the Philosophy of Culture*. New York: Oxford UP, 1992.

Aristotle. *Art of Rhetoric*. Trans. J. H. Freese. Cambridge, MA: Harvard UP, 1991.

Armah, Ayi Kwei. *The Beautyful Ones Are Not Yet Born*. London: Heinemann, 1969.

———. *Two Thousand Seasons*. Chicago: Third World P, 1979.

Ashcroft, Bill, Gareth Griffiths, and Helen Tiffin. *The Empire Writes Back: Theory and Practice in Post-Colonial Literatures*. London: Routledge, 1989.

Asiegbu, Johnson U. J. *Nigeria and Its British Invaders, 1851–1920: A Thematic Documentary History*. New York: NOK International, 1984.

Awoonor, Kofi. *This Earth, My Brother*. London: Heinemann, 1972.

Azikiwe, Nnamdi. *My Odyssey: An Autobiography*. New York: Praeger, 1970.

Babalola, C. A. "A Reconsideration of Achebe's *No Longer at Ease*." *Phylon* 47.2 (1986): 139–47.

Bacon, Katie. "An African Voice." *Atlantic Monthly* (August 2, 2000). Available online at http://www.theatlantic.com/unbound/interviews/ba2000-08-02.htm.

Baines, Jocelyn. *Joseph Conrad: A Critical Biography*. New York: McGraw-Hill, 1960.

Bakhtin, Mikhail M. *The Dialogic Imagination*. Ed. Michael Holquist. Trans. Caryl Emerson and Michael Holquist. Austin: U of Texas P, 1981.

Bamgbose, Ayo. *The Novels of D. O. Fagunwa*. Benin City, Nigeria: Ethiope P, 1974.

Bamiro, Edmund O. "The Social and Functional Power of Nigerian English." *World Englishes* 10.3 (1991): 275–86.

Basden, G. T. *Among the Ibos of Nigeria*. 1921. London: Frank Cass, 1966.

———. *Niger Ibos*. 1938. London: Frank Cass, 1966.

Bastian, Misty. "Irregular Visitors: Narratives about *Ogbaanje* (Spirit Children) in Southern Nigerian Popular Writing." *Readings in African Popular Fiction*. Ed. Stephanie Newell, Bloomington: Indiana UP, 2001. 59–67.

Beier, Ulli. "Fagunwa, a Yoruba Novelist." *Black Orpheus* 17 (1965): 51–56.

Beilis, Viktor. "Ghosts, People, and Books of Yorubaland." *Research in African Literatures* 18 (1987): 447–57.

Ben-Amos, Paula. *The Art of Benin*. New York: Thames and Hudson, 1980.

Benson, Peter. *"Black Orpheus," "Transition," and Modern Cultural Awakening in Africa*. Berkeley: U of California P, 1986.

Bhabha, Homi K. *The Location of Culture*. London: Routledge, 1994.

Bishop, Alan. *Joyce Cary: Gentleman Rider*. Oxford: Oxford UP, 1989.

Boehmer, Elleke. *Colonial and Postcolonial Literature: Migrant Metaphors*. New York: Oxford UP, 1995.

Booker, M. Keith. *The African Novel in English: An Introduction*. Portsmouth, NH: Heinemann, 1998.

———. "Marxist Literary Criticism." *A Practical Introduction to Literary Theory and Criticism*. New York: Longman, 1996. 71–88.

———. "Multicultural Approaches to *Heart of Darkness*." *A Practical Introduction to Literary Theory and Criticism*. New York: Longman, 1996. 219–25.

———. *Ulysses, Capitalism, and Colonialism: Reading Joyce after the Cold War*. Westport, CT: Greenwood P, 2000.

———. "Writing for the Wretched of the Earth: Frantz Fanon and the Radical African Novel." *Rereading Global Socialist Cultures after the Cold War: The Reassessment of a Tradition*. Ed. Dubravka Juraga and M. Keith Booker. New York: Praeger, 2002. 115–48.

———, and Dubravka Juraga. *The Caribbean Novel in English: An Introduction*. Portsmouth, NH: Heinemann, 2001.

Booth, James. *Writers and Politics in Nigeria*. New York: Africana Publishing Company, 1981.

Booth, Wayne. *The Rhetoric of Fiction*. 2nd ed. Chicago: U of Chicago P, 1983.

Brennan, Timothy. *At Home in the World: Cosmopolitanism Now*. Cambridge, MA: Harvard UP, 1997.

———. *Salman Rushdie and the Third World*. New York: St. Martin's P, 1989.

Brown, Lloyd W. "Cultural Norms and Modes of

Perception in Achebe's Fiction." *Research in African Literatures* 3.1 (1972): 21–35.

———. "The Historical Sense: T. S. Eliot and Two African Writers." *The Conch* 3.1 (1971): 59–70.

Buchan, John. *The Four Adventures of Richard Hannay (The Thirty-Nine Steps, Greenmantle, Mr. Standfast, The Three Hostages)*. 1933. Boston: David R. Godine Publishers, 1988.

Burke, Kenneth. *Language as a Symbolic Action: Essays on Life, Literature, and Method*. Berkeley: U of California P, 1966.

Carroll, David. *Chinua Achebe: Novelist, Poet, Critic*. 2nd ed. Houndmills, UK: Macmillan, 1990.

———. *George Eliot and the Conflict of Interpretations: A Reading of the Novels*. New York: Cambridge UP, 1992.

———, ed. *George Eliot: The Critical Heritage*. New York: Barnes and Noble, 1971.

———, ed. *Middlemarch*, by George Eliot. New York: Clarendon P–Oxford UP, 1986.

Cary, Joyce. *Mister Johnson*. 1939. New York: W. W. Norton, 1989.

Caute, David. *Frantz Fanon*. New York: Viking, 1970.

Chinweizu, Onwuchekwa Jemie, and Ihechukwu Madubuike. *Toward the Decolonization of African Literature: African Fiction and Poetry and Their Critics*. Washington, DC: Howard UP, 1983.

Chukwuka, Angus Obinna. *To Restore the Dignity of Man: The Challenge of the University of Nigeria*. Enugu, Nigeria: Jemesie Associates, 1998.

Cobham, Rhonda. "Making Men and History: Achebe and the Politics of Revisionism." Lindfors, *Approaches to Teaching Achebe's Things Fall Apart* 91–100.

Colmer, Rosemary. "The Start of Weeping Is Always Hard: The Ironic Structure of *No Longer at Ease*." *The Literary Half-Yearly* (Guest Editor: Bruce King.) 21.1 (1980): 121–35.

Cook, David, and Michael Okenimkpe. *Ngugi wa Thiong'o: An Exploration of His Writings*. London: Heinemann, 1983.

Coquery-Vidrovitch, Catherine. *Africa: Endurance and Change South of the Sahara*. Trans. David Maisel. Berkeley: U of California P, 1988.

Criswell, Stephen. "Colonialism, Corruption, and Culture: A Fanonian Reading of *Mister Johnson* and *No Longer at Ease*." *Literary Griot* 10.1 (1998): 43–64.

———. "Okonkowo as Yeatsian Hero: The Influence of W. B. Yeats on Chinua Achebe's *Things Fall Apart*." *Literary Criterion* 30.4 (1995): 1–14.

Crowder, Michael. *Nigeria: An Introduction to Its History*. London: Longman, 1979.

———. *The Story of Nigeria*. 4th ed. London: Faber, 1977.

Curtin, Philip D. *The Image of Africa: British Ideas and Action, 1780–1850*. Madison: U of Wisconsin P, 1964.

Dasenbrock, Reed Way. "Creating a Past: Achebe, Naipaul, Soyinka, Farah." *Salmagundi* 68 (1986): 312–32.

Dash, J. Michael. "The Outsider in West African Fiction: An Approach to Three Novels." *The Literary Half-Yearly* (Guest Editor: Bruce King.) 21.1 (1980): 19–29.

Dathorne, O. R. "Amos Tutuola: The Nightmare of the Tribe." *Introduction to Nigerian Literature*. Ed. Bruce King. London: Evans, 1971.

Davidson, Basil. *The Black Man's Burden: Africa and the Curse of the Nation-State*. New York: Times Books–Random House, 1992.

———. *Let Freedom Come: Africa in Modern History*. Boston: Little, Brown, 1978.

———. *The Search for Africa: History, Culture, Politics*. New York: Times Books–Random House, 1994.

Davis, Richard S. "In Search of Agency among Colonized Africans: Chinua Achebe's *No Longer at Ease* and Joyce Cary's *Mister Johnson*." *Journal of Commonwealth and Postcolonial Studies* 2.1 (1994): 12–26.

Diamond, Larry Jay. *Class, Ethnicity, and Democracy in Nigeria: The Failure of the First Republic*. Basingstoke: Macmillan, 1988.

Dirlik, Arif. *The Postcolonial Aura: Third World Criticism in the Age of Global Capitalism*. Boulder, CO: Westview P, 1997.

Dow, Miriam. "A Postcolonial Child: Achebe's Chike at the Crossroads." *Children's Literature Association Quarterly* 22.4 (Winter 1997–1998): 160–65.

Eagleton, Terry. *Marxism and Literary Criticism*. Berkeley: U of California P, 1976.

———, and Drew Milne, eds. *Marxist Literary Theory: A Reader*. Oxford: Blackwell, 1996.

Echeruo, M.J.C. Introduction. *The Sacrificial Egg and Other Short Stories*. By Chinua Achebe. Onitsha, Nigeria: Etudo Limited Onitsha, 1962. 3–6.

Echeruo, Michael. *Igbo-English Dictionary: A Comprehensive Dictionary of the Igbo Language, with an English-Igbo Index*. New Haven, CT: Yale UP, 1998.

Egejuru, Phanuel A. *Chinua Acehbe: Pure and Simple, An Oral Biography*. Lagos: Malthouse P, 2002.

Ehling, Holger G., ed. *Critical Approaches to Anthills of the Savannah*. Amsterdam: Rodopi, 1991.

Ekwe-Ekwe, Herbert. *The Biafra War: Nigeria and the Aftermath*. Lewiston, NY: Mellen, 1990.

Elder, Arlene A. "The Paradoxical Characterization of Okonkwo." Lindfors, *Approaches to Teaching Achebe's* Things Fall Apart 58–64.

Elimimian, Isaac I. *The Poetry of J. P. Clark Bekederemo*. Ikeja, Nigeria: Longman Nigeria, 1989.

Ellmann, Richard. *Yeats: The Man and the Masks*. New York: Macmillan, 1948.

Elugbe, Ben Ohiomamhe, and Augusta Phil Omamor. *Nigerian Pidgin: Background and Prospects*. Ibadan, Nigeria: Heinemann Educational Books, 1991.

Emecheta, Buchi. *The Bride Price*. New York: Braziller, 1976.

Emenyonu, Ernest N. "Chinua Achebe's *Things Fall Apart*: A Classic Study in Diplomatic Tactlessness." Petersen and Rutherford, *Chinua Achebe* 83–88.

———. "(Re)Inventing the Past for the Present: Symbolism in Chinua Achebe's *How the Leopard Got His Claws.*" *Bookbird: A Journal of International Children's Literature* 36.1 (Spring 1998): 6–11.

———. *The Rise of the Igbo Novel.* Ibadan: Oxford UP, 1978.

Esonwanne, Uzoma, ed. *Critical Essays on Christopher Okigbo.* New York: G. K. Hall, 2000.

Ezenwa-Ohaeto. *Chinua Achebe: A Biography.* Oxford: James Currey; Bloomington: Indiana UP, 1997.

Fabre, Michel. "Chinua Achebe on *Arrow of God.*" Lindfors, *Conversations with Chinua Achebe.*

Fanon, Frantz. *Black Skin, White Masks.* Trans. Charles Lam Markmann. New York: Grove P, 1967.

———. *The Wretched of the Earth.* Trans. Constance Farrington. New York: Grove P, 1968.

Faraclas, Nicholas. *Nigerian Pidgin.* New York: Routledge, 1996.

Feinstein, Alan. *African Revolutionary: The Life and Times of Nigeria's Aminu Kano.* Rev. ed. Enugu, Nigeria: Fourth Dimension P, 1987.

Feldman, Gayle. "Chinua Achebe: Views of Home From Afar." *Publishers Weekly* (July 3, 2000). Available online at http://publishersweekly.reviewsnews.com/index.asp?layout=article&articleid=CA168436.

Ferris, William R., Jr. "Folklore and the African Novelist: Achebe and Tutuola." *Journal of American Folklore* 86 (1973): 25–36.

Forsyth, Frederick. *The Biafra Story: The Making of an African Legend.* 1969. London: Leo Cooper, 2001.

Gagiano, Annie. *Achebe, Head, Marechera: On Power and Change in Africa.* Boulder, CO: Lynne Rienner, 2000.

Gibbs, James. *Wole Soyinka.* New York: Grove P, 1986.

Gikandi, Simon. "Chinua Achebe and the Poetics of Location: The Uses of Space in *Things Fall Apart* and *No Longer at Ease.*" *Essays on African Writing 1: A Re-Evaluation.* Ed.

Abdulrazak Gurnah. Portsmouth, NH: Heinemann, 1993. 1–12.

———. *Maps of Englishness: Writing Identity in the Culture of Colonialism.* New York: Columbia UP, 1996.

———. *Ngugi wa Thiong'o.* New York: Cambridge UP, 2001.

———. *Reading Chinua Achebe: Language and Ideology in Fiction.* Portsmouth, NH: Heinemann, 1991.

———. *Reading the African Novel.* Portsmouth, NH: Heinemann, 1987.

———. *Writing in Limbo: Modernism and Caribbean Literature.* Ithaca, NY: Cornell UP, 1992.

———, ed. *Encyclopedia of African Literature.* New York: Routledge, 2002.

Goldie, Terry. "A Connection of Images: The Structure of Symbols in *The Beautyful Ones Are Not Yet Born.*" *Kunapipi* 1.1 (1979): 94–107.

Gordimer, Nadine. *Burger's Daughter.* 1979. New York: Penguin, 1980.

———. *A Sport of Nature.* London: Penguin, 1988.

———. "A Tyranny of Clowns." *New York Times* (February 2, 1988): 26.

Granqvist, Raoul, ed. *Travelling: Chinua Achebe in Scandinavia, Swedish Writers in Africa.* Umea, Sweden: Umea UP, 1990.

Greene, Graham. *The Heart of the Matter.* 1948. London: Penguin, 1971.

Gruesser, John Cullen. *White on Black: Contemporary Literature about Africa.* Urbana: U of Illinois P, 1992.

Gugelberger, Georg M., ed. *Marxism and African Literature.* London: James Currey, 1985.

Haggard, H. Rider. *Diary of an African Journey: The Return of Rider Haggard.* Ed. with an Introduction and Notes by Stephen Coan. Pietermaritzburg: U of Natal P, 2000.

Hall, Robert A., Jr. *Pidgin and Creole Languages.* Ithaca, NY: Cornell UP, 1966.

Hammond, Dorothy, and Alta Jablow. *The Myth of Africa.* (rev. ed. of *The Africa That Never Was*). New York: Library of Social Science, 1977.

Harlow, Barbara. " 'The Tortoise and the Birds': Strategies of Resistance in *Things Fall Apart*." Lindfors, *Approaches to Teaching Achebe's* Things Fall Apart 38–44.

Harris, Michael T. *Outsiders and Insiders: Perspectives of Third Word Culture in British and Post-colonial Fiction*. New York: Peter Lang, 1994.

Harris, Wilson. "The Frontier on which *Heart of Darkness* Stands." *Research on African Literatures* 12 (1981): 86–92.

Hawkins, Hunt. "Conrad's Critique of Imperialism in 'Heart of Darkness.' " *PMLA* 94.2 (1979): 286–99.

———. "The Issue of Racism in *Heart of Darkness*." *Conradiana* 14.3 (1982): 163–71.

Hegel, G.W.F. *Phenomenology of Spirit*. Trans. A. V. Miller. New York: Oxford UP, 1977.

———. *The Philosophy of History*. Trans. J. Sibree. New York: Dover, 1956.

Hill, Alan. *In Pursuit of Publishing*. London: John Murray in association with Heinemann Educational Books, 1988.

Hogan, Patrick Colm. "Understanding *The Palm-Wine Drinkard*." *Ariel: A Review of International English Literature* 31.4 (October 2000): 33–58.

Horton, Robin. "Stateless Societies in the History of West Africa." *History of West Africa*. Vol. 1, 3rd ed. Ed. J.F.A. Ajayi and Michael Crowder. New York: Longman, 1985.

Hortons, Oke. *A Man of the People*. Comic strip in *The New Nigerian*, Kaduna, 1974–1975.

Huggan, Graham. *The Postcolonial Exotic: Marketing the Margins*. London: Routledge, 2001.

———. "Prizing 'Otherness': A Short History of the Booker." *Studies in the Novel* 29.3 (1997): 412–33.

Hyde, Lewis. *Trickster Makes This World: Mischief, Myth, and Art*. New York: Farrar, Straus and Giroux, 1998.

Igwe, G. E. *Igbo-English Dictionary*. Ibadan: University Press PLC, 1999.

Ihekweazu, Edith, ed. *Eagle on Iroko: Selected Papers from the Chinua Achebe International Symposium, 1990*. Ibadan, Nigeria: Heinemann Educational Books, 1996.

Innes, C. L. Arrow of God: *A Critical View*. London: Collins, 1985.

———. *Chinua Achebe*. New York: Cambridge UP, 1990.

———. *The Devil's Own Mirror: The Irishman and the African in Modern Literature*. Washington, DC: Three Continents P, 1990.

———. *A History of Black and Asian Writing in Britain, 1700–2000*. Cambridge: Cambridge UP, 2002.

———. *Woman and Nation in Irish Literature and Society, 1880–1935*. Athens: U of Georgia P, 1993.

———, and Bernth Lindfors, eds. *Critical Perspectives on Chinua Achebe*. Washington, DC: Three Continents P, 1978.

Inyama, Nnadozie F. "Genetic Discontinuity in Achebe's *No Longer at Ease*." *The Gong and the Flute: African Literary Development and Celebration*. Ed. Kalu Ogbaa. Westport, CT: Greenwood P, 1994.

Irele, Abiola. *The African Experience in Literature and Ideology*. Bloomington: Indiana UP, 1990.

———. "Tradition and the Yoruba Writer: D. O. Fagunwa, Amos Tutuola and Wole Soyinka." *Odu* 11 (1975): 75–100.

———. "The Tragic Conflict in Achebe's Novels." *Introduction to African Literature: An Anthology of Critical Writing from* Black Orpheus. Ed. Ulli Beier. London: Longman, 1967.

Isichei, Elizabeth. *A History of the Igbo People*. London: Macmillan, 1976.

———. *A History of Nigeria*. London: Longman, 1983.

Izevbaye, D. S. "Death and the Artist: An Appreciation of Okigbo's Poetry." *Research in African Literatures* 13.1 (1982): 44–52.

Jameson, Fredric. "Third-World Literature in the Era of Multinational Capitalism." *Social Text* 15: 65–88.

JanMohamed, Abdul R. "The Economy of Manichean Allegory: The Function of Racial Difference in Colonialist Literature." *"Race," Writing, and Difference*. Ed. Henry Louis Gates Jr. Chicago: U of Chicago P, 1986. 78–106.

———. *Manichean Aesthetics: The Politics of Literature in Colonial Africa*. Amherst: U of Massachusetts P, 1983.

———. "Sophisticated Primitivism: The Syncretism of Oral and Literate Modes in Achebe's *Things Fall Apart*." *Ariel: A Review of International English Literature* 15.4: 19–39.

Jeffries-Jones, Rhodri. *The C.I.A. and American Democracy*. New Haven, CT: Yale UP, 1989.

Jeyifo, Biodun. "For Chinua Achebe: The Resilience and the Predicament of Obierika." Petersen and Rutherford, *Chinua Achebe* 51–70.

———. *Ngugi wa Thiong'o*. London: Pluto, 1990.

———. "Okonkwo and His Mother: *Things Fall Apart* and Issues of Gender in the Constitution of African Postcolonial Discourse" *Callaloo* 16.4 (1993): 847–58.

———, ed. *Perspectives on Wole Soyinka: Freedom and Complexity*. Jackson: UP of Mississippi, 2001.

Jones-Quartey, K.A.B. *A Life of Azikiwe*. Baltimore: Penguin, 1965.

Joseph, Michael Scott. "A Pre-Modernist Reading of 'The Drum': Chinua Achebe and the Theme of the Eternal Return." *Ariel: A Review of International English Literature* 28.1 (January 1997): 149–66.

July, Robert W. *An African Voice: The Role of Humanities in African Independence*. Durham, NC: Duke UP, 1987.

Jussawala, Feroza. *Conversations with V. S. Naipaul*. Jackson: UP of Mississippi, 1997.

Kane, Cheikh Hamidou. *Ambiguous Adventure*. Trans. Katherine Woods. 1963. Portsmouth, NH: Heinemann, 1988.

Karl, Frederick R. *Joseph Conrad: The Three Lives*. New York: Farrar, Straus and Giroux, 1979.

Katrak, Ketu H. *Wole Soyinka and Modern Tragedy: A Study of Dramatic Theory and Practice*. Westport, CT: Greenwood P, 1986.

Kesteloot, Lilyan. *Black Writers in French: A Literary History of Négritude*. Washington, DC: Howard UP, 1991.

Killam, Douglas, and Ruth Rowe, eds. *The Companion to African Literatures*. Bloomington: Indiana UP, 2000.

Killam, G. D. *Africa in English Fiction, 1874–1939*. Ibadan, Nigeria: Ibadan UP, 1968.

———. *An Introduction to the Writings of Ngugi*. London: Heinemann, 1980.

———. *The Writings of Chinua Achebe*. London: Heinemann, 1977.

Kinnamon, Keneth, ed. *James Baldwin: A Collection of Critical Essays*. Englewood Cliffs, NJ: Prentice-Hall, 1974.

Kline, Reamer. *Education for the Common Good: A History of Bard College—the First 100 Years, 1860–1960*. Annandale-on-Hudson, NY: Bard College, 1982.

Klooss, Wolfgang. "Chinua Achebe: A Chronicler of Historical Change in Africa." *Essays on Contemporary Post-Colonial Fiction*. Ed. Hedwig Bock and Albert Wertheim. Munich: Max Hueber, 1986. 23–45.

Knipp, Thomas. "English-Language Poetry." *A History of Twentieth-Century African Literatures*. Ed. Oyekan Owomoyela. Lincoln: U of Nebraska P, 1993. 105–37.

Kolawole, M.E.M. "Gender and Changing Social Vision in the Nigerian Novel." Afonja and Aina, *Nigerian Women in Social Change* 193–205.

Larson, Charles R. "The Film Version of Achebe's *Things Fall Apart*." *Africana Journal* 13.1–4 (1982): 104–10.

Lazarus, Neil. "Pessimism of the Intellect, Optimism of the Will: A Reading of Ayi Kwei Armah's *The Beautyful Ones Are Not Yet Born*." *Research in African Literatures* 18 (Summer 1987): 137–75.

Leeming, David. *James Baldwin: A Biography*. New York: Knopf, 1994.

Lévi-Strauss, Claude. "The Structural Study of Myth." *Journal of American Folklore* 68 (1955): 428–44.

Lindfors, Bernth. "Achebe's African Parable." *Présence Africaine* 66 (1968): 130–36.

———. "Amos Tutuola." *Dictionary of Literary Biography* 125 (1993): 332–46.

———. *African Textualities: Texts, Pre-texts and Contexts of African Literature*. Trenton, NJ: Africa World P, 1997.

———. "*The Blind Men and the Elephant*" and

Other Essays in Biographical Criticisms. 1987. Rev. and expanded edition. Trenton, NJ: African World P, 1999.

———. *Early Nigerian Literature.* New York: Africana, 1982.

———. *Folklore in Nigerian Literature.* New York: Africana, 1973.

———. *Loaded Vehicles: Studies in African Literary Media.* Trenton, NJ: Africa World P, 1996.

———. *Long Drums and Canons: Teaching and Researching African Literatures.* Trenton, NJ: Africa World P, 1995.

———. *Popular Literatures in Africa.* Trenton, NJ: Africa World P, 1991.

———, ed. *Approaches to Teaching Achebe's Things Fall Apart.* New York: Modern Language Association, 1991.

———, ed. *Conversations with Chinua Achebe.* Jackson: UP of Mississippi, 1997.

———, ed. *Critical Perspectives on Amos Tutuola.* London: Heinemann, 1980.

Lindqvist, Sven. *Exterminate All the Brutes.* Trans. Joan Tate. New York: New P, 1996.

Little, J. P. "Autofiction and Cheikh Hamidou Kane's *L'Aventure ambiguë.*" *Research in African Literatures* 31.2 (2000): 71–90.

Lizarríbar Buxó, Camille. "Something Else Will Stand beside It: The African Writers Series and the Development of African Literature." Diss. Yale U, 1998.

Lugard, Frederick John Dealtry, Lord. *The Dual Mandate in Tropical Africa.* 1922. London: F. Cass, 1965.

———. *Political Memoranda: Revision of Instructions to Political Officers on Subjects Chiefly Political and Administrative, 1913–1918.* London: F. Cass, 1919.

Macey, David. *Frantz Fanon: A Biography.* New York: Picador, 2001.

MacKenzie, John M. *Orientalism: History, Theory, and the Arts.* Manchester: Manchester UP, 1995.

Madiebo, Alexander A. *The Nigerian Revolution and the Biafran War.* Enugu, Nigeria: Fourth Dimension Publishers, 1980.

Mamdani, Mahmood. *When Victims Become Killers: Colonialism, Nativism, and the Genocide in Rwanda.* Oxford: James Currey, 2001.

Maughan-Brown, David A. "*Anthills of the Savannah* and the Ideology of Leadership." Petersen and Rutherford, *Chinua Achebe* 139–48.

Mazrui, Ali A. *The Trial of Christopher Okigbo.* Portsmouth, NH: Heinemann, 1971.

Mba, Nina Emma. *Nigerian Women Mobilized: Women's Political Activity in Southern Nigeria, 1900–1965.* Berkeley: U of California Institute of International Studies, 1982.

Mbembe, Achille. *On the Postcolony.* Berkeley: U of California P, 2001.

McCall, John C. *Dancing Histories: Heuristic Ethnography with the Ohafia Igbo.* Ann Arbor: U of Michigan P, 2000.

McLellan, David. *Karl Marx: His Life and Thought.* New York: Harper and Row, 1973.

McDaniel, Richard Bryan. "The Python Episodes in Achebe's Novels." *International Fiction Review* 3 (1976): 100–106.

Mellanby, Kenneth. *The Birth of Nigeria's University.* London: Methuen, 1958.

Millar, Heather. *The Kingdom of Benin in West Africa.* New York: Benchmark, 1996.

Miller, Christopher. *Blank Darkness: Africanist Discourse in French.* Chicago: U of Chicago P, 1985.

Miller, James. "The Novelist as Teacher: Chinua Achebe's Literature for Children." *Children's Literature: Annual of the Modern Language Association Division on Children's Literature and the Children's Literature Association* 9 (1981): 7–18.

Mitchell, W.J.T. "Postcolonial Culture, Postimperial Criticism." *Transition* 56 (1992): 11–19.

Moore, Gerald. *Seven African Writers.* Oxford: Oxford UP, 1962.

———. *Twelve African Writers.* Bloomington: Indiana UP, 1980.

Moore-Gilbert, Bart. *Postcolonial Theory: Contexts, Practices, Politics.* London: Verso, 1997.

Moses, Michael Valdez. *The Novel and the Globalization of Culture.* New York: Oxford UP, 1995.

Mphalele, Es'kia (Ezekiel). *The African Image*. London: Faber and Faber, 1962.

————. *Afrika My Music: An Autobiography 1957–1983*. Johannesburg: Ravan, 1984.

Mudimbe, V. Y. *The Idea of Africa*. Bloomington: Indiana UP, 1994.

————. *The Invention of Africa: Gnosis, Philosophy, and the Order of Knowledge*. Bloomington: Indiana UP, 1988.

Naipaul, V. S. *An Area of Darkness*. London: Penguin, 1968.

————. 1979. *A Bend in the River*. London: Penguin, 1980.

————. *The Enigma of Arrival*. New York: Knopf, 1987.

Najder, Zdzislaw. *Joseph Conrad: A Chronicle*. New Brunswick, NJ: Rutgers UP, 1983.

Narayan, Shyamala. Review of *The Vintage Book of Indian Writing: 1947–1997* by Salman Rushdie and Elizabeth West. *Ariel: A Review of International English Literature* 29.1 (January 1998): 263–267.

National Portrait Gallery. *David Livingstone and the Victorian Encounter with Africa*. London: National Portrait Gallery, 1996.

Ngara, Emmanuel. "Achebe as Artist: The Place and Significance of *Anthills of the Savannah*." Petersen and Rutherford, *Chinua Achebe* 113–29.

————. *Art and Ideology in the African Novel: A Study of the Influence of Marxism on African Writing*. London: Heinemann, 1985.

Ngugi wa Thiong'o. *Barrel of a Pen: Resistance to Repression in Neo-Colonial Kenya*. Trenton, NJ: Africa World P, 1983.

————. *Decolonising the Mind: The Politics of Language in African Literature*. London: James Currey, 1992.

————. *Detained: A Writer's Prison Diary*. London: Heinemann, 1981.

————. *Devil on the Cross*. 1980. Trans. from the Gikuyu by the Author. Portsmouth, NH: Heinemann, 1988.

————. *A Grain of Wheat*. 1967. London: Heinemann, 1986.

————. *Homecoming: Essays on African and Caribbean Literature, Culture, and Politics*. New York: Lawrence Hill, 1972.

————. *Matigari*. Trans. Wangui wa Goro. London: Heinemann, 1989.

————. *Moving the Centre: The Struggle for Cultural Freedoms*. London: James Currey, 1993.

————. *Petals of Blood*. London: Heinemann, 1977.

————. *The River Between*. London: Heinemann, 1965.

————. *Secret Lives and Other Stories*. London: Heinemann, 1975.

————. *Weep Not, Child*. 1964. London: Heinemann, 1987.

————. *Writers in Politics*. London: Heinemann, 1981.

————, and Micere Githae Mugo. *The Trial of Dedan Kimathi*. London: Heinemann, 1977.

————, and Ngugi wa Mirii. *I Will Marry When I Want*. Translated from the Gikuyu by the authors. London: Heinemann, 1988.

Nixon, Rob. *London Calling: V. S. Naipaul, Postcolonial Mandarin*. New York: Oxford UP, 1992.

Njaka, Mazi Elechukwu Nnadibuagha. *Igbo Political Culture*. Evanston, IL: Northwestern UP, 1974.

Nkosi, Lewis. "Conversation with Chinua Achebe." *Africa Report* 9.5 (1964): 19–21.

————. "Ezekiel Mphahlele at 70." *Southern African Review of Books* (February/May 1990. Accessible online at www.uni-ulm.de/~rturrell/antho4html/Nkosi1.html.

————. *Tasks and Masks: Themes and Styles of African Literature*. Harlow, Essex: Longman, 1981.

Nnolim, Charles E. "The Form and Function of the Folk Tradition in Achebe's Novels." *Ariel: A Review of International English Literature* 14.1 (1983): 35–47.

Nwachuckwu-Agbada, J.O.J. "Chinua Achebe: The Celebration of Igbo Tradition of Politics in His Novels." *The Igbo and the Tradition of Politics*. Ed. U. D. Anyanwu and J.C.U. Aguwa. Enugu, Nigeria: Fourth Dimension Publishing, 1993. 121–33.

Nwankwo, Chimalum Moses. *The Works of Ngugi wa Thiong'o: Towards the Kingdom of*

Woman and Man. Okeja: Longman Nigeria, 1992.

Nwankwo, Nkem. *Danda*. 1964. London: Heinemann, 1970.

Nwoga, Donatus Ibe. "The Concept and Practice of Satire among the Igbo." *The Conch* 3.2 (1971): 30–45.

———. *Critical Perspectives on Christopher Okigbo*. Washington, DC: Three Continents P, 1984.

———. "Onitsha Market Literature." *Readings in African Popular Fiction*. Ed. Stephanie Newell. Bloomington: Indiana UP, 2001. 37–43.

———, ed. *Rhythms of Creation*. Enugu: Fourth Dimension, 1982.

Obiechina, Emmanuel. *An African Popular Literature: A Study of Onitsha Market Pamphlets*. Cambridge: Cambridge UP, 1973.

———. "Chinua Achebe's *No Longer at Ease*." *Okike* 13 (1979): 124–44.

———. *Culture, Tradition, and Society in the West African Novel*. Cambridge: Cambridge UP, 1975.

———. *Language and Theme: Essays on African Literature*. Washington, DC: Howard UP, 1990.

———. "Narrative Proverbs in the African Novel." *Oral Tradition* 7.2 (1992): 197–230.

———, Chukwuemeka Ike, and John Anenechukwu Umeh, eds. *The University of Nigeria, 1960–1985: An Experiment in Higher Education*. Nsukka, Nigeria: U of Nigeria, 1986.

Obilade, Tony. "The Stylistic Function of Pidgin English in African Literature." *Research in African Literatures* 9 (1978): 433–44.

Ogbaa, Kalu. *Gods, Oracles, and Divination: Folkways in Chinua Achebe's Novels*. Trenton, NJ: Africa World P, 1992.

———. *Understanding* Things Fall Apart*: A Student Casebook to Issues, Sources, and Historical Documents*. Westport, CT: Greenwood P, 1999.

Ogbalu, F. C., and E. N. Emenanjo, eds. *Igbo Language and Culture*. Ibadan, Nigeria: UP Limited, 1982.

Ogede, Ode. *Achebe and the Politics of Representation*. Trenton, NJ: Africa World P, 2001.

Ogunyemi, Chikwenye Okonjo. "Women and Nigerian Literature." *Perspectives on Nigerian Literature: 1700 to the Present*. Vol. 1. Lagos: Guardian Books, 1988. 60–67.

Ohale, Christine Nwakego. *From Ritual to Art: The Aesthetics and Cultural Relevance of Igbo Satire*. Lanham, MD: UP of America, 2003.

Ojinmah, Umelo. *Chinua Achebe: New Perspectives*. Ibadan: Spectrum Books, 1991.

Okafor, Nduka. *The Development of Universities in Nigeria: A Study of the Influence of Political and Other Factors on University Development in Nigeria, 1868–1967*. London: Longman, 1971.

Okechukwu, Chinwe Christiana. *Achebe the Orator: The Art of Persuasion in Chinua Achebe's Novels*. Westport, CT: Greenwood P, 2001.

Okpaku, Joseph. "A Novel for the People." *Journal of the New African Literature* 2 (Fall 1966): 76–80.

Olaniyan, Richard, ed. *Nigerian History and Culture*. Harlow, Essex: Longman, 1985.

Omotoso, Kole. *Achebe or Soyinka? A Study in Contrasts*. London: Hans Zell, 1996.

Opara, Chioma. "From Stereotype to Individuality: Womanhood in Achebe's Novels." Ed. Leonard Podis and Yakubu Saaka. *Challenging Hierarchies: Issues and Themes in Colonial and Post-independent Literature*. New York: Peter Lang, 1998. 113–23.

Opata, Damian U. "Eternal Sacred Order versus Conventional Wisdom: A Consideration of Moral Culpability in the Killing of Ikemefuna in *Things Fall Apart*." *Research in African Literatures* 18.1 (1987): 71–79.

Osei-Nyame, Kwadwo, Jr. "Gender, Nationalism and the Fictions of Identity in Chinua Achebe's *A Man of the People*." *Commonwealth Novel in English* 9–10 (Spring–Fall 2001): 242–62.

———. "Love and Nation: Fanon's African Revolution and Ayi Kwei Armah's *The Beautyful Ones Are Not Yet Born*." *The Journal of Commonwealth Literature* 33.2 (1998): 97–107.

Ouologuem, Yambo. *Le devoir de violence*. Paris:

Éditions de Seuil, 1968. (English trans. by Ralph Mannheim as *Bound to Violence*. London: Secker and Warburg, 1971.)

Owomoyela, Oyekan. *Amos Tutuola Revisited*. New York: Twayne, 1999.

———. *Yoruba Trickster Tales*. Lincoln: U of Nebraska P, 1997.

Oyegoke, Lekan. "Misreading Simon Gikandi's *Reading Chinua Achebe*." Rev. of *Reading Chinua Achebe: Language and Ideology in Fiction*, by Simon Gikandi. *The Literary Griot: An International Journal of Black Expressive Cultures* 5 (1993): 65–74.

Palmer, Eustace. *The Growth of the African Novel*. London: Heinemann, 1979.

———. *An Introduction to the African Novel*. New York: Africana, 1972.

Parry, Benita. "Problems in Current Theories of Colonial Discourse." *Oxford Literary Review* 9.1–2 (1987): 27–58.

Pedler, F. J. *West Africa*. London: Methuen, 1951.

Peek, Andrew. "Betrayal and the Question of Affirmation in Chinua Achebe's *No Longer at Ease*." *The Literary Half-Yearly* (Guest Editor: Bruce King) 21.1 (1980): 112–20.

Pelton, Robert D. *The Trickster in West Africa: A Study of Mythic Irony and Sacred Delight*. Berkeley: U of California P, 1980.

Perham, Margery Freda. *Lugard*. 2 vols. London: Collins, 1956–1960.

Petersen, Kirsten Holst, and Anna Rutherford. "Working with Chinua Achebe: The African Writers Series, James Currey, Alan Hill and Keith Sambrook in Conversation with Kirsten Holst Petersen." Petersen and Rutherford, *Chinua Achebe* 149–59.

———, eds. *Chinua Achebe: A Celebration*. Oxford: Heinemann, 1990.

Pieterse, Cosmo, and Dennis Duerden, eds. *African Writers Talking: A Collection of Radio Interviews*. New York: Africana, 1972.

Porter, Horace A. *Stealing the Fire: The Art and Protest of James Baldwin*. Middletown, CT: Wesleyan UP, 1990.

Post, K.W.J. Introduction to *Arrow of God*. New York: Anchor-Doubleday, 1969. vii–xiv.

Priebe, Richard K. "Kofi Awoonor's *This Earth, My Brother* as an African Dirge." *Ghanaian Literatures*. Ed. Richard K. Priebe. Westport, CT: Greenwood P, 1988. 265–78.

———. *Myth, Realism, and the West African Writer*. Trenton, NJ: Africa World P, 1988.

———. Review of *The Trickster in West Africa: A Study of Mythic Irony and Sacred Delight*, by Robert D. Pelton. *Research in African Literatures* 14 (1983): 401–5.

———. Teaching *Things Fall Apart* in a Criticism Course." Lindfors, *Approaches to Teaching Achebe's* Things Fall Apart 123–28.

Radin, Paul. *The Trickster: A Study in American Indian Mythology*. 1956. New York: Schocken, 1972.

Ranger, Terence. "The Invention of Tradition in Colonial Africa." *The Invention of Tradition*. Ed. Eric Hobsbawm and Terence Ranger. 1983. Cambridge: Cambridge UP, 1992.

Ravenscroft, Arthur. *Chinua Achebe*. Ed. Ian Scott-Kilvert. London: Longmans, 1969.

———. "The Nigerian Civil War in Nigerian Literature." *Commonwealth Literature and the Modern World*. Ed. Hena Maes-Jelinek. Bruxelles: Librairie Marcel Didier, 1975. 105–13.

Ray, Keith, and Rosalind Shaw. "The Structure of Spirit Embodiment in Nsukka Igbo Masquerading Traditions." *Anthropos: International Review of Anthropology and Linguistics* 82.4–6 (1987): 655–60.

Riddy, Felicity. "Language as a Theme in *No Longer at Ease*." Innes and Lindfors, *Critical Perspectives on Chinua Achebe* 150–59.

Robinson, Ronald E., and John A. Gallagher, with Alice Denny. *Africa and the Victorians: The Official Mind of Imperialism*. London: Macmillan, 1961.

Robson, Clifford B. *Ngugi wa Thiong'o*. London: Macmillan, 1979.

Rogers, Philip. "*No Longer at Ease*: Chinua Achebe's 'Heart of Whiteness.' " *Postcolonial Literatures: Achebe, Ngugi, Desai, Walcott*. Ed. Michael Parker and Roger Starkey. New York: St. Martin's, 1995. 53–63.

Rushdie, Salman. "The Empire Writes Back with a Vengeance." *London Times* (July 3, 1982): 8.

———, and Elizabeth West, eds. *The Vintage Book of Indian Writing: 1947–1997*. London: Vintage–Random House, 1997.

Sackey, Edward. "Oral Tradition and the African Novel." *Modern Fiction Studies* 37.3 (1991): 389–407.

Said, Edward. *Beginnings: Intention and Method.* New York: Columbia UP, 1985.

———. *Culture and Imperialism.* New York: Knopf, 1993.

———. *Joseph Conrad and the Fiction of Autobiography.* Cambridge, MA: Harvard UP, 1966.

———. *Orientalism.* New York: Vintage Books, 1979.

———. *The World, the Text, and the Critic.* Cambridge, MA: Harvard UP, 1983.

———. "Yeats and Decolonization." *Nationalism, Colonialism, and Literature.* Ed. Seamus Deane. Minneapolis: U of Minnesota P, 1990. 69–95.

Samantrai, Ranu. "Caught at the Confluence of History: Ama Ata Aidoo's Necessary Nationalism." *Research in African Literatures* 26.2 (Summer 1995): 140–57.

San Juan, E., Jr. *Beyond Postcolonial Theory.* New York: St. Martin's, 1998.

Saro-Wiwa, Ken. *On a Darkling Plain: An Account of the Nigerian Civil War.* London: Saros International, 1989.

Saunders, Frances Stonor. *The Cultural Cold War: The CIA and the World of Arts and Letters.* New York: New P, 1999.

Saunders, John Tennant. *University College, Ibadan.* Cambridge: Cambridge UP, 1960.

Sembène, Ousmane. *Les bouts de bois de Dieu.* Paris: Le Livre Contemporain, 1960. (English translation by Francis Price as *God's Bits of Wood.* New York: Doubleday, 1962.)

Sicherman, Carol M. *Ngugi wa Thiong'o: The Making of a Rebel: A Source Book in Kenyan Literature and Resistance.* London: Hans Zell, 1990.

Singh, Frances. "The Colonialistic Bias of *Heart of Darkness.*" *Conradiana* 10 (1978): 41–54.

Smith, Janet Adam. *John Buchan: A Biography.* Oxford: Oxford UP, 1985.

Smith, Jeanne Rosier. *Writing Tricksters: Mythic Gambols in American Ethnic Literature.* Berkeley: U of California P, 1997.

Soyinka, Wole. *The Interpreters.* London: Deutsch, 1965.

Sprinker, Michael, ed. *Edward Said: A Critical Reader.* Oxford: Basil Blackwell, 1992.

Stiebel, Lindy. *Imagining Africa: Landscape in H. Rider Haggard's African Romances.* Westport, CT: Greenwood P, 2001.

Stock, A. G. "Yeats and Achebe." *The Journal of Commonwealth Literature* 5 (1968): 105–11.

Stratton, Florence. *Contemporary African Literature and the Politics of Gender.* London: Routledge, 1994.

Sutherland, Efua T. *The Marriage of Anansewa and Edufa.* 1967. Harlow, Essex: Longman, 1987.

Taiwo, Oladele. *Culture and the Nigerian Novel.* New York: St. Martin's, 1976.

Tamuno, Tekena N., ed. *Ibadan Voices: Ibadan University in Transition.* Ibadan, Nigeria: Ibadan UP, 1981.

Taylor, Charles. *Hegel.* New York: Cambridge UP, 1975.

Ten Kortenaar, Neil. "Beyond Authenticity and Creolization: Reading Achebe Writing Culture." *PMLA* 110.1 (1995): 30–42.

———. "Only Connect: *Anthills of the Savannah* and the Trouble with Nigeria." *Research in African Literatures* 24.3 (1993): 59–72.

Thelwell, Michael. Introduction to Amos Tutuola, *The Palm-Wine Drinkard and His Dead Palm-Wine Tapster in the Dead's Town.* New York: Grove P, 1984. v–viii.

Todd, Richard. *Consuming Fictions: The Booker Prize and Fiction in Britain Today.* London: Bloomsbury, 1998.

Tucker, Robert C., ed. *The Marx-Engels Reader.* 2nd ed. New York: Norton, 1978.

Turner, Margaret E. "Achebe, Hegel, and the New Colonialism." Petersen and Rutherford, *Chinua Achebe* 31–40.

Tutuola, Amos. *Feather Woman of the Jungle.* 1962. San Francisco: City Lights, 1988.

———. *The Palm-Wine Drinkard and His Dead Palm-Wine Tapster in the Dead's Town.* London: Faber and Faber, 1952. Reprinted, Grove P, 1984.

Uchendu, Victor C. *The Igbo of Southeast Nige-*

ria. New York: Holt, Rinehart, and Winston, 1965.

Udumukwu, Onyemaechi. "Ideology and the Dialectics of Action: Achebe and Iyayi." *Research in African Literatures* 27.3 (Fall 1996): 34–49.

Ugonna, Nnabuenyi. "Igbo Satiric Art: A Comment." Ogbalu and Emenanjo, *Igbo Language and Culture.* Vol. 2. 65–79.

Ukadike, Nwachukwu Frank. *Black African Cinema.* Berkeley: U of California P, 1994.

Vassanji, M. G. *The Gunny Sack.* Oxford: Heinemann, 1989.

Walsh, William. *A Manifold Voice: Studies in Commonwealth Literature.* New York: Barnes and Noble, 1970.

Watt, Ian. *Conrad in the Nineteenth Century.* Berkeley: U of California P, 1979.

Watts, Cedric. " 'A Blood Racist': About Achebe's View of Conrad." *Yearbook of English Studies* 13 (1983): 196–209.

Webster, Wendy. "Elspeth Huxley: Gender, Empire and Narratives of Nation, 1935–1964." *Women's History Review* 8.3 (1999): 527–45.

Wilentz, Gay. "The Politics of Exile: Ama Ata Aidoo's *Our Sister Killjoy.*" *Arms Akimbo: Africana Women in Contemporary Literature.* Ed. Janice Lee Liddell and Yakini Belinda Kemp. Gainesville: UP of Florida, 1999. 162–75.

Wilson, Roderick. "Eliot and Achebe: An Analysis of Some Formal and Philosophical Qualities of *No Longer at Ease.*" Innes and Lindfors, *Critical Perspectives on Chinua Achebe* 160–68.

Wise, Christopher. "The Garden Trampled: or, The Liquidation of African Culture in V. S. Naipaul's *A Bend in the River.*" *College Literature* 23 (1996): 58–72.

Wren, Robert M. *Achebe's World: The Historical and Cultural Context of the Novels of Chinua Achebe.* Washington, DC: Three Continents P, 1980.

———. *J. P. Clark.* Boston: Twayne, 1984.

———. "*Mister Johnson* and the Complexity of *Arrow of God.*" *Health and the Human Condition: Perspectives on Medical Anthropology.* Ed. Michael H. Logan and Edward E. Hunt. North Scituate, MA: Duxbury, 1978. 50–62.

———. "*Things Fall Apart* in Its Time and Place." Lindfors, *Approaches to Teaching Achebe's* Things Fall Apart 38–44.

———. *Those Magical Years: The Making of Nigerian Literature at Ibadan, 1948–1966.* Washington, DC: Three Continents P, 1991.

Wright, Derek. "Scatology and Eschatology in Kofi Awoonor's *This Earth, My Brother.*" *International Fiction Review* 15.1 (1988): 23–26.

———. *Wole Soyinka Revisited.* New York: Twayne, 1992.

Yankson, Kofi. "Use of Pidgin in *No Longer at Ease* and *A Man of the People.*" *Asõemka* 1.2 (1974): 68–80.

Zabus, Chantal. "The Ancestor of Relexification: Calquing in Amos Tutuola's *The Palm Wine Drinkard.*" *The African Palimpsest: Indigenization of Language in the West African Europhone Novel.* By Zabus. Atlanta: Rodopi, 1991. 108–21.

Index

Note: Page numbers in **bold** refer to main entries in the encyclopedia. Major works by Chinua Achebe are listed under "Achebe, Chinua."

About the Contributors

CORA AGATUCCI teaches writing, literature, and humanities (including a course introducing African cultures, orature, literature, and film) at Central Oregon Community College in Bend, Oregon. She has published articles on Michelle Cliff, Eric Walrond, contemporary African American women writers, and timelines of ancient Africa and African empires. Her web sites on "African Timelines" and "African Authors: Chinua Achebe" have earned national recognition.

M. KEITH BOOKER is Professor of English at the University of Arkansas, Fayetteville. He is the author of numerous books and articles on postcolonial and other forms of modern literature and culture, including *The African Novel in English: An Introduction* and *The Caribbean Novel in English: An Introduction* (co-authored with Dubravka Juraga).

NICHOLAS BROWN is Assistant Professor in the Department of English at the University of Illinois at Chicago. He is at work on a book entitled *Utopian Generations: African Fiction and British Modernism*.

DEBRA RAE COHEN is Visiting Assistant Professor in the Department of English at the University of Arkansas, Fayetteville. A specialist in modern British literature, she is the author of *Remapping the Home Front: Locating Citizenship in British Women's Great War Fiction*.

PHANUEL AKUBUEZE EGEJURU is Professor of English at Loyola University in New Orleans. In addition to the recent biography (based on oral accounts) *Chinua Achebe: Pure and Simple*, she is the author of several books on African literature and culture, including *NWANYIBU: Womanbeing and African Literature* and *Towards African Literary Independence*. She is also the author of a novel, *The Seed Yams Have Been Eaten*.

JAMES GIBBS was educated at the universities of Bristol and Leeds in the United Kingdom and American University in Washington, D.C. He has taught at universities in Ghana, Malawi, Nigeria, and Belgium and is currently a senior lecturer at the University of the West of England, Bristol. His recent editorial commitments have included working on a handbook for African writers (with Jack Mapanje) and on Ghanaian literature, theater, and film (with Kofi Anyidoho). He is an editorial advisor for publications in the Netherlands, Nigeria, and Malawi, reviews editor for *African Literature Today*, and one of the joint editors of the African Theatre series, published in the United Kingdom by James Currey.

SIMON GIKANDI is Robert Hayden Professor of English Language and Literature at the University of Michigan, Ann Arbor. He is the recipient of awards from organizations such as the American Council of Learned Societies, the Mellon Foundation, and the Guggenheim Foundation. He is the author of several books on African and postcolonial literature and culture, including, most recently, *Maps of Englishness: Writing Identity in the Culture of Colonialism* and *Ngugi Wa Thiong'o*. He is the general editor of the *Encyclopedia of African Literature*.

JOSEF GUGLER is Professor of Sociology and Director of the Center for Contemporary African Studies at the University of Connecticut. Previously, he served as Director of Sociological Research at the Makerere Institute of Social Research, Uganda, and as Professor of Development Sociology at Bayreuth University, Germany. He has held visiting appointments in the Congo (Kinshasa), Germany, Tanzania, and the United States. His research has taken him to Cuba, India, Kenya, Nigeria, and Tanzania. He has widely published on urbanization in Africa and more recently on literature and film in Africa. His *African Film: Re-Imagining a Continent* is to appear in 2003.

BARBARA HARLOW is the Louann and Larry Temple Centennial Professor of English Literature at the University of Texas at Austin. She is the author of *Resistance Literature* (1986), *Barred: Women, Writing, and Political Detention* (1992), and *After Lives: Legacies of Revolutionary Writing* (1996), and co-editor with Mia Carter of *Imperialism and Orientalism: A Documentary Source-book* (1999). She is currently working on an intellectual biography of the South African activist Ruth First.

HUNT HAWKINS is Professor and Chair of the English Department at Florida State University, where he teaches modern British and postcolonial literatures. A past-President of the Joseph Conrad Society of America, he co-edited the book *Teaching Approaches to Joseph Conrad's* Heart of Darkness *and* The Secret Sharer, which is forthcoming. He has published articles on Conrad, Achebe, Césaire, Joyce, Forster, and Twain in such journals as *PMLA*, the *Journal of Modern Literature*, *CLA Journal*, *Conradiana*, and *New England Quarterly*.

FARHAD B. IDRIS is Assistant Professor of English at Frostburg State University in Frostburg, Maryland. He teaches Asian and African literatures and has published articles on V. S. Naipaul and Salman Rushdie.

C. L. INNES teaches at the University of Kent in Canterbury, United Kingdom. Innes was earlier a colleague of Achebe at the University of Massachusetts at Amherst, and has collaborated with him on such projects as the volumes *African Short Stories* and *Contemporary African Short Stories*, which they co-edited, and the journal *Okike*, of which she served as an assistant editor from 1974 to 1990. In addition to numerous articles and reviews in books and journals, her book-length publications include *Arrow of God: A Critical View*; *The Devil's Own Mirror: The Irishman and the African in Modern Literature*; *Chinua Achebe: A Critical Study*; *Woman and Nation in Irish Literature and Society, 1880–1935*; and *A History of Black and Asian Writing in Britain, 1700–2000*.

DAVID JEFFERESS recently completed his Ph.D. dissertation "Changing the Story:

Postcolonial Studies and Resistance" at McMaster University, Canada. His recent publications include postcolonial critiques of child rights discourse, the marketing practices of development agencies, and discourses of Canadian identity in relation to the Third World.

DOUGLAS KILLAM is retired from the Department of English at Guelph University, where he was professor and chair. A pioneering scholar of African literature, he is the author of such books as *Africa in English Fiction*, *The Writings of Chinua Achebe*, and *An Introduction to the Writings of Ngugi*. More recently, he co-edited *The Companion to African Literatures*.

CAMILLE LIZARRÍBAR BUXÓ received her Doctor of Philosophy degree from Harvard University, where she wrote a dissertation on the Heinemann African Writers Series and its place in the development of African literature.

THOMAS J. LYNN is Assistant Professor of English at Penn State Berks–Lehigh Valley College. His scholarly and teaching interests include literature of Africa and the Diaspora, postcolonial literature, world literature (ancient and modern) modernism, and folklore. His article "Hybridity and Ambivalence in Postcolonial West African Literature" appeared in the 2002 volume of *The Literary Griot*. His brief discussion of postcolonial literature appeared in the December 2000 issue of *PMLA*, while his article "Trickster and Carnival in *Things Fall Apart*," appeared in the Spring 1997 issue of *Publications of the Arkansas Philological Association*. He is currently writing a book on the trickster figure in West African literature. His non-academic interests include various volunteer activities, including long-standing participation with Amnesty International.

JULIE MCGONEGAL is a Ph.D. candidate in the Department of English at McMaster University, Canada. She is currently working on her dissertation, an examination of twentieth- and twenty-first-century discourses of postcolonial forgiveness and reconciliation in the contexts of Canada, South Africa, Australia, and India. She is also teaching in the area of globalization and is a Research Fellow with the Institute on Globalization and the Human Condition at McMaster University. Her publications include articles in *Essays on Canadian Writing* and *Women's Writing*.

ABDUL-RASHEED NA'ALLAH is Associate Professor of Comparative Literature (African and African Diaspora Literature, African Performance, Folklore, and Cultural Theory and Practice) at the Western Illinois University Department of African American Studies. He took his Ph.D. in Comparative Literature from the University of Alberta, Canada, and his B.A. (Hons) degree in English and Education and M.A. degree in Literature-in-English from the University of Ilorin, Nigeria, where he also taught English and African oral literature and performance from 1989 to 1994. Among his books are *Introduction to African Oral Literature*, *Ogoni's Agonies: Ken Saro-Wiwa and the Crisis in Nigeria*, *Almajiri: A New African Poetry*, and *The People's Poet: Emerging Perspectives on Niyi Osundare*.

CHRISTINE NWAKEGO OHALE, née Oti, was born in Ihiala, near Onitsha, in Anambra State of Nigeria and is a graduate of the University of Nigeria, Nsukka. She has been educated in Nigeria and the United States and holds two Masters degrees in English and a Ph.D. in African literature. Professor Ohale was, until her relocation to the United States, a Senior Lecturer in English at the University of Nigeria at Nsukka, a career that spanned roughly two decades, from 1981 to 2000. She is currently Associate Professor of English at Chicago State University. She has published essays in international journals in Africa, Europe, and the United States. Her new book is entitled *From Ritual to Art: The Aesthetics and Cultural Relevance of Igbo Satire.* Her research interests are mainly in the areas of African literature and African oral traditions.

KWADWO OSEI-NYAME JR. has a D.Phil. in African literature from the University of Oxford and lectures in African literature and cultural studies at the School of Oriental and African Studies, University of London. He has published a number of articles on African literature in such journals as *Ariel, Commonwealth: Essays and Studies, Current Writing, Journal of Commonwealth Literature, Kunapipi,* and *Research in African Literatures.*

RACHEL R. REYNOLDS is Assistant Professor in the Department of Culture and Communication at Drexel University in Philadelphia. Her current research focuses on the development of an ethnography based on field work within Igbo immigrant communities in the United States. She recently contributed a chapter about Igbo-speaking people to *Ethnolinguistic Chicago: Language and Literacy in Chicago Neighborhoods.*

SUSAN WILLIAMS is completing a dissertation on Edmund Spenser and T. E. Lawrence at the University of Arkansas, Fayetteville. Her interest in and knowledge of African literature stem from her teaching experience as a lecturer at the University of Ibadan in the early 1980s, as well as from a National Endowment for the Humanities (NEH) Summer Seminar on the African Novel, directed by Bernth Lindfors, and from an NEH Summer Institute in Ghana, co-directed by Abiola Irele.

CHRISTOPHER WISE was formerly Assistant Professor of English at Western Washington University. He currently works for the Jordanian-American Commission for Educational Exchange in Amman, Jordan.